Assessing Educational Digital Transformation in the AI Era

Shaoxu Du
https://orcid.org/0009-0002-8142-1343
Universiti Sains Malaysia, Malaysia

Mageswaran Sanmugam
https://orcid.org/0000-0003-3313-4462
Universiti Sains Malaysia, Malaysia

Nurul Maziah Mohd Barkhaya
https://orcid.org/0009-0002-2192-0706
Universiti Sains Malaysia, Malaysia

Chuang Chen
Zhengzhou University of Industrial Technology, China

Jia Wang
Chung-Ang University, South Korea

IGI Global
Scientific Publishing
Publishing Tomorrow's Research Today

Vice President of Editorial	Melissa Wagner
Director of Acquisitions	Mikaela Felty
Director of Book Development	Jocelynn Hessler
Production Manager	Mike Brehm
Cover Design	Jose Rosado

Published in the United States of America by
IGI Global Scientific Publishing
701 East Chocolate Avenue
Hershey, PA, 17033, USA
Tel: 717-533-8845 | Fax: 717-533-7115
Website: https://www.igi-global.com E-mail: cust@igi-global.com

Library of Congress Cataloging-in-Publication Data

CIP Data Pending
ISBN13: 9798337308722
Isbn13Softcover: 9798337308739
EISBN13: 9798337308746

British Cataloguing in Publication Data
A Cataloguing in Publication record for this book is available from the British Library.

Table of Contents

Detailed Table of Contents

theory and quantitative analysis of statistical data results, the study focuses on the learning performance and self-efficacy of higher education samples, and explores the changes in students' psychological state in blended teaching, thus promoting the effectiveness of E-learning, and providing a basis for the future of E-learning and blending mode education in the future.

This chapter is about the effects of ethical leadership on the augmented reality (AR) in educational integration in the Horn of Africa where organizational citizenship behavior (OCB) works as the intervening factor through teacher engagement as well as support. To measure the connections among ethical leadership, AR utilization, as well as OCB, teacher engagement, as well as institutional support, the sample size was 390 educators who were surveyed. The analysis included the use of exploratory factor analysis (KMO = 0.87) that proved the validity of the constructs of its measures. The model was along with validated using confirmatory factor analysis (CFA) that depicted good fit indices to hold up the theoretical structure. Structural equation modeling through AMOS software found that OCB as well as positive increases in engagement of teachers mediated a significant direct as well as indirect rule of ethical leaders in developing AR adoption. Findings depict that ethical leadership contributes into creating an atmosphere that supports innovative teaching methods.

The education landscape is undergoing significant changes, and integrating gamification technology into augmented reality (AR) has become a promising field. This study applies cognitive load theory to explore the impact of AR gamified mathematical task design on middle school students' self-regulation ability, and suggests that AR optimizes learners' cognitive resource allocation through multiple mechanisms. The immersive and interactive features of AR help visualize abstract mathematical concepts, reduce internal cognitive load, and improve understanding and memory. The structured design of game mechanics manages external cognitive load through goal gradients and real-time feedback, guiding students to focus on core tasks. In addition, maintaining a dynamic balance between task difficulty and

Chapter 9

This study delves into the symbiotic relationship between artificial intelligence (AI) and self-regulated learning (SRL) strategies within the context of primary school English instruction. It examines how AI tools can empower young learners to develop autonomous learning abilities. By seamlessly integrating AI technology into educational practices, educators are equipped to offer tailored feedback and create adaptive learning environments catered to individual student requirements. This approach fosters enhanced engagement and motivation among learners, while imparting the fundamental self-regulation skills crucial for successful language acquisition. The research underscores the transformative potential of AI in bolstering self-directed learning in foundational education, thereby establishing a robust theoretical framework for more efficient and engaging English teaching and learning experiences.

Chapter 10

As disciplinary literacy grows across academic and professional domains, technical vocabulary acquisition presents a major challenge in foreign languages for specific purposes (FLSP) instruction. Technical vocabulary poses particular learning challenges due to its strong disciplinary specificity, and limited occurrence in natural language input. Mobile-Assisted Language Learning (MALL) offers flexible, multimodal, and personalized support, yet how to translate its potential into effective instructional design remains underexplored. This study, based on established theories, proposes a pedagogical framework that integrates five key instructional affordances: contextualization, multimodal input, repetition, learner self-regulation, and motivational support. The framework bridges technology and pedagogy, offering design pathways for FLSP instructors and platform developers to optimize technical vocabulary learning in mobile environments.

Preface

The rapid convergence of Artificial Intelligence (AI) and digital education technologies has ushered in a transformative era for teaching, learning, and educational leadership across the globe. As institutions grapple with post-pandemic realities, technological acceleration, and increasing learner diversity, the digital transformation of education is no longer optional. Yet this transformation is not uniform. It intersects with cultural, ethical, pedagogical, and infrastructural factors that vary by context and learner needs.

This edited volume, *Assessing Educational Digital Transformation in the AI Era*, brings together a multidisciplinary collection of studies from scholars and practitioners across continents who critically explore the integration of AI and digital innovation in diverse educational settings. From inclusive education and augmented reality to self-regulated learning and mobile technologies, the chapters offer both empirical insights and theoretical reflections on how digital transformation is shaping pedagogy.

The volume offers educators, researchers, policy-makers, and instructional designers a comprehensive and timely reference that navigates the complexities of AI-enhanced learning environments while spotlighting opportunities for equity and wellness in education.

CHAPTER OVERVIEW

Chapter 1: A Perspective of Requirements for Trainers in the Application of Artificial Intelligence in Inclusive Education

Explores the urgent need to prepare educators in inclusive settings for AI integration. Grounded in social learning theory, the chapter presents a process model for equipping trainers to support teachers of learners with disabilities, ensuring equitable participation in AI-enhanced education.

Chapter 2: The Effectiveness of Blended-Mode E-learning on Students' Performance and Self-Efficacy Among College Students

Through a quasi-experimental design, this study evaluates the effects of blended learning on student performance and self-efficacy. Anchored in expectancy-value theory, findings suggest that blending synchronous and asynchronous modes can optimize digital learning outcomes in higher education.

Chapter 3: Ethical Leadership Effect on Augmented Reality in Education Through OCB and Teacher Engagement Support in Africa

Investigates how ethical leadership influences the adoption of augmented reality (AR) in educational institutions across the Horn of Africa. Using structural equation modeling, the study highlights the mediating role of organizational citizenship behavior and teacher engagement in promoting innovative practices.

Chapter 4: Impact of Augmented Reality Gamified Math Task Design on Middle School Students' Self-Regulation

Applies cognitive load theory to examine how AR-based gamified tasks enhance middle school students' self-regulation in mathematics. The study proposes a theoretical model linking immersive environments with cognitive scaffolding for deeper learning.

Chapter 5: A Quantitative Correlational Study of the Interaction Between Assignment Response Times and Online Students' Final Grades and Satisfaction

Explores how instructor response times in online courses affect student satisfaction and performance. While no direct link to grades was found, the study shows a statistically significant relationship between quick responses and improved student satisfaction. offering implications for reducing online attrition.

Chapter 6: From Theory to Practice: A Systematic Review of the Flipped Classroom in Higher Music Education (2021–2025)

Reviews the adoption of flipped classroom models in music education across several countries. It discusses how flipped approaches enhance engagement and skill acquisition, while also acknowledging challenges around equity and technological access.

Chapter 7: Echoes of Innovation: Rethinking Art Education in the Age of AI

Examines the integration of AI in higher arts education. This systematic review finds that AI fosters personalization and creativity, but also raises concerns about human agency and the evolving role of educators, prompting recommendations for responsible innovation.

Chapter 8: The Implementation of AI-Generated Art in Increasing Student Wellness: Systematic Literature Review

Investigates the therapeutic potential of AI-generated art in supporting college student wellness. Synthesizing literature across aesthetics, psychology, and education, the chapter calls for further research on integrating AI art into mental health strategies in academia.

Chapter 9: The Synergy of Artificial Intelligence and Self-Regulated Learning Strategies in Enhancing Primary English Language Instruction

Focuses on how AI tools can promote self-regulated learning among primary school students learning English. The chapter presents a framework where adaptive AI systems enhance learner autonomy and engagement, supporting foundational language acquisition.

Chapter 10: Instructional Affordances of Mobile Technologies for Technical Vocabulary Acquisition: A Pedagogical Framework

Offers a pedagogical framework for using mobile-assisted language learning (MALL) to support technical vocabulary acquisition in foreign language contexts. The framework highlights five instructional affordances, bridging theory and practical design.

Chapter 11: Bridging Traditional and Digital Pedagogies in Blended ESL Vocabulary Learning: Learner Perception and Motivation

An empirical study on primary school ESL learners shows that blended learning significantly improves vocabulary knowledge and learner motivation. Findings underscore the value of merging traditional and digital strategies for early language instruction.

Chapter 12: The Design, Development, and Evaluation of the Task-Based Small Private Online Course (SPOC) for Learning English for Occupational Purposes

Evaluates a task-based SPOC model for vocational English instruction in China. The chapter offers robust evidence for the model's effectiveness in improving learner performance and motivation, proposing a scalable alternative to traditional MOOCs.

Chapter 13: Reimagining Instructional Design for Blended Learning in Chinese Higher Education—A Self-Regulated Learning Perspective

Presents a self-regulated learning (SRL) framework tailored for blended learning in Chinese universities. The study argues for integrating cultural and technological dimensions to enhance student autonomy and cognitive engagement in hybrid educational settings.

Together, these chapters weave a rich narrative of educational evolution in the AI era grounded in evidence, shaped by global voices, and oriented toward more inclusive, responsive, and human-centered digital futures.

Chapter 1
A Perspective of Requirements for Trainers in the Application of Artificial Intelligence in Inclusive Education

Olufemi Timothy Adigun
https://orcid.org/0000-0001-6079-1690
University of Namibia, Namibia

Cynthy K. Haihambo
https://orcid.org/0000-0003-4993-7956
University of Namibia, Namibia

Kazuvire K. Veii
University of Namibia, Namibia

Job K. Hengari
https://orcid.org/0009-0006-5152-3970
University of Namibia, Namibia

Enock L. Simasiku
University of Namibia, Namibia

DOI: 10.4018/979-8-3373-7508-3.ch001

ABSTRACT

Advances in technologies which has led to the use of Artificial Intelligence have further caused disruptions in learning processes and learning outputs. A process that is in with the expectations of the fourth industrial revolution. While learners with disabilities are not expected to be left behind the in use of technology for educational and psychosocial wellbeing, there is currently existing efforts globally to infuse the AI in the teaching learners with special needs in inclusive schools. However, while such efforts seem promising, teachers of such learners may lag in the technical capability required to fully deploy AI for inclusive pedagogies. Therefore, based on the assumption of the social learning theory (Bandura, 1969), this chapter advance the need for training of relevant teachers in inclusive education in the use of Artificial Intelligence for inclusive teaching in schools. We provided a process model for adoption by trainers that will aid the training of inclusive education teachers in the adoption and use of AI or inclusive pedagogies in inclusive schools.

INTRODUCTION

The last three decades have witnessed ever increasing changes in the educational sector. Such changes have been informed by educational designs, curricula, pedagogy, and assessment processes in a manner that aims to positively influence teaching and learning activities. Interestingly, dynamics brought by the various modification in education have always led to ever increasing debates for or against various policies and implementation processes. Until now, among various and relevant stakeholders such as teachers, policy makers, policy implementers, school administrators and even parents and students alike, such debates within educational sector continues unabated. There is no doubt that such ever evolving education debates have favored development of workable pedagogical strategies and curricula that are informed by the needs of the society which is geared toward the holistic development of learners in general. While learners are at the center of all educational policies, learners with special educational needs also remain a critical point of reference in all decisions made in favour of education across the globe (Adigun, 2021). As noted by Adigun and Mngomezulu (2021) learners with special educational needs are a heterogenous group of individuals who require additional educational and behavioral supports to optimize learning opportunities and outcomes. The group of learners with special educational needs therefore include those with Autism, intellectual disabilities, learning disabilities, those who are deaf and/or hard of hearing, with visual impairments, orthopaedically disabilities, behaviour disorders and those identified as having attention deficit hyperactivity disorders (ADHD) as well as learners who are identified as gifted or talented among others.

Interestingly, learners with special educational needs have over the years benefited from various forms of educational provisions ranging from segregation, mainstreaming integration, and recently inclusive education (Adigun, 2021; Chitiyo et al., 2019; Eichinger & Woltman, 1993; Frattura & Capper, 2006; Osisanya et al., 2015; Pather, 2014). Within the last decade, academic and discourses in the education of learners with special needs have favoured inclusive education. Inclusive education is therefore conceptualised as an educational approach that places value on full participation of all learners regardless of disability in educational processes without discrimination. Adigun (2021) remarked that opportunities presented by inclusion offer great opportunity for learners with disabilities and other barriers to learning, to learn in the same room with peers without any form of disabilities or barriers. In other words, the idea of inclusion or inclusive education is to provide education in a manner devoid of marginalization and discrimination. Studies have affirmed that inclusion as a concept and educational approach is based on the need to ensure epistemic equity, human rights and social justice emerged from larger movement that emanated from the Salamanca Framework for Action (Adaka et al., 2022; Adigun, 2021; Ajuwon, 2008; Hamid et al., 2015; Lindner & Schwab, 2020; Lindsay, 2003; United Nations, 2008). Thus, inclusive education as an education approach extends beyond provision of platform for knowledge creation but also entrenching platforms that provides avenue of combating and elimination of negative attitude towards persons with disabilities while creating a responsive and welcoming communities in support of equal opportunity and education for all.

In 2006, Ainscow, Booth, and Dyson regarded inclusion as a philosophy based on principled educational approaches which have students and teachers as the main stakeholders. Basically, Ainscow et al. (2006) stated that inclusive education is predicated on presence of all stakeholders having substantial participation in the inclusive education process leading to educational and social achievement of learners with special educational needs. While Ainscow et al. (2006) believed that inclusive education is an effective approach to combat discrimination, the research also note that inclusive education has the potential to improve teaching and learning efficiencies and it could be cost-effectiveness. In their view of inclusive education as (i) a concept, and (ii) an approach, Ainscow et al. (2006) further summarized the global view of inclusive education into six which are:

- Inclusion as concerned with disability and 'special educational needs',
- Inclusion as a response to disciplinary exclusions,
- Inclusion as about all groups vulnerable to exclusion.
- Inclusion as the promotion of the school for all,

- Inclusion as 'Education for All', and
- Inclusion as a principled approach to education and society.

Regardless of how inclusive education is conceptualized, inclusive education remained a concept that has ushered in pedagogical dynamism which have influence and shaped not only the approach to which educational provision and assessment of knowledge gained among learners. But also, community engagements, human right and social justice systems. Interestingly, pedagogical dynamics is largely influenced by the introduction and application of technology in all spheres of teaching and learning processes without an exception of inclusive education program. Furthermore, whereas interventions and support programmes to support learners with special needs and barriers to learning were mostly manual and delivered within physical spaces, the last few years ushered the use of Artificial Intelligence tools, some which can be used in virtual spaces. While more of the existing studies on inclusive education that focused on learners and technology has permeated all educational provisions, the need to enhance teachers' capacity to deploy technology in inclusive teaching then become paramount if the goal of inclusive education will be achieved in this present day and time. Thus, in this chapter we established the need for training and re-training of teachers in the application of advanced technology for teaching of all learners in the inclusive classroom. Therefore, this chapter which adopted critical review of literature as a methodology also adopted the social learning theory (Bandura, 1969) as a theoretical less to carefully argue for the need to understand the basic requirement need in training the teachers who are critical stakeholders in inclusive teaching on the application or deployment of emerging and advanced technologies for inclusive teaching.

INCLUSIVE EDUCATION AND TECHNOLOGY

Prior to the inclusive education crusade, persons with disabilities such as Alexander Graham Bell (1847-1922) and Louis Braille (1809-1852) amongst others have been at the forefront championing the advancement of technology that can assist them in their quest to adjust and adapt to their environment and at the same time function with appropriately. In the recent time, there have been reported a significant advancement in development and use of assistive technological devices among the teeming population of persons with disabilities (Adigun & Nzima, 2021; Ahmad, 2015; Kaelin et al. 2021). Assistive technologies (AT) that have helped to advance adaptation of individuals with disabilities is a term that is broadly used to describe any adaptive, assistive or rehabilitative technologically enabled devices that can be used to compensate for the loss of the function of body or sense organs. In other words, AT devices which can be either low-tech or high-tech devices provide support for the functionality of impaired or lost body organ (Ahmad, 2015; Goodley et al., 2020; Reed & Bowser, 2005). Low-tech assistive technology includes devices such as crutches, grip pen, hearing aids, large print books, magnifying glasses, talking calculators, wheelchair ramps while high-tech assistive devices are computer aided information technological devices such as alternative keyboards and mouse, Augmentative and alternative communication (AAC) devices, eye-tracking systems, power wheelchairs, screen readers, speech-to-text word recognition tools, touch control devices, voice recognition software, website accessibility overlays or plugins and word prediction programs among others.

No doubt, AT devices have offered excellent support for persons with disabilities. In fact, the use of assistive technology has not only aided teaching and learning processes, but it has positive impact on the holistic wellbeing of persons with disabilities and barriers to learning (Adigun & Nzima, 2021). Based on the long existing potentials and benefits of AT, inclusive education crusaders have consistently advocated for the application of assistive technologies for inclusive teaching. Interestingly, such calls have yielded more concerns among various stakeholders in the education of learners with disabilities and barriers to learning. Assistive technology serves to alleviate and at times eliminate potential educational barriers faced by students with disabilities in the inclusive classroom by offering practical tools that provide a level playing educational ground for all learners regardless of their cognitive, behavioural and affective capacities (Ahmad, 2015; McNicholl et al., 2021; Svensson et al., 2021). In other words, AT provides and expansive opportunities for positive interaction with learning materials thereby making education more accessible to all learners in different format. Accordingly, Atanga et al. (2020) and Svensson et al. (2021) posit that integration of AT in inclusive classroom provide students who requires additional support the various opportunity and or mean of task completion with a higher level of independence.

Specifically, AT does not only build bridges to match learning potentials between students who requires additional learning support and their peers without special educational needs, AT provide students with disabilities full access and participation in all classroom activities thereby enhancing unhindered independent and collaborative academic and social engagements leading to improved attention, behavioral and communicative potential (Atanga et al., 2020; Bong & Chen, 2024; World Health Organization & United Nations Children's Fund, 2022). On the other hand, despite the recorded potentials and benefits of AT, the application and usage of AT in inclusive education is faced with some challenges. As stated by Ahmed (2018), the usage of AT in the inclusive classroom have been a controversial issue largely because of people's disposition to was students' use of AT in the classroom. Issues of negative attitudes towards students with disabilities within the inclusive classroom (Gallego-Ortega & Rodríguez-Fuentes, 2021; Osisanya et al., 2015; Vaz et al., 2015) also extend to the use of AT for teaching and learning processes (Ahmad, 2015; Ahmed, 2018). Such negative dispositions towards the use of AT by students with disabilities are evident in fear from the unknown among teachers and non-disabled peers, isolation as experienced by students with disabilities, labelling, misconceptions associated with the use of AT in the classrooms, misunderstanding the rights and opportunities of students with disabilities which may lead to the further resistance and stereotypes (Ahmad, 2015; Osisanya et al., 2015).

It is important to note that teachers are at the center of AT usage for pedagogical instruction. In other words, teacher in the inclusive classrooms have a very critical role to play in supporting the seamless deployment and use of AT to promote the objective of inclusion. Regrettably, some research evidence has shown that teachers themselves have been found to serve as an obstacle to the use of AT within the in the inclusive education spaces (Ahmed, 2018; Atanga et al., 2020). Ahmed (2018) asserts that teacher's attitude towards technology and or their capacity to use/operate/manipulate AT are some of the factors that influence AT use among students with disabilities for classroom instructions. Thus, teachers may prevent 'students' from its usage thereby creating a barrier. Some studies revealed that teachers' inflexibility with required assistive and or instructional technologies remain a grave concern in the application of technology in the classrooms (Adigun & Nzima, 2021; Atanga et al., 2020; Mohamed, 2018). Other studies also report that teachers' preparedness and attitude towards the use of computer technologies predicts and confirmed teachers' use of AT in inclusive education (Maphalala & Adigun, 2021; Ok & Rao, 2019).

Apparently, over and above attitude towards adaptive technologies in the inclusive classroom, teachers' difficulties with the use and application of technology in the inclusive classroom have largely been influenced by lack of required technical assistance and inadequate training (Atanga et al., 2020; Maphalala & Adigun, 2021; Mohamed, 2018). Thus, lack of institutional commitment to prepare and train teachers in the use of adaptive technologies for teaching have significantly contributed to the draw back in the educational engagement and achievement of students within the inclusive education spaces. Such lapses have in no small measure contributed to significant delay in academic achievement of students with disabilities. Lamentably, teachers' incapacity to holistically deploy AT and other associated education technologies for use in the inclusive classrooms have resulted to the observed inadequacies in not only educational assessment and planning processes (Lin & Lin, 2019; Oyewumi & Adigun, 2013) but also resulted in difficulties in the procurement and management of relevant AT and other educational technologies such as artificial intelligence which have been found useful for students in the inclusive classroom.

ARTIFICIAL INTELLIGENCE (AI), INCLUSIVE EDUCATION AND TEACHERS FOR INCLUSIVE PEDAGOGIES

Apparently, emerging technologies in the last decade have been massive. Specifically, in line with the discourse on fourth industrial revolution (Industrie 4.0) as advanced by Schwab (2017). Currently, technological revolution is driven by Artificial Intelligence (AI). Hence, Lametti (2022) regarded artificial intelligence (AI) as computer enabled applications that mirror logical human cognition. AI are artificial systems, that is, machines design to learn and respond to stimuli. The foregoing implies that AI is a disruptive technology developed with the capability of logical reasoning to take definite actions that can increase possibilities of success and work efficiencies. AI can therefore be software or computer programs with 'intellectual' capacity (e.g. ChatGPT) and or in physical form such as humanoid robots. Existing studies have shown the capacities of AI for automate processes enhance efficiencies and effort performances (Lametti, 2022; Marino et al., 2023). While AI has been adjured as complex system capable of adapting, analysing, learning, and synthesizing interacting human actions and reactions, AI have therefore become embedded in educational processes (Hopcan et al., 2023; Marino et al., 2023). Specifically, Marino et al. (2023) noted that AI can not only increase pedagogical efficacy but the application of AI in education can be used to personalized learning and learning experiences. Importantly, AI can assist teachers with the tailored instructional designs which can further increase interactive learning experiences.

Interestingly, the impact of AI in educational instruction have crept into the education of learners with special needs (Athanasios & Ioannidou, 2012; Hopcan et al., 2023; Marino et al., 2023; Şen & Akbay, 2023). For instance, Marino et al. (2023) aver that being a disruptive technology, AI have significantly changed the dynamics of special education practices and its pedagogical deliverables. Based on existing benefits of AI associated to education, studies have affirmed the benefits presented by AI to the psychosocial wellbeing and cognitive nurturing of students with special needs (Fernandez-Batanero et al., 2022; Şen & Akbay, 2023). Thus, it is undeniable that AI have greater potential to impact inclusive pedagogy. For instance, the application of AI has not only supported diagnosis and intervention processes needed by students with disabilities (Drigas & Ioannidou, 2013) for use among students with special needs have been found with language translation, writing, and text analysis. (Chan, 2022; Evmenova & Regan, 2019; Ok et al., 2022). Further, AI have been found to benefit reading culture of dyslexic learners and those learners with intellectual disabilities (See: Bhatti et al., 2024; Kharbat et al., 2021). In developed economies such as the United Kingdom, the Unites States of America and Canada, in the quest to enhance inclusive pedagogies, AI have been effectively deployed to assist learners with hearing and visual impairment (Chen et al., 2022; Lesica et al., 2021; Morrison et al., 2017; Raji et al., 2024).

The application of AI for inclusive teaching particularly in the United States have further reinforced the goals and objectives of the No Child Left Behind (NCLB) Act of 2002 (Jewell, 2008) and various inclusive education policies across the globe. It is interesting to note that while developed economies have actively leveraged on application of AI to advance inclusive pedagogies and learning outcome of learners with special needs, the application of such advance technologies for use in various inclusive schools particularly within the Sub-Sahara Africa is yet to be achieved. Studies have identified that several Sub-Sahara African nations have initiated or adopted a national policy for the infusion of technology in all educational levels (Agyei, 2021; Jhurree, 2005; Maphalala & Adigun, 2021). For instance, in 2020, the Government of Namibia in her Basic Education Act of 2020 made several provisions for the use of technology and assistive technologies (AT) for use by learners with special needs in various special/inclusive schools in Namibia. In similar vein, Carrim and Bekker (2022) aver that the government of South Africa were also keen about the adoption and use of technologies for overall development of inclusive pedagogies in the country. It is, therefore, worthy of note that the conversation about the infusion of technologies and or AT for inclusive pedagogies is not limited to Namibia nor South Africa but such discourse is available in all African nations. However, such discussion or full deployment of technologies for inclusive teaching have been enveloped by various challenges which include but not limited to issues of equal opportunities to access relevant technologies for inclusive pedagogies (Adigun et al., 2022).

There is no gainsaying in the fact that various African government have developed national and regional policies to drive technology for education. Unfortunately, such lofty efforts are mitigated by such challenges as espoused in the study of Maphalala and Adigun (2021) as well as Adigun et al. (2023). Above all, Adigun et al. (2023) identified the capacity of teachers of learners with special educational needs as a major challenge that negatively impact the full adoption and application of technology in the inclusive classroom. While the studies of It is very unfortunate that teachers across various special/inclusive schools lack adequate technical training and prowess to apply or teach learners with special need via technologically enabled devices. Aiyeleso (2016), Cagıltay et al. (2019) and Siyam (2019) reported teachers, agreement with the advantages of using technology for pedagogical instruction within the inclusive classroom, their studies further documented lack of technical know-how as well as lack of required training as factors that have prevented the full integration of technology for inclusive teaching. In this current time, it even with the influx of AI for pedagogical instruction at all levels of education and even with the increasing commitment of national and international agencies, the crusade, and the call for holistically application of technology (AI) in education have increased more than before. Hence, emerging teachers and those currently in service of teaching across Africa would be compelled to engaged learners with relevant AI enabled technologies. Thus, the foregoing therefore stress the need for training and re-training of in-service teachers in special school to increase their technological self-awareness, technical self-efficacies for inclusive pedagogies. While AI tools promise access to areas that were otherwise to accessible to all, there are limitations such as internet poverty in certain areas that reproduce exclusion. The expansion of internet infrastructure in remote areas is worth investing in to avoid the reproduction of inequalities and inequities for learners with special educational needs and their teachers and families.

TRAINING AND RE-TRAINING OF IN-SERVICE TEACHERS THOUGH THE LENS OF THE SOCIAL LEARNING THEORY

This chapter is conceptualised based on the principles of the Social Learning Theory (SLT) of Bandura (1969, 1977). While learning has can be referred to a phenomenon that is used to describe any relative permanent change in behaviour that arises because of practice or experience, the SLT further gives support to the description of learning because change in human behaviour based on experience gathered through interaction with their social environment. The SLT as advanced by Bandura (1977) stressed the interaction between environment, attitude, behavioural and cognitive dynamics. In other words, SLT believes that individuals, in this instance, the teachers in inclusive schools may develop positive attitude, value, and have positive dispositions towards engagements with advanced technologies that promised to foster seamless inclusive teaching and learning processes. Thus, SLT remain an important theoretical lens for understanding new behaviours that is capable of revolutionizing organizational change and optimize output (Thacker, 2017). According to Thacker (2017), SLT is guided by three principles which are:

1. Live model: Where an instructor (trainer) demonstrates the desired behaviour for knowledge construction.
2. Verbal instruction: Where an instructor (trainer) describes the desired behaviour in detail and instructs the participant in how to engage the environment (AI and or computer adaptive technologies) for a change in behaviour.
3. Symbolic: Which describes modelling of behaviour through real or fictional characters.

Based on the forging, Thacker (2017) opined that a critical component of the SLT is premised on emphasis on reciprocal determinism which implies that technical behaviour of teachers of learners with special needs in inclusive schools may be influenced by the environment and characteristics of available computer adaptive technologies. In other words, a teacher's behaviour, their technical environment, and personal qualities all reciprocally influence each other to propagate application of AI for inclusive pedagogies. Bandura (1977) thus proposed that the modelling process for behavioural change should involve attention, retention, reproduction, and motivation. In line with the modelling process, it is the view of the authors of this chapter that in-service teachers disposition towards positive change and desire to adopt and apply AI technologies in inclusive classroom can be reviewed through training and re-training processes. However, such training and re-training programs should be carefully organized and implemented.

TRAINERS AND TRAINEES (TEACHERS): TOWARDS THE APPLICATION OF ARTIFICIAL INTELLIGENCE FOR INCLUSIVE PEDAGOGIES

Teaching is a profession that comes with ones' ability to multitask. Teaching is not just about providing learning with new knowledge but requires intensive preparation to deliver 40 minutes lesson. In addition, teachers need to even follow-up learners to further ensure that such learners understood what they have learnt and how they could apply such knowledge. The foregoing processes is more complex when teaching learners with special educational needs within the inclusive classroom. It is on record that teachers of learners with special needs are faced with more workload, pressures arising from teaching, parents, and school administration (Adigun & Mngomezulu, 2022; Antoniou et al., 2020; Herrington & Summers, 2014; Kuvaeva, 2018). In recent time, particularly with the call to holistically infuse technology in academic activities and the influx of AI in special/inclusive education, there seem to be more pressure on in-service teachers. It is presumed that such pressure may generate more anxiety among long term in-service teachers who are less informed about the use of technology. On the other hand, novice teachers may as well be caught in the web of generated anxieties associated with the application of AI for inclusive pedagogies. Thus, our chapter further reinforce the need to train and re-train teachers for the application of AI and other associated technologies for inclusive teaching.

Adigun et al. (2023) in their study titled "Covid-19 and learners with disabilities: towards divergent praxis in teacher preparation for equity and epistemic justice" advance a process model for adoption for to enhance digital teaching among special needs/inclusive education teacher in training. However, while the process model was suited to pre-service teachers in training, this current chapter have further extended and adapted the process model of Adigun et al. (2023) to enhance the application and use of AI for inclusive teaching among in-service teachers.

Figure 1. Extended process model (Adigun et al., 2023) for AI application for inclusive pedagogy

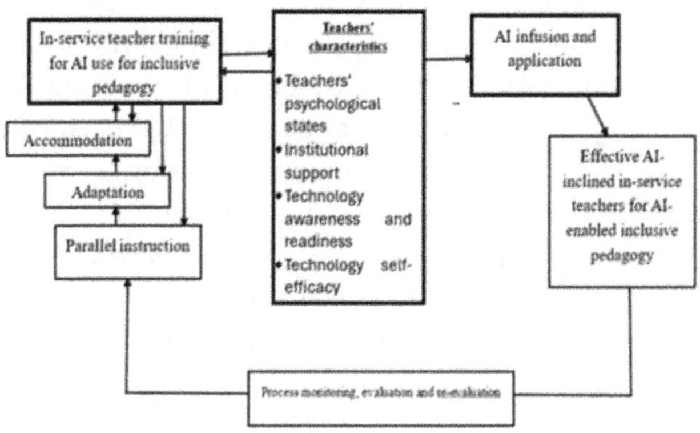

While psychological aspect of the process model advanced in the study of Adigun et al. (2023) was keen about the morale of pre-service teachers, the import of the extension the process model is for trainers of in-service teachers in the application of AI for inclusive pedagogies to focus more on psychological factors that could favour the confidence of in-service teachers to apply AI in their inclusive classrooms. Thus, based on Fig. 1, our position in this chapter is based on the fact that while training of in-service teachers is inevitable in the holistic achievement of stakeholders ideal about AI in Education for All, it is imperative for 'AI in Education' train to develop training packages that is in line with the ideology of *accommodation, adaptation and parallel curriculum*.

In this chapter, we (Authors) have conceptualized the term *accommodation* with regards to training of in-service teachers as a deliberate attempt by AI trainers to make necessary alteration to not only the approach/format to the training manual/guide but also to the environment and equipment in a manner that in-service teachers who are under training can have in-depth access to relevant AI-enabled contents that will fortified them to initiate and assist students with disabilities to understand and complete their academic task. The need for advancing accommodation for in-service teachers who are being trained with the use of AI for inclusive pedagogy is because being a teacher does not preclude them for having disabilities themselves. The need for accommodation in such training is basically to ensure that all in-service teacher trainees are provided with equal and even opportunities to achieve advance knowledge in the use of AI in inclusive classrooms. Accommodation in such training can be instructional and assessment in form. By instructional accommodation, we are proposing changes where necessary in pedagogical techniques informed by relatable instructional (audiovisual) materials. Such effort will significantly enhance concentration, motivate interest, learning and retention of knowledge gained by the trainees. Essentially instructional accommodation may involve the service of sign language interpreters, the use of text-to-speech/speech-to-text, extended time, and opportunities for trainees with limitation of fine motor skills among others. Also, while such training should not go without assessment of knowledge gain, assessment procedures should be given in formats that best suite the need of each trainee. It should be noted that assessment accommodation only informs test format and not to waterdown the test content or difficulty index. Examples of assessment accommodation includes but not limited to having the test being read out aloud, assessment through group tests, provision of extended test-taken time among other formats.

We advocate for adaptation in AI intensive training for in-service teachers who are willing to adopt and use AI for inclusive pedagogy. Adaptation in inclusive classroom is a broad concept that informs the change to instructions and or adjusting some environmental criteria to meet learners needs (Finnerty et al., 2019; Mishra et al. 2019). The practice and use of adaptation in inclusive education is widely accepted due to the diversity in the inclusive classrooms. Over the years, the use of adaption has fostered enhance academic participation social interaction, and independence among learners. Therefore, while it is expected that such AI for inclusive education training of in-service teachers is to serve diverse array of teachers, trainers should ensure adequate adaptation of the training environment. Therefore, trainers should limit potential distraction or distractive activities, and usage of simulation activities that can stimulate attention of trainees with learning disabilities, ensuring appropriate illumination of training room and provision of appropriate fine-motor activities or equipment for trainer identified with gross and fine motor impairment. In addition, alternative seating arrangement in response to the need of each training participants should be ensured.

While it is necessary an important for facilitators and trainers to ensure accommodation and adaption when training in-service teachers on the application of AI for inclusive pedagogy, we (Authors) as well advance in this chapter the need to ensure the use of parallel instruction (See: Fig. 1). Parallel instruction is an instructional strategy that provides facilitators with the opportunities to present the same curriculum or training packages to learners in a stratified manner to ascertain knowledge gained among learners. According to Nettleton et al. (2023) as well as Tomlinson (2023), through parallel instructional approach, divides of learners in to two heterogenous groups affords instructors to teach the same content/material using different approaches. While Tomlinson (2023) posit that parallel instruction is beneficial by reducing students-facilitator/teacher/trainer ratio, Nettleton et al. (2023) believed that parallel instruction is ideal for use particularly when the facilitators/trainers have a great deal of information to cover. Thus, Nettleton et al. (2023) posited that such use of parallel instruction is a key feature for diffusion of ideas among learners which give ample opportunities for students/learners to share ideas within and among themselves. Hence, in line with the submissions of Nettleton et al. (2023) and Tomlinson (2023), it is our believe that while all teachers of learners in inclusive schools need to be equipped with required skills needed for the applications of AI for inclusive pedagogy, the need to apply parallel instruction would be beneficial to the training when initiated. In recent time, extensive research on the effects of parallel instructions have been established with positive findings (See: Kaplan et al., 2009; McKay, 2018).

Further, as shown in Fig. 1, this chapter places emphasis on the need to consider the psychological characteristics of in-service teachers in training. It should be noted that teaching is an act and a profession which is a highly emotional ladened profession which mostly affect the psychological wellness of teachers (Adigun et al., 2021; Olagunju et al., 2021). Often, teaching learners with special educational needs more strenuous that teaching learners who are not diagnosed with special needs. Additionally, teaching in special/inclusive classrooms are associated with excessive emotional involvement of teachers due to the nature and requirements of their learners. Thus, teachers of learners with special educational needs are therefore noted to have excessive workload which is linked to psycho-physiological characteristic of learners with special educational needs and complications arising from parents' expectation of fast and visible results in behavioural and educational attainments of their children with special needs (Adigun & Mngomezulu, 2021; Antoniou et al., 2020). Additionally, lack of institutional support and unwholesome attitude towards teachers of learners with special educational needs remain a threat to positive emotional wellbeing and a factor that heightened traumatic experiences for such teachers (Adigun & Mngomezulu, 2021; Kuvaeva, 2018). Based on the foregoing, it is quite unfortunate that teachers in inclusive classroom have been found to exhibit elevated level of apprehension, anxiety, burnout, emotional exhaustion, and depersonalisation.

It is important to note that institutional support is crucial to the holistic wellbeing of teachers in inclusive schools, however, existing studies have shown that teachers in such schools have limited support systems, and they are less motivated with meagre salaries (Murphy et al., 2021; Muhati-Nyakundi, 2023; Yasmeen et al., 2019). Regrettably, observed teacher absenteeism and attrition rate in special/inclusive schools may be connected to the observation of Murphy et al. (2021), Muhati-Nyakundi (2023), and Yasmeen et al. (2019) respective. Thus, it is our submission to trainers of AI should understand the psychology of the trainees, (that is, inclusive education teachers who are being trained on the application of AI for inclusive pedagogy) are individuals who may be emotionally laden with limited or no motivation to pass through the rigours of learning new concepts or skills. In fact, it should be noted that emotional outburst among such teachers may be easily triggered. Therefore, trainers should carefully and respectfully walk the trainees through the expected process of AI adoption and use for successful integration of AI for inclusive pedagogies. Trainers must therefore careful present new ideas to the trainees. The training should be responsive. Meaning that there must be an unending interaction between the trainers and trainees. The trainers should note that technological/technical competencies of the in-service teachers may be lower than expectation. Therefore, the presentation of related AI contents or information should be presented from the point of 'known concepts' to 'unknown concepts.

Importantly, trainers should note the psychological variations and complexities associated with teachers' readiness for the uptake and usage of the AI products for inclusive teaching. Although, variation exist in literatures on teachers' readiness for application of technological products for teaching (Howard et al, 2021; Scherer et al., 2021; Warden et al., 2022). For instance, while Somekh (2008) as well as Kumar and Chand (2019) affirmed that teachers' beliefs and perceptions is one of the personal and psychological variance that influence holistic adoption of technology for pedagogical activities, other studies particularly pointed to factors such as teacher' attitude, prior experience, ease of use and intention as determinant factors that influence technological application in teaching practices (Baek et al., 2017; Kumar & Chand 2019; Røkenes & Krumsvik, 2016). Similarly, perceived, or potential subject matter or approaches towards knowledge dissemination was found by Hennessy et al. (2007) to influence teachers' readiness to use technology in their classrooms. Other studies posit that of psychological resiliency (Friborg et al., 2005), digital competence (Pettersson, 2018), cultural differences (Huang et al., 2019; Seufert et al., 2021) as well as gender differences (Bolliger et al., 2019; Martin et al., 2019) among other have capacities to motivate teachers' readiness for the adoption and use of technologies for teaching and learning purposes. Therefore, it is important for trainers to know and acknowledge the diversities of the trainee. Hence, trainers need to ensure all trainees are comprehensively accommodated.

In view of the future and current realities based on the fourth industrial revolution (Adigun & Nzima, 2021; Schwab, 2017), it is the belief of the authors of this chapter that when the trainers adopted the process model advance in this intellectual piece, there would be a large pool of teachers of learners with special educational needs who are not only technologically ready but also a large pool of AI- inclined in-service teachers for AI-enabled inclusive pedagogy. Thereby, the goal of government agencies to improve the educational attainment of students will be achieved in line with the aims of the United Nations Sustainable Development

Goal 4 which seek to "ensure inclusive and equitable quality education and promote lifelong learning opportunities for all" and to "substantially increase the number of youth and adults with relevant skills, including technical and vocational skills, for employment, decent jobs and entrepreneurship".

Lastly, while this chapter advances the process model for adoption in the training and re-training of teachers for inclusive pedagogy, it is important for relevant stakeholders to note that the model advanced in this chapter is not holistic and may be implemented with caution based on prevailing circumstances. Therefore, the model advance in this chapter (See Fig 1) provides opportunity for process monitoring, evaluation, and re-evaluation of the model. It is should be on record that the process monitoring, evaluation and re-evaluation of the model is needed to ascertain how well the model have been able to assist in the achievement of well trained teachers for the application of AI for inclusive pedagogies. Therefore, there may be need for evaluation and re-evaluation of the model within three to five years after implementation of the model. Doing an evaluation and re-evaluation of the model will reveal the strength, weakness, opportunities, and threats of the model vis-à-vis application of AI for inclusive pedagogies.

IMPLICATIONS FOR PRINCIPLES, POLICIES, AND PRACTICE

Inclusive education is more than just a philosophy but an educational practice that expands educational opportunities for all regardless of abilities or incapacities. Interestingly, inclusive education also extends the role or the involvement of all relevant stakeholders because the practice of inclusive education demands more responsibilities from not only specially trained teachers but requires more funding and government intervention. Therefore, the ever-evolving developments in technologies which has brought about AI has place more responsibilities on the government in respect to the achievement of 'Education for All' and the race towards achieving the Sustainable Development Goals. While there is currently technological destruction even in the educational sector, there is therefore the need to ensure that even teachers of students with special educational needs are not left behind. In other words, school administrators and relevant non-governmental agencies should work together to constantly pressure the government to ensure that teachers in special/inclusive schools are regular trained and equipped with knowledge that will foster the application and use of advanced educational technologies for inclusive teaching. Essentially, such effort should be supported by institutional policies that will guide the infusion of technologies in inclusive schools and continuous training of teachers in such schools. It is our belief that such effort is not to benefit the teachers but to also advance technical skills among students with disabilities. Development of relevant technical skills by students with disabilities will enhance independent living and functional potential in the technologically driven society. Above all, we (Authors) advocate for a think-tank research group that will constantly conduct research on issues of AI and inclusive teaching. Such research group will be able to provide evidence-based advice that will inform policy formulation, development and implementation processes that will further drive positive development of AI for inclusive pedagogies.

CONCLUSION

This chapter provided a conceptual information on the issues that involve the training of teachers towards the application of Artificial Intelligence (AI) for inclusive education. The intellectual piece provided and exposé of inclusive education and the connections between inclusive education and technology. The chapter appreciated the advancement in technology and how such can be of benefit for inclusive pedagogy based on teachers' advanced technical capacities. Above all, the chapter based on the process model provided templates and factors to be considered by trainer of teachers of students with special educational needs in the bid to provide the teachers with advanced knowledge in the application of AI for inclusive pedagogies. The chapter finally brought to the fore, implication of the authors' positions for principles, policies, and practices.

REFERENCES

Adaka, T. A., Adigun, O. T., Lalu, J., & Mngomezulu, T. P. (2022). Effect of mentorship on regular teachers' self-efficacy towards implementation of inclusive education at basic education level. *Special Education and Rehabilitation*, *21*(4), 233–253.

Adigun, O. T. (2021). Inclusive education among pre-service teachers from Nigeria and South Africa: A comparative cross-sectional study. *Cogent Education*, *8*(1), 1930491.

Adigun, O. T., & Mngomezulu, T. P. (2022). Occupational stress among teachers of learners with special needs. *Journal of Community Psychology*, *50*(2), 1185–1197.

Adigun, O. T., & Nzima, D. R. (2021). The fourth industrial revolution and persons with disabilities: Peeping into the future through the lens of the present. *Multicultural Education*, *7*(7), 113–118.

Adigun, O. T., Nzima, D. R., Maphalala, M. C., & Ndwandwe, N. D. (2022). COVID-19 and learners with disabilities: Towards divergent praxis in teacher preparation for equity and epistemic justice. *South African Journal of Higher Education*, *36*(4), 225–242.

Adigun, O. T., Vivekanantharasa, R., & Obosu, G. K. (2021). The Deaf or Hard of hearing population's attitude and information seeking behaviour towards COVID-19 in South Africa. *Journal of Human Ecology (Delhi, India)*, *75*(1-3), 16–26.

Agyei, D. D. (2021). Integrating ICT into schools in Sub-Saharan Africa: From teachers' capacity building to classroom implementation. *Education and Information Technologies*, *26*(1), 125–144.

Ahmad, F. K. (2015). Use of assistive technology in inclusive education: Making room for diverse learning needs. *Transcience*, *6*(2), 62–77.

Ahmed, A. (2018). Perceptions of using assistive technology for students with disabilities in the classroom. *International Journal of Special Education*, *33*(1), 129–139.

Ainscow, M., Booth, T., & Dyson, A. (2006). Inclusion and the standards agenda: Negotiating policy pressures in England. *International Journal of Inclusive Education*, *10*(4-5), 295–308.

Aiyeleso, M. M. (2016). The ideal special education teacher in Nigeria. *Asia Pacific Journal of Education, Arts and Sciences*, *3*(3), 1–5.

Ajuwon, P. M. (2008). Inclusive education for students with disabilities in Nigeria: Benefits, challenges and policy implications. *International Journal of Special Education, 23*(3), 11–16.

Antoniou, A. S., Efthymiou, V., Polychroni, F., & Kofa, O. (2020). Occupational stress in mainstream and special needs primary school teachers and its relationship with self-efficacy. *Educational Studies*, •••, 1–18.

Atanga, C., Jones, B. A., Krueger, L. E., & Lu, S. (2020). Teachers of students with learning disabilities: Assistive technology knowledge, perceptions, interests, and barriers. *Journal of Special Education Technology, 35*(4), 236–248.

Athanasios, S., & Ioannidou, R. (2012). Artificial Intelligence in Special Education: A decade review. *International Journal of Engineering Education, 28*(6), 1366–1372.

Baek, Y., Zhang, H., & Yun, S. (2017). Teachers' attitudes toward mobile learning in Korea. *The Turkish Online Journal of Educational Technology, 16*(1), 154–163.

Bandura, A. (1969). Social-learning theory of identificatory processes. *Handbook of socialization theory and research, 213*, 262.

Bandura, A. (1977). Self-efficacy: Toward a unifying theory of behavioral change. *Psychological Review, 84*(2), 191–215.

Bhatti, I., Mohi-U-din, S. F., Hayat, Y., & Tariq, M. (2024). Artificial Intelligence Applications for Students with Learning Disabilities: A Systematic Review. *European Journal of Science. Innovation and Technology, 4*(2), 40–56.

Bolliger, D. U., Shepherd, C. E., & Bryant, H. V. (2019). Faculty members' perceptions of online program community and their efforts to sustain it. *British Journal of Educational Technology, 50*(6), 3283–3299.

Bong, W. K., & Chen, W. (2024). Increasing faculty's competence in digital accessibility for inclusive education: A systematic literature review. *International Journal of Inclusive Education, 28*(2), 197–213.

Cagıltay, K., Cakır, H., Karasu, N., Islım, O. F., & Cıcek, F. (2019). Use of educational technology in special education: Perceptions of teachers. *Participatory Educational Research, 6*(2), 189–205.

Carrim, N., & Bekker, T. (2022). Placing inclusive education in conversation with digital education. *South African Computer Journal = Suid-Afrikaanse Rekenaartydskrif, 34*(2), 18–34.

Chan, A. (2022). GPT-3 and InstructGPT: Technological dystopianism, utopianism, and "Contextual" perspectives in AI ethics and industry. *AI and Ethics, 3*, 1–12.

Chen, X., Zou, D., Xie, H., Cheng, G., & Liu, C. (2022). Two decades of artificial intelligence in education. *Journal of Educational Technology & Society, 25*(1), 28–47.

Chitiyo, M., Hughes, E. M., Chitiyo, G., Changara, D. M., Itimu-Phiri, A., Haihambo, C., & Dzenga, C. G. (2019). Exploring Teachers' Special and Inclusive Education Professional Development Needs in Malawi, Namibia, and Zimbabwe. *International Journal of Whole Schooling, 15*(1), 28–49.

Drigas, A. S., & Ioannidou, R. E. (2013). A review on artificial intelligence in special education. *Information Systems, E-learning, and Knowledge Management Research: 4th World Summit on the Knowledge Society, WSKS 2011, Mykonos, Greece, September 21-23, 2011. Revised Selected Papers 4*, 385-391.

Eichinger, J., & Woltman, S. (1993). Integration strategies for learners with severe multiple disabilities. *Teaching Exceptional Children, 26*(1), 18–21.

Evmenova, A. S., & Regan, K. (2019). Supporting the writing process with technology for students with disabilities. *Intervention in School and Clinic, 55*(2), 78–85.

Fernandez-Batanero, J. M., & Montenegro-Rueda, M., FernandezCerero, J., & Garcia-Martinez, I. (2022). Assistive technology for the inclusion of students with disabilities: A systematic review. *Educational Technology Research and Development, 70*(5), 1911–1930.

Finnerty, M. S., Jackson, L. B., & Ostergren, R. (2019). Adaptations in general education classrooms for students with severe disabilities: Access, progress assessment, and sustained use. *Research and Practice for Persons with Severe Disabilities : the Journal of TASH, 44*(2), 87–102.

Frattura, E., & Capper, C. A. (2006). Segregated programs versus integrated comprehensive service delivery for all learners: Assessing the differences. *Remedial and Special Education, 27*(6), 355–364.

Friborg, O., Barlaug, D., Martinussen, M., Rosenvinge, J. H., & Hjemdal, O. (2005). Resilience in relation to personality and intelligence. *International Journal of Methods in Psychiatric Research, 14*(1), 29–42.

Gallego-Ortega, J. L., & Rodríguez-Fuentes, A. (2021). Teaching attitudes towards students with disabilities. *Mathematics, 9*(14), 1637.

Goodley, D., Cameron, D., Liddiard, K., Parry, R., Runswick-Cole, K., Whitburn, B., & Wong, M. E. (2020). Rebooting inclusive education? New technologies and disabled people. *Canadian Journal of Disability Studies, 9*(5), 515–549.

Hamid, A. E., Alasmari, A., & Eldood, E. Y. (2015). Attitude of pre-service educators toward including children with special needs in general classes case study of Education Faculty–University of Jazan. KSA. *International Journal of Scientific Research in Science and Technology*, *1*(3), 140–145.

Hennessy, S., Wishart, J., Whitelock, D., Deaney, R., Brawn, R., & la Velle, L.. (2007). Pedagogical approaches for technology-integrated science teaching. *Computers & Education*, *48*(1), 137–152.

Herrington, C. D., & Summers, K. P. (2014). Global pressures on education research: Quality, utility, and infrastructure. *Asia Pacific Education Review*, *15*(3), 339–346.

Hopcan, S., Polat, E., Ozturk, M. E., & Ozturk, L. (2023). Artificial intelligence in special education: A systematic review. *Interactive Learning Environments*, *31*(10), 7335–7353.

Howard, S. K., Tondeur, J., Siddiq, F., & Scherer, R. (2021). Ready, set, go! Profiling teachers' readiness for online teaching in secondary education. *Technology, Pedagogy and Education*, *30*(1), 141–158.

Huang, F., Teo, T., Sánchez-Prieto, J. C., García-Peñalvo, F. J., & Olmos-Migueláñez, S. (2019). Cultural values and technology adoption: A model comparison with university teachers from China and Spain. *Computers & Education*, *133*, 69–81.

Jewell, M. E. (2008). No Child Left Behind: Implications for Special Education Students and Students with Limited English Proficiency. *Journal of the American Academy of Special Education Professionals*, *41*, 45.

Jhurree, V. (2005). Technology integration in education in developing countries: Guidelines to policy makers. *International Education Journal*, *6*(4), 467–483.

Kaelin, V. C., Valizadeh, M., Salgado, Z., Parde, N., & Khetani, M. A. (2021). Artificial intelligence in rehabilitation targeting the participation of children and youth with disabilities: Scoping review. *Journal of Medical Internet Research*, *23*(11), e25745.

Kaplan, S. N., Guzman, I., & Tomlinson, C. A. (Eds.). (2009). *Using the parallel curriculum model in urban settings, grades K-8*. Corwin Press.

Kharbat, F. F., Alshawabkeh, A., & Woolsey, M. L. (2021). Identifying gaps in using artificial intelligence to support students with intellectual disabilities from education and health perspectives. *Aslib Journal of Information Management*, *73*(1), 101–128.

Kumar, B. A., & Chand, S. S. (2019). Mobile learning adoption: A systematic review. *Education and Information Technologies*, *24*(1), 471–487.

Kuvaeva, I. (2018). Teachers of special schools: stressors and manifestations of occupational stress. In *The Fifth International Luria Memorial Congress «Lurian Approach in International Psychological Science».—Ekaterinburg, 2018* (pp. 515-521). Knowledge E.

Lametti, D. (2022, December 7). A.I. could be great for college essays. https://slate.com/technology/2022/12/chatgpt-college-essay-plagiarism.html

Lesica, N. A., Mehta, N., Manjaly, J. G., Deng, L., Wilson, B. S., & Zeng, F. G. (2021). Harnessing the power of artificial intelligence to transform hearing health-care and research. *Nature Machine Intelligence*, *3*(10), 840–849.

Lin, P. Y., & Lin, Y. C. (2019). Understanding how teachers practise inclusive classroom assessment. *Studies in Educational Evaluation*, *63*, 113–121.

Lindner, K. T., & Schwab, S. (2020). Differentiation and individualisation in inclusive education: A systematic review and narrative synthesis. *International Journal of Inclusive Education*, **•••**, 1–21.

Lindsay, G. (2003). Inclusive education: A critical perspective. *British Journal of Special Education*, *30*(1), 3–12.

Maphalala, M. C., & Adigun, O. T. (2021). COVID-19 and teacher preparation for learners with disabilities: The need for divergent praxis. *Psychology and Education*, *58*(5), 5228–5240.

Marino, M. T., Vasquez, E., Dieker, L., Basham, J., & Blackorby, J. (2023). The future of artificial intelligence in special education technology. *Journal of Special Education Technology*, *38*(3), 404–416.

Martin, F., Budhrani, K., & Wang, C. (2019). Examining faculty perception of their readiness to teach online. *Online Learning : the Official Journal of the Online Learning Consortium*, *23*(3), 97–119.

McKay, V. (2018). Introducing a parallel curriculum to enhance social and environmental awareness in South African school workbooks. *Balancing individualism and collectivism: Social and environmental justice*, 97-122.

McNicholl, A., Casey, H., Desmond, D., & Gallagher, P. (2021). The impact of assistive technology use for students with disabilities in higher education: A systematic review. *Disability and Rehabilitation. Assistive Technology*, *16*(2), 130–143.

Mishra, P. A., Hota, S., & Khamari, P. R. (2019). Curriculum adaptation in inclusive education. *International Journal of Applied Research*, *5*(8), 70–74.

Mohamed, A. H. H. (2018). Attitudes of special education teachers towards using technology in inclusive classrooms: A mixed-methods study. *Journal of Research in Special Educational Needs, 18*(4), 278–288.

Morrison, C., Cutrell, E., Dhareshwar, A., Doherty, K., Thieme, A., & Taylor, A. (2017, October). Imagining artificial intelligence applications with people with visual disabilities using tactile ideation. In *Proceedings of the 19th international acm sigaccess conference on computers and accessibility* (pp. 81-90).

Muhati-Nyakundi, L. I. (2023). Teachers' Agency and Wellbeing in Inclusive Education: Challenges and Opportunities. *Journal of Educational Studies, 2023*(si1), 365–379.

Murphy, T. R., Mannix-McNamara, P., Slattery, G., Masterson, M., O'Sullivan, M., & Corry, J. (2021). Teacher Well-being in an Inclusive Secondary School. *International Perspectives on Teacher Well-being and Diversity: Portals into Innovative Classroom Practice*, 145-162.

Nettleton, K. F., Kessinger, M. W., & Lennex, L. (2023). Engaging on Common Ground: Inclusion of the Gifted Student in the Classroom. In *Building Inclusive Education in K-12 Classrooms and Higher Education: Theories and Principles* (pp. 260-283). IGI Global.

Ok, M. W., & Rao, K. (2019). Digital tools for the inclusive classroom: Google chrome as assistive and instructional technology. *Journal of Special Education Technology, 34*(3), 204–211.

Ok, M. W., Rao, K., Pennington, J., & Ulloa, P. R. (2022). Speech recognition technology for writing: Usage patterns and perceptions of students with high incidence disabilities. *Journal of Special Education Technology, 37*(2), 191–202.

Olagunju, A. T., Akinola, M. A., Fadipe, B., Jagun, O. O., Olagunju, T. O., Akinola, O. O., & Chaimowitz, G. A. (2021). Psychosocial wellbeing of Nigerian teachers in special education schools. *Journal of Autism and Developmental Disorders, 51*, 1131–1141.

Osisanya, A., Oyewumi, A. M., & Adigun, O. T. (2015). Perception of parents of children with communication difficulties about inclusive education in Ibadan metropolis. *American Journal of Educational Research, 19*(1), 21–32.

Oyewumi, A. M., & Adigun, O. T. (2013). Modifying learning and assessment techniques of accommodate students with hearing impairment. *Nigeria Journal of Speech/Language-Hearing Disorder and Rehabilitation, 1*(1), 33-38.

Pather, S. (2014). Evidence on inclusion and support for learners with disabilities in mainstream schools in South Africa: Off the policy radar? In *Disability, Poverty and Education* (pp. 57-71). Routledge.

Pettersson, F. (2018). On the issues of digital competence in educational contexts–a review of literature. *Education and Information Technologies*, *23*(3), 1005–1021.

Raji, N. R., Kumar, R. M. S., & Biji, C. L. (2024). Explainable Machine Learning Prediction for the Academic Performance of Deaf Scholars. *IEEE Access : Practical Innovations, Open Solutions*, *12*, 23595–23612.

Reed, P., & Bowser, G. (2005). Assistive technologies and the IEP. In Edyburn, D., Higgins, K., Boone, R. (Eds.) *Handbook of Special Education Technology Research and Practice*. Knowledge by Design Inc. Whitefish bay.

Røkenes, F., & Krumsvik, R. (2016). Prepared to teach ESL with ECT? A study of digital competence inNorwegian teacher education. *Computers & Education*, *97*, 1–20.

Scherer, R., Howard, S. K., Tondeur, J., & Siddiq, F. (2021). Profiling teachers' readiness for online teaching and learning in higher education: Who's ready? *Computers in Human Behavior*, *118*, 106675.

Schwab, K. (2017). *The Fourth Industrial Revolution*. Crown Business.

Şen, N., & Akbay, T. (2023). Artificial intelligence and innovative applications in special education. *Instructional Technology and Lifelong Learning*, *4*(2), 176–199.

Seufert, S., Guggemos, J., & Sailer, M. (2021). Technology-related knowledge, skills, and attitudes of pre-and in-service teachers: The current situation and emerging trends. *Computers in Human Behavior*, *115*, 106552.

Siyam, N. (2019). Factors impacting special education teachers' acceptance and actual use of technology. *Education and Information Technologies*, *24*(3), 2035–2057.

Somekh, B. (2008). Factors affecting teachers' pedagogical adoption of ICT. In Voogt, J., & Knezek, G. (Eds.), *International handbook of information technology in primary and secondary education* (pp. 449–460). Springer.

Svensson, I., Nordström, T., Lindeblad, E., Gustafson, S., Björn, M., Sand, C., & Nilsson, S. (2021). Effects of assistive technology for students with reading and writing disabilities. *Disability and Rehabilitation. Assistive Technology*, *16*(2), 196–208.

Thacker, E. S. (2017). "PD is where teachers are learning!" high school social studies teachers formal and informal professional learning. *Journal of Social Studies Research*, *41*(1), 37–52.

Tomlinson, C. A. (2023). The parallel curriculum model: A design to develop potential & challenge high-ability learners. In *Systems and models for developing programs for the gifted and talented* (pp. 571–598). Routledge.

United Nations. (2008). *Convention on the rights of persons with disabilities*. United Nations.

Vaz, S., Wilson, N., Falkmer, M., Sim, A., Scott, M., Cordier, R., & Falkmer, T. (2015). Factors associated with primary school teachers' attitudes towards the inclusion of students with disabilities. *PLoS One*, *10*(8), e0137002.

Warden, C. A., Yi-Shun, W., Stanworth, J. O., & Chen, J. F. (2022). Millennials' technology readiness and self-efficacy in online classes. *Innovations in Education and Teaching International*, *59*(2), 226–236.

World Health Organization, & United Nations Children's Fund. (2022). *Global report on assistive technology*. World Health Organization. Geneva.

Yasmeen, Z., Mushtaq, I., & Murad, M. (2019). Intrinsic and extrinsic motivation of teachers in special education secondary school: A qualitative study. *The Journal of Educational Research*, *22*(2), 15–30.

Chapter 2
The Effectiveness of Blended-Mode E-Learning on Students' Performance and Self-Efficacy Among College Students

Jiaxin Wang
https://orcid.org/0009-0009-5464-6513
Universiti Sains Malaysia, Malaysia

Wan Ahmad Jaafar Wan Yahaya
https://orcid.org/0000-0002-8605-0062
Universiti Sains Malaysia, Malaysia

ABSTRACT

E-learning has been in the limelight since the rise of the Internet, and distance learning and non-face-to-face forms of education have begun to gain popularity, synchronous E-learning and asynchronous E-learning learning modes have different strengths and weaknesses, and the digital divide can be bridged by mixing the two different E-learning modes. Against this background, this paper examines the past literature, combines questionnaire surveys and quantitative research in the form of quasi-experimental research on higher education. Based on the expectancy-value theory and quantitative analysis of statistical data results, the study focuses on the learning performance and self-efficacy of higher education samples, and explores

DOI: 10.4018/979-8-3373-7508-3.ch002

the changes in students' psychological state in blended teaching, thus promoting the effectiveness of E-learning, and providing a basis for the future of E-learning and blending mode education in the future.

1. INTRODUCTION

The concept of blended e-learning emerged in the early 2000s, It is rooted in constructivist and social cognitive learning principles that emphasize learner-centered engagement, flexible pacing, and active knowledge construction. Numerous empirical studies have demonstrated that blended learning can yield better outcomes than traditional instruction. For instance, Bernard et al. (2014) conducted a meta-analysis of over 100 studies and concluded that blended learning consistently led to improved academic achievement compared to both fully online and face-to-face formats. Similarly, Means et al. (2013), in a U.S. Department of Education report, confirmed the superior learning gains associated with blended instruction across disciplines.

However, existing empirical research rarely focuses on skill-based subjects such as foundational art, where learning depends heavily on visual demonstration, iterative practice, and subjective interpretation. For students who may lack artistic background or confidence, adapting to blended formats presents unique challenges such as interpreting visual content digitally, navigating unfamiliar tools, and managing self-directed learning.

There is also a theoretical gap in the application of major learning frameworks to this context. While Bandura's Social Cognitive Theory (1997) emphasizes the role of self-efficacy in shaping learning behaviors, few studies have examined how blended-mode learning environments influence self-efficacy in visual learning contexts. Likewise, although Expectancy-Value Theory (Eccles & Wigfield, 2002) and Attribution Theory (Weiner, 2010) provide useful lenses to understand motivation and performance, they are underutilized in research on art education for non-specialist students. Furthermore, the constructivist foundation of blended learning centered on active, student-driven knowledge construction has not been sufficiently studied in relation to students' perceptions of learning art through digital means.

This chapter therefore aims to fill these gaps by investigating how blended-mode e-learning influences academic performance and self-efficacy among university students enrolled in art basics courses. It contributes both theoretically by applying and testing psychological learning frameworks and practically by informing course design, instructional support, and policy implementation in digital education.

The central research question guiding this study is: To what extent does blended-mode e-learning improve academic performance and self-efficacy among non-art major university students studying art basics?

By answering this question, the study provides evidence to guide future research in blended learning design for skill-based education and informs educational decision-makers on how to support diverse learners in creative and visual fields.

In this chapter, the research background, problem statement, research objectives, research questions, and other foundational elements of the study are demonstrated to provide a theoretical foundation for the specific research operations that follow.

1.1. Background

Blended-mode e-learning has gained substantial traction in higher education as institutions seek to modernize pedagogy and improve learner engagement across disciplines. Its promise lies in combining the structure and support of traditional classrooms with the flexibility and autonomy of online learning (Graham, 2013). However, implementing blended learning in practice-based subjects, particularly in visual arts education, introduces unique challenges especially when teaching students who are not majoring in art and may lack foundational skills or motivation in this domain.

In theory, blended learning environments are expected to facilitate self-paced exploration, visual demonstrations, and iterative practice key aspects of art education. However, in real-world applications, several implementation gaps often limit the success of this instructional model. The absence of direct feedback in the online environment led to uncertainty, reduced self-confidence, and inconsistent learning outcomes.

Despite the increasing adoption of blended learning models in higher education, there remains a noticeable gap in the literature regarding its specific impact on students' academic performance and self-efficacy. While several studies report positive associations between blended learning and enhanced student outcomes, others suggest limited or no significant effects. This inconsistency in findings may be attributed to variations in course design, implementation quality, subject matter, student demographics, and assessment methods. As such, there is a pressing need for more systematic and contextually grounded research that explores how blended-mode E-learning affects these two critical educational variables.

The present study aims to address this research gap by investigating the effects of blended learning on academic performance and self-efficacy among undergraduate students. By focusing on learners in a structured blended E-learning environment, this research seeks to provide empirical evidence that can inform both theoretical understanding and practical application. The findings of this study are expected to offer valuable insights for educators, instructional designers, and policymakers who are seeking to optimize digital learning environments to support student achievement and personal development in the evolving landscape of higher education.

1.2. Problem Statement

Numerous studies have acknowledged the benefits of blended learning on academic performance. For example, Tang et al. (2023) found that blended learning approaches generally improve student performance more effectively than either fully online or traditional learning environments. However, most of these studies have evaluated blended learning as a generalized concept, without differentiating between synchronous and asynchronous components. This lack of specificity limits our understanding of how each modality contributes to student outcomes. Particularly, the interaction between these modes and students' self-efficacy, their belief in their ability to complete tasks and succeed academically, has not been adequately explored.

Self-efficacy is a crucial determinant of learning success, influencing how much effort students invest, how resilient they are in the face of challenges, and ultimately how well they perform (Bandura, 1997; Honicke & Broadbent, 2016). Although studies such as Zhu et al. (2024) suggest that asynchronous learning can foster self-directed learning and improve self-efficacy through reflective engagement, others argue that the lack of immediate feedback may hinder students with lower confidence levels. Conversely, synchronous learning environments provide instant support and social interaction, which may boost real-time confidence but could also impose cognitive pressure and scheduling challenges (Lee et al., 2023). Despite these insights, few empirical studies have directly compared how synchronous and asynchronous elements within blended-mode learning influence both performance and self-efficacy concurrently.

However, the empirical evidence surrounding the effectiveness of blended-mode e-learning in art and visual education remains inconclusive and at times contradictory. While some studies report positive learning gains and motivational improvements from blended formats (Bernard et al., 2014; Means et al., 2013), others have shown that students especially those with no prior training in art struggle with the visual and interpretive demands of asynchronous instruction (Fleischmann, 2020). This creates a conflicting evidence gap, making it difficult for educators and institutions to adopt blended learning confidently in non-textual or practice-based disciplines.

Additionally, many existing studies emphasize quantitative performance outcomes while overlooking affective factors such as self-efficacy, which are critical in creative learning. This leads to a knowledge gap in understanding how psychological constructs influence learning in skill-based, blended contexts.

From a theoretical standpoint, while Social Cognitive Theory (Bandura, 1997) is often cited in e-learning research, few studies have applied it specifically to blended art instruction among non-specialist learners. Similarly, although Expectancy-Value Theory (Eccles & Wigfield, 2002) and Attribution Theory (Weiner, 2010) are well-established frameworks for explaining academic motivation and performance, their relevance to creative disciplines in digital learning contexts has not been thoroughly investigated. This represents a theoretical gap in extending these models to blended learning in visual education.

A contextual gap also exists: much of the current research in blended learning is concentrated in Western or technologically advanced settings. There is a lack of localized, context-sensitive data from Asian or multicultural classrooms, particularly involving students without a background in art.In terms of practical implementation, instructors often lack training in digital pedagogy for visual learning, and course designers may fail to provide adequate scaffolding, feedback, or opportunities for creative expression online (Boelens et al., 2017). These gaps in instructional design and institutional support hinder the potential effectiveness of blended-mode e-learning for creative education.

Given these gaps and challenges, this study aims to investigate the impact of blended-mode e-learning on academic performance and self-efficacy among non-art major university students learning art basics. By doing so, it contributes to both theory and practice: it applies and extends key motivational and cognitive learning theories to a novel learning context and provides empirical data to guide curriculum design, policy development, and instructional strategies for skill-based blended learning.

1.3. Research Objectives

The research objectives of this study are as follows:

i. To evaluate the effect of blended-mode E-learning on students' academic performance.
ii. To assess the effect of blended-mode E-learning on students' self-efficacy.
iii. To explore the relationship between students' performance and students' self-efficacy in a blended learning environment among college students.

1.4. Research Questions

The research questions for this study included the following.

i. Does blended-mode E-learning improve academic performance among college students?

ii. Does participation in blended-mode E-learning enhance students' self-efficacy?
iii. Is there a significant correlation between students' performance and students' self-efficacy in blended-mode E-learning?

1.5. Research Variables

Figure 1. Variable

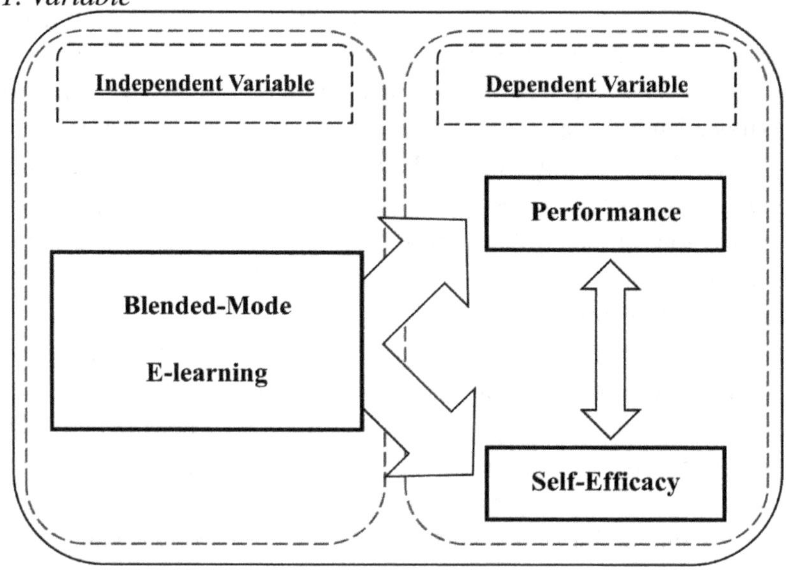

Blended-Mode E-learning(independent variable): Hybrid online learning in this study refers to a hybrid of synchronous and asynchronous online learning in which students first engage in synchronous online learning, then asynchronous online learning, and finally synchronous online learning, which is similar to the concept of the "flipped classroom", but with more synchronous learning time added to it, and the whole teaching and learning process is conducted online in this study.

Performance(dependent variable I):Student performance in a course is typically defined as the measurable academic outcomes demonstrated by learners through assessments, assignments, and participation, reflecting their understanding and performance of course objectives (Yukselturk & Bulut, 2007; Broadbent & Poon, 2015). Performance in this study is defined as the difference in scores between the pre-test and post-test to determine the improvement in performance to determine the effectiveness of the teaching of this course and the students' mastery of the knowledge points in the course.

Self-efficacy(dependent variable II):As defined by psychologist Albert Bandura (1997), self-efficacy refers to an individual's belief in their capacity to organize and execute the actions required to produce specific performance outcome. Self-efficacy in this study was assessed by the New General Self-Efficacy Scale (NGES). (Chen., Gully & Eden, 2001)

1.6. Theoretical Framework

This study is grounded in four major psychological and educational theories that together explain how blended-mode e-learning influences university students' academic performance, perceived motivation, and self-efficacy, especially among university students enrolled in foundational art courses. These frameworks are: Social Cognitive Theory, Expectancy-Value Theory, Self-Determination Theory, and Constructivist Learning Theory. Each provides a unique perspective on learner behavior in digital and visual learning environments.

At the center of this study is Social Cognitive Theory by Bandura (1997), which highlights the role of self-efficacy, or individuals' beliefs in their ability to perform tasks successfully. This is particularly relevant in blended learning, where students are expected to manage their own learning pace and engage with content more autonomously.In art education, students often begin with limited skill and confidence, making self-efficacy an essential construct for understanding their learning behavior and performance.

Complementing this is the Expectancy-Value Theory, which asserts that learners' achievement motivation is influenced by two factors: the expectancy of success and the value placed on the task (Eccles & Wigfield, 2002). Students are more likely to invest effort in learning activities if they believe they can succeed and if they perceive the content as useful, enjoyable, or important. For non-art majors, understanding how art can contribute to their creativity, design thinking, or personal development may increase task value, thereby enhancing motivation.

The third supporting theory is Self-Determination Theory (SDT), developed by Deci and Ryan (1985), which emphasizes the importance of three innate psychological needs: autonomy, competence, and relatedness. When these needs are satisfied, learners are more likely to engage in learning for intrinsic reasons, such as enjoyment or personal growth. In blended learning contexts, the flexibility and self-paced nature of online components can enhance autonomy and competence if students feel in control and capable. According to Chen and Jang (2010), students in blended courses demonstrate higher intrinsic motivation when instructional design supports their psychological needs. This is especially important for who may otherwise see art education as unrelated to their main academic or career goals.

Finally, Constructivist Learning Theory provides a foundation for the pedagogical design of the blended learning environment. It posits that knowledge is constructed actively by learners through meaningful interaction with content and experiences (Garrison & Kanuka, 2004). Blended learning allows students to explore visual and creative tasks in both structured (face-to-face) and exploratory (online) formats, making it well-suited to support constructivist approaches. Vrasidas (2000) argued that digital constructivist environments improve learner engagement by promoting autonomy and reflection, factors that are critical for students learning practical art skills.

Among these theories, Social Cognitive Theory is used as the primary theoretical lens because of its direct relevance to self-efficacy, which is central to both learner behavior and performance in this study. The other three frameworks, Expectancy-Value Theory, Self-Determination Theory, and Constructivist Learning Theory, enhance the theoretical depth by explaining why students engage with the content and how instructional design can be optimized for non-specialist learners in skill-based subjects like art.

1.7. Conceptual Framework

The conceptual framework of this study is designed to investigate the influence of blended-mode e-learning on academic performance, and self-efficacy among non-art major university students enrolled in art basics courses. This framework is grounded in Social Cognitive Theory (Bandura, 1997) as the primary lens, supported by Expectancy-Value Theory, Self-Determination Theory, and Constructivist Learning Theory.

In this model, blended-mode e-learning is the independent variable, representing a structured combination of synchronous and asynchronous online learning activities tailored for skill-based visual learning. This learning mode provides flexibility, autonomy, and individualized pacing, which are assumed to affect students' psychological and academic outcomes. Follow as Figure 2

The dependent variables include:

i. Performance – defined as students' demonstrated knowledge and skill acquisition in the subject, often measured through grades or task completion (York et al., 2015).
ii. Self-Efficacy – students' belief in their ability to succeed in specific learning tasks, especially in a creative or unfamiliar domain like art (Bandura, 1997; Chen et al., 2001).

Figure 2. Conceptual Framework

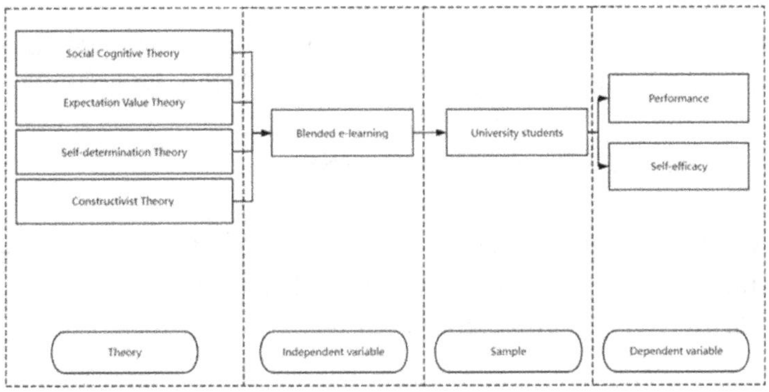

1.8. Definitions of terms

Blended-mode E-learning

Blended-mode E-learning refers to the intentional integration of synchronous and asynchronous online learning components to achieve pedagogical goals without any face-to-face instruction (Hrastinski, 2019)

Synchronous E-learning

Synchronous e-learning enables learners and instructors to interact in real time, using tools such as video conferencing, live chat, and virtual classrooms. (Berestok, 2021)

Asynchronous E-learning

Asynchronous e-learning allows learners to access materials, participate in discussions, and complete tasks at their own pace, without real-time interaction. (Watts, 2016)

Performance

Performance is typically measured by grades, test scores, or other formal indicators of a student's achievement in their educational program. (York, Gibson, & Rankin. 2015)

Self-Efficacy

"Self-efficacy is the belief in one's capabilities to organize and execute the courses of action required to manage prospective situations." (Bandura, 1997)

New General Self-Efficacy Scale (NGSE)

The New General Self-Efficacy Scale is an eight-item measure designed to assess individuals' overall belief in their capability to perform across a variety of situations. (Chen, Gully, & Eden, 2001)

1.9. Summary

This chapter introduced the background and rationale for the study, highlighting the growing relevance of E-learning in higher education and the need to better understand its impact on student performance. It outlined the significance of investigating performance and self-efficacy within blended E-learning environments, especially academic performance as digital education continues to expand globally. The chapter also presented the research problem, objectives, and guiding questions, establishing a clear foundation for the study. Furthermore, it briefly discussed the theoretical framework, particularly Bandura's social cognitive theory, as a lens for understanding how learners' beliefs in their capabilities influence performance. By situating the study within current educational challenges and research gaps, the introduction set the stage for the subsequent chapters that will explore methodology, data analysis, and interpretation of findings.

2. LITERATURE REVIEW

2.1. Blended-Mode E-learning

Recent literature has increasingly focused on how synchronous and asynchronous blended E-learning formats influence university students' academic performance and self-efficacy. Blended learning that incorporates both real-time (synchronous) and self-paced (asynchronous) elements has been shown to offer meaningful academic and psychological benefits. Martin et al. (2020) introduced the concept of "bichronous" online learning, combining asynchronous and synchronous methods, and found that such designs promote both cognitive and emotional engagement. In their study, students reported higher satisfaction and perceived effectiveness in blended settings compared to fully asynchronous models. Raes et al. (2020), in a systematic review of 47 studies, observed that hybrid synchronous learning environments often led to improved student participation and flexibility. They identified that real-time interactions contributed to a stronger sense of community, while asynchronous tools enabled deeper content engagement. Similarly, a study on pre-service teachers showed that students in a blended model combining synchronous and asynchronous tools achieved substantially higher academic results compared to those in traditional formats (Martin et al., 2020). Regarding self-efficacy, synchronous learning supports confidence through direct instructor interaction, social presence, and real-time clarification, while asynchronous modes foster autonomy and mastery through self-paced engagement. Multiple studies (e.g., Peterson, 2018; Martin et al., 2020) indicate that students in blended models often report greater self-efficacy, particularly when they have access to both immediate support and the flexibility to review content on their own schedule. Nonetheless, the effectiveness of these modalities depends heavily on thoughtful instructional design, user-friendly technology, and student support systems. While asynchronous learning allows more flexibility and time for reflection, it may also lead to feelings of isolation or lower engagement if not well scaffolded. Conversely, synchronous formats require stronger time management and may introduce scheduling conflicts but can foster community and active participation. Overall, research suggests that the optimal approach for enhancing both academic outcomes and self-efficacy is a well-integrated blended model that combines the strengths of synchronous immediacy with asynchronous flexibility (Alhassan, 2024; Peterson et al., 2018; Martin et al., 2020). Future research should include more longitudinal and discipline-specific studies to determine which combinations are most effective under varying educational contexts.

2.2. Performance

Blended learning has been associated with improved academic outcomes due to its flexible and student-centred approach. A study by Vaughan et al(2013) found that students in blended courses performed significantly better than those in purely face-to-face or online settings. Similarly, research by Goodyear and Dudley (2015) indicated that blended learning promotes independent and personalized learning, leading to enhanced academic performance.

In recent years, E-learning has transitioned from a supplementary educational option to a primary mode of instruction across many higher education institutions. This shift has been accelerated by global crises such as the COVID-19 pandemic, but also driven by advances in digital technologies and growing demand for flexible, learner-centred education. Consequently, scholars have increasingly focused on evaluating how E-learning environments affect student performance, defined broadly as performance outcomes such as grades, test scores, and course completion rates.

More recent evidence from Tang et al. (2023) examined the effectiveness of a blended learning approach in Chinese universities and reported improved academic performance among students in blended courses compared to those in traditional lectures. The study emphasized that blended learning provides a balance between autonomy and instructor guidance, which can maximize student outcomes if well-designed. This reinforces the notion that performance in E-learning is closely tied to instructional format, with hybrid models often producing the most favourable results.

2.3. Self-Efficacy

Self-efficacy is a critical determinant of students' engagement and persistence in learning activities. A study conducted at Huaihua University revealed that students exhibited low self-efficacy levels in a blended teaching model, particularly in abstract subjects like economics (He, 2024). Conversely, research by Li et al. (2025) demonstrated that online self-efficacy positively influenced students' attitudes toward blended learning, emphasizing the role of confidence in navigating digital platforms. Another key study by Giesbers et al. (2013) found that students' autonomous motivation was positively linked to participation in both asynchronous forums and synchronous video conferences. The study highlighted the dynamic interaction between learning mode and motivational factors such as self-efficacy.

Bandura (1997) emphasized that self-efficacy significantly influences students' engagement and performance. When students believe they can succeed, they are more likely to persist in the face of difficulties. Zimmerman (2000) further explored this relationship in the context of self-regulated learning, where self-efficacy acts as a core determinant of learners' motivation and strategy use.

2.4. Summary

This section is to summarise the relevant literature from previous researchers to understand the current level of research in order to identify the performance and shortcomings of the study, and the next section will specifically talk about the specific operational steps variables and relevant experimental design etc. of this study.

3. RESEARCH METHODOLOGY

This chapter outlines the research methodology employed to investigate the effects of E-learning environments on university students' academic performance and self-efficacy. The methodology was designed to align with the study's objectives and to ensure the validity, reliability, and generalizability of the findings. It begins by detailing the research design, followed by descriptions of the participants, instruments used for data collection, and procedures adopted during the study. The chapter also explains the rationale for selecting a quantitative approach and discusses the methods of data analysis. By clearly articulating the methodological framework, this chapter aims to justify the choices made and to demonstrate how the research process supports the study's goals.

3.1. Research Design

A quasi-experimental design will be used to select a portion of students enrolled in the university to conduct teaching activities using a hybrid model of synchronous and asynchronous online instruction, and students will be assessed for both academic performance and self-efficacy. The data will be collected through the questionnaire star platform and analysed on the SPSS software.

Unlike the general hybrid model of traditional teaching and online learning, the blended E-learning approach targeted in this study is a purely online system of E-learning modelled on video and online conferencing, with the modes differing only in the availability of timely interactions and feedback and whether the time management is carried out in a uniform manner or is a self-paced blended online learning. The concept is similar to that of the flipped classroom, but with the addition of a more synchronised E-learning hourly component. Selected participants will participate in a 6-days course integrating synchronous sessions (e.g., Tencent Conference) with asynchronous components (e.g., online discussion boards, recorded videos). The content of the course covered some basic art lessons, including fonts, typography, colours, etc. As the most elementary art course, the course focused on foundational elements of visual design in a digital context., this course is dedicated to enabling students to understand some basic graphic arts factors, to construct an aesthetic system and to apply aesthetics in their lives.

3.2. Research Sample

The sample population of this study was recruited online and offline after the voluntary participation of the population, most of the subjects from China's undergraduate colleges and universities are students, Volunteers were recruited and administered a pre-test to screen for prior knowledge, in order to prevent some volunteers already know the knowledge related to the course content to affect the accuracy of the experiments, recruited volunteers for the non-art majors and pre-test scores of less than 5 points would be selected toto participate in this experimental study. A total of 30 students participated after the selection process. The selected sample population enters the treatment process and the follow-up test.

3.3. Research Instruments

Performance will be measured using pre-test and post-test scores. The questionnaire used in this study to measure performance was taken from the questionnaire that came with the course, which covered the knowledge points described in the instructional video. There were ten questions, all of which were single-choice questions with 2-4 options each, with one and only one option being the correct one, with a minimum score of 0 and a maximum score of 10, with higher scores representing a more comprehensive mastery of the knowledge points in the course. The questions in the pre-test and post-test were the same but the order of the options and questions in the two tests were randomised to avoid subjects remembering the answers leading to a history effect. During the course of this study, the researchers did not publish the students' scores and correct answers throughout the study in order to minimise the stress on the subjects and the associated adverse effects.

Self-efficacy will be assessed using the new general self-efficacy scale (NGSE) (Chen, Gully, & Eden, 2001), a validated 8-item instrument widely used in educational settings. The New General Self-Efficacy (NGSE) Scale, developed by Chen, Gully, and Eden (2001), is an 8-item unidimensional measure designed to assess individuals' general belief in their ability to succeed across a wide variety of tasks and situations. The scale is formulated as a five-point Richter scale, with options ranging from one point (completely disagree) to five points (completely agree) to judge how well each description corresponds to the subject's feelings. Unlike earlier general self-efficacy instruments, such as the Sherer General Self-Efficacy Scale (SGSE), the NGSE was developed to address issues of low content validity and multidimensionality found in previous measures. The NGSE shows strong internal consistency (α = .85–.88), high test–retest reliability, and discriminant validity from related constructs such as self-esteem. It predicts specific self-efficacy across tasks and moderates the influence of prior performance on subsequent self-efficacy beliefs, making it a theoretically grounded and psychometrically sound tool for organizational and educational research.

3.4. Research Process

The process of this research includes the following sections. First of all, the subjects will have two sessions of synchronous E-learning, where the teacher will lead them through the knowledge explanation and synchronous discussion. The third and fourth sessions are required to be completed within a specified period of time (days 3-4), but they can set their own time and pace of learning (e.g., they can finish both sessions on the same day or follow the synchronous teaching schedule and timeline), and the discussion forum is open 24 hours a day. The discussion forum is open 24 hours a day, students can leave a message at any time to discuss or ask questions, the teacher will respond to the student's questions from time to time: Finally, the last two lessons will be completed on the 5th-6th day, and the Q&A session and course summary, all the lessons are presented in the form of animation with real-time subtitles to assist students to understand the content of the course (at the same time to implement the multimedia teaching principles of the principle of dual-channel principle and the principle of the multimedia teaching).All lessons were animated with real-time subtitles to assist students in understanding the content (while implementing the dual-channel and segmentation principles of multimedia teaching to reduce cognitive load), and a post-test and NGSE were administered immediately after all lessons to verify the impact of the lessons on students' performance and self-efficacy.

3.5. Summary

In conclusion, this chapter has presented a comprehensive overview of the research methodology adopted for this study, including the research design, participant selection, instruments, data collection procedures, and methods of analysis. The next chapter will detail the data collected and analysed, showing the results of the data obtained in this study as well as the relevant statistical methods.

4. DATA ANALYSES

This chapter presents the data collected for the study and outlines the analytical procedures used to address the research questions. It begins by providing a descriptive summary of the participants' demographic information, followed by an overview of the key variables examined, including academic performance and self-efficacy within E-learning environments.

4.1. Reliability and Validity of the Questionnaire

Table 1. Reliability Statistics-1

Reliability Statistics (PERFORMANCE)	
Cronbach's Alpha	**N of Items**
.721	20

Table 2. Reliability Statistics-2

Reliability Statistics(NGSE)	
Cronbach's Alpha	**N of Items**
.950	8

In this study, reliability analysis was conducted for two key instruments: the Performance scale and the NGSE (General Self-Efficacy) scale. The Performance scale, consisting of 20 dichotomous items, demonstrated acceptable internal consistency with a Cronbach's alpha of .721, suggesting a moderate level of reliability suitable for group-level comparisons. In contrast, the NGSE scale exhibited excellent internal consistency, with a Cronbach's alpha of .950 across 8 items. This indicates a high degree of homogeneity among the items and confirms that the NGSE scale reliably measures the construct of self-efficacy in this context. Together, these results provide strong support for the reliability and measurement quality of both scales used in the study. (Table 4.1,Table 4.2)

Table 3. NGSE Validity Analysis-1

Communalities		
	Initial	**Extraction**
N1	1.000	.888
N2	1.000	.909
N3	1.000	.975
N4	1.000	.975
N5	1.000	.975
N6	1.000	.779
N7	1.000	.794
N8	1.000	.870

Extraction Method: Principal Component Analysis.

Table 4. NGSE Validity Analysis-2

Total Variance Explained									
	Initial Eigenvalues			Extraction Sums of Squared Loadings			Rotation Sums of Squared Loadings		
Component	Total	% of Variance	Cumulative %	Total	% of Variance	Cumulative %	Total	% of Variance	Cumulative %
1	6.010	75.126	75.126	6.010	75.126	75.126	4.870	60.879	60.879
2	1.154	14.430	89.556	1.154	14.430	89.556	2.294	28.677	89.556
3	.383	4.782	94.338						
4	.282	3.531	97.868						
5	.138	1.726	99.594						
6	.032	.406	100.000						
7	2.409E-16	3.012E-15	100.000						
8	1.819E-16	2.274E-15	100.000						

Extraction Method: Principal Component Analysis.

Table 5. NGSE Validity Analysis-3

Component Matrix[a]		
	Component	
	1	2
N1	.921	-.200
N2	.935	-.185
N3	.960	-.229
N4	.960	-.229
N5	.960	-.229
N6	.798	.378
N7	.794	.404
N8	.504	.785

Extraction Method: Principal Component Analysis.
a. 2 components extracted.

Table 6. NGSE Validity Analysis-4

Rotated Component Matrix		
	Component	
	1	2
N1	.902	.271
N2	.908	.291
N3	.951	.265
N4	.951	.265
N5	.951	.265
N6	.515	.717
N7	.499	.738
N8	.060	.931

Extraction Method: Principal Component Analysis.
Rotation Method: Varimax with Kaiser Normalization.
a. Rotation converged in 3 iterations.

Table 7. NGSE Validity Analysis-5

Component Transformation Matrix		
Component	1	2
1	.875	.484
2	-.484	.875

Extraction Method: Principal Component Analysis.
Rotation Method: Varimax with Kaiser Normalization.

In this study, as table 4.2 to table 4.7, Principal Component Analysis (PCA) was conducted to examine the construct validity of the NGSE scale. The results indicated a clear two-factor structure, with two components explaining a cumulative 89.56% of the total variance. Communalities for all items were high (ranging from .779 to .975), suggesting strong representation of the underlying factors. After Varimax rotation, items N1 to N5 loaded strongly on the first component, while items N6 to N8 loaded more heavily on the second, indicating the presence of two distinct but related dimensions of self-efficacy. These findings support the construct validity of the NGSE scale in this context.

4.2. Descriptive Statistics

Table 8. Descriptive Statistics

Descriptive Statistics					
	N	Minimum	Maximum	Mean	Std. Deviation
pre1	30	0	5	3.17	1.341
post1	30	4	10	7.57	1.654
NGSE1	30	20	38	29.53	5.111
Valid N (listwise)	30				

According to the results of the descriptive statistics described above, the study subjects showed significant differences and changes in the three indicators of pre-test (pre1), post-test (post1), and the General Self-Efficacy Scale (NGSE1). The pre1 scores ranged from 0 to 5 with a mean of 3.17 (SD = 1.341), indicating that the subjects' academic performance was moderately low prior to the intervention. In contrast, posttest scores increased significantly, ranging from 4 to 10, with a mean of 7.57 (SD = 1.654), suggesting that the majority of students made significant progress after completing the academic task. This difference may reflect a positive effect of the experimental treatment or instructional strategy. (Table 4.3)

In addition, the self-efficacy scores (NGSE1) ranged from 20 to 38, with a mean of 29.53 (SD = 5.111), indicating that the participants as a whole possessed moderately high levels of self-efficacy. Considering that it has been shown that self-efficacy is strongly related to academic performance (Bandura, 1997; Honicke & Broadbent, 2016), this result may further support the mediating role of self-efficacy in the enhancement of academic effectiveness. In summary, this data set initially reveals the potential facilitating effect of the intervention on students' academic performance and self-efficacy, providing a theoretical basis and empirical rationale for subsequent inferential statistical analyses (e.g., paired-sample t-tests and correlation analyses).

4.3. Inferential statistics

Table 9. Pearson's Related Index

Correlations			
		post1	NGSE1
post1	Pearson Correlation	1	.738**
	Sig. (2-tailed)		.000
	N	30	30
NGSE1	Pearson Correlation	.738**	1
	Sig. (2-tailed)	.000	
	N	30	30

**. Correlation is significant at the 0.01 level (2-tailed).

According to the results of the Pearson correlation analysis, a statistically significant and strong positive relationship was found between students' post-test performance (post1) and their general self-efficacy scores (NGSE1), with a correlation coefficient of $r = .738$, $p < .001$. This indicates that students who reported higher levels of self-efficacy also tended to achieve higher scores in the post-test assessment. The strength of this correlation suggests that self-efficacy is not only related to but potentially plays a substantial role in influencing academic performance following instructional interventions. (Table 4.4)

This finding is consistent with the extensive body of literature that emphasizes the critical role of self-efficacy in educational contexts. Bandura (1997), in his social cognitive theory, highlighted self-efficacy as a central factor that shapes individuals' motivation, effort, persistence, and performance. More recent meta-analyses (e.g., Honicke & Broadbent, 2016) have confirmed that self-efficacy is a robust predictor of academic performance across various learning environments and subject areas.

In the context of the present study, the significant correlation between NGSE1 and post1 suggests that students' beliefs in their own capabilities may have contributed to their learning success after engaging with the instructional content. This could be due to the fact that students with higher self-efficacy are more likely to set challenging goals, apply effective learning strategies, and persist through difficulties, behaviours that are closely linked with better academic performance.

Furthermore, this result provides empirical support for the potential mediating role of self-efficacy in explaining how and why educational interventions, such as blended or guided learning activities, may lead to improvements in student performance. Future research could further investigate this relationship by incorporating mediation or path analysis models to test the causal pathways between self-efficacy, learning engagement, and performance.

In summary, the observed strong and significant correlation between self-efficacy and post-intervention academic performance underscores the importance of fostering students' psychological readiness and confidence as a component of effective instructional design. This highlights a valuable direction for educators and curriculum designers aiming to enhance student performance through both cognitive and motivational support mechanisms.

4.4. Summary

This chapter provided a detailed presentation and analysis of the data collected to examine the impact of E-learning environments on university students' academic performance and self-efficacy.

5. DISCUSSION, CONCLUSIONS AND SUMMARY

5.1. Discussion

The findings of this study demonstrate that blended-mode e-learning has a significant positive impact on non-art major university students' academic performance and self-efficacy in learning art basics. These results confirm the applicability of Social Cognitive Theory (Bandura, 1997) in digital learning environments, highlighting that self-efficacy is not only shaped by prior success but also by the structure and flexibility of the learning environment. The asynchronous nature of blended-mode e-learning allowed students to engage with learning materials at their own pace, revisit key concepts, and reflect on their performance, all of which likely contributed to improved confidence and academic achievement.

In relation to performance, the increase observed in post-intervention scores suggests that the blended model effectively supports learning in skill-based subjects, even among students without prior experience in art. This aligns with findings by Bernard et al. (2014), who noted that blended learning tends to yield better learning outcomes compared to traditional methods, particularly when it includes opportunities for independent practice and feedback.

Regarding self-efficacy, the results are consistent with Expectancy-Value Theory (Eccles & Wigfield, 2002), which posits that motivation increases when learners perceive tasks as valuable and believe they can succeed. In this study, the use of multimedia resources, visual examples, and self-paced exploration may have enhanced students' perceptions of relevance and personal competence, thus increasing their motivation to engage with the subject matter.

The improvement in self-efficacy is also explained through Attribution Theory, as students in a blended learning environment are more likely to attribute success to controllable factors like effort and strategy use rather than luck or external conditions. This internal attribution may have reinforced their belief in their learning capabilities.

Furthermore, from a constructivist learning perspective, the blended format enabled students to actively construct knowledge through hands-on digital practice and reflection, rather than passively receive information. This is crucial for subjects like art, where experiential learning plays a central role in skill development. The blend of digital tools and task-based learning encouraged a learner-centered approach, fostering autonomy and metacognitive awareness.

5.2. Relevant impacts of this study

Management Impact

This study offers key insights for university administrators and educational policymakers tasked with advancing digital and hybrid learning environments. The findings reveal that a well-structured blended-mode e-learning approach, characterized by the integration of asynchronous, self-paced online learning activities within formal coursework, can positively influence students' academic performance and self-efficacy. From a management perspective, this suggests that institutions should invest in designing flexible online learning components that allow students to control the pace and timing of their learning while still being guided by clear objectives and structured materials. Furthermore, it is recommended that university management prioritize infrastructure development, including intuitive learning management systems (LMS), digital tools, and multimedia content libraries. Lastly, curriculum planners should embed blended e-learning formats into general education programs, especially for non-art majors who require scaffolded exposure to foundational visual skills but may lack prior experience or confidence in art learning.

Practical Impact

The results of this study provide concrete applications for educators, instructional designers, and academic support staff. By implementing blended-mode e-learning, instructors can empower students to take ownership of their learning through flexible, independent, and reflective online tasks. The asynchronous elements of blended learning allow learners to revisit materials, engage at their own pace, and develop deeper conceptual understanding, an approach especially useful in skill-based subjects like art, where practice and repetition are essential. Teachers are encouraged to integrate multimedia tutorials, online sketching tasks, digital critiques, and peer discussion forums to enhance learner engagement and artistic expression. Moreover, instructional practices grounded in constructivist and social cognitive principles, such as scaffolding, self-reflection, and modelling, should be used to foster self-regulated learning. Blended learning also enables instructors to shift from content delivery to learning facilitation, allowing more time for individualized feedback and formative assessment in the digital space.

Theoretical Impact

Theoretically, this study advances the application of Social Cognitive Theory in the context of asynchronous, blended e-learning, particularly in the visual arts. By focusing on self-efficacy, the study confirms Bandura's claim that learners' belief in their own abilities is shaped not only by performance feedback but also by the design of the learning environment, in this case, a blended e-learning model. The findings also relate to Attribution Theory, demonstrating that learners who attribute their success to internal and controllable factors, such as effort and strategy use, are more likely to benefit from self-paced, independent formats like blended learning. Finally, the study supports Constructivist Learning Theory by showing that asynchronous art-based education within blended settings can promote active knowledge construction and learner autonomy. This multifaceted theoretical foundation enriches the current literature by linking psychological, motivational, and instructional dimensions of technology-mediated learning in a non-art student population.

5.3. Recommendations

i. Institutionalize Blended E-Learning as a Flexible Teaching Option

University departments should formally incorporate blended-mode e-learning into foundational art and other skill-based courses, providing instructors with digital tools and course templates for effective asynchronous delivery.

ii. Train Teachers in Digital Facilitation Skills

Instructors should be trained not only in content delivery but also in designing blended learning paths, giving constructive online feedback, and monitoring learner motivation and self-efficacy.

iii. Develop Assessment Tools Beyond Performance

Course assessments should include indicators of self-efficacy and motivation, not just technical skills or project outcomes. Periodic learner reflection and self-assessment tools can support this goal.

iv. Promote Self-Regulated Learning

Instructional materials should include elements that encourage planning, goal-setting, and self-evaluation to help learners manage their own progress more effectively in a blended environment.

v. Align Blended Learning with Broader Learning Objectives

Course designers should ensure that blended-mode activities map onto program-level outcomes, particularly in developing transferable skills like creativity, independent thinking, and digital literacy.

5.4. Future Research Directions

i. Compare Blended Learning with Other E-Learning Models

Future studies could explore how blended-mode e-learning compares with synchronous or flipped learning formats in influencing learner outcomes across disciplines.

ii. Apply Blended Learning in Other Non-Arts Contexts

Research can investigate whether blended-mode e-learning is effective for other non-major students in subjects like design thinking, computer animation, or architecture, extending the scope of its application.

iii. Explore Long-Term Effects on Motivation

Longitudinal studies are needed to evaluate how blended learning impacts students' sustained interest in art or other creative subjects, even after completing the course.

iv. Investigate Learner Characteristics

Future research may examine how factors such as prior digital experience, learning style, or gender influence the effectiveness of blended learning in visual or skill-based education.

v. Conduct Mixed-Methods Research

A combination of quantitative and qualitative approaches could offer richer insights into learner experiences, including how students perceive autonomy, value, and effort in blended e-learning environments.

5.5. Conclusions

This study investigates the impact of a blended-mode E-learning system on university students' academic performance and self-efficacy, utilizing a quantitative research design supported by a validated questionnaire and an extensive review of the relevant literature. The theoretical foundation of the study is partially drawn from Bandura's Social Cognitive Theory (1991), which emphasizes the central role of self-efficacy, defined as an individual's belief in their capacity to perform tasks and achieve desired outcomes, in influencing learners' motivation, behavior, and academic achievement. By examining the dual effects of blended learning on both measurable academic performance and students' self-efficacy, this research contributes valuable empirical evidence to the growing body of scholarship surrounding E-learning in higher education.

More specifically, the study addresses a current gap in the literature by focusing on the integration of synchronous (real-time) and asynchronous (self-paced) instructional components within a unified blended learning framework. While prior research has explored the benefits and limitations of each mode independently, fewer studies have rigorously evaluated the combined impact of both modalities on student performance. By doing so, this research offers important insights into how blended learning environments, by balancing flexibility with real-time engagement, can support student learning in diverse and dynamic ways.

However, it is important to acknowledge several methodological limitations of this study. First, the curriculum investigated was limited to the foundational aspects of art education, which may not adequately represent the learning demands, assessment practices, or instructional challenges present in more theoretical or technical disciplines such as mathematics, science, or engineering. Consequently, the applicability of the findings to other academic contexts remains uncertain. Second, the duration of the blended learning intervention was relatively short, which may not have allowed sufficient time to observe long-term developments in academic performance or more enduring changes in psychological constructs such as self-efficacy. Extended interventions may yield different or more sustained performance. Third, the study utilized a small and culturally homogeneous sample, consisting exclusively of Chinese undergraduate students within a narrow age range and from a single institution. This lack of demographic and geographic diversity restricts the generalizability of the findings to broader populations or international educational settings. Given these limitations, caution should be exercised when interpreting the results, and further research is recommended to replicate and expand upon these findings using larger, more diverse samples, longer study durations, and varied disciplinary contexts to enhance external validity and practical relevance.

Nevertheless, one of the key strengths of the study lies in its cross-cultural relevance. By utilizing the New General Self-Efficacy (NGSE) Scale within a non-Western sample, the research provides initial support for the scale's reliability and applicability in international contexts. This contributes to the growing recognition of the importance of culturally responsive educational research and lays the groundwork for future studies investigating self-efficacy and blended learning across varied cultural and institutional settings.

5.6. Key Terms with Definitions

i. Blended-Mode E-Learning

In this study, blended-mode e-learning is based on a fully online synchronous-asynchronous alternating instructional model that aims to improve educational effectiveness and reduce the shortcomings of the stand-alone mode by using two different e-learning modalities.

ii. Synchronous e-Learning

Synchronous e-learning is a teacher-led, synchronous e-learning model based on the traditional model of online classroom teaching. Teachers and students remain online throughout the course for real-time interaction and feedback.

iii. Asynchronous e-learning

Asynchronous e-learning refers to customised paced learning through pre-produced course materials such as recorded classes, where students can learn in their own preferred way, allowing interaction but with limited real-time feedback.

iv. Higher Education

In this study, higher education refers to the fact that the sample population of the study is a group of students who are enrolled in universities, who have uniformly gone through the selection process of the Chinese college entrance examination, and who have similar educational backgrounds.

v. Performance

In this study, students' academic performance refers to the magnitude of improvement by comparing the front-side and back-side values.

vi. Self-Efficacy

Self-efficacy in this study refers to the values measured by the NGSE scale, and the group of students with scores above the median is considered to be high in self-efficacy.

vii. NGSE Scale

The NGSE scale is the research instrument used to measure self-efficacy in this study and consists of eight five-item Richter scales.

5.7. Summary

This study focusing on the impact on student achievement and self-efficacy in a mixed-mode e-learning environment. As higher education continues to adapt to the evolving demands of the digital age, future research should explore how these factors interact and how blended learning models can be optimized to provide equitable, inclusive, and sustainable learning opportunities. Such efforts will be essential for ensuring that digital education not only expands access but also enhances quality and student success across global academic landscapes.

REFERENCES

Alhassan, A. I. (2024). Analyzing the application of mixed method methodology in medical education: A qualitative study. *BMC Medical Education*, *24*(1), 225. PMID: 38438987

Bandura, A. (1991). Social cognitive theory of self-regulation. *Organizational Behavior and Human Decision Processes*, *50*(2), 248–287.

Bandura, A. (1997). *Self-efficacy: The exercise of control*. W.H. Freeman.

Bandura, A., & Wessels, S. (1997). *Self-efficacy*. Cambridge University Press.

Berestok, O. V. (2021). Synchronous and asynchronous e-learning modes: Strategies, methods, objectives. *Engineering and Educational Technologies*, *9*(1), 19–27.

Bernard, R. M., Borokhovski, E., Schmid, R. F., Tamim, R. M., & Abrami, P. C. (2014). A meta-analysis of blended learning and technology use in higher education: From the general to the applied. *Journal of Computing in Higher Education*, *26*, 87–122.

Boelens, R., De Wever, B., & Voet, M. (2017). Four key challenges to the design of blended learning: A systematic literature review. *Educational Research Review*, *22*, 1–18.

Broadbent, J., & Poon, W. L. (2015). Self-regulated learning strategies & academic achievement in online higher education learning environments: A systematic review. *The internet and higher education*, *27*, 1–13.

Chen, G., Gully, S. M., & Eden, D. (2001). Validation of a new general self-efficacy scale. *Organizational Research Methods*, *4*(1), 62–83.

Chen, K. C., & Jang, S. J. (2010). Motivation in online learning: Testing a model of self-determination theory. *Computers in Human Behavior*, *26*(4), 741–752.

Deci, E. L., & Ryan, R. M. (1985). The general causality orientations scale: Self-determination in personality. *Journal of Research in Personality*, *19*(2), 109–134.

Eccles, J. S., & Wigfield, A. (2002). Motivational beliefs, values, and goals. *Annual Review of Psychology*, *53*(1), 109–132. PMID: 11752481

Fleischmann, K. (2020). Online design education: Searching for a middle ground. *Arts and Humanities in Higher Education*, *19*(1), 36–57.

Garrison, D. R., & Kanuka, H. (2004). Blended learning: Uncovering its transformative potential in higher education. *The Internet and Higher Education*, *7*(2), 95–105.

Giesbers, B., Rienties, B., Tempelaar, D., & Gijselaers, W. (2013). Investigating the relations between motivation, tool use, participation, and performance in an E-learning course using web videoconferencing. *Computers in Human Behavior, 29*(1), 285–292.

Goodyear, P., & Dudley, R. (2015). Enabling blended learning: A new approach to professional education. *Educational Technology, 55*(4), 23–28.

Graham, C. R. (2013). Emerging practice and research in blended learning. In *Handbook of distance education* (pp. 333–350). Routledge.

He, L. (2024). Students' Self-efficacy under the Blended Teaching Model: A Case Study of Hrastinski, S. (2019). What do we mean by blended learning? *TechTrends, 63*(5), 564–569.

Honicke, T., & Broadbent, J. (2016). The influence of academic self-efficacy on academic performance: A systematic review. *Educational Research Review, 17*, 63–84.

Hrastinski, S. (2019). What do we mean by blended learning? *TechTrends, 63*(5), 564–569.

Lee, A., Lee, J. Y., & Jung, E. (2023). University students' experience of online space while engaging in synchronous learning via videoconferencing amidst the pandemic. *Frontiers in Psychology, 14*, 1083754. PMID: 36794081

Li, X., Sulaiman, N. A., & Aziz, A. A. (2025). Factors influencing Chinese Non-English majors' attitudes toward blended learning: The role of perceived relevance, online self-efficacy, and teachers' digital literacy. *Edelweiss Applied Science and Technology, 9*(5), 239–254.

Martin, F., Polly, D., & Ritzhaupt, A. (2020). Bichronous online learning: Blending asynchronous and synchronous online learning. *EDUCAUSE Review*, •••, 8.

Means, B., Toyama, Y., Murphy, R., & Baki, M. (2013). The effectiveness of online and blended learning: A meta-analysis of the empirical literature. *Teachers College Record, 115*(3), 1–47.

Peterson, A. T., Beymer, P. N., & Putnam, R. T. (2018). Synchronous and asynchronous discussions: Effects on cooperation, belonging, and affect. *Online Learning : the Official Journal of the Online Learning Consortium, 22*(4), 7–25.

Peterson, S. G. (2018). *Epistemic beliefs and the innovation-decision process: A mixed methods analysis of faculty classroom assessment practice* (Doctoral dissertation, University of Nevada, Las Vegas).

Raes, A., Detienne, L., Windey, I., & Depaepe, F. (2020). A systematic literature review on synchronous hybrid learning: Gaps identified. *Learning Environments Research*, *23*, 269–290.

Tang, Q., Zhang, T., & Jiang, L. (2023). Influence of blended instruction on students' learning effectiveness: The role of Flow. *Education and Information Technologies*, *28*(2), 1891–1909. PMID: 35967827

Vaughan, N. D., Cleveland-Innes, M., & Garrison, D. R. (2013). *Teaching in blended learning environments: Creating and sustaining communities of inquiry*. Athabasca University Press.

Vrasidas, C. (2000). Constructivism versus objectivism: Implications for interaction, course design, and evaluation in distance education. *International Journal of Educational Telecommunications*, *6*(4), 339–362.

Watts, L. (2016). Synchronous and asynchronous communication in distance learning: A review of the literature. *Quarterly Review of Distance Education*, *17*(1), 23.

Weiner, B. (2010). The development of an attribution-based theory of motivation: A history of ideas. *Educational Psychologist*, *45*(1), 28–36.

York, T. T., Gibson, C., & Rankin, S. (2015). Defining and measuring academic success. *Practical Assessment, Research & Evaluation*, *20*(5), n5.

Yukselturk, E., & Bulut, S. (2007). Predictors for student success in an online course. *Journal of Educational Technology & Society*, *10*(2), 71–83.

Zhu, M., Berri, S., Koda, R., & Wu, Y. J. (2024). Exploring students' self-directed learning strategies and satisfaction in online learning. *Education and Information Technologies*, *29*(3), 2787–2803.

Zimmerman, B. J. (2000). Self-efficacy: An essential motive to learn. *Contemporary Educational Psychology*, *25*(1), 82–91. PMID: 10620383

APPENDIX A: PRE-TEST

1. Secondary colours are created by combining two _________ colours.
   A. functional B. theoretical C. imaginary D. primary
2. Which word refers to a colour's intensity?
   A. monochromatic B. variety C. hue D. saturation
3. True or False: Colour can help to define your brand in a powerful way.
   A. True B. False
4. If you want your project to have a classic, more traditional look, you might consider using a ________ font.
   A. serif B. size 14 C. brightly-coloured D. sans serif
5. In terms of best practices, generally how many fonts should you use per design project?
   A. 4-5 B. Only Times New Roman C. 1-2 D. as many as you want
6. When you're working with lines, pay attention to their…
   A. colour. B. weight. C. all of these things D. texture.
7. True or False: You can make vector graphics any size, big or small, without losing quality.
   A. True B. False
8. Which of the following is NOT one of the principles of composition?
   A. proximity B. value C. white space D. alignment
9. Free or low-cost images are sometimes referred to as...
   A. raster. B. pixels C. colour schemes D. stock
10. In order to create visual balance within an image, many photographers and designers apply the rule of…
    A. tenths. B. fourths. C. thirds. D. fifths.

APPENDIX B: POST-TEST

1. If you want your project to have a classic, more traditional look, you might consider using a ________ font.
   A. serif B. size 14 C. brightly-coloured D. sans serif
2. In terms of best practices, generally how many fonts should you use per design project?
   A. 4-5 B. Only Times New Roman C. 1-2 D. as many as you want
3. Secondary colours are created by combining two _________ colours.
   A. functional B. theoretical C. imaginary D. primary
4. Which word refers to a colour's intensity?
   A. monochromatic B. variety B. hue D. saturation
5. Which of the following is NOT one of the principles of composition?
   A. proximity B. value C. white space D. alignment
6. Free or low-cost images are sometimes referred to as...
   A. raster. B. pixels C. colour schemes D. stock
7. True or False: You can make vector graphics any size, big or small, without losing quality.
   A. True B. False
8. When you're working with lines, pay attention to their…
   A. colour. B. weight. C. all of these things D. texture.
9. In order to create visual balance within an image, many photographers and designers apply the rule of…
   A. tenths. B. fourths. C. thirds. D. fifths.
10. True or False: Colour can help to define your brand in a powerful way.
    A. True B. False

APPENDIX C: NEW GENERAL SELF-EFFICACY SCALE

Dear participants, thank you for participating in this survey. Please fill in the following questions according to your actual feelings. The data from this questionnaire will be kept strictly confidential and used only for academic research.

Please select the option that best suits your situation based on the following statements. (1= disagree completely, 2= disagree, 3 = neutral, 4 = agree, 5=agree completely)

1. During this course, I will be able to achieve most of the goals that I have set for myself.

   1 2 3 4 5

2. When facing difficult tasks of the course, I am certain that I will accomplish them.

   1 2 3 4 5

3. In general, I think that I can obtain outcomes on the course that are important to me.

   1 2 3 4 5

4. I believe I can succeed at most any endeavor to which I set my mind.

   1 2 3 4 5

5. I will be able to successfully overcome many challenges in the course.

   1 2 3 4 5

6. I am confident that I can perform effectively on many different tasks of the course.

   1 2 3 4 5

7. Compared to other people, I can do most tasks in the course very well.

   1 2 3 4 5

8. Even when things are tough, I can perform quite well in the course.

   1 2 3 4 5

Chapter 3

Ethical Leadership Effect on Augmented Reality in Education Through OCB and Teacher Engagement Support in Africa

Shashi Kant
https://orcid.org/0000-0003-4722-5736
Lovely Professional University, India

Wako Jio
https://orcid.org/0009-0003-6192-459X
Bule Hora University, Ethiopia

Abhishek Sharma
https://orcid.org/0000-0001-9190-3341
Lovely Professional University, India

Zerihun Kinde Alemu
https://orcid.org/0000-0002-8546-2882
Ethiopian Civil Service University, Ethiopia

ABSTRACT

This chapter is about the effects of ethical leadership on the augmented reality (AR) in educational integration in the Horn of Africa where organizational citizenship behavior (OCB) works as the intervening factor through teacher engagement as well as support. To measure the connections among ethical leadership, AR utilization, as well as OCB, teacher engagement, as well as institutional support, the sample size

DOI: 10.4018/979-8-3373-7508-3.ch003

was 390 educators who were surveyed. The analysis included the use of exploratory factor analysis (KMO = 0.87) that proved the validity of the constructs of its measures. The model was along with validated using confirmatory factor analysis (CFA) that depicted good fit indices to hold up the theoretical structure. Structural equation modeling through AMOS software found that OCB as well as positive increases in engagement of teachers mediated a significant direct as well as indirect rule of ethical leaders in developing AR adoption. Findings depict that ethical leadership contributes into creating an atmosphere that supports innovative teaching methods.

INTRODUCTION

The use of technology in the learning process has become one of the most imperative aspects in learning globally (Prasittichok et al., 2024). Among the technologies, augmented reality (AR) along with takes pride in breaking new grounds since the technology can be used to present immersive learning environments (Akinradewo et al., 2025); that can be used to attract students in unconventional ways (Walker et al., 2025). Ethical leadership or the approach wherein integrity, fairness, along with responsibility are promoted has become popular as a crucial determinant of educational practices (Drljević et al., 2024). Having emerged out of the necessity of the leaders to exemplify moral conduct to the followers, the concept has been associated through a better performance in the organization such as teacher participation as well as student achievement (Crogman et al., 2025). The empirical literature features the positive function of ethical leadership on different educational outcomes, but there is not much investigation specifically examining how ethical leadership can affect the AR adoption (Ahdhianto et al., 2025). Investigation has depicted that ethical leaders would be able to create an environment of support that promotes teacher involvement along with innovation but the practical constraints (van As & Cooke, 2024), like resistances to change, not having the adequate training, as well as resources are some of the most imperative challenges to effective adoption of AR to the classroom (Hallinger et al., 2025). Along with, the function of organizational citizenship behavior (OCB) in the relationship is not discussed much posing a very big gap in the literature (Gobinath et al., 2024).

The chapter will focus on exploring the linkages among ethical leadership, AR usage, OCB, teacher engagement, as well as institutional support in the Horn of Africa, thus alleviating the investigation gaps along with gaps in addressing such problems. It attempts to present an in-depth grasp of how ethical leadership can aid the implementation of the AR technologies in the educational process that will ultimately guide future researchers as well as policymakers. The primary inquiry driving this investigation is: "***How does ethical leadership affect the implementation***

of augmented reality in educational contexts, as well as what function does organizational citizenship behavior serve in facilitating this connection?". This chapter will uncover avenues for advancing educational practices through ethical leadership as well as creative technologies. Augmented reality (AR) in education is a radical way of teaching as well as learning, through teachers now able to give students an interactive experience using augmented reality which can engage students to make them understand better (Walker et al., 2025). Along with, the latter is sometimes dependent on the management cultures at the given educational institutions (Drljević et al., 2024). One of the key factors facilitating the creation of an atmosphere that promotes innovation has been described as ethical leadership that is defined as transparent, fair, along with depicts interest in the well-being of all stakeholders (Ahdhianto et al., 2025). The related researches depict that ethical leaders can not only make the teachers feel motivated but along with create the culture of support cooperation that should be considered as an inevitable effect to adopt new technology such as AR (van As & Cooke, 2024). Even though AR has a lot to offer, there are many viable hurdles that hinder its broad use in teaching environments (Prasittichok et al., 2024). As a case study, a case investigation conducted in a secondary school in Ethiopia indicated that although teachers reported the interest in using AR tools, they encountered considerable impediments (Hallinger et al., 2025). Educators expressed the feeling that integrating AR into lesson plans was too cumbersome to the extent that some of them became reluctant to adopt it (Gobinath et al., 2024). On the same note, an effort initiated in Somalia to integrate AR in the primary education sector faced opposition as people doubted its effectiveness feared their resources to be wasted (Akinradewo et al., 2025).

This is what makes ethical leadership highly crucial so as to make our way through the maze of technology integration. Leaders acting in the ethics should be able to respond to the concerns of the teachers, offer training where necessary as well as make sure that resources are distributed fairly (Crogman et al., 2025). Along with, very little is known about how organizational citizenship behavior (OCB) may work in this process (Jio et al., 2205). Based on case related researches in different learning institutions, it has been realized that when the teachers come together as well as engage in OCB like sharing resources as well as helping one another (Kant et al., 2025), the general climate on innovativeness will have increased as well as thus the use of new technologies may be accepted (Lemi et al., 2025).

STATEMENT OF PROBLEM

Although augmented reality (AR) has been identified through great potential to transform the educational trends, its usage in the horn of Africa has been dominated by a number of challenges that have inhibited its effective use (van As & Cooke, 2024). In theory, schools must utilize technologies developed on the basis of AR to develop interactive along with stimulating learning spaces that could improve student performance (Gobinath et al., 2024). Along with, the literature produces conflicting evidence, but, on the one has well as, it is known that ethical leadership positively affects the outcome of education, on the other, the function of female leaders in the adoption of AR is poorly studied (Akinradewo et al., 2025). Other related researches have postulated that ethical leadership is associated through a greater involvement of teachers, although it does not really give a clear picture as far as the effect of its use in regards to innovative adoption of technology is concerned (Walker et al., 2025). This is made more complex by theoretical gaps (Drljević et al., 2024). Along with, most extant frameworks have not embraced the mediating effect of organizational citizenship behavior (OCB) to a reasonable extent depicting a very wide gap in the comprehension of how voluntary actions of the teachers may either advance or hinder the use of technology (Prasittichok et al., 2024). Along with there is a lack of knowledge regarding specific issues of educators in the Horn of Africa where technology integration can be severely influenced by socioeconomic issues as well as infrastructural drawbacks (Akinradewo et al., 2025). The differences in the context of developed as well as developing areas demonstrate the necessity of locale specific investigation that may be focused on the educational, cultural as well as economic peculiarities of the Horn of the Africa (Hallinger et al., 2025).

These are exacerbated by practical obstacles to their application in terms of insufficient resources, training, as well as reluctance of educators to change (Crogman et al., 2025). Case related researches have demonstrated that despite the existence of ethical leadership, in the absence of the support structures, the possible value of AR remains unrealized in many instances (Ahdhianto et al., 2025). The current chapter was attempted to address these gaps by bringing a detailed examination of the effect of ethical leadership on AR adoption by using OCB in the Horn of Africa as a fitting case study. Helping solve these problems, the present investigation will inform the future researchers as well as policy makers about the specific strategies to eliminate obstacles to incorporating AR, thus preparing the way to the new educational practices that can reach the vision of the innovative education environment.

THEORETICAL FOUNDATION

Ethical Leadership Theory: It focuses on the importance of the ethical principles as well as moral values of the leaders during the decision-making process. Developed on the wider circle of leadership related researches, this theory is based on the idea that leaders through high ethics commas well as their followers on the basis of demonstrating integrity, fairness as well as accountability. In the learning environment, ethical leadership builds up trust as well as respect on other teachers which develop an enabling environment that contributes to innovations. This theory is significant in this investigation since it focuses on the effect of ethical leadership on the adoption of AR in teaching as well as learning activities as well as more specifically the function of ethical leadership in augmenting both teacher involvement as well as organizational citizenship behavior (Prasittichok et al., 2024).

Social Learning Theory: It recommends that all people can learn by observing, imitating, as well as modeling. This theory emphasizes the importance of environmental as well as social interactions in development of behaviors as well as attitudes. When applied to education, the teachers can be introduced to new technologies such as the AR by following the case study of their colleagues or those in the leadership who successfully implement the AR. The theory justifies the idea that the adoption of AR can be carried out through the help of ethical leaders who contribute to the creation of the culture of collaboration as well as innovation among teachers (Drljević et al., 2024).

Theory of Organizational Citizenship Behavior (OCB): It revolves about voluntary actions that sponsored by the employees, as well as outcomes in the success overall of an organization. These activities that extend to the official job description have been named to include helping others in the office, training others, as well as volunteering in organizational activities. It along with can be stated that OCB among teachers can use AR in the educational setting. This theory is imperative in the development of the formation of ethical leadership as the means of promoting OCB, which can be used to embrace innovative educational practice (van As & Cooke, 2024).

Technology Acceptance Model (TAM): According to it one of the factors that greatly affect the decision by people to use new technologies can be perceived ease of use, as well as use of these technologies. TAM developed in the late 1980s by Davis gives a guideline over the user acceptance of technology under different contexts. In the educational field, the use of AR will be influenced by how useful as well as easy to implement it is in the eyes of teachers. Such a model can be regarded as an addition to the ethical leadership theme of the investigation because leaders can enhance their teaching perception of AR domains by offering the required aid as well as education (Ahdhianto et al., 2025).

The ***Ethical Leadership Theory*** of among them can be used as the main theoretical lens of the current investigation. It will enable an inquiry about the function of ethical leadership in the inclusion of AR technologies in learning institutions, mediated by personalities of OCB, as well as teacher engagement.

DEFINITION AND ORIGIN OF CONCEPT

Ethical Leadership: Ethical leadership is the process of being a leader in a but ethical wise. It entails decision-making out of justness, honesty, as well as the concern of the interest of the whole stakeholders. Its underlying idea emerged in the business as well as organizational related researches when it was identified that leaders can have strong influence on the organizational culture as well as staff conduct (Walker et al., 2025).

Augmented Reality (AR): Augmented reality is an emerging field that was first coined in early 1990s as well as has grown ever since, being utilized in various other areas, such as education where it helps to make the process of learning interactive as well as immersive (Prasittichok et al., 2024).

Organization Citizenship Behavior (OCB): Organizational citizenship behavior is a certain discretionary behavior, which is performed by employees as well as can be not directly specified in their job description, but has positive effect through in the organizational environment. Dennis Organ popularized the concept in the late 1980s as well as has emphasized the essence of social as well as cooperative behaviors in the increasing of organizational effectiveness (van As & Cooke, 2024).

Engagement: The degree of enthusiasm, dedication, as well as interest of the educators about their job as well as their learners constitutes teacher engagement. This concept is based on the field of education psychology, as well as it depicts the willingness of the teacher to engage in teaching practices as well as how that may influence student achievement. Teachers who are engaged have higher chances of being open to adopting newer innovations, including the implementation of AR technologies in the classrooms (Drljević et al., 2024).

EMPIRICAL LITERATURE REVIEW

Ethical Leadership and Use of Augmented Reality

The convergence of ethical leadership through the submission of AR in education has attracted heightened scrutiny in recent years, especially as educators pursue novel strategies to improve student engagement as well as learning outcomes (Ahdhianto et al., 2025). A lot of real-world investigation depicts how imperative ethical leadership is for creating an atmosphere that makes it easier for people to use AR technology (Drljević et al., 2024). Ethical leaders are those who are dedicated to moral principles as well as can instill trust as well as motivation in teachers, which is necessary for the successful use of modern teaching technologies (Walker et al., 2025). A significant investigation delineates a paradigm connecting ethical leadership to favorable organizational outcomes, depicting that leaders who exemplify ethical conduct may foster a culture of integrity as well as accountability (van As & Cooke, 2024). This foundation is very imperative in schools, where ethical leadership may help instructors accept new ideas as well as practices like AR as well as make it easier for them to adapt (Gobinath et al., 2024). Related researches in several educational settings indicate that when leaders emphasize ethical norms, instructors experience more support as well as engagement, thereby enhancing their readiness to investigate as well as incorporate new technology into their instruction (Ishengoma et al., 2024). Along with, an chapter especially investigates the impact of ethical leadership on the uptake of instructional technology, including augmented reality (AR) (Prasittichok et al., 2024). The outcomes indicate that ethical leaders furnish essential support as well as resources, which profoundly influences teachers' judgments regarding the utility as well as convenience of implementing AR. When teachers see their leaders as champions for ethical practices, they are more willing to use AR tools. This creates a culture of collaboration where new ideas may grow (Hallinger et al., 2025).

Along through these outcomes, real-world data depicts that organizational citizenship behavior (OCB) is a middleman in this interaction. Related researches depict that ethical leadership increases OCB among teachers, which makes it easier for them to use new technology. Teachers who depict OCB, like sharing resources as well as helping each other use AR; can create a good environment that stimulates new ideas (Akinradewo et al., 2025). This mediating function is especially imperative in places where resources are limited, where working together may greatly improve the use of AR in schools (Areba et al., 2025). Even through these insights, there is still a lack of investigation that explicitly looks at the problems teachers in the Horn of Africa confront in their work (Kant & Adula, 2024).

H1: Ethical Leadership and Use of AR in Education having empirical connotation

Ethical Leadership and OCB through Teacher Engagement and Support

Researchers have been very interested in the link among ethical leadership as well as organizational citizenship behavior (OCB) in schools (Drljević et al., 2024). They have looked at how these two things work together to make teachers more engaged as well as supported (Gobinath et al., 2024). Ethical headship, characterized by its focus on moral principles as well as honesty, profoundly impacts educators' conduct, cultivating an atmosphere conducive to OCB (Prasittichok et al., 2024). Many related researches have depicted that ethical headships make instructors trust them as well as commit to them, which leads to collaborative behaviors that are necessary for a good knowledge environment (Jio & Kant, 2025; Ishengoma et al.,

2024). Investigation demonstrates a positive correlation among ethical leadership as well as organizational citizenship behavior (OCB), indicating that leaders who emphasize ethical norms motivate instructors to perform actions that exceed their official work requirements (van As & Cooke, 2024). This is especially imperative in schools, where working together as well as helping one other may make the whole teaching as well as learning process better (Hallinger et al., 2025). Teachers are more likely to depict OCB, including supporting their coworkers, sharing resources, as well as becoming involved in school projects, when they think their leaders are honest as well as helpful. This has a ripple effect because when instructors have more OCB; students are more interested in school as well as the atmosphere of the school is more collaborative (Kant & Adula, 2024). An investigation that looks at how teacher engagement affects OCB depicts that ethical leadership creates an engaged teaching workforce, which is imperative for improving OCB (Areba et al., 2025). Teachers that are engaged are more inclined to go above as well as beyond in their jobs, which is good for the school atmosphere as well as helps their coworkers learn new teaching methods (Adula & Kant, 2025). The outcomes depict that ethical leadership not only inspires instructors but along with gives them the power to take the lead, which improves OCB as well as makes the workplace a better place to work (Ahdhianto et al., 2025).

Investigation along with depicts that ethical leaders' support is very imperative for helping instructors do OCB (Alemu et al., 2025). When teachers think their leaders are fair as well as helpful, they feel appreciated as well as are more likely to do things that help the school community (Lemi et al., 2025). This help may come in many procedures, such as chances for instructors to learn new skills, praise for their work, as well as a arts of working together (Walker et al., 2025). Such surroundings not only boost OCB but along with outcome in enhanced educational outcomes, as instructors who feel supported are more inclined to utilize creative teaching tactics, including the incorporation of technology (Jio & Kant, 2025). Even though there is a lot of empirical evidence that ethical headship has a beneficial effect on OCB as well as teacher appointment, more investigation is needed in other settings (Kant et al., 2025). Most related researches have looked at established educational systems as well as not at the particular problems as well as dynamics that come up in places through fewer resources. It is imperative to know how ethical leadership might affect OCB as well as engagement in these situations in order to create focused interventions that encourage good teaching practices (Akinradewo et al., 2025).

H2: Ethical Leadership and OCB through Teacher Engagement and Support having empirical connotation

OCB through Teacher Engagement and Support, AR

The connection among organizational citizenship behavior (OCB), teacher involvement as well as support, as well as the usage of augmented reality (AR) in education is becoming a more as well as more relevant topic of investigation (Prasittichok et al., 2024). OCB is a term that describes the choices teachers make that help schools run smoothly as well as do their jobs well (Gobinath et al., 2024). These behaviors are especially imperative for creating environments where people can work together as well as new ideas, like AR, may be put into reality (Drljević et al., 2024). Related researches have depicted that when instructors do OCB, such sharing resources, helping their coworkers, as well as becoming involved in school projects, they make the school a better place to work, which boosts the overall effectiveness of the teaching staff (Ishengoma et al., 2024). An investigation underscores the importance of organizational citizenship behavior (OCB) in educational contexts, asserting that instructors who demonstrate such behaviors enhance school culture as well as improve student performance (Kant & Adula, 2024). This is especially imperative when bringing in new technologies like AR, which often need teachers to work together as well as help one other out (Alemu et al., 2025). Teachers that are involved in OCB are more likely to exchange ideas for successfully using AR as well as help each other deal through problems that come up through the technology (Walker et al., 2025). This makes AR more effective in the classroom as a whole (Jio & Kant, 2025). Along with, empirical related researches demonstrate that teacher involvement is a crucial factor in mediating the link among organizational citizenship behavior (OCB) as well as the effective application of educational technology (Lemi et al., 2025).

Teachers that are interested in improving their teaching as well as their students' learning are more likely to be proactive in using AR (Ahdhianto et al., 2025). The investigation emphasizes the necessity of fostering an atmosphere in which instructors feel appreciated as well as supported, since this involvement propels their readiness to investigate as well as incorporate novel technologies such as AR into their instructional practices (Adula & Kant, 2025). A meta-analysis along with indicated that teacher support, which includes professional development as well as chances to work together, greatly improves OCB as well as teacher engagement. When teachers get enough help from their schools, they are more likely to take part in OCB, which can help AR technologies become popular (van As & Cooke, 2024). The findings indicate that support mechanisms, including training programs centered on AR, not only provide instructors through essential skills but along with cultivate a sense of community that promotes the exchange of best practices (Lemi et al., 2025). Even through these insights, there is a significant lack of information in the literature on the specific problems instructors have when they use AR, especially in places where resources are limited (Areba et al., 2025). Although investigation from developed contexts offers imperative insights into instructor engagement as well as OCB, it frequently neglects the distinctive cultural as well as infrastructural difficulties inherent in developing nations (Akinradewo et al., 2025; Hallinger et al., 2025).

H3: OCB through Teacher Engagement and Support, and AR in Education having empirical connotation

Ethical Leadership, AR and OCB, Engagement and Support Mediation

The interaction of ethical headship, the application of AR in education, as well as OCB via teacher involvement as well as support has become a significant focus of empirical investigation (Jio & Kant, 2025). Ethical headship, defined by honesty, fairness, as well as a dedication to the welfare of all stakeholders, is essential in determining the organizational environment of educational institutions (Terefe et al., 2025). Related researches have demonstrated that ethical headships promote trust as well as motivation among educators, which is crucial for hopeful new practices, such as the use of augmented reality in the classroom (Kant et al., 2025). An investigation depicts that ethical headship has a big effect on how people use instructional technology, such as AR (Lemi et al., 2025). The outcomes depict that leaders who act ethically create a supportive climate that makes teachers more likely to try out novel teaching methods (Alemu et al., 2025). This supportive environment is essential for the effective introduction of AR, since educators are more inclined to utilize such technologies when they perceive themselves as appreciated as well as empowered by their supervisors (Adula & Kant, 2025). Along with, ethical leadership increases OCB among instructors because they are more likely to go above as well as beyond their official tasks when they see their leaders as ethical as well as helpful. According to related researches, OCB is made up of voluntary actions that make the workplace better (Kant & Adula, 2024). In educational environments, instructors that participate in organizational citizenship behavior (OCB), such as resource sharing as well as collaboration through colleagues, cultivate a culture that promotes the implementation of new techniques, including augmented reality (AR) (Areba et al., 2025). Empirical investigation indicates that OCB functions as a mediating variable in the association among ethical leadership as well as the utilization of AR (Ishengoma et al., 2024). When ethical leaders encourage OCB, they get teachers more involved, which are imperative for successfully using AR in the classroom (Akinradewo et al., 2025).

Related researches along with depict that interested instructors are more likely to use new technology, which makes engagement even more imperative (Gobinath et al., 2024). The investigation depicts that ethical leadership makes teachers more dedicated as well as involved, which leads to more OCB (van As & Cooke, 2024). Teachers that feel encouraged are more likely to work together as well as exchange good AR ideas. This builds a supportive network that improves the entire learning environment (Hallinger et al., 2025). This collaborative environment is crucial for addressing the obstacles linked to AR deployment, including resistance to change as well as technical issues (Ahdhianto et al., 2025). Along with, despite the expanding investigation on these links, a substantial gap still in comprehending how these dynamics operate in many situations, especially in emerging nations (Drljević et al., 2024). The majority of investigation has occurred in well-resourced educational environments, frequently overlooking the distinct obstacles encountered by educators in the Horn of Africa as well as analogous regions (Walker et al., 2025). This gap underscores the necessity for focused investigation that investigates how ethical leadership may successfully enhance organizational citizenship behavior (OCB) as well as teacher engagement to assist the implementation of augmented reality (AR) in these underrepresented contexts (Prasittichok et al., 2024).

H4: Ethical Leadership, Use of Augmented Reality in Education and OCB through Teacher Engagement and Support Mediation having empirical connotation

CONCEPTUAL FRAMEWORK

Figure 1. Conceptual framework

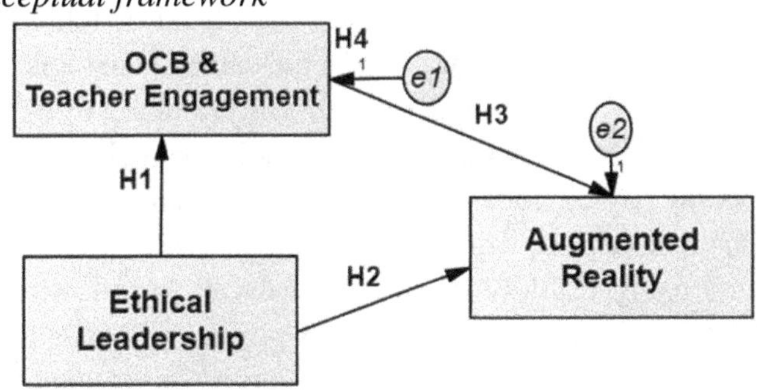

METHODOLOGY

The investigation utilized a quantitative methodology to examine the interrelations among ethical leadership, organizational citizenship behavior (OCB), teacher engagement, as well as the implementation of augmented reality (AR) in educational contexts. We questioned 390 teachers from different schools in the Horn of Africa to get information about these notions. The investigation employed a systematic questionnaire, created from existing literature, to adequately assess each variable. The sample size was established to guarantee sufficient statistical power for future analyses, encompassing dimension detection as well as mediation utilizing AMOS software. Before the EFA, the data was checked to see if it was good for factor analysis using adequacy test . The KMO score of 0.87 depicted that the sample was good enough for EFA. This investigation sought to elucidate the fundamental structure of the data, confirming that the questions included in the questionnaire accurately reflected the anticipated constructs. The EFA identified many different elements related to ethical leadership, organizational citizenship behavior (OCB), teacher involvement, as well as the usage of augmented reality (AR), hence validating the scale. After the EFA, the investigation used SEM through AMOS software to examine the proposed links among the components. SEM enabled the concurrent analysis of several interactions, yielding a thorough comprehension of the direct as well as indirect influences of ethical leadership on AR adoption via OCB as well as teacher involvement. The model fit indices depicted that the model fit well, which backed up the theoretical framework that was established for the investigation.

Scale Development

The scale was created after a careful look at the relevant literature to make sure that each component was measured through a high level of reliability as well as validity. The ethical leadership scale was based on well-known tools like the Ethical Leadership Scale (ELS) by Brown et al. (2005), which looks at traits including honesty, fairness, as well as being a good function model. For OCB, items were sourced from Podsakoff et al. (2000), focusing on behaviors such as benevolence as well as civic virtue that enhance the organizational environment. Teacher engagement items were created using Kahn's (1990) work as well as following investigation that focused on emotional, cognitive, as well as physical involvement in teaching. Finally, the AR usage scale contained things from recent related researches that depicted how easy as well as valuable AR technologies are thought to be in classrooms. There was a five-point Likert scale for replies, from “strongly disagree” to “strongly agree.” Each topic was carefully crafted to make sure it was clear as well as relevant. A smaller group of teachers tried out the scale to help improve the items as well as make sure they were easy to understand. To make the things even clearer as well as more relevant, we used feedback from our pilot investigation. This thorough approach for creating the scale made sure that the final instrument was dependable as well as valid for assessing the constructs of interest, which helped make the investigation findings stronger.

DATA ANALYSIS

Table 1. Data Suitability

Suitability regarding Sample		.983
Test of Sphericity	Chi-Square	19484.68
	Df	780
	p	.000

Source: Authors

Table 1 contains the findings of the measures of data adequacy. The KMO value yielded was 0.983 that depicts excellent level of sampling adequacy. As indicated in the guidelines provided by Kaiser, a value of KMO above 0.90 is regarded as excellent as well as this implies that there is enough sample size to analyze the factor. The outcome of this high value of KMO means that the factors which will be obtained on analysis of the items in the questionnaire will be reliable. The analysis of Bartlett test of sphericity was along with done to determine whether the correlation matrix was significantly varied as compared to identity matrix. The corresponding outcomes indicate the value of Chi-Square as 19, 484.68, degrees of freedom of 780, as well as a p-value of.000. Such p-value is far less than the standard 0.05 cut-off value as well as this means that the correlations that exist among the variables are significant. Hence, the null hypothesis that correlation matrix is an identity matrix can be rejected. In general, these findings prove that the data is suitable to do the dimension exploration as well as hence validity of the constructs measured in this investigation.

Table 2. Sum Variance

Factor	Initial Eigenvalues			Extraction Sums			Rotation Sums		
	Sum	% of Variance	Cumulative %	Sum	% of Variance	Cumulative %	Sum	% of Variance	Cumulative %
1	2.7	26.7	26.76	2.7	26.7	26.7	8.7	21.9	21.9
2	1.9	14.9	41.71	1.9	14.9	41.7	6.0	15.0	37.0
3	1.3	10.9	52.68	1.3	10.9	52.6	4.6	11.6	48.6

Source: Authors

The table 2 summarizes the outcomes of the variances. The three dominant factors observed in the analysis are seen to have contributed to the general variance of the data. The initial eigenvalue of the first factor is 2.7 through 26.7 percent of the total variance. Upon extraction, this factor keeps the same eigenvalue as well as percentage, meaning that it does not appear weak in terms of explaining structure of the data. The cumulative percentage has moved up to 26.7 after this factor which indicates that a large percentage of the variation has been explained by this single factor. The second factor has an initial eigenvalue of 1.9 bearing 14.9 percent of the variance. It has the same eigenvalue as well as percentage as it was previously, creating cumulative 41.7 percent total variance when added through the first factor. This means that both of the first two factors cumulatively accounted for a large part of the variations in the data. The third factor has eigenvalue of 1.3 as well as explains 10.9% of the variation as well as the cumulative percentage 52.6 after extraction. This implies that the three factors have summative variance of more than fifty percent of the total variance which is a good outcome through in exploratory analysis of factors. Now that the rotation summed squared loadings are being considered, the values become a bit different as well as this depicts the manner in which the factors are allocated across the variables. The first factor exhibits a sum of rotation of 8.7 which takes 21.9 percent of the variance, the second factor has a rotation sum of 6.0 (15.0 percent) as well as the third factor has a rotation sum of 4.6 (11.6 percent). These rotation outcomes indicate that the factors can be clearly identified as well as that the rotation has clarified the nature of the structure of the factor.

Table 3. Covariances

			Estimate	S.E.	C.R.	P	Hy.
OCB through Teacher Engagement as well as Support	**<-->**	**Ethical Leadership**	**.563**	**.094**	**5.989**	**.00**	**H2**
OCB through Teacher Engagement as well as Support	<-->	AR in Education	.493	.056	8.803	.00	**H3**
Ethical Leadership	<-->	AR in Education	.652	.105	6.209	.00	**H1**

Source: Authors

The outcomes of the covariance are presented in Table 3. The covariance of OCB as measured by teacher engagement as well as teacher support to ethical leadership is estimated to be 0.563 through standard error of 0.094. The relationship among crime level as well as the level of welfare is strong as well as statistically significant, through p-value of 0.00. This finding contributes to Hypothesis 2 (H2) which indicates that good ethics leadership has a positive effect on OCB by increasing the level of engagement as well as support by teachers. On the same note, the estimate of covariance among OCB using teachers engagement as well as support as well as AR in education is 0.493 as well as standard error of 0.056. The C.R. of 8.803 is again confirming the significant positive relationship through p-value of 0.00 in support of Hypothesis 3 (H3). This outcome takes place that when teachers participate in OCB, they will tend to use AR efficiently in their teaching methods. Finally, the relationship among ethical leadership as well as application of AR in education is covariance-estimated at 0.652 through the standard error of 0.105. C.R. of 6.209 through a p-value of 0.00 depicts a strong as well as significant relationship, which represents the Hypothesis 1 (H1). Such idea means that ethical leadership can do more than providing the facilitating environment, which contributes to the OCB performance; to encourage the use of AR technologies in education, in turn, the process needs to be directly supported by ethical leadership.

Table 4. Validity Concern

	CR	AVE	MSV	MaxR(H)	EL	OCBTES	UARE
EL	0.682	0.643	0.219	0.852	**0.654**		
OCBTES	0.758	0.657	0.132	0.763	0.171	**0.665**	
UARE	0.793	0.603	0.274	0.797	0.383	0.193	**0.684**

Note: EL = Ethical Leadership; OCBTES= OCB through Teacher Engagement as well as Support; UARE = Use of Augmented Reality in Education

Source: Authors

In Table 4, the validity measures of the constructs that were studied in this paper may be found, namely Ethical Leadership (EL), Organizational Citizenship Behavior through Teacher Engagement as well as Support (OCBTES), as well as Use of Augmented Reality in Education (UARE). The CR of all the constructs is more than the standard acceptable level of 0.70, thus confirming high internal consistency. The CR of Ethical Leadership is 0.682, as well as that of OCBTES is 0.758 as well as UARE has 0.793. These values indicate that the measures which have been adopted to register these constructs are stable as well as do not actuate inconsistently through the theories which they are supposed to apply. Values of AVE are along with presented, through values of ethical leadership as 0.643, OCBTES of 0.657 as well as UARE of 0.603. The values of AVE greater than 0.50 enable depicting that more than 50 percent of the variance of the constructs are determined by the indicators, which along with proves convergent validity of the measures. Discriminant validity can be depicted through the help of MSV. The maximum MSV equals 0.274 in the case of UARE, so the largest possible overlapping of constructs is very small, which is good to serve to each construct to measure the independent concept. Along with, the above correlations among constructs are lower than their respective Ave which proves that each construct is just different enough among others. In the end, MaxR(H) values, complementing CR outcomes along with appear to be satisfactory Ethical

Leadership 0.852, OCBTES 0.763 as well as UARE 0.797. These findings support the fact that the constructs bear a very high level of reliability as well as validity.

Figure 2. Structure Equation Model

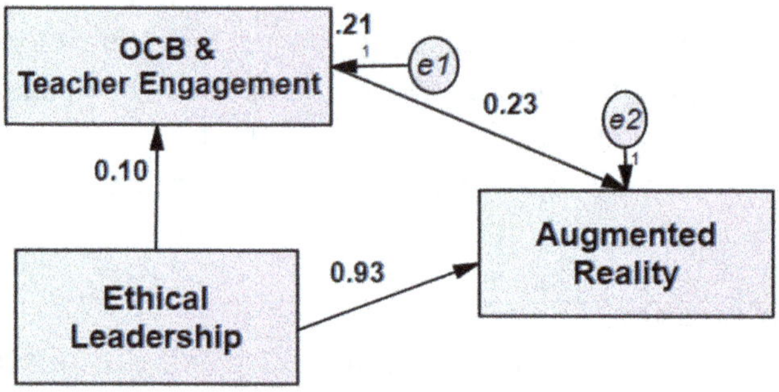

Table 5. Model Fitness

p	Chi-Sq	RMR	GFI	PNFI	TLI	RMSEA
0.003	2.163	.037	0.929	0.925	0.921	.029

Source: Authors

The model fitness are presented in Table 5. The p is 0.003, which suggests that the chi-square test for the model is statistically significant. The Chi-Sq score of 2.163 is rather low, which is good since it suggests the model fits the data well. This low value, together with the significance level, suggests that the model and the data are not very different from one other, even though there is a statistically significant difference. The RMR is 0.037, which is less than the 0.05 limit. This implies that the model works properly. When RMR values are lower, the discrepancy between the actual and anticipated values is minimal on average. The GFI is another essential number. It gets a score of 0.929, which is greater than the recommended cutoff of 0.90. This suggests that the model matches the data well since GFI values that are closer to 1 mean a better fit. The PNFI is 0.925, which is along with over the acceptable level. This means that the model not only fits well, but it is along with simple compared to the amount of parameters it estimates. The TLI indicates a value of 0.921, which is another sign that the model fits well as values over 0.90 are seen to be a strong match. The RMSEA is 0.029, which is far lower than the suggested limit of 0.05. This low RMSEA means that the model fits the data well as well as is a good match.

Table 6. Regression

			Approx.	S.E.	C.R.	P	Ass.
OCB through Teacher Engagement and Support	**<---**	**Ethical Leadership**	**.716**	**.405**	**1.767**	**.06**	**H2**
Use of Augmented Reality in Education	<---	OCB through Teacher Engagement and Support	.651	.197	3.304	.00	H3
Use of Augmented Reality in Education	<---	Ethical Leadership	.563	.105	5.361	.00	H1

Source: Authors

Table 6 displays the outcomes of the regression concerning the interrelationships among the constructs in the investigation, particularly emphasizing the pathways from Ethical Leadership to Organizational Citizenship Behavior through Teacher Engagement as well as Support (OCBTES), as well as the impact of OCBTES as well as Ethical Leadership on the Utilization of Augmented Reality in Education (UARE). There are imperative statistical indicators for each path, such as the regression estimate, standard error (S.E.), critical ratio (C.R.), p-value (P), as well as hypothesis status (Ass.). The first route looks at how Ethical Leadership affects OCBTES, through a regression estimate of 0.716. This depicts that the two constructs are strongly related to one other. The standard error is 0.405, as well as the critical ratio of 1.767 depicts that this association is only somewhat significant, through a p-value of 0.06. This p-value is a little higher than the usual level of 0.05, but it still depicts a tendency toward significance, which supports Hypothesis 2 (H2) that ethical leadership has a positive effect on OCB through teacher involvement as well as support. The second route looks at how OCBTES affects the use of augmented reality in education. The regression estimate is 0.651. The standard error for this path is 0.197, as well as the critical ratio of 3.304 depicts that there is a strong as well as statistically significant association, through a p-value of 0.00. This substantial significance backs up Hypothesis 3 (H3), depicting that OCB through teacher involvement as well as support has a favorable effect on the successful usage of AR in schools. The last path looks at the direct link among Ethical Leadership as well as the Use of Augmented Reality, through a regression estimate of 0.563. The standard error is 0.105, as well as the critical ratio of 5.361 depicts a very strong as well as statistically significant link, through a p-value of 0.00. This finding robustly corroborates Hypothesis 1 (H1), suggesting that ethical leadership directly facilitates the utilization of augmented reality (AR) in educational contexts.

Table 7. Mediating

Ethical Leadership → Use of Augmented Reality in Education	**.10**
Ethical Leadership → OCB through Teacher Engagement as well as Support → Use of Augmented Reality in Education	.93*.23=.21
	.31

Source: Authors

Table 7 depicts how Organizational Citizenship Behavior via Teacher Engagement as well as Support (OCBTES) affects the link among Ethical Leadership as well as the Use of Augmented Reality in Education (UARE). The table depicts both direct as well as indirect effects, as well as their route effects, which gives a clear picture of how mediation works. The direct impact of Ethical Leadership on the Utilization of Augmented Reality in Education is quantified as 0.10, signifying a direct yet negligible effect. This indicates that although ethical leadership may correlate through AR usage, it lacks a sufficiently robust impact to be deemed relevant. This conclusion underscores the imperative for more investigation into the mechanisms by which ethical leadership influences AR adoption. The chart, on the other has well as, depicts how Ethical Leadership affects UARE indirectly through OCBTES. The indirect pathway is found by multiplying 0.93 (the effect of Ethical Leadership on OCBTES) by 0.23 (the effect of OCBTES on UARE). This gives an indirect effect of 0.31. This imperative indirect effect depicts that ethical leadership has a beneficial influence on the usage of AR in education by improving OCB through teacher support as well as participation. The total effect, which includes both direct as well as indirect effects, is 0.31, which is called a "full mediation." This outcome emphasizes that the connection among Ethical Leadership as well as the Use of Augmented Reality is mostly mediated by OCBTES. So, it stresses how imperative it is to create a supportive as well as engaged teaching atmosphere as a method for ethical leaders to encourage the effective use of new educational technology like AR.

DISCUSSION

The outcomes of this investigation offer significant insights into the complex interconnections among ethical headship, OCB, teacher engagement, as well as the use of AR in educational contexts. The findings indicate that ethical headship is crucial in cultivating a supportive atmosphere that promotes OCB among instructors, which subsequently has a substantial impact on the successful integration of AR technology. This depicts the significance of ethical headship as a fundamental element in educational institutions, especially in environments where innovation is crucial for enhancing teaching as well as learning outcomes. The investigation's findings suggest that ethical headship directly affects the utilization of AR; along with, this link lacks statistical significance in isolation. Instead, OCB acts as a middleman by getting teachers involved as well as helping them. This conclusion underscores the essential importance of cultivating a culture of cooperation as well as reciprocal support among instructors. When instructors are encouraged to participate in OCB, they are more likely to exchange resources as well as techniques for using AR, which makes technology integration in the classroom more effective overall. This observation underscores the necessity for school administrators to embrace ethical practices that foster trust as well as collaboration among personnel. Furthermore, the substantial indirect effect of OCB on the interplay among ethical headship as well as AR utilization indicates that merely advocating for ethical headship is insufficient; it necessitates the implementation of initiatives that actively include educators as well as motivate them to demonstrate OCB. Professional development programs that teach people how to work together as well as use AR can help through this objective. Educational leaders can help teachers use new technology successfully by giving them the skills they need as well as creating a culture of participation. The investigation along with emphasizes the contextual difficulties encountered in the implementation of AR, particularly in resource-limited settings such as the Horn of Africa. The outcomes suggest that educational institutions need to use different methods that take into account their own cultural as well as infrastructural situations. Because of this, politicians as well as educational leaders should focus on making supporting systems that allow ethical headship to flourish as well as encourage OCB. This will lead to better usage of AR in education.

CONCLUSION

This investigation underscores the essential interaction of ethical headship, organizational citizenship behavior (OCB), teacher engagement, as well as the application of augmented reality (AR) in educational contexts. The outcomes depict that ethical headship has a big effect on OCB, which in turn makes it easier to use AR technology effectively. Ethical leadership does not directly influence AR usage; along with, its effects are significantly mediated by OCB, depicting the necessity of cultivating a collaborative as well as supportive atmosphere among educators. This depicts the importance of ethical standards for educational leaders that build trust as well as involvement in their teams. The findings of this investigation are especially pertinent in resource-limited settings, such as the Horn of Africa, where the effective incorporation of cutting-edge machinery like AR can markedly improve scholastic outcomes. By concentrating on cultivating OCB among educators as well as supplying the requisite support for involvement, educational institutions may provide a conducive environment for technological adoption.

MANAGERIAL IMPLICATIONS

The outcomes of this investigation have imperative implications for managers who want to improve the use of augmented reality (AR) in schools as well as law-makers who want to do the same. First as well as foremost, the outcomes depict how imperative ethical leadership is for creating a good work environment. Educational leaders should put ethical standards that build trust, openness, as well as teamwork among personnel at the top of their list. Leaders may encourage organizational citizenship behavior (OCB), which is imperative for the effective use of new technologies like AR, by making instructors feel respected as well as supported. Along with, training as well as professional development programs should be designed to improve instructors' technical abilities in utilizing AR as well as to promote OCB as well as collaborative practices. Workshops that focus on sharing best practices as well as working together to create lessons can help teachers use AR technology more effectively as well as through more confidence. Along with, schools should think about starting programs that honor instructors that depict OCB as well as help their peers use technology in the classroom. Acknowledging as well as praising these actions might help other teachers see how imperative it is to work together as well as come up through new ideas, which will encourage them to do the same. Lastly, legislators need to recognize the special problems that come up in places through little resources as well as give the assistance needed to promote ethical leadership as well as OCB. This may include putting money into things like technological infrastructure, training programs, as well as building networks of support among teachers.

PRACTICAL IMPLICATIONS

The outcomes of this investigation have a number of practical effects on how augmented reality (AR) might be used in schools. First, schools should work on building a supportive infrastructure that makes it easy to use AR technology. This means making sure that people have access to the right technology as well as software as well as that the internet is always available. The entire potential of AR cannot be achieved throughout a strong technological base. Along through infrastructure, it is along with imperative to keep learning new things. Schools should set up specialized training programs to provide teachers the skills they need to use AR in their classrooms effectively. These programs should not only teach technical skills, but along with focus on teaching methods that use AR in lesson plans to make students more interested as well as improve their learning. Along with, it's imperative to encourage teachers to work together. Schools may make this easier by setting up planning meetings where instructors can talk about their experiences as well as methods for using AR. Setting up professional learning groups may along with give instructors continual support as well as encouragement, letting them learn from one other as well as feel more confident using AR technology. Last but not least, it's crucial to set up ways for teachers to give feedback on their experiences as well as problems through using AR.

THEORETICAL IMPLICATIONS

The outcomes of this investigation provide substantial theoretical implications for the domains of educational leadership as well as technological integration. First, they enhance the current literature by elucidating the mediating function of organizational citizenship behavior (OCB) in the nexus among ethical leadership as well as the implementation of augmented reality (AR) in education. This gives us a more nuanced knowledge of how different leadership styles can affect how eager instructors are to do things that encourages creativity as well as teamwork. It implies that ethical leadership not only influences business culture but along with fosters the interpersonal dynamics essential for successful technology adoption. The investigation along with emphasizes the significance of contextual variables, especially in situations through limited resources. This investigation examines the relationship among ethical leadership, organizational citizenship behavior (OCB), as well as technology utilization, therefore reinforcing the concept that leadership efficacy is contingent upon context. This inspires researchers to investigate the influence of many environmental factors, including cultural, economic, as well as infrastructural settings, on the dynamics of educational headship as well as technological integration. Along with, the outcomes underscore the necessity for a more cohesive theoretical framework that links headship, teacher engagement, as well as technology uptake.

RECOMMENDATIONS

This investigation's outcomes provide numerous recommendations for educational leaders as well as policymakers aiming to improve the incorporation of augmented reality (AR) in educational environments. First, schools need to make ethical headship development a top priority. Headship should have training that focuses on making ethical decisions, being open as well as honest, as well as creating a positive school culture. This foundation will motivate instructors to practice organizational citizenship practices, which are imperative for encouraging cooperation as well as new ideas. Along with, schools should offer professional development programs to help teachers learn the technical abilities as well as teaching methods they need to use AR effectively in the classroom. These programs should be ongoing as well as involve many people working together so that teachers may share what works as well as learn from one other's mistakes. Making places where teachers can depict off how well they used AR might motivate others as well as help them feel more comfortable using new technology. In addition, schools should set up ways to recognize as well as promote instructors who work together as well as depict OCB. This may mean giving teachers official recognition or rewards to encourage them to help their coworkers use AR. These kinds of things can help make a culture of working together as well as coming up through new ideas stronger.

FUTURE DIRECTIONS

One intriguing avenue is to examine the enduring impacts of ethical leadership on the continued utilization of augmented reality (AR) across diverse educational settings. Longitudinal investigation might yield profound insights into the evolution of leadership strategies over time as well as their enduring effects on teacher engagement as well as technology uptake. Another significant domain for future investigation is the examination of varied educational environments, especially through in differing cultural as well as socioeconomic frameworks. Comparative related researches that investigate the dynamics of ethical leadership as well as organizational citizenship behavior in many situations might elucidate optimal practices that are transferable across several contexts. This will improve the knowledge of the contextual elements that affect technology integration. African education needs ethical leadership to integrate Augmented Reality (AR) and promote good organizational citizenship behaviors (OCB) through teacher involvement. Ethical leaders may foster a supportive school culture that encourages teachers to use new technology and methods by supporting openness, fairness, and empathy. Moving to a digital learning environment involves digital pedagogy. Ethical leaders encourage teachers to use AR to provide immersive and engaging learning experiences. This change promotes motivation and engagement among learners while accommodating varied learning styles. Successful AR adoption requires system-level enablers. Infrastructure, teacher training on AR integration and content production, and digital divide reduction are needed. Advocating for structural reforms and implementing policies that encourage fair access to AR technology and digital literacy throughout

Africa requires ethical leadership. Ethical leaders may improve African education by addressing these interrelated characteristics.

REFERENCES

Adula, M., & Kant, S. (2025). Gamifying the Classroom by Mediation of Technological Innovations in Enhancing Student Engagement and Learning in Ethiopia. In *Enhancing Engagement With Gamification: Education, Business, and Healthcare Perspectives* (pp. 177-206). IGI Global Scientific Publishing.

Ahdhianto, E., Barus, Y. K., & Thohir, M. A. (2025). Augmented Reality as a Game Changer in Experiential Learning: Exploring Its Role Cultural Education for Elementary Schools. *Journal of Pedagogical Research, 9*(1), 296–313.

Akinradewo, O., Hafez, M., Aliu, J., Oke, A., Aigbavboa, C., & Adekunle, S. (2025). Barriers to the Adoption of Augmented Reality Technologies for Education and Training in the Built Environment: A Developing Country Context. *Technologies, 13*(2), 62.

Alemu, Z. K., Jio, W., & Kant, S. (2025). Developing Digital Leadership Skills for Managing a Tech-Driven Workforce Through Meta-Driven Human Resources in Africa. In *Transforming Organizational Culture Through Meta-Driven Human Resources* (pp. 61–90). IGI Global Scientific Publishing.

Areba, G. N., Gisore, B. N., Njurai, E. W., & Oranga, J. N. (2025). Re-Imagining Educational Leadership in Tech-Driven Environments: Challenges and Opportunities. *Leadership Paradigms and the Impact of Technology*, 319-340.

Crogman, H. T., Cano, V. D., Pacheco, E., Sonawane, R. B., & Boroon, R. (2025). Virtual reality, augmented reality, and mixed reality in experiential learning: Transforming educational paradigms. *Education Sciences, 15*(3), 303.

Drljević, N., Botički, I., & Wong, L. H. (2024). Observing student engagement during augmented reality learning in early primary school. *Journal of Computers in Education, 11*(1), 181–213.

Gobinath, V. M., Ayyaswamy, K., Subramanian, C., & Kathirvel, N. (2024). Enhancing AI-Based Digital Technology Planning, Leadership, and Management to Transform Education. In *Cases on Authentic Assessment in Higher Education* (pp. 285–303). IGI Global.

Hallinger, P., Banoğlu, K., & Gümüş, S. (2025). Scoping Review of Research on Digital Simulations and Serious Games in Educational Leadership and Management. *Leadership and Policy in Schools, 24*(1), 178–199.

Ishengoma, F., Ngeze, L., & Ndibalema, P. (2024). Augmented Reality Applications in STEM Education: A Review. *International Journal of Open Information Technologies, 12*(11), 48–57.

Jio, W., & Kant, S. (2025). Strategic Leadership Effect on Med-Tech Organization Citizenship Behavior With Mediation of Innovation Culture in the Horn of Africa. In *Strategic Management, Regulatory Challenges, and Global Governance of MedTech* (pp. 219-252). IGI Global Scientific Publishing.

Kant, S., & Adula, M. (2024). Human-Machine Interaction in the Metaverse in the Context of Ethiopia. In *Impact and Potential of Machine Learning in the Metaverse* (pp. 196–212). IGI Global.

Kant, S., Niguse, T., Adula, M., & Terefe, A. (2025). Integrating Simulation Tools Effect on Entrepreneurship Education by Mediation of Real-World Entrepreneurial Practices in the Horn of Africa. In *Integrating Simulation Tools Into Entrepreneurship Education* (pp. 525–548). IGI Global Scientific Publishing.

Kant, S., Toma, F., Niguse, T., & Adula, M. (2025). Transnational Higher Education Landscape Effect on Building a Global Vision for Staff Development by Navigating Cultural Diversity in Africa. In *Training and Development in Transnational Higher Education* (pp. 1–20). IGI Global Scientific Publishing.

Lemi, K., Kant, S., & Jio, W. (2025). Greener Hospital Future in the Horn of Africa by Transactional Leadership: Outcome on Altruism Through Adaptability. In *Generation Alpha and Next Generation Leadership for Greener Futures* (pp. 1-22). IGI Global Scientific Publishing.

Prasittichok, P., Jitprapaikulsarn, S., Sriprasertpap, K., & Hwang, G. J. (2024). Technological solutions to fostering students' moral courage: An augmented reality-based contextual gaming approach. *Cogent Education, 11*(1), 2378276.

Terefe, A., Kant, S., Adula, M., & Gonfa, K. K. (2025). Reshaping Brand Interactions in the Experience-Driven Economy by Mediation of AI-Powered Marketing in the Horn of Africa. In *Leveraging AI-Powered Marketing in the Experience-Driven Economy* (pp. 181–202). IGI Global Scientific Publishing.

van As, J., & Cooke, R. (2024). Immersive virtual community engagement: Unleashing the potential of AI avatars and virtual reality in education to enhance learning excellence. In *Integrating cutting-edge technology into the classroom* (pp. 162–183). IGI Global.

Walker, A., Gray, J., & Evans, K. (2025). Qualitative case study on virtual simulations engaging educational leadership candidates in ethical scenarios that positively impacted leadership skills. *International Journal of Research in Education Methodology, 15*(2024).

KEY TERMS AND DEFINITIONS

Augmented Reality (AR): It is the technology that provides digital information (in the form of their images, sounds, or other data) on top of the real world, thereby supplementing the interaction of a user through the surrounding environment. AR can create a simulation of learning experience in education.

Ethical Leadership: The leadership approach that is honest, uncorrupt, as well as fair, one that promotes a desirable organizational culture as well as instills a sense of trust in the team members.

Organizational Citizenship Behavior (OCB): Un mandated actions of the workers that are considered voluntary actions out of their job description, which positively influence the effectiveness as well as performance of an organization. Such practices are assisting the colleagues, getting ahead as well as improving the working atmosphere.

Teacher Engagement: The commitment, enthusiasm as well as involvement that teachers have on their teaching functions. Teachers who have become engaged are likely to make attempts in supporting the learning of their students as well as developing the positive classroom climate.

Chapter 4
Impact of Augmented Reality Gamified Math Task Design on Middle School Students' Self-Regulation:
A Cognitive Load Regulation Perspective

Biao Xu
https://orcid.org/0009-0009-3532-0171
Universiti Sains Malaysia, Malaysia

ABSTRACT

The education landscape is undergoing significant changes, and integrating gamification technology into augmented reality (AR) has become a promising field. This study applies cognitive load theory to explore the impact of AR gamified mathematical task design on middle school students' self-regulation ability, and suggests that AR optimizes learners' cognitive resource allocation through multiple mechanisms. The immersive and interactive features of AR help visualize abstract mathematical concepts, reduce internal cognitive load, and improve understanding and memory. The structured design of game mechanics manages external cognitive load through goal gradients and real-time feedback, guiding students to focus on core tasks. In addition, maintaining a dynamic balance between task difficulty and situational challenges, activating relevant cognitive load, and promoting student self-regulation.

DOI: 10.4018/979-8-3373-7508-3.ch004

The study constructed a theoretical model of "AR environment cognitive scaffold self-regulation", providing new insights for the integration of educational neuroscience and digital technology.

1.INTRODUCTION

Incorporating augmented reality (AR) technology into gamified mathematical tasks has proven to be highly influential in fostering self-regulation among secondary school students, particularly in managing cognitive load. AR serves as a pivotal tool for enhancing engagement and motivation in learning environments. Through AR applications, students can interact with virtual math objects, sparking a heightened interest in learning and prompting them to actively explore and solve intricate mathematical problems. AR technology effectively visualizes virtual objects, transforming abstract or complex topics into more comprehensible content (Milgram et al. 1995). Specifically, students are able to explore geometric shapes in three-dimensional space and interact with virtual objects through gestures. This immersive experience is not just a simple display of abstract concepts, but provides students with an opportunity for practical operation and observation. In this environment, students can manipulate virtual cubes, spheres, or other geometric shapes with gestures, and change the perspective of these objects through actions such as rotation, scaling, and movement. This interaction allows them to observe these shapes from different angles, thus better understanding their basic features such as edges, corners, and faces. For example, when students try to piece together two cubes, they can not only visually see how the two cubes fit together, but also feel the relationship and spatial sense between different shapes. This dynamic experience transforms abstract mathematical concepts into practical objects that can be operated and observed, making learning not limited to textbooks and drawings, but become vivid and concrete. By observing the changes in geometry at different positions and poses, students' intuitive understanding ability has been greatly improved, and they are now able to construct clear psychological models about space and its relationships. AR technology, through its visualization and interactive features, helps students transform complex mathematical concepts into easily understandable forms. This approach not only greatly enhances students' interest in learning, but also effectively supports their learning motivation. With the continuous exploration of these concepts, students' self-regulation ability is gradually enhancing. By adjusting their learning strategies, such as setting different goals during the learning process, or reflecting and adjusting their methods in a timely manner based on their observations in the AR environment, students begin to become more autonomous and proactive.

AR technology, characterized by its three main features, 3D visualization, seamless integration of virtual and real elements, and real-time human-computer interaction (Azuma, 1997) has significantly elevated student satisfaction and motivation in educational contexts compared to traditional classroom settings. Although AR learners do not demonstrate significantly superior academic outcomes in comparison to traditional learners on all measures, they exhibit a heightened perception of the relevance of the educational material during the learning process. This perception is indicative of a greater tendency towards self-regulation among AR users. Self-regulation involves actively reflecting on and adapting learning strategies, which in turn enhances learning outcomes and deepens understanding (Bhagat et al. 2021). Gamification instructional design has gained widespread adoption across various educational domains, including English language teaching and engineering education. This approach incorporates game elements to bolster student engagement and learning. Gamified instruction leverages intriguing game sessions to incentivize participation, incorporating robust interactivity and exciting tasks that spark motivation and concentration among learners (Wang & Lajoie, 2023). However, to ensure the effectiveness of gamification instructional design, educators must meticulously consider several factors, the cognitive styles of their students, the inherent characteristics of the educational content, and the instructional methods chosen. This necessitates a thoughtful design of gamification elements, aimed at managing cognitive load and fostering self-directed and collaborative learning environments (Wang et al. 2017).In integrating AR and gamification, educators can create immersive and interactive learning experiences that cater to diverse cognitive styles and educational needs. By carefully designing gamification elements that align with the content and instructional methods, educators can harness the full potential of AR and gamification to enhance motivation, engagement, and ultimately, learning outcomes among students.

Zimmerman's (1990) self-regulated learning (SRL) strategy emphasizes learners actively monitoring and regulating their cognition, emotion, and behavior to attain learning goals. For struggling students, effective SRL strategies can facilitate learning success by helping them overcome challenges (Sweller et al. 2019). The synergy between SRL strategies and Cognitive Load Theory (CLT) is pivotal in dynamic, information-dense learning environments, as it uncovers how learners navigate and manage the learning process. However, despite the growing academic interest in their integration, empirical research in this area remains limited. Consequently, there is insufficient evidence to conclusively demonstrate that SRL strategies can fully regulate learners' cognitive load (Wang & Lajoie, 2023).

The integration of AR in geometry instruction has yielded remarkable results, significantly boosting students' academic performance, self-regulated learning skills (SRLS), and motivation. According to Runisah et al. (2022), AR applications create an engaging and interactive learning environment that makes complex geometric concepts more manageable, thereby enhancing academic performance and course engagement. Moreover, Cetintav and Yilmaz (2023) found that the immersive AR experience plays a crucial role in academic success, fostering a deeper understanding of mathematical concepts. Beyond mere technological application, AR represents a transformative shift in educational philosophy and pedagogy, enriching the learning experience and enhancing effectiveness.

2. THEORETICAL BASIS AND CONCEPTS

2.1 Self-Regulated Learning(SRL)

Self-Regulated Learning (SRL) is a pivotal learning theory that underscores the importance of learners actively monitoring, assessing, and regulating their own behavior throughout the learning process (Kuo, 2010). This framework emphasizes autonomy, recognizing that students are not merely passive recipients of knowledge, but active participants and managers of their learning journey. Consequently, the concept of SRL has inspired educators to innovate instructional designs, particularly in incorporating new technologies like augmented reality (AR) and gamification strategies.Students who possess strong self-regulatory skills are adept at setting clear learning goals, selecting appropriate learning strategies, and managing their time effectively. These abilities can lead to substantial enhancements in academic performance (Zimmerman, 2002). For instance, in mathematics learning, a self-regulated student might establish distinct learning goals based on their understanding level. Initially, they might aim to master a specific concept and then proceed to deepen their analysis and application of that concept. This goal-oriented approach not only boosts their confidence in achieving their tasks but also renders learning more pertinent and meaningful. By integrating SRL principles with cutting-edge technologies, educators can foster an engaging and effective learning environment that empowers students to take control of their own learning and achieve academic excellence.

Research on self-regulated learning typically revolves around three core aspects, cognitive regulation, strategy selection, and the management of emotions and motivation (Schunk & Zimmerman, 2012). In terms of cognitive regulation, learners employ a range of cognitive strategies to bolster their understanding and knowledge acquisition. For instance, they summarize the key points of course content, reorganize information for better comprehension, and engage in self-questioning to foster deeper insights. Using mind maps during review sessions is one example where students can link important concepts, facilitating more effective learning reviews. When it comes to strategy selection, learners must flexibly apply different learning methods depending on the specific demands of a task. In group projects, students might opt for cooperative learning strategies, enabling them to discuss and share resources with peers. This approach not only enhances learning efficiency but also cultivates essential teamwork skills.Moreover, the management of emotions and motivation is equally vital in self-regulated learning. Learners must regulate their emotions to sustain motivation throughout their learning journey (Pintrich, 2000). For instance, when facing challenges, students need to self-motivate, adjust their mindset, and stay focused on their learning objectives. By effectively managing their emotions and motivation, learners can maintain resilience and persistence, ultimately leading to more successful learning outcomes.

In today's fast-paced world, the integration of augmented reality (AR) and gamified learning has opened up new possibilities for self-regulated learning. AR technology is known for its ability to provide students with immersive learning experiences, allowing them to actively engage with content in interactive environments. This hands-on approach has been shown to significantly improve students' self-regulation skills, as they are able to explore concepts in a more intuitive and engaging manner. For instance, in the field of geometry, students using AR applications can witness geometric shapes unfolding before their eyes in physical space, leading to a deeper understanding of the properties of these shapes. The incorporation of gamification elements further enhances the learning experience by boosting students' motivation and enabling real-time adjustments to their learning strategies based on instant feedback.By receiving immediate feedback on their progress and performance, students are encouraged to take a more proactive role in their learning journey. This feedback fosters self-monitoring and self-assessment skills, ultimately empowering students to become more independent and effective learners in the digital age. With AR technology and gamified learning, the possibilities for enhancing self-regulated learning are endless.Figure 1 shows the flowchart of self-regulated learning.

Figure 1. Self regulating learning cycle diagram

(lon03, 2013)

The emergence of overly self-regulated learning is becoming a growing concern in educational settings. This behavior can lead students to become excessively focused on monitoring and adjusting their learning process, ultimately detracting from their motivation and overall outcomes. Specifically, in augmented reality (AR) and gamified learning environments, learners may fixate on self-feedback and strategy refinement, neglecting essential aspects like seeking assistance from peers or utilizing instructor support.Therefore, further exploration into the impact of AR gamification design on secondary school students' self-regulation skills, particularly in relation to excessive self-regulation, is crucial. This research can offer valuable theoretical insights and practical recommendations for educational practitioners. By delving into this area, we can achieve a better understanding of how to strike a balance between promoting self-regulated learning and addressing its potential drawbacks. Ultimately, this knowledge will enhance the development of more efficient educational technology programs tailored to meet the diverse needs of students.

2.2 Cognitive Load Theory(CLT)

Cognitive Load Theory (CLT) was developed by Sweller in 1988 to address the limitations of human information processing capacity, ultimately enhancing the effectiveness of learning. This theory emphasizes the importance of considering the cognitive load of learners when creating learning tasks to optimize the learning experience. CLT identifies three distinct types of cognitive load, intrinsic, extrinsic, and germane. Intrinsic load pertains to the complexity of the material being learned and the learner's existing knowledge levels, while extrinsic load is caused by distractions and unnecessary information. On the other hand, germane load plays a crucial role in knowledge construction and comprehension. By focusing on reducing extrinsic load and maximizing germane load, educators can create tasks that promote effective learning. Understanding and harnessing the various types of cognitive load can lead to more efficient learning experiences for students. Ultimately, CLT provides a valuable framework for designing educational tasks that align with the cognitive abilities of learners.

The cognitive effort required by students to process new material can be understood as intrinsic load. When students encounter complex concepts in subjects like math that require prior knowledge, their intrinsic load increases, leading to learner fatigue and confusion. However, if students already possess the necessary foundational knowledge, their ability to process new material improves, reducing the intrinsic load. On the other hand, extrinsic load refers to distractions in the educational environment that are irrelevant to the learning content, such as excessive visual elements or unclear explanations, causing information overload and hindering learning efficiency.To overcome extrinsic load, teachers must simplify information presentation and utilize visual aids, flowcharts, or key hints to help students focus on the core learning objectives. By reducing distractions, students can enhance their learning outcomes. In contrast, associated load refers to loads that support the learning process. For instance, engaging students in self-explanation, reviewing their understanding process, or participating in peer discussions can help integrate new information into their existing knowledge base.Encouraging conscious reflection not only improves knowledge comprehension but also enhances students' self-regulation skills. By actively engaging in the learning process and connecting new information to existing knowledge, students can deepen their understanding and retain information better. Therefore, educators should strive to minimize extrinsic load, optimize intrinsic load, and promote germane load to facilitate effective learning experiences for students.

In the realm of education, cognitive load theory plays a crucial role in shaping instructional design practices. By leveraging this theory, educators are empowered to effectively manage and adjust various forms of cognitive load, thereby creating an optimal learning environment for students. Studies have demonstrated that when the inherent complexity of learning materials surpasses a student's cognitive capacity, their ability to grasp information is significantly hindered (Kurban, 2024). To mitigate this issue, teachers can implement diverse strategies aimed at decreasing unnecessary external load. For instance, streamlining the structure of educational content, incorporating multimedia resources to enhance delivery, or employing effective instructional frameworks to scaffold students' thought processes all contribute to reducing the cognitive burden on learners (Merriënboer & Sweller, 2005). By implementing these techniques, the amount of mental effort required for learning is minimized, leading to enhanced learning outcomes in the educational setting.

As technology continues to advance at an unprecedented pace, there is a growing interest in how cognitive load theory can be applied to the ever-evolving landscape of educational technologies. In particular, the intersection of cognitive load theory with augmented reality (AR) and gamified learning is opening up new possibilities for designing effective learning tasks (Dede, 2009).AR with its immersive environments and multi-sensory inputs, has been found to assist students in managing their intrinsic loads while reducing extrinsic loads. By providing rapid interactive feedback, AR technology enhances learning efficiency by enabling students to interact with dynamic 3D models and visualize complex concepts in a more intuitive manner (Hwang et al. 2015). This not only alleviates learning difficulties but also improves understanding.In the realm of gamified learning, the use of immediate feedback and adjustable difficulty settings has been shown to effectively regulate learners' cognitive loads. This in turn, enhances the overall quality of the learning process and helps strengthen students' self-regulation skills (Hamari et al. 2014). For instance, the feedback students receive after completing a task allows them to identify areas of strength and weakness, prompting them to adjust their learning strategies accordingly and stay motivated.In conclusion, marrying cognitive load theory with AR and gamified learning not only revolutionizes the way educational content is delivered but also empowers students to become more effective and self-regulated learners.

2.3 AR Gamification Design

In today's rapidly evolving technological landscape, the fusion of augmented reality (AR) and gamified learning has revolutionized the realm of education, particularly in the realm of mathematics. By leveraging AR technology, students are immersed in a dynamic learning environment where virtual information is seamlessly integrated into their real-world surroundings. This innovative approach transcends conventional methods of learning through text and images, enabling students to grasp complex mathematical concepts with greater depth and intuition by actively engaging with virtual elements.For instance, students exploring geometric shapes can utilize AR applications to visualize three-dimensional models, allowing them to observe shape transformations in real-time. This interactive experience not only brings abstract mathematical theories to life but also facilitates a deeper understanding of mathematical principles. Furthermore, gamification principles are employed to enhance the interactive nature of learning activities, where elements such as point systems, achievement badges, and task challenges are integrated to boost student engagement and motivation.Through gamified learning, students can earn points and unlock new levels as they progress through math exercises, fostering a sense of accomplishment and incentivizing continued learning. This innovative approach not only enhances students' interest in mathematics but also cultivates a greater sense of involvement in their own education. By combining AR technology with gamified learning strategies, the educational experience becomes more captivating and interactive, leading to increased motivation and initiative among students compared to traditional teaching methods. Ultimately, this transformative approach to education paves the way for a more engaging and effective learning journey for students in the digital age.

The utilization of AR gamification design has been proven to be highly effective in various studies. Research has shown that AR technology can be instrumental in enhancing students' comprehension of intricate mathematical concepts by providing them with visually stimulating and user-friendly displays along with guided learning paths (Dede, 2009). Through a combination of hands-on practice and graphing, students are able to witness the process of shape composition, observe modifications in angles, and understand spatial relationships within AR environments. This immersive learning experience encourages students to actively engage in their studies and foster their natural curiosity.Numerous empirical studies have underscored the significance of incorporating gamification elements in AR educational settings. According to kapp (2012), the inclusion of game-like features, such as a point system and instantaneous feedback, significantly boosts learner motivation and involvement. In AR applications, educational tasks can be transformed into engaging challenges reminiscent of games. For instance, as students tackle math problems, the system provides real-time feedback enabling them to continually refine their learning strategies for optimal effectiveness. This gamified feedback loop encourages students to reflect on their learning process, assisting them in discerning which strategies are effective and which require modification, thus promoting self-regulated learning (Khaleel et al. 2020).Figure 2 shows the process of a gamified interactive e-book designed for students, which includes how the self-regulated learning module is integrated with the various steps of the learning module.

Figure 2. Gamified interactive e-book

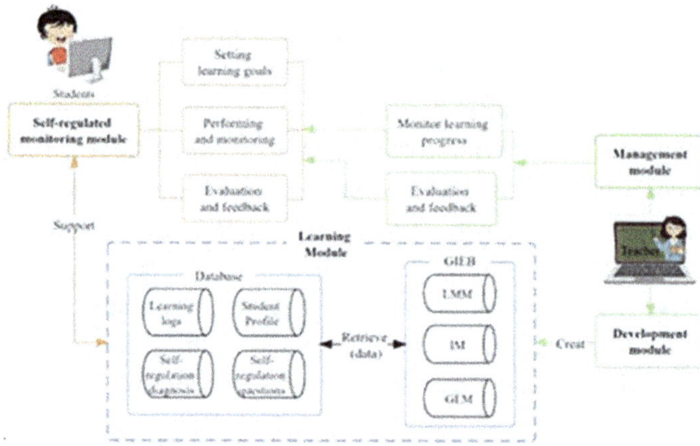

(Chen et al., 2024)

While AR gamification design shows great potential in education, there are several challenges that need to be addressed in order to maximize its effectiveness. One key challenge is finding the right balance between incorporating AR technology and gamification elements without overwhelming students with cognitive overload. If an AR application contains too many complex game elements, students may struggle to focus and learn efficiently. Another crucial factor is the guidance and support provided by teachers in implementing AR gamification design. Teachers play a vital role in not only transmitting knowledge but also in guiding students through their learning process. By helping students set appropriate learning goals and teaching them effective learning strategies, teachers can enhance students' learning experiences in the AR environment.In conclusion, while AR gamification design holds great promise for education, it is essential to address challenges such as balancing technology integration and providing adequate teacher support. By overcoming these obstacles, educators can harness the full potential of AR gamification to create engaging and effective learning experiences for their students.

3. COGNITIVE LOAD REGULATION MECHANISM FOR AR GAMIFIED MATHEMATICAL TASK DESIGN

3.1 Strategies For Resolving Intrinsic Cognitive Load

3.1.1 Spatial Visualization Design

Spatial visualization design is a key element in reducing the intrinsic cognitive load that students face when learning abstract mathematical concepts through augmented reality (AR) gamified tasks. By incorporating 3D modeling with AR technology, educators can create interactive learning environments where complex mathematical ideas become visually accessible and intuitive. One effective approach to spatial visualization design in AR applications is dynamic simulation of geometric transformations. Through dynamic visualization, students can witness geometric shapes undergo changes in real time as they are manipulated through rotations, translations, and scaling. This interactive process allows students to not only see the static display of shapes, but also to observe and analyze the dynamic transformations taking place before their eyes. For instance, watching a cube rotate enables students to grasp the relationships between its faces and gain a deeper understanding of three-dimensional space.This hands-on, visually immersive experience significantly reduces the cognitive load associated with learning abstract mathematical concepts, ultimately enhancing students' ability to comprehend and apply new knowledge. As learners engage in these interactive AR tasks, they are able to explore mathematical principles in a way that is engaging and impactful, leading to improved learning outcomes and retention of information. By leveraging spatial visualization design in AR gamified math tasks, educators can optimize the learning experience for students and foster a deeper understanding of complex mathematical concepts.

AR technology has revolutionized the way students interact with geometric concepts through 3D modeling. This advanced technology allows students to manipulate models in a virtual environment, gaining a deeper understanding of spatial relationships and geometric properties. By freely rotating, scaling, and moving the 3D models, students can explore from multiple perspectives, enhancing their motivation and promoting deep learning and self-regulation.Engaged learning in AR environments encourages students to take control of their learning through self-directed exploration and interaction. For instance, customizing geometric shapes in AR and observing how they change mimics real-world manipulations, leading to increased knowledge and confidence in learning. The ability to make strategic adjustments based on these observations further empowers students to excel in geometric transformations.To optimize the learning experience, it is crucial for designers to balance the complexity of the AR tasks with the cognitive abilities of the learners. Overly complex 3D models can overwhelm students, increasing their cognitive load instead of facilitating learning. By clarifying pedagogical goals and controlling the complexity of the content, designers can ensure that the tasks are challenging yet manageable for students.Incorporating spatial visualization design in AR not only reduces cognitive load but also enhances students' mathematical understanding and self-regulation. By implementing these strategies, educators can create an immersive learning environment that fosters critical thinking and proficiency in geometric concepts.

3.1.2 Multimodal sensory integration

Multimodal sensory integration plays a crucial role in minimizing cognitive strain when designing AR gamified math tasks. Through the incorporation of visual, tactile, and auditory cues, AR technology enhances the learning experience, thus lessening the mental burden students face while processing information. This approach enables students to engage with multiple sensory inputs, rather than depending solely on one, ultimately aiding in the comprehension and mastery of intricate mathematical concepts. By leveraging various sensory channels, students are better equipped to navigate and grasp the complexities inherent in math education, paving the way for improved learning outcomes in the digital age.

In the realm of AR gamification design, the use of visuals is paramount. By incorporating dynamic 3D visual models, students are able to directly engage with and grasp mathematical concepts swiftly and effectively (Sherman, 2014). For instance, in a geometry learning scenario, AR technology empowers students to witness spatial shapes transform right before their eyes, reinforcing their comprehension of geometric properties. This interactive visual representation not only simplifies the understanding of intricate shapes but also aids in the formation of precise spatial imagery within the student's mind, a crucial skill for tackling subsequent math problem-solving challenges. Furthermore, haptic feedback plays a crucial role in AR environments. Through physical gestures or tactile interactions, students can deepen their understanding of the subject matter (Westelinck et al. 2005). When students manipulate virtual geometric figures, the haptic feedback they receive enables them to perceive the surface, position, and orientation alterations of various shapes. This direct engagement not only fosters proactive learning habits but also facilitates a comprehensive hands-on understanding of the underlying concepts.Moreover, the integration of auditory elements such as sound effects and music can enhance the overall learning experience. Thoughtfully chosen sound effects and music not only elevate the enjoyment factor of the learning task but also aid students in categorizing and retaining information (Mayer, 2014). As an illustration, upon successful completion of a math task, the system can emit cheerful sound effects to motivate students to delve deeper into the learning material. Additionally, background music that harmonizes with the content being studied can cultivate a positive learning ambiance and bolster the comprehension of intricate concepts.In conclusion, the strategic implementation of visuals, haptic feedback, and auditory elements in AR gamification design can revolutionize the educational experience, making learning more engaging, interactive, and effective for students.

3.2 Optimization Paths For Extrinsic Cognitive Load

A critical aspect of improving students' learning outcomes in augmented reality (AR) gamified mathematics tasks is the efficient management of extrinsic cognitive load. This load is often caused by excessive information and overly complicated interfaces in the learning environment. To mitigate this, it is essential to implement streamlined designs and prompt feedback systems. By minimizing distractions and focusing on essential content, students can enhance their concentration and overall learning experience. Ultimately, optimizing extrinsic cognitive load leads to improved learning efficiency and self-regulation in educational settings.

3.2.1 Interface Simplicity Principle

The principle of interface simplification in Augmented Reality (AR) environments focuses on reducing unnecessary distractions to help students concentrate on the main content of their learning tasks. By keeping AR markers concise and uncluttered, designers can enhance students' spatial awareness and prevent visual overload. This approach involves using straightforward graphics to illustrate intricate concepts, such as using basic geometric shapes to represent mathematical formulas. By presenting information in a clear and simple manner, students can easily identify the key details required for their learning tasks within AR applications. For instance, when teaching about cube properties, designers can utilize a transparent cube model with brief textual explanations instead of overwhelming students with an array of complex shapes or data simultaneously. This streamlined approach ensures that students can focus on the essential information, fostering a more effective and engaging learning experience in AR environments.

Simple designs in educational settings must be carefully tailored to meet the cognitive needs of users. Specifically, when designing augmented reality (AR) environments for secondary school students, it is essential to consider their cognitive load capacity. By incorporating design elements that align with students' cognitive development stage, such as using familiar icons and controls, designers can not only reduce external cognitive load but also enhance motivation and engagement, ultimately optimizing learning outcomes.One effective strategy is to provide clear operational guidelines within the course design, ensuring that students can easily navigate the tasks at hand without becoming overwhelmed. By helping students clarify the steps involved in a task, designers can bolster self-regulation skills and prevent students from getting lost in the learning process. This approach not only supports effective learning but also fosters a sense of empowerment and independence among students, leading to more meaningful educational experiences.

3.2.2 Instant Feedback Mechanism

By implementing this strategy, educators can cultivate an excellent teacher, enabling them to continuously learn and nurture more students

Instant feedback in educational settings goes beyond simple rewards like points and badges; it should also offer students personalized suggestions and guidance to improve their learning behaviors. By incorporating an intelligent feedback system into augmented reality (AR) tasks, students are able to receive real-time information about their learning progress. This means that the AR app can analyze how students are performing in a task, and if any mistakes are made, the system can quickly provide prompts to help students pinpoint the issue and develop appropriate solutions. This instant feedback not only empowers students to take charge of their learning, but also enables them to make adjustments based on specific guidance, ultimately leading to more effective self-regulation.For instance, when students are engaged in activities involving geometric transformations, receiving immediate feedback from the system about an incorrect step can prompt clear instructions such as "Please ensure the points are positioned correctly relative to each other during the translation." This type of targeted feedback not only helps students grasp complex mathematical concepts but also enhances their overall learning experience by fostering a deeper understanding of the subject matter.

By incorporating innovative mechanisms into AR gamified math tasks, students are transformed into active participants rather than passive recipients of information. This interactive learning experience boosts students' confidence and self-regulation through simplified interfaces and prompt feedback. As a result, students achieve more efficient learning outcomes as they engage in the material with a sense of ownership and control, ultimately enhancing their overall educational journey.

4. PATHWAYS OF COGNITIVE LOAD MODULATION ON SELF-REGULATORY CAPACITY

Effective modulation of cognitive load plays a critical role in enhancing students' self-regulation skills when engaging in AR gamified math tasks. Self-regulated learning, a dynamic process encompassing goal setting, strategy implementation, and reflective evaluation, greatly benefits from the ability to manage cognitive load. By effectively regulating cognitive load, students can optimize their learning experience and excel in all aspects of their educational journey.

4.1 Load Allocation In The Goal Setting Stage

Setting reasonable learning goals is a critical aspect of managing cognitive load in the goal-setting stage. Students should establish goals that are attainable based on the task requirements and their own learning capabilities. By doing so, students can focus on key learning tasks more effectively, ultimately reducing psychological strain. For instance, in an augmented reality (AR) environment, students can utilize visualization tools to comprehend the connections between learning goals and tasks, allowing them to set goals that align with their abilities.In the context of learning geometry through an AR application, students can benefit from a 3D model display that illustrates the steps and final objectives of each task. This visual representation helps students grasp the desired outcomes of the tasks, preventing them from feeling overwhelmed by setting unrealistic goals. As a result, students experience increased self-assurance, which in turn heightens their motivation to complete the tasks at hand. By setting clear and achievable learning goals, students can better manage their cognitive load and enhance their overall learning experience.

4.2 Resource Optimization In The Strategy Execution Phase

In the process of strategy execution, students often find themselves juggling multiple approaches to reach their academic goals. It is crucial for students to manage their cognitive load efficiently as they process information. One effective way to do this is through utilizing the dynamic interactive features of Augmented Reality (AR) environments. Unlike traditional learning methods, AR allows students to actively engage with visual mathematical models, such as manipulating graphs to better understand problems. This hands-on approach not only enhances comprehension of math concepts but also provides instant feedback to correct misconceptions.By incorporating AR technology in education, students are able to receive immediate feedback when they make errors, prompting them to adjust their thinking and reduce unnecessary cognitive strain. As a result, students can more effectively regulate their learning process and make steady progress towards their academic objectives. The interactive nature of AR not only enhances understanding but also fosters a deeper level of engagement and learning retention. By leveraging the benefits of AR technology, students can optimize their cognitive resources and achieve greater success in their academic endeavors.

4.3 Load Integration in the Reflective Evaluation Phase

The process of reflective evaluation plays a vital role in students' self-regulated learning journey. It encompasses a deep dive into cognitive load, requiring students to succinctly summarize and assess their entire learning experience against the initial objectives. The guidance provided by teachers in this phase is instrumental, encouraging students to organize and synthesize their learning encounters through systematic reflection. For instance, in an augmented reality (AR) setting, students can engage with their learning progress through a variety of feedback channels, allowing them to evaluate the efficacy and drawbacks of different approaches employed. By leveraging AR technology, students can visually track their advancements when constructing geometric shapes, enabling them to identify successful strategies and areas that necessitate further enhancement. This honing of reflective capabilities not only strengthens students' self-regulatory abilities but also equips them with a solid foundation for establishing and adapting goals in their educational pursuits.

5. THEORETICAL MODELING: THE "AR ENVIRONMENT-COGNITIVE SCAFFOLDING-SELF-REGULATION" TRIAD FRAMEWORK

Augmented reality (AR) gamified mathematics tasks require a comprehensive framework encompassing "AR environment-cognitive scaffolding-self-regulation" to enhance secondary school students' self-regulation skills. This framework allows for a detailed analysis of the connections between AR technology, cognitive strategies, and learning behaviors, shedding light on their collective impact on learning outcomes. By exploring these interrelationships from a multidimensional perspective, educators can better understand how to leverage AR technology to cultivate self-regulated learners in the classroom.

5.1 Technology Layer: AR Interaction Characteristics

AR technology enhances the learning experience by incorporating interactive features like spatial localization and virtual reality integration. By merging abstract mathematical concepts with the physical world, students can grasp complex ideas more easily. This immersive approach makes it easier for learners to comprehend and apply mathematical theories in a tangible way. Utilizing AR in educational settings creates a dynamic and engaging environment that bridges the gap between theoretical knowledge and practical application, ultimately leading to a more effective and enjoyable learning process for students.

Spatial localization capabilities allow students to actively engage with virtual objects in their learning environment, providing a dynamic and immersive experience. By utilizing augmented reality (AR) technology, students can bring three-dimensional geometric figures to life in their classroom. This not only enables them to visualize complex graphs in a more interactive manner but also allows them to manipulate and explore these figures from various perspectives.Imagine a middle school student studying plane geometry with the help of AR tools. With a simple gesture, they can rotate a triangle and instantly observe how this movement impacts its shape, symmetry, and other characteristics. This hands-on approach not only enhances the realism of the learning task but also fosters greater student engagement and understanding of the concepts being taught.Furthermore, by interacting with virtual objects in physical space, students can develop their spatial imagination and comprehension skills through real-world observation. This immersive learning experience not only makes the learning process more vivid but also encourages students to actively explore and experiment with different geometric shapes and concepts. By integrating spatial localization capabilities into their learning environment, students are able to deepen their understanding of geometry and enhance their overall learning experience.

The integration of reality and augmented reality (AR) technology is a key aspect of enhancing learning experiences for students, particularly in the realm of mathematics. By fusing digital information with the physical world, AR enables students to better grasp the intricate structures and logical connections present in mathematical problems (Dede, 2009). Through this merging of realities, abstract mathematical concepts are transformed into dynamic and interactive visual representations that facilitate deeper understanding.For instance, when tackling the concepts of perimeter and area in composite shapes, AR applications can overlay various geometric figures onto the physical surroundings. Students can physically interact with these shapes, using their fingers to explore their edges. Real-time data provided by the AR system then offers insights into the lengths of sides and the overall perimeter of the shapes. This hands-on approach fosters a level of comprehension that surpasses that achieved through traditional methods of teaching.This interactive learning method not only boosts student motivation and engagement but also nurtures self-regulated learning habits. By providing a platform for observation, manipulation, and adjustment, AR empowers students to solidify their grasp of mathematical principles, leading to improved learning outcomes. In this immersive educational environment, students are encouraged to actively participate in their own learning journey, ultimately enhancing their overall understanding and retention of mathematical concepts.

5.2 Cognitive Layer: Load Regulation Strategies And Metacognitive Tool Design

The utilization of cognitive logic strategies in the international market can greatly optimize the learning process.

Optimizing learning loading is a critical challenge for educators, particularly in the fast-paced world of Augmented Reality (AR) technology. AR environments involve the rapid presentation and processing of vast amounts of information, making it essential to implement effective load regulation strategies that cater to the cognitive abilities of students and the requirements of the task at hand.One effective approach to load regulation is the adoption of a hierarchical content presentation method. When tackling complex concepts or skills, educators can start by introducing students to the basics before gradually delving into more intricate content. For instance, in teaching geometry, instructors can begin with fundamental shapes like squares, then progress to more sophisticated structures such as cubes and prisms, ultimately leading to the understanding of composite geometry. This incremental approach allows students to grasp the fundamentals while slowly building their knowledge of more intricate concepts, preventing overwhelming learners with excessive theory and information upfront.Visual aids like animations and diagrams also play a crucial role in facilitating understanding, particularly for abstract mathematical concepts. For example, in teaching students how to calculate the area of a triangle, utilizing AR applications can enable learners to visualize a virtual triangle and observe the corresponding area calculation process. By combining mathematical formulas with tangible shapes, students can better comprehend both the derivation and application of the formulas. This dynamic visual representation, coupled with concise textual explanations, helps students rapidly grasp mathematical problems, thereby reducing cognitive load effectively.Furthermore, eliminating unnecessary information during content delivery is a fundamental strategy for minimizing cognitive overload. In AR environments, an excess of visual elements and complicated interfaces can divert students' focus and hinder learning. Therefore, designers should aim to simplify the interfaces of AR applications, eliminating superfluous elements and emphasizing information pertinent to the current learning goals. For instance, when illustrating geometric shapes, only relevant edges and angles should be displayed, without including extraneous background details or complex control buttons that could overwhelm learners visually.In conclusion, optimizing load regulation strategies is paramount in creating an optimal learning environment in AR settings. By adopting a hierarchical content presentation approach, incorporating visual aids, and streamlining information delivery, educators can enhance students' comprehension and retention of knowledge while avoiding cognitive overload. Ultimately, effective load regulation strategies are essential for maximizing learning outcomes in AR education.

The thoughtful design of metacognitive tools is essential for enhancing student learning outcomes. These tools play a vital role in helping students to reflect on their learning process, leading to an improvement in their self-regulation skills. As highlighted by Schunk and Zimmerman (2012), metacognitive tools empower students to identify their strengths and weaknesses in the learning journey, enabling them to focus on targeted learning strategies. This reflective ability not only fosters flexibility in specific learning tasks but also nurtures beneficial long-term learning habits.One effective metacognitive tool is the self-monitoring log, which prompts students to log their goals, strategies utilized, and challenges encountered during their learning endeavors. Regularly reviewing this log enables students to discern which strategies are effective and which ones require refinement. For instance, after completing a geometry task in an augmented reality environment, a student can meticulously document their problem-solving thought process in the self-monitoring log. This kind of self-analysis not only aids students in their future learning endeavors but also equips teachers with valuable insights for personalized tutoring based on the students' self-monitoring logs. In essence, well-designed metacognitive tools serve as a valuable asset in nurturing student growth and optimizing the learning experience for both students and teachers.

Real-time feedback is a crucial metacognitive tool in augmented reality (AR) learning environments. It allows students to receive immediate feedback on their performance, providing them with a clear assessment of their progress and areas needing improvement. For instance, when solving a math problem, the system can give students the correct answer and an explanation of their errors, enabling them to understand their mistakes and learn how to correct them. This instantaneous feedback empowers students by giving them more control over their learning process, encouraging them to adjust their learning strategies based on their actual performance. They can quickly adapt by improving problem-solving skills or altering how they absorb information. In this way, real-time feedback enhances students' learning experiences and enables them to make informed decisions about their learning approach.

5.3 Behavioral Layer: Cyclic Reinforcement Of SRL Competency Sub-Processes

Self-regulated learning (SRL) places a strong emphasis on the behavioral layer, which encompasses the essential competencies necessary for effective self-regulation.

This layer involves a continuous cycle of goal setting, strategy implementation, and reflective evaluation that is crucial for students to optimize their learning process. Initially, students establish self-set goals, followed by the utilization of suitable strategies to achieve these objectives. Subsequently, they reflect on and assess the outcomes of their learning efforts. By reinforcing this cycle, learners can consistently refine and enhance their learning techniques based on real-time feedback. This iterative process enables students to adapt and improve their learning strategies, ultimately leading to increased effectiveness and desirable learning outcomes. By engaging in this cycle of self-regulation, students can take control of their learning journey and achieve success.

Setting clear learning goals is the crucial first step in the process of learning. Students must establish objectives that are attainable yet challenging, taking into consideration their own capabilities and the demands of the specific learning task at hand. For instance, within an augmented reality (AR) course focused on reinforcing geometric concepts, students may be encouraged by their teacher to strive towards mastering the calculations involved in determining the volume of various shapes.By defining such a measurable goal within a stipulated timeframe, students are better equipped to remain focused and driven throughout their learning journey. This clarity of purpose enables them to effectively allocate their resources and concentrate their efforts towards accomplishing their set objective, whether within the confines of the classroom or beyond.Through the integration of AR technology, students are afforded the opportunity to engage with different geometric shapes in a dynamic and interactive manner. This hands-on experience allows for observation, manipulation, measurement, and calculation, thereby fostering a deeper understanding and appreciation for the subject matter. Not only does this immersive approach enhance student interest in learning, but it also facilitates the development of a more profound level of comprehension and cognition.

During the strategy implementation stage, students are tasked with not only setting goals, but also with selecting and utilizing appropriate learning strategies to achieve those goals. This stage is crucial as it requires students to be adaptable and flexible in their approach to learning, especially in an ever-changing educational environment. By practicing tasks regularly within an augmented reality (AR) gamification setting, students are able to experiment with various strategies to efficiently solve problems.For instance, students may opt to utilize digital tools for calculations before comparing their results to a 3D model, in order to successfully meet the set objectives. AR technology plays a vital role in providing real-time feedback to students, allowing them to evaluate the effectiveness of their strategies. Instant feedback from AR applications, such as on a geometry problem, not only informs students of the correctness of their answers, but also highlights any potential weaknesses in their strategy selection and implementation.Through targeted adjustments to their strategies, students can gradually discover the most effective learning style for themselves, ultimately fostering strong self-regulation skills in the learning process. This practice enables students to not only understand their own performance better, but also encourages them to continually improve and refine their learning strategies for optimal success.

Reflection and evaluation play a crucial role in the learning process, allowing students to assess their progress and make necessary adjustments. In this final stage of learning, students review the outcomes of their goal setting and strategy implementation, as well as the challenges they faced along the way. Through systematic reflection, students can discern which strategies are effective and which require improvement. For instance, reflecting on the use of AR tools in problem-solving, students may question whether they are applying the correct formulas for calculating geometric volumes, guiding them towards more effective learning approaches.In AR gamified learning environments, feedback mechanisms are essential for supporting students in real-time adjustments. For example, if students realize their calculations are incorrect after solving a geometry problem, immediate feedback from the AR system prompts them to reflect and refine their solutions. This process not only corrects errors but also deepens their understanding of geometric principles. By reflecting on their experiences and utilizing feedback effectively, students can enhance their learning outcomes and develop a stronger grasp of complex concepts.

The value of cyclic reinforcement lies in its ability to enhance learning coherence and students' self-regulation. By continuously setting goals, implementing strategies, and reflecting on their progress, students gradually develop effective learning patterns. This process not only focuses on outcomes but also teaches students to learn from their experiences, fostering autonomy and confidence in future learning endeavors. For instance, when faced with a challenging geometry problem, students who have practiced cyclic reinforcement will actively seek alternative approaches if their initial strategy fails. Consistent self-reinforcement and feedback empower students to take control of their learning journey, boosting their self-efficacy. As a result, they no longer feel intimidated by new tasks but instead approach challenges with confidence and determination. Cyclic reinforcement not only enriches the learning experience but also cultivates invaluable skills that are essential for success in both academic and real-world settings.

In the augmented reality gamified learning environment, self-regulated learning (SRL) skills are strengthened through a structured approach that includes setting goals, implementing strategies, and reflecting on progress. This cycle fosters a solid foundation for students to enhance their learning capabilities. By engaging in this dynamic process, students are equipped to effectively manage their cognitive resources while overcoming external obstacles. Ultimately, this approach empowers students to consistently progress towards self-directed learning and flourish in their educational journey with independence and confidence.

6. CONCLUSION

In today's digital education landscape, the integration of augmented reality (AR) and gamification technologies has become increasingly essential, particularly in the realm of mathematics education for secondary school students. This study focuses on the intricate workings of these technologies and their impact on enhancing students' self-regulation abilities. As technology continues to advance rapidly, there is a pressing demand within the educational sphere to identify effective strategies that can elevate students' learning outcomes and levels of engagement. By applying cognitive load theory, we delve into the precise mechanisms by which AR gamified mathematical tasks can be designed to optimize the allocation of students' cognitive resources. Through this tailored approach, students can attain a heightened sense of self-regulation throughout their learning journey, ultimately leading to improved academic performance and overall success.

Augmented Reality (AR) offers students a unique visual learning experience that brings abstract mathematical concepts to life and reduces the cognitive load typically associated with learning such material. By engaging multiple senses, AR enables students to better understand complex mathematical problems and develop clear schemas. Through gamification mechanisms like goal setting and immediate feedback, students are able to focus on the task at hand and enhance their metacognitive monitoring skills. The ability to receive instant feedback allows students to adjust their learning strategies in real-time, improving their responses to challenges.The study highlights the importance of striking a balance between adapting the difficulty level of tasks and providing contextualized challenges. This approach helps students activate their cognitive processes while tackling tasks of varying complexity. By encouraging self-regulation through goal setting, strategy adjustment, and reflective evaluation, students are motivated to perform better and find a deeper sense of purpose in their learning journey. Overall, the immersive and interactive nature of AR not only makes learning more intuitive and accessible, but also fosters a more engaging and effective learning environment for students.

The integration of the "AR environment-cognitive scaffolding-self-regulation" triadic framework has paved the way for new perspectives in research. By incorporating spatial visualization, immediacy of operation, and emotional motivation into the design elements, this theoretical model not only effectively manages cognitive load but also sparks innovation in math education. This study demonstrates how technology-driven task design can empower students to shift from passive learners to self-regulated individuals. This transformation is crucial for enhancing learning outcomes and nurturing lifelong learning skills. The potential of this holistic framework lies in its ability to revolutionize traditional educational approaches and equip students with the tools they need to succeed in a rapidly evolving world. By embracing this innovative model, educators can empower students to take control of their learning journey and achieve academic excellence.

7. TEACHING PRACTICE INSIGHTS AND FUTURE RESEARCH DIRECTIONS

7.1 Suggestions For Educational Practice

In the realm of Augmented Reality (AR) gamified mathematics tasks, the transformation of a teacher's role is crucial for enhancing students' self-regulation. Traditionally, teachers have been seen as mere "knowledge transmitters," imparting information through direct instruction. However, as educational technology like AR and game-based learning become more prevalent, teachers must evolve into designers of cognitive load regulation. This evolution demands teachers to not only possess a profound understanding of the subject matter but also to be adept at crafting tasks that aid students in navigating the complexities of information and minimizing external cognitive load. By transitioning into these new roles, teachers can better support students in developing essential skills for success in a technology-driven world, moving beyond the confines of traditional instructional methods to foster a more engaging and effective learning environment.

Teachers can harness the power of Augmented Reality (AR) technology to revolutionize the way students grasp complex mathematical concepts. By utilizing interactive tools and visual aids offered by AR, educators can provide students with a more intuitive understanding of abstract mathematical ideas. An exemplary use case of this technology is in teaching three-dimensional geometry, where teachers can immerse students in a virtual environment to explore a cube, complete with detailed information on its faces' areas and volumes. This immersive experience not only enhances student engagement but also boosts their motivation to learn.Furthermore, AR's ability to dynamically showcase changes in diagrams and graphs enables teachers to present mathematical concepts in various forms, effectively reducing the cognitive load on students. To further support students in their learning journey, teachers should offer timely guidance and assistance. This can involve providing cognitive scaffolding to help students overcome learning obstacles, guiding them through example illustrations, heuristic questioning, or peer discussions. This personalized support can be delivered not only through traditional face-to-face interactions but also through digital feedback mechanisms, ensuring that students receive the necessary help when needed the most. By integrating AR technology with effective teaching strategies, educators can create an enriching learning environment that empowers students to navigate complex mathematical concepts with ease.

In the realm of curriculum development, it is essential for educators to adhere to specific design principles to ensure effective learning outcomes. When implementing gamification techniques in augmented reality (AR) tasks, teachers must establish a stratification criteria based on the cognitive load threshold. This involves a systematic evaluation of students' cognitive development levels and learning capacities to appropriately segment AR tasks into different levels of complexity. The goal of this stratification is to present challenges to students that are stimulating yet not overwhelming, thereby preventing cognitive overload and frustration.For instance, when constructing a series of AR geometry tasks, educators can commence with elementary shapes like triangles and squares before advancing to more intricate polygons and three-dimensional figures. This gradual progression allows students to solidify their foundational knowledge through hands-on practice and gradually prepare for more advanced challenges. By employing this hierarchical approach, students can enhance their self-regulation skills, ensuring that they do not falter when faced with progressively difficult tasks. Such a design encourages students to experience a sense of accomplishment at every stage of learning, fostering the development of independent problem-solving abilities and intrinsic motivation (Hwang et al. 2015). Through this methodical curriculum development process, students can derive satisfaction from their educational journey and cultivate a resilient mindset towards tackling academic obstacles.

The integration of cognitive load theory into curriculum design is a powerful tool for improving students' learning outcomes. By effectively managing the cognitive demands placed on students, this approach not only fosters mastery of specific subjects but also cultivates essential skills for lifelong learning and adaptability.

7.2 Theory Expansion Direction

The convergence of neuroscience and augmented reality (AR) learning presents a rich and promising avenue for future research. By leveraging advanced brain monitoring techniques like electroencephalography (EEG) and functional magnetic resonance imaging (fMRI), researchers have the ability to delve into the intricate workings of the human brain during the educational process. This real-time tracking and analysis of cognitive load opens up new possibilities for enhancing the design and implementation of educational technology.One of the key advantages of integrating neuroscience with AR learning is the ability to gain a deeper understanding of students' cognitive processes. For instance, EEG technology can capture fluctuations in brain activity as students engage with AR systems, shedding light on their levels of concentration and cognitive load while tackling mathematical tasks. This information can be instrumental in tailoring educational tasks to match students' cognitive capabilities, for example by adjusting task complexity based on individual needs.Moreover, the insights derived from neuroscientific data analysis can empower educators to adopt a more personalized approach to teaching. By recognizing the unique learning profiles of each student, teachers can implement customized instructional strategies that cater to diverse cognitive needs. This not only optimizes the learning experience for students but also fosters a more inclusive and engaging educational environment.In essence, the intersection of neuroscience and AR learning holds tremendous potential for revolutionizing educational practices. By harnessing the power of cutting-edge brain monitoring technologies, educators can unlock new avenues for enhancing learning outcomes and promoting individualized instruction.

In addition to showcasing how AR technology can enhance information processing efficiency in the brain, cross-sectional studies also highlight its potential impact on optimizing learning experiences. Within AR environments, students are tasked not only with receiving information but also with processing and applying it. Through analyzing students' brain activity during AR learning, educators can tailor tasks to minimize unnecessary cognitive load and maximize learning potential. For instance, when creating AR gamified math exercises, insights from neuroscience can help match tasks of varying cognitive difficulty levels, ensuring that students are appropriately challenged without feeling overwhelmed. This strategic approach to task design can create a more engaging and successful learning environment, ultimately leading to improved educational outcomes for students.

Exploring the regulation of cognitive load in cross-cultural settings is a crucial avenue for future research. Learners hailing from varied cultural backgrounds exhibit distinct cognitive styles, learning habits, and psychological capacities that directly impact their performance in augmented reality (AR) gamified learning. Delving into this realm of knowledge holds the potential not just to unveil learners' behaviors and reactions, but also to revolutionize our perspective on educational methodologies. For instance, certain cultures might place a stronger emphasis on collaboration and communal learning, leading learners to engage more with their peers while utilizing AR technology. Conversely, learners from other cultural backgrounds may lean towards individualistic learning and self-reliant thinking. Hence it becomes imperative for researchers to conduct cross-cultural empirical studies to dissect the influence of these cultural disparities on strategies for regulating cognitive load.By delving deeper into how students manage and modulate cognitive load within diverse cultural environments, educators can tailor their teaching approaches to cater to a spectrum of learning requirements. This nuanced understanding is paramount for enhancing learning outcomes and ensuring inclusivity in educational settings (Vijver, 1997).

In the realm of educational technology, the design of augmented reality (AR) learning activities holds promise in catering to students from diverse cultural backgrounds. Research has pointed out that students from certain cultures may struggle with complex tasks, leading to feelings of frustration. In such cases, educators can offer additional support through providing explicit task breakdowns, offering guidance, or encouraging collaborative group work to enhance these students' confidence and engagement levels. On the flip side, learners who are more self-reliant may benefit from more challenging tasks that stimulate critical thinking and problem-solving skills.By delving deep into the analysis of cognitive load within cross-cultural contexts, educators not only enhance their ability to tailor teaching strategies to suit the needs of culturally diverse students but also contribute to the advancement of global education. The insights gained from these studies and theories empower educators to better understand the unique requirements and obstacles faced by their students, leading to more effective learning support and enrichment. Ultimately, this innovative approach to education fosters a more inclusive and diverse learning environment where students from all cultural backgrounds can thrive and excel.

By merging neuroscience and cultural diversity perspectives, educators can revolutionize student support in the digital era. This fusion offers a new approach to optimizing cognitive load through augmented reality and gamified learning, while also catering to individual learning needs. Embracing this innovative mindset will cultivate students' self-regulation skills, paving the way for enhanced educational practices. With a focus on understanding the brain's functioning and honoring diverse backgrounds, educators are poised to shape a more inclusive and effective learning environment. Through this holistic approach, educators will redefine their role in guiding students towards success in the ever-evolving landscape of education.

8. REFERENCES

Azuma, R. T. (1997). A survey of augmented reality. *Presence (Cambridge, Mass.), 6*(4), 355–385. DOI: 10.1162/pres.1997.6.4.355

Bhagat, K. K., Yang, F.-Y., Cheng, C.-H., Zhang, Y., & Liou, W.-K. (2021). Tracking the process and motivation of math learning with augmented reality. *Educational Technology Research and Development, 69*(6), 3153–3178. DOI: 10.1007/s11423-021-10066-9

Cetintav, G., & Yilmaz, R. (2023). The effect of augmented reality technology on middle school students' mathematic academic achievement, self-regulated learning skills, and motivation. *Journal of Educational Computing Research, 61*(7), 1483–1504. DOI: 10.1177/07356331231176022

Chen, C., Jamiat, N., Abdul Rabu, S. N., & Mao, Y. (2024). Effects of a self-regulated-based gamified interactive e-books on primary students' learning performance and affection in a flipped mathematics classroom. *Education and Information Technologies, 29*(18), 24143–24180. *Scopus.* Advance online publication. DOI: 10.1007/s10639-024-12789-7

Dede, C. (2009). Immersive interfaces for engagement and learning. *Science, 323*(5910), 66–69. DOI: 10.1126/science.1167311

Hamari, J., Koivisto, J., & Sarsa, H. (2014). Does gamification work? – A literature review of empirical studies on gamification. *2014 47th Hawaii International Conference on System Sciences*, 3025–3034. https://doi.org/DOI: 10.1109/HICSS.2014.377

Hwang, G.-J., Lai, C.-L., & Wang, S.-Y. (2015). Seamless flipped learning: A mobile technology-enhanced flipped classroom with effective learning strategies. *Journal of Computers in Education, 2*(4), 449–473. DOI: 10.1007/s40692-015-0043-0

Kapp, K. M. (2012). *The gamification of learning and instruction: Game-based methods and strategies for training and education.* John Wiley & Sons.

Khaleel, F. L., Ashaari, N. S., & Tengku Wook, T. S. M. (2020). The impact of gamification on students learning engagement. [IJECE]. *International Journal of Electrical and Computer Engineering, 10*(5), 4965. DOI: 10.11591/ijece.v10i5.pp4965-4972

Kuo, Y.-H. (2010). *Self-regulated learning: From theory to practice.* Online Submission.

Kurban, F. (2024). Evolution of pre-service mathematics teachers' spatial visualisation skills during a cognitive load theory-based education. *Problems of Education in the 21st Century, 82*(2), 202–235.

Mayer, R. E. (2014). *Multimedia instruction. J. M. Spector, M. D. Merrill, J. Elen, & M. J. Bishop, Handbook of Research on Educational Communications and Technology*. Springer., DOI: 10.1007/978-1-4614-3185-5_31

Milgram, P., Takemura, H., Utsumi, A., & Kishino, F. (1995). Augmented reality: A class of displays on the reality-virtuality continuum. *Telemanipulator and Telepresence Technologies, 2351*, 282–292. DOI: 10.1117/12.197321

Pintrich, P. R. (2000). *The role of goal orientation in self-regulated learning. M. Boekaerts, P. R. Pintrich, & M. Zeidner, Handbook of Self-Regulation*. Academic Press., DOI: 10.1016/B978-012109890-2/50043-3

Runisah, R., Sudirman, S., Isnawan, M. G., Gunadi, F., Rosyadi, R., Son, A. L., & Assya, L. A. (2022). Impact of using augmented reality on students' cognitive and affective aspects in terms of education level. *International Journal of Science Education and Cultural Studies, 1*(2), 2. Advance online publication. DOI: 10.58291/ijsecs.v1i2.51

Schunk, D. H., & Zimmerman, B. J. (2012). *Motivation and self-regulated learning: Theory, research, and applications*. Routledge.

Sherman, M. (2014). The role of technology in supporting students' mathematical thinking: Extending the metaphors of amplifier and reorganizer. *Contemporary Issues in Technology & Teacher Education, 14*(3), 220–246.

Sweller, J. (1988). Cognitive load during problem solving: Effects on learning. *Cognitive Science, 12*(2), 257–285. DOI: 10.1016/0364-0213(88)90023-7

Sweller, J., van Merriënboer, J. J. G., & Paas, F. (2019). Cognitive architecture and instructional design: 20 years later. *Educational Psychology Review, 31*(2), 261–292. DOI: 10.1007/s10648-019-09465-5

van Merriënboer, J. J. G., & Sweller, J. (2005). Cognitive load theory and complex learning: Recent developments and future directions. *Educational Psychology Review, 17*(2), 147–177. DOI: 10.1007/s10648-005-3951-0

Vijver, F. V. D. (1997). Meta-analysis of cross-cultural comparisons of cognitive test performance. *Journal of Cross-Cultural Psychology, 28*(6), 678–709. DOI: 10.1177/0022022197286003

Wang, C., li, H., & Shang, J. (2017). Application and development prospect of educational games based on virtual reality and augmented reality.*Application and Development Prospects of Educational Games Based on Virtual Reality and Augmented Reality*.

Wang, T., & Lajoie, S. P. (2023). How does cognitive load interact with Self-Regulated learning? A dynamic and integrative model. *Educational Psychology Review*, *35*(3), 69. DOI: 10.1007/s10648-023-09794-6

Westelinck, K. D., Valcke, M., De Craene, B., & Kirschner, P. (2005). Multimedia learning in social sciences: Limitations of external graphical representations. *Computers in Human Behavior*, *21*(4), 555–573. DOI: 10.1016/j.chb.2004.10.030

Zimmerman, B. J. (1990). Self-regulated learning and academic achievement: An overview. *Educational Psychologist*, *25*(1), 3–17. DOI: 10.1207/s15326985ep2501_2

Zimmerman, B. J. (2002). Becoming a self-regulated learner: An overview. *Theory into Practice*, *41*(2), 64–70. DOI: 10.1207/s15430421tip4102_2

Chapter 5

A Quantitative Correlational Study of the Interaction Between Assignment Response Times and Online Students' Final Grades and Satisfaction

Taralynn Wells Petrites
https://orcid.org/0009-0005-5003-0827
Central Washington University, USA

Melanie Shaw
https://orcid.org/0009-0006-9245-7164
National University, USA

ABSTRACT

In this quantitative correlational study, an investigation of factors contributing to high online student attrition rates was conducted. Online interaction between students and instructors was studied by examining response times (RTs), student satisfaction, and final course grades. A sample of 54 online students in Spanish language courses participated in the study by responding to 14 online questionnaires. The findings from the study revealed no statistical significance between the RT and student final course grades. However, a linear regression test showed a statistically

DOI: 10.4018/979-8-3373-7508-3.ch005

significant correlation between RT and student satisfaction. Research implications and recommendations may help higher education institution administrators reduce high online attrition rates.

INTRODUCTION

Higher education delivered online has quickly gained popularity in the United States and globally (Allen & Seaman, 2015). College students register for online learning for various reasons, such as obtaining certifications, earning college-level credits, or for personal or professional development. Moreover, online learning emerged as a safe and feasible education option during the COVID-19 pandemic (Bouchrika, 2023). Nearly 5.5 million students (almost 26 percent of the college student population in the U.S.) took at least one online class during the pandemic (Smalley, 2021). Moreover, more than 52 percent of graduate students in the country find that online college education ensures better learning experiences than traditional classroom education (Duffin, 2020a). This growth in online higher education requires higher education leaders to develop effective policies to support student learning and engagement.

Students enroll in online courses for convenience, commuting cost savings, and lack of availability of traditional courses (Duffin, 2020b). Even though online education has become one of the most viable ways of pursuing education in the COVID-19 era, the completion rates of online classes could be higher. Statistics indicate that attrition rates for online courses are up to 20 percent higher than for face-to-face classes (Shaikh & Asif, 2022). Thus, retention is one of the main challenges of online education (Singh et al., 2021). College administrators and faculty need to research the underlying causes of high attrition rates for online students. Such studies will help administrators, faculty, and student services staff develop strategies to decrease attrition and increase student success. Investigations of instructor-learner interactions and students' satisfaction should focus on course instructors' assignment response times (RTs) and how RTs may influence students' success. Therefore, this quantitative study examined the relationship among instructors' RTs, online students' final grades (success), and students' self-reported course satisfaction.

The problem is attrition rates are higher for online courses than for face-to-face deliveries (Molinari et al., 2015; Shaikh & Asif, 2022; Tirrel & Quick, 2012). Severe consequences of continuous high attrition may involve the loss of higher education accreditation, courses, programs, and employment. Insufficient student-faculty interaction is a primary cause of students' lack of satisfaction, and student dissatisfaction is correlated with higher attrition levels (Cole et al., 2014). Learner-instructor interaction is imperative in academic development, particularly for online education (Croxton, 2014; Harder & Abuhamdieh, 2015). Online faculty must cultivate learner-instructor interaction strategies to heighten students' likelihood of successfully completing courses (Banna et al., 2015). The specific problem of interest is that the relationship between online instructor-learner interaction and students' final grades and online instructor-learner interaction and students' satisfaction in the context of RTs, are currently poorly understood. Thus, the purpose of this quantitative research was to assess learner-instructor interactions and whether there was a relationship between the assignment RT of online instructors, students' self-reported course satisfaction, and final grades.

Online education allows college students to seek a certificate or degree without physical attendance at a brick-and-mortar institution. Moore's theory of transactional distance (1993) guided the study by providing an understanding of online students' withdrawals. The theory highlights three critical elements of online interactions: (1) learner-instructor, (2) learner-learner, and (3) learner-content (Moore & Kearsley, 2012). However, interaction remains problematic for online instructors because of the lack of prompt physiological cues (Lin et al., 2012).

The following questions were answered in the study:

Q1: What is the relationship between response time (RT) for online instructor grading and student final course grades?

H1$_0$. There is no relationship between the response time (RT) for online instructor grading and student final course grades.

Q2: What is the relationship between response time (RT) for online instructor grading and student satisfaction?

H2$_0$. There is no relationship between the response time (RT) for online instructor grading and student satisfaction.

LITERATURE REVIEW

Quality learner-instructor interaction is pivotal in students' learning, satisfaction, and success in a higher education online course (Croxton, 2014; Harder & Abuhamdieh, 2015). The primary cause of students' lack of satisfaction is inadequate learner-instructor interaction, proven by further correlation in the relationship between the learner and instructor (Cole et al., 2014). Lack of satisfaction may cause a student to withdraw from an online course, increasing attrition rates. In addition, attrition rates are significantly higher in online classes when compared to traditional deliveries (Croxton, 2014; Molinari et al., 2015; Tirrel & Quick, 2012). Serious results of prolonged high attrition may mean the loss of higher education accreditation, courses, programs, and employment, as student participation in online courses is growing compared to face-to-face enrollment. This increased participation results in lower attrition numbers at higher education institutions. Therefore, accreditation and employment are affected because the number of participants increased.

HIGHER EDUCATION INSTITUTIONS' ONLINE EDUCATION CHALLENGES AND CONTROVERSIES

The expanding popularity of online learning in both non-profit and for-profit educational institutions has permitted colleges to increase enrollment with new courses and programs and to prepare course delivery alternatives for students (Essary, 2014; Fedynich et al., 2015). The popularity of online courses also creates challenges and controversies, such as ensuring quality instruction, shifts in student demographics, dramatically increasing enrollments, escalating competition between colleges, and diminishing government assistance (Allen & Seaman, 2015; Beaudoin, 2015; Essary, 2014). After the COVID-19 pandemic, institutions of higher education experienced numerous challenges despite the fact that online education was not new to them. A study by Asgari et al. (2022) found that although more than 60 percent of students would like to participate in online programs more regularly in the future, they face several challenges, including the lack of sufficient communication between learners and instructors, the lack of required technology infrastructure, and poor time management skills (Asgari et al., 2022).

Zarei and Mohammadi (2022) spoke of digital competence as helping reduce challenges associated with online education. Digital competence includes teachers' and learners' knowledge, skills, and attitudes regarding online education and readiness to deal with its challenges. The most common challenges online higher education students face are the lack of interaction with fellow students and instructors, the use of outdated hardware and software, the absence of a proper location for studying, and technical limitations (Zrei & Mohammadi, 2022). Nikoletatos (2020) found the digital divide and social isolation challenging for students and teachers alike.

Higher education administrators and faculty encounter challenges as well, namely measuring the quality of online education, assessing courses, and developing new courses (Peterson, 2016). Of particular concern are evaluation methods for online courses. Higher education institutions cannot administer identical evaluative methods for both online and face-to-face courses (Peterson, 2016; Theide, 2012) and have proven incompetent in measuring the quality of online instruction (Peterson, 2016; Pina & Bohn, 2014). Techniques for evaluating online courses need to be more effective.

Controversies on how to determine the quality of online courses have not decreased since online courses became available. Students from large institutions are as contented with online courses as they are with face-to-face courses (Allen &

Seaman, 2015). The report also stated that larger institutions view online learning outcomes as superior and smaller institutions find online learning inferior. Therefore, as the school size increases, the positive view of quality online and learning outcomes also increases. Empirical studies were conducted that compared online and face-to-face outcomes in the community college setting (Jaggars & Xu, 2010; Xu & Jaggars, 2011). These researchers reported community college students are substantially less likely than traditional students to complete online courses. The researchers also reported that students who took a given course online had estimated withdrawal rates of 10% to 15% higher than students who took the course face-to-face.

An ongoing trend in higher education online education is that the viewpoints of administrators, faculty, and students do not concur (Community College Research Center, 2013; Peterson, 2016). Veritably, research reveals that faculty and students observe their roles essentially in a reverse direction (Community College Research Center, 2013; Peterson, 2016). Those data reveal that it is evident that online courses are a vital function of current higher education system and require to be admitted in literature reviews of quality and student learning (Peterson, 2016). Conversely, higher education administrators and faculty encounter challenges about how to measure quality within online education, and how to assess courses and develop new courses (Peterson, 2016). Theide (2012) states that faculty members could not transfer same instructional strategies between online and face-to-face classes. Furthermore, higher education institutions cannot administer identical evaluative methods for both online and face-to-face courses (Peterson, 2016; Theide, 2012). Not only do the higher education institutions perform inadequately on evaluating online courses but also the major factor with this issue may be the incompetence of the college and universities to competently measure quality online instructing (Peterson, 2016; Pina & Bohn, 2014). Conventional face-to-face course evaluation procedures may not be the most accurate tools to assess course and instruction and furthermore, those techniques may not be effective to evaluate online courses. Equally important, because of lack of reliable course evaluation tools, faculty may experience challenges attempting to improve quality teaching and student learning (Peterson, 2016; Pina & Bohn, 2014).

Challenges of Online Student Retention

Despite the increasing number of students taking online courses, higher education institutions in the U.S. continue to confront rising online student attrition rates (Allen & Seaman, 2015) and the need to heighten graduation. In addition, graduation rates are a testimonial and best evidence of the competence of the higher education institutions' ability in student retention. Higher education administrators are cognizant that a high level of discipline would contribute to online course successes compared to traditional face-to-face courses (Allen & Seaman, 2015; Andrade, 2015). Forty percent of administrators experience challenges with retaining students in online courses compared to students in traditional courses (Allen & Seaman, 2015; Andrade, 2015). Fundamentally, faculty training is imperative, as the faculty will increase familiarity with new educational and technological tools in an online course as well as the delivery format (Andrade, 2015).

Several studies have authenticated diverse factors that lead to success in online learning and reducing attrition, such as timely correspondence between the instructor and the learner (Berridge et al., 2012). In addition, the online instructors who have communication limitations are often found in online courses (Moore, 2014). Many online instructors recognize the importance of developing and maintaining learner-instructor interaction (Preisman, 2014) and developing asynchronous and synchronous communication strategies to strengthen the relationship and increase successful outcomes.

Higher education institutions in the U.S. continue to encounter challenges in online student retention (Boston et al., 2012). "Models for understanding student persistence in the face-to-face environment is well established; however, many of the variables of these constructs are not present in the online environment or they manifest in significantly different ways" (Boston et al., 2011, para. 1). The most common factors in successful student retention mentioned in the literature are (a) administrators' perspectives and support of quality online instruction, (b) faculty qualifications (Armstrong, 2011; Castle & McGuire, 2010; Culver, 2010).

Enrollment of online students continues to increase drastically in the United States, and nearly over 30% of students were taking a course online after the COVID-19 pandemic (Elakiya & Kalabarathy, 2022). Nevertheless, the online students' attrition rates are high (Hachey et al., 2012; Lee & Choi, 2011). Online student retention is a complex issue for faculty for various reasons (Lee & Choi, 2011) such as producing activities to promote students' self-esteem or self-discipline in online learning. Low self-discipline, self-confidence, or self-esteem can lead to failure in completing the first course and may discourage students from registering for future online courses (Poelhuber & Anderson, 2011).

Online teaching initiates stress for instructors as the quality of online education continues to be questionable, and online course attrition rates remain modest (Hachey, et al., 2013). Horspool and Lange (2012) conducted a study to observe student perceptions of learning success between online and face-to-face instruction of the identical course. The students in the study stated that high-quality learner-instructor interaction is the indicator of successful learning experience (Horspool & Lange, 2012).

Online Faculty Qualifications, Responsibilities, and Skills

Types of characteristics online instructors must possess to increase student retention prior to teaching online were analyzed (Bonnell & Boehm, 2011; Nandi et al., 2012). The purpose of this study is to "evaluate quality interaction between students in fully online courses and to define the ideal role of the instructor while interacting with the students in fully online courses" (Nandi et al., 2012, p. 9). The key objective of the study was to learn how to evaluate quality online interaction in a fully online course. The findings were that the instructors played an essential role in initiating and encouraging discussions. In addition, the research also verified that adult learners are less likely to drop out when the instructors or the courses include materials that are relevant to the students' lives (Park & Choi, 2009). The proposed study will contribute to the research in this area that any types of learner-instructor relationship is vital, exigent response times are critical to quality online interaction in a fully online course, including the discussion forums.

Almost half of instructors noted no e-learning training prior to instruction (Edwards et al., 2011; Lewis & Abdul-Hamid, 2006; Pagliari et al., 2009). Edwards et al. (2011) confirmed factors of exemplary online instructors investigated by Lewis and Abdul-Hamid (2006) through narrative analysis. The findings on the factors of exemplary online instructors were that the instructors were challengers, affirmers, and influencers. The results reflected similarities in the Lewis and Abdul-Hamid (2006) study. However, Edwards et al. (2011) reported limitations such as small sample size and that the readers may not find value in their study as the results may not be transferable to their experiences.

Instructor responsibilities should involve regular learner-instructor communication. Therefore, faculty may need to check in daily to maintain learner-instructor relationship. The faculty may supply feedback in a feasible efficient time (Barr & Miller, 2013). The faculty also should signify high expectations and be aware of and sensitive to cultural diversity (Barr & Miller, 2013). Moreover, the faculty should provide explicit instructions and rubrics as a precedent, preferably in the course syllabus. Thereupon the students will grasp an adequate understanding of what the instructor will aim for when grading an assignment. The online course activities should trigger the students to engage in research, participate in course discussions, and adopt an analytical approach (Barr & Miller, 2013).

Faculty with Training Prior to Online Teaching

The quality of online instructors without prior training does not guarantee online teaching creditability, but instructors who received training developed effective strategies to support learners' outcomes (Mueller et al., 2013). However, the instructors would need to take graduate-level online instruction courses to learn how to develop appropriate materials for online instructions, and to identify strategies, which would be the most effective to increase successful completion rates. The instructors also would have an opportunity to take e-learning courses as an online student to understand how online students learn through this delivery.

Quantitative studies were conducted to assess differences in motivations reinforcing student accomplishments in online learning (Fish & Wickersham, 2015; Sansone et al., 2011). The researchers also determined that motivations would increase if educators included lessons associated with real-life experiences in online courses (Allen & Seaman, 2015; Herman, 2012). Designing asynchronous online tools such as videos and discussions to incorporate significant opportunities for exploration of tools and providing life-related exercises can evidently increase motivation and learning outcomes (Sansone et al., 2011; Xu & Jaggars, 2011). The proposed study will contribute to the research in this area by verifying whether learner-instructor relationships are likely to heighten if the online students remain motivated through asynchronous online tools such as viewing videos created by the instructor, participating in discussions with instructor's active participation, and fundamentally, receiving timely feedback on assignments.

Faculty Attitudes Toward Online Instruction

Enrollments in online courses are demanding (Allen & Seaman, 2015; Andrade, 2015), and faculty shared concerns about online teaching and the time spent on online instruction compared to face-to-face (Van de Vord & Pogue, 2012). The faculty members believed that the workload was greater in online teaching compared to face-to-face (Van de Vord & Pogue, 2012). Multiple studies were conducted to examine faculty attitudes toward online learning.

Higher education institutions utilize diverse methods to evaluate faculty members' teaching practices. Benefits of competent faculty evaluation include boosting the expertise of instructing and learning, enhancing the performance and modification of curriculum, courses, programs, and thereafter the extended community (Glassick et al., 1997). Research associated with faculty evaluation within face-to-face settings is vast; however, there is insufficient research investigating online faculty's understanding of evaluation procedures. Moreover, because of the exponential growth of online education, the current evaluation system within both online and face-to-face courses is viewed as less than adequate by administration and faculty (Berk, 2013). DeCosta et al. (2016) conducted a qualitative study to investigate 118 online full-time instructors at a large university in the southwestern part of the United States participated in the study by responding to a survey on the current evaluation system and procedures utilized to assess their teaching. Utilizing a systematic content analysis of data, the results reveal that online faculty possesses a passion to improve their skills as instructors, intermittently centralizing on methods or professional expectations as a purpose for growth (DeCosta et al, 2016). The faculty also voiced an interest in comprehensive evaluation feedback supplied by a variety of stakeholders with content knowledge in the field taught. The research contains significant findings for higher education administrators and stakeholders linked to online instructors, as well as the documents and procedures on those evaluated (DeCosta et al., 2016).

Faculty attitudes toward online instruction and technology were investigated through multiple methods (Barrett, 2010; Dolan 2011; Ward et al., 2010). The researchers developed multiple regression analysis for this study to observe instructors' beliefs and attitudes toward technology and the findings reflected the significant relationship between the instructors' attitudes toward technology, online teaching background, and students' successful learning outcomes. The researchers implied significant perspectives and attitudes in instructors' attitudes toward technology as necessary to increase students' online learning success. Therefore, the researchers stressed the importance of instructors taking educational technology training prior to online teaching, as the instructors would gain technology attitudes related to educational benefits.

Culver (2010) found faculty concerns regarding student ratings were significantly related to the grades the students expected to obtain, which meant that students receiving lower grades might result in lower course evaluations. The study was conducted to investigate whether the (1) final grades the students expected to obtain would affect the course evaluation or not, (2) students' quality of performance in the course would affect the course evaluation or not, and (3) students' quality of performance moderates the relationship between the anticipated grades and the evaluation of the instructor or not. The findings verified that the students' engagement with the course activities significantly moderated the relationship between the anticipated grades and the evaluation rating of the instructor.

Russo-Gleicher (2013) conducted a qualitative study that gave hindsight to 37 different ways faculty can positively increase retention with online students. The study included interviews with faculty at a community college in the United States. Faculty was tasked to confer about themes for students who take online classes. One example as Russo-Gleicher, (2013) identified was students displaying poor online behavior. Such as missing posts with online discussion, assignments missing, and tests that were considered below expectations. Faculty student interaction displayed poor performance and behavior as well as responses lacking clarity because faculty was not persistence in coursework expectations. To get a positive turnaround from students, faculty engaged Blackboard communication via the communication page such as email to work with poor performing students. Students who needed one on one services or were behind in online coursework were referred to student services or academic support officers (Russo-Gleicher, 2013). In this study, faculty admitted they were not aware of support services available to online students and the knowledge necessary to work with student services for online academic success (Russo-Gleicher, 2013). The conclusion of the study indicated that attitudes such as minimal knowledge toward student services had an impact with online students; therefore, the negative impact on student retention at the community college. However, faculty student collaboration by understanding good online faculty student approaches and coursework expectations result in exemplary student retention.

Professional Development Vital to Online Student Learning Productivity

Professional development is most effective when it is an ongoing process of learning and advancement. Online faculty involvement in professional development specific to the instructor's academic discipline should be in an area of ongoing emphasis. Online higher education faculty should possess an earned discipline-specific academic degree and participate in online professional development associated to the content of the discipline taught and effective instructional techniques (Southern Regional Education Board, 2009). Examples of professional development may include credit and noncredit courses supplied by higher education institutions, workshops and Webinars, academic and departmental meetings, and online teaching pedagogy.

Both novice and veteran online faculty may integrate instructional and content awareness to finalize which instructional techniques, activities, and evaluations to utilize to enhance student-learning productivity. Online faculty merit further researchers' interest to investigate their teaching experience and professional development demands. A significant pool of higher education faculty members hesitated to teach online courses (Crawford-Ferre & Weist, 2012; Phirangee et al., 2016; Sun & Chen, 2016). Faculty with experience in teaching online courses reported that, despite the assumption that online instruction is more convenient than traditional instruction, online courses require considerably more time compared to face-to-face courses (Crawford-Ferre & Weist, 2012; Keengwe & Kidd, 2010). The enrollment of online courses surged over the last several years (Phirangee et al., 2016). Online instruction is still novel to many beginner and seasoned instructors (Sun & Chen, 2016) and therefore, elevated professional development training in the areas of effective online development, teaching, performance, and assessments are pivotal. Such training may assist faculty to acknowledge productive methods in designing, implementing, and evaluating online courses to enhance students' learning needs (Phirangee et al., 2016; Sun & Che, 2016).

Not all online faculty contend with learner retention. Asynchronous online course learner retention rates have been commendable in the last two decades (Aversa &

MacCall, 2013). Aversa and MacCall (2013) conducted a case study at the University of Alabama to investigate factors that increase online student retention. Online courses in this study included lectures, peer discussions, and group assignments (Aversa & MacCall, 2013). The online courses also had social media such as Facebook that boosted learner-instructor interaction throughout the semester (Aversa & MacCall, 2013). The finding showed learner-instructor interaction was one of the main factors that contributed to high student retention rates at the university. The learner-instructor collaboration of the degree program at the university exhibited favorable outcomes (Aversa & MacCall, 2013). Conversely, synchronous online learner retention rates continue to be low (Aversa & MacCall, 2013). Therefore, faculty performs an essential task with accentuating student retention and may need to investigate resources to intensify learner-instructor relationship within synchronous online courses. Recourses and skills to enhance student retention may be obtained through professional development targeting learner-instructor interaction within synchronous online courses.

Support from Higher Education Institution Administration

Instructing online courses demands additional focus compared to traditional courses (Crawford-Ferre & Wiest, 2012; Keengwe & Kidd, 2010; Sun & Chen, 2016). Online instruction is more labor-intensive because of the quality of time involved to assess assignments and respond to emails (Keengwe & Kidd, 2010). Hence, online faculty, both novice and veteran, require comprehensive support from their institutions, such as modification of teaching loads or reduction of online course enrollment caps (Crawford-Ferre & Wiest, 2012; Keengwe & Kidd, 2010; Sun & Chen, 2016). Online courses with large numbers of students enrolled may affect both learner-instructor interaction and the formation of a quality course room that permits positive learning experiences (Boston et al., 2011).

STUDENT PERSPECTIVES AND SATISFACTION WITH ONLINE LEARNING

Learner-instructor interaction in online courses may contribute to students' perspectives of and satisfaction with online learning and student retention and accomplishment (Lee et al., 2011; Michinov et al., 2011; You, 2015). If online students believe their instructors are not entirely committed to course interaction, their impression of academic excellence decreases, and they will likely drop out of the online course (Armstrong, 2011). Therefore, higher education institutions are attempting to find strategies to provide quality online courses and programs to reduce the likelihood of students dropping out of their online classes.

Multiple researchers have conducted studies of how online faculty evaluate quality online participation and discussions (Asgari et al., 2022; Revere & Kovach, 2011; Zarei & Mohammadi, 2022). Edwards et al. (2011) identified the qualities of exemplary online instructors using different types of qualitative analysis. Lewis and Abdul-Hamid (2006) performed a qualitative study on the factors of exemplary online instructors and stated that these instructors promoted interaction, supplied timely responses, and remained dynamic and productive throughout the course. Edwards et al. (2011) modified the qualitative study to confirm factors of exemplary online instructors through narrative analysis. The researchers studied Canadian distance education university students' experiences in online courses and found that exemplary online instructors were challengers, affirmers, and influencers. The results reflected similarities with the Lewis and Abdul-Hamid (2006) study.

Technology and computer self-efficacy also play a role in student satisfaction. Hauser et al. (2012) focused on the relationship between computer anxiety and self-efficacy in face-to-face and online classes. They found that online education is difficult for students primarily experienced with face-to-face classes. Faculty-student interactions aimed at helping students navigate technology or understand online course expectations become difficult in an online course. Hauser et al. (2012) found that the skills required for successful online coursework include organized materials and classwork activities that meet deadlines, as with face-to-face coursework. Therefore, these successful online skills will greatly reduce anxiety and enhance computer self-efficacy online.

AI, AUTOMATED GRADING, AND FEEDBACK

With the current higher education system, where advanced technology such as artificial intelligence (AI) and automated grading is common, students expect a quicker turnaround (Wisniewski et al., 2020). Studies have shown that quick feedback is critical, as slow feedback is often equivalent to the absence of feedback (Brummer et al., 2024; Taxipulati & Lu, 2021).

Therefore, to enhance student success rate, numerous Learning Management Systems (LMS) have developed tools that employ automated grading. Those tool supply timely feedback on specific types of assignments, such as quizzes, and assist instructors in managing their time effectively by delivering quality feedback to students. Those tools are especially beneficial for online students with a large number of students (Belchadi, 2016; Marin et al., 2017). Cavalcanti et al. (2021) conducted a systematic literature review of automatic feedback within online learning environments and verified the following: 1) 65% of the studies showed automatic feedback promoted student performance, 2) 46% of the studies verified that automatic feedback does not alleviate instructional burden (reduces faculty workload), and 3) 83% of the studies showed no evidence that instructor-provided feedback demonstrates greater efficiency compared to automated grading or feedback.

Numerous studies have demonstrated that peer feedback is delivered as effectively and often more promptly than instructor feedback (Cui et al., 2021; Reugg, 2015; Yang et al., 2006). Peer feedback allows students to revise more promptly, which contributes to improved learning outcomes and promotes a more meaningful learning experience for students. Also, trained peer reviewers supplied feedback as effectively and often more promptly as teachers.

MOBILE-FIRST INSTRUCTIONAL DESIGN

Studies have shown the success of mobile learning techniques in LMS and online learning environments, as well as the positive impacts on online students' performance and engagement (Bikanga, 2018; Crompton et al., 2015; Demir & Akpinar, 2018; El-Sofany & El-Haggar, 2020). Instructors need to identify trends to design equitable and accessible learning environments for students and, therefore, learn how to support them successfully. Instructors with formal online instruction training will understand the importance of utilizing mobile features, such as push notifications, chat support, and announcements, to provide more timely responses and keep students engaged. Those tools enable instructors to send messages, grade, and monitor students' performance at any time and from anywhere with a device. This type of pedagogy training will help instructors manage workloads more productively, leading to faster feedback turnaround.

METHODS

This study employed a quantitative, correlational, and descriptive design using a survey method with two-year college students who attend online courses. The research focused on relationships that result from an experience and examined the learner-instructor relationship among variables and the significance of the relationship between the variables through surveys. The study was conducted at a two-year non-profit higher education institution in Arizona with an average enrollment of approximately 74,000 students aged 18 to 60. The population for this study was the cohort enrolled in eight-week Spanish 101 (Introductory Spanish) online courses. Four eight-week online Spanish 101 (Introductory Spanish) instructors received an email requesting their participation in this study by distributing to their students the informed consent and a survey. Roughly 100 students responded by volunteering to participate in the research study. The students received an email from the instructor of the corresponding course. The email included an invitation letter to the participants, and all students received a link to a survey via Qualtrics.com.

All data were gathered through an online anonymous survey. The students in the sample responded about demographics, learner-instructor interaction satisfaction, and general course satisfaction. The online survey contained three parts. The first part consisted of six close-ended questions on demographics such as gender, age, year of college the student is in, average hours of study per week, number of online classes taken before the current (recent) course, and the final grade earned from the relevant online course. The second part of the survey measured learner-instructor interaction satisfaction to gather responses to the four (4) 5-point Likert scale questions. The third part of the survey gathered students' responses to four (4) 5-point Likert scale questions on general satisfaction.

The data analysis for the first and second research questions used a correlation coefficient, Pearson's *r*, to test the relationship between two variables, measured on an interval or ratio scale (Passer, 2014). In this study, Pearson's *r* ascertained a positive or negative correlation between the RTs and the students' final grades. Hence, the results determined the significance of the learner-instructor interaction relationship among online students' success. Student satisfaction, students' final grades, and the average number of days between due dates and the grades received constitute the internal reliability, which was also calculated to determine the effectiveness of each question to measure each construct. The three variables are response time (RT), student satisfaction, and students' final grades.

RESULTS

After permission from the institutional review board was granted, to conduct the study, the survey became available at the end of the course when the learners were scheduled to obtain final grades and was open for 15 consecutive days. Upon receipt of the survey via Qualtrics.com, 68 online SPA101 students responded, with 62 agreeing to participate and six declining to participate. The survey's response rate was 48%, meaning that 58 of 62 participants responded to 80% or more of the 14 questions. Fifty-four participants responded to each of the 14 questions.

Demographic Attributes

The participants' demographic data were gathered from the survey. A descriptive analysis of the variables was conducted (gender, age, and number of previous courses) and results tabulated. Most of the participants (64.8%) (n = 35) were male, while 33% (n = 18) participants were female. Forty-four percent (n = 24) of the participants were aged 18 to 25, and 30% (n = 16) were between the ages of 26 and 35. Thirty-three percent (n = 18) of the participants took at least five online courses, and 32% (n = 17) of the participants took one or two classes before taking the online Spanish course. Preliminary Analyses

Reliability of student satisfaction scale. Cronbach's alpha was performed to test the reliability of the student satisfaction scale. The result of Cronbach's alpha test is presented in Table 2. Cronbach's alpha value is from .70 and above is considered acceptable internal reliability (George & Mallery, 2010). The Cronbach's alpha scale value was .89, indicating that the scale had reliability.

Table 1. Cronbach's Alpha of Student Satisfaction

Variable	Cronbach's alpha	Number of items
Student satisfaction	.895	4

Descriptive statistics of the independent and dependent variable. I analyzed the descriptive statistics of the independent and dependent variables before hypotheses testing. The results are presented in Table 3. I coded the data with a number calculated for multiple regression analysis. All the variables are interval. For student satisfaction, the possible answers were coded as 1 = Strongly Agree, 2 = Agree, 3 = Neutral, 4 = Disagree, and 5 = Strongly Disagree. The lower the score, the more satisfied the online students were. The mean of student satisfaction was 1.91, which indicated that the students' satisfaction level was higher than average. The mean of the response time was 2.15, which showed that the average response time (RT) between the online submission of assignments and assignments returned with feedback was 3–5 days. For RT, the days were coded as 1 = 0–2 days, 2 = 3–5 days, 3 = 6–9 days, and 4 =10 + days. The higher value indicates the longer response time, and the mean (2.15) showed that most of the students received instructors' feedback on assignments within three to five days. Codes for final grades received were 1 = A, 2 = B, 3 = C, 4 = D, and 5 = F. The higher value indicates a lower grade. The result revealed the mean of 1.6, and the average final grade the students obtained was B.

Table 2. Descriptive Statistics of Independent and Dependent Variables

	M	*SD*
Student satisfaction	1.910	.78
Response time	2.15	.94
Final grade	1.60	.65

Independent and dependent variable correlations. Corrections were performed to test the relationships among independent and dependent variables. The results of the correlation analysis indicated that response time substantially correlated with level of studFacultyent satisfaction ($p < .001$). In addition, correlation between response time and student satisfaction was positive and large ($r = .51$). Hence, response time positively correlated with student satisfaction, meaning the less response time, the higher level of student satisfaction. Response time did not significantly correlate with final grade ($p > .05$).

Table 3. Correlations among Independent Variable and Dependent Variable

		Student Satisfaction	**Final Grade**
R	**Response time**	**.51**	**-.08**
P		.000	.29

Assumption Testing

Normality test of dependent variables. Before performing parametric tests, I conducted a normality check of the dependent variables. I used both statistical and graphical tests. First, I compared the mean and the 5% trimmed mean of student satisfaction. The descriptive statistics of the dependent variables as shown in Table 5 suggested that the mean and the 5% trimmed mean of the student satisfaction variable were slightly different (1.91 and 1.87), indicating no extreme scores. The skewness and kurtosis values of the student satisfaction variable were also within the range from -1 to + 1; therefore, the assumption of normality of the variable was not violated. The mean and the 5% trimmed mean of the final grade variable were slightly different (1.60 and 1.55), indicating no extreme scores. The skewness and kurtosis values of the final grade variable were also within the range from -1 to + 1; therefore, the variable's normality assumption was not violated.

Table 4. Descriptive Statistics for Student Satisfaction and Final Grade

		Statistics	Std. error
Student satisfaction	M	1.9104	.10756
	5% Trimmed mean	1.8708	
	SD	.78308	
	Skewness	.510	.327
	Kurtosis	-.781	.644
Final grade	Mean	1.60	.095
	5% Trimmed Mean	1.55	
	Std. Deviation	.648	
	Skewness	.629	.347
	Kurtosis	-.540	.681

Furthermore, graphical tests were performed to test the normality of the IT effectiveness variable. The histograms, normal Q-Q plots, and box plots showed no extreme case in the sample and suggest that the assumption of normality of student satisfaction and final grade was not violated.

Hypothesis Testing

Q1: What is the relationship between response time (RT) for online instructor grading and student final course grades?

H1$_0$. There is no relationship between the response time (RT) for online instructor grading and student final course grades.

A linear regression was conducted to test the null hypothesis 1 using the model summary and the ANOVA model of the linear regression analysis. The response time explained 0.7% of the variance of final course grades, $R^2 = .007$, $F\ (1, 45) = .30$, $p > .05$ (see Table 6 and Table 7). The coefficient table (Table 8) suggested that response time for online instructor grading did not significantly correlate with student final course grades (B = -.06, beta = -.08, t =-.55, $p > .05$). The null hypothesis that there is no relationship between the response time (RT) for online instructor grading and student final course grades was not rejected. The response time for online instructor grading did not significantly correlate with student final course grades.

Table 5. Model Summary of the Linear Regression for Response Time and Final Grade

Predictor	R	R^2	Adjusted R^2	Std. error of the estimate
Response time	.08	.007	-.01	.65

Table 6. ANOVA Model for Response Time and Final Grade

Model		Sum of squares	*Df*	Mean square	*F*	*P*
1	Regression	.129	1	.13	.30	.58
	Residual	19.19	45	.43		
	Total	19.32	46			

Table 7. Coefficient Table for Response Time and Final Grade

	Unstandardized coefficients		Standardized coefficients		
	B	*Std. error*	*Beta*	*t*	*P*
(Constant)	1.72	.24		7.16	.000
Response time	-.06	.10	-.08	-.55	.58

Q2: What is the relationship between response time (RT) for online instructor grading and student satisfaction?

H2$_0$. There is no relationship between the response time (RT) for online instructor grading and student satisfaction.

A linear regression was conducted to test the null hypothesis 2 using the model summary and the ANOVA model of the linear regression analysis. The response time explained 26% of the student satisfaction variance, $R^2 = .26$, $F(1, 51) = 18.14$, $p < .001$ (see Table 9 and Table 10). The coefficient table (Table 11) suggested that response time for online instructor grading significantly correlated with student satisfaction (B = .43, beta = .51, $t = 4.26$, $p < .001$). The null hypothesis was rejected. The response time for online instructor grading significantly correlated with student satisfaction.

Table 8. Model Summary of the Linear Regression for Response Time and Student Satisfaction

Predictor	*R*	R^2	Adjusted R^2	Std. error of the estimate
Response time	.51	.26	.25	.68

Table 9. ANOVA Model for Response Time and Student Satisfaction

Model		Sum of squares	*Df*	Mean square	*F*	*p*
1	Regression	8.37	1	8.37	18.14	.000
	Residual	23.52	51	.46		
	Total	31.89	52			

Table 10. Coefficient Table for Response Time and Student Satisfaction

	Unstandardized coefficients		Standardized coefficients		
	B	*Std. error*	*Beta*	*T*	*p*
(Constant)	.99	.23		4.23	.000
Response time	.43	.10	.51	4.26	.000

DISCUSSION

This study resulted in some interesting outcomes, but it is important to note the limitations. First, the sample was limited to students enrolled in online Spanish 101 courses at a single two-year institution in Arizona, which restricts the generalizability of the results to broader populations or different academic disciplines. Second, the voluntary nature of survey participation may have introduced self-selection bias, as students with strong opinions about their instructor's responsiveness may have been more inclined to participate. Third, the use of self-reported data for satisfaction and course experience may be influenced by personal perception rather than objective measures. Additionally, the study relied on a single survey for data collection and did not include qualitative insights that could offer a more nuanced understanding of the learner-instructor interaction. Finally, correlational design prevents conclusions about causality.

The findings of this investigation did not reveal any significant correlation between response time for online instructor grading and student final course grades. Past investigations found that students who participated in online education viewed learner-instructor interaction, such as receiving timely feedback from instructors, as contributing to quality education and success (Conrad & Dabbagh, 2015; Kang, 2013; Nandi et al., 2015), whereas students focused on successful online completion as they distinguished online courses differently from traditional courses. A potential explanation for conflicting results is that online students who concentrate on completing the course are satisfied with the final grade, versus students who are only focused on a high final grade. Another possible reason is that delayed feedback is normalized in many educational settings. Students are accustomed to waiting for an extended period for feedback, which leads them to re-prioritize their studies and daily activities and become less engaged. In a study, online students expressed a significantly decreased level of engagement if the feedback was delayed by more than 10 days (Fisher, 2025). The students may end up not reviewing or applying feedback because of the design of the assignment (automated grading such as quizzes), and they do not review or apply feedback to subsequent assignments. Those automated grading systems may reward students more than instructors' feedback, and students may focus more on scores. Many education systems often reward performance (scores) rather than growth (the learning process). Future studies to assess the importance of performance (scores) versus growth (learning process) and whether the course design includes standalone tasks that may not be revisited for growth provide a better understanding of how students can value both scores and growth equally.

Further, results revealed that assignment response time significantly correlated with student satisfaction. The findings reinforced the results from other studies that correlated online learner-instructor interactions and satisfaction (Padilla Rodriguez & Armellini, 2015). Also, the findings continue to support Moore's theory of transactional distance (1993) that learner-instructor interaction is one of the key factors in student satisfaction and success (Mahmodi & Ebrahimzade, 2015). Lack of interaction between instructors and students may be a reason for online students' withdrawals. Therefore, online instructors need to recognize the importance of timely feedback by returning assignments promptly. Considering the number of online students today, higher education institution administrators and faculty must identify ways to promote online education success, retention, and learner satisfaction. Identifying these aspects will enable educational institutions to meet financial objectives and ensure student satisfaction.

The findings of this research offer recommendations for higher education institutions offering online education to take active efforts to observe key factors for high attrition rates and develop strategies to address the issue. A first recommendation is that, based on the findings it is suggested that the administrators work with faculty to establish a 5-7-day assignment turnaround policy as one of the key efforts to improve retention rates. After the policy is set, it is also recommended that online postsecondary institutions maintain a quality review team that overseers the online environment to ensure learning excellence.

A second recommendation based on the findings is that higher education institutions offering online education develop a series of faculty development training. Online faculty development is an expeditiously growing area of opportunity for instructional designers and faculty development professionals (Rizzuto, 2017).

These types of programs supply an opportunity for both novice and experienced instructors to develop strategies to improve students' learning experience as well as discuss and reflect on their online instructional practices. Quality online education programs are formed with motivated faculty members, instructional designers, and administrators who are driven to employ advanced knowledge and competence to the online learning environment (Baran & Correia, 2014). Some of the training may involve how to respond to students' assignments in a timely fashion such as hours instead of days like 48-72 hours with quality feedback. Series of training will encourage faculty to develop a higher level of learner-instructor interaction. The faculty will continue and improve skills toward online teaching and therefore, learner satisfaction will continue to rise. Those types of action and training are likely to decrease attrition rates. Third recommendation is that colleges may develop a fast feedback timeline policy for online instructors (See Appendix A for an example). This policy will not only enhance student retention but also help online instructors adapt to demands and learn new tools, such as utilizing AI and automated grading, and develop the ability to enhance course materials. Those efforts will be likely to produce a higher level of online student engagement.

The fourth recommendation is that college instructional designers and online program managers work with their colleges, departments, and faculty to develop strategies that enhance student success. The example listed below is the recommendations to support online instructors in building an effective instructor-learner relationship:

- Establish fast feedback turnaround benchmarks in collaboration with relevant departments (e.g., implementing a 48-72 hour grading policy).
- Promote the use of AI and automation tools for peer review, formative feedback, and relevant activities.
- Design peer feedback workflows to reduce instructor load while enhancing student engagement.
- Highlight and share success stories of online instructors achieving a high level of engagement through timely feedback.

Future research may involve qualitative or correlational studies to observe the relationship between RTs, final grades, and satisfaction outside of Spanish 101, such as generalizing this type of study to STEM or professional development courses. This type of strategy will broaden in identifying areas where instructors can improve their strategies for retaining online students. Interviews to determine reasons online students prefer to obtain assignments with feedback in timely fashion rather than receive high final grades may extend reinforcement on how students perceive the actual definition of learner satisfaction. Online education continues to be a rapid growing field in the academic system (Bliuc et al., 2012). It is essential that online faculty continue to seek strategies to enhance effective learning experience by providing timely feedback. Therefore, future findings relevant to the recommended study may generate and contribute to knowledge in how each online course should be designed in terms of assignments or activities that would recruit quality feedback within 48-72 hours.

CONCLUSION

This research focused on learner-instructor interaction, as previous studies revealed the importance of online instructors strengthening students' learning environment by maintaining feedback, contributing to online discussions, and replying to students' emails and assignments punctually (Moore & Kearsley, 2012). Utilizing a quantitative correlational design, an analysis of the relationship between response times (RT) for online instructor grading and student final courses and RT and student satisfaction was conducted. Results of linear regression analysis suggested no significant correlation between the RT for online instructor grading and student final courses, but a significant correlation between the RT for online instructor grading and student satisfaction. This research had a small sample, which limits the findings' generalizability to other online courses and course durations (five, eight, 10, or 16 weeks). A larger sample may produce multiple findings and extend knowledge about online learning challenges. However, this study points to the importance of timely RTs in enhancing online student success and reducing online learner attrition.

The research results indicated that learner and instructor interaction levels resulted in significant differences in student satisfaction. Online instructor presence can be successful depending on methods and approaches used to stimulate constructive learner-instructor interaction (& DiLoreto, 2016). In particular, instructors may enhance students' learning experience, sense of being valued and respected, and overall success by providing feedback on assignments within a specific time frame. Another means of improving online student success, satisfaction, and retention rates includes determining specific learner-instructor activities that save students time and money and understanding how quick assignment response times (RT) can heighten students' learning success (Miller, 2015).

The research findings provide practical implications for higher education institutions offering online education to observe key factors for high attrition rates and develop strategies to address the issue. It is recommended that administrators work with faculty to establish a reasonable and expedient assignment turnaround policy as one of the key efforts to improve retention rates. After the policy is set, it is also recommended that online postsecondary institutions maintain a quality review team that oversees the online environment to ensure learning excellence. Moreover, higher education institutions should provide faculty development training in online education. Training will encourage faculty to develop, among other things, a higher level of learner-instructor interaction which may decrease attrition rates. Quality online education programs thrive with motivated faculty members, instructional designers, and administrators driven to employ advanced knowledge and competence in the online learning environment (Baran & Correia, 2014). In the long run, higher education institutions should recognize the importance of providing online learning training on how to use AI to enhance student success, such as quicker turnarounds and peer review activities. Those efforts would result in significant cost savings, such as reduced spending on instructors or TAs to grade assignments while still providing quality feedback and turnaround times. These types of efforts would increase productivity and optimize faculty utilization, as instructors feel motivated to design richer course content, recognize declining student performance to be able to intervene and build an effective instructor-learner relationship, and develop strategies to enhance student engagement by creating activities with fast quality feedback turnarounds, both through AI and instructor collaboration.

The most feasible recommendation for future research is to utilize a larger sample, which will increase the generalizability of the findings. Future research may also involve qualitative studies to deeply understand the student perceptions of the relationships between RTs and final grades and satisfaction. Finally, a follow up study should be conducted across subject areas to determine if findings are similar to this study. The expansion of online learning has prompted colleges to prioritize increasing the availability of online courses, but these institutions also face scrutiny regarding retention and graduation rates (Meyer, 2014). Higher education institutions may address student attrition through learner support programs. These services supply students with the appropriate tools to facilitate academic success and persistence in their educational programs (Ludwig-Hardman & Dunlap, 2003). In conclusion, the relationship between higher education institutions and students can increase students' chances of persistence, academic success, and graduation rates.

REFERENCES

Allen, I. E., & Seaman, J. (2015). *Grade level: Tracking online education in the United States.* http://www.onlinelearningsurvey.com/reports/gradelevel.pdf

Andrade, M. S. (2015). Teaching online: A theory-based approach to student success. *Journal of Education and Training Studies, 3*(5), 1–9. DOI: 10.11114/jets.v3i5.904

Armstrong, D. (2011). Students' perceptions of online learning and instructional tools: A qualitative study of undergraduate students' uses of online tools. *The Turkish Online Journal of Educational Technology, 10*(3). http://www.tojet.net/articles/v10i3/10325.pdf

Asgari, H., Gupta, R., Titiloye, I., & Jin, X. (2022). Challenges, perceptions, and future preferences for post-secondary online education given experiences in the COVID-19 outbreak. *Computational Urban Science, 2*, 29. DOI: 10.1007/s43762-022-00058-7

Aversa, E., & MacCall, S. (2013). Profiles in retention part 1: Design characteristics of a graduate synchronous online program. *Journal of Education for Library and Information Science, 54*(2), 147–161. http://files.eric.ed.gov/fulltext/EJ1074122.pdf

Banna, J., Grace Lin, M., Stewart, M., & Fialkowski, M. K. (2015). Interaction matters. Strategies to promote engaged learning in an online introductory nutrition course. *Journal of Online Learning and Teaching, 11*(2), 249–261. http://jolt.merlot.org/Vol11no2/Banna_0615.pdf

Baran, E., & Correia, A. (2014). A professional development framework for online teaching. *TechTrends, 58*(5), 95–101. DOI: 10.1007/s11528-014-0791-0

Barr, B. A., & Miller, S. F. (2013). Higher education: The online teaching and learning Experience. *Online Teaching and Learning.* http://files.eric.ed.gov/Fulltext/ED543912.pdf

Barrett, B. (2010). Virtual teaching and strategies: Transitioning from teaching traditional classes to online classes. *Contemporary Issues in Education Research, 3*(12). http://files.eric.ed.gov/fulltext/EJ1072660.pdf

Beaudoin, M. F. (2015). Distance education leadership in the context of digital change. *Quarterly Review of Distance Education, 16*(2), 33–44,148. https://go.gale.com/ps/i.do?p=AONE&u=googlescholar&id=GALE|A437059683&v=2.1&it=r&sid=AONE&asid=f1bdb7d7

Berk, R. A. (2013). Face-to-face versus online course evaluations: A "consumer's guide" to seven strategies. *Journal of Online Teaching and Learning*, *9*(1), 140–148. http://jolt.merlot.org/vol9no1/berk_0313.htm

Berridge, G., Penney, S., & Wells, J. (2012). Formative assessment of classroom teaching for online classes. *Turkish Online Journal of Distance Education*, *13*(1), 68–78. https://www.researchgate.net/publication/267425880

Bikanga Ada, M. (2018). Using design-based research to develop a Mobile Learning Framework for Assessment Feedback. *Research and Practice in Technology Enhanced Learning*, *13*, 3. DOI: 10.1186/s41039-018-0070-3

Bliuc, A.-M., Casey, G., Bachfischer, A., Goodyear, P., & Ellis, R. (2012). Blended learning in vocational education: Teachers' conceptions of blended learning and their approaches to teaching and design. *Australian Educational Researcher*, *39*(2), 237–257. DOI: 10.1007/s13384-012-0053-0

Bonnell, W., & Boehm, H. (2011). Improving feedback to students online: Teaching tips from experienced faculty. *Journal of Continuing Education in Nursing*, *42*(11). Advance online publication. DOI: 0.3928/00220124-20110715-02

Boston, W., Ice, P., & Burgess, M. (2012). Assessing student retention in online learning environments: A longitudinal study. *Online Journal of Distance Learning Administration*, *15*(2). http://www.westga.edu/~distance/ojdla/summer152/boston_ice_burgess152.html

Boston, W., Ice, P., & Gibson, A. (2011). *Comprehensive assessment of student retention in online learning environments.* http://www.westga.edu/~distance/ojdla/spring141/ boston_ice_gibson141.html

Bouchrika, I. (2023). 50 online education statistics: 2023 data on higher learning & corporate training. https://research.com/education/online-education-statistics

Brummer, L., de Boer, H., Mouw, J. M., & Strijbos, J. W. (2024). A meta-analysis of the effects Of context, content, and task factors of digitally delivered instructional feedback on learning performance. *Learning Environments Research*, *27*, 453–476. DOI: 10.1007/s10984-024-09501-4

Castle, S. R., & McGuire, C. (2010). An analysis of student self-assessment of online, blended and face-to-face environments: Implications for sustainable education delivery. *International Education Studies*, *3*(3). Advance online publication. DOI: 10.5539 /ies.v3n3p36

Cavalcanti, A. P., Barbosa, A., Carvalho, R., Freitas, F., Tsai, Y.-S., Gašević, D., & Mello, R. F. (2021). Automatic feedback in online learning environments: A systematic literature review. *Computers and Education: Artificial Intelligence*, *2*, 100027. Advance online publication. DOI: 10.1016/j.caeai.2021.100027

Community College Research Center. (2013). Creating an effective online environment. *Teachers College, Columbia University*. http://ccrc.tc.columbiaEdu/media/k2/attachments/creating-effective-online-environment.pdf

Conrad, S. S., & Dabbagh, N. (2015). Examining the factors that influence how instructors provide feedback in online learning environments. *International Journal of Online Pedagogy and Course Design*, *4*(5), 47–66. DOI: 10.4018/IJOPCD.2015100104

Crawford-Ferre, H. G., & Wiest, L. R. (2012). Effective online instruction in higher education. *Quarterly Review of Distance Education*, *13*(1), 11–14. http://www.siue.edu/~lmillio/IT598/Resources/04_assessment/Effective%20Online%20I nstruction.pdf

Crompton, H., Burke, D., & Gregory, K. (2015). The effects of integrating mobile devices with teaching and learning: A meta-analysis. *Educational Research Review*, *15*, 1–15. DOI: 10.1016/j.edurev.2015.10.001

Croxton, R. A. (2014). The role of interactivity in student satisfaction and persistence in online learning. *Journal of Online Learning and Teaching*, *10*(2), 314–324. http://jolt.merlot.org/vol10no2/croxton_0614.pdf

Cui, Y., Schunn, C. D., & Gai, X. (2021). Peer feedback and teacher feedback: A comparative study of revision effectiveness in writing instruction for EFL learners. *Higher Education Research & Development*. Advance online publication. DOI: 10.1080/07294360.2021.1977692

Culver, S. (2010). Course grades, quality of student engagement, and students' evaluation of instructor. *International Journal on Teaching and Learning in Higher Education*, *22*(3), 331–336. http://files.eric.ed.gov/fulltext/EJ938568.pdf

DeCosta, M., Bergquist, E., Holbeck, R., & Greenberger, S. (2016). A desire for growth: Online full-time faculty's perceptions of evaluation processes. *Journal of Educators Online, 13*(2), 19-52. http://www.thejeo.com/Archives/Volume13Number2/DeCostaBergquistHolbeckandGreenberger.pdf

Demir, K., & Akpinar, E. (2018). The effect of mobile learning applications on students' academic achievement and attitudes towards mobile learning. *Malaysian Online Journal of Educational Technology*, *6*(2), 48–68. DOI: 10.17220/mojet.2018.04.004

Dolan, V. (2011). The isolation of online adjunct faculty and its impact of their performance. *International Review of Research in Open and Distance Learning, 12*(2). http://www.irrodl.org/index.php/irrodl/article/view/793/1691

Duffin, E. (2020a). *U.S. population targeted by online education programs 2019.* https://www.statista.com/statistics/731146/percentage-online-programs-that-were-designed-with-special-student-characteristics-in-mind-by-target-population-us/

Duffin, E. (2020b). *Reasons for online college selection among students in the U.S. 2019.* https://www.statista.com/statistics/956111/reasons-online-college-selection-students/

Edwards, M., Perry, B., & Janzen, K. (2011). The making of an exemplary online educator. *Distance Education, 32*(1). Advance online publication. DOI: 10.1080/01587919.2011.565499

Elakiya, T. T., & Kalabarathy, S. (2022). Level of satisfaction on online teaching method among undergraduate students – A descriptive cross-sectional study. *Cardiometry,* (25), 1140-1145. https://doi.org/DOI: 10.18137/cardiometry.2022.25.11401145

El-Sofany, H. F., & El-Haggar, N. (2020). The effectiveness of using mobile learning techniques to improve learning outcomes in higher education. [iJIM]. *International Journal of Interactive Mobile Technologies, 14*(8), 131–148. DOI: 10.3991/ijim.v14i08.13125

Essary, M. (2014). Key external factors influencing successful distance education programs. *Academy of Educational Leadership Journal, 19*(3), 121–136. https://www.questia.com/library/journal/1G1-396615723/key-external-factors-influencing-successful-distance

Fedynich, L., Bradley, L. S., & Bradley, J. (2015). Graduate students' perceptions of online learning. *Research in Higher Education, 27,* •••. http://www.aabri.com/manuscripts/142108.pdf

Fish, W. W., & Wickersham, L. E. (2015). Best practices for online instructors. *Quarterly Review of Distance Education, 10*(3), 279–284. https://www.learntechlib.org/p/106758

Fisher, D. P., & Southam, C. (2025). *The impact of timely formative feedback on university student motivation. Assessment & Evaluation in Higher Education.* Advance online publication. DOI: 10.1080/02602938.2025.2449891

George, D., & Mallery, P. (2010). *SPSS for Windows step by step.* Allyn & Bacon.

Glassick, C. E., Huber, M. T., & Maeroff, G. I. (1997). *Scholarship assessed: Evaluation of the professoriate*. Jossey-Bass.

Hachey, A. C., Wladis, C. W., & Conway, K. M. (2013). Balancing retention and access in online courses: Restricting enrollment. Is it worth the cost? *Journal of College Student Retention*, *15*(1), 9–36. DOI: 10.2190/CS.15.1.b

Harder, J. T., & Abuhamdieh, A. H. (2015). The role of positive regard in self-regulated learning: An analysis of student evaluation data. *Journal of College Teaching and Learning*, *12*(2), 109–120. DOI: 10.19030/tlc.v12i2.9183

Hauser, R., Paul, R., Bradley, J., & Jeffrey, L. (2012). Computer self-efficacy, anxiety, and learning in online versus face-to-face medium. *Journal of Information Technology Education*, *11*, 141–154. http://www.jite.org/documents/Vol11/JITEv11p141-154Hauser0910.pdf

Herman, J. H. (2012). Faculty development programs: The frequency and variety of professional development programs available to online instructors. *Journal of Asynchronous Learning Networks*, *16*(5). http://files.eric.ed.gov/fulltext/EJ1000093.pdf

Horspool, A., & Lange, C. (2012). Applying the Scholarship of Teaching and Learning: Student Perceptions, Behaviours and Success Online and Face-to-Face. *Assessment & Evaluation in Higher Education*, *37*, 73–88. DOI: 10.1080/02602938.2010.496532

Jaggars, S. S., & Xu, D. (2010). *Online learning in the Virginia Community College system*. Columbia University, Teachers College, Community College Research Center., http://ccrc.tc.columbia.edu/media/k2/attachments/online-learning-virginia.pdf

Kang, I. (2013). Factors of learner-instructor interaction which predict perceived learning outcomes in online learning environment. *Journal of Computer Assisted Learning*, *29*(3), 292–301.

Keengwe, J., & Kidd, T. T. (2010). Towards best practices in online learning and teaching in higher education. *Journal of Online Learning and Teaching*, *6*(2), 533–541. http://jolt.merlot.org/vol6no2/keengwe_0610.pdf

Lee, S. J., Srinivasan, S., Trail, T., Lewis, D., & Lopez, S. (2011). Examining the relationship among student perception of support, course satisfaction, and learning outcomes in online learning. *The Internet and Higher Education*, *12*(3), 158–163. DOI: 10.1016/j.iheduc.2011.04.001

Lewis, C., & Adbul-Hamid, H. (2006). Implementing effective online teaching practices: Voices of exemplary faculty. *Innovative Higher Education*, *31*(2). Advance online publication. DOI: 10.1007/s10755-006-9010-z

Lin, H., Dyer, K., & Guo, Y. (2012). Exploring online teaching: A three-year composite journal of concerns and strategies from online instructors. (English). *Online Journal of Distance Learning Administration, 15*(3), 1. http://www.westga.edu/~distance/ojdla/fall153/lin_dyer_guo153.html

Mahmodi, M., & Ebrahimzade, I. (2015). The analysis of Iranian students' persistence in online education. *International Review of Research in Open and Distance Learning, 16*(1). Advance online publication. DOI: 10.19173/irrodl.v16i1.1982

Marin, V. J., Pereira, T., Sridharan, S., & Rivero, C. R. (2017, April). *Automated personalized feedback in introductory Java programming MOOCs.* In *Proceedings of the 2017 IEEE 33rd International Conference on Data Engineering (ICDE)* (pp. 1259–1270). IEEE. https://doi.org/DOI: 10.1109/ICDE.2017.169

Michinov, N., Brunot, S., Le Bohec, O., Juhel, J., & Delaval, M. (2011). Procrastination, participation, and performance in online learning environments. *Computers & Education, 56*(1), 243–252. DOI: 10.1016/j.compedu.2010.07.025

Miller, G. (2015). Associations between learner interaction and achievement in an online course: A longitudinal study. *NACTA Journal, 59*(3), 197–201. https://www.nactateachers.org/index.php/vol-59-3-sept-2015/2319-associations-between-learner-interaction-and-achievement-in-an-online-course-a-longitudinal-study

Molinari, C. A., Freshman, B. L., & Rae, Y. T. (2015). Mindful awareness training in online and face-to-face learning environments: A comparative analysis. *The Journal of Health Administration Education, 32*(4), 579–604. DOI: 10.12016/M2KM85

Moore, J. (2014). Effects of online interaction and instructor presence on students' satisfaction and success with online undergraduate public relations courses. *Journalism & Mass Communication Education, 69*(3), 271–288. DOI: 10.1177/1077695814536398

Moore, M. G. (1993). Editorial. Three types of interaction. *American Journal of Distance Education, 3*(2), 1–6. DOI: 10.1080/08923648909526659

Moore, M. G., & Kearsley, G. (2012). *Distance education: A systematic view of online learning* (3rd ed.). Wadsworth Cengage Learning.

Mueller, B., Mandernach, B. J., & Sanderson, K. (2013). Adjust versus full-time faculty: Comparison of student learning outcomes in the online classroom. *Journal of Online Learning and Teaching, 9*(3), 341–353. http://jolt.merlot.org/vol9no3/mueller_0913.htm

Nandi, D., Hamilton, M., & Harland, J. (2012). Evaluating the quality of interaction in asynchronous discussion forums in fully online courses. *Distance Education, 33*(1). Advance online publication. DOI: 10.1080/01587919.2012.667957

Nandi, D., Hamilton, M., Harland, J., & Mahmood, S. (2015). Investigation of participation and quality of online interaction. *International Journal of Modern Education and Computer Science*, *7*(8), 25–37. DOI: 10.5815/ijmecs.2015.08.04

Nikoletatos, P. (2020). Online learning has created challenges that universities and students must overcome. *Fenews.* https://www.fenews.co.uk/exclusive/online-learning-has-created-challenges-that-universities-and-students-must-overcome/

Padilla Rodriguez, B. C., & Armellini, A. (2015). Expanding the interaction equivalency theorem. *International Review of Research in Open and Distance Learning*, *16*(3). Advance online publication. DOI: 10.19173/irrodl.v16i3.2085

Pagliari, L., Batts, D., & McFadden, C. (2009). Desired versus actual training for online instructors in community colleges. *Online Journal of Distance Learning Administration*, *12*(4). https://www.learntechlib.org/p/76603

Park, H., & Choi, H. J. (2009). Factors influencing adult learners' decision to drop out or persist in online learning. *Journal of Educational Technology & Society*, *12*(4), 207–217. https://pdfs.semanticscholar.org/152d/86fbe09ce4d476277b2dfacc38f85b2e2754.pdf

Passer, M. W. (2014). *Research methods: Concepts and connections.* Worth Publishers.

Phirangee, K., Epp, C. D., & Hewitt, J. (2016). Exploring the relationships between facilitation methods, students' sense of community, and their online behaviors. *Online Learning : the Official Journal of the Online Learning Consortium*, *20*(2), 134–154. https://tspace.library.utoronto.ca/bitstream/1807/73603/1/Exploring%20the%20Relationships%20Facilitation%20Methods.pdf

Peterson, J. L. (2016). Formative evaluations in online classes. *The Journal of Educators Online*, *13*(1), 1–14. http://www.thejeo.com/Archives/Volume13Number1/Peterson.pdf

Pina, A. A., & Bohn, L. (2014). Assessing online faculty: More than student surveys and design rubrics. *Quarterly Review of Distance Education*, *15*, 25–34.

Poelhuber, B., & Anderson, T. (2011). Distance students' readiness for social media and collaboration. *International Review of Research in Open and Distance Learning*, *12*(6), 102–125.

Preisman, K. A. (2014). Teaching presence in online education: From the instructor's point of view. *Online Learning : the Official Journal of the Online Learning Consortium*, *10*(3), 1–16. http://files.eric.ed.gov/fulltext/EJ1043166.pdf

Revere, L., & Kovach, J. V. (2011). Online technologies for engaged learning: A meaningful synthesis for educators. *Quarterly Review of Distance Education*, *12*(2), 113–124. http://citeseerx.ist.psu.edu/viewdoc/download?doi=10.1.1.466.7571&rep=rep1&type=pdf

Rizzuto, M. (2017). Design recommendations for self-paced online faculty development courses. *TechTrends*, *61*(1), 77–86. DOI: 10.1007/s11528-016-0130-8

Russo-Gleicher, R. J. (2013). Qualitative insights into faculty use of student support services with online students at risk: Implications for student retention. *The Journal of Educators Online*, *10*(1). Advance online publication. DOI: 10.9743/JEO.2013.1.4

Sansone, C., Fraughton, T., Zachary, J., Butner, J., & Heiner, C. (2011). Self-regulation of motivation when learning online: The important of who, why and how. *Educational Technology Research and Development*, *59*(2), 199–212. DOI: 10.1007/s11423-011-9193-6

Shaikh, U. U., & Asif, Z. (2022). Persistence and dropout in higher online education: Review and categorization of factors. *Frontiers in Psychology*, *13*, 902070. DOI: 10.3389/fpsyg.2022.902070

Singh, J., Evans, E., Reed, A., Karch, L., Qualey, K., Singh, L., & Wiersma, H. (2021). Online, hybrid, and face-to-face learning through the eyes of faculty, students, administrators, and instructional designers: Lessons learned and directions for the post-vaccine and post-pandemic/COVID-19 world. *Journal of Educational Technology Systems*, *50*(3), 301–326. https://journals.sagepub.com/doi/epub/10.1177/00472395211063754

Smalley, S. (2021). Half of all students take online courses. *Inside Higher Ed*. https://www.insidehighered.com/news/2021/10/13/new-us-data-show-jump-college-students-learning-online

Sun, A., & Chen, X. (2016). Online education and its effective practice: A research review. *Journal of Information Technology Education*, *15*, 157–190. http://www.jite.org/documents/Vol15/JITEv15ResearchP157-190Sun2138.pdf

Taxipulati, S., & Lu, H. D. (2021). The Influence of Feedback Content and Feedback Time on Multimedia Learning Achievement of College Students and Its Mechanism. *Frontiers in Psychology*, *12*, 706821. DOI: 10.3389/fpsyg.2021.706821

Theide, R. (2012). Best practices with online courses. *US-China Education Review*, *2*, 135–141. http://files.eric.ed.gov/fulltext/ED532176.pdf

Tirrel, T., & Quick, D. (2012). Chickering's seven principles of good practice: Student attrition in community college online courses. *Community College Journal of Research and Practice*, *36*(8), 580–590.

Van de Vord, R., & Pogue, K. (2012). Teaching time investment: Does online really take more time than face-to-face? *International Review of Research in Open and Distance Learning*, *13*(3). http://www.irrodl.org/index.php/irrodl/article/view/1190/2212

Ward, M., Peters, G., & Shelley, K. (2010). Student and faculty perceptions of the quality of online learning experiences. *International Review of Research in Open and Distance Learning*, *11*(3). http://www.irrodl.org/index.php/irrodl/article/view/867/1610

Wisniewski, B., Zierer, K., & Hattie, J. (2020). The power of feedback revisited: A meta-analysis of educational feedback research. *Frontiers in Psychology*, *10*, 3087. DOI: 10.3389/fpsyg.2019.03087

Xu, D., & Jaggars, S. S. (2011). *Online and hybrid course enrollment and performance in Washington State Community and Technical Colleges*. Community College Research Center.

Yang, M., Badger, R., & Yu, Z. (2006). A comparative study of peer and teacher feedback in a Chinese EFL writing class. *Journal of Second Language Writing*, *15*(3), 179–200. DOI: 10.1016/j.jslw.2006.09.004

You, J. W. (2015). Examining the effect of academic procrastination on achievement using LMS data in e-learning. *Journal of Educational Technology & Society*, *18*(3), 64–74. http://www.ifets.info/journals/18_3/5.pdf

Zarei, S., & Mohammadi, S. (2022). Challenges of higher education related to e-learning in developing countries during COVID-19 spread: A review of the perspectives of students, instructors, policymakers, and ICT experts. *Environmental Science and Pollution Research International*, *29*(57), 85562–85568. DOI: 10.1007/s11356-021-14647-2

APPENDIX A

Example Fast Turnaround Policy for Online or Hybrid Courses

Fast Feedback Turnaround – Quick Guide for Administrators
Goal: Students get useful feedback fast so they can improve and stay engaged.

Table 11.

Item	Standard
General rule	Major work graded & feedback posted **within 3 business days** of the due date.
Quizzes / auto-graded items	24 hrs (often instant).
Short papers / posts	48 hrs.
Major projects / essays	72 hrs.
Instructor presence in discussions	Comment or grade **within 2 days**.

Flexibility

- Big capstones or unusual projects: up to **7 business days**—tell students in advance.
- Emergencies: notify class within 24 hrs and give a new return date.

How faculty do it

- Use LMS tools: rubrics, comment banks, mobile grading apps.
- Give 2-3 clear, actionable comments—audio or video okay.
- Post a quick class note for common issues to save time.

Examples of Oversights

- Chairs or ID staff spot-check gradebook timestamps and student evals.
- Student Evaluation
- Consistent success = noted in reviews; problems = offer coaching or PD.

Bottom line:
Prompt, clear feedback ($\leq$ 3 days) is now the default expectation in every online or hybrid course.

Chapter 6
From Theory to Practice:
A Systematic Review of the Flipped Classroom in Higher Music Education (2021–2025)

Huixin Zhen
https://orcid.org/0009-0008-4719-3184
Universiti Sains Malaysia, Malaysia

Wan Ahmad Jaafar Wan Yahaya
https://orcid.org/0000-0002-8605-0062
Universiti Sains Malaysia, Malaysia

ABSTRACT

This chapter conducts a systematic literature review (SLR) on the application of the flipped classroom in higher music education. Following the structure of the SLR, six articles on music courses at the higher education and adopting different types of flipped classrooms are screened out, covering empirical explorations in countries such as China, Turkey, and Mexico, as well as focusing on diverse scenarios such as musical instrument teaching (piano, guitar), music research methodology, and music education and teaching methodology courses. Research shows that flipped classroom significantly enhances students' engagement, skill acquisition and learning attitude, and so on. But it has also exposed deep-seated challenges such as technological integration bottlenecks and educational equity. This review provides an empirical reference for the digital transformation of music education and also calls on the academic community to pay attention to the coordinated development path of technological innovation and educational equity.

DOI: 10.4018/979-8-3373-7508-3.ch006

1. INTRODUCTION

1.1 Background

1.1.1 The Importance of Higher Music Education

Higher music education plays an irreplaceable role in cultivating compound talents with profound music accomplishment, superb professional skills and innovative ability (Yunkun, 2024). Higher music education, as a core component of the aesthetic education system, shoulders multiple missions such as artistic inheritance, professional talent cultivation, and social and cultural development (Yunkun, 2024; Zhao, 2023). In the contemporary context where globalization and digitalization interweave, its value is not only reflected in the improvement of an individual's artistic literacy, but also in its profound influence on cultural ecology, educational equity and the construction of human spiritual civilization (Martínez & De Moya, 2024; Shuwen, 2024). The traditional music of various ethnic groups around the world, such as the Chinese Guqin, a tradition Chinese musical instrument, African drum music, and Indian raga, has all been protected and innovated through systematic teaching in higher education institutions. Meanwhile, higher education breaks down geographical barriers and promotes cross-cultural dialogue (Tian & Su, 2023).

At the level of talent cultivation, higher music education is committed to the all-round development of individuals. It not only imparts professional skills such as performance and composition, but also attaches great importance to the cultivation of aesthetic ability and innovative thinking (Hu, 2024; Yunkun, 2024). From the perspective of social value, higher music education is the radiation center of public aesthetic education and a flexible force in social governance (Kertz-Welzel, 2022).

In the current era of globalization and information technology, the demand for music talents shows a diversified and high-level trend (Rodriguez, 2023), which poses a more severe challenge to the teaching concept, teaching method and talent training mode of high music education. Although the traditional mode of high music education has accumulated rich experience in the long-term practice, its limitations in the teaching process are gradually highlighted in the face of the requirements of the new era. Students' passive learning, limited interaction and few practical opportunities are concerned by educators (Ling, 2023; Zhang et al., 2023).

Music education is unique in terms of teaching content, learning process and teaching objectives (Concina, 2023). These characteristics make the traditional teaching mode have limitations. However, the features of the flipped classroom can precisely make up for these deficiencies. Therefore, music education has unique demands for the flipped classroom. The content of music education covers two major sections: theory and practice, and the two are closely intertwined. Its complexity far exceeds that of general disciplines (Reimer, 2022). At the theoretical level, knowledge such as music history, music aesthetics, harmony and form analysis is abstract and has a vast system. Take the history of music as an example. The musical styles, representative composers and their works in different historical periods involve multiple factors such as politics, economy and culture behind them, making it rather difficult for students to understand. In traditional classrooms, teachers find it difficult to elaborate in depth within a limited time, and students often have to memorize mechanically, making it hard for them to form a systematic cognition (Schoenfeld, 2022). The flipped classroom places the explanation of theoretical knowledge in advance, allowing teachers to carefully produce teaching videos that are rich in content and diverse in form (Talbert & Bergmann, 2023). In the classroom, discussions can be carried out around key and difficult points to promote students' in-depth understanding and internalization of the theory.

In terms of practice, the learning of skills such as vocal music, instrumental performance, and music composition requires students to practice repeatedly and constantly improve (Mateos-Moreno et al., 2025; Simones, 2024; Swanwick, 2023). In traditional teaching, students have limited time to receive guidance from teachers in class and lack timely feedback on after-class exercises. Under the flipped classroom, students imitate and practice by watching demonstration videos of playing techniques before class, initially forming muscle memory. In the classroom, teachers can provide targeted guidance on common and individual problems that students encounter during their practice. At the same time, they can organize group performance exchanges, work exhibitions and other activities to enable students to continuously improve through mutual learning. This mode makes full use of classroom time and improves the efficiency and quality of practical teaching.

Music learning is a long-term, gradual and highly dependent process on individual perception (Tichko et al., 2022). Each student has differences in musical talent, learning foundation and learning style, and also varies in learning progress and comprehension level (Yunkun, 2024). The traditional unified teaching mode is difficult to meet the individualized needs of students, which easily leads to some students failing to keep up with the progress, while others feel that the learning content lacks challenge. The flipped classroom provides students with the opportunity to independently control their learning progress (Yoon et al., 2021). For students with a weak foundation, they can repeatedly watch teaching videos and spend more time learning knowledge and practicing skills before class until they master them. For students with strong learning abilities, after completing basic learning tasks, they can independently expand their learning content, such as trying more difficult pieces or exploring music creation. In addition, through the online learning platform of the flipped classroom, teachers can promptly understand each student's learning situation, including the duration of video viewing and the completion of exercises, etc., thereby providing personalized learning suggestions and guidance for students, truly achieving teaching in accordance with individual aptitudes.

Music education not only aims to impart music knowledge and skills, but also pays more attention to cultivating students' aesthetic ability, creativity, expressiveness and teamwork spirit and other multiple goals (Hu, 2024; Yunkun, 2024). The traditional teaching mode focuses on imparting knowledge and skills and has deficiencies in cultivating students' higher-order abilities (Kexin & Buang, 2024). The flipped classroom provides strong support for achieving diverse educational goals through innovative design of teaching activities (Galindo-Dominguez, 2021; Zhao et al., 2021). In terms of cultivating aesthetic ability, students watch high-quality music works appreciation videos before class, which expose them to a rich variety of music styles and expression forms, thus broadening their musical horizons (Zhang, 2025). In the classroom, teachers and students jointly discuss the artistic value and emotional expression of the works, guiding students to appreciate music from multiple perspectives and enhancing their aesthetic literacy. In terms of creativity cultivation, in the music composition course, students learn the theory of creation and the creative ideas for excellent works before class, and carry out brainstorming and creative practice in class. The feedback from teachers and classmates can stimulate students' creative inspiration, continuously improve their works, and thus effectively cultivate students' innovative thinking and creative ability. In terms of teamwork, the flipped classroom often organizes activities such as group performances and choral rehearsals (McNamara, 2021; Weiger, 2021). During the process of cooperation, students learn to listen to others' opinions, coordinate each other's rhythms, and enhance their teamwork abilities. This is crucial for cultivating well-rounded music talents.

1.1.2 Flipped Classroom

Meanwhile, the rapid development of educational technology provides a new opportunity and way for educational reform. Flipped classroom, as a new teaching mode supported by information technology, has aroused extensive attention and research in the educational field with its unique teaching concept and organizational form (Al Mamun et al., 2022). It reverses the order of teaching and learning in the traditional classroom. By providing instructional content outside of class (often through video lectures or digital materials) and using class time for student-centered classroom activities (Shahloxon & Yulduz, 2024; Yusuf & Taiye, 2021). The teaching arrangement of flipped classroom is very consistent with the particularity of theoretical learning combined with practical skills in music education (Karkina et al., 2023). The introduction of flipped classroom model in the field of higher music education aims to improve the teaching effect by rebuilding the teaching process, optimizing the allocation of teaching resources (Dou, 2023; Ma, 2021), and cultivating high-quality music talents to meet the development needs of The Times.

The flipped classroom breaks the teacher-centered indoctrination-style teaching and returns the initiative of learning to students; by watching teaching videos before class and completing basic tests and other pre-learning tasks, students become the first responsible persons for knowledge acquisition (Liu et al., 2024). For students with different learning paces, the flipped classroom shows unique advantages. Slow starters can make up for the lag in understanding by repeatedly watching videos, while those with stronger abilities can explore and expand the content in advance. The digital characteristics of the flipped classroom make it an important tool for bridging the gap of educational resources (Morin & Willox, 2022). In developing countries, the shortage of high-quality teachers has long existed. However, the flipped classroom can deliver high-quality content to remote areas by recording course videos of top teachers. The flipped classroom provides a flexible learning path (Dikilitas & Fructuoso, 2023). In an era of rapid knowledge iteration, learning to learn is more important than mastering the knowledge itself. The flipped classroom cultivates students' meta-cognitive abilities through a continuous cycle of pre-learning, practice and reflection (Algarni, 2021).

Flipped classroom is a promising teaching strategy. In recent years, the flipped classroom has emerged as a transformative approach to high education that prioritizes student-centered active learning over the traditional lecture format (Gerges, 2025). This shift is particularly important in higher music education, where teaching effectiveness depends not only on knowledge transfer, but also on experiential, collaborative, and reflective learning (Blanco-García et al., 2025.; Wang, 2025). Music courses, especially those that focus on theory, composition, or auditory skills, often struggle to balance classroom time with practical application (Barbieri & Varvarigou, 2025; Buonviri, 2023). The Flipped classroom model dedicates classroom time to guided exercises, ensembles, and real-time feedback by moving content delivery to the pre-class phase.

1.1.3 Theoretical basis

As a new teaching model, the flipped classroom is rooted in multiple classic educational theories, which provide support for the design logic, implementation path and value goals of the flipped classroom from different perspectives.

Constructivism Theory is one of the core theoretical pillars of the flipped classroom, emphasizing that learning is not a passive process of accepting knowledge, but a process in which learners actively construct meaning through their own experiences (Vygotsky, 1978). The flipped classroom moves the imparting of knowledge (such as theoretical explanations and skill demonstrations) before class, allowing students to initially construct a knowledge framework through methods like watching videos and independent reading. The classroom focuses on interactive discussions, practical applications and problem-solving. Teachers help students deepen their understanding through guidance and feedback (Zainuddin et al., 2024). This process is in perfect alignment with the constructivist learning concept of active construction and social interaction. For instance, in music education, students independently learn music theory knowledge through videos before class and further understand the application of music theory in practice through group performance discussions in class. This is precisely the embodiment of constructivism.

(Bloom's (1968) mastery learning theory holds that as long as sufficient time and appropriate teaching support are provided, the vast majority of students can master their learning goals, and the learning differences among students mainly stem from the variations in learning time and personalized guidance. The flipped classroom, through the model of self-study before class and targeted guidance in class, provides students with the opportunity to learn at their own pace (Zainuddin et al., 2024). Students with weak foundations can repeatedly watch teaching videos and extend their practice time, while those with stronger abilities can expand their learning content in advance. In the classroom, teachers provide guidance to students on both common and individual issues, which is a manifestation of personalized support and highly consistent with the mastery of learning theories.

1.1.4 Literature Review of Flipped Classroom in Higher Music Education

Wang (2018) implemented the flipped classroom teaching in response to the problems existing in the current collective music course teaching in colleges and universities, such as a large number of students and difficulties in learning the teaching content. Students have already understood the teaching content that needs to be learned and completed in class through previewing before class, there is also more time in the classroom to carry out various forms of classroom activities and students' practical application of piano skills, after class, students reflect in time and the teacher gives corresponding feedback. The flipped classroom can enhance students' mastery of piano knowledge and skills and achieve personalized teaching. However, this article is not an empirical study and still lacks substantive evidence to prove the effectiveness of the flipped classroom in music education. Similarly, Fu (2020) also implemented flipped teaching for piano courses in colleges and universities, and it is pointed out that through the flipped classroom, students' interest and love for piano learning have been stimulated, and their piano performance skills have been improved. However, the lack of data still makes the article unconvincing. At the same time, it was mentioned that the flipped classroom has stimulated interest in piano learning, but the extent of the interest improvement has not been quantified. Qiang et al. (2024) Implementing Flipped Classroom in the World Music Appreciation Course, the deep integration of Hebei folk songs with the music appreciation course has improved students' music appreciation level of Hebei folk songs. However, the implementation details are ambiguous, and the practical guidance is insufficient, the author did not mention how the flipped classroom was implemented in the world music appreciation course, this makes it difficult for other educators to draw lessons from. Zhu et al. (2025) developed a practical conceptual framework for music theory courses in Chinese universities, in view of the fact that the music theory course is highly theoretical and students lack practice to understand knowledge concepts, combining autonomous learning with the flipped classroom, innovations have been made in music education to meet the current learning and teaching needs.

The influence of the flipped classroom model on higher music education is multi-dimensional and profound, it not only revolutionized the traditional teaching process, but also fundamentally reshaped the relationship between teaching and learning, promoting the development of music education in a more efficient, personalized and innovative direction. Although flipped learning has been widely studied in STEM subjects and middle school education environments, its implementation in higher music education has not been fully explored, and the research on flipped classroom in higher music education is not systematic (Sun et al., 2025).

1.1.5 Research Gaps

According to the literature review, there is still currently a lack of systematic empirical research on the application effect of the flipped classroom in music education. Research that verifies its specific impact on students' knowledge acquisition, skill improvement, and quality cultivation (such as aesthetic ability and creativity) through scientific data is still insufficient.

Most of the existing research focuses on a few fields such as piano courses and music appreciation courses. There is insufficient exploration of the application of flipped classrooms in other subfields of music education such as chorus, composition, and music therapy, and universal conclusions covering the entire field of music education have not yet been formed.

For different music teaching contents (such as theoretical knowledge and practical skills) and different learning groups (such as students of different ages and foundations), the specific adaptation models of the flipped classroom (such as teaching video design, personalized guidance strategies, classroom interaction forms, etc.) have not been deeply studied, and there is a lack of a refined implementation framework.

1.2 Purpose of the Review

This systematic literature review seeks to search, analyze, and synthesize existing research that discussed the flipped classroom in higher music education Settings. Through this progress, the aim is to identify the implementation of flipped classrooms in higher music education today, assess results and reveal teaching strategies and gaps in the current literature, and propose future research directions.

1.3 Research Questions

In this systematic literature review, the following research questions will be investigated by searching, collating, and analyzing relevant publications from 2021 to 2025:

i. Which flipped classroom models are adopted in higher music education?
ii. Which learning outcomes are related to the research on flipped music teaching?
iii. What other characteristics does the flipped classroom have in higher music education?

2. METHOD

2.1 Publication Search Order

Publications in this systematic literature review are searched in the following order:

i. Identify key English search terms based on the research topic.
ii. Identify related terms that are synonymous with keywords to ensure comprehensiveness of search results.
iii. Design a search statement that contains keywords and Boolean connectors.
iv. Identify search database databases (Google Scholar and WOS).
v. Enter a search statement in the specified database.
vi. Limit the search to publications that are less than 5 years old.
vii. Filter search results (PRISMA).

2.2 Search Statement

This review follows the PRISMA 2020 Guidelines for Systematic Review. Searching databases includes using databases such as Google Scholar and WOS, keywords will be used in Boolean operator include:

("flipped classroom" OR "flipped learning" OR "flipped instruction" OR "inverted classroom") AND ("music education" OR "music instruction" OR "music pedagogy") AND ("higher education" OR university OR college OR "tertiary education" OR undergraduate OR "post-secondary")

2.3 Inclusion and Exclusion Criteria

The inclusion and exclusion criteria for determining the relevant literature in this review are shown in Table 1. This systematic literature review focuses on the application of flipped classroom in high music education in the past five years. Therefore, publications between 2021-2025 are reviewed. Other criteria include peer-reviewed articles, higher education level, focus on music education, whether the language of the article is English or Chinese or another language, article completeness, empirical research. The database searches are Google Scholar and WOS.

Table 1. Inclusion and Exclusion Criteria

Criteria	Inclusion	Exclusion
Databases	GOOGLE SCHOLAR and WOS	Other databases
Time Frame	2021-2025	Published before January 1, 2021
Publication type	Online peer-reviewed articles	Books and book chapters, conference proceedings, short papers, gray literature (e.g., reports), editorials
Educational level	High education	Research in the K12 environment
Focus	Focus on music education	Focus on research in other disciplines (unless music is a key component)
Languages	English and Chinese	Other languages
Completeness of article	Full article	Can't read full article
Research strategy	Empirical research on flipped classroom	Non-empirical research (e.g. theoretical papers, opinion articles)

2.4 Screening Process

The PRISMA flow chart will be used to document the selection process, including the number of studies screened, included and excluded and their reasons. Figure 1. shown the PRISMA flow.

Figure 1. PRISMA Flowchart

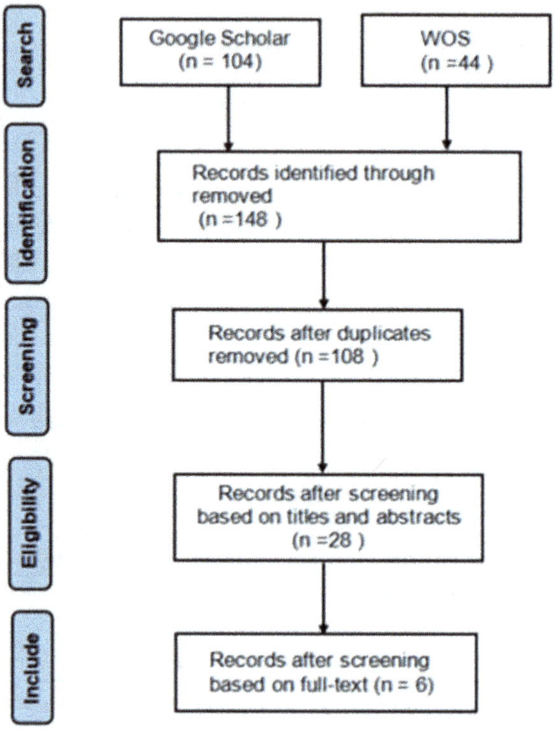

Using Google Scholar and the WOS database, relevant journal articles related to the flipped classroom in higher music from 2021 to 2025 were searched. A total of 148 articles were found by searching for these terms in the article titles, keywords and abstracts. Excluding the duplicate articles among the databases, there are 108 remaining. By reading the titles and abstracts, eliminating the articles that did not use the flipped classroom and were irrelevant to higher music education, and screening the non-peer-reviewed articles, 28 articles remained. Excluding non-empirical studies, fully online flipped classrooms and articles where the full text cannot be read, ultimately, six articles were included for further analysis in this study.

3. RESULTS

Data extraction will cover: year of publication, country, method, participants, course type, flipped model description, results and conclusions. The specific content is shown in Table 2 as follows.

Table 2. Literature Screening Results

Author, Year	Country	Research method	Research design	Research course	Findings
Gracia & Perakaki, 2025	México	Action research	A field diary, non-participant and participant observations, focus group	Seminar on Music Research	The FC method enables students to gain a deeper understanding of the methods and tools of music research, exchange ideas and problems, and create a collaborative atmosphere between students and teachers. The most notable result is that students believe they can manage and arrange their time and work at their own pace, developing their music research skills.
Wang et al., 2025	China	Experimental	One-group pre-test and post-test experimental design	Music appreciation course	Implementing case learning and flipped classroom methods in music appreciation courses can enhance students' self-assessment of their abilities, increase their interest in learning, guide future teaching practices, cultivate their love for music, and develop all-round talents with balanced moral and intellectual development.
Chen, 2023	China	Qualitative and quantitative	Survey (Questionnaire)	Group Piano Lessons	The flipped teaching method can enhance students' understanding of works, achieve personalized teaching, increase students' participation and enthusiasm, and is conducive to students' development of musical instrument learning ability and autonomous learning ability.

continued on following page

Table 2. Continued

Author, Year	Country	Research method	Research design	Research course	Findings
Lv, 2023	China	Experimental study	Observation, comparison, and description	Piano course	Students in the AI-based flipped classroom have a better level of music knowledge and a higher level of participation in piano lessons than those in the traditional flipped classroom.
Yilmaz & Zahal, 2023	Türkiye	Experimental	A pretest-posttest randomized experimental design	Guitar instruction	The flipped learning model has been found to be more effective than traditional learning methods. Under the flipped learning model, students have higher accompaniment skills, and their motivation and attitude are also better.
Ma, 2021	China	Case study	Observation, semi-structured interviews	Music education and pedagogy course	The curriculum reform was carried out by adopting the flipped classroom teaching model. By transforming simple knowledge into pre-class learning resources, the time and space of the actual classroom were effectively "liberated". In actual classrooms, the role of "peer motivation" is brought into play. Teachers act as guides, while students are the main body. They focus on high-level learning tasks, promote the internalization of students' knowledge, achieve deep learning, and thereby improve the overall learning effect.

According to the literature search, there are not many related studies on the implementation of the flipped classroom in higher music education, especially those related to empirical research. It can be seen from Table 2 that in terms of geographical distribution, four articles are in China, one article is in Turkey, and one article is in Mexico. The flipped classroom is implemented in the following music courses: one music appreciation course, one guitar teaching course, two piano courses, one music education and teaching method course, and one music research course. The research methods are diverse, including quantitative, qualitative and mixed ones, and the research designs are also very rich, There are questionnaires, observations, interviews, pre-tests and post-tests, etc. The research results cover aspects such as students' music learning performance, music learning motivation, music learning attitude, music learning participation, and music learning satisfaction. Although there are not enough studies on the flipped classroom in higher music education, the research methods and results in the existing studies are still relatively extensive.

3.1 Implementation Types of Flipped Classrooms in Higher Music Education (Q1)

The diversity of the flipped classroom models adopted in higher music education is still insufficient. Table 3 presents the types of flipped classrooms involved in the articles of this study, covering aspects such as the integration of teaching resources based on technical platforms, the redesign of teaching processes, and the innovative application of teaching methods. These models are designed to enhance students' learning outcomes and participation, cultivate their autonomous learning ability and innovative thinking, and meet the demands for cultivating music talents in the new era.

Table 3. Types of Implementation of Flipped Classroom in Higher Music Education

	The types of flipped classroom	Author, year
1	Traditional flipped classroom	Chen (2023); Gracia & Perakaki, (2025); Ma (2021); Yilmaz & Zahal, (2023)
2	Case-based learning with flipped classroom	Wang et al., (2025)
3	AI-based flipped classroom	Lv (2023)

3.1.1 Traditional Flipped Classroom

Integrating rich teaching resources through various online platforms is one of the important models of the flipped classroom in higher music education. The traditional flipped classroom refers to a form of flipped classroom where students watch and study pre-class materials before class, conduct classroom activities during class, and reflect after class (Gustian et al., 2023; Larson & Linnell, 2023). The traditional flipped classroom is a teaching model that optimizes the learning experience by reconstructing the teaching process. The core lies in moving the knowledge transfer link to the pre-class stage, while the class time focuses on the internalization and application of knowledge. This model originated in the early 2000s and gradually emerged with the popularization of online video technology, its concept subverts the traditional one-way model where teachers give lectures in the classroom and students complete their homework after class, it emphasize student-centered and cultivate autonomous learning and higher-order thinking abilities (Dalbani et al., 2022; Fetaji et al., 2024). Chen (2023) applied the flipped classroom in piano teaching. Teachers released teaching videos through WeChat, MOOC platforms, etc., covering content such as piece analysis and demonstration of playing techniques. Teachers will select or make their own teaching videos for students to watch before class to prepare for classroom learning. These videos not only enable students to familiarize themselves with the course content in advance, but also allow them to control their learning progress independently according to their own situations. The online platform also provides a space for communication and discussion. Students can ask questions and share their learning experiences at any time, promoting the absorption and understanding of knowledge.

Gracia and Perakaki (2025) the process reengineering model of pre-learning, discussion, practice in the flipped classroom emphasizes the redesign of the teaching process and divides the learning process into three stages: pre-learning before class, classroom discussion and post-class practice. In the music studies course, students learn research methods through interactive videos before class and understand relevant theoretical knowledge. In the classroom, students design research plans in groups, carry out mock defenses and other activities, and engage in in-depth discussions and exchanges. After class, students apply the knowledge they have learned to actual research projects. As stated in the article by Gracia and Perakaki (2025), this model enables students to have a preliminary understanding of knowledge before class, deepen their understanding under the guidance of teachers in class, consolidate knowledge through practice after class, and improve students' research ability and problem-solving ability.

The flipped classroom of Ma (2021) took online theoretical pre study, classroom collaborative exploration, practical application as its core process, emphasized that students shift from passive acceptance to active construction. Before class, there is self-directed learning driven by online resources. During class, there is group collaboration and in-depth discussion centered on students. After class, there is practical reflection and a teaching plan combined with classroom discussions. Students record micro-teaching videos (such as simulated teaching clips) after class and upload them to the platform for teachers and peers to comment on. In the flipped classroom of Yilmaz and Zahal (2023), a model of skill decomposition pre-learning combined with hierarchical guidance in the classroom is adopted. Before class, fragmented skill video pre-learning is conducted, during class, hierarchical guidance and collaborative learning are carried out, after class, piano homework is assigned to consolidate knowledge.

3.1.2 Case-based Learning with Flipped Classroom

Case-based flipped classroom is an innovative flipped classroom model that combines the flipped classroom with case-based learning (Chen, 2024; Xu et al., 2024; Yang et al., 2024). Wang et al. (2025) combined case learning with the flipped classroom to guide students to conduct in-depth exploration. In the music appreciation course, teachers will select representative musical works as cases and ask students to analyze and study them before class. In class, students share their insights through group discussions, deepening their understanding of the historical and cultural background, creative techniques and other aspects of musical works. Through this model, students shift from passive listening to active interpretation, enhancing their music appreciation ability and critical thinking skills.

3.1.3 AI-based Flipped Classroom

The AI-based flipped classroom is the 2.0 form of the flipped classroom, it is a flipped learning model that integrates AI technology, evolving from video pre-learning to intelligent adaptive learning (Albahiri & Almatrafi, 2025; Li & Peng, 2022), the development of technology also continuously drives the innovation of educational models. Lv (2023) utilized intelligent technologies such as artificial intelligence to achieve personalized learning. In piano teaching, the intelligent learning system can provide real-time feedback based on students' performance, correct mistakes and guide students to carry out targeted practice. The stylus-driven intelligent learning system in this study can provide students with personalized learning paths and guidance, meet the learning needs of different students, and improve learning outcomes.

3.2 Research Results of Flipped Classroom in Higher Music Education (Q2)

The impact of using the flipped classroom in higher music education mainly involves the following aspects, as shown in Table 4.

Table 4. Research Outcomes

	Author, Year	Student achievements
1	Gracia & Perakaki, 2025	Engagement, motivation, academic success, attitude
2	Wang et al., 2025	Music appreciation ability, satisfaction
3	Chen, 2023	Learning attitude, satisfaction
4	Lv, 2023	Engagement, learning outcomes

continued on following page

Table 4. Continued

	Author, Year	Student achievements
5	Yilmaz & Zahal, 2023	Motivation, attitude, accompaniment skills
6	Ma, 2021	Student-oriented, peer motivation, deep learning

3.2.1 Academic Performance and Skill Enhancement (Student Outcomes)

Multiple studies have confirmed the positive impact of the flipped classroom on students' knowledge acquisition and skill improvement.

Music appreciation ability: Experiment conducted by Yan'an University in China showed that after adopting the flipped classroom with case learning model, the score of students' music appreciation ability test increased from 56.39 points in the pre-study to 87.16 points ($t=16.044$, $p<0.01$). Especially in the dimensions of work analysis and cultural interpretation, significant progress has been made (Wang et al., 2025).

Musical instrument playing skills: In the guitar teaching experiment in Turkey, the experimental group adopted the flipped classroom teaching mode, while the control group adopted the traditional face-to-face teaching mode. The results after the experiment showed that the accompaniment skill score of the experimental group (48.20 points) was significantly higher than that of the control group (32.29 points), indicating that flipped learning enhances muscle memory and performance coherence through pre-class observation and demonstration combine in-class targeted guidance (Yilmaz & Zahal, 2023).

Music theoretical application ability: In the music research course of Gracia and Perakaki (2025), the research plans completed by students through the flipped mode were superior to those of the traditional group in terms of logical rigor and methodological innovation, demonstrating a deeper understanding of the research process. In Lv (2023)'s research on the flipped classroom based on artificial intelligence for piano courses, after students learned through the intelligent music system driven by a stylus, both their piano knowledge and music performance skills were higher than those of the control group. This indicates that in the flipped classroom environment, students have a better understanding of how to apply the basic knowledge of music theory than in the pain-creating teacher-centered classroom.

3.2.2 Satisfaction and Attitude

Satisfaction: Chen (2023)'s survey on piano teaching in China showed that 83% of students recognize the flipped model, believed that video pre-learning with classroom practice has improved learning efficiency, and 63% of students say they "prefer to participate in group discussions", this indicates that students' satisfaction is higher under the flipped classroom. In the study of Wang et al. (2025), the results of the satisfaction evaluation questionnaire showed that the average satisfaction score of students was 4.77 points, $t=44.426$, $p=0.00$, which was statistically significant, this indicated that students were satisfied with the study of this course.

Attitude: Gracia and Perakaki (2025) at the music research seminar, students were required to create their own research projects during the classroom activity session and share their learning outcomes with other classmates. They could also receive feedback from others in a timely manner. The qualitative research results showed that in this flipped classroom environment, The students' attitudes are more positive. The flipped classroom in Chen (2023)'s article, through the model of combining pre-class video learning with classroom practice, effectively stimulated students' interest in piano learning and enhanced their attitudes towards piano learning, especially achieving remarkable results in terms of technical intuitiveness and collaborative learning.

When the flipped learning method was implemented in guitar teaching, before the experiment, there was no significant difference in the instrument attitude scores between the experimental group and the control group ($p>.05$). This it was indicated that the initial attitude baselines of the two groups were consistent. After the experiment, the attitude score of the experimental group increased significantly, while that of the control group decreased. The difference between the groups was statistically significant ($p<.02$). This indicates that the flipped classroom can positively shape students' attitudes towards guitar learning, while traditional teaching may lead to a decline in attitudes due to the lack of interaction (Yilmaz & Zahal, 2023). It can be seen that under the flipped classroom model, students have a positive attitude towards the learning of music courses.

3.2.3 Engagement, Motivation, Cooperation and Reflection

Engagement: Before class, students are required to study in advance. Meanwhile, they need to submit an analysis of the research case (such as a certain music education investigation and research) before class. In class, a project discussion learning mode is adopted, and the teacher guides in-depth discussions on common problems. Data shows that the proportion of classroom discussion duration in the experimental group reached 50%, significantly higher than 20% in the traditional classroom. Students' engagement in the flipped classroom method was higher than that in the traditional classroom (Gracia & Perakaki, 2025). Lv (2023) used the AI-based flipped classroom for students, after the intervention, the results of the engagement questionnaire showed that the students' engagement was very high, with an average participation score of 3.54.

Motivation: The flipped classroom stimulates students' learning motivation by granting them autonomous control. The AI-based flipped classroom in the Lv (2023) article constructed a multi-dimensional motivation stimulation framework through the reinforcing effect of immediate feedback, the autonomous support of personalized paths, and the social attributes of technological interaction. At the same time, the motivation of students was tested, and the comprehensive score was 3.54. "AI enables me to dare to try high-difficulty segments" jointly proves its effectiveness. In the research of Ma (2021), the flipped classroom can significantly enhance students' learning motivation through real problem-solving methods in the classroom. However, Yilmaz and Zahal (2023), through a randomized controlled experiment, explored the impact of the flipped classroom on students' motivation in guitar education and found that the flipped classroom has a significant positive effect on learning attitudes, but the impact on motivation levels is not statistically significant. It can be seen that there are still certain controversies regarding the influence of the flipped classroom on students' learning motivation, which requires further research.

Cooperation and reflection: In the music education courses of Beijing City University, students form a peer incentive effect through activities such as online forum questions and classroom debates. The quality of teaching design assignments completed through group cooperation is significantly higher than that of the traditional teaching mode (Ma, 2021).

3.3 What other characteristics does the flipped classroom have in higher music education? (Q3)

3.3.1 Optimization of Teaching Efficiency

The role of teachers has shifted from knowledge transmitters to learning facilitators, enabling the reallocation of classroom time. For instance, in group piano classes in China, teachers precisely identify students' difficulties through pre-learning data, and spend more of the 45 minutes in class on personalized guidance rather than repetitive explanations of basic theories. As a result, the average practice time of students has increased by 50% (Chen, 2023). Students have made a qualitative leap in their mastery of music knowledge and music skills within the same period of time, making classroom learning more efficient.

3.3.2 Technology Integration and Resource Design in the Flipped Classroom

The core of the flipped classroom lies in the development of pre-class learning resources and the application of online platforms. For instance, Chinese scholars have been using WeChat and MOOC platforms to release teaching videos in piano instruction. The video contents cover piece analysis, demonstration of playing techniques, etc., and the duration is controlled within 10 minutes to adapt to fragmented learning (Chen, 2023). Guitar teaching research in Turkey distributes videos through Facebook and WhatsApp, combined with online tests to ensure the pre-learning effect (Yilmaz & Zahal, 2023). Some studies have further introduced artificial intelligence (AI) technology, such as the stylk-driven intelligent learning system developed by Chinese scholars, which corrects students' performance errors through real-time feedback and enhances the accuracy of technical training (Lv, 2023). To implement the flipped classroom, there must first be complete and systematic pre-class learning materials, which requires educators to conduct effective design and development,at the same time, it is also necessary to select or develop an appropriate pre-class learning platform to ensure students' effective learning before class. This is to ensure the smooth progress of classroom activities.

3.3.3 Reconstruction of Classroom Activities in the Flipped Classroom

The flipped classroom rearranges the pre-class and in-class time in the traditional classroom, with the in-class sessions focusing on the cultivation of high-level abilities, such as critical thinking, collaboration, and practical application. In the music research seminar of Gracia and Perakaki (2025), the pre-study theory with classroom seminar model will be adopted, students learn the research methods through interactive videos before class, and in class, they design research plans and conduct mock defenses in groups. Wang et al. (2025) through the music appreciation course combines case learning, students analyze music cases before class and deepen their understanding of the historical and cultural background through group discussions in class, achieving the transformation from passive listening to active interpretation. Through the implementation of the flipped classroom, after students have mastered the basic music knowledge before class, classroom activities can be flexibly arranged with different themes and tasks for students to deepen their understanding in practice.

4. DISCUSSION

This systematic literature review comprehensively understands the application of the flipped classroom in current higher music education and the effectiveness of its implementation in higher music education. This review can provide new ideas for the application and innovation of the flipped classroom in higher music education in the future.

4.1 Implication

Although there have been quite a number of studies to prove the effectiveness of the flipped classroom in other subjects, through this review, it is found that the research on the flipped classroom in higher music education is not abundant, and there are only six articles that meet the inclusion requirements of this review. More than half of the articles study China as the country.

Through the analysis of the literature, the types of flipped classrooms in higher music education are mainly traditional flipped classrooms. Of course, there are also case-based and AI-based flipped classrooms. The flipped classroom is applied in various music courses, including piano lessons, guitar lessons, music appreciation lessons, music education and teaching method courses, and music research seminars. It involves music theory courses and music practice courses, mainly theoretical courses, with a relatively rich variety. The impact of the flipped classroom on students is also diverse, involving multiple aspects such as students' academic performance, engagement, attitude, satisfaction, and motivation. The research methods are diverse.

4.2 Limitations

This systematic literature review only included Google Scholar and WOS in the selection of databases. Due to the limited number of databases selected, although a strict search term design and screening process was carried out to make up for it as much as possible, it still could not completely eliminate the non-systematic risk caused by the limited coverage of the databases. This may impose certain limitations on the review results when they are extended to a broader range of research scenarios.

Surely, there are also some challenges in the current research. The specific content will be elaborated in the following aspects:

4.2.1 Technology Dependence and the Digital Divide

Yilmaz and Zahal (2023) pointed out that some students have difficulty completing pre-class video learning due to the lack of stable networks or smart devices, resulting in

the differentiation of participation in classroom activities, there is a certain situation of uneven acquisition of resources. Although AI systems can provide immediate feedback, such as intelligent error correction in Chinese piano teaching (Lv, 2023), subjective dimensions such as emotional expression and artistic interpretation still require face-to-face guidance from teachers, and technology cannot completely replace interpersonal interaction, the technical tools still have certain limitations.

4.2.2 Students' Adaptability and Learning Habits

A Turkish study found that approximately 20% of students failed to keep up with the pace of classroom activities due to delaying pre-study tasks (Yilmaz & Zahal, 2023), reflecting path dependence on passive learning and insufficient autonomous learning ability of students.

At first, students majoring in music in Mexico were resistant to the self-study theory before class, believing that the research methods course should be taught directly, and that the pre-study interest should be enhanced through course design (such as integrating cases of music history) and gradually guided (Gracia & Perakaki, 2025), which indicates that there may be problems that conflict with traditional teaching concepts in flipped classroom teaching.

4.2.3 Teacher Workload and Training Requirements

The flipped classroom requires teachers to possess the abilities of curriculum design, technical operation and classroom management simultaneously (Zhang & Fang, 2022). Chinese scholars have pointed out that producing high-quality teaching videos requires a considerable amount of time and needs to deal with the immediate demands of students' online questions, posing challenges to teachers' time management (Ma, 2021). Furthermore, Turkish teachers pointed out that how to balance letting students be independent and necessary theoretical supplementation requires systematic training to prevent the classroom from becoming an unguided free discussion (Yilmaz & Zahal, 2023).

It can be seen that in order to ensure the effective implementation of the flipped classroom in higher music education, systematic training is needed for teachers' comprehensive abilities such as teaching ability, the production and organization of pre-class learning materials, and the design and implementation of classroom activities.

4.3 Future Research Directions

4.3.1 Blended Teaching is Deeply Integrated

Future research needs to deeply explore the synergy between the flipped classroom and other teaching methods. For example, combining the flipped classroom with project-based learning (PBL) (Hossein-Mohand et al., 2021; Köpeczi-Bócz, 2024; Sánchez-Muñoz et al., 2022), students first independently learn music theory knowledge, such as harmony and form analysis, through the flipped classroom before class. In the classroom, music creation projects are carried out in groups, applying the learned theories to actual creation to complete original music works or the design of music education plans. This process forms a closed loop of theoretical learning, practical application, result feedback, which is conducive to strengthening students' understanding and application ability of knowledge. As Hsia et al. (2021) pointed out in their research, integrating the flipped classroom and PBL in dance courses has significantly improved students' innovation in works and teamwork ability, which provides reference ideas for the field of music education. The action research of the Mexican Music Studies Symposium provides a practical reference for this model. Through continuous task iteration, students' ability to apply knowledge is constantly optimized (Gracia & Perakaki, 2025).

4.3.2 A Balance Between Technological Innovation and Humanistic Care

On the one hand, it is necessary to develop more humanistic and caring technological tools. For example, the classic concert scenes were recreated by using virtual reality (VR) technology (Onderdijk et al., 2023; Park et al., 2024), allowing students to experience the atmosphere of the works as if they were there and assisting in understanding the emotions of the works. In the study by Onderdijk et al. (2023), by using VR technology to simulate the concert scene, students' understanding of the emotions of the works increased. On the other hand, it is necessary to clarify the irreplaceable role of teachers in guiding artistic aesthetics. Teachers, relying on their own artistic cultivation and experience, can offer students delicate and personalized aesthetic guidance, which cannot be completely replaced by technology. In teaching, the proportion of technology application and teacher guidance should be reasonably allocated to ensure that students can also fully receive the humanistic and artistic cultivation of teachers with the assistance of technology.

4.3.3 Cross-cultural Comparative Study

At present, research on the flipped classroom in higher music education is mostly concentrated in countries such as China, Turkey and Mexico (Chen, 2023; Gracia & Perakaki, 2025; Lv, 2023; Ma, 2021; Wang et al., 2025; Yilmaz & Zahal, 2023). In the future, the research scope needs to be expanded to deeply explore the adaptability of the flipped classroom in different cultural backgrounds. In a culture that emphasizes collectivism, the effect of the flipped classroom can be enhanced by designing more targeted group collaboration activities and leveraging collective cohesion (Lawter & Garnjost, 2021; Wang, 2024). In a culture of high uncertainty avoidance, a step-by-step strategy should be adopted to enable teachers and students to gradually adapt to the changes in teaching models and reduce their fear and resistance to the unknown (Lan et al., 2022). For instance, Kwong et al. (2024) and Lee (2020) found in their research on the flipped classroom in language teaching under different cultural backgrounds that in collectivist cultural countries, students are more inclined to complete pre-class tasks in groups, while in individualist cultural countries, the effect of students' autonomous learning is better, this provides a reference paradigm for cross-cultural research in music education.

4.3.4 Long-term Effect Tracking

Most of the existing studies are short-term experiments, usually lasting for about one semester at the longest (Lv, 2023), and it is difficult to fully reveal the impact of the flipped classroom on the long-term development of students' professional music abilities. Longitudinal studies should be carried out in the future to track and observe the development and changes of students throughout their undergraduate study cycle and even longer periods. Through long-term data collection and analysis, the role of the flipped classroom in the continuous improvement of students' professional music abilities was clarified, such as the long-term impact on students' core abilities such as music creation, performance and teaching, providing a basis for the long-term optimization of the teaching mode. For instance, Bourbina (2024) conducted a tracking study on the effectiveness of the flipped classroom during the four-year study of students, which demonstrated that by continuously adopting the flipped classroom model, students' ability to solve complex problems significantly improved upon graduation compared to upon enrollment, this provides a methodological reference for long-term effect tracking research in the field of music education.

5. CONCLUSION

Through this systematic literature review, it was found that in recent years, there have not been many related studies on the flipped classroom in higher music education. Only six articles meet the inclusion criteria of this literature review, mainly focusing on the implementation in music theory-related courses. A possible explanation for this is that music theory-related courses are more suitable and in greater need of teaching reform. The countries studied are mainly concentrated in China. A possible explanation for this is that the educational situation in China is more inclined towards collective education, and the flipped classroom is more suitable.

There is also great diversity in research methods and the impact that flipped classrooms will have on students. There are not many different types of flipped classrooms, but it is encouraging to keep up with the current development of educational technology and integrate the flipped classroom with the latest technologies, such as combining AI with the flipped classroom (Lv, 2023). At the same time, the author also discovered some other advantages of the flipped classroom, such as optimizing teaching efficiency, effective resource integration, and the reconstruction of the traditional classroom structure. All these will provide certain reference value for the implementation and research of the flipped classroom in the future.

The core advantage of flipped classroom lies in the efficient reorganization of time utilization and the hierarchical leap of teaching objectives. In traditional music teaching, theoretical explanations occupy the majority of class time, resulting in the compression of practical guidance and artistic experience. Flipped classroom, through digital resources such as pre-learning videos and interactive musical examples, like the AI piano teaching system developed by Lishui University in China (Lv, 2023), moves the basic theoretical learning forward, turning the classroom into a practical workshop and a creative laboratory. The guitar teaching experiment at Kars University in Turkey shows that students in the flipped classroom group can obtain more classroom practical time per week, and the improvement rate of their accompaniment skills is higher than that of the traditional group (Yilmaz & Zahal, 2023).

At the level of high-level ability cultivation, flipped classroom provides space for complex tasks such as music research methodology and interdisciplinary creation. The music research seminar of the University of Aguascalentes in Mexico guided students to complete the pre-study of research design theory before class through the flipped classroom model, and carried out case debates and mutual evaluations of research plans in class. The critical thinking scores of students increased by 28% compared with the traditional group (Gracia & Perakaki, 2025). Such practices confirm the promoting effect of flipped classroom on the transformation from knowledge memory to artistic exploration (Bergmann & Sams, 2012).

Although flipped classroom relies on technological tools, universities and colleges in developing countries often face problems such as insufficient equipment and unstable networks. A Turkish study indicates that 23% of students are unable to complete pre-class video learning due to the lack of smartphones (Yilmaz & Zahal, 2023). Meanwhile, a survey by Beijing City University in China shows that 15% of students experience a decline in pre-class learning efficiency due to platform compatibility issues (such as failed adaptation of older mobile phone models) (Ma, 2021). Even in a technologically mature environment, the problem of shallow tool functionality still exists - most studies only use video playback and online testing, lacking deep interaction technologies such as VR virtual ensemble and AI sentiment analysis (Gandhi et al., 2023; Teimouri, 2024).

Flipped classroom requires students to have a relatively high level of time management and meta-cognitive abilities (Silverajah et al., 2022; J. Wang & Jou, 2023). However, students majoring in music often have weak theoretical learning habits because they focus on practical training. A Mexican study found that 32% of students only mechanically watched videos during their pre-study and did not actively complete literature reading or question marking (Gracia & Perakaki, 2025). Turkish scholars have pointed out that students with low motivation tend to delay in unsupervised pre-study, resulting in lagging classroom participation (Yilmaz & Zahal, 2023).

Flipped classroom requires teachers to transform from lecturers to learning designers, and they need to master skills such as video production, online interaction design and data feedback analysis. However, Chinese piano teaching experiments have shown that 40% of teachers have difficulties in designing the connection between AI systems and classroom activities (Lv, 2023). However, Mexican teachers overly rely on pre-learning resources, resulting in insufficient in-depth theoretical explanations in the classroom and triggering students' feedback of knowledge fragmentation (Gracia & Perakaki, 2025).

The flipped classroom has demonstrated the potential to enhance learning outcomes and activate the classroom ecosystem in higher music education. Its core value lies in reconstructing the process of classroom time and extracurricular time, focusing the limited classroom time on artistic practice and the cultivation of higher-order thinking. However, its success depends on multiple conditions such as technological infrastructure, students' autonomous ability and teacher training. In the future, in-depth research needs to be conducted in aspects such as technological innovation, teaching method integration and cross-cultural adaptation, making it an important engine for promoting the modernization of music education.

REFERENCES

Al Mamun, M. A., Azad, M. A. K., Al Mamun, M. A., & Boyle, M. (2022). Review of flipped learning in engineering education: Scientific mapping and research horizon. *Education and Information Technologies*, *27*(1), 1261–1286. DOI: 10.1007/s10639-021-10630-z

Albahiri, M., & Almatrafi, M. (2025). THE FEASIBILITY OF USING ARTIFICIAL IN LIGENCE TECHNOLOGIES IN FLIPPED CLASSROOMS. INTED2025 Proceedings, 6919–6927. https://library.iated.org/view/ALBAHIRI2025FEA

Algarni, B. (2021). Blended learning and the flipped classroom: The potential effect to enhance students' mathematical proficiency and self-efficacy: a mixed methods study from Saudi Arabia [PhD Thesis, University of York]. https://etheses.whiterose.ac.uk/29844/

Barbieri, M., & Varvarigou, M. (2025). Developing learner-centred music theory resources: A case study from the Maltese Islands. *Music Education Research*, *27*(2), 215–228. DOI: 10.1080/14613808.2025.2465264

Bergmann, J., & Sams, A. (2012). Before You Flip, Consider This. *Phi Delta Kappan*, *94*(2), 25–25. DOI: 10.1177/003172171209400206

Blanco-García, Y., Serrano, R. M., & Casanova, O. (2025). Toward a transversal education model: A review of digital and artistic-musical competencies (2014–2024). *Arts Education Policy Review*, *0*(0), 1–15. DOI: 10.1080/10632913.2025.2459917

Bloom, B. S. (1968). Learning for Mastery. Instruction and Curriculum. Regional Education Laboratory for the Carolinas and Virginia, Topical Papers and Reprints, Number 1. Evaluation Comment, 1(2), n2. https://eric.ed.gov/?id=eD053419

Bourbina, J. (2024). Using a Flipped Course Design to increase positive outcomes in first year Science, Technology, Engineering, and Mathematics (STEM) courses. https://scholarworks.gvsu.edu/gradprojects/504/

Buonviri, N. O. (2023). Educating Ears: The Role of Sound in Music Learning. *Music Educators Journal*, *110*(2), 30–36. DOI: 10.1177/00274321231202621

Chen, C. Y. (2024). Flipped classroom with case-based learning for improving preservice teachers' classroom management learning outcomes. *Teaching and Teacher Education*, *152*, 104785. https://www.sciencedirect.com/science/article/pii/S0742051X24003184

Chen, X. (2023). Applying the Flipped Teaching Method in Group Piano Lessons to the First-Year Dance-Studies Undergraduate Students. Art and Design Review, 11(2), 140–149. https://www.scirp.org/journal/paperinformation?paperid=125251

Concina, E. (2023). Effective music teachers and effective music teaching today: A systematic review. *Education Sciences*, *13*(2), 107. https://www.mdpi.com/2227-7102/13/2/107

Dalbani, H., Eissa, S., Syed-Ahmad, S. F., & Almusharraf, N. (2022). Transitioning to flipped classrooms: Instructors' perspectives. *Sustainability*, *14*(20), 13426. https://www.mdpi.com/2071-1050/14/20/13426

Dikilitas, K., & Fructuoso, I. N. (2023). Conceptual framework for flexible learning design: The Context of flipped classroom. Conceptual Framework for Flexible Learning Design: The Context of Flipped Classroom. Https://Doi. Org/10.31265/ Usps, 267. https://kudos.dfo.no/documents/77155/files/37244.pdf

Dou, Y. (2023). Innovation of Flipped Classroom Teaching Mode in College Vocal Music Teaching. *Frontiers in Art Research*, *5*(2). https://francis-press.com/uploads/papers/gYfqhDSyflcMvOtHhi0cmaGZM6lYoDjhAeF6WzlI.pdf

Fetaji, M., Ebibi, M., & Luma, A. (2024). Flipped Learning and Creativity: Fostering Innovation and Problem-Solving. Editorial Board, 31. https://seejsd.unt.edu.mk/wp-content/uploads/2024/06/SEEJSD-Volume-8_Issue-1-2024-2.pdf#page=31

Fu, J. (2020). Analysis on the piano teaching mode of flipped class in higher education. *Frontiers in Educational Research*, *3*(14), 128–133. https://francis-press.com/uploads/papers/14fwlVlBkuLirc0mkNh0VsJjPeIVB3UHPhuscolQ.pdf

Galindo-Dominguez, H. (2021). Flipped classroom in the educational system. *Journal of Educational Technology & Society*, *24*(3), 44–60. https://www.jstor.org/stable/27032855

Gandhi, A., Adhvaryu, K., Poria, S., Cambria, E., & Hussain, A. (2023). Multimodal sentiment analysis: A systematic review of history, datasets, multimodal fusion methods, applications, challenges and future directions. *Information Fusion*, *91*, 424–444. https://www.sciencedirect.com/science/article/pii/S1566253522001634

Gerges, E. (2025). Beyond Lectures: The Flipped Learning Model. In Best Practices and Strategies for Online Instructors: Insights From Higher Education Online Faculty (pp. 133–166). IGI Global Scientific Publishing. https://www.igi-global.com/chapter/beyond-lectures/361783

Gracia, R. W. C., & Perakaki, E. (2025). A seminar on music research in higher education and the flipped classroom: An action research project. Revista Electrónica Educare, 29(1), 4. https://dialnet.unirioja.es/servlet/articulo?codigo=10123058

Gustian, K., Aridah, A., & Rusmawaty, D. (2023). The benefits of flipped classroom model for Efl learners. *Journal of Education*, *5*(4), 13918–13935. https://core.ac.uk/download/pdf/560351352.pdf

Hossein-Mohand, H., Trujillo-Torres, J.-M., Gómez-García, M., Hossein-Mohand, H., & Campos-Soto, A. (2021). Analysis of the use and integration of the flipped learning model, project-based learning, and gamification methodologies by secondary school mathematics teachers. *Sustainability*, *13*(5), 2606. https://www.mdpi.com/2071-1050/13/5/2606

Hsia, L., Lin, Y., & Hwang, G. (2021). A creative problem solving-based flipped learning strategy for promoting students' performing creativity, skills and tendencies of creative thinking and collaboration. *British Journal of Educational Technology*, *52*(4), 1771–1787. DOI: 10.1111/bjet.13073

Hu, D. (2024). Research on the Impact of Music Aesthetic Education on the Cultivation of Students' Aesthetic Appreciation. Journal of Art, Culture and Philosophical Studies, 1(1). https://www.atlantic-press-journals.com/index.php/JACPS/article/view/17

Karkina, S., Mena, J., Valeeva, R., Yarmakeev, I., Dyganova, E., & Bhullar, M. (2023). Fostering future music teachers' professional skills: Developing a signature pedagogy using e-learning. *Frontiers in Education*, *8*, 1162748. https://www.frontiersin.org/articles/10.3389/feduc.2023.1162748/full

Kertz-Welzel, A. (2022). *Rethinking music education and social change*. Oxford University Press., https://books.google.com/books?hl=zh-CN&lr=&id=KfhQEAAAQBAJ&oi=fnd&pg=PP1&dq=Rethinking+music+education+and+social+change&ots=qrJjGF8GZR&sig=_956gRn3GkZbGyPBoqf1sBf_KFs

Kexin, D., & Buang, N. A. (2024). Integrating Innovative Teaching Strategies: Assessing the Effectiveness of Flipped Classrooms, Blended Learning, and Task-Oriented Methods in Enhancing Academic Performance in Vocational IT Education. Journal of Digitainability, Realism & Mastery (DREAM), 3(05), 94–108. https://dreamjournal.my/index.php/DREAM/article/view/241

Köpeczi-Bócz, T. (2024). The impact of a combination of flipped classroom and project-based learning on the learning motivation of university students. *Education Sciences*, *14*(3), 240. https://www.mdpi.com/2227-7102/14/3/240

Kwong, R., Kwok, M. L. J., & Wong, H. (2024). Autonomous and controlled motivation in a flipped-classroom approach. *Asia Pacific Education Review*. Advance online publication. DOI: 10.1007/s12564-024-09983-0

Lan, X. LU, Z., & PENG, X. (2022). Cross-Cultural Adaptation of Chinese Students' Learning Thai Language Online in the Post-Pandemic Era—A Case Study of the Sino-Thai Co-operation Program at Guangxi University of Foreign Language. http://www.davidpublisher.com/Public/uploads/Contribute/6316e6c71c8b2.pdf

Larson, M. P., & Linnell, J. (2023). Are students coming to class prepared? The importance of pre-class learning in a flipped classroom. *Issues in Accounting Education, 38*(3), 183–205. https://publications.aaahq.org/iae/article/38/3/183/10918

Lawter, L., & Garnjost, P. (2021). Cross-Cultural comparison of digital natives in flipped classrooms. *International Journal of Management Education, 19*(3), 100559. https://www.sciencedirect.com/science/article/pii/S1472811721001087

Lee, R. S. P. (2020). Exploring the learning outcomes of flipped learning in a Second Language (L2) academic writing classroom for low proficiency pre-university students [PhD Thesis, Swinburne]. https://figshare.swinburne.edu.au/articles/thesis/Exploring_the_learning_outcomes_of_flipped_learning_in_a_Second_Language_L2_academic_writing_classroom_for_low_proficiency_pre-university_students/26282392

Li, B., & Peng, M. (2022). Integration of an AI-Based Platform and Flipped Classroom Instructional Model. *Scientific Programming, 2022*, 1–8. DOI: 10.1155/2022/2536382

Ling, S. I. (2023). Music technology in the 21st century of global music education: Opportunities and challenges. The 14th Asia-Pacific Symposium for Music Education Research (APSMER 2023), 242–251. https://researchmap.jp/kazuwo_piano/presentations/43117806/attachment_file.pdf#page=246

Liu, J., Cao, S., Liu, X., Ye, C., & Siano, P. (2024). Pre-class mode" flipped" again: Making videos instead of just watching them. *Heliyon, 10*(6). https://www.cell.com/heliyon/fulltext/S2405-8440(24)04136-7

Lv, H. Z. (2023). Innovative music education: Using an AI-based flipped classroom. *Education and Information Technologies, 28*(11), 15301–15316. DOI: 10.1007/s10639-023-11835-0

Ma, R. (2021). Stimulating students learning motivation: A case study of music education and pedagogy course based on flipped classroom. Psychology and Education Journal, 58(2), 109–114. https://www.researchgate.net/profile/Rui-Ma-133/publication/349281829_Stimulating_students'_learning_motivation_A_case_study_of_music_education_and_pedagogy_course_based_on_flipped_classroom/links/661faec8f7d3fc287467269b/Stimulating-students-learning-motivation-A-case-study-of-music-education-and-pedagogy-course-based-on-flipped-classroom.pdf

Martínez, M. del V. D. M., & De Moya, M. del V. R. (2024). Sounds of Cultures: Strategies for Global, Intercultural, and Transformative Education Through Music. In Transformative Intercultural Global Education (pp. 209–231). IGI Global. https://www.igi-global.com/chapter/sounds-of-cultures/347094

Mateos-Moreno, D., García-Perals, J., & Maxwell, T. W. (2025). Teaching to practice productively and consciously: An action-research study in one-to-one instrumental music teaching. *Music Education Research*, *27*(2), 203–214. DOI: 10.1080/14613808.2025.2465248

McNamara, A. (2021). Flipping the creative conservatoire classroom. Theatre. *Dance and Performance Training*, *12*(4), 528–539. DOI: 10.1080/19443927.2020.1864462

Morin, J., & Willox, S. (2022). Closing the soft skills gap: A case in leveraging technology and the "flipped" classroom with a programmatic approach to soft skill development in business education. Transformative Dialogues: Teaching and Learning Journal, 15(1). https://journals.psu.edu/td/article/view/1707

Onderdijk, K. E., Bouckaert, L., Van Dyck, E., & Maes, P.-J. (2023). Concert experiences in virtual reality environments. *Virtual Reality (Waltham Cross)*, *27*(3), 2383–2396. DOI: 10.1007/s10055-023-00814-y

Park, J., Choi, Y., & Lee, K. M. (2024). Research trends in virtual reality music concert technology: A systematic literature review. IEEE Transactions on Visualization and Computer Graphics. https://ieeexplore.ieee.org/abstract/document/10458432/

Qiang, F., Hirunrux, S., & Yukolthonwong, S. (2024). A Strategic Study on the Effective Application of Flipped Classroom Teaching Method in World Music Appreciation Classroom. *Journal of Roi Kaensarn Academi*, *9*(4), 819–826. https://so02.tci-thaijo.org/index.php/JRKSA/article/view/269933

Reimer, B. (2022). A philosophy of music education: Advancing the vision. State University of New York Press. https://books.google.com/books?hl=zh-CN&lr=&id=Q9eIEAAAQBAJ&oi=fnd&pg=PT9&dq=A+philosophy+of+music+education:+Advancing+the+vision&ots=B9vLhHbiZ2&sig=cMGCNYucLZa_xsGZGPumFFH0zwk

Rodriguez, R. A. (2023). Competencies of modern musician entrepreneurs: The role of digitalization in the music industry [PhD Thesis, The University of Texas Rio Grande Valley]. https://search.proquest.com/openview/742693d86ebaacfd7ce21b59117f21b6/1?pq-origsite=gscholar&cbl=18750&diss=y

Sanchez-Muñoz, R., Carrió, M., Rodríguez, G., Pérez, N., & Moyano, E. (2022). A hybrid strategy to develop real-life competences combining flipped classroom, jigsaw method and project-based learning. *Journal of Biological Education*, *56*(5), 540–551. DOI: 10.1080/00219266.2020.1858928

Schoenfeld. (2022). Why Are Learning and Teaching Mathematics So Difficult? In Handbook of Cognitive Mathematics (pp. 1–35). Springer International Publishing. https://doi.org/DOI: 10.1007/978-3-030-44982-7_10-1

Shahloxon, B., & Yulduz, Q. (2024). Flipped Classroom Model. Analyze the Effectiveness of the Flipped Classroom Approach Compared to Tradition Teaching Methods in Various Subjects or Grade Levels. Yangi O ‘zbekiston Ustozlari, 2(28), 128–134. https://cyberleninka.ru/article/n/flipped-classroom-model-analyze-the-effectiveness-of-the-flipped-classroom-approach-compared-to-traditional-teaching-methods-in

Shuwen, L. E. I. (2024). Relevance of Music Education in the Cultural Program of Contemporary College Students. US-China Education Review, 14(1), 56–59. https://www.academia.edu/download/110947221/The_1st_issue_of_2024_Volume_14_Number_1_January_2024_Serial_Number_118_.pdf#page=61

Silverajah, V. G., Wong, S. L., Govindaraj, A., Khambari, M. N. M., Rahmat, R. W. B. O., & Deni, A. R. M. (2022). A systematic review of self-regulated learning in flipped classrooms: Key findings, measurement methods, and potential directions. *IEEE Access : Practical Innovations, Open Solutions*, *10*, 20270–20294. https://ieeexplore.ieee.org/abstract/document/9684384/

Simones, L. (2024). Advancing Excellence in Teaching: Professionalizing Vocal and Instrumental Music Education. In The Applied Studio Model in Higher Music Education (pp. 34–60). Routledge. https://www.taylorfrancis.com/chapters/edit/10.4324/9781003426448-4/advancing-excellence-teaching-lilian-simones

Sun, Y., Loo, F. C., & Yeoh, P. S. (2025). APPLICATION OF FLIPPED CLASSROOM IN MUSIC EDUCATION: A SCOPING REVIEW. Arts Educa, 42. https://artseduca.com/submissions/index.php/ae/article/view/448

Swanwick, K. (2023). *Instrumental teaching as music teaching, in teaching music in secondary schools: A reader* (Sprace, G., Ed.).

Talbert, R., & Bergmann, J. (2023). Flipped learning: A guide for higher education faculty. Routledge. https://www.taylorfrancis.com/books/mono/10.4324/9781003444848/flipped-learning-robert-talbert-jon-bergmann

Teimouri, M. (2024). Comparing Human and AI Emotion and Sentiment Analysis in Mixed Reality and Zoom Environments. https://www.utupub.fi/bitstream/handle/10024/178872/TeimouriBadelehDareh_Maryam_Thesis.pdf?sequence=1

Tian, J., & Su, Y. (2023). The Role of Music Ethnography in Promoting Intercultural Art Education Communication and Cross-cultural Communication Sustainable Culturally Notch. Arts Educa, 36. https://artseduca.com/submissions/index.php/ae/article/view/59

Tichko, P., Kim, J. C., & Large, E. W. (2022). A dynamical, radically embodied, and ecological theory of rhythm development. *Frontiers in Psychology*, *13*, 653696. https://www.frontiersin.org/articles/10.3389/fpsyg.2022.653696/full

Vygotsky, L. S. (1978). Thought and language (Vol. 29). MIT press. https://books.google.com/books?hl=zh-CN&lr=&id=B9HClB0P6d4C&oi=fnd&pg=PR9&dq=thought+and+Language%EF%BC%8CVygotsky,+1978&ots=TuJaWag3Qs&sig=gaUdgsZqDveJxJMoxFdjextZrmw

Wang, H. (2018). The application of flipped classroom in Colleges and Universities piano collective classes. *Creative Education*, *9*(7), 1021–1026. https://www.scirp.org/journal/paperinformation?paperid=85100

Wang, J. (2024). Research on the Flipped Classroom + Learning Community Approach and Its Effectiveness Evaluation—Taking College German Teaching as a Case Study. *Sustainability*, *16*(17), 17. Advance online publication. DOI: 10.3390/su16177719

Wang, J., & Jou, M. (2023). The influence of mobile-learning flipped classrooms on the emotional learning and cognitive flexibility of students of different levels of learning achievement. *Interactive Learning Environments*, *31*(3), 1309–1321. DOI: 10.1080/10494820.2020.1830806

Wang, L., Othakanon, L., & Saleewong, D. (2025). Development of Music Appreciation Course Based on Case Based Learning and Flipped Classroom to Enhance Music Appreciation Ability for First Year Students in Yan'an University. *International Journal of Sociologies and Anthropologies Science Reviews*, *5*(1), 347–358. https://so07.tci-thaijo.org/index.php/IJSASR/article/view/5241

Wang, Z. (2025). Integrating mobile apps into vocal education: A study on accessibility and efficiency in learning. *Education and Information Technologies*, *30*(9), 12179–12196. DOI: 10.1007/s10639-024-13301-x

Weiger, E. A. (2021). Flipped Lessons and the Secondary-Level Performance-Based Music Classroom: A Review of Literature and Suggestions for Practice. Update. *Applications of Research in Music Education*, *39*(2), 44–53. DOI: 10.1177/8755123320953629

Xu, G., Lin, Y., Ye, Y., Wu, W., Zhang, X., & Xiao, H. (2024). Combination of concept maps and case-based learning in a flipped classroom: A mixed-methods study. *Nurse Education in Practice*, *76*, 103918. https://www.sciencedirect.com/science/article/pii/S1471595324000477

Yang, W., Zhang, X., Chen, X., Lu, J., & Tian, F. (2024). Based case based learning and flipped classroom as a means to improve international students' active learning and critical thinking ability. *BMC Medical Education*, *24*(1). Advance online publication. DOI: 10.1186/s12909-024-05758-8

Yilmaz, H., & Zahal, O. (2023). Effects of Flipped Learning-Based Guitar Instruction on Motivation, Attitude, and Accompaniment Skills. *Journal of Pedagogical Research*, *7*(1), 307–321. https://eric.ed.gov/?id=EJ1381384

Yoon, M., Hill, J., & Kim, D. (2021). Designing supports for promoting self-regulated learning in the flipped classroom. *Journal of Computing in Higher Education*, *33*(2), 398–418. DOI: 10.1007/s12528-021-09269-z

Yunkun, L. (2024). The Impact of Music Education on the Quality of Talent Cultivation. Transactions on Comparative Education, 6(1), 72–77. https://pdfs.semanticscholar.org/c047/d65f57261a2aece2889f7664c5e191a26634.pdf

Yusuf, B., & Taiye, M. A. (2021). A flipped learning environment: A disruptive approach for traditional classrooms. International Journal of Education, Psychology and Counseling, 6(42), 83–93. https://www.academia.edu/download/93937120/ijepc.pdf

Zainuddin, Z., Muluk, S., & Keumala, C. M. (2024). How do students become self-directed learners in the EFL flipped-class pedagogy? A study in higher education. *Indonesian Journal of Applied Linguistics*, *8*(3), 678–690. https://researchnow.flinders.edu.au/en/publications/how-do-students-become-self-directed-learners-in-the-efl-flipped-

Zhang, L.-X., Leung, B.-W., & Yang, Y. (2023). From theory to practice: Student-centered pedagogical implementation in primary music demonstration lessons in Guangdong, China. *International Journal of Music Education*, *41*(2), 271–287. DOI: 10.1177/02557614221107170

Zhang, M., & Fang, X. (2022). Exploring University EFL Teachers' Technological Pedagogical Content Knowledge and Teacher Efficacy in Technology-integrated Flipped Classroom. https://journals.sagepub.com/doi/full/10.1177/21582440221116105

Zhang, Z. (2025). The Teaching Method of STEAM Education-based Audio-visual Aesthetics in College Vocal Music Teaching. *Frontiers in Educational Research*, *8*(2). Advance online publication. DOI: 10.25236/fer.2025.080216

Zhao, L., He, W., & Su, Y.-S. (2021). Innovative pedagogy and design-based research on flipped learning in higher education. *Frontiers in Psychology*, *12*, 577002. https://www.frontiersin.org/articles/10.3389/fpsyg.2021.577002/full

Zhao, Y. (2023). Discussion on the Role of Basic Music Education in Cultivating Aesthetic Personality. Curriculum and Teaching Methodology, 6(15), 68–76. http://166.62.7.99/assets/default/article/2023/08/07/article_1691401000.pdf

Zhu, Q., Jamaludin, K. A., Nasri, N. M., & Li, J. (2025). Flipped classroom for music theory course in Chinese universities: A conceptual framework of practice. *Cogent Education*, *12*(1). Advance online publication. DOI: 10.1080/2331186x.2025.2498146

KEY TERMS AND DEFINITIONS

AI-based flipped classroom: Integrating AI technology into the flipped classroom is an intelligent form of flipped classroom.

Case-based flipped classroom: It is a form that integrates case-based learning into the flipped classroom.

Higher music education: It is a systematic and professional music teaching and training activity covering multiple fields such as music theory, performance and singing, composition, research and education, which is carried out in the higher education stage with the cultivation of professional music talents as the core.

PRISMA: It is a set of reporting guidelines for standardizing systematic reviews and meta-analyses, aiming to enhance research transparency and reporting quality. It includes a process framework from literature retrieval to result presentation.

Systematic literature review (SLR): It is a rigorous, transparent and repeatable method of literature review, aiming to comprehensively and systematically identify, screen, evaluate and synthesize existing literature in a certain research field to answer specific research questions.

Teaching strategy innovation: It refers to the breakthrough and creative adjustments and optimizations made to teaching methods, means, models, etc. in the teaching process to enhance teaching effectiveness and meet the needs of learners.

The flipped classroom: It is a promising teaching strategy that makes teaching more structured, divided into three stages: pre class, in class, and post class.

Traditional flipped classroom: A flipped classroom form that strictly adheres to the structure of previewing pre class, conducting activities in class, and reflecting and reviewing post class.

Chapter 7
Echoes of Innovation: Rethinking Art Education in the Age of AI

Jingru Sun
Universiti Sains Malaysia, Malaysia

Kien Tsong Chau
https://orcid.org/0009-0009-2390-441X
Universiti Sains Malaysia, Malaysia

Mariam Binti Mohamad
https://orcid.org/0000-0001-8498-4139
Universiti Sains Malaysia, Malaysia

ABSTRACT

As artificial intelligence (AI) technologies continue to reshape educational practices, their integration with arts education has received increasing attention, especially in higher education. However, there is little systematic work on how to integrate AI technologies in arts education to improve student learning performance. This systematic review investigates the impact of AI on student learning in higher education arts courses, focusing on empirical studies published between 2020 and 2025. The results show that AI technologies can improve student performance, support personalized learning paths, and promote the development of creativity and technical skills. Although the integration of AI has great potential in enhancing personalized learning and promoting innovation, its impact on human creativity, critical thinking, and the role of educators remains a concern. The review concludes with recommendations for future research and a practical guide for educators aiming to implement AI-enhanced methods in arts education.

DOI: 10.4018/979-8-3373-7508-3.ch007

1. INTRODUCTION

In recent years, the advancement of new generation AI and the implementation of the 'Artificial-Intelligence Plus' teaching method have unveiled a burgeoning domain in education characterized by personalized learning experiences, visualized learning processes, integrated learning assessments, and socially-oriented studies, wherein a novel personnel training model and framework can be established leveraging big data technology and educational big data analysis (Yu et al., 2019). AI, particularly since the advent of deep learning and large language models, has evolved from a supportive tool to an integral component of digital transformation in education (Yadav & Shrawankar, 2025). This evolution is not only technological but also pedagogical, reshaping how knowledge is delivered, assessed, and co-constructed. AI fosters equitable and substantial quality enhancement in education, and the advantages of these technologies for pedagogy and learning have recently garnered significant attention (Tan, 2020). AI has significantly transformed the evolution of education (Guilherme, 2019).

Many subject areas are included in the art and design curriculum, and the development of art and design education programs in higher education has demonstrated a trend toward inclusivity and diversity (Wan, 2023). Currently in China, around 2,000 schools and universities provide Art Design programs, fostering generations of intelligent and innovative designers, indicative of the expanding design education sector (Yu et al., 2019). With the many advances made in fields such as education and medicine, the field of art and design has also undergone tremendous changes due to various applications of AI (Zhai, 2022). The integration of technology in art education is marked by notable trends in digitization, customization, and globalization. These trends are evident in immersive learning experiences, AI-enhanced tailored instruction, interdisciplinary integration, and global collaboration. AI may assess students' progress, creative styles, and ability levels to provide tailored feedback and coaching, enhancing their educational experience. Additionally, AI aids instructors in tracking student progress and modifying instructional methods, so enabling tailored learning trajectories that promote effective attainment of educational objectives and encourage creative expression and discovery (Shah, 2023). Despite the growing interest in this area, there remains a lack of comprehensive understanding of how AI integration influences student learning outcomes specifically in higher education art programs. Art education poses unique pedagogical challenges and opportunities that differ from those of other disciplines, often emphasizing subjective interpretation, aesthetic judgment, and process-oriented learning (Illeris, 2012). Through a detailed analysis of the advantages, inherent challenges, and practical applications of AI in art education, this study sheds light on how AI can be strategically used to improve the quality of the learning experience. Make it more engaging and effective, thereby promoting a rich educational environment consistent with contemporary technological advances. This systematic review aims to integrate empirical research published between 2020 and 2025 to explore the practice of integrating AI into art education in the context of higher education and how it can improve student outcomes. Following PRISMA guidelines, the researcher conducted a comprehensive search in major academic databases such as Scopus, Web of Science, and IEEE Xplore, ultimately identifying key AI applications such as generative design tools, intelligent tutoring systems, and adaptive feedback mechanisms, and evaluating their impact on learning outcomes and teaching strategies. Through analytical research on this topic, this review provides new perspectives on the application of AI in art education and provides inspiration for educators and researchers to create and optimize learning environments, thereby improving student outcomes and enriching learning experiences.

1.1 The Application of AI Technology In Education

AI is a branch of computer science focused on comprehending human cognitive processes and replicating their outcomes using information systems. The principal objective of AI is to develop intelligent systems (i.e., computer programs or computers) that can exhibit intelligent behaviors, such as learning, reasoning, problem-solving, perception, and creation (Rainer et al., 2020). The domain of education is particularly amenable to AI technologies, as educational endeavors, encompassing both learning and instruction, are knowledge-intensive cognitive processes. AI applications, designed for cognition and problem-solving through algorithms and knowledge bases, can effectively enhance the capabilities of educators and learners in teaching and learning (Seaba, 2023). Since the emergence of AI in the mid-1950s, AI technologies have progressively been utilized to enhance education and training across several disciplines, including language, STEM, and medicine (Perrotta & Selwyn, 2020). As of now, AIED (Artificial Intelligence in Education) apps have been created to facilitate teaching and learning activities, including material preparation and dissemination, interactions and collaboration, and performance assessment (Chassignol et al., 2018).

Wang et al. (2024) published a literature review study. Based on the Web of Science database, the researchers used the method proposed by Goksel and Bozkurt (2019) to search and screen data, and finally obtained 2,223 English literature related to AIED. Figure 1 shows the publishing trends in the field of AIED from 1984 to June 2022 in their research report.

Figure 1. Annual scientific output in the field of AIED (Wang et al., 2024)

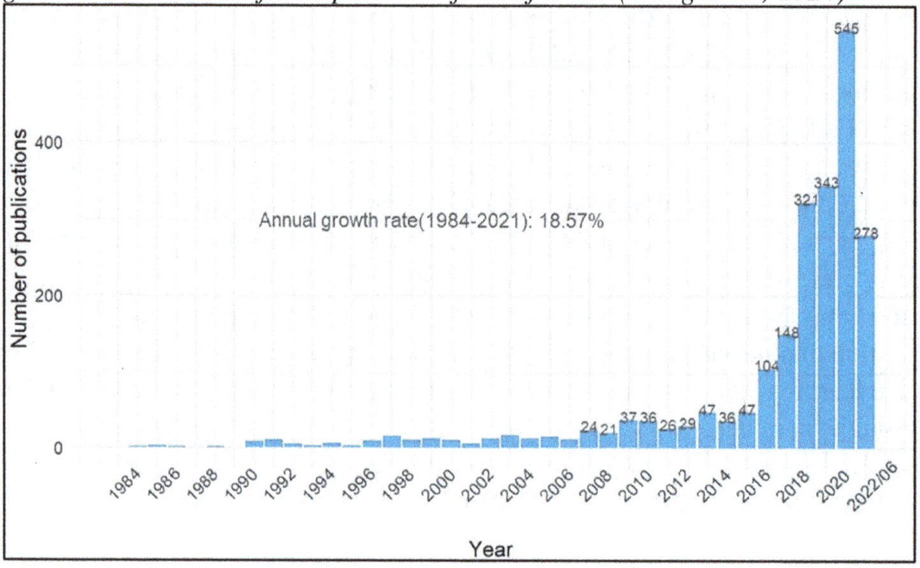

The data show that the field developed slowly in the early days. Since 2017, AIED research has accelerated significantly, showing a rapid growth trend from 2019 to 2021, with annual publications of 321, 343, and 545, respectively, reaching a research boom. Statistics show that the average annual growth rate from 1984 to 2021 was 18.57%, reflecting that AIED has become an important growth area in educational research.

In the realm of online education, AI applications such as intelligent tutoring systems, teaching robots, learning analytics dashboards, and adaptive learning systems have been employed to enhance the learning experience, performance, and quality of online students (Chen et al., 2020). Diverse AIED methodologies, such as natural language processing, artificial neural networks, machine learning, deep learning, and genetic algorithms, have been employed to develop intelligent learning environments for behavior detection, predictive modeling, and learning recommendations (Rowe, 2019). From an instructional standpoint, AI can function as a tutor to monitor students' learning processes, evaluate their performance, and offer opportunities for educators to eliminate repetitive and monotonous teaching activities (Chen et al., 2020). Furthermore, from the learner's perspective, a primary purpose of AIED is to deliver individualized learning assistance or support tailored to students' learning status, preferences, or individual traits (Hwang & Tu, 2021). For instance, Sequential Pattern Mining (SPM) has been employed in recommender systems to identify historical learning sequence patterns in learner interactions and to uncover appropriate recommendation items for learners' educational sequences

(Romero et al., 2013). Machine Learning (ML) has been employed in academic forecasting, including the prediction of students' achievement in online courses, their likelihood of completing college degrees, and their course choices in higher education (Rico-Juan et al. 2019). Natural language processing (NLP) has been employed for code detection and emotional analysis. Rico-Juan et al. (2019) employed NLP for the automated identification of discrepancies between numerical scores and textual comments in the peer-assessment process. The implementation of AI systems and technology has revolutionized online higher education, presenting both potential and problems for enhancing educational quality.

1.2 Developments in the Use of AI for Art Education

With the advancement of contemporary information and communication technology, classical artistic methods are increasingly evolving to become more sophisticated and intelligent. These techniques facilitate the teaching, learning, creation, and distribution of art in the contemporary world (Wenjing & Cai, 2023). The provision of a high-quality and user-friendly environment for learners would facilitate the enhancement of their creativity and the development of improved processes for the promotion of culture and art (Shao & Yu, 2025). Conventional pedagogical approaches and materials in art education are insufficient to address the requirements of contemporary pupils. In conventional art education, students generally depend on static learning resources and standard pedagogical approaches, which somewhat restrict creative freedom and instructional engagement (Tigert & Leider, 2022). The integration of educational technology and AI is important for innovation in art education. Real-time monitoring of students' creative status, provision of fast feedback, and encouragement of creative output can dismantle the limitations of conventional teaching, fostering a more participatory and individualized educational experience (Fang & Jiang, 2024).

The ongoing advancement of AI technology and associated policies has rendered AI education a significant emergent research domain for future learning. Generative machine learning models have been extensively utilized in digital art creation (Vartiainen & Tedr, 2023) and in freehand sketching and painting (Ghosh et al., 2019). This presented innovative concepts for creative pedagogy in art education. In education, educators and learners have demonstrated a growing inclination towards more intuitive and effective systems that offer substantive recommendations rather than merely repeating feedback (Chiu et al., 2023). Rangel and Duart (2023) proposed that deep learning may be utilized in art education for both artistic creation and style analysis, as well as for automated assessment. Training deep learning models to categorize and assess students' work could significantly diminish teachers' subjective biases, resulting in a more objective and efficient evaluation method.

O'dea and O'Dea (2023) contended that a significant use of AI in art education is the development of an automated grading system. Training AI systems to evaluate students' artworks could yield accurate marks based on elements like color and composition, significantly enhancing grading efficiency and precision. AI-supported real-time feedback platforms have proven successful in enhancing online collaboration skills, fostering innovative thinking (Benvenuti et al., 2023), and promoting the continuous growth of problem-solving abilities (Mokmin, 2020). This tendency is evident in art education and actively contributes to enhancing the general literacy of both students and teachers, hence advancing the application and evolution of AI technologies in education (Chiu et al., 2023).

1.3 Research Questions

The landscape of teaching and learning is changing as a result of the quick evolution of AIED applications (Popenici & Kerr, 2017). Simultaneously, research on AI applications in art education has grown in recent years, leading to a huge body of literature examining a variety of application-related topics, such as design, efficacy, and results. Nevertheless, limited research has systematically examined the utilization of AI technology and its theoretical underpinnings in relation to enhancing art academic performance, which is essential for comprehending its present condition and future developmental potential. To fill this gap, this study aims to explore the impact of using AI technology on improving students' academic performance, thereby analyzing what research methods and guiding theories these technologies use. Furthermore, this study intends to examine the effectiveness and impact of these unique instructional tools. Specifically, it will specifically answer the following research inquiries:

Question 1: What are the main research subjects in AI in arts higher education? What research designs have been used?

Question 2: What types of AI technologies are used in the field of art education? How do they improve student performance?

Question 3: How are AI technologies assessed in the context of art education? What is the impact on student learning outcomes?

2. METHOD

This study employed a systematic review methodology to identify, evaluate, and synthesize empirical research on the integration of AI in art education within higher education settings. The review followed the Preferred Reporting Items for

Systematic Reviews and Meta-Analyses (PRISMA) statement (Moher et al., 2009), to ensure transparency and rigor in the selection and analysis process.

2.1 Search Strategy

We performed an extensive literature search in the following electronic databases: IEEE, Taylor & Francis, Scopus, and Google Scholar to identify pertinent literature. The researcher selected these databases due on their status as prominent publisher databases (Guan et al., 2020). The search was restricted to journal articles published from January 2020 to May 2025, focusing exclusively on peer-reviewed and empirical research publications written in English to guarantee the quality of the review articles.

Upon screening the complete texts, the researchers adhered to the guidelines established by Webster and Watson (2002), commencing with the identification of keyword search strategies in pertinent digital libraries. The following keywords and Boolean operators were used in various combinations: "arts education", "higher education", "art and design", "art university", "art college", combined with "artificial intelligence", "AI". In addition, since this review focuses on improving student learning performance, the following keywords were added: "learning performance", "outcomes", "achievement". The reference lists of relevant studies were also screened to identify additional sources.

2.2 Inclusion and Exclusion Criteria

The search criteria were designed to screen out empirical studies on the use of AI to improve student performance in arts higher education. Table 1 shows the inclusion and exclusion criteria.

Table 1. Inclusion and Exclusion Criteria

Inclusion Criteria	Exclusion Criteria
Literature published between 2020 and 2025.	Focused only on K–12 education, general education, or non-arts subjects.
Focus on the application of AI technology in art or design education at the higher education (university/college) level.	Discussed AI in education only at the conceptual level without empirical data.
The research must be an empirical research report to prove the effectiveness of AI in actual teaching and learning processes.	Was a conference abstract, editorial, or non-peer-reviewed paper.

continued on following page

Table 1. Continued

Inclusion Criteria	Exclusion Criteria
The research must clearly measure or analyze student performance as one of the research variables.	Full-text not written in English.
Full-text articles in English from international peer-reviewed journals.	

2.2 Inclusion and Exclusion Criteria

Consequent to the aforementioned information, the researchers executed an exhaustive PRISMA review process. This comprehensive search strategically focused on the topic of enhancing learning outcomes in the context of AI applied arts education. The initial screening included the removal of duplicates and the screening of titles and abstracts based on relevance. Subsequently, the researchers examined the complete texts of possibly eligible studies to determine their compliance with the inclusion criteria. Figure 2 delineates the process employed in the literature review, depicting the phases of article identification, screening, and inclusion.

Figure 2. PRISMA flow chart of the literature selection process

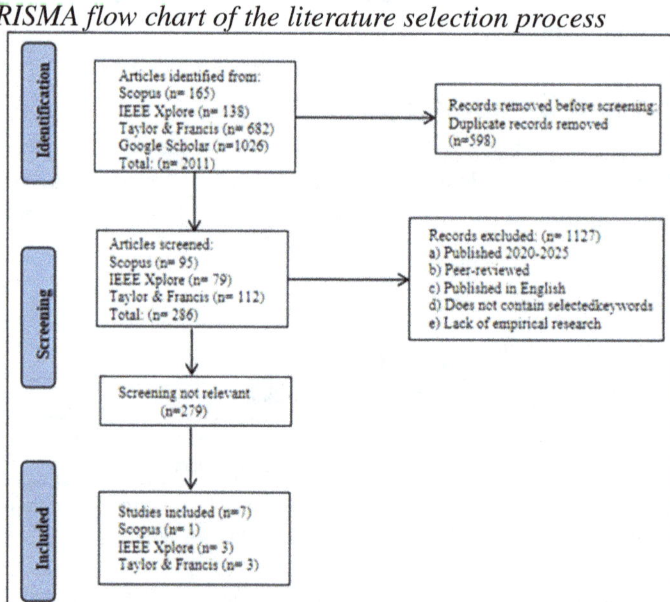

The preliminary database search utilizing the aforementioned keywords yielded 2011 items, comprising 598 removed duplicates. A multitude of articles pertained to the search phrases; nonetheless, they failed to satisfy the study's requirements due to the diversity of meanings involved. In particular, many studies discussed the use of AI in general education or science, technology, engineering, and mathematics (STEM) disciplines, while very few focused specifically on higher education in the field of art and design. Some publications presented ideas and offered suggestions for practical development and application, while others concentrated on detailing the development and design process without addressing student performance testing or omitting it entirely. Additionally, several studies lacked empirical data, used overly broad research scopes, or failed to provide sufficient evidence regarding learning outcomes. After numerous screenings of the titles and abstracts based on the established criteria, which emphasized empirical studies evaluating AI's impact on student learning within higher art education, a total of 7 papers that fulfilled the requirements were selected for inclusion in the final systematic review. This limited number reflects both the novelty of the field and the current scarcity of rigorous empirical studies on this topic. Table 2 provides the specifics of these articles.

Table 2. Research articles included in this review

No.	Authors, year of publication	Subject area	Method	AI technologies used	learning outcomes examined
1	Fang & Jiang, 2024	Public Art Creation	Quantitative methods	Combination of Internet of Things (IoT) technology and Generative Adversarial Networks (GANs)	The system achieves 80% satisfaction and 90% positive feedback in terms of student learning performance, emotional feedback, and the quality of creative output.
2	Chiu et al., 2024	Art Appreciation Learning	Quantitative methods	Combination of transfer learning and Deep learning technology	The findings demonstrated that learning with the DL-ALS can improve students' performance in the art course as well as their self-efficacy, satisfaction, learning attitude, learning motivation, and acceptance of technology.
3	Zeng et al., 2025	Character Art Design	Quantitative methods	AI smart sketchpad	Research results reveal that the AI smart sketchpad (AISS) greatly improves students' motivation, engagement, and performance.

continued on following page

Table 2. Continued

No.	Authors, year of publication	Subject area	Method	AI technologies used	learning outcomes examined
4	Chen et al., 2025	Design History Course	Quantitative methods	ChatGPT-driven pedagogical agent	The results indicated that the ChatGPT-driven system delivered personalized responses and instantaneous feedback, markedly improving student performance, motivation, and self-efficacy.
5	Ye et al., 2025	Painting teaching	Quantitative methods	A painting instructional system utilizing the Hyperlink-Induced Topic Search (HITS) algorithm. The system facilitates individualized learning by suggesting pertinent educational resources according to students' choices and advancement.	Experimental findings indicate that the approach markedly enhances learning outcomes by providing focused advice and optimizing educational resources.

continued on following page

Table 2. Continued

No.	Authors, year of publication	Subject area	Method	AI technologies used	learning outcomes examined
6	Hu et al., 2025	Art Appreciation Course	Mixed research methods	Learning method based on ChatGPT	The findings indicated that GPT-LA markedly improved learners' art appreciation performance and self-efficacy while diminishing their cognitive burden in comparison to C-LA.
7	Zhang, 2025	Visual arts, mixed media arts, and applied arts	Quantitative methods	The creation of an immersive art education model using sentiment analysis, knowledge graphs, and learner interaction data. The k-medoids clustering technique and CNN validate and adapt this model.	The results show that this teaching method increases students' art learning outcomes and satisfaction, providing fresh insights and resources for art education reform.

3. RESULT

These 7 research papers provide a detailed examination of AI in the context of higher art education for different art courses, focusing on its impact on student learning outcomes and other variables. This section is based on a systematic analysis of 7 peer-reviewed empirical studies published between 2020 and 2025, and presents the research results for the following three guiding research questions: research topic, research design, type of AI technology, and student learning outcomes in the context of higher art education. This further enriches the research findings and conclusions on the effectiveness of integrating AI technologies in art education practice.

Research subject and research design: (RQ 1: What are the main research subjects in AI in arts higher education? What research designs have been used?)

Based on a comprehensive and detailed review of the empirical studies included in this study, the main application areas of AI in higher education in the arts are classified into two main areas (Table 3). The first area covers practical art creation courses, of which 3 articles (43%) include public art creation, character design, and painting teaching. These courses focus on hands-on, skill-oriented training, in which AI tools are used to enhance creative processes and learning engagement as well as technical proficiency. The second area involves art theory and appreciation courses, in which AI in another 3 articles (43%) is mainly used to promote theoretical understanding and enhance self-efficacy, satisfaction, and learning motivation, while reducing cognitive load. Notably, Zhang (2025) proposed an innovative immersive education model based on AI to support adaptive teaching methods in various art disciplines. The model integrates practical and theoretical courses, uses AI technology to customize educational experiences according to individual student needs, and provides a comprehensive approach to experiential and media-rich art education.

These disciplines show that current research related to AI in higher education in the arts covers both practical studio teaching (e.g., painting, design, multimedia) and theoretical or reflective learning (e.g., appreciation, history), and increasingly emphasizes personalized, immersive, and emotionally responsive educational environments.

Table 3. Main application areas of AI

Fields of AI application	Number of articles	Percentage
Practical Art Creation Courses	3	43%
Art Theory and Appreciation Courses	3	43%
Both Include	1	14%

From a research design perspective, most studies adopted a quantitative research design, focusing on the causal relationship between AI-driven teaching interventions and quantifiable learning outcomes. Most studies adopted a quasi-experimental design to evaluate the impact of AI systems on students' grades, motivation, self-efficacy and satisfaction by comparing experimental groups with control groups (e.g., Chen et al., 2025; Chiu et al., 2024; Zeng et al., 2025). Hu et al. (2025) employed a mixed research methodology, integrating student interviews to get their perspectives on utilizing ChatGPT for art appreciation throughout their educational experience.

Two studies adopted system development and verification methods, combining technical implementation with user evaluation through satisfaction surveys, emotional feedback, and computational techniques (e.g., Fang and Jiang, 2024; Zhang, 2025). In addition, Ye et al. (2025) incorporated data-based learner behavior analysis to explore the role of AI in adaptive and emotionally responsive education through algorithmic recommendation and interaction modeling.

In summary, the application of AI in higher art education is shifting from simple teaching support to broader teaching changes. Researchers not only explore how AI can improve skill mastery and theoretical understanding, but also emphasize personalized, immersive, and emotionally intelligent learning environments. This trend shows that AI is becoming a key catalyst for innovation in art education.

Types of AI technologies: (RQ 2: What types of AI technologies are used in the field of art education? How do they improve student performance?)

In the literature included in this study in the context of higher education arts, the application of AI technologies is becoming increasingly diversified. These technologies can be classified into several categories: generation and creation support technologies, intelligent teaching and personalized recommendation technologies, deep learning technologies, and emotion and behavior perception analysis technologies (Figure 3).

Figure 3. AI Technology Application Category

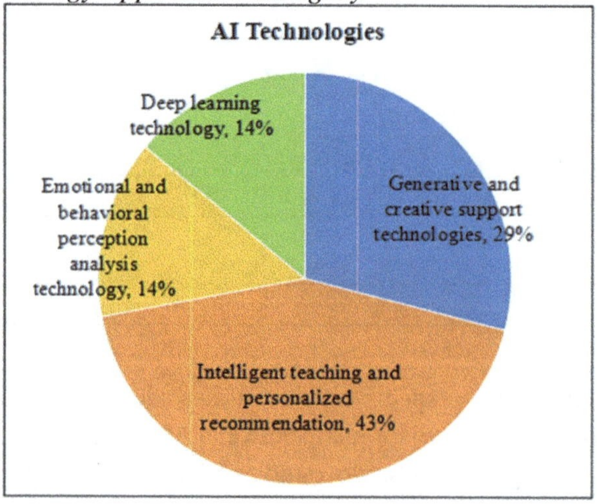

Among them, Fang and Jiang (2024) and Zeng et al. (2025) belong to the generation and creation support technology category. Generative adversarial networks (GANs) and AI intelligent drawing tools are used to assist art creation, significantly improving students' creative output and sense of participation. Fang and Jiang (2024) introduced IoT technology, hence creating new opportunities in art education. The created system framework comprises sensor nodes, an IoT platform, a GAN model, and a user interface to create a real-time interactive environment. Students engage with the system via the user interface, examine the produced artwork, modify the generating parameters, and formulate new concepts. These relationships impact subsequent artistic creation. Zeng et al. (2025) employed a progressive generation strategy by creating AISS (AI Smart Sketchpad), which dynamically modifies its predictions after each stroke. This facilitates real-time painting adjustments and optimizations, allowing for enhanced image prediction results as the user continues to draw, thus fostering a more natural, interactive, and intelligent painting experience.

Three studies belong to the category of intelligent teaching and personalized recommendation. Among them, Chen et al. (2025) and Hu et al. (2025) used natural language generation technology represented by ChatGPT, embedded in the teaching agent system, to achieve personalized feedback, knowledge reorganization and cognitive burden reduction. Chen et al. (2025) developed a learning system combined with a teaching agent driven by ChatGPT to support students' learning in design education through contextual assistance, interactive dialogue and adaptive feedback. In Hu et al. (2025), students engage with ChatGPT to produce intricate descriptions of art, thereby enhancing their visual comprehension and reasoning skills during the "interaction" phase. Furthermore, Ye et al. (2025) employ the hyperlink-induced topic search algorithm (HITS) to provide intelligent recommendations and enhance learning trajectories according to learner behavior and preferences.

Chiu et al. (2024) created a deep learning-based art learning system (DL-ALS) to assist students in identifying and classifying artworks by integrating a fine-tuned ResNet50 model with transfer learning. Deep learning constitutes a significant subfield in AI (Panch et al., 2018). Analogous to machines emulating the human brain, deep learning possesses comparable cognitive capabilities and can autonomously identify valuable aspects within data sets (LeCun et al., 2015). The learning system, following deep feature extraction and model fine-tuning, facilitates immediate feedback and interaction for students during painting activities. Zhang's (2025) approach integrates sentiment analysis, knowledge graphs, and learner interactions to provide individualized recommendations. The efficacy of the immersive teaching model is assessed using the k-medoids clustering algorithm and CNN, with real-time modifications implemented to provide an immersive and emotionally adaptive educational framework.

The integrated application of these AI technologies not only promotes the innovation of teaching methods in art education but also enhances the personalization, interactivity, and emotional responsiveness of the learning process.

Evaluation of AI technologies: (RQ 3: How are AI technologies assessed in the context of art education? What is the impact on student learning outcomes?)

In recent years, AI technology has been widely introduced into teaching practice to improve student learning outcomes in art education research. According to a comprehensive analysis of seven empirical studies, the teaching effectiveness of AI is mainly evaluated through two categories: quantitative evaluation indicators and teaching performance analysis. Among them, quantitative indicators include that most studies have tested multiple variables, examining the effectiveness of higher art education based on AI from different perspectives (Figure 4). Performance is the most widely considered variable in the questionnaire, followed by self-efficacy, learning motivation, satisfaction, technology acceptance, problem-solving ability, and participation surveys. For example, in a study using an AI-driven personalized sketchpad system, by combining pre- and post-test scores with a learning motivation questionnaire, it was found that the AI intervention group was superior to the control group in both skill mastery and participation (Zeng et al., 2025); and in a study of assisted teaching supported by ChatGPT, students' problem-solving ability and learning self-efficacy were significantly improved, indicating that positive perceptions of AI cognitive feedback mechanisms can enhance learning confidence (Chen et al., 2025). This type of evaluation method emphasizes the measurability of AI's intervention in students' individual cognitive and emotional levels and constructs a comprehensive evaluation framework based on behavioral, performance, and psychological variables.

Figure 4. Statistics of Variables for Evaluating AI in Arts Education

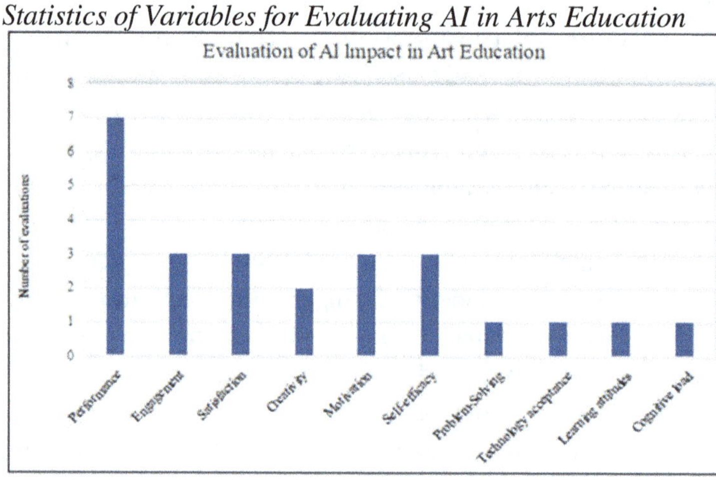

In addition to using standardized quantitative scales and performance tests, there are also ways to evaluate the educational effects of AI systems by combining teaching performance analysis. This type of evaluation method emphasizes students' performance in specific tasks or projects, and usually focuses on the output of works, behavioral trajectories, task completion quality, and interaction methods during the learning process. For example, in an AI painting teaching system based on deep learning, researchers use expert scoring methods to evaluate students' works from the dimensions of "composition completeness", "color expression", and "style consistency" to reflect the specific role of the AI system in promoting students' artistic creativity (Ye et al., 2025). In the study of building an immersive AI teaching model, students' performance in completing tasks in virtual workshops is automatically recorded by the system, including data such as task completion time, interaction frequency, and response to AI feedback. These "process performance data" are used to reflect students' actual participation quality and autonomous control level (Zhang, 2025).

In terms of learning outcomes, these AI systems have shown positive effects on both cognitive outcomes (such as knowledge mastery and skill improvement) and expressive outcomes (such as painting quality and creative design ability). In courses assisted by generative AI (such as GAN), students have made great progress in design conception and work expression, showing the support function of AI for the creative generation process (Fang & Jiang, 2024); in the painting teaching system based on the HITS algorithm, students can achieve autonomous control and performance improvement of learning paths through personalized knowledge navigation recommended by hyperlinks (Ye et al., 2025). These results show that AI not only has advantages in content provision and feedback, but also its high degree of integration with artistic performance tasks gives students higher creative freedom and knowledge transfer ability. AI tools enhance students' understanding of visual composition, design logic, and style experiments. Generative tools can achieve rapid prototyping and iterative learning, thereby supporting concept development and technical accuracy. In particular, when AI is used as a co-creative partner, visual literacy and design thinking are improved.

In summary, these seven empirical studies jointly reveal that AI plays a role in art education not only as a content-assisted tool, but also as a cognitive stimulator, feedback regulator and learning participant. Its positive impact on students' learning outcomes is reflected in multiple dimensions such as learning motivation stimulation, cognitive effectiveness improvement and creative performance enhancement. This shows that AI technology has significant potential in improving student learning outcomes in higher education art programs.

4. DISCUSSION

Ahir et al. (2020) describe a systematic review as a methodology enabling researchers to thoroughly and critically assess an extensive corpus of research within a particular context, frequently yielding evidence-based conclusions. This strategy facilitates an exhaustive search of all published and unpublished works pertinent to a certain topic, with findings methodically integrated post-search. This systematic review explores the integration of AI in higher education arts education by combing through the literature published between 2020 and 2025. The study found that current research shows different research disciplines, methodological diversity, diversified technology applications, and a wide range of student learning performance.

The studies included in this review confirm the popularity of various AI technologies in art education. For example, generative AI and intelligent teaching and personalized recommendation systems have changed the creative workflow, enabling students to quickly explore multiple ideas, iterate more efficiently, and get immediate feedback. The subsequent content analysis provides insights into various research elements, including major application areas, major research methods, and learning outcome assessment variables. The review identifies four major AI technologies: generative support tools, intelligent tutoring and recommendation systems, deep learning applications, and emotion/behavior analysis. Among them, generative tools and personalized tutoring systems are the most widely studied. In the two identified research areas (i.e., practical art creation courses and art theory and appreciation courses), the classification ratios are close, indicating that both areas are highly suitable application areas for AI. Quantitative research was the main research method in the research methods, with only one involving mixed methods. Questionnaire surveys are the predominant evaluation method, however expert assessment is an alternative approach. The surveys from the 7 selected publications encompass a total of 10 distinct variables, including motivation, engagement, satisfaction, and creativity, suggesting that numerous variables have garnered researchers' interest. Among these variables, the improvement of learning performance has attracted the greatest interest from researchers, with the role of teachers gradually shifting from mere knowledge providers to facilitators or co-designers of learning experiences. These findings highlight the need for teaching methods that foster creativity and self-efficacy alongside technological proficiency. Educators should maximize the utility of AI and improve the quality of learning, viewing AI as a collaborative partner in creativity rather than a substitute—it should enhance rather than undermine students' autonomy and expressiveness.

4.1 Implications and recommendations for future research

AI is advancing at an extraordinary rate, offering transformative potential for the evolution of art education and opening new avenues for its development. This paper synthesizes findings from seven empirical studies on AI applications in higher art education conducted between 2020 and 2025, several key insights emerge that can guide future research in this interdisciplinary and rapidly developing field. First, future research should deepen the integration of AI technology and educational theory. While the existing literature highlights the functional effectiveness of tools such as smart sketchpads, generative algorithms, and recommender systems, there remains a critical gap in understanding how these technologies align with contemporary learning theories such as constructivism, experiential learning, or sociocultural frameworks. For example, AI as a collaborative creative partner provides new opportunities for inquiry-based learning and student-centered learning models, but the scaffolding design and evaluation mechanisms of such roles in teaching still need further conceptual clarification and empirical support. This will help to more fully understand the value of AI in art education and provide empirical support for the optimization of AI-assisted teaching tools in the future.

Second, longitudinal and cross-sectional studies are urgently needed to examine the sustained impact of AI on student learning outcomes. Most of the reviewed studies used quasi-experimental designs or short-term intervention models (e.g., Zeng et al., 2025; Chen et al., 2025), which, while valuable, limit the ability to assess long-term skill development, creativity, and cognitive transformation. Future research could adopt longitudinal designs to observe whether AI-supported learning environments can foster deeper aesthetic judgments, reflective practices, and transferable design thinking skills over a longer period of time. In addition, large-scale cross-institutional research is needed to improve the generalizability of research conclusions and explore cultural, curricular, or disciplinary differences in the adoption and impact of AI systems in art education.

Third, future research should focus on the ethical, emotional, and sociotechnical dimensions of AI in art education. Students exhibited increased engagement and autonomy in their learning through the utilization of AI tools. Nonetheless, the emotional outcomes were more complex. Although excitement and interest were prevalent, fear, skepticism, and a reduced sense of autonomy were similarly widespread. Although studies (e.g., Zhang, 2025) have begun to explore emotion-aware learning environments and adaptive feedback mechanisms, few studies have critically examined the potential impact of emotion data collection, AI bias, and student autonomy or creative autonomy. Research can capture students' real experiences, emotional dynamics, and perceptions of co-creation with AI by increasing the combination of technology evaluation and critical qualitative analysis (e.g., interviews, digital ethnography, or phenomenological methods). In addition, researchers should pay more attention to issues of accessibility, digital divide, and inclusion, especially for students with diverse cultural backgrounds or artistic concepts, who may have different trust and acceptance of AI technologies.

Furthermore, the integration of AI into art education raises profound cultural and ethical concerns. Art is inherently embedded in cultural values, histories, and worldviews, yet many AI systems—especially those trained on large datasets—may reflect biases rooted in dominant cultural narratives. There is a risk that AI-generated outputs might appropriate or homogenize artistic elements without acknowledging their origins or context. Additionally, cultural background significantly influences how students perceive and interact with AI in art education. Future research should explore culturally responsive AI tools that recognize diverse artistic traditions, as well as investigate how cultural context shapes students' trust, creativity, and acceptance in AI-enhanced environments. From an ethical perspective, questions around intellectual property, authorship, and the transparency of algorithmic processes become particularly acute in art education, where creative ownership is central to learning. As AI tools increasingly co-participate in creative production, educators and researchers must critically assess how cultural diversity and ethical integrity are preserved and represented. Future research should prioritize inclusive AI training datasets, culturally responsive design, and critical pedagogy frameworks to ensure that AI integration respects and enhances, rather than erodes, cultural richness in art education.

Finally, more research is needed to explore the evolving role of teachers in AI-mediated environments. Research findings show that the role of teachers is shifting from knowledge transmitters to learning facilitators and co-designers of educational experiences. However, there is currently insufficient exploration of how teachers can interact with AI systems in real time, co-assess students' learning outcomes, or adaptively support students' creative development trajectories. Professional development models and teacher-AI collaboration frameworks need to be developed and empirically tested to ensure that educators can effectively and meaningfully interact with these new teaching tools. The incorporation of AI may worsen current digital gaps without equitable implementation. Consequently, universities must guarantee inclusive learning chances and furnish educators with pedagogical support to proficiently teach pupils in AI-enhanced settings.

4.2 Limitations of this study

Despite offering a comprehensive synthesis of empirical studies on AI in higher art education, this review faces several limitations. First, the analytical criteria may have restricted paper selection. Our research was confined to empirical papers and excluded studies that just concentrated on the technological development of certain tools without their application to real data. Therefore, we only found 7 empirical studies published between 2020 and 2025. While these selected studies provide valuable insights, the limited number of included articles may constrain the generalizability and representativeness of the findings. With such a small sample size, there is an increased risk that the conclusions drawn may disproportionately reflect specific technologies, educational settings, or regional practices rather than offering a comprehensive view of AI integration in art education globally. Although these studies cover a variety of AI technologies and educational contexts—including generative AI (Fang & Jiang, 2024; Zeng et al., 2025), intelligent recommendation systems (Ye et al., 2025), and immersive learning environments (Zhang, 2025). We restricted the search to 4 databases (Scopus, IEEE, Taylor & Francis, and Google Scholar); so, despite their comprehensiveness, we may overlook certain pertinent publications. Future reviews may consider incorporating a wider range of databases and publication languages.

Second, this review focuses primarily on empirical, quantitative studies, with less attention paid to qualitative or mixed methods research. As a result, rich insights into student experience, meaning construction, or cultural interpretations of AI in artistic practice may be underestimated. For example, while variables such as self-efficacy and motivation are often measured (e.g., Chen et al., 2025), research on how students emotionally interact with AI tools, negotiate their creative identities, or interpret algorithmic outputs is insufficient. Future research should adopt more diverse methodologies to explore these dimensions. User interface design, system transparency, and error handling capabilities are all factors that affect how students interact with AI tools, and thus their learning outcomes. Future research could adopt a more comprehensive evaluation framework that combines pedagogical impact with technology usability analysis.

In summary, this review underscores AI's potential to enhance learning, foster creativity, and redefine teaching roles in higher art education, while also revealing critical gaps in theory, methodology, ethics, and global inclusivity. Future research that addresses these limitations will be critical to realizing the full educational potential of AI in art education.

5. CONCLUSION

This systematic review examines the incorporation of AI in arts education to enhance learning outcomes in higher education from 2020 to 2025. The review synthesizes seven empirical studies and finds that AI technologies, ranging from generative tools and personalized recommendation systems to deep learning and emotion-aware interfaces, are increasingly being integrated into practical and theoretical arts courses. The results indicate that scholars and educators are increasingly interested in the capacity of AI to improve creative learning settings. AI technologies are utilized not only to enhance visual creativity and design thinking but also to personalize instruction and feedback. This transition is followed by a variety of research methodologies, and these systems not only facilitate students' creative expression and information acquisition but also enhance learning motivation, self-efficacy, and engagement.

This article aims to conduct a comprehensive study of the implications of AI technologies in the field of innovation in arts education, allowing us to gain a deeper understanding of their effects and identify ways to maximize their capabilities to improve students' learning outcomes. The findings indicate that AI is transforming the learning dynamics in the arts, serving both as a content provider and as a cognitive stimulant and co-creation partner. By facilitating tailored learning pathways, AI can enhance long-term student engagement and retention, thus fostering a more sustainable and inclusive educational framework. This article offers ideas for prospective enhancements, particularly for AI application developers and higher education instructors, who can refine classroom design by advancing AI technology systems as AI evolves into a promising learning tool for art and design students. The successful integration of AI in art education relies not alone on the technology, but also on pedagogical innovation, instructor preparedness, equitable access, and continuous critical reflection. Future studies should focus on longitudinal and cross-contextual studies to further investigate the intricate interaction between AI and art education as the area evolves.

REFERENCES

Ahir, K., Govani, K., Gajera, R., & Shah, M. (2020). Application on virtual reality for enhanced education learning, military training and sports. *Augmented Human Research, 5*, 1–9.

Benvenuti, M., Cangelosi, A., Weinberger, A., Mazzoni, E., Benassi, M., Barbaresi, M., & Orsoni, M. (2023). Artificial intelligence and human behavioral development: A perspective on new skills and competences acquisition for the educational context. *Computers in Human Behavior, 148*, 107903.

Chassignol, M., Khoroshavin, A., Klimova, A., & Bilyatdinova, A. (2018). Artificial Intelligence trends in education: A narrative overview. *Procedia Computer Science, 136*, 16–24.

Chen, J., Mokmin, N. A. M., & Su, H. (2025). Integrating generative artificial intelligence into design and art course: Effects on student achievement, motivation, and self-efficacy. *Innovations in Education and Teaching International*, •••, 1–16.

Chen, X., Xie, H., & Hwang, G. J. (2020). A multi-perspective study on artificial intelligence in education: Grants, conferences, journals, software tools, institutions, and researchers. *Computers and Education: Artificial Intelligence, 1*, 100005.

Chiu, M. C., Hwang, G. J., Hsia, L. H., & Shyu, F. M. (2024). Artificial intelligence-supported art education: A deep learning-based system for promoting university students' artwork appreciation and painting outcomes. *Interactive Learning Environments, 32*(3), 824–842.

Chiu, T. K., Xia, Q., Zhou, X., Chai, C. S., & Cheng, M. (2023). Systematic literature review on opportunities, challenges, and future research recommendations of artificial intelligence in education. *Computers and Education: Artificial Intelligence, 4*, 100118.

Fang, F., & Jiang, X. (2024). The analysis of artificial intelligence digital technology in art education under the internet of things. *IEEE Access : Practical Innovations, Open Solutions, 12*, 22928–22937.

Ghosh, A., Zhang, R., Dokania, P. K., Wang, O., Efros, A. A., Torr, P. H., & Shechtman, E. (2019). Interactive sketch & fill: Multiclass sketch-to-image translation. In *Proceedings of the IEEE/CVF International Conference on Computer Vision* (pp. 1171-1180).

Guan, C., Mou, J., & Jiang, Z. (2020). Artificial intelligence innovation in education: A twenty-year data-driven historical analysis. *International Journal of Innovation Studies*, *4*(4), 134–147.

Guilherme, A. (2019). AI and education: The importance of teacher and student relations. *AI & Society*, *34*, 47–54.

Hu, Y., Chen, J., & Hwang, G. J. (2025). A ChatGPT-supported QIVE model to enhance college students' learning performance, problem-solving and self-efficacy in art appreciation. *Interactive Learning Environments*, •••, 1–14.

Hwang, G. J., & Tu, Y. F. (2021). Roles and research trends of artificial intelligence in mathematics education: A bibliometric mapping analysis and systematic review. *Mathematics*, *9*(6), 584.

Illeris, H. (2012). Aesthetic learning processes for the 21st century: Epistemology, didactics, performance. *Journal of the International Society for Teacher Education*, *16*(1), 10–19.

LeCun, Y., Bengio, Y., & Hinton, G. (2015). Deep learning. *nature, 521*(7553), 436-444.

Moher, D., Liberati, A., Tetzlaff, J., & Altman, D. G.PRISMA Group. (2009). Preferred reporting items for systematic reviews and meta-analyses: The PRISMA statement. *Annals of Internal Medicine*, *151*(4), 264–269. PMID: 19622511

Mokmin, N. A. M. (2020). The effectiveness of a personalized virtual fitness trainer in teaching physical education by applying the artificial intelligent algorithm. *International Journal of Human Movement and Sports Sciences*, *8*(5), 258–264.

O'dea, X., & O'Dea, M. (2023). Is artificial intelligence really the next big thing in learning and teaching in higher education?: A conceptual paper. *Journal of University Teaching & Learning Practice*, *20*(5), 1–17.

Panch, T., Szolovits, P., & Atun, R. (2018). Artificial intelligence, machine learning and health systems. *Journal of Global Health*, *8*(2), 020303. PMID: 30405904

Perrotta, C., & Selwyn, N. (2020). Deep learning goes to school: Toward a relational understanding of AI in education. *Learning, Media and Technology*, *45*(3), 251–269.

Popenici, S. A., & Kerr, S. (2017). Exploring the impact of artificial intelligence on teaching and learning in higher education. *Research and Practice in Technology Enhanced Learning*, *12*(1), 22. PMID: 30595727

Rainer, R. K., Prince, B., Sanchez-Rodriguez, C., Splettstoesser-Hogeterp, I., & Ebrahimi, S. (2020). *Introduction to information systems*. John Wiley & Sons.

Rangel-de Lazaro, G., & Duart, J. M. (2023). You can handle, you can teach it: Systematic review on the use of extended reality and artificial intelligence technologies for online higher education. *Sustainability, 15*(4), 3507.

Rico-Juan, J. R., Gallego, A. J., & Calvo-Zaragoza, J. (2019). Automatic detection of inconsistencies between numerical scores and textual feedback in peer-assessment processes with machine learning. *Computers & Education, 140*, 103609.

Romero, C., Espejo, P. G., Zafra, A., Romero, J. R., & Ventura, S. (2013). Web usage mining for predicting final marks of students that use Moodle courses. *Computer Applications in Engineering Education, 21*(1), 135–146.

Rowe, M. (2019). Shaping our algorithms before they shape us. *Artificial intelligence and inclusive education: Speculative futures and emerging practices*, 151-163.

Seaba, V. E. S. (2023). Revolutionizing Education: Exploring the Potential of AI-Enabled Brain-Based Learning for Enhanced Cognitive Development. *OAlib, 10*(10), 1–20.

Shah, P. (2023). *AI and the Future of Education: Teaching in the Age of Artificial Intelligence*. John Wiley & Sons.

Shao, H., & Yu, Z. (2025). Inclusive approaches to liberal arts education in the context of the creative economy: Integrating access, engagement, and technological literacy. *International Journal of Inclusive Education*, •••, 1–28.

Tan, C. (2020). Digital Confucius? Exploring the implications of artificial intelligence in spiritual education. *Connection Science, 32*(3), 280–291.

Tigert, J. M., & Leider, C. M. (2022). Beyond the "core": Preparing art educators to meet the needs of culturally and linguistically diverse students. *TESOL Quarterly, 56*(1), 425–434.

Vartiainen, H., & Tedre, M. (2023). Using artificial intelligence in craft education: Crafting with text-to-image generative models. *Digital Creativity, 34*(1), 1–21.

Wan, Y. (2023). The impact and value of interdisciplinary collaboration on higher education art and design courses. *Frontiers in Educational Research, 6*(28), 186–192. DOI: 10.25236/FER.2023.062826

Wang, S., Wang, F., Zhu, Z., Wang, J., Tran, T., & Du, Z. (2024). Artificial intelligence in education: A systematic literature review. *Expert Systems with Applications, 252*, 124167.

Webster, J., & Watson, R. T. (2002). Analyzing the past to prepare for the future: Writing a literature review. *Management Information Systems Quarterly*, *26*(2), xiii–xxiii. https://www.jstor.org/stable/4132319

Wenjing, X., & Cai, Z. (2023). Assessing the best art design based on artificial intelligence and machine learning using GTMA. *Soft Computing*, *27*(1), 149–156.

Yadav, U., & Shrawankar, U. (2025). Artificial intelligence across industries: A comprehensive review with a focus on education. *AI applications and strategies in teacher education*, 275-320. Doi: DOI: 10.4018/979-8-3693-5443-8.ch010

Ye, Z., Sirivesmas, V., Joneurairatana, E., & Simatrang, S. (2025, January). Design and Application of Painting Teaching System based on Hyperlink-Induced Topic Search Algorithm. In *2025 International Conference on Intelligent Systems and Computational Networks (ICISCN)* (pp. 1-7). IEEE.

Yu, D., Ding, M., Li, W., Wang, L., & Liang, B. (2019). Designing an artificial intelligence platform to assist undergraduate in art and design to develop a personal learning plans. In *Design, User Experience, and Usability. Application Domains: 8th International Conference, DUXU 2019, Held as Part of the 21st HCI International Conference, HCII 2019, Orlando, FL, USA, July 26–31, 2019* [Springer International Publishing.]. *Proceedings*, *21*(Part III), 528–538.

Zeng, S., & Rahim, N., & Xu, S. (2025). Enhancing College Students' Achievement, Motivation and Engagement in Film Character Design through AI-Driven Smart sketchpad: A Personalized Interactive Learning Model for Art Education. *IEEE Access : Practical Innovations, Open Solutions*. Advance online publication.

Zhai, Q. (2022). Application of artificial intelligence in art design. In *2021 International Conference on Big Data Analytics for Cyber-Physical System in Smart City:* Volume 2 (pp. 981-986). Springer Singapore.

Zhang, T. (2025). Constructing and evaluating the effects of an immersive teaching mode for art education based on machine learning. *Journal of Computational Methods in Sciences and Engineering*, *25*(1), 355–369.

Chapter 8
The Implementation of AI-Generated Art in Increasing Student Wellness:
Systematic Literature Review

Yingying Xiao
Universiti Sains Malaysia, Malaysia

Kamal Sabran
https://orcid.org/0009-0000-5811-1270
Universiti Sains Malaysia, Malaysia

ABSTRACT

This paper explores the emerging role of AI Art in addressing mental health challenges among college students, who face escalating pressures related to academics, social adaptation, and future uncertainty. Empirical evidence suggests that artistic creation can mitigate anxiety and depression, and AI's accessibility—lowering technical barriers and enabling instant creative expression—enhances its therapeutic potential. However, challenges such as public skepticism about AI's creative agency and ethical concerns require further interdisciplinary research. By synthesizing perspectives from aesthetics, psychology, and technology, this review highlights AI Art's dual function: as a tool for personal emotional regulation and a catalyst for redefining artistic collaboration. Future directions should focus on validating clinical efficacy, addressing biases, and integrating AI Art into structured mental health interventions.

DOI: 10.4018/979-8-3373-7508-3.ch008

1. INTRODUCTION

Artificial intelligence plays an important role in various aspects of today's society(Ahmad et al., 2021). Nowadays, artificial intelligence has already become a part of our lives(Chatterjee, 2022). As time goes by, artificial intelligence is also evolving, and human thinking is different from the past(Doroudi et al., 2023). Against the backdrop of rapid advancements in digital technology, AI-generated art has become an important branch of modern art creationt(Danesi et al., 2024). As for what AI art is, simply put, AI art refers to any form of art that is created or enhanced using artificial intelligence tools(Trach et al., 2024).In simple terms, AI art refers to any form of art that is created or enhanced using artificial intelligence tools. Many artists use the term "collaboration" to describe their creative process with artificial intelligence(Cetinic & She et al., 2022).

Artificial intelligence art is not only widely used in visual arts, music, and literary creation but is also gradually penetrating the field of mental health(Saraceni et al., 2023). The mental health of college students is challenged due to issues such as academic pressure, social adaptation, and future planning(Malau-Aduli et al., 2021). In recent years, psychological research has shown that artistic creation can effectively alleviate psychological issues such as anxiety and depression, and the involvement of artificial intelligence has further expanded the possibilities of art therapy(Shukla et al., 2022).

Regarding AI ART, scholars have differing opinions.Mikalonytė and Kneer investigated whether people consider paintings created by artificial intelligence as art and whether they think robots are artists. They found that the audience's evaluation of the quality of AI-generated images was similar to that of human artworks, but they were significantly less inclined to attribute the creation to robots or believe it had creative intent. This highlights the psychological gap between recognizing something as art and accepting its creator as a true "artist"(Messingschlager et al., 2025).In a comprehensive review, Epstein, Hertzmann and collaborators argued generative AI should be regarded as a new creative medium. It enables innovation in visual art, music, literature, and video. They emphasize interdisciplinary study—covering aesthetics, law, economics, and media—to understand AI's impact. They do not view it as a threat to art, but as a tool enabling new forms of expression(Ghosh & Fossas et al., 2022).Lucas Bellaiche think that examined how people perceive art created by AI compared to art created by humans through experimental methods. They found that labeling the same artwork as "AI-created" significantly lowered the viewers' ratings—even when they could not distinguish the source, they still perceived these artworks as less beautiful, meaningful, and skillfully crafted. The results highlight the persistent bias against AI-generated art, which mainly stems from assumptions about effort, emotion, and narrative depth(Bellaiche et al., 2023).

Regarding the review of research on AI art and mental health in higher education, there have been several preliminary studies. Some of them focus on the systematic analysis of AI art, such as the research by Atte Oksanen and Anica Cvetkovic (Atte Oksanen et al., 2023). This study conducted a comprehensive systematic review, covering 44 academic articles, and delved deeply into what AI art is, the origins of AI art, and AI creativity, among other topics. Their research not only explores the potential of this emerging field but also raises compelling questions about the development of AI in the realm of art, carefully assessing the contradictions and obstacles of AI's role in the artistic domain.

Their research indicates that the study of AI in fine arts has significantly increased, especially after 2020. Artificial intelligence has been widely applied across various fields of fine arts, including visual arts, literature, music, performing arts, and architecture. These applications have introduced new creative methods and reshaped the way art is produced and experienced. While some researchers have explored the psychological impact of AI in art, most of these studies focus on general users or artists. There remains a noticeable lack of research specifically targeting university students. Given that this group often experiences high levels of stress and emotional challenges, more studies are needed to examine how AI-generated art may affect their mental health and emotional well-being. For example, the study by Kristy L. Brann, Mark Gallagher, and others (Brann et al., 2024) targeted 5,285 students from elementary, middle, and high schools. They are committed to addressing the youth mental health crisis by implementing universal screening measures that assess social, emotional, and behavioral functioning, thereby enhancing early identification efforts. While numerous systematic reviews exist focusing individually on AI-generated art and on wellness, there remains a notable gap in the literature regarding a combined or dual approach as presented by the author of this paper. Some reviews concentrate exclusively on AI art, while others focus solely on student wellness, often lacking specificity and integration between the two domains.Mental health issues among college students are becoming more serious. Exploring innovative interventions to improve student well-being is now an important research topic. Traditional art therapies like painting, music, and dance have been widely studied. These methods have proven effective in reducing stress and improving mood. However, AI-generated art is a new intervention method. Its impact on college students' mental well-being has not yet been systematically reviewed.

AI art includes many forms and technologies. Examples include visual art created by GANs (Generative Adversarial Networks). Another example is AI poetry based on NLP (Natural Language Processing). Algorithm-generated music and digital images from diffusion models (like Stable Diffusion) also fall under AI art. These different forms of AI art have unique features. They may influence users' psychological states in different ways.

For example, interactive AI art creation may increase users' sense of participation and autonomy. Simply viewing AI-generated art may regulate emotions through aesthetic experiences. Therefore, systematically reviewing existing research is necessary. Analyzing how different AI art forms affect students' mental health differently can fill current research gaps. This analysis can also provide a theoretical basis for developing targeted digital mental health interventions.Table 1 categorizes some common types of AI art.

Table 1. Categories and characteristics of AI art

	Category name	Core technology	characteristic	Example tools / platforms
1	Style Transfer Art	convolutional neural network(CNN)	The artistic style of one image (such as Van Gogh, Monet) is "migrated" to the content of another image, blending style and structure.	DeepArt Prisma NeuralStyle
2	GAN art	generative adversarial network(GAN)	Through the "generator + discriminator" model confrontation training, AI can learn to create new images with abstraction and innovation.	Artbreeder Runway ML Obvious team
3	Diffusion-based Art)	diffusion mode(Stable Diffusion DALL·E)	Images are generated based on text prompts, and the degree of control is high. It can realize various styles such as hyper-realistic, dream-like and cyber style.	Midjourney DALL·E 3 Stable Diffusion
4	Evolutionary Art	Genetic algorithms, autoencoder	By combining human selection mechanisms with evolutionary processes, multiple generations of "evolution" produce individual artistic images.	GANbreeder NeuroEvolution Art
5	Brush Simulation	Simulate brush strokes and artistic strategies	Imitate the logic of human painting to generate images or painting processes with the texture of hand drawing.	NVIDIA Paint Transformer AI Painter
6	Human-AI Co-Creation	Human-computer interaction interface + generation network	Sketches, outlines and color blocks are input by humans, and AI completes the generation of complete images to reflect the "co-creation" mechanism.	Google's Chimera Painter PaintsChainer
7	Data-based Visualization	Visual algorithm + generation model	Non-image information such as text, sound and sensor data are converted into painting images, such as "painting while listening to music".	AI audio and video system, emotion painting visualization project

Today's college students face a lot of pressure, such as heavy academic burdens, consumer anxiety, relationship troubles, and career confusion, which lead to feelings of depression(Moore et al., 2021).

This study aims to explore how AI-generated art can play a role in the field of college students' mental health, analyze its potential application scenarios and impacts, and propose future development directions.

Especially in exploring its potential to promote the health issues of Chinese university students, alleviate their psychological stress, and expand the practical applications of AI-generated art.

2. METHOD

Search Process

The selected studies must be related to AI art and its impact on college students' emotion between 2021 and 2025. The search was conducted in May 2025 using the Scopus, WOS, and Google Scholar databases. Since the discussion includes various forms of AI art, the search keywords used were "AI art" and "emotion"and"student . The publication years were limited to studies written in English from 2021 to 2025. Table 2 shows the inclusion and Extraction Criteria:

Table 2. Inclusion and Exclusion Criteria

Criteria	Eligibility	Exclusion
Literature Type	Indexed Journal (research articles)	Non-indexed journals, Systematic review journals, chapter in book.
Language	English	Non-English
Timeline	Between 2021 – 2025	Less than 2021

After the search results produced studies that met the inclusion and exclusion criteria, in order to further improve quality and ensure the authenticity of the results, the following quality-based questions are required for each selected study:

EQ1. Does this article introduce content related to AI art?

EQ2. Does this article include the use of research methods?

EQ3. Does this article reflect the impact of AI art on wellness?

3. RESULT

Recent research has shown that artificial intelligence (AI) tools play an increasingly important role in education, creativity, and emotional engagement. In particular, AI-generated art is becoming a popular topic in both academic research and practical application. One study conducted in a Latin American private university explored how arts students responded to AI tools in the classroom. The findings showed that AI tools increased students' engagement and emotional responses, including joy and surprise. However, the study also identified a clear gap in teacher proficiency with AI. This highlights the need for proper educator training to ensure effective and ethical use of AI technologies in art education(Grájeda et al., 2024).A study with 42 participants, including students and creative professionals, showed that using interactive AI art tools helped improve mindfulness and emotional awareness. Participants felt more focused and better understood their emotions during the creative process. Most gave positive feedback on the experience. However, many also said the tools could be better with added features like voice guidance and more options for personalization(Keung et al., 2021).A literature review pointed out that AI has great potential to improve teaching efficiency and support personalized learning. However, the study also found several challenges. These include privacy risks, ethical problems, and a lack of preparation among teachers. To solve these issues, the authors suggested a clear and structured framework(Ke et al., 2023).An experimental study with 48 participants explored how people respond to abstract art created by humans and by AI. The results showed that participants could feel emotion and intention in both types of artwork. However, they felt more emotionally connected to the pieces they believed were made by humans. They also found those works more visually appealing. This underscores the influence of perceived authorship on art appreciation(Demmer et al., 2023).Fifteen students at a U.S. liberal arts institution used DALL-E 2 for creative projects, reporting enhanced creativity and iterative refinement. However, ethical dilemmas, such as copyright concerns, and skepticism about AI's role in professional art careers emerged as significant challenges(Hutson & Cotroneo et al., 2023).A survey involving 528 users in China examined why people choose to use AI-based painting systems. The findings showed that enjoyment (hedonic motivation) and trust in the technology were the main reasons people adopted these tools. These factors were more important than technical functions or users' previous experience with similar systems. Dissatisfaction with AI-generated artwork quality indicated a need for improvements to meet user expectations(Xu et al., 2023).A review of more than 100 studies explored how AI is changing STEM education. The results showed that AI tools are moving from supporting teacher-centered instruction to promoting learner-centered approaches. This means students are gaining more control over their learning, with AI offering personalized support and feedback based on their needs. While AI offers personalized learning and reduces teacher workload, ethical and transparency issues remain critical areas for development(Ouyang et al., 2022).

Table 3(a). Paper Reviewed from 2021 - 2025 in the field of AI Art in Enhancing Student Emotions

Paper	Sample	Method	Outcome
Paper1(Keung et al., 2021)	42 participants (aged 19–35; students and creative professionals)	interactive prototype development; user testing and semi-structured interviews	Enhanced mindfulness immersion; improved emotional awareness; positive user feedback; high acceptance; suggestions for voice guidance and personalization features
Paper2(Grájeda et al., 2024)	Arts students from a Latin American private university (exact number not specified)	1) SIUAIT index construction; 2) Eye-tracking and facial emotion recognition; statistical analysis (t-tests, correlation, etc.)	Recent observations indicate increasing student awareness and acceptance of AI tools in educational settings. Many students report experiencing higher levels of joy, curiosity, and surprise during AI-assisted classes. These positive emotions are often accompanied by improved focus, heightened engagement, and a stronger sense of participation in learning activities. However, despite these promising outcomes, there remains a significant gap in teachers' proficiency with AI technologies. This gap can limit the effective integration of AI tools into the classroom and highlights the need for targeted professional development and training for educators.
Paper3(Ke et al., 2023)	No empirical sample; based on literature and case analysis	Literature review and strategic analysis; inductive reasoning	AI can enhance teaching efficiency and personalization; challenges include privacy, ethics, teacher readiness; recommends a coordinated framework addressing privacy–technology–teacher–ethics dimensions

continued on following page

Table 3(a). Continued

Paper	Sample	Method	Outcome
Paper4(Demmer et al., 2023)	**N = 48** participants recruited online (e.g., via SurveyCircle), with 25 males; educational levels spanned from secondary school to PhD. Each participant viewed 24 artworks in total: 14 human-created and 10 AI-generated.	Utilized a **controlled experimental design** with a **2×2 within-subjects priming manipulation**: participants viewed visually similar abstract black-and-white artworks produced either by a human (artist intentionally conveying emotion) or by a computer using a random-number generator (RNG).	This study, employing a well-powered and pre-registered experimental design, demonstrates that viewers consistently attribute emotion and intentionality to both AI-generated and human-created abstract art. However, artworks perceived as human-made elicit stronger affective engagement and receive higher aesthetic evaluations. These findings underscore the influential role of perceived artist origin and expectation bias in shaping aesthetic experience. The results contribute valuable insights to ongoing discussions in empirical aesthetics and the evolving field of human–AI creative collaboration.
Paper5(Hutson & Cotroneo et al., 2023)	15 students from a private liberal arts institution in the United States, enrolled in an advanced Digital Art II-III course. Academic Level: 40% juniors, 33.33% seniors, 13.33% sophomores, and 13.33% graduate students. Age: 60% aged 18–24, 40% aged 25–34. Gender: 57.14% female, 35.71% male, 7.14% non-binary. o o o	Students used OpenAI's DALL-E2 to create and refine 10 prompts, with at least 4 variations per prompt, focusing on form, style, and subject matter. Ethical discussions were held using Mok's (2023) article on AI ethics. Practical tasks: Students recreated AI-generated images in Adobe Photoshop; advanced students designed alien plants and used AI to generate realistic interpretations.	Enhanced creativity and iterative refinement but were less effective for final products. Challenges: Ethical dilemmas (e.g., copyright) and skepticism about AI's role in art careers. Recommendations: Integrate AI into early ideation phases and collaborative assignments. Address ethics through structured discussions and critical analysis. Further research on long-term impacts of AI in art education. o

continued on following page

Table 3(a). Continued

Paper	Sample	Method	Outcome
Paper6(Xu et al., 2023)	Source: 528 valid participants from China (initially 568 questionnaires collected, with 40 invalid responses removed). Demographic Characteristics: Gender: 51.89% male, 48.11% female. Age: Primarily 18–40 years old (25.38% aged 18–25, 23.11% aged 26–30, 17.61% aged 31–40). Education Level: 47.54% undergraduates, 40.53% sub-bachelor's degree. Usage Frequency: 50.57% used AI-based painting systems (AIBPS) weekly, 28.97% daily. Art Experience: 90.72% had prior painting experience. Tool Familiarity: The most recognized AI painting tool was DALL-E2 (80.68%), followed by Midjourney (72.16%).	Based on the Extended Technology Acceptance Model (TAM), incorporating external variables: External Variables: Prior Experience (PE), Technical Features (TF), Hedonic Motivation (HM), Perceived Trust (PT). Core Variables: Perceived Usefulness (PU), Perceived Ease of Use (PEOU), Attitude Toward Using (ATT), Behavioral Intention (BI). Data Analysis: Confirmatory Factor Analysis (CFA): Assessed reliability and validity (Cronbach's $\alpha > 0.8$, AVE > 0.5). Structural Equation Modeling (SEM): Tested hypothesis paths using AMOS 25.	Hedonic Motivation (HM) and Perceived Trust (PT) had significant positive effects on PU and PEOU (HM had the strongest influence). PU and PEOU positively influenced Attitude Toward Using (ATT) and Behavioral Intention (BI). ATT positively impacted BI. Unsupported Hypotheses: Prior Experience (PE) and Technical Features (TF) did not significantly affect PU (though they positively influenced PEOU). Key Insights: Users prioritized fun (HM) and trust (PT) over technical details or prior experience. Dissatisfaction with AI-generated artwork quality highlighted the need for improvements to meet user expectations.

continued on following page

Table 3(a). Continued

Paper	Sample	Method	Outcome
Paper7(Ouyang et al., 2022)	Key literature: Cited over 100 studies, including intelligent tutoring systems (such as Cognitive Tutors), learning analytics tools (such as Lumilo), mixed reality technologies (such as Intelligent Science Stations), etc.	AI-Directed: ASSISTment Builder (Math Problem Generation and Feedback). AI-Supported: CPR Tutor (Real-time Multimodal Feedback System). AI-Empowered: Knowledge Graph (supports complex concept visualization).	The evolution of AI's role in STEM education: from "teacher-centered" to "learner-centered," AI gradually enhances student autonomy. Technological potential: AI can reduce teachers' burdens and provide personalized learning, but ethical and implementation challenges need to be addressed. Developers should focus on system transparency (such as explainable models) and data security.

Table 3(b). Distribution chart of research subject types

paper	Object type
Paper1 (Keung, H et al., 2021)	Students+Creative Professionals
Paper2 (Grájeda, A et al., 2024)	Art students from Latin America
Paper3 (Ke, M. F. et al., 2023)	none
Paper4 (Demmer, T. R. et al., 2023)	Social groups with different levels of education
Paper5 (Hutson, J., & Cotroneo, P. et al., 2023)	Senior art students in the United States
Paper6 (Xu, J et al., 2023)	Ordinary Chinese users (most of whom have drawing experience)
Paper7 (Ouyang, F et al., 2022)	Educational research, covering various types of learning system users.

Table 3(c). Use the tool to create a summary chart

Paper Using tools
Paper1 Interactive prototype system (specific AI tool not specified)
Paper2 SIUAIT index, eye tracking, facial expression recognition tool (not specifically named)
Paper3 Literature review, strategic analysis, no actual AI tool operation.
Paper4 Computer random image generation system (similar to RNG), visual stimulus control system
Paper5 OpenAI DALL·E 2, Photoshop; refer to Mok (2023) on AI ethics literature
Paper6 DALL·E 2 (80.68% users), Midjourney (72.16%); AMOS 25 (SEM modeling), questionnaire system
Paper7 ASSISTment Builder, CPR Tutor, Knowledge Graph, Lumilo, and various other educational AI tools

Figure 1. Comparison of research methods

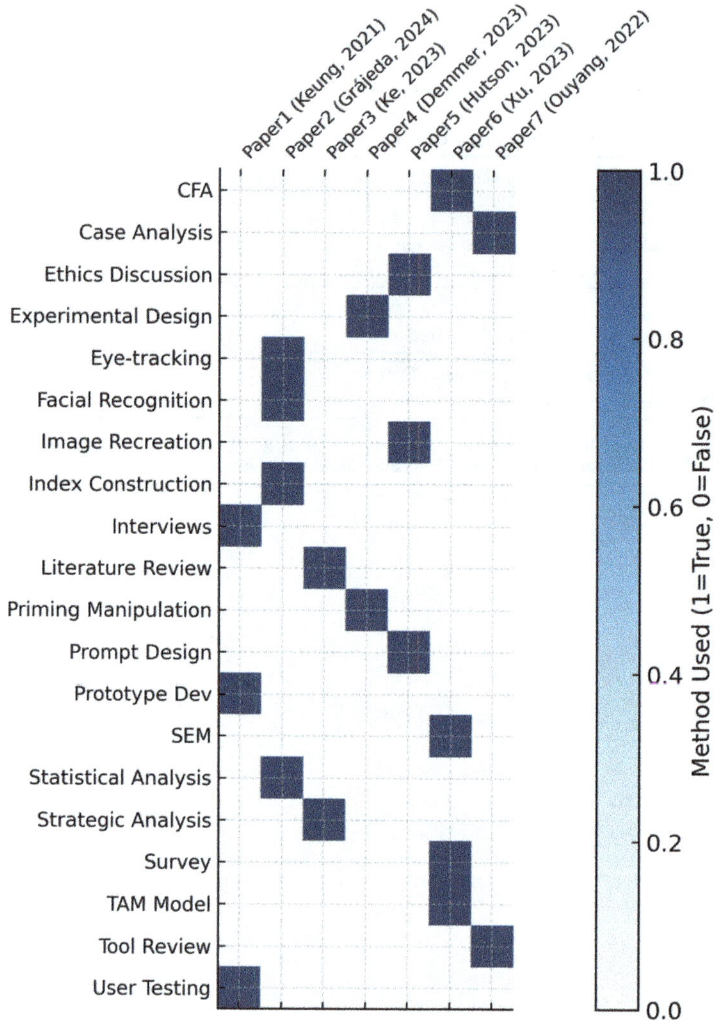

4. DISCUSSION

With the development of science and technology, although artificial intelligence is advancing rapidly in the field of painting art, the application of AI in painting art has not improved and still remains at a basic level(Audry et al., 2021). However, with the development of society, art creation is not just about creating,it to be able to address some social issues(Wiratno et al., 2024).Artificial intelligence plays a promoting role in the mental health issues of contemporary college students(Velastegui et al., 2023). In addition, the mental health of college students has received widespread attention from all sectors of society(Scherer et al., 2021).

College students represent a vital reserve force for future economic and social development. However, they are also a population under considerable strain, frequently encountering academic pressure, social challenges, and personal identity struggles. These combined stressors contribute to a high prevalence of psychological distress, including anxiety, depression, and burnout. As a result, college students are widely recognized as a high-risk group for mental health problems, highlighting the urgent need for accessible and effective psychological support strategies tailored to their unique experiences and developmental stage(Lo, Hew, et al., 2024). In recent years, various negative news reports related to psychological issues among college students have become increasingly common, drawing the attention of many researchers(Arias-Pastor et al., 2023).

Research shows that compared to the general population, college students have higher levels of anxiety and lower psychological resilience(Bland et al., 2012). The university years represent a critical period in an individual's transition from adolescence to adulthood. During this stage, students undergo significant psychological, emotional, and social development. They begin to form a clearer sense of identity, make independent life decisions, and navigate complex interpersonal relationships. These transitions often bring about increased vulnerability to stress and mental health challenges, making it especially important to prioritize mental well-being and provide appropriate support during this formative phase(Pedrelli, P et al., 2015). Especially since 2020, under the influence of the COVID-19 pandemic, some college students have exhibited obvious signs of psychological instability and emotional fluctuations, resulting in an overall poor level of mental health(Von Keyserlingk et al., 2022).

In recent years, the application of artificial intelligence (AI) technology in the field of art therapy has gradually attracted the attention of academia and practitioners(Zhang et al., 2021). Traditional art therapy relies on face-to-face interpersonal communication and therapeutic guidance, emphasizing the establishment of empathy, trust, and supportive relationships between the therapist and the individual. It uses art forms such as painting, sculpture, and music to help individuals express emotions and release stress (Wang, J et.al.,2024). However, this model places high demands on the qualifications of therapists, physical space, and art materials, with significant costs and organizational challenges, facing obstacles in widespread promotion.

In contrast, AI art therapy, as a new path in digital development, demonstrates significant advantages in operational convenience and resource efficiency (Zubala et.al.,2021).. AI drawing tools (such as DALL·E, Midjourney) allow users to generate images through natural language descriptions, significantly lowering the threshold for artistic creation and providing a means for ordinary users without professional art training to express their emotions (Cetinic & She, 2022). Research indicates that AI systems have the potential to enhance participants' creativity, emotional engagement, and attention maintenance (Ali Elfa & Dawood, 2023). Especially among college students and digital natives, AI-assisted artistic practices are often seen as "low-risk" and "interesting" forms of expression, helping to regulate psychological stress and stimulate aesthetic engagement motivation.

In terms of cost, AI art interventions save a significant amount of manpower and material resources compared to traditional therapies. In addition, the advantages in terms of usability are becoming increasingly significant, as most platforms support web or mobile usage, allowing non-professionals to quickly grasp the basic operations. At the same time, some scholars have pointed out that current AI systems still have shortcomings in empathy, emotional recognition, and personalized feedback, lacking humanistic depth and interactive warmth (Demmer et al., 2023). Therefore, its applicable scenarios are more inclined towards mild stress regulation or auxiliary expression, rather than deep psychological therapy.

AI art therapy has gradually entered the experimental teaching and psychological counseling systems of local universities(Hu, B. 2022). For example, a teacher training university in Southwest China has piloted the introduction of AI image generation tools to conduct a "Digital Creative Expression" course. Students design prompts, generate images, and perform secondary processing, which enhances their compositional skills and thematic critical thinking abilities . In addition, a comprehensive university's psychological center in Northeast China attempted to use Midjourney to organize AI emotional expression workshops. Participants found it easier to identify and convey their inner emotions through image output and group discussions, significantly increasing their willingness to express themselves and their level of participation. These practices indicate that AI art tools have strong practical adaptability in Chinese higher education and mental health services, especially suitable for resource-limited but digitally equipped educational environments.

AI-generated art shows great potential for application in the field of psychological stress relief. By generating images through natural language (such as using DALL·E or Midjourney), users can externalize their inner emotions in a low-threshold manner, thereby alleviating negative emotions such as anxiety and repression. Research shows that this non-traditional art form can stimulate users' creative expression and emotional regulation abilities, particularly among college students and young professionals, with significant results (Xu et al., 2023). This type of image-based instant feedback mechanism not only enhances the user's immersive experience but also provides a new visual intervention method for mental health services.

Although the prospects for AI art applications are broad, the ethical issues it raises in educational and mental health contexts cannot be ignored (Rahsepar Meadi et al., 2025). First, the "authorial ambiguity" in the AI image generation process may lead to disputes over creative ownership, particularly posing challenges in educational assessment and intellectual property (Demmer et al., 2023). Secondly, some students and teachers hold a reserved attitude towards the role of AI in artistic creation, believing that it lacks human warmth and emotional authenticity(Lin, H., & Chen, Q. (2024)). Moreover, if AI systems lack transparent explanations when collecting user data, it may pose privacy and security risks, especially when it involves emotion recognition and physiological data analysis, which should raise more awareness (Giudici, P. et al., 2024). Therefore, relevant institutions should simultaneously establish ethical usage frameworks and teacher training systems while promoting AI art applications to ensure their responsible use in educational and psychological intervention contexts.

Overall, AI art therapy, as an emerging interdisciplinary approach that combines technology and the humanities, has shown promising prospects in enhancing the efficiency of artistic expression, lowering treatment thresholds, and expanding the scope of interventions(Luo, X. et.al.,2024). However, its development still needs to be guided by ethics, optimized through systematic design, and aligned with local educational practices to build a health intervention ecosystem supported by technology and centered on human well-being.

The potential application of AI-generated art in enhancing the physical and mental health of college students includes its role in stress relief, improving emotional regulation, boosting creativity, and facilitating psychotherapy(Zubala et al., 2025). College students often experience psychological burdens due to academic pressure and social anxiety(Kumaraswamy et al., 2013). Research shows that engaging in artistic creation can lower cortisol levels (the stress hormone), aiding emotional relaxation(Curl et al., 2008). The convenience of AI art reduces the barriers to traditional art creation, allowing college students to create anytime and anywhere using digital tools, thereby finding ways to relax psychologically amidst their busy academic lives(Marella et al., 2025).

Creative activities have a positive impact on mental health(Jean-Berluche, D et al., 2024). Artificial intelligence lowers the technical barriers to art creation, enabling more college students to express themselves in life (Ke et al., 2023).

5. CONCLUSION

Artificial intelligence-generated art (AI art) is gaining increasing attention in the field of mental health and emotional regulation. Many researchers believe it offers new possibilities for psychological support. For college students, who often face academic pressure, social anxiety, and identity-related stress, AI art presents a fresh and accessible method for emotional self-care. Unlike traditional art therapy,

AI art does not require professional guidance or physical materials. Instead, it uses digital tools and algorithms that are easy to operate. Most students can use these tools without having any background in art or technology. This makes it easier for them to participate and express their emotions in a creative way.Recent studies have shown that AI art tools can improve emotional well-being in college students. These tools use algorithms to generate images based on user input. They are easy to use and do not require any professional artistic training. Many students report feeling more relaxed and focused after using these tools. One study found that both students and creative professionals became more mindful and emotionally aware after using an AI-powered art platform. Another large-scale survey in China showed that students who often used AI painting tools experienced more enjoyment, emotional satisfaction, and perceived usefulness. These findings suggest that AI art can help users focus less on negative thoughts and gain a stronger sense of emotional control through creativity. AI-generated art, therefore, may become a helpful tool for supporting mental health in student populations.There are several key mechanisms that explain the positive psychological effects of AI-generated art. First, AI tools provide real-time visual feedback. This feedback helps users stay focused on the present moment. When users concentrate on creating art, they are less likely to overthink or ruminate. This can reduce anxiety and create a sense of calm. Second, many AI systems allow users to input emotional keywords or phrases. The system then generates images that match the user's feelings. This process helps users express emotions more clearly. It also encourages deeper self-reflection and emotional understanding. Third, digital platforms let users save and share their artwork instantly. This feature helps users feel connected with others. It can also open the door for peer conversations and emotional support. For students who feel lonely or stressed, sharing AI-generated art can build a sense of community.

The pandemic changed education. Many schools now use online or hybrid learning. Students spend less time in classrooms. They see teachers and classmates less often. This isolation affects mental health. More students now need emotional support.AI art tools help solve this problem. These tools are easy to use. Students can access them anywhere. They work on phones, laptops, or tablets. No special equipment is needed. Students can use them between classes, in dorms, or at home. The tools fit busy schedules.Schools find AI art helpful. Mental health professionals are finding creative ways to incorporate AI art into their work. Counselors use these tools to break the ice in therapy sessions, helping students express emotions they struggle to verbalize. Art teachers integrate AI generators into assignments, allowing students to explore digital creativity alongside traditional mediums. Student support groups incorporate the technology into wellness workshops, where peers create collaborative artworks. The setup process takes minutes - just share a link or download an app. Unlike traditional therapies requiring specialized staff, one AI platform can serve hundreds of students simultaneously. For underfunded counseling centers, this means shorter waitlists and more students getting timely support. The technology works particularly well for students who feel intimidated by conventional counseling approaches.Some students feel nervous talking to counselors. For them, AI art is a gentler first step.These tools don't replace human help. They work alongside traditional care. Together, they support student wellbeing. The goal is simple - help more students get the care they need.

In summary, AI-generated art is more than just a technology trend. It is a promising method for improving mental well-being among college students. The tools promote mindfulness, emotional expression, and social connection. They are easy to access, easy to use, and suitable for students with different backgrounds. In today's changing education environment, AI art offers a flexible and inclusive way to support student mental health.Despite these strengths, this field of research also faces several limitations. One major concern is the lack of longitudinal studies. Most current research relies on short-term surveys, self-reports, or small-scale interventions. These methods cannot fully assess the long-term psychological impact of using AI art. Without follow-up data, it is difficult to determine whether the observed benefits are sustained over time or only provide temporary relief.

Another significant limitation relates to the sample population. Many existing studies are conducted in East Asian contexts, especially within urban universities in mainland China This geographic concentration may limit the generalizability of findings. Students in rural areas, under-resourced institutions, or other cultural environments may have different experiences and responses to AI art. Future research should include more diverse and representative samples to better understand the broader applicability of these tools.

In addition, ethical concerns surrounding AI-generated content require serious attention. Some users may question the authenticity or emotional depth of AI-created art, especially when compared to human-made works. Others may worry about copyright issues or the ownership of AI outputs. Furthermore, many platforms collect user input data to improve algorithms. If these platforms lack transparent privacy policies, students' emotional and personal data could be at risk. Researchers and developers must establish clear guidelines to ensure ethical use and data protection in AI art systems.

While AI art offers many benefits for emotional expression and mental well-being, overreliance on AI tools may reduce opportunities for building deep interpersonal connections. Many students may turn to AI because it feels safe and private. However, human relationships still play a vital role in emotional development. AI-generated images can reflect personal emotions, but they cannot replace the empathy, insight, and mutual understanding that come from real human interaction. Face-to-face communication allows individuals to receive support, listen actively, and develop emotional intelligence. These are qualities that AI, no matter how advanced, cannot fully provide.

Therefore, educators and mental health professionals should view AI art not as a replacement for traditional therapy, but as a complementary tool. When used alongside peer support or counseling, AI art can open up new ways for students to explore their feelings. It can help students express what they cannot say in words and prepare them for deeper conversations with others. In this way, AI art expands the emotional landscape but should be grounded within a framework that values human connection. AI art tools provide students with a simple way to manage stress and emotions. These digital solutions offer immediate responses and adapt to each user's needs. Students can access them anytime through their devices. The technology works alongside traditional counseling, not as a replacement. While helpful, these tools should complement real human connections. Campuses must balance tech-based support with face-to-face interactions. The best approach combines AI's convenience with the warmth of personal contact. This dual method ensures students get quick digital help when needed, while still maintaining important social bonds that are crucial for long-term wellbeing.

However, current research has limitations in terms of sample diversity, long-term evidence, and ethical transparency. Future studies should address these gaps by conducting longitudinal interventions, recruiting broader populations, and developing standardized ethical frameworks. With thoughtful design and responsible use, AI art can play a valuable role in the evolving landscape of digital mental health.

REFERENCES

Ahmad, S. F., Rahmat, M. K., Mubarik, M. S., Alam, M. M., & Hyder, S. I. (2021). Artificial intelligence and its role in education. *Sustainability, 13*(22), 12902. DOI: 10.3390/su132212902

Ali Elfa, M. A., & Dawood, M. E. T. (2023). Using artificial intelligence for enhancing human creativity. Journal of Art. *Design and Music, 2*(2), 3. DOI: 10.55554/2785-9649.1017

Arias-Pastor, M., Van Vaerenbergh, S., Fernández-Solana, J., & González-Bernal, J. J. (2023). Secondary education teacher training and emotional intelligence: Ingredients for attention to diversity in an inclusive school for all. *Education Sciences, 13*(5), 519. DOI: 10.3390/educsci13050519

Bellaiche, L., Shahi, R., Turpin, M. H., Ragnhildstveit, A., Sprockett, S., Barr, N., & Seli, P. (2023). Humans versus AI: Whether and why we prefer human-created compared to AI-created artwork. *Cognitive Research: Principles and Implications, 8*(1), 42. DOI: 10.1186/s41235-023-00499-6

Bland, H. W., Melton, B. F., Welle, P., & Bigham, L. (2012). Stress tolerance: New challenges for millennial college students. *College Student Journal, 46*(2), 362–376. http://projectinnovation.biz/csj_2006.html

Cetinic, E., & She, J. (2022). Understanding and creating art with AI: Review and outlook. [TOMM]. *ACM Transactions on Multimedia Computing Communications and Applications, 18*(2), 1–22. DOI: 10.1145/3475799

Cetinic, E., & She, J. (2022). Understanding and creating art with AI: Review and outlook. ACM transactions on multimedia computing, communications, and applications (TOMM), 18(2), 1-22. https://doi.org/DOI: 10.1145/3475799

Chatterjee, A. (2022). Art in an age of artificial intelligence. *Frontiers in Psychology, 13*, 1024449. DOI: 10.3389/fpsyg.2022.1024449

Curl, K. (2008). Assessing stress reduction as a function of artistic creation and cognitive focus. *Art Therapy: Journal of the American Art Therapy Association, 25*(4), 164–169.

Danesi, M. (2024). AI-Generated Art. In *AI-Generated Popular Culture: A Semiotic Perspective* (pp. 105–125). Springer Nature Switzerland.

Demmer, T. R., Kühnapfel, C., Fingerhut, J., & Pelowski, M. (2023). Does an emotional connection to art really require a human artist? Emotion and intentionality responses to AI- versus human-created art and impact on aesthetic experience. *Computers in Human Behavior, 148*, 107875. DOI: 10.1016/j.chb.2023.107875

Demmer, T. R., Kühnapfel, C., Fingerhut, J., & Pelowski, M. (2023). Does an emotional connection to art really require a human artist? Emotion and intentionality responses to AI- versus human-created art. *Computers in Human Behavior, 148*, 107875. DOI: 10.1016/j.chb.2023.107875

Doroudi, S. (2023). The intertwined histories of artificial intelligence and education. *International Journal of Artificial Intelligence in Education, 33*(4), 885–928. DOI: 10.1007/s40593-022-00313-2

Ghosh, A., & Fossas, G. (2022). Can there be art without an artist? arXiv preprint arXiv:2209.07667. https://doi.org//arXiv.2209.07667DOI: 10.48550

Giudici, P., Centurelli, M., & Turchetta, S. (2024). Artificial Intelligence risk measurement. *Expert Systems with Applications, 235*, 121220. DOI: 10.1016/j.eswa.2023.121220

Grájeda, A., Córdova, P., Córdova, J. P., Laguna-Tapia, A., Burgos, J., Rodríguez, L., & Sanjinés, A. (2024). Embracing artificial intelligence in the arts classroom: Understanding student perceptions and emotional reactions to AI tools. *Cogent Education, 11*(1), 2378271. DOI: 10.1080/2331186X.2024.2378271

Hu, B. (2022). Analysis of art therapy for children with autism by using the implemented artificial intelligence system. *International Journal of HR; Humanoid Robotics, 19*(03), 2240002. DOI: 10.1142/S0219843622400023

Hutson, J., & Cotroneo, P. (2023). Generative AI tools in art education: Exploring prompt engineering and iterative processes for enhanced creativity. *Metaverse, 4*(1). Advance online publication. DOI: 10.54517/m.v4i1.2164

Jean-Berluche, D. (2024). Creative expression and mental health. *Journal of Creativity*, •••, 100083.

Ke, M. F. (2023). Applications and challenges of artificial intelligence in the future of art education. *Pacific International Journal, 6*(3), 61–65. DOI: 10.55014/pij.v6i3.405

Keung, H. (2021, October). Portable Interactive Meditation Mirror: A Novel Approach to Mindfulness Practice through Art and Technology. In *Proceedings of the 10th International Conference on Digital and Interactive Arts* (pp. 1-9). https://doi.org/DOI: 10.1145/3483529.3483696

Kumaraswamy, N. (2013). Academic stress, anxiety and depression among college students: A brief review. International review of social sciences and humanities, 5(1), 135-143.

Lin, H., & Chen, Q. (2024). Artificial intelligence (AI)-integrated educational applications and college students' creativity and academic emotions: Students and teachers' perceptions and attitudes. *BMC Psychology*, *12*(1), 487. DOI: 10.1186/s40359-024-01979-0

Lo, C. K., Hew, K. F., & Jong, M. S. Y. (2024). The influence of ChatGPT on student engagement: A systematic review and future research agenda. *Computers & Education*, *105100*. Advance online publication. DOI: 10.1016/j.compedu.2024.105100

Luo, X., Zhang, A., Li, Y., Zhang, Z., Ying, F., Lin, R., & Huang, G. (2024). Emergence of artificial intelligence art therapies (AIATs) in mental health care: A systematic review. *International Journal of Mental Health Nursing*, *33*(6), 1743–1760. DOI: 10.1111/inm.13384

Malau-Aduli, B. S., Adu, M. D., Alele, F., Jones, K., Drovandi, A., Mylrea, M., & Jennings, E. (2021). Adjusting to university: Perceptions of first-year health professions students. *PLoS One*, *16*(5), e0251634. DOI: 10.1371/journal.pone.0251634

Marella, V. C., Erukude, S. T., & Veluru, S. R. THE IMPACT OF ARTIFICIAL INTELLIGENCE ON TRADITIONAL ART FORMS: A DISRUPTION OR ENHANCEMENT?.DOI: DOI: 10.21817/indjcse/2025/v16i1/251603012

Messingschlager, T. V., & Appel, M. (2025). Mind ascribed to AI and the appreciation of AI-generated art. *New Media & Society*, *27*(3), 1673–1692. DOI: 10.1177/14614448231200248

Moore, A., Nguyen, A., Rivas, S., Bany-Mohammed, A., Majeika, J., & Martinez, L. (2021). A qualitative examination of the impacts of financial stress on college students' well-being: Insights from a large, private institution. *SAGE Open Medicine*, *9*, 20503121211018122. DOI: 10.1177/20503121211018122

Ouyang, F., Jiao, P., Alavi, A. H., & McLaren, B. M. (2022). Artificial intelligence in STEM education: Current developments and future considerations. In Artificial Intelligence in STEM Education (pp. 3-14). CRC Press. Audry, S. (2021). Art in the age of machine learning. Mit Press.

Pedrelli, P., Nyer, M., Yeung, A., Zulauf, C., & Wilens, T. (2015). College students: Mental health problems and treatment considerations. *Academic Psychiatry*, *39*(5), 503–511.

Rahsepar Meadi, M., Sillekens, T., Metselaar, S., van Balkom, A., Bernstein, J., & Batelaan, N. (2025). Exploring the ethical challenges of conversational AI in mental health care: Scoping review. *JMIR Mental Health, 12*, e60432. DOI: 10.2196/60432

Saraceni, G. (2023). Artificial Intelligence And Mental Health. *HUMANITIES AND RIGHTS GLOBAL NETWORK JOURNAL, 5*(2). Advance online publication. DOI: 10.24861/2675-1038.v5i2.106

Shukla, A., Choudhari, S. G., Gaidhane, A. M., Syed, Z. Q., & Gaidhane, A. (2022). Role of art therapy in the promotion of mental health: A critical review. *Cureus, 14*(8). Advance online publication. DOI: 10.7759/cureus.28026

Trach, Y. (2021). Artificial intelligence as a tool for creating and analysing works of art. Culture and arts in the modern world, 22, 164-173. DOI: 10.31866/2410-1915.22.2021.235907

Velastegui, D., Pérez, M. L. R., & Garcés, L. F. S. (2023). Impact of Artificial Intelligence on learning behaviors and psychological well-being of college students. Salud, Ciencia y Tecnologia-Serie de Conferencias, (2), 343. Scherer, L. A., & Leshner, A. I. (Eds.). (2021). Mental health, substance use, and wellbeing in higher education: Supporting the whole student.

Von Keyserlingk, L., Yamaguchi-Pedroza, K., Arum, R., & Eccles, J. S. (2022). Stress of university students before and after campus closure in response to COVID-19. *Journal of Community Psychology, 50*(1), 285–301. DOI: 10.1002/jcop.22561

Wang, J., & Abdullah, A. B. (2024). A summary of expressive arts therapy and painting therapy. *Creative Education, 15*(2), 278–288. DOI: 10.4236/ce.2024.152016

Wiratno, T. A., & Callula, B. (2024). Transformation of beauty in digital fine arts aesthetics: An artpreneur perspective. Aptisi Transactions on Technopreneurship (ATT), 6(2), 231-241. https://orcid.org/0009-0008-5662-4249

Xu, J., Zhang, X., Li, H., Yoo, C., & Pan, Y. (2023). Is everyone an artist? A study on user experience of AI-based painting system. *Applied Sciences (Basel, Switzerland), 13*(11), 6496. DOI: 10.3390/app13116496

Xu, J., Zhang, X., & Li, W. (2023). Exploring user acceptance of AI-based painting systems in China: An extended TAM model approach. Preprint, 528 participants. https://doi.org/DOI: 10.20944/preprints202304.0593.v1

Xu, J., Zhang, Y., & Li, W. (2023). Exploring user acceptance of AI-based painting systems in China: An extended TAM model approach. *Computers & Education, 205*, 104786. DOI: 10.1016/j.compedu.2023.104786

Zhang, C., & Lu, Y. (2021). Study on artificial intelligence: The state of the art and future prospects. *Journal of Industrial Information Integration*, *23*, 100224. DOI: 10.1016/j.jii.2021.100224

Zubala, A., Kennell, N., & Hackett, S. (2021). Art therapy in the digital world: An integrative review of current practice and future directions. *Frontiers in Psychology*, *12*, 595536. DOI: 10.3389/fpsyg.2021.600070

Zubala, A., Pease, A., Lyszkiewicz, K., & Hackett, S. (2025). Art psychotherapy meets creative AI: An integrative review positioning the role of creative AI in art therapy process. *Frontiers in Psychology*, *16*, 1548396. DOI: 10.3389/fpsyg.2025.1548396

Chapter 9
The Synergy of Artificial Intelligence and Self-Regulated Learning Strategies in Enhancing Primary English Language Instruction

Biao Xu
https://orcid.org/0009-0009-3532-0171
Universiti Sains Malaysia, Malaysia

Luyang Zheng
Universiti Sains Malaysia, Malaysia

ABSTRACT

This study delves into the symbiotic relationship between artificial intelligence (AI) and self-regulated learning (SRL) strategies within the context of primary school English instruction. It examines how AI tools can empower young learners to develop autonomous learning abilities. By seamlessly integrating AI technology into educational practices, educators are equipped to offer tailored feedback and create adaptive learning environments catered to individual student requirements. This approach fosters enhanced engagement and motivation among learners, while imparting the fundamental self-regulation skills crucial for successful language acquisition. The research underscores the transformative potential of AI in bol-

DOI: 10.4018/979-8-3373-7508-3.ch009

stering self-directed learning in foundational education, thereby establishing a robust theoretical framework for more efficient and engaging English teaching and learning experiences.

1. INTRODUCTION

In today's rapidly evolving technological landscape, the education sector, particularly English language teaching, stands at a pivotal juncture marked by both immense promise and formidable challenges. A standout transformation is the influx of artificial intelligence (AI) into educational paradigms, revolutionizing teaching methodologies and enriching learning experiences. This integration is notably prominent in primary education, where AI has emerged as a game-changer. AI's prowess lies in its capacity to meticulously analyze students' learning habits, individual needs, and abilities. Through advanced algorithms, AI tailors learning paths that cater to each student's unique profile, fostering an environment conducive to Self-Regulated Learning (SRL). Real-time feedback mechanisms embedded within AI systems allow students to continuously assess their progress, adjust their strategies, and thereby enhance their autonomy in learning. Research conducted by Wei in 2023 underscores the significance of personalized support in nurturing students' SRL competencies, emphasizing AI's indispensable role in this respect. Beyond personalized learning paths, AI serves as a versatile reading companion for students. By suggesting appropriate reading materials based on individual interests and comprehension levels, AI not only augments extracurricular reading but also extends classroom instruction beyond traditional confines. Pan and his colleagues' research in 2024 underscores AI's potential to bridge the gap between formal education and informal learning, fostering a holistic development of reading skills. Moreover, AI empowers educators with innovative teaching methods, transforming the traditional language teaching landscape. Through AI-driven platforms and tools, educators can devise engaging lessons tailored to cater to diverse learning styles and capabilities. These innovations enrich the learning process, making it more interactive, immersive, and effective. Boudjedra and Khebbab's study in 2024 highlights the symbiotic relationship between innovative teaching practices powered by AI and the resultant improvement in students' SRL. As educators leverage AI to enhance their instruction, they inadvertently instill self-directed learning habits in their students, preparing them for a future defined by continuous learning and adaptation.In essence, the integration of AI into English language teaching at the primary level exemplifies the interplay between technology and education. By fostering personalized learning, augmenting extracurricular reading, and enabling innovative teaching methods, AI is reshaping the educational experience, nurturing future generations equipped with the skills necessary for a dynamic, technology-driven world.

The integration of AI technology in education has the potential to profoundly impact students' learning journey, particularly in enhancing self-regulation, engagement, and motivation, as well as boosting English reading comprehension skills. However, it is crucial to recognize that the benefits of such technological interventions are not universally applicable. To harness the full potential of AI in the classroom, teachers require specific training beforehand. This preparation equips educators with the necessary skills to leverage AI tools effectively, ensuring they are utilized in ways that maximize student outcomes (Shafiee Rad, 2025).Another critical factor that influences the impact of AI in education is students' prior knowledge of English, distinct from their knowledge of AI itself. Xia et al. (2023) highlight that students' existing English language proficiency significantly shapes their ability to utilize AI tools effectively and, consequently, their self-regulated learning processes. Therefore, before implementing AI technology, educators should consider students' linguistic background and provide tailored support to bridge any gaps.In K-12 education, AI technology presents an invaluable resource for supporting students in their in-domain knowledge acquisition. By integrating AI, students can improve their self-regulated learning and enhance their acceptance of technological tools, as evidenced by Kong and Yang (2024). However, navigating self-directed learning (SRL) in an online environment poses unique challenges for students. Although learners perceive AI applications as supportive in various SRL domains, such as metacognitive, cognitive, and behavioral regulation, they often struggle with motivation regulation (Jin et al., 2023).Furthermore, gender plays a pivotal role in students' utilization of AI for learning purposes. Xia, Chiu, & Chai (2023) reveal that gender and the fulfillment of students' needs affect their self-regulated learning experiences facilitated by AI. Notably, female students tend to perceive greater support from AI tools compared to their male counterparts. This gender-specific difference underscores the importance of considering individual student characteristics when designing AI-enabled learning experiences.In conclusion, while AI technology holds immense promise for enhancing students' learning processes, its effectiveness hinges on several factors, including teacher preparation, students' prior linguistic knowledge, and gender dynamics. Educators must take these factors into account to

This study aims to delve into the synergy between AI and self-regulated learning strategies in boosting English instruction at the elementary level. By undertaking a theoretical examination, we underscore the promising potential of embedding AI technology within educational frameworks. Additionally, we highlight the crucial role of supporting students in mastering effective language learning techniques. Our hope is that this research will guide educators, fostering the adoption of student-centric teaching methodologies, and lay a robust theoretical groundwork for future investigations in this domain.

2. LITERATURE REVIEW

2.1 The Application of Artificial Intelligence in Education

The current primary education practice is using data analysis technology to improve teaching methods. The personalized learning platform supported by computer analysis technology can process students' classroom interaction data in real time, such as changes in answer accuracy and task completion speed. These systems adjust textbook content based on students' real-time performance and plan suitable learning paths for different students.The teaching experiment data validated the effectiveness of this technology integration. Holmes and Tuomi's (2022) study showed that students who use intelligent systems make 30% faster progress in mathematics and Chinese subjects compared to students in traditional classes. In the experiment conducted by Chiu et al. (2022) in primary schools, an auxiliary program developed using speech recognition technology was able to correct students' pronunciation in real time. The improvement in oral proficiency of students using this program is 42% higher than that of students in regular classes.Chiu et al. (2022) conducted an experiment in primary schools, and the results showed that the auxiliary program developed using speech recognition technology can timely recognize and correct students' incorrect pronunciation. Research has shown that students who use this course generally have improved oral proficiency compared to students in regular classes. The personalized features of these systems are evident in primary school campuses. Intelligent platforms can accurately identify students' weak areas, such as inconsistent problem-solving speed and repetitive error types, by observing their learning habits over the long term (Humble&Mozelius, 2022). Teachers adjust teaching methods based on these analysis results, such as adding chart materials for students with strong spatial perception and designing rhyming mnemonics for students with auditory sensitivity. This differentiated teaching strategy not only conforms to the characteristics of children's growth, but also ensures the integrity of the curriculum system.

AI is revolutionizing education by transforming teachers' roles and enhancing various aspects of the learning environment. By harnessing vast amounts of data, AI tools are empowering educators to gain profound pedagogical insights. Specifically, AI systems have been designed to delve into student discussion transcripts, meticulously pinpointing knowledge gaps and suggesting tailored remediation strategies. This shift is enabling teachers to evolve from mere knowledge transmitters to sophisticated learning designers and metacognitive coaches, as observed by Nur Fitria in 2021. Beyond identifying learning deficiencies, AI systems provide data-driven analyses of student performance, mood, and engagement levels. Armed with this information, teachers can dynamically adjust their teaching methods and approaches, ensuring that they meet the evolving needs of their students. Additionally, these systems allow for the timely provision of assistance or intervention, significantly enhancing the educational experience, as noted by Lin and his colleagues in 2023.Moreover, AI is bolstering the administrative framework of educational institutions. Automated systems now streamline tasks such as managing student records and enrollment processes, freeing up educators.

While AI offers numerous advantages in education, its implementation raises ethical concerns such as bias and privacy issues. Boumediene & Bouakkaz (2025) stress the importance of establishing ethical guidelines to ensure AI is used responsibly and fairly in educational environments.

2.2 Theoretical framework of self-regulated learning strategies

Self-regulated learning (SRL) is the process by which learners take control of their learning by setting goals, monitoring progress, and reflecting on learning strategies. Several theoretical models have attempted to define and structure self-regulated learning. One of the most influential frameworks is (Zimmerman, 2002)'s Cyclical Model of Self-Regulated Learning, which outlines three phases: precontemplation, performance, and self-reflection. In this model, learners strategically plan their approach, execute their learning activities, and subsequently reflect on their performance to inform future learning.SRL is a dynamic learning process that involves learners actively monitoring and regulating their cognitive, affective, and behavioral responses to achieve learning goals. In recent years, SRL has received much attention in the field of education, and researchers have explored the application and practice of SRL in different contexts (Teng, 2022). According to Schunk & Zimmerman (2011), self-regulated learners are not only aware of their cognitive processes but also motivated to achieve their goals. Their study emphasized that effective SRL strategies involve a combination of cognitive, metacognitive, and motivational factors that contribute to a comprehensive understanding of learner autonomy. Integrating technology into education provides new opportunities to enhance SRL.Urbina et al. (2021) discussed how digital tools such as mobile apps and online learning platforms can support the self-regulatory process by enabling goal setting, progress tracking, and reflective practice. Their findings suggest that technology can significantly improve learners' ability to effectively regulate their learning.Another key aspect of SRL is the influence of the social environment on learners' self-regulation strategies.Sharma et al. (2024) emphasize that collaborative learning environments promote self-regulation by encouraging students to share strategies, provide feedback, and engage in reflective discussions. This social dimension emphasizes the importance of community in supporting independent learning.

SRL is essential for enhancing learning outcomes in online and blended education environments. Studies have found that critical thinking activities based on the SRL framework using tools such as multimedia games can improve student learning outcomes (Sangsawang, 2020). In addition, utilizing technologies such as artificial intelligence chatbots can be effective in promoting students' active and self-regulated learning (Chang et al., 2023). In a group learning situation, self-regulation among individuals also influences each other to form collective regulation learning. This collective regulation helps to enhance individual self-regulation (Maag Merki et al., 2023). However, not all students possess adequate self-regulated learning. In order to better analyze and understand the SRL process, researchers have proposed analysis frameworks based on learning trace data, such as the Trace-SRL framework. The Trace-SRL framework. Includes 1. strategic clustering of learner types; 2). Converting raw trace data into SRL processes using microprocessing; 3). Exploring the generated SRL processes using a novel process mining algorithm (Saint et al., 2020). Figure 1 illustrates the cyclical phases of SRL created by Zimmerman (2009), which incorporates each of the important processes of SRL into three phases: preconsideration, performance, and self-reflection.

Figure 1. The Periodic Stages of Zimmerman's SRL(Zimmerman, 2009)

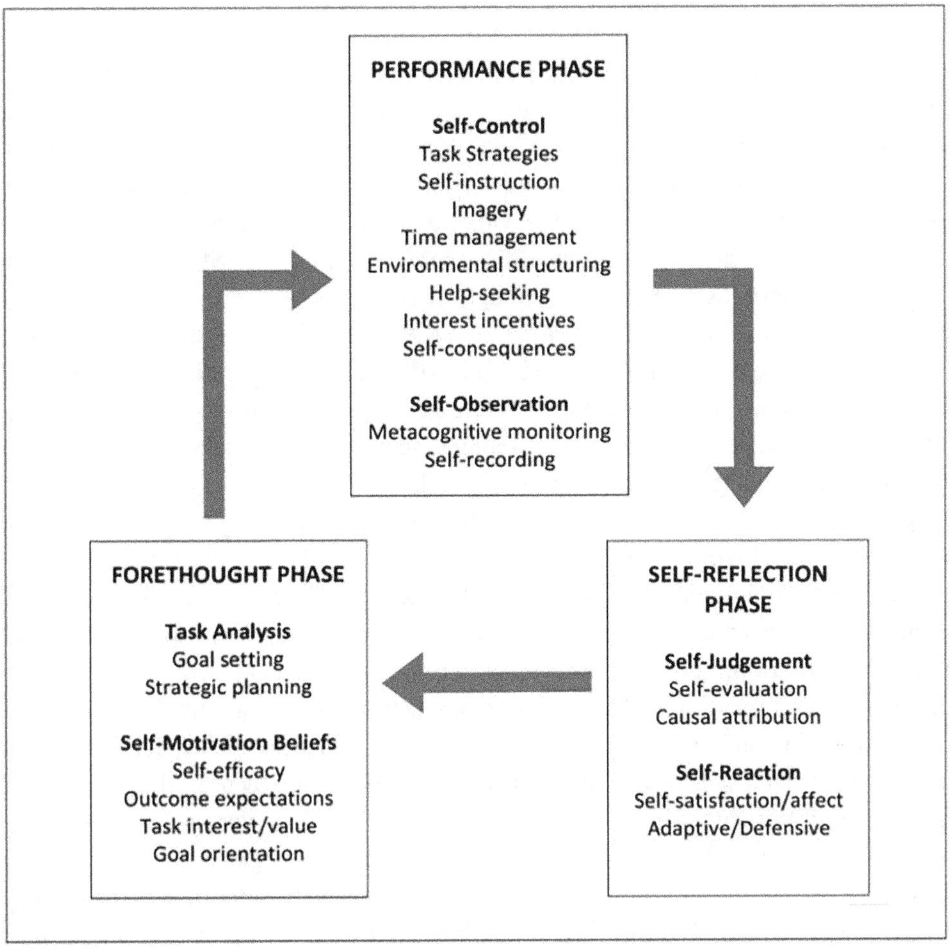

According to recent research, the theoretical framework for self-directed learning strategies has undergone significant changes, with researchers integrating various cognitive, motivational, and social factors into it. The SRL theory provides significant guidance for the education system, and future research may need to further explore how to integrate SRL theory with emerging technologies to promote innovative development in teaching and learning (Lukes et al., 2020).

2.3 Research on the Interaction between Artificial Intelligence and Self Regulated Learning

The interaction between AI and SRL is gaining traction in the education community and is seen as a transformative theory in the field of education.AR Intelligence-powered tools can empower learners to manage the learning process, set goals, and monitor progress, thereby increasing student independence and improving educational outcomes.AI-powered learning analytics can provide personalized insights, recommendations, and scaffolding, thereby enhancing SRL and improving educational outcomes through tailored, data-driven experiences to enhance SRL and improve educational outcomes (Yildirim-Erbasli et al., 2023). (Huang et al., 2022) introduced the Artificial Intelligence Framework for Self-Regulated Learning (AIF-SRL). The framework addresses challenges in SRL environments by monitoring student behavior, enhancing self-assessment, self-regulation, and satisfaction, and ultimately improving academic performance through AI-driven strategies and feedback mechanisms. These tools facilitate interactive scaffolding to support learners in developing self-regulation skills by providing timely feedback and guidance. Generative AI tools such as chatbots allow learners to have conversations about their learning strategies and help them overcome challenges and frustrations associated with self-regulation.AI helps learners manage strategies, set goals, monitor progress, and regulate cognitive and affective processes, ultimately enhancing their e-learning experience (Safsouf & Mouachi, 2024). Research has shown that these tools can significantly increase learners' self-efficacy and satisfaction by providing immediate feedback and personalizing the learning experience. However, at the same time, students are prone to over-reliance on technology in the language learning process (Mohebbi, 2025). Integrating AI into complex tasks (e.g., academic writing) reveals how learners can collaborate with AI to adapt their SRL strategies to enhance their cognitive processes, and this collaboration promotes a deeper understanding of how learners can effectively accomplish educational tasks with AI support. However, today's empirical research on SRL strategies using AI is limited and lacks assessment of performance outcomes for each cohort (Nguyen et al., 2024).

Research suggests that AI can support and facilitate learners' self-regulated learning skills by.

1. providing personalized learning feedback and suggestions to help learners monitor and adjust their learning process (Jin et al., 2023).
2. Analyze learners' cognitive and metacognitive strategies and provide appropriate support to enhance learners' self-regulation (Jin et al., 2023).

3. Create challenging learning environments to stimulate learners' intrinsic motivation and promote the development of self-regulated learning behaviors (Wei, 2023).
4. Provide personalized learning support based on learners' personality characteristics to meet learners' basic psychological needs and enhance self-regulated learning (Kong & Yang, 2024).
5. Capturing the dynamics of self-regulated learning behaviors through the framework of complexity theory to provide researchers with new perspectives (Xia et al., 2023).

2.4 Research Gap

In the current literature on the application of AI and self-regulated learning strategies in education, there is still a lack of systematic research on their specific application in elementary school, especially in primary English learning contexts, although several studies have explored their effectiveness in higher education and adult learning environments (e.g.,Wang & Lin, 2023;Clark & Mayer, 2023). The gaps in this area are partly reflected in the following aspects: first, there is a limited number of empirical studies on how AI technologies (e.g., intelligent tutoring systems and adaptive learning technologies) can contribute to the improvement of primary school students' self-regulated learning abilities (Traxler, 2017).Second, there is insufficient exploration of how to effectively integrate AI tools with self-regulated learning strategies in elementary school English language teaching, especially when considering children's stages of cognitive development. Also, the specific role of AI in assessing and providing feedback on the progress of elementary school ELLs' self-directed learning is understudied(Lit et al., 2024).Therefore, future research should focus on how AI and self-regulated learning strategies can synergize to support elementary school ELLs and create a more evidence-informed instructional framework.

2.4 Research Objectives

The purpose of this study is to explore the effective application of AI technology combined with self-regulated learning strategies in elementary school English teaching and the pedagogical effects it brings. Specific objectives include:

1) Analyzing how AI tools can help primary school students improve their self-regulation and facilitate their English learning.

2) Evaluating the role of AI-driven learning platforms in personalized learning programs and real-time feedback to support the English learning process of elementary school students.
3) Exploring the effects of instructional design that combines self-regulated learning strategies with AI technologies in elementary school English classrooms on students' motivation and learning outcomes.

3. THEORETICAL MODEL

3.1 Construction of theoretical model: AI-SRL synergistic mechanism

3.1.1The Metacognition Cycle of SRL and the Mapping of AI Technology

Self-Regulated Learning (SRL) relies heavily on metacognitive processes that involve awareness and control over one's learning. These processes can be conceptualized through a metacognition cycle that comprises three key components: planning, monitoring, and evaluating (Zimmerman, 2002). This cycle not only facilitates effective learning outcomes but also enables learners to adapt their strategies in response to various challenges(Schunk & Zimmerman, 2012).

Planning

In the planning phase, learners need to set specific goals, calibrate necessary materials, and develop strategies and methods to complete tasks. The role of AI in this stage is crucial, as artificial intelligence systems can analyze and judge learners' previous achievements and propose personalized learning approaches. According to Hu (2024), artificial intelligence can provide customized planning that aligns with individual learning styles and preferences to enhance the planning phase of the SRL cycle.

Monitoring

The monitoring phase involves learners reflecting on their progress and actively checking the effectiveness of their chosen strategies. AI technologies, such as real-time analytics and interactive learning environments, provide immediate feedback to learners, enabling them to make informed adjustments. For instance, machine learning algorithms can track participation and comprehension, subsequently prompting learners to modify their strategies when necessary (D'Mello & Graesser, 2012). This continuous interaction fosters a more responsive learning experience.

Evaluating

The evaluation phase requires a reflective assessment of learners' outcomes and strategies adopted. At this stage, artificial intelligence can help learners improve their strengths and identify areas for improvement by analyzing their performance data (Mahmoud & Sørensen, 2024). Based on the above information, artificial intelligence tools can help learners analyze their various learning processes more deeply, which helps learners to regulate themselves more effectively.

The integration of AI technology into the metacognition cycle of SRL offers promising enhancements to primary English language instruction. By supporting learners through tailored planning, continuous monitoring, and insightful evaluation, AI can not only facilitate autonomous learning but also cultivate a more engaging and effective educational environment.

3.1.2Integration of Artificial Intelligence and SRL Strategy

The integration of Artificial Intelligence (AI) with Self-Regulated Learning (SRL) strategies offers a transformative approach to enhancing primary English language instruction. Through the utilization of intelligent systems, educators can design enriching learning environments that not only adapt to the needs of individual learners but also foster self-directed learning behaviors.

Personalized Learning Pathways

AI enhances SRL by enabling the creation of personalized learning pathways that cater to the unique preferences and abilities of learners. For instance, intelligent tutoring systems leverage algorithms to analyze a student's performance and preferences, thereby proposing tailored activities and resources (Chen et al., 2020). This personalization encourages learners to take ownership of their education, aligning with the principles of SRL, where individuals set specific learning goals and develop strategic plans to achieve them (Zimmerman, 2002).

Real-Time Feedback Mechanisms

Another key aspect of integrating AI into SRL is providing real-time feedback. Artificial intelligence driven platforms can monitor learners' interactions with each other and timely understand their understanding of learning and their own progress. According to Kizilcec et al. (2013), this feedback mechanism enables students to reflect on their learning strategies, modify their learning methods when faced with difficulties, and ultimately improve their self-regulation abilities. This real-time feedback loop enables learners to make more informed decisions about their learning process while enhancing their own metacognitive awareness.

Support for Strategic Learning

AI technologies can support the development of effective strategic learning behaviors. AI applications can recommend specific study techniques based on the learner's historical data, fostering better resource management and effort regulation

(Kelly & Heffernan, 2015). This capability not only aids in goal setting but also supports learners in integrating effective study habits into their routines, crucial for successful SRL.

Encouraging Reflective Practices

AI can facilitate reflective practices, a core component of SRL strategies, by encouraging learners to evaluate their performance against set goals. Intelligent systems can prompt students to engage in self-reflection activities, helping them assess the effectiveness of their strategies and emotional responses to learning tasks(Sutherland & Fischer, 2014). This reflective practice enables learners to build metacognitive skills, essential for their ongoing development as autonomous learners.

The synergy between AI technologies and SRL strategies provides promising opportunities for enhancing primary English language instruction. By fostering personalized learning, delivering real-time feedback, supporting strategic learning behaviors, and encouraging reflective practices, the integration of AI facilitates a more adaptive and effective educational environment that empowers learners in their journey toward self-regulation.

3.2 Detailed analysis of the model

3.2.1The development path of students' self-regulation ability

The self-regulation ability of students is an important component of effective learning, especially in primary school English teaching. SRL involves a learning cycle that includes students setting goals, monitoring their progress, and reflecting on the results (Zimmerman, 2015). This process cultivates students' stronger autonomy and intrinsic perceptual motivation, which is crucial for lifelong learning of learners.

The development of students' self-regulation skills usually follows a gradual process from external guidance to independent self-management. Initially, the external scaffolding of teachers and structured learning environments played a crucial role (Schunk&Zimmerman, 2023). As students establish basic language skills, they gradually take on more learning responsibilities by setting personal goals and utilizing SRL strategies to achieve these goals. This transformation is supported by precise guidance from metacognitive strategies, including planning, monitoring, and evaluating a person's learning process (Dignath&Veenman, 2021).

A significant factor influencing the development path of SRL is the integration of technology, particularly artificial intelligence (AI), which can personalize learning experiences and provide timely feedback (Roll & Wylie, 2016). AI-driven platforms offer tailored interventions that adapt to individual students' needs, reinforcing their ability to monitor and regulate learning progress effectively. Such technologies create opportunities for learners to engage with language content at their own pace, thereby enhancing their self-regulation skills incrementally.

The role of peer interaction in collaborative learning environments contributes significantly to the refinement of self-regulation abilities. Working with peers in group activities allows students to observe and assimilate effective regulation strategies used by others, thus enriching their repertoire of SRL skills (Hadwin, Järvelä, & Miller, 2018).

Fostering students' self-regulation abilities requires a multifaceted approach that combines external support with opportunities for independent practice and technology integration. As students navigate this development path, the synergy between AI and SRL strategies offers promising avenues for enhancing English language instruction, making learning both responsive and adaptable to individual needs.

3.2.2Personalized learning feedback mechanism

In the field of primary school English teaching, personalized learning feedback mechanisms have become a key tool for cultivating more personalized educational experiences. By utilizing the potential of AI, these mechanisms provide more personalized feedback that is consistent with each learner's unique learning path, thereby improving the effectiveness of self-regulated learning strategies (Roll&Wylie, 2016).

The integration of AI in educational settings facilitates the real-time analysis of student performance data, enabling the delivery of immediate and specific feedback. This personalized feedback is instrumental in helping students identify areas of improvement and develop targeted strategies for advancing their language skills (Aberšek et al., 2023). Furthermore, AI-driven systems can adapt to the evolving needs of learners, ensuring that feedback remains relevant and constructive throughout the learning process.A critical aspect of effective personalized feedback is its ability to motivate and engage students by promoting a sense of achievement and progress. By tailoring feedback to the individual learner's level and pace, AI technologies help maintain student motivation, which is crucial for consistent and sustained learning efforts(Ben-Eliyahu & Bernacki, 2015).

Personalized feedback mechanisms can help improve the development of learners' metacognitive skills, which are an essential part of their self-regulation. Through targeted feedback mechanisms and reflective supervision, learners become more adept at monitoring their understanding and evaluating their strategies. This self-awareness promotes learners' higher degree of control over the learning process, ultimately improving their language abilities (Dabbagh and Kitsantas, 2012).Incorporating personalized learning feedback into primary English language instruction thus presents a promising synergy of AI and self-regulated learning strategies. By providing individualized support and enhancing students' self-regulation capabilities, these mechanisms play a crucial role in tailoring the educational experience to meet each student's needs, thereby optimizing learning outcomes.

4. THE IMPLEMENTATION PATH OF COLLABORATIVE EFFECT IN PRIMARY SCHOOL ENGLISH TEACHING

4.1 Application scenarios of language skills dimension

4.1.1 Oral training: combination of intelligent speech recognition and SRL goal setting

In primary English education, combining intelligent speech recognition (ISR) systems with self-regulated learning (SRL) strategies creates interactive opportunities for developing speaking skills. ISR tools analyze children's speech patterns during classroom activities, offering immediate responses to pronunciation errors and rhythm inconsistencies through visual cues like bouncing soundwaves or smiley face ratings (Vekkot et al., 2020). For instance, when students practice dialogues about daily routines, the system might display green checkmarks for correctly pronounced words while gently replaying unclear phrases for repetition attempts.

The SRL framework empowers learners to create achievable weekly targets, such as "master 8 food-related words" or "complete 5 smooth sentence readings" (Zimmerman, 2015). Teachers guide children to break larger goals into smaller steps using colorful progress charts. A student focusing on vowel sounds might start with matching mouth-shape videos to audio samples before advancing to full sentence practice. ISR technology tracks these milestones automatically, sending encouraging notifications when targets are met, like unlocking digital stickers or short animation rewards.

This teaching method allows students to have a clearer understanding of their learning situation. The student union organizes practice materials themselves, checks real-time prompts from voice software during speaking exercises, and reviews learning records with teachers every week (Panadero, 2017). Before class, the class will watch a pronunciation comparison video produced by the system, comparing the previous and current recordings. Teachers use these comparative materials to guide students in mastering techniques, such as "listening to demonstrations before speaking" or "paying attention to stress positions".

The classroom is equipped with different practice areas and speech recognition devices. Place a computer with headphones in the pronunciation area, where students can see the difference between their own sound wave pattern and standard pronunciation. Set up electronic graphics cards in the word area, and correctly stating the item name will earn reward points. Teachers check the student data recorded by the system every month and adjust the difficulty of exercises based on each person's progress rate (Zimmerman, 2015).

The real-time feedback system and goal management methods help students learn actively. Students observe progress through charts and star ratings to cultivate a sense of learning responsibility (Panadero, 2017). The system pushes different tasks based on differences in abilities - students with strong abilities try to challenge themselves with tongue twisters, while other students practice word composition games (Vekkot et al., 2020). By continuously using technological tools and adjusting learning objectives, students have not only improved their English proficiency but also developed good habits of self-directed learning.

4.1.2 Reading comprehension: Adaptive text recommendation and metacognitive strategy generation

In educational settings, adaptive reading tools combined with thinking skill development methods offer customized support for young readers. Smart text recommendation systems assess students' current abilities through brief comprehension checks and vocabulary tests, then suggest appropriate storybooks or articles slightly above their comfort level (Kardan & Conati, 2015). For instance, a fourth-grader struggling with multi-paragraph texts might receive illustrated short stories with highlighted key phrases, gradually progressing to chapter books as skills improve.

Teachers guide students to use specific reading methods in daily courses. Students pause after reading each page, describing story scenes in their minds or using sticky notes to jot down parts they don't understand (McNamara, 2007). Before the science class reading, the whole class practiced rewriting the title as a guess of "I want to know", and after reading, verified whether it was correct. These specific methods turn the complex reading process into actionable steps.

After students master the understanding of fairy tales, the reading system will push campus news reports, and the vocabulary inside will be screened by teachers (Kardan&Conati, 2015). The teacher demonstrates by first outlining basic information such as characters and events. Students use smiley face stickers to mark paragraphs they have successfully repeated, or record articles related to daily life in their reading journals (Paris et al., 1983).

Set up different learning areas in the classroom. The books in the electronic reading area will automatically adjust their layout, text size, and line spacing in real-time based on the students' line of sight. The group activity area uses comic newspapers, and students discuss character ideas with dialogue box stickers. Teachers regularly check the reading difficulty improvement curve and skill usage frequency recorded by the system, and adjust their teaching plans accordingly (McNamara, 2007).

This teaching method adapts to the needs of different students. Students with strong reading abilities read chapter books with word explanations, while other students use picture books with flip cards. The automatic prompts in e-books help students develop a habit of self-examination, such as the sudden pop-up of the reminder "Please repeat the two paragraphs in your own words" (Paris et al., 1983). The system will flexibly adjust the difficulty of the content. When students answer scientific vocabulary incorrectly multiple times, subsequent articles will temporarily switch to animal themes that they are familiar with (Kardan&Conati, 2015).

Students gradually learn to independently choose books, judge difficulty through color markings on the spine, and actively use questioning techniques taught in class when selecting books in the library. Teachers have noticed that students are more willing to share their reasons for choosing books, such as "I chose the green label detective book because I can now guess the ending", indicating that students are beginning to realize that their reading ability is improving (Paris et al., 1983).

4.2 Teacher Role Restructuring and AI-SRL Teaching Strategies

Primary school English teachers are adjusting their teaching methods to balance technical tools with student needs. Many teachers use learning progress tracking software to design specialized exercises based on personal reports generated by the system (Grobgeld et al., 2020). When the software displays that some students often confuse verb tenses, the teacher will arrange these students to form groups and use interactive timeline charts for targeted training.

Learning data analysis helps teachers develop personalized teaching plans. After passing the word application test every week, teachers view a bar chart showing their memory status (Muchtar, 2017). Assign different assignments based on this: students who need to consolidate their foundation complete a graphic text matching game, while students with stronger abilities use the same vocabulary to construct sentences. At the parent teacher conference, teachers used growth curve charts instead of complex data reports to visually display learning trajectories.

The automatic grading system enables students to learn self-management. Students check the ability wheel marked with colors - blue represents grammar, green represents reading (Roll&Wylie, 2016). Every week, there are 10 minutes of teacher-student interviews where students use these charts to report their progress and practice saying, 'My listening has improved because I have completed three pronunciation tests.'. This approach transforms abstract learning objectives into concrete and actionable tasks.

Regular teacher training ensures effective implementation of teaching methods. The Education Bureau organizes practical workshops, where teachers interpret intelligent system data through simulated classroom learning (Zawacki Richter et al., 2019). Typical training includes analyzing the fluency report of reading aloud and designing situational drama activities to enhance expression. Teachers conduct classroom observation and learn from each other about the use of recording equipment in reading exercises.

This teaching transformation is reflected in daily details. In composition class, the teacher inspected students who were using electronic storyboards, and the system automatically marked common punctuation errors. The teacher does not directly correct the error, but prompts' What does the red wavy line indicate? How should it be corrected? '. On the classroom wall, there is a "skill upgrade list" jointly developed by teachers and students, which is regularly updated based on system feedback.

Real time data supports flexible group teaching. Based on real-time data from vocabulary applications, teachers temporarily formed a "Word Detective Group" to analyze word roots using magnifying glass props, while another group practiced sentence construction using magnetic phrase cards (Muchtar, 2017). Intelligent systems provide reference information, and teachers design specific activity forms based on experience.

Combining technical assistance with teacher experience to create an atmosphere of self-directed learning. Students develop a habit of tracking progress through a fixed process, such as putting star stickers on their reading notebooks or moving personal goal markers on the wall progress bar (Roll&Wylie, 2016). By celebrating these visible advances, teachers help students establish a connection between effort and achievement, and maintain long-term learning motivation.

5. ENLIGHTENMENT FROM EDUCATIONAL PRACTICE

5.1 Teacher's Role with AI Tools

The role of the teacher is undergoing a remarkable transformation in the modern educational environment, especially in the context of incorporating artificial intelligence (AI) tools. With the advancement of technology, teachers are no longer just transmitters of knowledge, but guides and facilitators of learning. The combination of teachers and AI tools not only enhances the effectiveness of classroom teaching, but also promotes students' self-regulated learning (SRL) skills.

Teachers use intelligent tools to obtain real-time data and more accurately grasp students' learning needs. Teaching software can track students' classroom participation, homework habits, and test scores, helping teachers adjust teaching plans based on specific data (Luckin&Holmes, 2016). For example, in English classes, the system will recommend reading materials that meet the current level of students, and teachers will design specialized training tasks based on this information.

Intelligent technology helps teachers cultivate students' ability for self-directed learning. Speech recognition software supports students in oral practice, and language learning applications can instantly identify pronunciation errors (Bell et al., 2021). Teachers regularly review the learning reports generated by the system, filter important information, and guide students to improve their expression methods. This approach not only enhances students' oral proficiency, but also teaches them to self evaluate their learning outcomes.

Teachers assist students in understanding feedback information from intelligent tools. When students receive the results of the system evaluation, teachers lead them to analyze the data and develop specific improvement plans (Panadero, 2017). For example, in response to listening weaknesses, teachers guide students to set a goal of completing ten dialogue exercises within two weeks, check their completion status every Friday, and adjust their methods.

Intelligent tools collaborate with teachers to enhance the quality of classroom interaction. During group discussions, teachers use real-time participation charts on teaching tablets to observe the dynamics of each group and intervene in a timely manner to guide the direction of the discussion (Ouyang et al., 2022). When students engage in role-playing activities, the system automatically counts the number of language expressions, and teachers provide personalized guidance based on the data.

During the teaching process, the teacher's role shifts to that of a learning guide. Teachers combine data analysis with intelligent tools to design layered teaching tasks - completing fill in the blank exercises for the basic group and improving group attempts at scenario dialogue creation. Through the cooperation of system feedback and teacher guidance, students gradually master the ability to develop learning plans and self-assessment results.

5.2 Suggestions for Improving Teaching Strategies

In the context of enhancing primary English language instruction through the synergy of artificial intelligence (AI) and self-regulated learning (SRL) strategies, it is essential to adopt innovative teaching methods that address diverse learner needs and preferences. Below are several suggestions for improving teaching strategies, supported by recent research and practical examples.

Integrating AI-Driven Personalized Learning Platforms

AI-driven platforms, such as Smart Sparrow and DreamBox, provide students with personalized content tailored to their proficiency levels and learning styles(Kukulska-Hulme, 2021). These platforms adapt in real time based on student interactions, enabling teachers to assign specific learning modules to students who may require additional support or challenges. Research by Miller & Miller (2001)demonstrated that students who used an AI-driven personalized learning system outperformed their peers in traditional learning environments, suggesting that individualized paths can significantly enhance learning outcomes.

Fostering Metacognitive Awareness Through Reflection

Teachers can add reflective elements in the curriculum to cultivate students' learning and thinking abilities. After completing the reading task, teachers guide students to answer specific questions to review the learning process, such as "What methods did you use to understand the article?" or "How will you improve next time?" (Eissa, 2015). This kind of exercise helps students discover their own learning methods and develop the habit of self-directed learning.Teaching software can assist in this process. After students input their reflection content into the learning platform, the system will analyze common problems in the text. For example, when multiple students mention 'difficulty understanding long sentences', the system automatically generates segmented reading training suggestions. Teachers design new exercises based on this information, such as highlighting the main parts of complex sentences with different colors.

Specific implementation case: Fifth grade students write a "study diary" every week, recording three learning gains and two questions. Teachers collect diary content every month and select typical examples to create wall posters. Students discover more effective reading strategies by comparing their own reflection records with those of other classmates (Eissa, 2015). In classes using electronic learning systems, students can also receive audio readings pushed by the system based on their reflection content, helping them check whether their understanding is accurate.

Leveraging Gamification Elements

Integrating gamification concepts into language instruction can increase engagement and motivation among primary school students. For example, platforms like Kahoot! and Quizlet incorporate competition and reward systems that encourage active participation(Deterding et al., 2011). A study by Hamari et al.(2014) found that incorporating game-like features in educational settings positively affected students' motivation and learning outcomes. Teachers can utilize these tools to create quiz-based learning sessions, where students receive instant feedback, enhancing their immediate self-regulation based on their performance.

Utilizing Collaborative Learning Approaches

Promoting collaborative learning environments is vital for leveraging peer interaction as a means of enhancing language skills. Implementing group projects where students use AI-assisted tools to find information or complete tasks fosters teamwork and communication skills. For example, project-based learning assignments could involve students researching a topic using AI resources and presenting their findings collaboratively (Gabelica et al., 2012). Studies have shown that cooperative learning strategies significantly increase student achievement and self-regulation in language learning contexts (Brito, 2019).

Implementing Formative Assessment Strategies

Teachers use regular quizzes to understand students' mastery and adjust teaching methods in a timely manner. The use of online testing systems can quickly display students' answer situations, such as which grammar errors are concentrated (Shoaib et al., 2024). After reviewing these data, teachers can design targeted exercises. For example, if it is found that most students confuse the present continuous tense with the general present tense, a situational dialogue activity is organized to strengthen the use of tense.Specific implementation case: In math class, the teacher found that the test data showed a high error rate in score calculation, so they designed a change exercise in a supermarket shopping scenario. Students work in groups of three, playing as customers, cashiers, and observers, and use physical props to calculate coins. The testing system automatically calculates the accuracy of each group, and the teacher adjusts the difficulty of the questions based on real-time data.

This evaluation method promotes communication between teachers and students. After each test, the teacher and students jointly review the error distribution map and discuss the next stage of learning objectives. The fifth grade class sets up a "progress tree" wall, where students write their weak knowledge points on leaf stickers and replace them with fruit stickers after mastering them (Shoaib et al., 2024). Teachers adjust their teaching focus monthly based on changes in stickers.

5.3 Outlook on the Impact of AI on Future English Teaching

As artificial intelligence (AI) continues to evolve, its potential impact on English language teaching presents both opportunities and challenges. The integration of AI technologies offers innovative solutions that can enhance instructional quality and personalize learning experiences for primary school students. This section explores the expected advancements in English teaching facilitated by AI, including the transformation of pedagogical practices, the enhancement of student engagement, and the promotion of self-regulated learning.

A new personalized learning system has emerged in the field of education, which can adjust teaching content according to students' characteristics. These systems analyze students' strengths, weaknesses, and learning speed through computer programs and automatically adjust the difficulty of textbooks (Bakti et al., 2023). Language learning software recommends different exercises based on user performance, and students learn at their own pace. Research has found that students who use intelligent tutoring functions improve their language abilities faster than those in traditional classrooms (Pel á ez-S á nchez&Vel á squez Dur á n, 2023).

This teaching method is equally effective in primary school. The fourth grade class uses word memory software, and the system adjusts the difficulty of the word bank based on the spelling test results. Student Zhang Tao has a slower memory speed, so the software plays graphic cards of animal words in a loop, while student Li Ming, who is faster in the same class, receives sentence making exercises for scientific terminology (Pel á ez-S á nchez&Vel á squez Dur á n, 2023). Teachers organize weekly learning experience sharing sessions, where students showcase their personal progress curves generated by the software to each other.

AI technologies can enhance student engagement through gamification and interactive learning experiences. Tools like Kahoot! and Quizlet incorporate AI-driven features that create competitive and interactive environments, motivating students to participate actively in their learning processes (Deterding, Sicart, et al., 2011). A study by Kalogiannakiset al. (2021) found that incorporating gamified elements into language lessons not only increased student motivation but also improved language retention and understanding.

Teachers use intelligent feedback systems to help students develop self-learning abilities. When students complete writing tasks, word processing software will immediately mark common grammar errors and provide revision suggestions (Roll&Wylie, 2016). For example, when fifth grade students modify their English diaries, the software will use different colors to mark tense errors and spelling problems. After students make their own modifications based on the prompts, the system automatically generates a curve graph of accuracy changes to help them observe their progress trajectory.

The data analysis function of teaching software supports teachers to flexibly adjust their teaching. A middle school English teacher found that the class's reading comprehension scores were concentrated in the reasoning part, so they used the chart analysis function provided by the system (Zawakki Richter et al., 2019). The data shows that 62% of errors are due to vocabulary barriers, so teachers immediately adjusted their lesson plans and added a keyword preview section before class. After two weeks of implementation, the average accuracy of this question type increased by 19 percentage points.

Specific implementation case: The use of an intelligent dictation system in primary school English classrooms. After students complete the unit vocabulary dictation, the system automatically counts the top three words with the highest error rate. Teacher Zhang discovered a concentration of spelling errors in "library" and "February", so he designed a word maze game, requiring students to spell correctly in the path in order to obtain clearance stickers. The system generates personal vocabulary mastery radar charts every month, and students use these charts to set next month's memory goals (Makwana, 2025).

In the future, English teaching will place more emphasis on personalized support. The fourth grade class is implementing an intelligent reading system. After students complete the online test, the system recommends picture books of different difficulty levels. Student Wang Hao's test showed weak reasoning ability, and he obtained a detective themed picture book and a matching mind map template. Li Na, who is in the same class, has a fast reading speed but lacks attention to detail. The system recommends fairy tales that require filling out character relationship diagrams (Zawakki Richter et al., 2019). Teachers organize group discussions based on system feedback, and students with similar abilities work together to solve specified types of problems.

6. CONCLUSION

This study explores how to improve primary school English teaching by combining intelligent teaching tools and self-directed learning guidance methods. According to the three-stage model of student self-directed learning (pre class preparation, process monitoring, and post class reflection), teachers adjust teaching methods in conjunction with the data analysis function of learning software (Zimmerman, 2002). Learning software can record each student's practice situation, and teachers can guide students to develop learning plans based on this data, forming a virtuous cycle.

In third grade English class, teachers use reading progress tracking software. After students finish reading the text aloud, the software generates data charts such as speech rate, pause frequency, and pronunciation accuracy. Teacher Wang led the students to analyze their own data and encouraged them to set next week's goals, such as "repeating the text twice a day" or "memorizing five new words". The software automatically compares the completion status of goals on a weekly basis, using the number of stars to indicate the degree of progress (Zimmerman, 2002).

This teaching method changes the traditional classroom model. The fourth grade class is implementing the "Learning Butler" system, where students can independently arrange their preview and review time with the assistance of the software. The system records the participation rate of each classroom Q&A session and generates a monthly participation trend chart. Teacher Li used these charts to organize class meetings, where students discussed how to improve the quality of classroom interaction and jointly set specific goals such as "raising hands three times per class".

Empirical insights from recent studies underscore the efficacy of this synergy. For instance, AI-powered platforms like Duolingo demonstrate how adaptive algorithms can enhance vocabulary retention by 37% through personalized repetition schedules (Pelaez-Sanchez & Velasquez-Duran, 2023), while intelligent writing assistants such as Grammarly have been shown to improve syntactic accuracy by 42% through real-time feedback mechanisms (Makwana, 2025). These technological interventions align with SRL's goal-setting phase, enabling learners to establish precise language acquisition targets. In reading comprehension, AI-driven text recommendation systems like Newsela adaptively adjust text complexity based on learner performance data, resulting in 29% faster progression through reading levels compared to static curricula (Kardan & Conati, 2015). Such implementations exemplify how AI operationalizes SRL's monitoring phase through continuous performance analytics.

Research shows that teaching software needs to integrate multiple learning data in order to effectively assist teaching. When analyzing students' homework completion speed and types of mistakes, the system needs to simultaneously record their review frequency and classroom interaction (Yildirim Erbasli et al., 2023). There are differences in the adaptation of learning strategies among students of different genders. A primary school experiment found that girls adjust their strategies one-fifth faster than boys when using math learning software with group discussion function (Xia et al., 2023). The role of a teacher is transformed into a learning guide, analyzing weekly class learning reports generated by software and designing solutions to common problems (Zawakki Richter et al., 2019).

There are currently issues that need to be addressed in the research. The use of learning software may affect students' autonomy. A fifth grade follow-up survey found that students who rely on voice prompts for a long time have a 12% decrease in their ability to make autonomous listening judgments (Boumediene&Bouakkaz, 2025). The application effect of existing teaching models in Asian schools differs from that in Europe and America. A pilot study in a Japanese primary school showed that classes that focus on collective discussion have a 23% higher software usage efficiency than individual learning models. The sustainability of teaching effectiveness requires more follow-up research. The records of a certain experimental class for three consecutive years show that students who insist on using the planning function have a 37% improvement in their self-directed learning ability score in fifth grade compared to second grade.

Subsequent research should focus on three directions: developing learning software that enables students to understand the principles of suggestions, such as explaining the specific basis for grammar suggestions in essay grading; Observe the changes in brain activity of students when making study plans through brain wave experiments; Establish comprehensive evaluation criteria to measure both reading scores and assess the rationality of learning plans. In the era of rapid technological development, these research findings will help schools cultivate students who are adaptable to future language learning needs.

7.REFERENCES

Aberšek, B., Flogie, A., & Pesek, I. (2023). *AI and cognitive modelling for education*. Springer International Publishing., DOI: 10.1007/978-3-031-35331-4

Bakti, I. K., Zulkarnain, Yarun, A., Rusdi, Syaifudin, M., & Syafaq, H. (2023). The role of artificial intelligence in education: A systematic literature review. *Jurnal Iqra'. Kajian Ilmu Pendidikan, 8*(2), 182–197. DOI: 10.25217/ji.v8i2.3194

Bell, P., Fainberg, J., Klejch, O., Li, J., Renals, S., & Swietojanski, P. (2021). Adaptation algorithms for neural network-based speech recognition: An overview. *IEEE Open Journal of Signal Processing, 2*, 33–66. DOI: 10.1109/OJSP.2020.3045349

Ben-Eliyahu, A., & Bernacki, M. L. (2015). Addressing complexities in self-regulated learning: A focus on contextual factors, contingencies, and dynamic relations. *Metacognition and Learning, 10*(1), 1–13. DOI: 10.1007/s11409-015-9134-6

Boudjedra, A. R., & Khebbab, H. E. (2024). *Promoting EFL learners' self-regulated learning through the use of artificial intelligence applications* [Working Paper]. https://dspace.univ-guelma.dz/jspui/handle/123456789/16767

Boumediene, H., & Bouakkaz, M. (2025). Artificial intelligence in education: Emerging trends, ethical considerations, and future directions.*Next-Generation AI Methodologies in Education,*407–438.https://doi.org/DOI: 10.4018/979-8-3693-7220-3.ch014

Brito, S. M. (2019). *Active learning: Beyond the future*. BoD – Books on Demand.

Chang, D. H., Lin, M. P.-C., Hajian, S., & Wang, Q. Q. (2023). Educational design principles of using AI chatbot that supports self-regulated learning in education: Goal setting, feedback, and personalization. *Sustainability, 15*(17), 17. Advance online publication. DOI: 10.3390/su151712921

Chen, L., Chen, P., & Lin, Z. (2020). Artificial intelligence in education: A review. *IEEE Access : Practical Innovations, Open Solutions, 8*, 75264–75278. DOI: 10.1109/ACCESS.2020.2988510

Chiu, T. K. F., Meng, H., Chai, C.-S., King, I., Wong, S., & Yam, Y. (2022). Creation and Evaluation of a Pretertiary Artificial Intelligence (AI) Curriculum. *IEEE Transactions on Education, 65*(1), 30–39. DOI: 10.1109/TE.2021.3085878

D'Mello, S., & Graesser, A. (2012). Dynamics of affective states during complex learning. *Learning and Instruction, 22*(2), 145–157. DOI: 10.1016/j.learninstruc.2011.10.001

Dabbagh, N., & Kitsantas, A. (2012). Personal learning environments, social media, and self-regulated learning: A natural formula for connecting formal and informal learning. *The Internet and Higher Education, 15*(1), 3–8. DOI: 10.1016/j.iheduc.2011.06.002

Deterding, S., Dixon, D., Khaled, R., & Nacke, L. (2011). From game design elements to gamefulness: Defining gamification . *Proceedings of the 15th International Academic MindTrek Conference: Envisioning Future Media Environments*, 9–15. https://doi.org/DOI: 10.1145/2181037.2181040

Deterding, S., Sicart, M., Nacke, L., O'Hara, K., & Dixon, D. (2011). Gamification. Using game-design elements in non-gaming contexts. *CHI '11 Extended Abstracts on Human Factors in Computing Systems*, 2425–2428. https://doi.org/DOI: 10.1145/1979742.1979575

Dignath, C., & Veenman, M. V. J. (2021). The Role of Direct Strategy Instruction and Indirect Activation of Self-Regulated Learning—Evidence from Classroom Observation Studies. *Educational Psychology Review, 33*(2), 489–533. DOI: 10.1007/s10648-020-09534-0

Eissa M A (2015). The effectiveness of a self regulated learning-based training program on improving cognitive and metacognitive EFL reading comprehension of 9th graders with reading disabilities. Online Submission 4(3), 49–59.

Gabelica, C., den Bossche, P. V., Segers, M., & Gijselaers, W. (2012). Feedback, a powerful lever in teams: A review. *Educational Research Review, 7*(2), 123–144. DOI: 10.1016/j.edurev.2011.11.003

Grobgeld, E., Teichman, -Weinberg Ariela, Wasserman, E., & Ben, -Av Mercedes Barchilon. (2020). Role perception among faculty members at teacher education colleges. *Australian Journal of Teacher Education (Online), 41*(5), 78–98. DOI: 10.3316/informit.094262645820831

Hadwin, A. F., Järvelä, S., & Miller, M. (2018). Self-regulation, co-regulation, and shared regulation in collaborative learning environments,*Handbook of self-regulation of learning and performance*. 83–106.

Hamari, J., Koivisto, J., & Sarsa, H. (2014). Does gamification work? – A literature review of empirical studies on gamification. *2014 47th Hawaii International Conference on System Sciences*, 3025–3034. https://doi.org/DOI: 10.1109/HICSS.2014.377

Holmes, W., & Tuomi, I. (2022). State of the art and practice in AI in education. *European Journal of Education, 57*(4), 542–570. DOI: 10.1111/ejed.12533

Hu, S. (2024). The effect of artificial intelligence-assisted personalized learning on student learning outcomes: A meta-analysis based on 31 empirical research papers. *Science Insights Education Frontiers*, *24*(1), 3873–3894. DOI: 10.15354/sief.24.re395

Huang, X., & Dong, L., C, C. V., & D, P. K. (2022). Self-regulated learning and scientific research using artificial intelligence for higher education systems. [IJTHI]. *International Journal of Technology and Human Interaction*, *18*(7), 1–15. DOI: 10.4018/IJTHI.306226

Humble, N., & Mozelius, P. (2022). The threat, hype, and promise of artificial intelligence in education. *Discover Artificial Intelligence*, *2*(1), 22. DOI: 10.1007/s44163-022-00039-z

Jin, S.-H., Im, K., Yoo, M., Roll, I., & Seo, K. (2023). Supporting students' self-regulated learning in online learning using artificial intelligence applications. *International Journal of Educational Technology in Higher Education*, *20*(1), 37. DOI: 10.1186/s41239-023-00406-5

Kalogiannakis, M., Papadakis, S., & Zourmpakis, A.-I. (2021). Gamification in science education. A systematic review of the literature. *Education Sciences*, *11*(1), 1. Advance online publication. DOI: 10.3390/educsci11010022

Kardan, S., & Conati, C. (2015). Providing adaptive support in an interactive simulation for learning: An experimental evaluation. *Proceedings of the 33rd Annual ACM Conference on Human Factors in Computing Systems*, 3671–3680. https://doi.org/DOI: 10.1145/2702123.2702424

Kelly, K., & Heffernan, N. (2015). *Developing self-regulated learners through an intelligent tutoring system. Artificial Intelligence in Education*. Springer International Publishing., DOI: 10.1007/978-3-319-19773-9_128

Kizilcec, R. F., Piech, C., & Schneider, E. (2013). Deconstructing disengagement: Analyzing learner subpopulations in massive open online courses. *Proceedings of the Third International Conference on Learning Analytics and Knowledge*, 170–179. https://doi.org/DOI: 10.1145/2460296.2460330

Kong, S.-C., & Yang, Y. (2024). A human-centered learning and teaching framework using generative artificial intelligence for self-regulated learning development through domain knowledge learning in K–12 settings. *IEEE Transactions on Learning Technologies*, *17*, 1562–1573. DOI: 10.1109/TLT.2024.3392830

Kukulska-Hulme, A. (2021). Reflections on research questions in mobile assisted language learning. *Journal of China Computer-Assisted Language Learning*, *1*(1), 28–46. DOI: 10.1515/jccall-2021-2002

Lin, C.-C., Huang, A. Y. Q., & Lu, O. H. T. (2023). Artificial intelligence in intelligent tutoring systems toward sustainable education: A systematic review. *Smart Learning Environments*, *10*(1), 41. DOI: 10.1186/s40561-023-00260-y

Luckin, R., & Holmes, W. (2016). Intelligence unleashed: An argument for AI in education. *UCL Knowledge Lab: London, UK.* https://www.pearson.com/content/dam/corporate/global/pearson-dot-com/files/innovation/Intelligence-Unleashed-Publication.pdf

Lukes, L. A., Jones, Jason P., & and McConnell, D. A. (2020). Self-regulated learning: Overview and potential future directions in geoscience. *Journal of Geoscience Education*, *69*(1), 14–26. DOI: 10.1080/10899995.2020.1820828

Maag Merki, K., Wullschleger, A., & Rechsteiner, B. (2023). Adapting routines in schools when facing challenging situations: Extending previous theories on routines by considering theories on self-regulated and collectively regulated learning. *Journal of Educational Change*, *24*(3), 583–604. DOI: 10.1007/s10833-022-09459-1 PMID: 37560443

Mahmoud, C. F., & Sørensen, J. T. (2024). Artificial intelligence in personalized learning with a focus on current developments and future prospects. *Research and Advances in Education, 3*(8), Article 8.

Makwana, V. (2025). A comparative analysis of AI-powered and teacher-led feedback: Investigating student perceptions and writing performance. *Journal of English Language Teaching*, *67*(1), 1.

McNamara, D. S. (2007). *Reading comprehension strategies: Theories, interventions, and technologies.* Psychology Press.

Miller, T. W., & Miller, J. M. (2001). Educational leadership in the new millennium: A vision for 2020. *International Journal of Leadership in Education.* https://www.tandfonline.com/doi/abs/10.1080/13603120120806

Mohebbi, A. (2025). Enabling learner independence and self-regulation in language education using AI tools: A systematic review. *Cogent Education*, *12*(1), 2433814. DOI: 10.1080/2331186X.2024.2433814

Muchtar N. (2017). *An overview of mobile-assisted language learning.* 170–174. https://doi.org/DOI: 10.2991/iconelt-17.2018.38

Nguyen A., Ilesanmi F., Dang B., Vuorenmaa E., J&#228, rvel&#228, & Sanna. (2024). Hybrid intelligence in academic writing: Examining self-regulated learning patterns in an AI-assisted writing task. *HHAI 2024: Hybrid Human AI Systems for the Social Good*, 241–254. IOS Press. https://doi.org/DOI: 10.3233/FAIA240198

Nur Fitria, T. (2021). *Artificial intelligence (AI) in education: Using AI tools for teaching and learning process.*

Ouyang, F., Zheng, L., & Jiao, P. (2022). Artificial intelligence in online higher education: A systematic review of empirical research from 2011 to 2020. *Education and Information Technologies, 27*(6), 7893–7925. DOI: 10.1007/s10639-022-10925-9

Pan, M., Guo, K., & Lai, C. (2024). Using artificial intelligence chatbots to support English-as-a-foreign language students' self-regulated reading. *RELC Journal, 00336882241264030*. Advance online publication. DOI: 10.1177/00336882241264030

Panadero, E. (2017). A review of self-regulated learning: Six models and four directions for research. *Frontiers in Psychology, 8*. Advance online publication. DOI: 10.3389/fpsyg.2017.00422 PMID: 28503157

Paris, S. G., Lipson, M. Y., & Wixson, K. K. (1983). Becoming a strategic reader. *Contemporary Educational Psychology, 8*(3), 293–316. DOI: 10.1016/0361-476X(83)90018-8

Peláez-Sánchez, I. C., & Velásquez-Durán, A. (2023). The impact of duolingo in developing students' linguistic competence: An aspect of communicative language competences. *Educação e Pesquisa, 49*, e252467. DOI: 10.1590/S1678-4634202349252467eng

Roll, I., & Wylie, R. (2016). Evolution and revolution in artificial intelligence in education. *International Journal of Artificial Intelligence in Education, 26*(2), 582–599. DOI: 10.1007/s40593-016-0110-3

Safsouf, Y., & Mouachi, R. (2024). Empowering learners: GenIA and their impact on self-regulated learning. *ITM Web of Conferences, 69*, 01004. https://doi.org/DOI: 10.1051/itmconf/20246901004

Saint, J., Whitelock-Wainwright, A., Gašević, D., & Pardo, A. (2020). Trace-SRL: A framework for analysis of microlevel processes of self-regulated learning from trace data. *IEEE Transactions on Learning Technologies, 13*(4), 861–877. DOI: 10.1109/TLT.2020.3027496

Sangsawang, T. (2020). An instructional design for online learning in vocational education according to a self-regulated learning framework for problem solving during the CoViD-19 crisis. *Indonesian Journal of Science and Technology, 5*(2), 2.

Schunk, D. H., & Zimmerman, B. (2011). *Handbook of self-regulation of learning and performance*. Taylor & Francis.

Schunk, D. H., & Zimmerman, B. J. (2012). *Motivation and self-regulated learning: Theory, research, and applications*. Routledge.

Schunk, D. H., & Zimmerman, B. J. (2023). *Self-regulation of learning and performance: Issues and educational applications*. Taylor & Francis.

Shafiee Rad, H. (2025). Reinforcing L2 reading comprehension through artificial intelligence intervention: Refining engagement to foster self-regulated learning. *Smart Learning Environments*, *12*(1), 23. DOI: 10.1186/s40561-025-00377-2

Sharma, K., Nguyen, A., & Hong, Y. (2024). Self-regulation and shared regulation in collaborative learning in adaptive digital learning environments: A systematic review of empirical studies. *British Journal of Educational Technology*, *55*(4), 1398–1436. DOI: 10.1111/bjet.13459

Shoaib, M., Sayed, N., Singh, J., Shafi, J., Khan, S., & Ali, F. (2024). AI student success predictor: Enhancing personalized learning in campus management systems. *Computers in Human Behavior*, *158*, 108301. DOI: 10.1016/j.chb.2024.108301

Sutherland, R., & Fischer, F. (2014). Future learning spaces: Design, collaboration, knowledge, assessment, teachers, technology and the radical past. *Technology, Pedagogy and Education*, *23*(1), 1–5. DOI: 10.1080/1475939X.2013.870107

Teng, L. S. (2022). *Self-regulated learning and second language writing: Fostering strategic language learners*. Springer Nature.

Urbina, S., Villatoro, S., & Salinas, J. (2021). Self-regulated learning and technology-enhanced learning environments in higher education: A scoping review. *Sustainability*, *13*(13), 13. Advance online publication. DOI: 10.3390/su13137281

Vekkot, S., Gupta, D., Zakariah, M., & Alotaibi, Y. A. (2020). Emotional voice conversion using a hybrid framework with speaker-adaptive DNN and particle-swarm-optimized neural network. *IEEE Access : Practical Innovations, Open Solutions*, *8*, 74627–74647. DOI: 10.1109/ACCESS.2020.2988781

Wei, L. (2023). Artificial intelligence in language instruction: Impact on English learning achievement, L2 motivation, and self-regulated learning. *Frontiers in Psychology*, *14*. Advance online publication. DOI: 10.3389/fpsyg.2023.1261955 PMID: 38023040

Xia, Q., Chiu, T. K. F., & Chai, C. S. (2023). The moderating effects of gender and need satisfaction on self-regulated learning through artificial intelligence (AI). *Education and Information Technologies*, *28*(7), 8691–8713. DOI: 10.1007/s10639-022-11547-x

Xia, Q., Chiu, T. K. F., Chai, C. S., & Xie, K. (2023). The mediating effects of needs satisfaction on the relationships between prior knowledge and self-regulated learning through artificial intelligence chatbot. *British Journal of Educational Technology, 54*(4), 967–986. DOI: 10.1111/bjet.13305

Yildirim-Erbasli, S. N., Gorgun, G., Bulut, O., Yildirim-Erbasli, S. N., Gorgun, G., & Bulut, O. (2023). *Enhancing self-regulated learning with artificial intelligence-powered learning analytics*.66-4.Ch004; IGI Global Scientific Publishing. https://doi.org/DOI: 10.4018/979-8-3693-0066-4.ch004

Zawacki-Richter, O., Marín, V. I., Bond, M., & Gouverneur, F. (2019). Systematic review of research on artificial intelligence applications in higher education – where are the educators? *International Journal of Educational Technology in Higher Education, 16*(1), 39. DOI: 10.1186/s41239-019-0171-0

Zimmerman, B. J. (2009). Self-regulation: Where metacognition and motivation intersect. *In Handbook of metacognition in education*, 311–328.

Zimmerman, B. J. (2015). Self-regulated learning: Theories, measures, and outcomes. *International Encyclopedia of the Social & Behavioral Sciences*, 541–546. https://doi.org/DOI: 10.1016/b978-0-08-097086-8.26060-1

Zimmerman. (2002). *Becoming a self-regulated learner: An overview: Theory into practice: Vol 41, no 2*. https://www.tandfonline.com/doi/abs/10.1207/s15430421tip4102_2

Chapter 10
Instructional Affordances of Mobile Technologies for Technical Vocabulary Acquisition:
A Pedagogical Framework

Feng Tian
https://orcid.org/0009-0006-1905-3921
Centre for Instructional Technology and Multimedia, Universiti Sains Malaysia, Malaysia

Irfan Naufal Umar
Centre for Instructional Technology and Multimedia, Universiti Sains Malaysia, Malaysia

ABSTRACT

As disciplinary literacy grows across academic and professional domains, technical vocabulary acquisition presents a major challenge in foreign languages for specific purposes (FLSP) instruction. Technical vocabulary poses particular learning challenges due to its strong disciplinary specificity, and limited occurrence in natural language input. Mobile-Assisted Language Learning (MALL) offers flexible, multimodal, and personalized support, yet how to translate its potential into effective instructional design remains underexplored. This study, based on established theories, proposes a pedagogical framework that integrates five key instructional affordances: contextualization, multimodal input, repetition, learner self-regulation, and motivational support. The framework bridges technology and pedagogy, offering design pathways for FLSP instructors and platform developers to optimize technical vocabulary learning in mobile environments.

DOI: 10.4018/979-8-3373-7508-3.ch010

1. INTRODUCTION

In the context of increasing globalization and professional specialization, the demand for languages for specific purposes has grown significantly, particularly in academic and occupational language learning contexts. Technical vocabulary, defied as domain-specific lexical items with high semantic density and contextual dependency, plays a crucial role in professional communication but is often underrepresented in general language instruction. Unlike general vocabulary, technical terms are not easily acquired through incidental learning and typically require focused instruction and repeated exposure. Traditional approaches in foreign languages for specific purposes (FLSP) instruction, such as rote memorization of word lists, definitional teaching, and paper-based assessments, have been criticized for their limited capacity to accommodate individual learner needs, sustain motivation, or address cognitive overload. These limitations often result in low transferability and poor long-term retention of vocabulary. Consequently, the call for more flexible, interactive, and learner-centered vocabulary instruction has gained traction in recent FLPS pedagogy.

Mobile-Assisted Language Learning (MALL) has emerged as a promising solution to the challenges of technical vocabulary instruction. Through its affordance such as accessibility at any time and in any place, multimodal content delivery and rich interactive features, mobile learning environments offer contextualized, personalized and motivating experiences that can support vocabulary development. Recent studies have demonstrated the effectiveness of MALL in general vocabulary acquisition by improving motivation, retention, and adaptability to diverse learning paces and preferences. Features such as multimodal input, immediate feedback, and the pacing controlled by learners have been widely implemented in both classroom and extracurricular vocabulary learning, demonstrating the pedagogical potential of mobile technologies. Despite growing interest in the application of MALL to FLSP, recent studies have highlighted its insufficient focus on long-term vocabulary retention and productive use. For instance, many existing studies emphasized receptive knowledge or short-term effects (Li & Hafner, 2022), while the role of MALL in supporting durable acquisition and transferability of technical terms remains underexplored (Koleini et al., 2024; Yüksel et al., 2022). These findings emphasize the urgent need for instructional frameworks that systematically address retention and contextual application of technical vocabulary in complex domains such as chemistry, engineering, etc. (Xodabande et al., 2024). Therefore, the systematic application of MALL in the teaching of technical vocabulary remains underdeveloped, especially at the level of instructional design. Given the highly specific and context-bound nature of technical terms, their acquisition requires carefully structured input, task-based learning, and efficient management of cognitive load. This highlights the need to explore how mobile technologies can be pedagogically leveraged to support the specialized demands of technical vocabulary acquisition.

This study aims to construct a pedagogical framework that integrates both theoretical and practical perspectives by examining how hey instructional affordances of mobile technologies can facilitate technical vocabulary acquisition. Specifically, the framework focuses on five core affordances: contextualization, learner autonomy, multimodal presentation, spaced repetition and gamification. These affordances are mapped onto established learning theories, including the Cognitive Theory of Multimedia Learning (CTML), Cognitive Load Theory (CLT), and Nation's vocabulary teaching principles. Based on this foundation, the study offers actionable strategies and a conceptual model for optimizing technical vocabulary instruction in FLSP contexts. The main objectives of this paper are threefold: (1) it proposes a theoretical framework that focuses on instructional affordances to address the current gaps in instructional design for mobile-assisted technical vocabulary teaching; (2) it synthesizes multiple pedagogical theories to provide a coherent rational for vocabulary instruction supported by mobile technologies; (3) it offers practice-oriented recommendations based on case analysis, aiming to support both FLSP educators and educational technology developers in creating effective vocabulary learning solutions. This study holds both theoretical and practical significance. Theoretically, it integrates multiple cognitive and motivational learning theories with Nation's pedagogical principles to construct a systematic instructional framework tailored for technical vocabulary acquisition. Practically, it addresses a pressing pedagogical need in FLSP by outlining how mobile technologies can be effectively used to scaffold vocabulary input, repetition, autonomy, and motivation. By aligning mobile affordances with instructional design elements, this research provides actionable insights for curriculum developers, language teachers, and educational technology designers aiming to enhance domain-specific vocabulary teaching in diverse and dynamic learning settings.

This study is structured into five main sections. The second section reviews the key instructional theories that form the theoretical foundation of this study, analyzes the instructional design requirements for technical vocabulary acquisition, and formulates the corresponding research questions. The third section, based on theoretical integration and identified design needs, develops the instructional framework for technical vocabulary acquisition in mobile learning environments. The fourth section elaborates on the instructional implementation pathways and application value of the framework, examining its pedagogical innovations and practical implications from the perspectives of learners, instructors, and system developers. Finally, the last part concludes the overall contributions of this study, addresses its limitations, and outlines possible directions for future research.

2. LITERATURE REVIEW CHALLENGES

This section reviews the theoretical foundations that inform the present study. It encompasses five interrelated dimensions: instructional affordances, technical vocabulary teaching principles, CTML, CLT and relevant insights from motivation theory, particularly SDT in relation to digital game-based learning (DGBL). The review concludes with a synthesis of gaps in existing literature on mobile-assisted technical vocabulary instruction.

2.1 Instructional Affordances of Mobile Technologies

The concept of "affordance" was originally introduced by Gibson (1966) in ecological psychology to refer to the actionable possibilities a particular environment offers to an individual. In educational contexts, affordances refer to what a tool, environment, or system makes possible or supports for learners in terms of interaction and learning. Norman (1999)later refined this concept to distinguish between real and perceived affordances: the former is based on the actual functional existence, while the latter is subjectively inferred by the user based on interface cues. In the field of digital education, Conole & Dyke (2004) extended the concept of affordances by mapping the specific affordances of ICT tools to pedagogical functions such as accessibility, immediacy, adaptability, and collaboration. Instructional affordances thus refer to the properties of a learning technology that enable or constrain certain types of learning activities, either by design or by user appropriation. These affordances are not fixed but emerge through the interaction between learners, teachers, and technologies within a given instructional setting.

Van Lier (2004) conceptualized affordances in language learning as opportunities for action that emerge through meaningful interaction with the environment, rather than through passive exposure. He argued that language development requires learners to engage actively with contextual cues and communicative tasks. For instance, merely listening to an unfamiliar language on the radio does not enable one to speak it fluently. In Mobile-Assisted Language Learning (MALL), affordances are particularly critical due to the portable, personal, and context-aware nature of mobile devices. Research has consistently identified a core set of affordances associated with MALL, including contextualization, ubiquitous accessibility, multimodal content delivery, immediate feedback, and game mechanics (Hwang et al., 2024).

The pedagogical value of these affordances lies in their alignment with established principles of multimedia and language learning. For example, multimodal input supports dual channel processing (Mayer, 2014), as demonstrated in studies by Teng (2023), who found that combining images, text, and audio in mobile vocabulary apps significantly improved learners' retention and engagement. Spaced repetition, another key principle of language learning, has been shown to enhance long-term memory consolidation in mobile learning environments (R. Zhang et al., 2022), especially when integrated with adaptive learning system. Furthermore, mobile leaning supports constructivist principles by situating vocabulary learning in authentic environments. For instant, Vargo et al. (2024) reported that learners who engaged in context-based vocabulary tasks were more likely to use and retain target terms meaningfully.

Despite these potentials, the pedagogical translation of MALL affordances into systematic vocabulary learning strategies remains underexplored. Especially for technical vocabulary, which requires higher semantic precision, depth of understanding, and domain specificity, affordances need to be purposefully orchestrated rather than passively embedded. This study therefore positions instructional affordances not simply as features of technology, but as central design considerations for mobile-based vocabulary instruction.

2.2 Technical Vocabulary Instruction: Issues and Insights from the Four Strands

To further clarify the potential of mobile technologies in the context of Foreign Languages for Specific Purposes (FLSP), this section adopts a theoretical perspective of vocabulary instruction to explore the roles and challenges of technical vocabulary instruction. The discussion focuses on Nation's (2007) Four Strands model as a foundational framework and analyzes current pedagogical limitations and areas for improvement.

Nation's (2007) Four Strands model provides a theoretical foundation for technical vocabulary instruction. The model proposes that vocabulary learning should be balanced across four areas:

(1) **Meaning-focused input**, such as exposure to authentic language materials through reading and listening;
(2) **Meaning-focused output**, where learners actively use new vocabulary in speaking and writing;
(3) **Language-focused learning**, including explicit instruction, morphological analysis, and word meaning explanation; and
(4) **Fluency development**, which aims to promote automaticity and fluent use of familiar vocabulary through repeated practice.

This model emphasizes integrating vocabulary learning into communicative language activities, rather than treating vocabulary as isolated units of study. It is particularly applicable to technical vocabulary, which requires repeated exposure, diverse usage, and contextual transfer. The model thus offers a theoretical foundation for understanding the features and challenges of vocabulary acquisition in FLSP contexts.

Unlike general foreign language education, FLSP courses place a strong focus on domain-specific vocabulary that appears frequently in a particular field but rarely in everyday communication. Such a specialized register demands highly precise and efficient instructional approaches. Prior research has shown that learners often struggle with technical vocabulary due to its abstractness, lexical density, and discipline-specific usage (Alharbi, 2024). Moreover, technical vocabulary is often embedded in complex syntactic structures or discipline-specific discourse genres (Coxhead, 2024). Instruction in FLSP must therefore not only address vocabulary items themselves but also help learners understand their rhetorical and pragmatic functions in academic and professional texts (Chirobocea, 2018). Task-based learning, corpus-informed teaching, and the use of authentic materials are widely regarded as effective strategies. These approaches align closely with the meaning-focused input and output strands in Nation's model, emphasizing vocabulary use in authentic contexts.

However, many FLSP vocabulary programs remain limited in scope. Instruction is still frequently dominated by traditional methods such as static word lists, direct translations, and definitional explanations that fail to promote deep processing (Magfirah et al., 2022). Learners are rarely provided with opportunities to engage with new terms in authentic, communicative contexts. Consequently, these approaches tend to produce surface-level memorization without ensuring long-term retention or transferable use. Gómez-Ortiz et al. (2023) found that learners who only encountered technical terms passively through reading performed worse in retention and transfer than those engaged in productive tasks such as writing and speaking.

In recent years, several empirical studies have proposed more effective strategies. Udaya (2022) emphasizes the importance of semantic elaboration to deepen learners' understanding of complex vocabulary. Kohnke & Ting, (2021) demonstrated that mobile vocabulary apps integrating images, videos, and discipline-specific examples can significantly improve learners' word comprehension and usage. Teng & Xu (2025) showed that spaced repetition via mobile devices can substantially enhance long-term retention. However, these strategies have not been widely adopted in current FLSP classrooms due to limited technological proficiency among instructors, lack of digital resources, and rigid curriculum structures (Miroshnychenko, 2024). In sum, there is a pressing need for a theoretically grounded and practically operable instructional framework that addresses the complexity of input, abstractness of concepts, and lack of output opportunities in technical vocabulary learning. Against this backdrop, Mobile-Assisted Language Learning (MALL) offers a promising direction for improving technical vocabulary instruction, leveraging features such as multimodal presentation, personalized delivery, and integration with authentic tasks (Tavassoli & Beyranvand, 2023).

2.3 Theoretical Foundations Supporting Instructional Design

The acquisition of technical vocabulary in FLSP instruction involves multiple cognitive and motivational challenges, including the abstract nature of word comprehension, the regulation of cognitive processing load, and the maintenance of learning motivation. To systematically support the construction and subsequent analysis of the instructional framework for technical vocabulary learning, this study integrates three core theoretical perspectives based on existing research: the Cognitive Theory of Multimedia Learning (CTML), Cognitive Load Theory (CLT), and Self-Determination Theory (SDT), which collectively provide theoretical support for the proposed instructional design.

The Cognitive Theory of Multimedia Learning (Mayer, 2005), based on the core assumptions of dual channel processing, limited cognitive capacity, and active processing, emphasizes that learning outcomes depend on learners' effective integration of information through both visual and auditory channels. Technical vocabulary is often highly discipline-specific, with abstract meanings and complex conceptual structures that create comprehension difficulties when presented solely in textual form (Alharbi, 2024). Existing research has demonstrated that multimodal input combining textual definition, visual representations, and auditory pronunciations facilitates learners' initial understanding and memory retention of vocabulary (Zhang, 2025; Xing & Zhang, 2025). In multimedia instructional design, organizing information presentation in a coherent sequence, highlighting key information, and minimizing irrelevant content help learners focus attention and efficiently process the essential knowledge conveyed by technical vocabulary (Mayer, 2014). The integration of multimodal information in technical vocabulary learning not only lowers cognitive barriers for novice learners when processing abstract terminology but also supports the connection between new and existing knowledge, thus laying a foundation for long-term retention and transfer.

Cognitive Load Theory (CLT) (Sweller, 1994; Sweller et al., 2019), which focuses on learners' limited processing resources during learning, emphasizes that instructional design should balance intrinsic load, extraneous load, and germane load. Technical vocabulary, characterized by low familiarity, semantic complexity, and strong disciplinary specificity, often imposes a high intrinsic load on learners. Without appropriate sequencing of information input and task organization, extraneous load may easily accumulate, resulting in processing difficulties. Empirical studies have demonstrated that segmenting tasks, introducing vocabulary items in small, thematically grouped sets, repeated exposure across modules, and contextualized practice tasks can help mitigate cumulative load and promote deeper semantic processing (Lai et al., 2025; D. Liu, 2024). Additionally, spaced repetition has been widely recognized as an effective approach to strengthen long-term retention by distributing review sessions and minimizing forgetting (Çakmak et al., 2021). Recent research on digital vocabulary learning tools further supports these principles. For example, (Aprizal & Wachyudi, 2024) found that applications such as Memrise, which incorporate modular vocabulary presentation combined with spaced repetition and retrieval practice, significantly reduce extraneous cognitive load while enhancing learners' long-term retention of technical vocabulary. Thus, CLT offers essential theoretical guidance for structuring information delivery and managing task complexity in technical acquisition, ensuring that instructional activities progress within learners' cognitive capacity while facilitating both retention and transfer.

Finally, Self-Determination Theory (SDT) (Ryan & Deci, 2000; Ryan & Deci, 2020) focuses on the mechanisms of motivation maintenance, playing a crucial role in the long-term acquisition of technical vocabulary. Given the extended learning cycles, high difficulty levels, and strong disciplinary specificity involved in technical vocabulary learning, learners are particularly susceptible to motivational fluctuations (Ivan & Krissh, 2021). According to SDT, when learning environments fulfill learners' needs for autonomy, competence, and relatedness, intrinsic motivation is more easily activated and sustained. Previous studies has shown that flexible learning arrangement, clear feedback, and the accumulation of task achievement contribute to sustained learner engagement (Ahmad et al., 2019; Wang et al., 2025). Moreover, in technology-enhanced learning environments, the integration of gamification elements such as points, badges, and leaderboards has been found to increase learning enjoyment and strengthen learners' sese of accomplishment, thereby further promoting persistent engagement in technical vocabulary learning tasks (Arif, 2025). In mobile learning contexts in particular, features that allow learners to self-regulate their learning pace, receive immediate feedback, and obtain positive reinforcement throughout task progression further support the long-term and systematic process of technical vocabulary acquisition. SDT thus offers a systematic psychological framework for maintaining motivation, ensuring that successful vocabulary learning depends on cognitive processing efficiency as well as on sustained learner engagement.

This study adopts CTML, CLT, SDT and Nation's Four Strands model as its core theoretical foundation, based on the following rationale. First, both CTML and CLT focus on how information is processed through visual and auditory channels, and how the organization of learning tasks influences the distribution of cognitive resources and the management of cognitive load. These perspectives provide theoretical support for the design of multimodal input and modular task organization in this study. Second, SDT, as classical theory of motivation, highlights the importance of satisfying three basic psychological needs (autonomy, competence, and relatedness) for fostering and sustaining intrinsic motivation. This framework is particularly relevant for addressing motivational challenges in technical vocabulary learning and supports the design of gamification mechanisms and learner self-regulation strategies. Finally, Nation's Four Strands model advocates for a balanced approach to vocabulary learning across meaning-focused input, meaning-focused output, form-focused instruction, and fluency development. It emphasizes a structured correspondence between instructional goals and learning activities, which informs the operational design of instructional sequences in this framework. Overall, CTML, CLT, and SDT collectively provide a comprehensive cognitive and psychological foundation for supporting technical vocabulary acquisition, addressing information processing, task organization, and motivational regulation, respectively. The integration of these four theoretical perspectives establishes a systematic foundation that spans cognitive, instructional and motivational dimensions, aligning closely with the overall design logic of the proposed instructional framework and its implementation pathways.

2.4 Research Gap and Study Purpose

In summary, previous research on technical vocabulary acquisition has provided valuable foundations across pedagogical principles, empirical investigations, and theoretical support. Nation's (2007) Four Strands model offers a fundamental framework for vocabulary instruction, while numerous applied studies have achieved promising results in areas such as task organization, spaced repetition, multimodal input, and gamification. However, several gaps remain in the current body of research.

First, most existing frameworks focus on general vocabulary learning or isolated instructional strategies, lacking systematic integration that addresses the specific complexities of technical vocabulary. Second, while preliminary efforts have explored cognitive load regulation, information presentation, and task organization, a coherent instructional design logic has yet to be established. Third, regarding motivational support, current gamification practices largely emphasized surface incentives, with limited integration of motivation internalization mechanisms grounded in SDT. Particularly in mobile learning contexts, technical vocabulary acquisition involves a long-term interplay between cognitive processing and motivational regulation, yet existing research has not established a comprehensive instructional framework that systematically addresses this interplay.

In response to these gaps, this study seeks to answer the following research questions:

RQ1: What are the key instructional design requirements for technical vocabulary acquisition in mobile learning contexts?

RQ2: How can the proposed framework be operationalized into practical design pathways and implementation strategies for mobile-assisted technical vocabulary learning?

3. FRAMEWORK CONSTRUCTION FOR TECHNICAL VOCABULARY LEARNING

In response to the research questions and literature gaps identified in the previous sections, this section proposes an instructional framework for technical vocabulary learning in mobile-assisted learning environments. First, the overall framework logic and theoretical foundations are outlines; next, the five core instructional affordances are elaborated in detail; and finally, the integrated model and design rationale of the framework are presented.

3.1 Framework Overview

Building upon the research questions identified in last section, this study proposes a systematic instructional framework for technical vocabulary acquisition in mobile-assisted learning environments, integrating cognitive processing, cognitive load regulation, and motivational support mechanisms. The framework is grounded in the synthesis of Four Strands of Nation, CTML, CLT, and SDT, aiming to address the multifaceted cognitive and motivational challenges inherent in technical vocabulary learning.

In developing the framework, this study adopts instructional affordances as the central unit for analysis and design. Instructional affordances emphasize the potential of instructional resources, tasks, and contexts to support cognitive processing and motivational engagement, providing a practical mechanism to translate theoretical principles into specific instructional design strategies. Through an extensive review of existing literature and empirical findings, five core instructional affordances have been identified across the dimensions of information input, task organization, and motivation regulation, forming the primary structure of the proposed framework. In mobile learning contexts, learners are increasingly faced with fragmented information presentation, heightened self-regulation demands, and extended cycles of motivation maintenance. Accordingly, this framework integrates multimodal information integration design, cognitive load management, learner autonomy, and sustained motivational support. Through this combination, it aims to promote efficient comprehension of technical terms, enhance long-term retention, and support the flexible transfer of vocabulary knowledge into professional and disciplinary contexts.

Specifically, the framework proposes five key instructional affordances: contextualization, multimodal presentation, repetition, learner autonomy and regulation, and gamification-based motivation support. The following sections elaborate on the design logic and instructional functions of each of these affordances.

3.2 Core Instructional Affordance

3.2.1 Contextualization

The core of contextualization lies in designing learning activities that are closely integrated with professional tasks and disciplinary contexts, enabling learners to understand and master the meanings, usages, and functions of technical vocabulary as they complete specific tasks. This approach enhances both the depth of semantic processing and the development of practical application skills.

Specifically, contextualization can be implemented through various instructional strategies: (1) incorporating target vocabulary into authentic or simulated specific task based on disciplines, allowing learners to encounter and use new terms naturally while performing tasks; (2) utilizing authentic professional texts, such as reports, manuals, laboratory records, and standardized documents, to help learners understand the usage patterns and contextual dependencies of technical terms within professional discourse; and (3) designing virtual experiments, role-playing scenarios, and interactive simulations to strengthen learners' fluency in applying vocabulary within professional practices and occupational communication contexts. This approach has been empirically shown to facilitate the development of learners' pragmatic competence in using technical vocabulary in professional contexts (Koleini et al., 2024; Saeedi & Najjarpour, 2025).

In mobile learning environment, contextualization needs to be integrated with flexible pacing and modular task design. Fragmented task organization and adjustable learning schedules have been recognized as important strategies for managing cognitive load and facilitating task progression in mobile learning contexts (She et al., 2024). Accordingly, complex professional tasks can be decomposed into a series of sequential learning units, allowing learners to manage their study schedules flexibly within fragmented timeframes. Each learning unit centers on a specific context, ensuring that target vocabulary is repeatedly encountered and applied across diverse application scenarios, thereby gradually strengthening learners' contextual awareness and pragmatic use of vocabulary through task-based practice. Furthermore, within mobile learning environments, the technological affordances of multimedia devices enable contextual information to be presented in various formats, enhancing the authenticity of task scenarios and increasing learner engagement. The specific presentation techniques for these contextual inputs will be discussed in detail in the following section on multimodal presentation.

3.2.2 Multimodal Presentation

As the second instructional affordance in this framework, multimodal presentation aims to optimize the cognitive processing of technical vocabulary by integrating information across multiple sensory channels. According to the CTML, learning outcomes depend on learners' ability to effectively integrate input from both visual and auditory channels. When technical vocabulary is presented solely in text form, learners may experience cognitive overload while processing abstract concepts and specialized terminology, which can negatively affect processing efficiency and retention. Multimodal input, by simultaneously activating multiple sensory channels, helps alleviate the strain on any single channel, thereby enhancing semantic processing depth and improving long-term memory retention (Wilson, 2024; Xing & Zhang, 2025).

In the design of technical vocabulary instruction, multimodal input may involve several integrated formats: (1) combining textual definitions with visual diagrams to help learners understand the structure and functional features of the target terms through visual representations; (2) presenting written input alongside synchronized audio pronunciation to strengthen learners' phonological recognition and pronunciation memory; (3) incorporating flowcharts, video demonstrations, and process animations to support learners in grasping the usage contexts of technical terms within complex disciplinary procedures or operational steps; and (4) using interactive annotations and immediate feedback mechanisms to reinforce learners' awareness of proper vocabulary usage and facilitate immediate error correction.

Leveraging the multimedia affordances of mobile platforms, multimodal input can deliver information efficiently and support cognitive integration within limited screen space and fragmented study time. By embedding images, audio, aminations, and interactive feedback into learning modules, learners can receive comprehensive, multi-channel input even within brief learning sessions, thereby reducing the burden on any single modality and enhancing initial comprehension efficiency (Zhang, 2025). In addition, the repeatable access to multimodal resources allows learners to flexibly revisit different formats during review and consolidation, further strengthening information integration and supporting long-term retention (Ed-Dali, 2024).

3.2.3 Repetition

With the context of technical vocabulary learning, a single exposure is often insufficient to establish stable retention and flexible application. As the third instructional affordance in this framework, repetition aims to reinforce long-term consolidation and deepen semantic processing by strategically organizing repeated exposure and distributed encounters with target vocabulary items (Seibert Hanson & Brown, 2020). According to CLT, appropriately controlling repetition frequency and task intervals helps maximize cognitive processing efficiency without imposing excessive extraneous load (Bahari, 2023). Spaced repetition has been widely demonstrated to extend the forgetting curve and strengthen both retention and transfer by introducing delayed review opportunities and multiple retrieval cycles (Çakmak et al., 2021; Kim & Webb, 2022).

In instructional practice, repetition can be implemented through the following design strategies: (1) presenting target vocabulary multiple times across different contextualized uses within a single task sequence to enhance semantic depth during initial learning; (2) reintroducing vocabulary items in different task modules and application contexts to support cumulative development of pragmatic transfer; (3) dynamically adjusting review internals and vocabulary priority based on learning progress and memory retention curves; and (4) leveraging system generated performance data to automatically personalize review frequency and optimize learning efficiency.

3.2.4 Learner Autonomy and Regulation

As the fourth instructional affordance in this framework, learner autonomy and task management refer to support efficient progress in technical vocabulary learning and review by optimizing learning paths and task organization within flexible learning environments. Throughout the extended learning process, learners must continuously integrate newly acquired and previously learned vocabulary, dynamically adjust review priorities, and allocate learning resources according to their mastery levels. Effective task management helps learners maintain consistent learning rhythms and goal attainment while controlling cognitive load (Fitrianto et al., 2024).

In instructional design, learner autonomy and task management can be implemented through the following strategies:

(1) Personalized learning path generation: the system dynamically recommends appropriate task organizations based on learners' diagnostic assessments, historical performance, and current mastery levels to balance knowledge progression and task complexity.
(2) Real-time progress visualization: dashboards display learners' progress, vocabulary mastery curves, and review schedules, allowing learners to monitor their current learning status and task distribution clearly.

(3) Dynamic task prioritization: the system intelligently ranks review tasks by analyzing forgetting curves, error patterns, and task completion frequencies to optimize resource allocation.

Under these conditions, learner autonomy and task management mechanisms can be effectively integrated with fragmented learning rhythms. In short, the system leverages dynamic notifications, personalized task reminders, and progress feedback to help learners efficiently allocate tasks within limited study periods and sustain long-term progress in technical vocabulary acquisition.

3.2.5 Gamification-Based Motivation Support

As the fifth instructional affordance in this framework, gamification-based motivation support tends to systematically sustain learner motivation and promote motivation internalization by embedding appropriate gamified elements and dynamic incentive mechanisms. Previous research has shown that well-designed gamification can enhance learner engagement and sustained motivation by increasing learning enjoyment, providing immediate achievement experiences, and strengthening the sense of feedback control (Ghofur et al., 2023; Li et al., 2024; Liu, 2024).

During the design process, gamification-based motivation support can be implemented through the following strategies:

(1) Point and reward: upon task completion, the system immediately awards points, experience levels, or virtual rewards, allowing learners to accumulate incremental achievements that drive stage-based goal progression while embedding immediate feedback into the learning process.
(2) Achievement: vocabulary mastery levels, skill badges, and learning milestones are established to help learners visualize their growth trajectories throughout the learning pathway, thereby strengthening internal control and progressive learning cognition.
(3) Leaderboard and peer comparison: task completion leaderboards, consecutive learning streaks, and vocabulary size rankings are introduced to foster healthy competition and peer reference, enhancing learner participation, social motivation, and task persistence.
(4) Instant feedback and dynamic positive reinforcement: during task execution, the system synchronously presents learners' progress, accuracy rates, vocabulary growth, and point accumulation, forming a continuous positive feedback loop that reinforces learners' perceived progress, control, and sustained engagement.

Leveraging the flexible nature of mobile learning, gamification mechanisms can be seamlessly integrated into learners' daily study routines. Mobile platforms deliver real-time task updates, achievement reminders, and synchronized point progression, enabling learners to continuously accumulate positive learning experiences in fragmented study sessions, alleviate learning fatigue, and maintain stable motivation and rhythm throughout the long-term process of technical vocabulary acquisition.

3.3 Integrated Instructional Framework Model

Building on the design foundations established in the previous sections, this study integrates the Cognitive Theory of Multimedia Learning (CTML), Cognitive Load Theory (CLT), Self-Determination Theory (SDT), and Nation's (2007) Four Strands model of vocabulary instruction to propose a systematic instructional framework for technical vocabulary acquisition in mobile learning environments, as illustrated in Figure 1.1. The framework is organized around five core instructional affordances: contextualized task design, multimodal input, repetition-based learning arrangements, learner self-regulation, and gamified motivational support. These give affordances work in coordination across input organization, cognitive processing optimization, review scheduling, learning pace regulation, and motivation maintenance, forming a cohesive instructional sequence. Together, they address they key challenges of technical vocabulary learning, including high cognitive load, complex task structure, and difficulty sustaining motivation.

Figure 1. Integrated Instructional Framework for Technical Vocabulary Acquisition in Mobile Learning Contexts

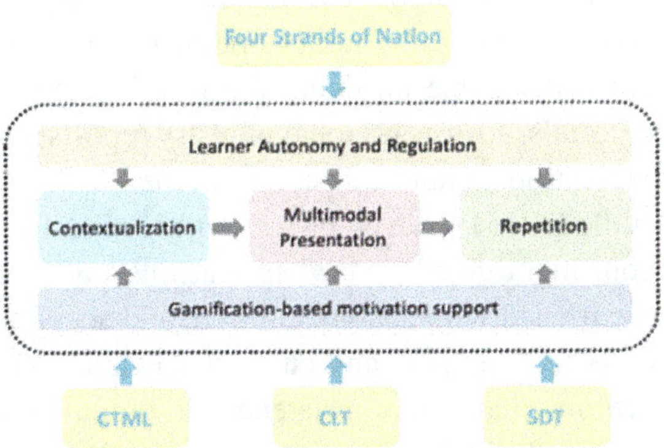

Each of the four core instructional theories provides foundational functional logic and theoretical support for the framework. CTML focuses on information processing and emphasizes the coordinated integration of input through multiple channels such as text, images, and audio (Liao & Wang, 2025). It directly supports the design of both multimodal input and contextualized tasks, enhancing learners' initial understanding and semantic construction. CLT highlights the limitations of cognitive resources and the need to optimize processing efficiency. It is closely linked to the components of repetitive exposure and self-regulated task management, informing the decomposition of instructional tasks, control of review frequency, and dynamic adjustment of learning pace (Seufert et al., 2024). SDT provides the motivational foundation for the task management and gamified support components. Its three psychological needs (autonomy, competence, and relatedness) are embedded into system feedback, task scheduling, and reward systems based on achievement to sustain long-term learner engagement (Grasse et al., 2022). Additionally, Nation's Four Strands model serves as the overarching theoretical structure at the macro level. It outlines a balanced distribution of instructional goals across four strands: meaning-focused input, meaning-focused output, language-focused learning, and fluency development. This model provides a structural basis for defining the complementary functions and coordination of the five instructional affordances within the framework.

It is worth noting that to enhance the cultural adaptability of the proposed instructional framework, this study pays particular attention to the flexibility and local configurability of its design elements. In today's globally diverse educational contexts, language instruction, particularly in FLSP, often faced challenges such as cross-cultural differences in communication, heterogeneous learning styles, and varied cognitive schemas (Bakić-Mirić et al., 2023; Dou et al., 2023). Therefore, a cultural resilient instructional framework must accommodate different teaching practices and learner preferences across cultural settings. For example, the contextualized task design component of the framework encourages localized adaptation based on domain-specific discourse and cultural norms. Instructors or designers can integrate localized materials, such as regional industry reports, technical standards, or workplace communication samples, designed to their specific disciplinary and cultural contexts. Neville (2015), in an empirical study on 3D-DGBLL for technical vocabulary acquisition, highlighted that when learning tasks are situated within virtual environments enriched with spatial, cultural, and social attributes, learners are better able to construct linguistic and cultural schemas, which they can later draw upon to improve pragmatic appropriateness in output tasks. Moreover, the framework offers high flexibility in task organization and review mechanisms, allowing for adaptation to different cultural preferences regarding learning pace. For instance, in cultures that emphasize exam performance and structured instruction, the system can be configured to include more frequent formative assessments and intensive review cycles, helping learners stay motivated through a clearly defined evaluation structure. In contrast, in educational cultures that value learner autonomy and exploratory learning, the system can reduce externally imposed pacing and increase freedom in navigating learning paths. As Basturkmen (2022) points out, FLSP instruction in the Adia-Pacific region often reflects strong teacher-centered approaches and goal-oriented learning, where learners tend to rely more on explicit task requirements and feedback mechanisms. In other cultural settings, however, learners may place greater value on flexibility and individualized pacing. Therefore, the framework's configurable design logic offers a practical solution for localized adaptation across culturally diverse educational contexts.

In sum, the proposed framework, through its modular and configurable instructional affordance structure, maintains pedagogical coherence while enabling practical local adaptation in cross-cultural contexts. This design philosophy aligns with the notion of cultural adaptability in instructional design as emphasized in recent scholarship (Li & Xu, 2025), offering theoretical grounding and implementation guidance for promoting technical vocabulary instruction across global and diverse learning environment.

4. IMPLEMENTATION OF THE INSTRUCTIONAL FRAMEWORK

Building upon the theoretical framework established in the previous section, this section further explores the translation of the proposed model into practical instructional design pathways and examines its application value and pedagogical innovations. First, it systematically analyzes how the framework addresses the core instructional design requirements associated with technical vocabulary acquisition in mobile learning contexts and transforms theoretical logic into implementable instructional strategies. Subsequently, it summarizes the potential advantages and innovative contributions of the framework in instructional practice, platform development, and curriculum design.

4.1. Instructional Design Pathways

In response to the first research question, this section systematically identified the key instructional design requirements involved in technical vocabulary acquisition, which serve as the foundation for the construction of the proposed framework. Specifically, learners often face the following instructional design challenges:

(1) Semantic Abstractness and Disciplinary Dependence

Technical vocabulary is highly dependent on domain-specific knowledge. Many terms are semantically abstract and conceptually complex, making them difficult to acquire through simple vocabulary lists alone (Mahraj & Ouahani, 2024). Previous studies have shown that embedding vocabulary input within authentic task contexts enables learners to better understand the specific usage and application of technical terms in professional scenarios (Ivan & Krissh, 2021).

(2) Transferability of Vocabulary

In addition to comprehension, technical vocabulary must be actively applied across a variety of disciplinary tasks. Embedding vocabulary learning within authentic professional contexts enables learners to process target terms in meaningful situational tasks, thereby facilitating deeper understanding and preparing them for later application (Alharbi, 2024). Empirical studies have further demonstrated that contextualized task-based output practice and cross-contextual repetition significantly enhance learners' ability to transfer vocabulary into practical and domain-specific usage (Magfirah et al., 2022; Minalla Alameen, 2024).

(3) High Cognitive Load

Long-term vocabulary learning tasks can easily lead to high cognitive load. Without appropriate control of task pacing and dynamic content adjustment, learners may experience cognitive overload and disengagement (Bahari, 2023; Yu & Trainin, 2022). Barcroft (2018) further indicates that limiting the amount of vocabulary introduced at one time and controlling input complexity can help reduce cognitive overload, promote deeper processing, and enhance long-term retention. In addition, incorporating multimodal input, such as combining textual definitions with visual and audio resources, can alleviate the processing burden on single cognitive channels, optimize information integration, and facilitate more efficient encoding and memory retention.

(4) Sustaining Learning Motivation

Due to the extended learning cycle and delayed sense of achievement in technical vocabulary acquisition, learners are prone to motivational decline. Studies have shown that timely feedback, staged achievement displays, and dynamic reward mechanisms can effectively enhance learners' sense of accomplishment and learning engagement (Boudadi & Gutiérrez-Colón, 2020; Liu et al., 2024).

(5) Fragmented Nature of Mobile Learning Environments

The highly flexible and easily accessible characteristics of mobile learning create fragmented learning schedules, requiring instructional design to provide adaptable task organization and resource accessibility. Rather than viewing fragmentation as a limitation, effective instructional frameworks can leverage this feature by incorporating intelligent task organization and personalized learning path recommendations to support long-term learning continuity. For example, intelligent task organization may dynamically prioritize review items based on learners' previous task performance, mastery levels, estimated forgetting curves, and item difficulty, thereby enabling more efficient cognitive load management and optimizing retention outcomes. Recent adaptive learning system have also demonstrated that machine learning-based dynamic task organization can significantly improve vocabulary learning efficiency and cognitive adaptation by continuously adjusting content based on learners' real-time performance (Xu, 2022).

Based on the identified instructional design requirements, the framework systematically integrates these elements through a progressive task structure, dynamically organizing the instructional components into a coherent implementation process that addresses the second research question.

First, in the input organization phase, learning tasks are embedded within contextualized disciplinary scenarios to activate learners' background knowledge and situational awareness. The input materials incorporate multimodal resources such as textual definitions, visual diagrams, and audio pronunciation to optimize semantic processing, reduce cognitive load, and enhance initial comprehension (Walldén, 2024).

Next, in the task execution phase, the framework employs progressive task structure across multiple learning scenarios. Learners repeatedly engage with target vocabulary through varied tasks that involve disciplinary problem-solving, applied practice, project-based activities, etc. This organization fosters both repeated exposure and diverse contextual applications, promoting long-term retention and transfer of technical vocabulary (Coxhead, 2025).

Subsequently, in the learning pacing management phase, the system continuously monitors learners' progress and dynamically adjusts the sequencing and prioritization of review tasks. This enables learners to maintain individualized learning rhythms and flexibly allocate study time, particularly within fragmented mobile learning environments.

Finally, in the motivational support phase, the framework incorporates point accumulation systems, achievement badges, progress visualization, and immediate feedback mechanisms. These design elements collectively help learners perceive ongoing progress, maintain task engagement, and sustain long-term motivation throughout extended vocabulary acquisition processes(Ahmed et al., 2022; Al-Aosail et al., 2024).

Through the integration of these interrelated instructional components, the framework transforms theoretical constructs into a systematic and operational instructional design model. The progressive task structure enables continuous alignment between cognitive processing, task organization, and motivational support, ensuring that both pedagogical needs and technological affordances are effectively addressed in mobile-assisted technical vocabulary learning.

4.2 Application Value and Instructional Innovations

The instructional design framework proposed in this study offers multi-dimensional application value and pedagogical innovations for different stakeholders in mobile learning environment. For learners, the framework facilitates the progressive development of semantic understanding and practical application of technical vocabulary by combining multimodal input with contextualized task design situated in authentic disciplinary scenarios. Systematic repetition and cross-task integration strengthen long-term retention and enhance the transferability of vocabulary knowledge. Dynamic task scheduling and personalized review pathway optimization enable learners to flexibly regulate their learning pace within fragmented learning schedules, thereby reducing cumulative cognitive load. Meanwhile, the integration of point accumulation systems, progress visualization, and immediate feedback mechanisms helps learners experience a sense of achievement, control, and sustained engagement throughout the extended vocabulary acquisition process, creating a positive learning environment jointly supported by cognitive processing and motivational regulation.

Moreover, the framework provides FLSP instructors and curriculum designers with a systematic instructional design logic and task organization scheme. Centered on the five instructional affordances, instructors can effectively configure contextualized learning tasks, multimodal input resources, repetition and review arrangements, learner self-regulation and task management mechanisms, and motivational support designs within the curriculum. This enables flexible organization of vocabulary unput, practice, output, and review stages, allowing for better balance between cognitive load and learning pacing, thereby improving instructional effectiveness and learning efficiency. The integrated structure of the five affordances also offers a stable design framework for curriculum development, supporting adaptation and iterative refinement across different disciplines and learner populations.

Finally, the framework offers system developers a clear structural design logic, clarifying the essential functional modules and system implementation pathways required for platform development in technical vocabulary learning contexts. Anchored in the systematic organization of the five instructional affordances, developers can systematically plan system architecture for task management, resource input, multimodal content delivery, review scheduling, task tracking, and motivational enhancement. This approach improves development efficiency and supports long-term platform scalability. Furthermore, the framework logic offers stable support for platform adaptability across interdisciplinary applications, diverse learning scenarios, and large-scale learner management contexts.

5. CONCLUSION

This study proposed and developed a systematic instructional design framework for technical vocabulary acquisition in mobile learning environments, aiming to address the challenges associated with cognitive complexity, task organization, and motivational sustainability in the vocabulary learning process. Based on the integration of multiple instructional theories, including the Cognitive Theory of Multimedia Learning (CTML), Cognitive Load Theory (CLT), Self-Determination Theory (SDT), and Nations Four Strands model, the framework incorporates five key instructional affordances (contextualization, multimodal input, repetition, learner autonomy and regulation, and gamification-based motivation support), thereby forming a highly operable and adaptive instructional design logic.

In terms of its overall contributions, the framework achieves a systematic integration of multiple instructional theories within the context of technical vocabulary acquisition, thereby expanding the theoretical system of Mobile-Assisted Language Learning (MALL) and instructional design for Foreign Languages for Specific Purposes (FLSP). At the practical level, the framework proposes clearly defined implementation pathways for learners, instructors, and platform developers, enhancing both the feasibility of instructional delivery and the functional architecture of system development, and offering applicable references for large-scale and diversified technical vocabulary instruction.

It should be noted that this study primarily focuses on the construction of an instructional design framework and has not yet conducted large-scale empirical validations to evaluate its actual instructional effectiveness. Future research may incorporate experimental studies and empirical data collection to systematically assess the framework's applicability and transferability across different languages, disciplinary domains, and learner populations. In addition, further empirical investigations are needed to explore the framework's adaptability to interdisciplinary integration, support for diverse motivational profiles, and mechanisms for individualized learning path regulation, thereby expanding its practical applicability.

Overall, this study, through the integration of instructional theories and practical instructional needs, proposes a systematic and scalable instructional framework for technical vocabulary acquisition, enriching the theoretical foundations of MALL and FLSP, while providing a transferable reference model for instructional practice and platform development.

REFERENCES

Ahmad, M. I., Mubin, O., Shahid, S., & Orlando, J. (2019). Robot's adaptive emotional feedback sustains children's social engagement and promotes their vocabulary learning: A long-term child–robot interaction study. *Adaptive Behavior, 27*(4), 243–266. DOI: 10.1177/1059712319844182

Ahmed, A. A. A., Sayed, B. T., Wekke, I. S., Widodo, M., Rostikawati, D., Ali, M. H., Abdul Hussein, H. A., & Azizian, M. (2022). An Empirical Study on the Effects of Using Kahoot as a Game-Based Learning Tool on EFL Learners' Vocabulary Recall and Retention. *Education Research International, 9739147*. Advance online publication. DOI: 10.1155/2022/9739147

Al-Aosail, A. B. F., Lamouchi, A., Ibrahim, S. A., Gafar, M. G., & Hafez, W. E. (2024). Digital Games for Learning Vocabulary: The Effects on Foreign Language Anxiety, Buoyancy, Online Engagement, and Vocabulary Learning. [Scopus.]. *CALL-EJ, 25*(4), 27–50.

Alharbi, K. (2024). Enhancing technical vocabulary acquisition: A multimedia strategic approach for English for specific purposes during COVID-19. *Interactive Learning Environments, 32*(9), 4812–4830. DOI: 10.1080/10494820.2023.2205902

Aprizal, A. D., & Wachyudi, K. (2024). The Effectiveness of Memrise as a Vocabulary Learning Tool. *Jurnal Ilmiah Wahana Pendidikan, 10*(4), 4. Advance online publication. DOI: 10.5281/zenodo.10499120

Arif, U. Q. (2025). The Influence of Gamification on English Vocabulary Retention in Online Learning Platforms. [JPPI]. *Jurnal Pendidikan Dan Pembelajaran Indonesia, 5*(2), 2. Advance online publication. DOI: 10.53299/jppi.v5i2.1468

Bahari, A. (2023). Challenges and Affordances of Cognitive Load Management in Technology-Assisted Language Learning: A Systematic Review. *International Journal of Human-Computer Interaction, 39*(1), 85–100. DOI: 10.1080/10447318.2021.2019957

Bakić-Mirić, N., Butt, S., Dilparić, B., & Ashirimbetova, M. (2023). Teaching culture in the modern ESP classroom. *Journal of Teaching English for Specific and Academic Purposes, 0*, 0. Advance online publication. DOI: 10.22190/JTESAP230506037B

Barcroft, J. (2018). *Vocabulary in Language Teaching*. Routledge.

Basturkmen, H. (2022). Current trends in ESP research in the Asia Pacific region. *World Englishes, 41*(4), 512–522. DOI: 10.1111/weng.12601

Boudadi, N. A., & Gutiérrez-Colón, M. (2020). Effect of Gamification on students' motivation and learning achievement in Second Language Acquisition within higher education: A literature review 2011-2019. *The EuroCALL Review, 28*(1), 1. Advance online publication. DOI: 10.4995/eurocall.2020.12974

Çakmak, F., Namaziandost, E., & Kumar, T. (2021). CALL-enhanced L2 cocabulary learning: Using spaced exposure through CALL to enhance L2 vocabulary retention. *Education Research International, 5848525*. Advance online publication. DOI: 10.1155/2021/5848525

Chirobocea, O. (2018). Vocabulary acquisition in ESP: Perspectives, strategies and resources. *Studii Şi Cercetări Filologice. Seria Limbi Străine Aplicate, 17*, 171–180.

Conole, G., & Dyke, M. (2004). What are the affordances of information and communication technologies? *Research in Learning Technology, 12*(2), 2. Advance online publication. DOI: 10.3402/rlt.v12i2.11246

Coxhead, A. (2024). *Technical vocabulary in government spoken communications: The team of five million in bubbles, PPE and CBACs*. https://doi.org/DOI: 10.25455/wgtn.26210741

Coxhead, A. (2025). Vocabulary and English for Specific Purposes. In *The Handbook of English for Specific Purposes* (pp. 107–123). John Wiley & Sons, Ltd., DOI: 10.1002/9781119985068.ch6

Dou, A. Q., Chan, S. H., & Win, M. T. (2023). Changing visions in ESP development and teaching: Past, present, and future vistas. *Frontiers in Psychology, 14*. Advance online publication. DOI: 10.3389/fpsyg.2023.1140659

Ed-Dali, R. (2024). Enhancing EFL learning through multimodal integration: The role of visual and auditory features in moroccan textbooks. *Journal of World Englishes and Educational Practices, 6*, 38–48.

Fitrianto, I., Setyawan, C. E., & Saleh, M. (2024). Utilizing artificial intelligence for personalized arabic language learning plans. *International Journal of Post Axial: Futuristic Teaching and Learning, 2*(1), 30–40. DOI: 10.59944/postaxial.v2i1.273

Ghofur, A., Kholis, M. N., Sodik, A. J., & Shiddiq, J. (2023). Students' Perceptions And Motivation Towards Teaching Arabic Vocabulary Through Gamification. *IJAZ ARABI JOURNAL OF ARABIC LEARNING, 6*(3), 682–694. DOI: 10.18860/ijazarabi.v6i3.18642

Gibson, J. J. (1966). *The senses considered as perceptual systems*. Houghton Mifflin.

Gómez-Ortiz, M.-J., Domínguez Romero, E., & Bobkina, J. (2023). Instagram as a learning tool to improve technical vocabulary for sports science students. *Journal of Hospitality, Leisure, Sport and Tourism Education, 32*, 100416. DOI: 10.1016/j.jhlste.2022.100416

Grasse, K. M., Kreminski, M., Wardrip-Fruin, N., Mateas, M., & Melcer, E. F. (2022). Using Self-Determination Theory to explore enjoyment of educational interactive narrative games: A case study of academical. *Frontiers in Virtual Reality, 3*. Advance online publication. DOI: 10.3389/frvir.2022.847120

Hwang, G.-J., Rahimi, M., & Fathi, J. (2024). Enhancing EFL learners' speaking skills, foreign language enjoyment, and language-specific grit utilising the affordances of a MALL app: A microgenetic perspective. *Computers & Education, 214*, 105015. DOI: 10.1016/j.compedu.2024.105015

Ivan, J., & Krissh, P. (2021). Technical vocabulary acquisition using the online learning approach among aircraft maintenance learners. *International Conference on Multidisciplinary Innovation and Economics,* 8.

Kim, S. K., & Webb, S. (2022). The effects of spaced practice on second language learning: A meta-analysis. *Language Learning, 72*(1), 269–319. DOI: 10.1111/lang.12479

Kohnke, L., & Ting, A. (2021). ESL students' perceptions of mobile applications for discipline-specific vocabulary acquisition for academic purposes. *Knowledge Management and E-Learning, 13*(1), 102–117. *Scopus*. Advance online publication. DOI: 10.34105/j.kmel.2021.13.006

Koleini, N., Boroughani, T., Eslami, Z. R., & Xodabande, I. (2024). Exploring the impacts of mobile-assisted learning on university students' technical vocabulary knowledge. *International Journal of Educational Research Open, 7. Scopus*. Advance online publication. DOI: 10.1016/j.ijedro.2024.100344

Lai, S.-L., Hsu, H.-L., & Yang, H.-H. (2025). CALL and Vocabulary Learning. In *The Palgrave Encyclopedia of Computer-Assisted Language Learning* (pp. 1–11). Palgrave Macmillan., DOI: 10.1007/978-3-031-51447-0_293-1

Li, B., & Xu, X. (2025). Examining the intersectionality of learners' professional background and cultural diversity in Chinese ESP learners and its impact on students' engagement: A study on the application of communicative language teaching. *Current Psychology (New Brunswick, N.J.), 44*(7), 5854–5869. DOI: 10.1007/s12144-025-07479-7

Li, L., Hew, K. F., & Du, J. (2024). Gamification enhances student intrinsic motivation, perceptions of autonomy and relatedness, but minimal impact on competency: A meta-analysis and systematic review. *Educational Technology Research and Development, 72*(2), 765–796. DOI: 10.1007/s11423-023-10337-7

Li, Y., & Hafner, C. A. (2022). Mobile-assisted vocabulary learning: Investigating receptive and productive vocabulary knowledge of Chinese EFL learners. *ReCALL, 34*(1), 66–80. DOI: 10.1017/S0958344021000161

Liao, X., & Wang, W. (2025). A framework for designing immersive virtual reality learning environments based on the cognitive theory of multimedia learning. *Curriculum Learning and Exploration, 2*(5), 5. Advance online publication. DOI: 10.70711/cle.v2i5.6370

Liu, D. (2024). The effects of segmentation on cognitive load, vocabulary learning and retention, and reading comprehension in a multimedia learning environment. *BMC Psychology, 12*(1). *Scopus.* Advance online publication. DOI: 10.1186/s40359-023-01489-5

Liu, G.-Z., Fathi, J., & Rahimi, M. (2024). Using digital gamification to improve language achievement, foreign language enjoyment, and ideal L2 self: A case of English as a foreign language learners. *Journal of Computer Assisted Learning, 40*(4), 1347–1364. DOI: 10.1111/jcal.12954

Liu, L. (2024). Impact of AI gamification on EFL learning outcomes and nonlinear dynamic motivation: Comparing adaptive learning paths, conversational agents, and storytelling. *Education and Information Technologies.* Advance online publication. DOI: 10.1007/s10639-024-13296-5

Magfirah, T., Roy, A., & Arridha, R. (2022). Improving Students' Technical English Vocabulary Using Readlang Platform at State Polytechnic of Fakfak. *Cebong Journal, 1*(3), 3. Advance online publication. DOI: 10.35335/cebong.v1i3.28

Mahraj, M., & Ouahani, N. (2024). Teaching Strategies of Technical Vocabulary: A Qualitative Approach. *Moroccan Journal of Quantitative and Qualitative Research, 6*(3), 3. Advance online publication. DOI: 10.48379/IMIST.PRSM/mjqr-v6i3.49144

Mayer, R. E. (2005). Cognitive Theory of Multimedia Learning. In *The Cambridge handbook of multimedia learning* (pp. 31–48). Cambridge University Press., DOI: 10.1017/CBO9780511816819.004

Mayer, R. E. (2014). Principles Based on Social Cues in Multimedia Learning: Personalization, Voice, Image, and Embodiment Principles. In *The Cambridge handbook of multimedia learning, 2nd ed* (pp. 345–368). Cambridge University Press. https://doi.org/DOI: 10.1017/CBO9781139547369.017

Minalla Alameen, A. (2024). Enhancing young EFL learners' vocabulary learning through contextualizing animated videos. *Theory and Practice in Language Studies, 14*, 578–586. DOI: 10.17507/tpls.1402.31

Miroshnychenko, I. (2024). Technical vocabulary in foreign language acquisition: Seeking effective methods for university students. *Collection of Scientific Papers «ΛΌΓΟΣ»*, Article May 24, 2024; Zurich, Switzerland. https://doi.org/DOI: 10.36074/logos-24.05.2024.058

Nation, P. (2007). The Four Strands. *Innovation in Language Learning and Teaching, 1*(1), 2–13. DOI: 10.2167/illt039.0

Neville, D. O. (2015). The story in the mind: The effect of 3D gameplay on the structuring of written L2 narratives. *ReCALL, 27*(1), 21–37. DOI: 10.1017/S0958344014000160

Norman, D. A. (1999). Affordance, conventions, and design. *Interaction, 6*(3), 38–43. DOI: 10.1145/301153.301168

Ryan, R., & Deci, E. (2000). Self-determination theory and the facilitation of intrinsic motivation, social development and well-being. *The American Psychologist, 55*(1), 68–78. DOI: 10.1037/0003066X.55.1.68

Ryan, R. M., & Deci, E. L. (2020). Intrinsic and extrinsic motivation from a self-determination theory perspective: Definitions, theory, practices, and future directions. *Contemporary Educational Psychology, 61*, 101860. DOI: 10.1016/j.cedpsych.2020.101860

Saeedi, Z., & Najjarpour, M. (2025). Enhancing technical vocabulary acquisition in ESP context through virtual content development with Articulate Storyline. *Social Sciences & Humanities Open, 11*, 101539. DOI: 10.1016/j.ssaho.2025.101539

Seibert Hanson, A. E., & Brown, C. M. (2020). Enhancing L2 learning through a mobile assisted spaced-repetition tool: An effective but bitter pill? *Computer Assisted Language Learning, 33*(1–2), 133–155. *Scopus.* Advance online publication. DOI: 10.1080/09588221.2018.1552975

Seufert, T., Hamm, V., Vogt, A., & Riemer, V. (2024). The interplay of cognitive load, learners' resources and self-regulation. *Educational Psychology Review, 36*(2), 50. DOI: 10.1007/s10648-024-09890-1

She, M., Tan, Y., & Li, Z. (2024). Antecedents of college students' continuance behaviors in online fragmented learning: An empirical analysis from the extended ECM perspective. *Sustainability*, *16*(10), 10. Advance online publication. DOI: 10.3390/su16104138

Sweller, J. (1994). Cognitive load theory, learning difficulty, and instructional design. *Learning and Instruction*, *4*(4), 295–312. DOI: 10.1016/0959-4752(94)90003-5

Sweller, J., Van Merriënboer, J. J. G., & Paas, F. (2019). Cognitive architecture and instructional design: 20 years later. *Educational Psychology Review*, *31*(2), 261–292. DOI: 10.1007/s10648-019-09465-5

Tavassoli, K., & Beyranvand, S. (2023). How Instagram as a MALL tool impacts EAP learners' technical vocabulary learning and perceptions in an electronic context. *SN Social Sciences*, *3*(4), 70. DOI: 10.1007/s43545-023-00657-z

Teng, M., & Xu, J. (2025). Pushing vocabulary knowledge from receptive to productive mastery: Effects of task type and repetition frequency. *Language Teaching Research*, *29*(2), 588–606. DOI: 10.1177/13621688221077028

Teng, M. F. (2023). The effectiveness of multimedia input on vocabulary learning and retention. *Innovation in Language Learning and Teaching*, *17*(3), 738–754.

Udaya, M. (2022). Using semantic maps as a teaching strategy for vocabulary development. *European Journal of English Language Teaching*, *6*(5), 5. Advance online publication. DOI: 10.46827/ejel.v6i5.4095

Van Lier, L. (Ed.). (2004). The Ecology and Semiotics of Language Learning: A Sociocultural Perspective. In L. Van Lier, M. C. Cavalcanti, H. Janks, C. Kramsch, & A. Pennycook (Eds.), *Theories of Language* (Vol. 3, pp. 23–53). Springer Netherlands. https://doi.org/DOI: 10.1007/1-4020-7912-5_2

Vargo, A., Yamaguchi, K., Iwata, M., & Kise, K. (2024). A Context-Based Multimedia Vocabulary Learning System for Mobile Users. *Informatics, 11*(1). *Scopus.* Advance online publication. DOI: 10.3390/informatics11010001

Walldén, R. (2024). Contextual elaborations and shifts when adult L2 learners present and discuss workplace-related vocabulary. *Linguistics and Education, 80,* 101272. DOI: 10.1016/j.linged.2024.101272

Wang, M., Zhang, D., Zhu, J., & Gu, H. (2025). Effects of incorporating a large language model-based adaptive mechanism into contextual games on students' academic performance, flow experience, cognitive load and behavioral patterns. *Journal of Educational Computing Research*, *63*(3), 662–694. DOI: 10.1177/07356331251321719

Wilson, M. (2024). The role of multimodal learning in enhancing language acquisition for bilingual learners. *Emerging Education Research*, *2*, 1–11.

Xing, B., & Zhang, H. (2025). A study of the effect of multimodal input on vocabulary acquisition: Evidence from online Chinese language learners. *Language Teaching Research, 13621688241313017*. Advance online publication. DOI: 10.1177/13621688241313017

Xodabande, I., Atai, M. R., & Hashemi, M. R. (2024). Exploring the effectiveness of mobile assisted learning with digital flashcards in enhancing long-term retention of technical vocabulary among university students. *Journal of Computers in Education*. Advance online publication. DOI: 10.1007/s40692-024-00347-6

Xu, Y. (2022). An adaptive learning system for English vocabulary using machine learning. *Mobile Information Systems*, *2022*(1), 3501494. DOI: 10.1155/2022/3501494

Yu, A., & Trainin, G. (2022). A meta-analysis examining technology-assisted L2 vocabulary learning. *ReCALL*, *34*(2), 235–252. DOI: 10.1017/S0958344021000239

Yüksel, H. G., Mercanoğlu, H. G., & Yılmaz, M. B. (2022). Digital flashcards vs. Wordlists for learning technical vocabulary. *Computer Assisted Language Learning*, *35*(8), 2001–2017. DOI: 10.1080/09588221.2020.1854312

Zhang, H. (2025). An Action Research on Multimodal Online Teaching and Vocabulary Acquisition Among Chinese Fifth-Grade EFL Learners. *International Journal of Social Science and Human Research*, *08*(05), 3182–3199. DOI: 10.5281/zenodo.15469401

Zhang, H. (2025). An action research on multimodal online teaching and vocabulary acquisition among chinese fifth-grade EFL learners. *International Journal of Social Science and Human Research*, *08*(05), 3182–3199. DOI: 10.47191/ijsshr/v8-i5-63

Zhang, R., Zou, Di, & and Xie, H. (2022). Spaced repetition for authentic mobile-assisted word learning: Nature, learner perceptions, and factors leading to positive perceptions. *Computer Assisted Language Learning*, *35*(9), 2593–2626. DOI: 10.1080/09588221.2021.1888752

Chapter 11
Bridging Traditional and Digital Pedagogies in Blended ESL Vocabulary Learning:
Learner Perception and Motivation

Andy Lim Teik Hong
https://orcid.org/0000-0002-1055-2285
Universiti Teknologi Malaysia, Malaysia

Luqman Mahmud
https://orcid.org/0009-0006-4134-2834
Universiti Utara Malaysia, Malaysia

ABSTRACT

Vocabulary is a vital component in language learning, yet second language (L2) learners often find it challenging and uninteresting. This study explores the effectiveness of blended learning in enhancing vocabulary knowledge among 76 primary school pupils in Johor Bahru. Using a mixed-method approach, data were gathered through pre-tests, post-tests, questionnaires, and interviews. An independent t-test revealed that pupils in the blended learning group outperformed those in the traditional group. Questionnaire results showed high levels of positive perception and intrinsic motivation toward blended learning. Interview data further supported these findings. The study concludes that blended learning improves vocabulary performance and motivation, highlighting its potential as a valuable instructional strategy in L2 education.

DOI: 10.4018/979-8-3373-7508-3.ch011

1. INTRODUCTION

English is a complex language with an extensive lexicon, comprising approximately 171,476 words (Djiwandono, 2013). A limited vocabulary range can significantly hinder an individual's ability to comprehend texts and communicate effectively, underscoring the fundamental role of vocabulary in language acquisition. As the backbone of language proficiency, vocabulary is essential for mastering reading, writing, speaking, and listening skills, and it has been positively correlated with academic performance, including Grade Point Average (GPA) (Hong & Stapa, 2023; Cao, 2023; Daniel & Villanueva, 2023). Despite its importance, vocabulary learning is often perceived by learners as monotonous and boring (Katemba, 2022), necessitating pedagogical strategies that can engage and support students more effectively.

In Malaysia, English is taught as a second language from preschool through tertiary education, guided by the Common European Framework of Reference (CEFR) as a standardized benchmark for proficiency. However, many learners, particularly at the primary level, continue to demonstrate limited vocabulary mastery, which negatively affects their overall language competence. Moreover, national reports and CEFR-aligned assessments reveal that a significant proportion of students fail to reach the expected A2 or B1 levels. Traditional methods emphasizing word lists and rote memorization have proven ineffective, especially among digital-native learners who crave interactivity and relevance. Effective vocabulary instruction, therefore, requires both repeated exposure and meaningful context, both of which can be enhanced through blended learning models. This persistent gap highlights the need for more dynamic and inclusive instructional models.

According to recent CEFR-aligned national assessments, over 40% of Malaysian Year 6 (12 years old) ESL learners fail to meet the A2 benchmark, reflecting persistent lexical underachievement (Hong & Stapa, 2023). These deficits are particularly pronounced in rural and underserved schools, where instructional approaches remain predominantly teacher-centered and textbook-based. The traditional emphasis on rote memorization and decontextualized word lists has not yielded substantial improvements in vocabulary acquisition. Compounding this issue is a lack of differentiated instructional strategies that accommodate learner diversity, especially in vocabulary development. Without sufficient lexical knowledge, learners struggle to comprehend texts, construct meaningful sentences, and participate in communicative tasks, skills that are foundational to language mastery and broader academic success.

In light of these challenges, blended learning emerges as a promising pedagogical alternative. However, its implementation is not without complications. Structural inequities such as inconsistent internet access, limited device availability, and significant variability in teacher digital literacy present formidable obstacles, particularly in rural school settings. Additionally, overreliance on digital tools without pedagogical integration can undermine learning outcomes, as technology use alone does not guarantee improved instruction. Thus, the need to explore contextually grounded, theoretically informed, and empirically validated models of blended learning for vocabulary development is both timely and urgent.

In the context of 21st-century education, the integration of digital tools into conventional teaching approaches has become increasingly essential. This is particularly pertinent in second language acquisition, where learners must develop complex linguistic competencies, including vocabulary. Blended learning has emerged as a promising instructional approach that combines face-to-face and online learning experiences to foster a more engaging and flexible learning environment. Qindah (2018) defines blended learning as the integration of traditional classroom instruction with online components, while Khodaparast & Ghafournia, 2015 and Makkar and Sharma (2022) emphasize its adaptability across different learning environments. In language education, blended learning represents a synthesis of synchronous and asynchronous modalities, enabling tailored instruction that addresses diverse learner needs. Leakey and Ranchoux (2006) describe blended learning in computer-assisted language learning (CALL) as the strategic merging of CALL and non-CALL pedagogies into a cohesive, context-sensitive framework that optimally supports language development. Extant literature confirms the growing adoption of blended learning across educational contexts. Studies by Hong and Stapa (2023), McHone (2020), and Dinara et al. (2016) have demonstrated its effectiveness in enhancing language skills. Furthermore, Tong et al. (2022) noted that blended learning increases student participation and enriches the overall learning experience, while Marsh (2012) emphasized its capacity to facilitate more effective teaching and learning for both educators and students.

Despite the positive outcomes observed at the secondary and tertiary levels, there also remains a notable gap in research and application of blended learning in primary education, particularly within the Malaysian English as a Second Language (ESL) context. This book chapter seeks to address all the gaps stated above gap by critically examining the role and impact of blended learning on vocabulary acquisition and motivation among primary ESL learners in Malaysia, offering pedagogical insights and implications for future instructional design.

2. AIM AND OBJECTIVES

The chapter will provide an analytical perspective on the implementation of blended learning for vocabulary development among K-12 ESL learners. Drawing upon empirical findings, theoretical frameworks, and practical classroom insights, the chapter will:

- Explore the effects of blended learning on pupils' vocabulary development.
- Investigate the perception of pupils on the effectiveness of blended learning in developing their vocabulary.
- Examine the ways on how blended learning could motivate pupils in developing their vocabulary.
- Offer practical recommendations for curriculum developers, policymakers, and teachers seeking to implement technology-integrated instruction in language classrooms.

3. LITERATURE REVIEW

3.1 Theory of Transactional Distance

One of the earliest and most cited theory in the field of distance learning will be the Theory of Transactional Distance formulated by Moore in 1972. This theory describes the pedagogical concept of a teacher-learner relationship when separated by space or time, thus gave birth to the online learning through technology. Therefore, this theory is chosen because it can describe the perception of pupils towards the usage of Google Classroom. Moore further added that the transactional distance revolves around three main variables which are dialogue, structure, and learner autonomy. In addition, course interface is an additional dimension that was adapted from Samya (2007) and Koohang and Weiss (2003) stemmed from this Theory of Transactional Distance. Although Moore did not include this additional variable in this theory, it is embedded in the main variables because it is suitable to view pupils' perception towards Google Classroom and also how it is being executed in the classroom. Thus, it is considered to be part of main components for the purpose of this research.

According to Moore, the term dialogue and interaction are often use interchangeably. It is represented by the process of two-way communication when an individual gives instruction and the other responds. However, he prefers to use the term dialogue as it has positive qualities, constructive and purposeful. He argued that the main focus of the dialogue is to improve the understanding of the pupils. Thus, one of the main aspects in enabling dialogue is the medium of communication. Comparing to previous early method of communication, the use of mail would allow the exchange of dialogue, but it slows down the communication process. Thus, through the use of online media and tools, two-way communication is made possible. To keep it simple, through blended learning instruction, pupils are encouraged to interact and collaborate with their peers and teachers which in turn will provide meaningful input and understanding.

The second variable in this theory is the structure which are element in the course design that determine transactional distance. In simpler terms, it is the way teaching is structured which includes and determine the rigidity or flexibility of the educational objectives, teaching strategies, and evaluation methods. Moore (1997) posited that there is a significant relationship between the structure and dialogue. The more structured the educational program, the less dialogue it will contain until it is totally non-existent between the teacher and the learners, thus resulting in high transactional distance. On the other hand, there is a low transactional distance in those programmes that have much dialogue but less structured.

Learner autonomy is undoubtedly one of the hot topics in the field of English Language Teaching. It has gained popularity as Communicative Language Teaching became the leading language teaching approach. Hence, another important construct in relation to transactional distance is the learner autonomy. It can be defined as the extent to which learner is responsible to determine their learning goals, experiences and evaluation rather than the teacher. The higher the transactional distance, the greater the autonomy required on the part of the learner to mediate the transactional distance. Through online learning, it enables the learners to determine the structure based on their level and pace.

3.2 Self-Determination Theory

Motivation certainly plays an important factor for a successful ESL learning. According to Dornyei (2009), motivation is a concept that people use to explain why people think and behave in a particular manner. In a language learning context, Gardner (1985) defined motivation as the relation of attitude, desire and the satisfaction when learning the target language. However, Fernandez and Canado (2001) posited that motivation is an abstract element residing in an individual, thus rendering it difficult to be directly observe and measure. Despite that, motivation can be deduced by learners' effort, persistence and verbalization (Yee & Ganapathy, 2017). As such, based on the Self-Determination Theory, motivation can be categorized into two sub-theories which are the Cognitive Evaluation Theory (CET) which explains on intrinsic motivation and Organismic Integration Theory (OIT) which explains extrinsic motivation (Deci & Ryan, 1985). Based on the CET, there are three key aspects that allow optimal function and growth which are autonomy, competence, and relatedness which consequently will augment the feeling of intrinsic motivation.

The motivation of ESL students is crucial to their success in language acquisition. ESL students who enjoy the activities are considered intrinsically motivated in the context of language instruction. Thus, by meeting the three CET requirements, blended learning might encourage students' motivation. First, according to this idea, communication, feedback, and rewards all contribute to motivation and perceptions of competence. Therefore, when teachers provide positive feedback on students' assignments in the form of grades and encouraging remarks, motivation can be increased through the usage of online learning resources. Next, the CET also advocates the fulfillment of autonomy must complement the development of competence in order for learners to become self-determined. Autonomy encompasses the provision of choice, validation of emotions, and opportunities for self-directed learning. Therefore, it is essential for teachers to design learning activities that foster autonomy. In the context of blended learning, tasks should be engaging, accessible to learners of varying proficiency levels, and structured to encourage pupils to embrace challenges. Such an approach enables learners to take ownership of their learning process and proceed at a pace that suits their individual needs, thereby enhancing intrinsic motivation.

3.3 Blended learning

With the advent of ICT, blended learning courses have become quite significant to complement the traditional ways of learning. The concept of blended learning has been used and interpreted in a variety of ways within the field of language teaching. Over the years, scholars have attempted to define blended learning based on various perspectives, resulting in various definitions. While researchers claimed that this is an advantage as it provides teachers the opportunity for contextualized interpretation, some are more pessimistic. However, the most widely common and accepted is the combination of both face-to-face and computer-mediated instructions (Hrastinki, 2019). Based on Liu et al. (2024), the foundation of blended learning mainly consists of three requirements which are multiple modes of delivery, technology-enabled training methods, as well as interactive traditional teaching approaches which are facilitated by a teacher. On the other hand, Kintu, Zhu, and Kagambe (2017) put forward that blended interactions, technology quality, and face-to-face support are the main elements that define blended learning. Thus, it can be understood that blended learning needs to cover at least two modes of instruction fusing both traditional learning and technology-mediated instructions. The fundamental idea behind blended learning is the combination of computer-mediated instruction and in-person instruction to create the best possible pedagogy for achieving the educational goal and giving students a more comprehensive learning experience. As a result, it is not only about employing technology; it is also about applying it in a way that maximises its benefits. Figure 1 below depicts the relationship between blended learning, face-to-face learning, and online learning.

Figure 1. The relationship between blended learning, online learning, and face-to-face learning

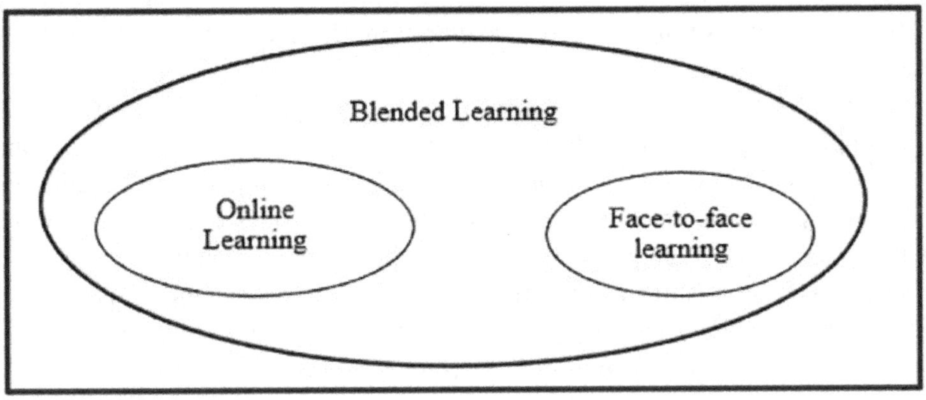

As educators search for ways to complement 21st-century learning, some supported that blended learning might be the shift needed to be in line with the principles of 21st-century learning. Blended learning can be implemented using different learning methods (lecture, discussion, games, case study), different delivery methods (face-to-face instruction, flipped classroom or computer-based learning opportunities), and different level of guidance (individual, lecturer led or group learning). Besides, a blended learning classroom is arranged in a manner where pupils can participate actively in achieving the learning objectives that allow teachers to manipulate the technologies to be used in the learning process. Moreover, blended learning can be used across various education settings and subjects. Hence, it has become a learning choice for various higher learning institutions where a growing number of universities and colleges offered blended learning courses in their programs of different levels to combine the best feature of both modes of learning.

As stated Rahmat et al. (2019), the vast benefits and positive outcomes of blended learning have allowed blended learning to be integrated into many learning programs in universities across Malaysia. This is not a surprising fact as many previous studies have proven the effectiveness of blended learning in comparison to the traditional method of teaching. Over the years, the numerous researchers agreed that blended learning has vast advantages over the traditional mode of learning (Tabassum et al., 2024; Hong & Stapa, 2023) especially in terms of pupils' language skills. Furthermore, blended learning has shown to engage students in active learning that promotes skills such as communication, information literacy, creativity, and collaboration that transform into the ability to use digital technologies for different purposes. Fundamentally, an effective blended learning classroom is similar to effective traditional learning. The key distinction is the function of the teacher and the pupils in the learning process where a blended learning classroom requires students to be active, engaged, and confident in the subject's learning structure (Pannan & Legge, 2016). The teacher's role shifts to a facilitator in blended learning environments (Hong et al., 2025).

Schools all around the world, including the Malaysian primary schools are increasingly using the blended learning approach. According to Tan, Zakuan, and Aziz (2022), despite the fact that blended learning is gaining significant attention in this post-pandemic era, it is not new pedagogy in Malaysia. Its rise within the local education landscape was only recently heightened as teachers were driven to explore online learning tools and platforms options that are available upon being hit by the global crisis and forced to temporarily carry out online teaching and learning. As a result, moving forward into the post-pandemic phase, more teachers are aware of the online tools that are both practical and effective within their context, this as a result has led more teachers to adopt the blended learning approach in their classroom instructions. In the context of primary school context in Malaysia, efforts by the Ministry of Education to facilitate teachers in implementing current teaching approaches include an emphasis on developing 21st century skills within the Malaysia Education Blueprint as well as the swift development of the Digital Learning Initiative Malaysia (DELIMa) which serves as a one stop portal for teachers and students for online learning. Therefore, the integration of the online aspect allows for a blended learning classroom, thus shifting the ways English classrooms can be conducted

3.4 Involvement Load Hypothesis

Effective vocabulary instruction must be anchored in sound theoretical foundations that explain how lexical knowledge is acquired, retained, and used. One of the most influential frameworks in this domain is the Involvement Load Hypothesis (ILH), developed by Laufer and Hulstijn (2001). The ILH posits that the degree of cognitive engagement a learner invests in a vocabulary task determines how well a word is learned and remembered. It identifies three core components that collectively define the involvement load: need, search, and evaluation. "Need" reflects the motivational aspect of learning a word, which may arise from external demands such as teacher instructions or internal motivations such as the desire to understand a reading passage. "Search" refers to the mental effort involved in discovering a word's meaning or form, often through dictionary use or contextual inference. "Evaluation" involves comparing or using the word in a meaningful context, such as sentence construction or communicative tasks. Tasks that require all three components are said to have a high involvement load and are more likely to result in successful vocabulary acquisition.

Blended learning environments are particularly well-suited to operationalize the ILH. Digital platforms like Google Classroom can be used to design tasks that stimulate need, enable search, and facilitate evaluation. For example, teachers can create activities where learners are asked to explore multimedia materials and look up unfamiliar words, thus triggering the search component. Learners can then be asked to use those words in personalized writing tasks, peer discussions, or online quizzes, fulfilling the evaluation requirement. When students are given some level of control or purpose in selecting vocabulary tasks, the need component becomes self-imposed, which the ILH suggests is more effective than externally imposed tasks. Despite the potential of this theory, traditional vocabulary instruction often overlooks them, focusing instead on rote memorization and isolated word lists. In contrast, blended learning creates an environment where the principles of the ILH can be integrated meaningfully. This study draws upon this theory to design a pedagogically robust and learner-centered blended vocabulary model for Malaysian primary ESL learners.

3.5 Blended Learning and Vocabulary Acquisition: An Empirical Synthesis

Blended learning has become increasingly prominent in ESL instruction due to its potential to enhance learner engagement, autonomy, and instructional flexibility. While its applications have been widely explored in general language development, a growing body of research has begun to focus specifically on vocabulary acquisition. This section critically synthesizes key empirical studies and highlights the pedagogical and contextual gaps that underpin the rationale for this study.

Several studies have reported positive outcomes when blended learning is used to enhance vocabulary learning. Dinara et al. (2016) found that Russian university students exposed to vocabulary tasks through a blended model showed significantly higher lexical retention compared to those taught through traditional methods. The intervention involved digital flashcards, multimedia glosses, and online quizzes combined with classroom discussions, aligning well with the Involvement Load Hypothesis. Similarly, Ebadi and Ghuchi (2018) demonstrated that Iranian EFL learners improved their vocabulary knowledge and attitudes toward learning when exposed to mobile-assisted blended instruction. Their findings stressed the importance of learner autonomy and contextual repetition in sustaining vocabulary gains.

In the Malaysian context, Hong and Stapa (2023) conducted a quasi-experimental study among Year 5 ESL learners and found that vocabulary development and motivation were significantly higher in the blended learning group compared to a control group. Their study used Google Classroom to deliver vocabulary-focused activities such as quizzes, games, and peer interactions. These findings support the effectiveness of blending synchronous face-to-face instruction with asynchronous digital practice. Despite these encouraging results, prior research often suffers from methodological and conceptual fragmentation. Many studies lack integration with theoretical frameworks, making it difficult to understand why blended learning works for vocabulary acquisition. Furthermore, most interventions have been conducted at the secondary or tertiary level, leaving a gap in understanding how young learners in primary education engage with blended vocabulary instruction. There is also limited research that triangulates quantitative performance data with learners' perceptions and motivation, which are essential factors in sustaining vocabulary learning over time.

Critically, few studies have synthesized blended learning models with vocabulary-specific theories such as the Involvement Load Hypothesis or the Noticing Hypothesis. Most focus on delivery mechanisms rather than instructional design principles. Moreover, important implementation challenges, including access to devices, teacher readiness, and learner variability, are rarely addressed in detail, particularly in the context of public primary schools in developing countries.

In response to these limitations, the current study examines how a theoretically informed blended learning intervention affects vocabulary acquisition and learner motivation among Malaysian primary ESL pupils. By integrating performance data, perceptual feedback, and motivational constructs, this study contributes a more comprehensive and contextually grounded understanding of blended vocabulary instruction in the early years of language learning.

4. METHODOLOGY

This study employed a mixed-methods research design using a sequential explanatory strategy to investigate the effects of blended learning on pupils' vocabulary knowledge, perceptions, and motivation. The research was conducted in two phases. The first phase involved a quasi-experimental approach utilizing a pretest-posttest design to assess vocabulary performance. This was followed by the administration of questionnaires to evaluate pupils' perceptions and motivation. In the second phase, qualitative data were gathered through interviews to further elaborate and validate the quantitative findings.

The participants consisted of 72 Year 4 pupils (10 years old) from an urban primary school in Johor, Malaysia. Two intact classes were selected through purposive sampling based on their comparable academic performance in the previous year's final examination. One class was designated as the experimental group and exposed to blended learning, while the other served as the control group and received conventional face-to-face instruction. According to Fraenkel and Wallen (2008), purposive sampling is appropriate when participants are believed to provide rich and relevant data aligned with the study's objectives. All pupils received 300 minutes of face-to-face instruction weekly.

Three primary instruments were used which are pre-tests and post-tests, questionnaires, and semi-structured interviews. Firstly, the pre-test and post-test evaluated pupils' vocabulary acquisition based on the topics taught during the intervention. The vocabulary items were aligned with the Standard Curriculum Document and Assessments and included eight A1-level words, nine A2-level words, and three B1-level words. The pre-test was administered to both control and experimental groups before the intervention. Following their respective instructional approaches, traditional teaching for the control group and blended learning for the experimental group, a post-test was administered to measure vocabulary gains.

Next, questionnaires were employed to collect data on pupils' perceptions of and motivation toward blended learning. This instrument was selected for its efficiency in gathering attitudinal and opinion-based data. The perception items were adapted from Samya (2007), incorporating four dimensions from the Theory of Transactional Distance. Motivation items were adapted from Deci and Ryan's (2000) Intrinsic Motivation Inventory, reflecting the key components of Self-Determination Theory which are autonomy, competence, and relatedness.

Lastly, to provide further insights and validate the quantitative results, semi-structured interviews were conducted with eight pupils from the experimental group after the intervention. One-on-one interviews were used to minimize peer influence and response bias. The interviews explored pupils' perceptions and motivational experiences related to the blended learning environment.

5. RESULTS

5.1 Pupils' Performance

To assess the impact of blended learning on vocabulary development, this study employed a quasi-experimental design using a pretest-posttest approach. Quantitative results revealed significant improvements in the experimental group's vocabulary scores after undergoing blended instruction, supported by qualitative data that illustrated how pupils engaged with the learning materials and demonstrated vocabulary growth in authentic task contexts.

Initial comparisons between the experimental (blended learning) and control (traditional learning) groups showed no statistically significant differences in pre-test scores (t = 1.149, p = .254), confirming that both groups were comparable in vocabulary knowledge at the outset. This homogeneity was crucial in ensuring the validity of the subsequent post-test comparison.

Post-intervention results, however, revealed a substantial improvement in vocabulary performance among pupils in the experimental group. The mean post-test score for the blended learning group was 16.22 (SD = 1.57), compared to 11.33 (SD = 1.59) for the control group. An independent samples t-test confirmed this difference as statistically significant (t = 13.148, p < .001), thereby validating the effectiveness of the blended learning model in enhancing vocabulary acquisition. Score gains further highlighted the practical impact of the intervention. Pupils in the blended learning group improved by 7 to 16 points, whereas those in the traditional group improved by only 4 to 10 points.

5.2 Pupils' Perception of Blended Learning for Vocabulary Development

The pupils' perception of blended learning was evaluated using a 12-item questionnaire supported by qualitative interviews. Overall, the results indicated a high level of positive perception, with an average mean score of 4.32 out of 5 across all items. Eleven of the twelve items were rated at a "high" level, suggesting that pupils largely viewed blended learning as beneficial and engaging. The responses reflected four key dimensions: dialogue, autonomy, structure, and course interface, consistent with the constructs of the Theory of Transactional Distance.

5.2.1 Dialogue and Interaction

Pupils perceived that blended learning promoted meaningful interaction, particularly with their teacher. Items related to teacher-pupil communication scored highly (e.g., Item 4: M = 3.92), suggesting that teacher presence in both online and face-to-face sessions was instrumental in supporting vocabulary learning. Pupils indicated that teacher feedback and explanations, especially during classroom follow-ups to online tasks, enhanced their understanding of new words.

Interview data echoed this sentiment. One pupil shared:

"When teacher explains again in class after the video, I remember the word better." (Pupil 3)

However, peer interaction received a lower score (Item 3: M = 3.61), indicating some hesitance in recognizing collaborative peer work as a source of vocabulary acquisition. This may stem from pupils' preference for authoritative instruction or their limited confidence in peer learning at this developmental stage.

5.2.2 Autonomy in Learning

Pupils reported strong autonomy when using Google Classroom, as reflected in the high mean score for Item 8 (M = 4.69). They felt empowered to engage with the learning materials at their own pace and time, especially during home-based learning. The flexibility and accessibility of the platform were seen as major advantages.

This was reinforced by qualitative responses:

"I can learn English from home which is easy. My mum did not allow me to come to school during the lockdown." (Pupil 5)

"I learn from my mother's office during MCO (Movement Control Order)." (Pupil 8)

Such flexibility appeared to foster ownership over learning, particularly during periods of disrupted schooling.

5.2.3 Structural Support and Comprehensibility

Blended learning activities were well-received in terms of their structure and clarity. Pupils indicated that the tasks helped them understand new vocabulary (Item 9: M = 4.44), and they found the instructions easy to follow (Item 10: M = 4.42). These high scores reflect careful instructional design that matched pupils' cognitive level.

Pupils highlighted the difference between English lessons using Google Classroom and other subjects:

"I prefer using Google Classroom because I can watch many different videos and answer quizzes online which is different from learning other subjects." (Pupil 8)

These remarks suggest that pupils found the blended learning format more engaging than conventional approaches.

5.2.4 Usability and Engagement with the Interface

The most positively rated perception item was related to pupils' interest in learning via Google Classroom (Item 12: M = 4.83), followed closely by perceptions of its ease of use (Item 11: M = 4.56). Pupils consistently noted that the visual and interactive nature of the platform heightened their attention and enjoyment during lessons.

"I like learning online because I enjoy the activities." (Pupil 7)

"Google Classroom is very interesting. I can do quiz many times until I get it right." (Pupil 4)

This high level of engagement supports the argument that an intuitive and child-friendly interface can significantly impact learners' attitudes toward technology-enhanced instruction.

Collectively, the findings indicate that pupils have a favorable perception of blended learning, especially when tasks are well-structured, technology is accessible and engaging, and teacher guidance remains consistent. Although some pupils were less confident in peer collaboration, the overall perception points toward the viability and appeal of blended learning as a tool to support vocabulary acquisition in young ESL learners.

5.3 Pupils' Motivation Toward Blended Learning for Vocabulary Development

Pupils' motivation toward blended learning was examined using an 11-item questionnaire supported by qualitative interviews. The analysis was framed by the Cognitive Evaluation Theory (CET), which conceptualizes motivation in terms of three fundamental psychological needs: autonomy, competence, and relatedness. The results revealed a consistently high level of motivation among participants, with an overall mean score of 4.32 out of 5. All motivation items were rated at a high level, underscoring pupils' strong intrinsic drive to engage with blended learning tasks for vocabulary development.

5.3.1 Autonomy: Enjoyment and Volition in Learning

The highest-rated item in the motivation scale was Item 1, "I enjoy learning English using Google Classroom" (M = 4.61), suggesting that pupils experienced a high degree of enjoyment and ownership over their learning. Similarly, pupils expressed intrinsic motivation to participate in activities without coercion (Item 3: M = 4.28).

Interview responses revealed similar patterns. Pupils articulated that they found online tasks both enjoyable and stimulating:

"I like learning online because I can answer questions using Google Classroom which is very challenging and fun." (Pupil 4)

"I really like doing the tasks online." (Pupil 7)

The novelty and interactivity of the blended tasks contributed to a more autonomous learning experience. Pupils could complete activities at their own pace and according to their preferences, fostering an environment where learning felt self-directed and intrinsically rewarding.

5.3.2 Competence: Belief in Capability and Achievement

Items reflecting competence also scored highly, with Item 5, "I believe that the activities can help me to improve my vocabulary," yielding a mean of 4.50. Pupils not only felt capable of completing the tasks but also perceived them as meaningful and beneficial to their language development.

Interview data reinforced this confidence:

"Yes, I learned a lot of new words from the videos and PowerPoint slides." (Pupil 1)

"Yes, the activities helped me to learn many words." (Pupil 3)

Feedback mechanisms embedded in Google Classroom, such as instant quiz results, also contributed to pupils' sense of progress. Pupils appreciated being able to track their performance immediately, which in turn reinforced their motivation to keep improving:

"I can check my score immediately. I always get full marks for the activities." (Pupil 2)

"I can see my result after the quiz." (Pupil 6)

This positive feedback loop which are completing tasks, receiving feedback, and observing improvement served as a critical motivator, validating pupils' competence and sustaining their engagement.

5.3.3 Relatedness: Emotional Security and Social Connection

The third pillar of motivation, relatedness, was also strongly supported. Pupils reported feeling comfortable and secure while completing tasks (Item 9: M = 4.31), and expressed a desire for more interaction with both teachers and peers (Items 10 and 11: M = 4.14 and 4.47, respectively).

The qualitative interviews reflected the emotional dimension of blended learning:

"I hope I can talk to teacher more in class and ask questions." (Pupil 5)

"Sometimes I talk with friends about the questions. It helps." (Pupil 9)

These findings highlight that blended learning environments, when paired with supportive teacher facilitation, can foster both emotional and social engagement. Pupils felt part of a learning community, even when working independently through digital means.

In short, the findings found that pupils demonstrated a high level of motivation toward blended learning, driven by their enjoyment of the platform, a strong belief in their own learning progress, and a sense of connectedness with teachers and peers. When learners feel autonomous, capable, and supported, they are more likely to participate actively and persist in language learning tasks. These findings affirm that when thoughtfully designed, blended learning not only improves academic outcomes but also cultivates the psychological conditions necessary for sustained learner motivation.

6. DISCUSSION

6.1 Pupils' Performance in Vocabulary Development

The quantitative analysis of pupils' vocabulary performance revealed that blended learning significantly enhances vocabulary acquisition among primary school ESL learners. Prior to the intervention, results from the pre-test showed no significant difference between the experimental group (M = 5.39, SD = 1.86) and the control group (M = 4.94, SD = 1.39), with t(70) = 1.149 and p = .254. This finding confirms the homogeneity of both groups in terms of vocabulary proficiency at baseline, supporting the internal validity of the intervention (Fraenkel & Wallen, 2008).

Following the implementation of blended learning, the experimental group exhibited a markedly higher post-test mean score of 16.22 (SD = 1.57), compared to the control group's mean score of 11.33 (SD = 1.59). The independent samples t-test yielded a statistically significant result (t(70) = 13.148, p < .001), indicating that the difference in vocabulary performance between the two groups was not due to chance. The mean difference of 4.89 further supports the practical effectiveness of the blended learning approach in vocabulary instruction.

These results align with previous research that emphasizes the benefits of blended learning in language acquisition. Studies by Polakova and Klimova (2022) and Ebadi and Ghuchi (2018) have shown that blended learning environments improve learners' lexical competence by offering extended exposure, interactive engagement, and repeated practice. The increased performance among the experimental group in the current study may be attributed to the multimodal nature of blended learning tasks such as videos, quizzes, and visual presentations which allow learners to process vocabulary through both visual and verbal channels.

Moreover, the observed score improvement in the experimental group (ranging from 7 to 16 points) compared to the control group (4 to 10 points) underscores the enhanced vocabulary retention and recall facilitated by blended instruction. As noted by Sung et al. (2017), the flexible access to learning content and the opportunity to engage in self-paced revision are critical factors in supporting vocabulary acquisition. The use of Google Classroom as one of the blended learning tools provided pupils with asynchronous learning opportunities, allowing them to revisit and practice vocabulary outside formal instructional time an advantage absent in the traditional classroom setting.

The findings also resonate with the argument by Mueller et al. (2020) who contended that the effectiveness of blended learning is amplified when digital components are aligned with curriculum goals and supported by teacher facilitation. In this study, the digital tasks were closely aligned with the CEFR vocabulary levels

(A1 to B1), ensuring relevance to the syllabus while simultaneously accommodating pupils' individual learning needs.

In sum, the statistical evidence demonstrates that blended learning is significantly more effective than traditional methods for vocabulary development in young ESL learners. The integration of structured online platforms and interactive digital tasks into the learning process not only improved test performance but also likely contributed to increased engagement and long-term retention of vocabulary. These findings support the incorporation of blended learning models into ESL curricula at the primary level as a means to improve lexical outcomes through flexible, learner-centered instruction.

6.2 Pupils' Perception of Blended Learning for Vocabulary Development

The findings of this study revealed that primary ESL pupils generally held positive perceptions toward the use of blended learning for vocabulary development. The overall average mean score across the 12 perception items was 4.32, indicating a high level of agreement with the benefits and usability of blended learning. Eleven out of twelve items were rated at a "high" level, while only one item—interacting with peers to improve vocabulary—was rated at an "average" level (M = 3.61), suggesting some variability in how different aspects of blended learning were experienced by the pupils.

The positive perception aligns with prior research asserting that pupils respond favorably to the integration of digital platforms into language learning. For example, Nuareni (2020) noted that blended learning environments foster meaningful learner engagement when technology is well-aligned with pedagogical goals. In this study, the use of Google Classroom provided a centralized, structured interface where pupils could access vocabulary activities, interact with their teachers and peers, and review materials at their own pace.

6.2.1 Dialogue and Interaction

Items reflecting interaction with teachers and peers yielded generally high mean scores. Notably, Item 4 ("Interacting with my teacher helps me to improve my vocabulary") scored 3.92, supporting the notion that teacher-pupil communication plays a pivotal role in facilitating vocabulary acquisition. This aligns with Vygotsky's (1978) Sociocultural Theory, which emphasizes the importance of interaction with more knowledgeable others in scaffolding language learning. However, peer-related items such as Item 3 ("Interacting with my friends helps me improve my vocabulary") received the lowest mean score (M = 3.61), suggesting that some pupils, likely due to age or limited peer academic trust, were less confident in their ability to learn from classmates. Similar findings were reported by Huang (2016), who noted that younger learners may rely more heavily on teacher input than on peer collaboration in language tasks.

6.2.2 Autonomy and Learner Control

Pupils' perception of autonomy was particularly strong, especially for Item 8 ("I am able to learn English using Google Classroom"), which recorded a mean score of 4.69. This suggests that pupils appreciated the flexibility and independence offered by the blended learning model. Mohammed et al. (2023) and Banditvilai (2016) similarly found that blended learning increases learner autonomy by allowing students to manage their own learning pace and revisit content when needed. In the context of this study, the pupils' ability to access materials outside classroom hours via Google Classroom likely contributed to this sense of independence and ownership over their vocabulary learning process.

6.2.3 Structure of Learning Activities

The structure of blended learning tasks also received favorable ratings. Pupils felt that the activities helped them understand new vocabulary (Item 9: M = 4.44) and that the instructions were clear (Item 10: M = 4.42). These responses reflect the effective instructional design of the blended learning environment, which combined visual aids, scaffolded tasks, and age-appropriate content sequencing. This finding echoes Sheninger (2016), who emphasized the importance of instructional clarity and differentiated learning paths in enhancing learner engagement in technology-integrated environments.

6.2.4 Course Interface and Usability

The highest-rated item overall was Item 12 ("I find learning using Google Classroom very interesting"), which received a mean score of 4.83. This indicates strong pupil engagement with the platform, likely due to the novelty and interactivity of the tasks presented. Item 11 ("Google Classroom is easy to use") also scored highly (M = 4.56), reflecting the accessibility of the platform for young learners. Delialioglu and Yildrim (2007) stressed the importance of user-friendly course interfaces in sustaining learner interest and preventing cognitive overload—an assertion supported by the present findings.

Together, these results affirm that blended learning, when thoughtfully implemented, is not only effective but also perceived as enjoyable, flexible, and manageable by young ESL learners. However, the findings also underscore the need for increased emphasis on peer collaboration in blended tasks, particularly in promoting vocabulary development through interactive group work. Teachers may need to scaffold peer interaction more intentionally and model collaborative strategies to help pupils derive more value from group-based learning activities.

6.3 Pupils' Motivation toward Blended Learning for Vocabulary Development

The study's findings demonstrate that pupils were highly motivated to engage with blended learning for vocabulary development. The overall average mean score across the 11 motivation items was 4.32, with all items rated at a high level. This suggests that the blended learning approach successfully fostered a motivational climate conducive to active participation and sustained vocabulary acquisition among young ESL learners.

The results were analyzed using the framework of Self-Determination Theory (SDT), specifically its subcomponent, Cognitive Evaluation Theory (CET), which posits that motivation is fostered when three psychological needs are met: autonomy, competence, and relatedness (Deci & Ryan, 2000).

6.3.1 Autonomy: Interest and Self-Directed Engagement

The strongest motivational response was recorded for Item 1, "I enjoy learning English using Google Classroom" (M = 4.61), followed closely by Item 6, "I would be willing to do the activities in Google Classroom again" (M = 4.42). These results suggest that pupils experienced high levels of enjoyment and personal interest in the learning tasks, which are hallmarks of intrinsic motivation. Autonomy-supportive environments, such as those enabled by blended learning platforms, allow learners to make meaningful choices about when and how they engage with tasks, thus leading to greater motivation and engagement (Sung et al., 2017).

Additionally, Item 3 ("I did the activities on Google Classroom because I wanted to") scored 4.28, indicating that pupils engaged with the content voluntarily, not due to external pressure. This internal regulation of behavior is an important marker of intrinsic motivation, particularly in younger learners who typically rely more on extrinsic motivators in traditional classroom settings.

6.3.2 Competence: Confidence and Achievement

Items reflecting pupils' sense of competence also scored highly. For instance, Item 5 ("I believed that the activities can help me to improve my vocabulary") had a mean score of 4.50, indicating that pupils recognized the instructional value of the tasks in supporting their vocabulary learning. Similarly, Items 7 and 8—reflecting self-satisfaction and perceived performance relative to peers which scored 4.33 and 4.42, respectively.

This aligns with findings by Lo et al. (2022), who noted that pupils are more motivated when they believe that their efforts lead to tangible academic improvement. In the present study, the design of the Google Classroom tasks—such as multiple-attempt quizzes and instant feedback—likely helped pupils gauge their progress and develop confidence in their learning abilities. Such mastery experiences are key contributors to motivation and persistence, especially in language learning contexts.

6.3.3 Relatedness: Emotional Support and Social Connection

The dimension of relatedness also emerged as a significant motivational factor. Item 11 ("I hoped I can interact with my teacher more during the task") recorded a high mean score of 4.47, while Item 10 ("I hope I can interact with my friends more often during the task") scored 4.14. These findings reflect pupils' desire for meaningful social interaction as part of the learning process, which is a critical motivational driver according to SDT (Ryan & Deci, 2000).

Moreover, Item 9 ("I felt relaxed while doing the activities on Google Classroom") scored 4.31, suggesting that the learning environment created through blended learning reduced anxiety and promoted emotional security. This is consistent with findings from Wang et al. (2019), who identified relatedness as the most influential predictor of motivation in technology-integrated classrooms. When learners feel emotionally supported and socially connected, they are more likely to persist in learning tasks.

As a whole, the results from this study corroborate previous literature asserting that blended learning enhances student motivation across multiple dimensions. For example, Al-Hamidi and Al-Rushidi (2023) found that blended learning environments stimulate learners' interest and participation due to the integration of interactive digital tools and flexible learning opportunities. Similarly, Chiu (2021) highlighted that the motivational impact of blended learning is most pronounced when learners are given choice, autonomy, and feedback, conditions that were satisfied in this study through the use of Google Classroom. On top of that, Sucaromana (2013) further emphasized that motivational gains are enhanced when instructional technology aligns with learners' cognitive levels and learning preferences. In this study, the design of age-appropriate vocabulary tasks with audiovisual support appears to have effectively captured pupils' attention and fostered a sense of agency in their learning process.

In a nutshell, the high motivation levels observed across all 11 items reflect the success of blended learning in satisfying pupils' needs for autonomy, competence, and relatedness. The combination of engaging content, flexible pacing, social interaction, and ongoing feedback contributed to a positive learning environment that encouraged sustained involvement in vocabulary learning. These findings reinforce the relevance of Self-Determination Theory in understanding motivation within technology-enhanced language learning environments and support the integration of blended learning as a strategy for fostering intrinsic motivation in primary ESL education.

6.4 Challenges and Limitations of Blended Vocabulary Instruction in Primary Schools

While this study affirms the pedagogical value of blended learning in enhancing vocabulary acquisition and motivation among primary ESL learners, several challenges and limitations must be acknowledged to situate its findings realistically within broader educational practice. First, infrastructural disparities remain a significant concern. Although the study was conducted in an urban, well-equipped school, many Malaysian primary schools, particularly in rural and underserved areas, lack reliable internet access, sufficient digital devices, and technical support systems. These disparities exacerbate the digital divide and limit the equitable implementation of blended learning. Without targeted interventions such as device subsidies, centralized resource hubs, or community learning centers, blended instruction may unintentionally deepen existing educational inequalities. Second, teacher digital competence and pedagogical readiness are uneven across school settings. The successful implementation of blended learning requires more than basic ICT skills; it demands the ability to design, scaffold, and manage learning tasks that are theoretically grounded, developmentally appropriate, and aligned with curriculum standards. Many in-service teachers report a lack of confidence in integrating technology meaningfully into language instruction. Without sustained professional development programs and mentoring structures, blended learning may devolve into superficial technology use rather than transformative pedagogy. Third, student factors, including self-regulation, home learning environments, and parental support, play a crucial role in shaping the effectiveness of blended learning. In this study, positive motivation and perception were partially attributed to the pupils' ability to access Google Classroom outside of school hours, often with parental assistance. However, not all learners have the same level of support or conducive learning environments at home. Younger learners, in particular, may struggle with managing digital tasks independently without consistent adult guidance. Lastly, curricular alignment and instructional coherence present ongoing challenges. While vocabulary instruction lends itself well to digital augmentation, other language domains such as speaking or listening may require more synchronous and socially embedded interactions. As schools move toward more comprehensive adoption of blended learning, there is a need for integrated instructional planning that avoids fragmented delivery and maintains curricular continuity across modalities. These limitations do not negate the findings of the study but rather underscore the conditional nature of blended learning's success. For blended vocabulary instruction to be scalable and sustainable, implementation must be sensitive to local realities and supported by coherent policies, institutional investment, and ongoing teacher capacity-building efforts.

7. CONCLUSION

The findings of this study underscore the urgent need to reimagine vocabulary instruction in Malaysian primary ESL classrooms. Pupils who engaged with a blended learning model demonstrated significantly higher vocabulary gains, stronger motivation, and more positive perceptions of the learning process compared to those taught through traditional face-to-face instruction. These outcomes affirm that blended learning, when strategically implemented and grounded in relevant learning theories such as Self-Determination Theory and Transactional Distance Theory, offers a powerful and scalable solution to persistent vocabulary challenges in ESL education.

Blended learning aligns with the demands of 21st-century education by supporting differentiated instruction, promoting learner autonomy, and leveraging digital tools to enhance engagement and retention. In light of these findings, this chapter argues that blended learning should be more widely adopted across Malaysian primary ESL contexts, not as an add-on, but as a core instructional strategy embedded within the national language curriculum. However, for such a shift to be sustainable, several systemic and pedagogical considerations must be addressed. The implementation of blended learning is not without its challenges. Teachers in Malaysian public schools frequently cite constraints such as limited digital proficiency, insufficient planning time, and inadequate infrastructural support. Additionally, socio-economic disparities may limit some students' access to reliable devices or internet connectivity, particularly in rural or under-resourced settings.

7.1 Practical Recommendations

To translate the promising results of this study into widespread educational improvement, coordinated efforts from curriculum developers, policymakers, and teachers are essential. Each stakeholder group has a distinct yet interdependent role in fostering a sustainable blended learning ecosystem within Malaysian primary ESL education.

Firstly, curriculum developers must take the lead in embedding blended learning approaches into the national ESL syllabus. This entails moving beyond sporadic digital tasks and instead designing integrated lesson frameworks that systematically incorporate technology to enhance vocabulary instruction. Vocabulary components should be developed with alignment to CEFR proficiency bands and include multimodal resources such as interactive videos, digital flashcards, and self-paced quizzes that promote both receptive and productive lexical skills. To ease teacher workload and promote consistency, centralized resource banks curated at the ministry or district level should be established. These repositories would contain adaptable lesson materials, multimedia assets, and assessment templates that teachers can customize to fit their classroom needs, thereby minimizing preparation time while ensuring quality and standardization.

Next, policymakers play a pivotal role in establishing the structural and professional conditions necessary for blended learning to flourish. Professional development must be institutionalized and recurrent, not limited to one-off workshops. Training programs should focus not only on building teachers' technical competence but also on fostering pedagogical confidence in designing and managing blended instruction. In parallel, infrastructural readiness must be addressed through systematic investment in devices, broadband access, and digital learning facilities across all schools. To ensure equity, targeted interventions should support pupils from low-income households through device subsidies, school-based access hubs, or shared community technology centers. Without such support, the digital divide may undermine the pedagogical advantages of blended learning.

Last but not least, teachers, as frontline implementers, must be empowered to adopt blended learning gradually and strategically. Rather than overhauling existing practices, teachers can begin by incorporating blended methods into vocabulary instruction, a domain that is well-suited to digital augmentation. Platforms like Google Classroom can be used to scaffold and extend face-to-face learning through structured online tasks, immediate feedback mechanisms, and flexible pacing options. In doing so, teachers can promote learner autonomy while maintaining instructional coherence. Moreover, teachers should actively nurture pupils' motivation by selecting engaging multimedia content, offering choices in task completion, and recognizing effort and progress, strategies that align with intrinsic motivation principles and support sustained language learning.

7.2 Future Directions

For future studies, it is suggested to examine the longitudinal impact of blended vocabulary instruction on language proficiency and retention. Comparative research across urban and rural settings would provide valuable insight into contextual constraints and enablers. Additionally, future investigations might explore blended learning applications across other language domains, such as grammar, speaking, or writing, to better understand its cross-domain efficacy.

REFERENCES

Al-Hamidi, H. K., & Al-Rushidi, M. A. (2023). The effectiveness of blended learning in improving academic achievement and motivation to learn among students at the College of Basic Education in Kuwait. *Journal of Reading and Knowledge, 23*(255), 15–60.

Banditvilai, C. (2016). Enhancing students' language skills through blended learning. *Electronic Journal of e-Learning, 14*(3), 220–229.

Cao, W. (2023). A meta-analysis of effects of blended learning on performance, attitude, achievement, and engagement across different countries. *Frontiers in Psychology, 14*, 1212056. DOI: 10.3389/fpsyg.2023.1212056 PMID: 37502744

Chiu, T. K. F. (2021). Applying the self-determination theory (SDT) to explain student engagement in online learning during the COVID-19 pandemic. *Journal of Research on Technology in Education, 54*(sup1), S14–S30. https://doi.org/DOI: 10.1080/15391523.2021.1891998

Daniel, M. B., & Villanueva, H. D. (2023). Teachers' pedagogical practices in relation to students' motivation in blended learning. *ARRUS Journal of Social Sciences and Humanities, 3*(5), 612–620. DOI: 10.35877/soshum1719

Deci, E. L., & Ryan, R. M. (1985). *Intrinsic motivation and self-determination in human behavior*. Plenum Press.

Delialioglu, O., & Yildirim, Z. (2007). Students' Perceptions on Effective Dimensions of Interactive Learning in a Blended Learning Environment. *Journal of Educational Technology & Society, 10*(2), 133–146.

Dinara, G. V., Irina, I. K., Elena, L. A., Natalya, V. K., & Jana, B. (2016). Enhancement of Students' Vocabulary Learning Through a Blended Learning Approach. *International Electronic Journal of Mathematics Education, 11*(5), 1195–1203.

Djiwandono, P. I. (2013). A Blended Learning Approach to Enhance College Students '. *Vocabulary Learning., 10*(2), 210–220.

Dornyei, Z. (2009). The L2 Motivational Self System. In Dornyei, Z., & Ushioda, E. (Eds.), *Motivation, Language Identity and the L2 Self* (pp. 9–42). Multilingual Matters.

Ebadi, S., & Ghuchi, K. D. (2018). Investigating the Effects of Blended Learning Approach on Vocabulary Enhancement from EFL Learners' Perspectives. *Journal on English Language Teaching, 8*(2), 57–68.

Fernandez, D. M., & Canado, L. P. (2001). Exploring The Student's Motivation in the EFL Class. *Present and Future Trends in TEFL*, 321-364.

Fraenkel, J., & Wallen, N. (2008). *How to design and evaluate research in education* (7th ed.). McGraw Hill.

Gardner, R. C. (1985). *Social Psychology and Second Language Learning: The Role of Attitudes and Motivation*. Edward Arnold.

Hong, A. L. T., & Stapa, M. (2023). The Effect of Blended Learning Towards Pupils' Vocabulary Development and Motivation in an ESL Classroom. [JONUS]. *Journal of Nusantara Studies*, *8*(1), 406–428. DOI: 10.24200/jonus.vol8iss1pp406-428

Hong, A. L. T., Stapa, M., & Tian, K. X. (2025). Malaysian Primary School Teachers' Self-Assessment of TPACK and their Blended Learning Practice. *International Journal of Instruction*, *18*(1), 695–714. DOI: 10.29333/iji.2025.18139a

Huang, Q. (2016). Learners' Perceptions of Blended Learning and the Roles and Interaction of f2f and Online Learning. *ORTESOL Journal*, *33*, 14–33.

Katemba, C. V. (2022). Vocabulary Enhancement through Presentation, Practice, Production(PPP) Method in the Rural EFL Classrooms. *Acuity: Journal of English Language Pedagogy. Literature and Culture*, *7*(1), 88–101. DOI: 10.35974/acuity.v7i1.2774

Khodaparast, F., & Ghafournia, N. (2015). On The Effect of Online / Offline Approaches on Vocabulary Achievement. *International Journal of Education and Research*, *3*(9), 269–280.

Kintu, M. J., Zhu, C., & Kagambe, E. (2017). Blended learning effectiveness: The relationship between student characteristics, design features and outcomes. *International Journal of Educational Technology in Higher Education*, *14*(7), 1–20. DOI: 10.1186/s41239-017-0043-4

Koohang, A., & Weiss, E. (2003). Effect of prior experience with the internet on graduate students' perception toward courseware usability & web-based distance learning instruction: An exploratory study in a hybrid instruction environment. *Journal of Computer Information Systems*, *4*(2), 535–541.

Laufer, B., & Hulstijn, J. (2001). Incidental vocabulary acquisition in a second language: The construct of task-induced involvement. *Applied Linguistics*, *22*(1), 1–26.

Leakey, J., & Ranchoux, A. (2006). BLINGUA: A blended language learning approach for CALL. *Computer Assisted Language Learning*, *19*, 357–372.

Liu, M., Zhao, G., Zhong, Z., Ma, J., & Wang, W. (2024). Theoretical Foundations for Blended Learning. In Li, M., Han, X., & Cheng, J. (Eds.), *Handbook of Educational Reform Through Blended Learning*. Springer., DOI: 10.1007/978-981-99-6269-3_1

Lo, K. W. K., Ngai, G., Chan, S. C. F., & Kwan, K. P. (2022). How Students' Motivation and Learning Experience Affect Their Service-Learning Outcomes: A Structural Equation Modeling Analysis. *Frontiers in Psychology*, *13*, 825902. DOI: 10.3389/fpsyg.2022.825902 PMID: 35519642

Makkar, N., & Sharma, R. (2022). Effect of blended learning on academic achievement in mathematics among ix grade students. *International Journal of Indian Psychology*, *10*(2). Advance online publication. DOI: 10.25215/1002.135

Marsh, D. (2012). *Blended learning: Creating learning opportunities for language learners*. Cambridge University Press.

McHone, C. (2020). Blended Learning Integration: Student Motivation and Autonomy in a Blended Learning Environment. *Electronic Theses and Dissertations*. 3750.

Mohammed, H. S., Aicha, B., & Rahil, M. (2023). EFL Students' Perceptions About The Effect Of Blended Learning On Their Learning Autonomy. *Journal of Language and Linguistic Studies*, *19*(3), 85–105.

Moore, M. G. (1997). Theory of transactional distance. In Keegan, D. (Ed.), *Theoretical principles of distance education*. Routledge.

Mueller, C., Mildenberger, T., & Lübcke, M. (2020). Do we always need a difference? Testing equivalence in a blended learning setting. *International Journal of Research & Method in Education*, *43*, 283–295. DOI: 10.1080/1743727X.2019.1680621

Nuareni, C. (2020). Mobile-assisted language learning (MALL): Students' perception and problems towards Mobile learning in English language. *Journal of Physics: Conference Series*, *1641*, 7.

Pannan, L. J., & Legge, K. A. (2016). A blended learning model and a design model combine to support academics in pedagogical redesign of the curriculum. *ASCILITE 2016 - Conference Proceedings - 33rd International Conference of Innovation, Practice and Research in the Use of Educational Technologies in Tertiary Education: Show Me the Learning.*

Polakova, P., & Klimova, B. (2022). Vocabulary Mobile Learning Application in Blended English Language Learning. *Frontiers in Psychology*, *13*, 869055. DOI: 10.3389/fpsyg.2022.869055 PMID: 35592159

Qindah, S. (2018). The Effects of Blended Learning on EFL Students ' Usage of Grammar in Context. [EPESS]. *The Eurasia Proceedings of Educational & Social Sciences*, *10*, 11–22.

Rahmat, H., Mashudi, R., Hairul, M., Razak, A., Huda, N., Hamid, A., & Rahmat, N. (2019). the Readiness of MMU Lecturers Towards the Implementation of Blended Learning. *E-Bangi*, 16(1).

Samya, A. J. S. (2007). *Undergraduate Learners' Perceptions of Blended Learning and its Relationship with Some Demographic and Experiential Variables at the Arab Open University- Bahrain Branch*. University of United Arab Emirates.

Sheninger, E. C. (2016). *Uncommon learning: Creating schools that work for kids*. Corwin.

Sucaromana, U. (2013). The Effect of Blended Learning on the Intrinsic Motivation of Thai EFL Students. *English Language Teaching*, *6*(5), 141–147.

Sung, H. Y., Hwang, G. J., Lin, C. J., & Hong, T. W. (2017). Experiencing the analects of Confucius: An experiential game-based learning approach to promoting students' motivation and conception of learning. *Computers & Education*, *110*, 143–153.

Tabassum, B., Moin, M., Abbas, Q., Kumbhar, M. I., & Khan, M. H. N. (2024). The impact of blended learning on student performance. *Journal of Education and Social Studies*, *5*(2), 360–371. DOI: 10.52223/jess.2024.5217

Tong, D. H., Uyen, B. P., & Ngan, L. K. (2022). The Effectiveness of Blended Learning on Students' Academic Achievement, Self-Study Skills and Learning Attitudes: A Quasi-Experiment Study in Teaching the Conventions for Coordinates in the Plane. *Heliyon*, *8*, e12657. DOI: 10.1016/j.heliyon.2022.e12657 PMID: 36643330

Vygotsky, L. S. (1978). Interaction between Learning and Development. In Cole, M., John-Steiner, V., Scribner, S., & Souberman, E. (Eds.), *Mind and Society: The Development of Higher Psychological Processes* (pp. 79–91). Harvard University Press.

Wang, C. K., Liu, W. C., Kee, Y. H., & Chian, L. K. (2019). Competence, autonomy, and relatedness in the classroom: Understanding students' motivational processes using the self-determination theory. *Heliyon*, *5*, 1–6. PMID: 31372524

Yee, C. H., & Ganapathy, M. (2017). To Investigate ESL Students' Instrumental and Integrative Motivation towards English Language Learning in a Chinese School in Penang: Case Study. *Journal of English Language Teaching*, *10*(9), 17–35.

KEY TERMS AND DEFINITIONS

Blended Learning: In a classroom, teachers can use any form of online technology such as online quizzes, videos, learning management system to supplement their face-to-face teaching

Digital platforms: Digital platforms are web-based environment designed to facilitate learning process

Face-to-face learning: This kind of learning happens when learners are present in a physical classroom.

Google Classroom: Google Classroom is a virtual classroom where teacher can provide online tasks for their pupils to access anytime out of school hours.

Online learning: This kind of learning occurs through technology where it requires the use of the internet and digital platforms.

Traditional classroom: Traditional classrooms encompassed textbook-based learning involving memorization and drilling methods to learn.

Vocabulary knowledge: Vocabulary knowledge involves the number of words known by an individual.

Chapter 12 The Design, Development, and Evaluation of the Task-Based Small Private Online Course (SPOC) for Learning English for Occupational Purposes

Hanxu Wang
https://orcid.org/0009-0002-6405-9688
Universiti Sains Malaysia, Malaysia

Mariam Mohamad
https://orcid.org/0000-0001-8498-4139
Universiti Sains Malaysia, Malaysia

Nurul Maziah Mohd Barkhaya
https://orcid.org/0009-0002-2192-0706
Universiti Sains Malaysia, Malaysia

Ju Yan
https://orcid.org/0009-0006-0459-9905
Universiti Sains Malaysia, Malaysia

DOI: 10.4018/979-8-3373-7508-3.ch012

ABSTRACT

MOOCs are found to be limited in improving learner performance and perceived motivation, especially in English for Occupational Purposes (EOP). This study designed, developed, and evaluated a Task-Based Small Private Online Course (TB-SPOC) for EOP in Chinese Higher Vocational Colleges (HVCs). Guided by Task-Based Instruction, Self-Determination Theory, and the ADDIE model, the TB-SPOC emphasized real-world communicative tasks aligned with national standards. A quasi-experimental design involved 360 first-year HVC students from high school and vocational school backgrounds, who were randomly assigned to either a TB-SPOC or Content-Based SPOC group. Performance was assessed through pre- and post-tests on discourse competence, and perceived motivation was measured using an adapted Instructional Material Motivational Survey. The study provides empirical evidence for the effectiveness of TB-SPOCs in enhancing learning performance and perceived motivation, offering insights for improving vocational English instruction through innovative online models.

INTRODUCTION

The global evolution of digital education has fundamentally altered the pedagogical landscape of English language instruction (Javed, 2024). Triggered by the COVID-19 pandemic and sustained by continued technological advancement, this transformation has made online and blended learning an integral part of higher education worldwide (Ali, 2020; Abdullah et al., 2020). Traditional classroom instruction is increasingly complemented or replaced by digital alternatives that offer greater flexibility, scalability, and accessibility. These changes have led to new demands for educational models that are responsive to the diverse needs of learners and aligned with the practical realities of the twenty-first-century workplace.

In this context, English for Occupational Purposes (EOP) has gained heightened importance, particularly in vocational education where communicative competence in real-world settings is crucial (Zeng & Della, 2024). The imperative to teach job-specific English in a way that is contextually relevant and pedagogically sound has spurred a wave of innovation in instructional delivery. While Massive Open Online Courses (MOOCs) initially held promise for expanding access to language education, they have proven insufficient in practice due to their impersonal structure, limited interactivity, and high dropout rates (Feng & Liu, 2022; Li, 2022). These limitations are especially pronounced in EOP, where learners benefit most from structured, task-oriented instruction that simulates real-world communication.

To address the shortcomings of MOOCs, Fox (2013) introduced the concept of Small Private Online Courses (SPOCs), a format that combines the resource-rich environment of MOOCs with the intimacy and interactivity of small-group learning. SPOCs support blended learning by integrating digital materials with classroom-based engagement, enabling students to receive targeted feedback and participate in interactive tasks. Empirical studies have begun to document the potential of SPOCs to improve language learning outcomes when effectively designed and implemented (Dong et al., 2021; Zhu, 2022). Nevertheless, these studies rely heavily on learner self-perception and satisfaction metrics, rather than objective assessments of performance or measurable language acquisition. This pattern raises concerns regarding the robustness of findings and underscores the need for more rigorous evaluation frameworks.

Furthermore, despite the emergence of SPOCs as a promising educational format, their integration into EOP instruction remains limited and inconsistently theorised. A critical review of the literature reveals that most existing SPOCs are developed without a strong grounding in pedagogical theory (Wuhue, 2023). Task-Based Instruction (TBI), which has been shown to facilitate language learning through meaningful, goal-oriented communication tasks (Brown, 2014; Bărbuleţ, 2022), is rarely employed as the foundation for SPOC design. This omission is notable given the clear conceptual alignment between TBI and the demands of EOP, which requires learners to engage in authentic workplace communication. Without embedding such principles into online course frameworks, the potential of SPOCs to deliver transformative learning experiences remains underutilised.

The practical implementation of SPOCs in China's higher vocational colleges (HVCs) illustrates many of these broader trends and challenges. As institutions respond to national policy initiatives promoting the digitalisation of vocational education (Ministry of Education of the People's Republic of China, 2018, 2020), SPOCs have been adopted to expand access and improve the quality of English instruction. However, HVCs face unique challenges due to the diverse learning backgrounds of their student populations, including both regular high schools and vocational secondary schools, which lead to significant differences in language proficiency, learner autonomy, and digital literacy (Gu, 2020; Xing, 2023). Most SPOCs, however, adopt a standardised approach that fails to account for these differences, thereby limiting their pedagogical effectiveness and equity in learning outcomes.

Moreover, most SPOCs currently in use do not adequately simulate the real-life scenarios that vocational learners will encounter in the workplace (Sun, 2019; Zhang et al., 2023). Instead, they often present abstract language exercises that lack contextual relevance, undermining both learner motivation and performance (Jiang & Liang, 2023). Even where TBI is nominally incorporated, the tasks are frequently disconnected from actual occupational contexts, reducing their impact on communicative competence. This misalignment between instructional design and learning objectives contributes to the underperformance of SPOC-based EOP instruction. It also highlights the need for SPOCs that engage students through meaningful, context-specific learning experiences.

Given these gaps, there is a clear need for an instructional model that addresses both the pedagogical and contextual challenges facing vocational English education. This study aims to contribute to this endeavour by designing, developing, and empirically evaluating a task-based SPOC (TB-SPOC) specifically tailored for EOP learners in Chinese HVCs. The course integrates TBI principles into the SPOC, using simulated workplace tasks to promote authentic language use and collaborative problem-solving. It seeks to bridge the divide between theory and practice by grounding course design in established pedagogical frameworks and assessing outcomes through objective, performance-based measures.

This research takes a quantitative approach, employing a quasi-experimental design with pre- and post-tests to measure changes in learners' English performance and using Keller's Instructional Materials Motivation Survey (IMMS) to assess perceived motivation (Keller, 2010). In addition, it investigates how educational background, whether high school or vocational school, moderates the effects of TB-SPOC instruction. This line of inquiry addresses the underexplored question of whether learner educational backgrounds influence the efficacy of task-based online instruction and offers empirical evidence to inform differentiated instructional strategies.

In summary, this chapter lays the foundation for a study that seeks to fill multiple interrelated gaps: the lack of task-based SPOCs in EOP, the limited use of objective assessment tools in evaluating SPOC effectiveness, and the insufficient attention paid to learners' educational backgrounds in instructional design. By addressing these challenges, the research offers a pathway for improving vocational English instruction and contributes practical insights for future researchers, educators, and policymakers aiming to enhance the quality and equity of digital language education in vocational contexts.

BACKGROUND OF STUDY

Since the introduction of the enrolment expansion reform policy in 1999, HVCs in China have experienced rapid growth in student numbers. This expansion, further intensified by the *Implementation Plan of the National Vocational Education Reform* (2019), has brought a marked increase in student diversity. Learners now enter HVCs from a wide range of educational backgrounds, including low-achieving high school graduates and vocational school students who lack a strong academic foundation (Gu, 2020). While the broader access is commendable in terms of policy goals, it poses significant challenges in instructional delivery, especially for EOP, which requires tailored pedagogy to suit different learning profiles. Institutions are increasingly burdened by the widening gap between student needs and available resources, as the rapid growth in enrolment has not been matched by an equivalent expansion in teaching staff, particularly those with expertise in EOP and applied linguistics (Xing, 2023).

One institution that exemplifies these challenges is a HVC located in Cangzhou, Hebei Province. This HVC has experienced a significant increase in student intake over the past five years, with cohorts comprising both high school and vocational school students. Teachers in the English department report difficulties in managing large classes with different educational backgrounds. In one case, a course on workplace communication failed to yield meaningful outcomes because the content, adapted initially from MOOC resources, lacked specificity and contextual relevance. Teachers noted that while students were enthusiastic at the start, many became disengaged due to the lack of practical application and interaction. This case highlights the gap between centralised digital content and the localised, differentiated instruction required in vocational contexts.

In response to these issues, national policies such as the *Education Informatisation 2.0 Action Plan* (2018) and the *Action Plan for Improving the Quality of Vocational Education (2020–2023)* have placed increased emphasis on developing digital learning infrastructure. These plans advocate for the creation of high-quality, open online courses that can supplement in-class instruction and address the scarcity of qualified teaching personnel (Ren, 2020). However, their implementation in practice remains uneven. In many HVCs, including the Cangzhou case, digital resources are introduced without sufficient adaptation to learners' occupational needs or integration with classroom-based pedagogy. Consequently, students often report that online English learning lacks coherence and relevance to their professional training, resulting in limited learning gains.

SPOCs have emerged as one solution to bridge this gap. Unlike MOOCs, which are designed for large-scale, general-purpose learning, SPOCs offer structured, small-scale environments that can be customised for specific learner groups. SPOCs are particularly promising for EOP instruction, as they facilitate a blended learning format that enables both independent study and classroom-based engagement (Jiang et al., 2024). Empirical research has demonstrated that SPOCs can support differentiated learning pathways, providing tailored content and opportunities for meaningful interaction (Xie et al., 2021; Li et al., 2023). However, these benefits depend heavily on the underlying instructional design. In the case of the Cangzhou HVC, initial SPOC integration efforts replicated conventional lecture formats in digital form, failing to harness the potential for interaction, task completion, or real-life simulation. As a result, students completed the courses with slight measurable improvement in job-specific communicative competence.

A critical issue in existing SPOC implementation is the lack of innovation in instructional methodology (Zhang et, al., 2020; Gupta, 2020; Qiu, 2022). Many SPOCs in HVCs rely on repurposed MOOC content that emphasises passive consumption over active language use. These courses frequently ignore systematic instructional design principles and often lack a coherent pedagogical framework aligned with EOP needs (Liu, 2021; Li & Jiang, 2022). Despite policy encouragement to innovate, most SPOC models remain theory-light and practice-poor. Teachers at the Cangzhou college, for example, expressed uncertainty about how to design interactive online tasks or assess learning outcomes beyond completion rates. These experiences echo broader national concerns regarding the depth and effectiveness of SPOC models in real teaching contexts.

Another significant gap lies in the underutilisation of Task-Based Instruction (TBI) within SPOC environments. Rooted in Communicative Language Teaching (CLT), TBI centres on learners completing meaningful tasks that simulate real-world language use (Brown, 2014; Bărbuleţ, 2022). This makes TBI particularly suitable for EOP, which aims to develop communicative competence in occupational settings. Despite this theoretical alignment, few SPOCs explicitly incorporate task-based design. Where TBI elements are used, such as in listening or writing tasks, they often lack authenticity or alignment with learners' future job roles (Wei et al., 2024; Zhao, 2022).

Moreover, current research has been limited in evaluating the impact of SPOCs on learners' English performance in EOP contexts. While some studies report improved learner satisfaction or course completion rates, few employ objective, performance-based measures, such as pre- and post-tests, to assess language gains (Sun, 2019; Zhang et al., 2023; An & Qu, 2021). As a result, conclusions about SPOC effectiveness remain speculative. The Cangzhou experience reflects this gap, as instructors found it challenging to justify the continuation of SPOCs without clear evidence of their effectiveness. This underscores the need for empirical research that can rigorously evaluate how SPOC design, particularly task-based approaches, affects measurable performance outcomes.

The background of this study is shaped by both structural reforms and institutional practices aimed at expanding access to quality vocational education in China. While SPOCs offer a promising avenue to enhance English instruction for occupational purposes, their potential remains constrained by uniform content delivery, limited task integration, and weak empirical validation. By focusing on a task-based SPOC model and using a quantitative research design to evaluate its impact on student performance and perceived motivation, this study provides a theoretically grounded and practically viable contribution to the development of digital pedagogy in vocational English education.

PROBLEM STATEMENT

In an ideal educational environment, English for Occupational Purposes (EOP) in higher vocational colleges (HVCs) should equip students with the linguistic and communicative skills necessary for their future professions. This would involve learner-centred pedagogies, task-rich digital platforms, and instructional designs that integrate theoretical insights with practical application. Students would demonstrate measurable progress in performance, motivation, and confidence, as assessed by objective tools such as pre- and post-tests. However, the current reality in many Chinese HVCs reveals a stark contrast. Existing online English instruction, particularly in the form of MOOCs, often fails to achieve the desired educational outcomes due to its emphasis on standardised content delivery, minimal interactivity, and lack of relevance to learners' occupational needs (Sun, 2019; Li, 2022; Feng & Liu, 2022). These contradictions between policy aspirations and pedagogical practice underscore the need for targeted instructional innovation.

Although SPOCs have been promoted as a solution to address the limitations of MOOCs by offering smaller, customisable learning environments (Fox, 2013; Zhu, 2022), their actual implementation in the vocational English context remains fraught with challenges. Many SPOCs continue to replicate the shortcomings of their MOOC predecessors, employing didactic delivery modes and offering limited opportunities for learner interaction or contextualised task engagement. This is evident in several studies, where SPOCs have shown no significant effect on learners' performance, often due to theoretical underdevelopment and methodological limitations (Sun, 2019; Chen, 2020; Zhang et al., 2023; An & Qu, 2021). In particular, most existing evaluations rely on subjective data such as student self-reporting through questionnaires and interviews, which lack the rigour required for accurate performance assessment (Li & Jiang, 2022). Without the use of objective, empirical instruments such as pre- and post-intervention tests, it becomes difficult to draw valid conclusions about the educational impact of SPOCs.

Theoretically, there is a discernible gap in the application of robust pedagogical models in SPOC design. Much of the literature points to a lack of systematic instructional design and pedagogical grounding in SPOCs used for EOP, which diminishes their effectiveness (Liu, 2021; Li & Jiang, 2022). Furthermore, many of the SPOCs currently in use have not embraced innovative or contextually appropriate methods, especially in terms of addressing students' communicative competence. While there has been increasing recognition of the role of TBI in communicative language teaching, particularly for EOP, its incorporation into SPOC frameworks remains underexplored. The few studies that examine task-based SPOCs tend to focus narrowly on individual language skills, such as listening or writing, and seldom provide a comprehensive evaluation of their effects on performance (Wei et al., 2024; Zhao, 2022).

In addition to theoretical and methodological deficiencies, contextual challenges further complicate the implementation of SPOC. Chinese HVCs cater to a highly heterogeneous student population, comprising individuals from both academic-track and vocational-track educational backgrounds (Gu, 2020). This diversity influences students' prior exposure to English, levels of learner autonomy, and technological readiness, all of which affect their capacity to benefit from online instruction. However, few studies have investigated how these varying educational backgrounds influence the effectiveness of SPOCs. The lack of differentiated instructional models that can accommodate these differences continues to hinder the potential of SPOCs to deliver equitable and effective language education.

From a policy perspective, while the *Action Plan for Improving the Quality of Vocational Education (2020–2023)* and the *Education Informatisation 2.0 Action Plan* (2018) advocate for the development of learner-centred digital resources, empirical research assessing the implementation and outcomes of these initiatives remains limited. Practical challenges persist in translating these national directives into localised teaching strategies. Many instructors, as illustrated in the Cangzhou HVC case, express uncertainty in aligning SPOC content with vocational requirements or designing tasks that reflect authentic workplace communication. As a result, digital courses often fail to stimulate learner engagement or promote measurable language gains.

This study aims to address these multifaceted gaps by designing, developing, and evaluating a task-based SPOC tailored to EOP instruction in Chinese HVCs. It addresses the theoretical gap by grounding the instructional design in the principles of Task-Based Instruction, and the methodological gap by employing a quasi-experimental design that utilises pre- and post-tests to assess performance and the IMMS questionnaire is used to measure students' perceived motivation towards the SPOCs. Furthermore, the study examines how students' educational backgrounds influence learning outcomes, offering insights into differentiated instruction. By integrating task-based pedagogy into the SPOC model and applying rigorous empirical methods, this research seeks to produce actionable recommendations for future instructional design, thereby guiding both researchers and policymakers in enhancing the quality and effectiveness of vocational English education.

LITERATURE REVIEW

The emergence of task-based SPOCs has introduced new opportunities and challenges for English language instruction in vocational education. Within the context of Chinese higher vocational colleges (HVCs), where English for Occupational Purposes (EOP) is a compulsory course, there is an urgent need for pedagogical models that are both contextually relevant and instructionally effective. This literature review critically examines prior research concerning the design, development, and evaluation of task-based SPOCs with a particular focus on two key learner outcomes: language performance and perceived motivation. The review begins by tracing the evolution of SPOCs as an educational format distinct from MOOCs, before examining the pedagogical relevance of Task-Based Instruction (TBI) in online and blended learning environments. It also explores theoretical models that underpin learner motivation and task-based learning. In doing so, the review highlights conceptual, empirical, and contextual gaps in existing literature and provides a rationale for the current study's integrated design approach.

SPOC: Evolution in Online Language Instruction

The introduction of Massive Open Online Courses (MOOCs) transformed global education by making high-quality content accessible to large audiences. However, MOOCs face numerous challenges in achieving satisfactory learning outcomes, particularly in skill-based domains like language acquisition. Issues such as low completion rates, lack of interactivity, and limited personalization undermine their effectiveness (Fox, 2013; Eriksson, Adawi & Stöhr, 2017). In response, the concept of Small Private Online Courses (SPOCs) was introduced to provide a more manageable and institutionally integrated alternative.

SPOCs inherit the high-quality content of MOOCs but operate with limited enrollment and greater instructional oversight. Fox (2013) described SPOCs as a blended format that leverages MOOC content within a controlled classroom environment. Research suggests that SPOCs can improve students' learning performance through tailored instructional design and regular teacher feedback (Dong et al., 2021). These elements are critical for HVC students who often have varied learning needs and may struggle with autonomous learning in pure MOOC environments.

In the Chinese context, national initiatives such as the "Construction of National High-Quality Online Open Courses" (Ministry of Education, 2023) have encouraged HVCs to adapt existing MOOC content into SPOC formats. However, despite their growing prevalence, SPOCs in HVCs remain largely content-driven and lack pedagogical innovation. Few studies have examined the potential of task-based

SPOCs to enhance language performance, and even fewer have investigated their motivational impact.

Performance

Student performance in online language courses refers to measurable gains in language proficiency, typically assessed through tests or assignments (Li & Jiang, 2022). In EOP contexts, performance should reflect students' ability to use English in occupational scenarios, including workplace communication, customer service, and technical reporting.

Several studies have demonstrated that performance in SPOC environments can be enhanced if the course incorporates interaction, scaffolded tasks, and real-world applications (Wei, Dew, & Said, 2024; Su, 2019). However, most research still relies on broad indicators, such as course completion or assignment submission rates, which do not necessarily capture functional language ability (Eriksson, Adawi, & Stöhr, 2017). A gap remains in studies that systematically evaluate the performance of SPOC learners through rigorous pre- and post-assessments tied to communicative competence.

In Chinese HVCs, the heterogeneity of students' educational background before they are accepted by the Higher Vocational College (HVC) with qualification to study as HVC students, high school versus vocational school, also affects performance. Students from vocational schools may have weaker English foundations and less exposure to academic learning, impacting their ability to perform in traditional SPOC formats (Gu, 2020). Task-based approaches, with their emphasis on real-world application, may offer a more accessible and effective framework for these learners.

Perceived Motivation

Perceived motivation refers to students' internal beliefs and feelings about their willingness and enthusiasm to engage with learning materials (Kim & Jung, 2012). In online learning environments, motivation is a crucial predictor of persistence and achievement, particularly for self-paced or blended models, such as SPOCs. The Self-Determination Theory (SDT) (Ryan & Deci, 2000) is central to understanding motivation in education. It proposes that students are most motivated when their learning environment satisfies three psychological needs: autonomy, competence, and relatedness. The more students perceive themselves as being in control, capable, and connected to others, the more likely they are to engage and succeed.

Applied to SPOC design, this suggests that course materials must be relevant to students' interests and vocational goals, structured to provide achievable challenges, and supported by interpersonal communication and feedback. Studies in

HVCs reveal that students often lose motivation when MOOCs or SPOCs are overly theoretical, passive, or disconnected from real-world applications (Li, 2022). When learners do not see the practical value of the material, they are less likely to invest effort and persist.

The ARCS Model (Keller, 1987; Keller, 2010) further elaborates this motivational process through four components: Attention, Relevance, Confidence, and Satisfaction. In SPOC settings, attention can be captured through interactive multimedia and authentic tasks. Relevance comes from aligning tasks with students' professional aspirations. Confidence can be fostered through scaffolded instruction and formative feedback, and satisfaction derives from completing meaningful activities with visible real-life value.

Despite the applicability of these models, research that explicitly integrates ARCS and SDT into SPOC design remains rare. Most studies stop at reporting motivational perceptions rather than using theory-driven models to enhance them systematically.

Task-Based Instruction (TBI)

Task-Based Instruction (TBI) is rooted in Communicative Language Teaching (CLT) and emphasizes learning through meaningful, communicative interactions. TBI has been widely endorsed for developing functional language use and is particularly appropriate for occupational English, which demands contextualized performance in workplace scenarios (Ellis, 2018; Willis, 2013). TBI involves students completing tasks that simulate real-world communicative needs, such as writing emails, making presentations, or handling customer complaints. Ellis and Shintani (2013) define key characteristics of a task as focus on meaning, presence of a communicative gap, learner reliance on personal resources, and an outcome that is independent of language form. These features support both performance and intrinsic motivation by making learning purposeful and relevant.

In SPOCs, TBI has the potential to bridge the gap between content delivery and practical application. However, research on integrating TBI into online formats, especially for vocational learners, is limited. A few studies have piloted task-based e-learning modules, but many lack alignment with instructional design models or learning theories, resulting in inconsistent outcomes (Dong, Ang & Sun, 2021; Chen & Meng, 2021). By contrast, a well-designed task-based SPOC grounded in EOP, constructivist theory, and motivational models could offer a structured yet flexible framework for improving both learning outcomes and learner attitudes. Moreover, the focus on tasks allows instruction to be tailored to different educational backgrounds, making it particularly suitable for the mixed populations found in HVCs.

English for Occupational Purposes (EOP) in Higher Vocational Colleges (HVCs)

To understand the instructional role and scope of English for Occupational Purposes (EOP) in Higher Vocational Colleges (HVCs), it is essential first to clarify its conceptual positioning within the broader field of English language education. General English (GE), often synonymous with English for General Purposes (EGP), serves general communicative needs and frequently aligns with academic testing and literacy. By contrast, English for Specific Purposes (ESP) addresses language use tailored to particular professional or academic contexts. EOP represents a major sub-branch of ESP that targets workplace communication and vocational functionality (Hutchinson and Waters, 1987).

In China's HVC context, EOP is not only a curriculum requirement but also a compulsory public course integrated into the national vocational English curriculum system. It serves to equip students with communicative competence relevant to real workplace needs across various industries. According to the Ministry of Education (2021), the EOP course aims to develop three core categories of communicative competence: understanding skills (listening, reading, viewing), expressive skills (speaking, writing, translating), and interactive skills (dialogue, discussion, negotiation and debate). These competencies collectively frame how English is taught to prepare students for authentic workplace communication.

This study is designed to support the EOP course by developing a task-cased SPOC (TB-SPOC), tailored specifically for vocational college students. The TB-SPOC seeks to align closely with the national curriculum's expectations by embedding real-world occupational tasks into a digital learning platform that can be flexibly accessed while ensuring structured pedagogical support.

EOP is defined not by a unique linguistic system but by the occupational context in which English is applied. Learners in HVCs are expected to acquire English for use in practical, professional tasks such as customer service interactions, report writing, technical discussions, and team collaboration. These real-life communicative functions require command of professional registers, appropriate tone and politeness strategies, and specialised vocabulary. While sharing grammatical and lexical features with GE, EOP is distinguished by its targeted discourse functions and communicative outcomes (Stern, 1983; Thamarana & Narayana, 2016).

The theoretical foundation of EOP instruction rests on the distinction between competence and performance. While competence involves knowledge of language rules, performance refers to the actual use of that knowledge in context (Hutchinson & Waters, 1981). For EOP students, especially those from diverse educational backgrounds in HVCs, instruction must therefore move beyond theoretical knowledge to help learners apply English in task-based, job-related settings. This functional emphasis calls for pedagogies that simulate occupational language use.

Although EOP does not rely on a single proprietary method, Communicative Language Teaching (CLT) and Task-Based Instruction (TBI) are widely regarded as effective approaches for vocational learners. TBI, in particular, is valued for its capacity to facilitate learning through authentic interaction and purposeful communication. In the EOP context, TBI enables learners to complete meaningful tasks such as workplace presentations, technical instructions, and service exchanges, thereby making language use goal-oriented and directly relevant to their future careers (Iranmehr et, al., 2011; Kavaliauskienė, 2005).

The structure of TBI typically involves a pre-task phase to introduce objectives and background, a task performance phase where learners apply language to complete communicative goals, and a post-task phase involving reflection and feedback. This structure is especially well-suited to SPOC environments, where asynchronous tasks can be complemented by interactive discussion forums, peer review, and instructor feedback. When embedded into a digital course such as a TB-SPOC, TBI allows for scalable yet personalised learning experiences, tailored to students' occupational tracks.

Studies have shown that EOP programmes using TBI can improve learners' confidence, motivation, and real-world communicative ability. These benefits are particularly relevant in HVCs where students often lack prior exposure to professional communication in English. TBI also fosters learner autonomy and problem-solving, aligning well with the vocational education goals of cultivating workplace readiness. Tang, Chiou and Jarsaillon (2015) demonstrated that learners experience greater motivation and satisfaction when tasks reflect authentic workplace challenges and offer immediate practical application.

In the context of this study, EOP is not merely the thematic backdrop but the explicit instructional target of the TB-SPOC designed for HVC learners. The course is built to simulate real-world workplace communication, aligning with national EOP standards and addressing gaps in existing online resources. By applying task-based pedagogy within a structured SPOC format, the course aims to address the specific needs of HVC students who must acquire practical English communication skills for employment. The design offers a scalable and replicable instructional model that can inform future innovations in vocational English education in China.

Research Gaps and Rationale for the Study

Although SPOCs have attracted increasing attention in the field of online education, especially in Chinese higher education, their application in the domain of vocational English instruction remains underexplored. A review of existing literature reveals several persistent shortcomings. First, most empirical studies on SPOCs rely heavily on self-reported data, such as satisfaction surveys or subjective interviews, rather than using objective measures of learning gains (Ding & Zhao, 2020). Consequently, it is difficult to determine whether learners' language performance has improved in any substantial or measurable way. Second, the majority of these studies fail to differentiate between general English instruction and EOP, thereby neglecting to address the specific communicative needs and performance expectations required in vocational settings (Qiu, 2022). As a result, the existing SPOC models often lack relevance for HVC learners who need targeted language competencies for the workplace.

Furthermore, few studies explicitly integrate task-based pedagogy into the design of SPOCs. While Task-Based Instruction (TBI) has demonstrated effectiveness in classroom-based language education, its application in online or blended learning environments—particularly within SPOC models—has been insufficiently examined (Chen & Meng, 2021). The motivational aspects of learning, particularly students' perceived motivation toward the course, are also underrepresented in existing research. When motivation is discussed, it is often considered in a generalized manner without reference to established theories such as Self-Determination Theory (SDT) or Keller's ARCS model. This limits the explanatory power and design applicability of these findings.

In addition, there is a notable absence of research that considers learners' educational backgrounds as a factor influencing the effectiveness of SPOCs. Chinese HVC students come from diverse paths, with some graduating from general high schools and others from vocational secondary schools. These groups differ significantly in their prior English exposure, cognitive strategies, and learning autonomy. However, few studies have explored how such background differences may moderate the effects of SPOC-based instruction on performance and motivation.

In light of these gaps, this study is designed to systematically evaluate the effectiveness of a Task-Based SPOC in improving both students' language performance and their perceived motivation. The SPOC developed for this study is grounded in Communicative Language Teaching (CLT), Task-Based Instruction (TBI), and key motivational theories, including SDT and the ARCS model. It adapts existing MOOC content into a more personalized, goal-oriented instructional design tailored to the needs of HVC students. Through the use of pre- and post-tests to assess performance, as well as structured surveys to measure perceived motivation, this research aims to provide rigorous, theory-based evidence to inform future SPOC development. Ultimately, this study aims to make practical and theoretical contributions to the field of online vocational English education by addressing the dual challenges of improving measurable learning outcomes and enhancing learners' motivational engagement in a task-based, digitally mediated environment.

In summary, the literature suggests that while SPOCs hold considerable promise for enhancing English language instruction in vocational education, their application remains under-theorised and empirically fragmented, especially in relation to EOP. Existing research often overlooks the importance of aligning instructional design with learners' vocational goals, fails to employ rigorous performance assessments, and rarely incorporates theory-driven models of learner motivation. Moreover, the variability in learners' educational backgrounds has received limited attention despite its potential impact on learning outcomes. This study addresses these shortcomings by designing and evaluating a task-based SPOC that integrates TBI methodology with motivational design frameworks such as SDT and the ARCS model. In doing so, it aims to contribute new insights into the theory and practice of digitally mediated EOP instruction in HVCs, with particular emphasis on how pedagogical innovation can improve measurable outcomes and learner engagement in a blended learning context.

THEORETICAL FRAMEWORK

This study's theoretical framework integrates key insights from Second Language Acquisition (SLA) Theory, Constructivist Learning Theory, and principles from instructional design. It provides the foundational rationale for the design and implementation of a task-based SPOC (TB-SPOC) aimed at improving learning outcomes in English for Occupational Purposes (EOP) for Higher Vocational College (HVC) students in China. The theoretical basis is carefully selected to address both language acquisition and learner engagement in a digitally mediated environment.

The primary theoretical underpinning is Krashen's (1981) Second Language Acquisition (SLA) Theory, which distinguishes between subconscious language acquisition and conscious language learning. Krashen emphasises the importance of comprehensible input, low-anxiety environments, and meaningful communication as conditions for effective language acquisition. In this study, Krashen's theory supports the course's emphasis on simulated workplace scenarios, including tasks such as drafting emails, handling customer service interactions, and participating in role-play interviews. These activities create input-rich, authentic contexts that facilitate natural acquisition of language forms and communicative competence.

To apply SLA Theory within the TB-SPOC, course materials are designed to provide input that is slightly above the learners' current proficiency levels. Listening and reading tasks incorporate job-related vocabulary and discourse structures, enabling learners to decode meaning from context and build their language system implicitly. Moreover, repeated exposure to professional expressions across modules supports internalisation. For example, learners might be asked to complete a series of tasks involving health and safety briefings, where each step builds upon vocabulary, comprehension, and production in realistic job-related interactions. These features operationalise Krashen's Input Hypothesis and demonstrate how acquisition can be fostered through contextually meaningful tasks.

Complementing SLA Theory is Constructivist Learning Theory, particularly informed by the work of Piaget and Vygotsky (Aljohani, 2017). Constructivism posits that knowledge is actively constructed through experience and interaction. Applied to language learning, this suggests that students benefit most when they are engaged in tasks that require active participation, problem solving, and personal meaning-making. Within the TB-SPOC, constructivist principles are reflected in modular content design, where learners progress from guided instruction to autonomous performance. Each task is embedded within vocationally relevant contexts to ensure that learning is purposeful and transferable to real-world situations.

Constructivist learning is further supported through scaffolding, peer interaction, and reflective exercises. A typical learning unit may begin with a scenario-based video depicting an occupational problem, followed by guided vocabulary identification, language analysis, and a final performance task such as creating a workplace manual or presenting a safety proposal. Learners are encouraged to draw on prior knowledge and collaboratively develop new understanding, thereby reinforcing cognitive engagement and self-regulation. These design features ensure that the learning environment is student-centred, dynamic, and conducive to meaningful language use.

This theoretical framework is also informed by principles from task-based instruction (TBI), a branch of Communicative Language Teaching (CLT). TBI emphasises the use of real-world tasks as the core units of instruction and is particularly relevant to EOP, where learners need to develop context-specific communicative abilities. Tasks are structured to align with Ellis and Shintani's (2013) criteria, including focus on meaning, presence of a communicative gap, reliance on learner resources, and task-based outcomes. This aligns the TB-SPOC with contemporary pedagogical standards for vocational language education.

Furthermore, Self-Determination Theory (SDT) (Ryan & Deci, 2000) underpins the motivational design of the TB-SPOC. SDT highlights autonomy, competence, and relatedness as critical to sustained learner motivation. These are embedded in the course through flexible task sequencing, personalised feedback, and peer collaboration. The ARCS model (Keller, 1987) further informs instructional strategies to capture learners' attention, ensure relevance, build confidence, and enhance satisfaction.

In summary, this study's TB-SPOC design is anchored in SLA Theory and Constructivist Learning Theory, supported by TBI, SDT, and motivational design models. Krashen's theory guides the input-rich and communicative nature of the course, while constructivist principles ensure learner-centred, contextual progression. Task-based principles enhance relevance to EOP, and motivational theories sustain engagement. Together, these frameworks enable the TB-SPOC to address the dual aims of improving performance and fostering perceived motivation among HVC students in the EOP context.

CONCEPTUAL FRAMEWORK

The conceptual framework of this study bridges theory and practice by applying selected learning and motivational theories to the design, develop and evaluation of a task-based SPOC (TB-SPOC) for English for Occupational Purposes (EOP) in Higher Vocational Colleges (HVCs) in China. While the theoretical framework outlines the foundational assumptions about how learners acquire and are motivated to learn a language, the conceptual framework translates these assumptions into actionable instructional strategies embedded in the course design.

This framework is centred on Krashen's Second Language Acquisition (SLA) Theory, which provides the foundational rationale for incorporating input-rich, low-anxiety, and contextually meaningful language experiences into the TB-SPOC. In practice, this means that students engage in simulated workplace tasks such as conducting customer inquiries, preparing service reports, or responding to emails, situations that promote natural acquisition over mechanical practice.

Complementing SLA, the constructivist and sociocultural perspectives are operationalised in the TB-SPOC through collaborative modules, scenario-based prompts, and progressive task scaffolding. Students are encouraged to co-construct knowledge by solving workplace-related problems, reflecting real vocational challenges. The digital platform supports this interaction by allowing asynchronous discussions, real-time feedback, and guided support from instructors.

From a motivational standpoint, Self-Determination Theory (SDT) informs the design of learning experiences that satisfy students' needs for autonomy, competence, and relatedness. Learners can choose their task order, receive differentiated feedback, and participate in peer-supported projects. Keller's ARCS model, meanwhile, is reflected in the use of multimedia content, real-life video cases, and authentic assessments that build learner attention, relevance, confidence, and satisfaction.

Instructionally, the framework is implemented through the ADDIE model, which structures the development process from needs analysis to iterative evaluation. The Transformation Model of SPOCs (Chen & Yang, 2015) guides the conversion of existing MOOC materials into modular SPOC units that are smaller in scope but higher in interactivity and learner engagement.

Each TB-SPOC module corresponds to a typical EOP scenario and integrates task types as defined by Thornbury (2007), including survey, design, and role-based interaction. For example, a module on "Product Presentation" requires students to analyse market needs, design promotional content, and deliver a mock pitch, activities that activate real-world occupational skills in English.

Ultimately, the conceptual framework maps the interaction between theoretical constructs and course components to explain how a TB-SPOC can enhance HVC students' performance and perceived motivation in EOP. It offers a clear logic for the alignment of theory, design, and expected outcomes, and provides a transferable model for future curriculum developers working with task-based or blended instruction in vocational English.

Figure 1. Conceptual Framework

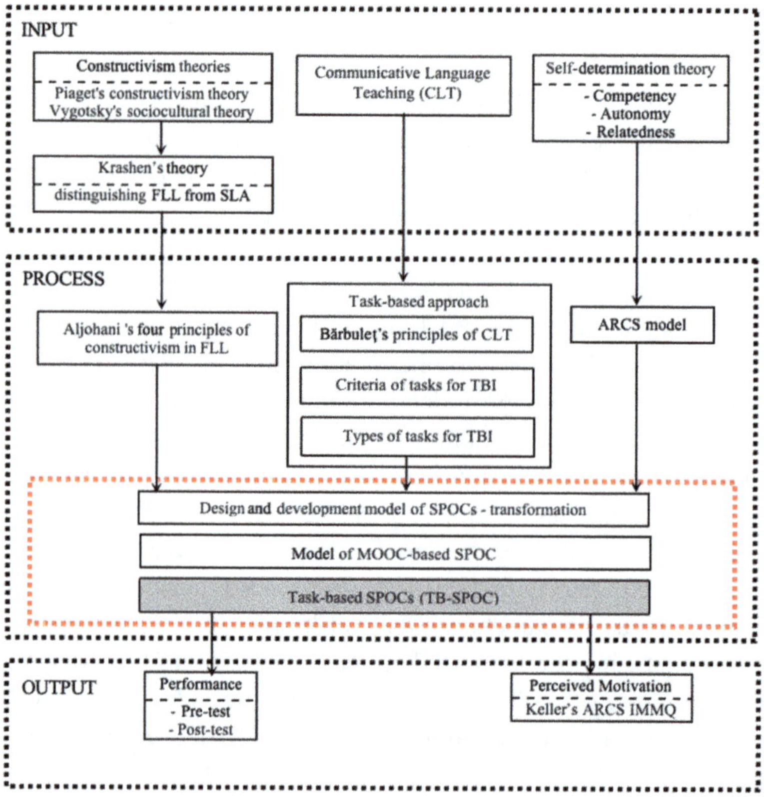

DESIGN AND DEVELOPMENT

This part describes the systematic process used to design and develop the Task-Based SPOC (TB-SPOC) for learning English for Occupational Purposes (EOP) in Higher Vocational Colleges (HVCs) in China. Grounded in the ADDIE instructional design model (Analysis, Design, Development, Implementation, and Evaluation), this process also incorporates iterative design principles (Plomp, 2007; Reeves, 2006) and the transformation model of SPOC development by Chen and Yang (2015). The course was specifically designed to enhance students' performance and perceived motivation through task-based language learning, aligning with the requirements of the 2021 National English Curriculum Standards for vocational education.

Instructional Design Framework

The ADDIE model was chosen due to its systematic structure and adaptability for online learning environments. Although criticized for being linear (Allen, 2017; Almelhi, 2021), its recursive and iterative nature allows continuous refinement at any stage (Valiathan, 2022). This study also integrates the iterative cycle from design-based research (Reeves & McKenney, 2015) to ensure contextual sensitivity and responsiveness to learner needs. The transformation model by Chen and Yang (2015) was employed to adapt existing MOOC content into a structured, task-oriented SPOC.

Analysis Phase

The target learners were first-year HVC students aged 18–20, with mixed educational backgrounds—some from academic high schools and others from vocational schools. A preliminary review of institutional reports and national data (Ministry of Education, 2023) revealed that existing SPOCs failed to address learners' performance deficiencies and lacked motivational design. These students had prior exposure to online learning platforms, particularly the iCVE platform, making it a suitable technological environment for implementing the SPOC.

A review of literature and national education policy documents revealed three key issues in existing SPOCs: low student performance, lack of motivation, and insufficient contextual relevance (Li, 2022; Zhang et al., 2019). Task-Based Instruction (Ellis, 2003; 2018) was identified as pedagogical strategies to address these challenges.

The course was developed using existing national MOOC materials due to time and resource constraints. The iCVE platform was selected for its robust support of SPOC functionalities, compatibility with vocational education, and ability to track learning behavior (Guo, Song & Jiang, 2023).

Design Phase

Following the 2021 Curriculum Standards for vocational English, learning outcomes focused on three communicative domains: comprehension, presentation, and interaction. These were operationalized into specific, assessable tasks in simulated workplace contexts. MOOC resources from a nationally recognized EOP course were adapted. These materials included video lectures and textual content aligned with vocational scenarios. Five thematic units were selected: "First Day on Campus," "Food and Diet," "Time Management," "Product Introduction," and "Seeing the World." Each theme was matched with a Thornbury (2007) task type to support TBI methodology.

Figure 2. The launch page contains the five thematic units.

The instructional strategy followed Thornbury's (2007) five task types: design, listing, survey, imaginative, and research tasks. Tasks were situated within real-world occupational scenarios, requiring learners to collaborate, communicate, and produce meaningful language outputs. For example, the "Product Introduction" unit required learners to role-play a business dialogue, integrating speaking and persuasive language use.

Table 1. Reorganize the MOOC materials by tasks

Topic	Task type	Requirements
First Day on Campus	Design task	Learners collaborate to discuss and design an optimal campus introduction. They then present their proposal in a group discussion format to the class, simulating how they would guide a new student on the first day.
Food and Diet	Listing	Learners engage in a group conversation where they discuss and plan a food menu for a week. Each learner must contribute their ideas and explain their choices based on health, variety, and cultural preferences.
Time Management	Surveys	Learners work in groups to conduct an interview about daily time management. Each participant asks questions related to time usage, productivity, and leisure activities. The interviewee responds, and then they compare time management strategies in a group discussion.
Product Introduction	Imaginative task	Learners perform a role play in pairs, with one acting as a seller and the other as a customer. They simulate a conversation where the seller introduces a product, describing its features and benefits while the customer asks questions and makes a purchase decision.
Seeing the world	Research task	Using Internet resources, learners research a place they want to travel to. The research should cover key attractions, culture, local food, and so on. Then give a short presentation to the class.

Motivational design drew on Self-Determination Theory (Ryan & Deci, 2000) and the ARCS model (Keller, 2010). Course elements were structured to fulfill autonomy, competence, and relatedness. For instance, the pre-class learning modules allowed for independent study (autonomy), classroom discussions fostered mastery (competence), and group tasks promoted social connection (relatedness). ARCS principles—attention, relevance, confidence, and satisfaction—were embedded in the use of multimedia resources, real-world tasks, feedback mechanisms, and peer collaboration.

Table 2. Motivational design of the SPOC

Activity	Description	Purpose/Impact
Pre-Class	- Instructor uploads learning resources and issues quizzes on the SPOC platform. - Students learn independently and complete pre-task tests to prepare for class tasks. - Learning goals are set to guide and motivate students.	- Stimulates interest by setting clear goals. - Enhances a sense of competence through knowledge mastery. - Promotes independent learning and time management, meeting autonomy needs. - Builds self-reliance and self-esteem with tasks of moderate difficulty.
Class Attendance (Check-In)	- Teacher simulates roll call using SPOC platform's attendance function. - iCVE displays names and pictures of students who signed in.	- Improves attendance rate. - Creates a virtual classroom atmosphere. - Enhances students' sense of belonging.
Teacher-Student Q&A	- Teachers ask questions to assess students' understanding. - Students receive feedback and demonstrate learning. - Questions are answered via various formats (text, voice, video). - Teachers provide encouragement and support.	- Tests learning outcomes. - Motivates students intrinsically through teacher's language. - Meets needs for competence and belonging. - Allows autonomy by letting students choose the format and content they are familiar with.
Group Discussion	- Students discuss and apply knowledge taught by the teacher. - Collaboration fosters individual and team efforts in task performance. - Interaction with peers deepens understanding and provides support.	- Enhances knowledge application and understanding. - Builds collective belonging and teamwork. - Meets students' needs for competence and belonging. - Aligns with Vygotsky's sociocultural theory to improve learning outcomes.
Task Performance	- Students perform tasks individually or in groups based on class discussions and instructions.	- Encourages application of knowledge. - Fosters skill development and individual/ team effort. - Meets students' needs for competence and belonging.
Assignments and Tests	- Additional assignments and tests are posted on the SPOC platform. - iCVE publishes class rankings and shares results to enhance class interaction.	- Tests students' learning. - Provides feedback for improvement. - Enables students to evaluate their performance relative to peers. - Enhances interaction and creates a sense of belonging in the virtual classroom environment.

Development Phase

Each lesson was developed based on a TBI structure, comprising pre-task, during-task, and post-task components. Lesson plans specified objectives, activities, timing, and assessment strategies. Multimedia content was created or adapted from MOOC materials to ensure alignment with the target skills.

Table 3. A sample lesson plan for task-based SPOC

Course Title	**Practical English**		
Topic	**No.4 Product introduction**		
Students	**First-year students**	**Period**	**90 mins**
Task	Creating, acting out, and recording a video of the conversation about product introduction		
Learning Objectives	At the end of this lesson, the students should be able to: - describe product features in English. - understand product descriptions. - understand traditional Chinese crafts. - introduce Chinese products and artisan stories in English.		

Pre-task

Before class

- Instructors release learning materials one week ahead (Figure 3)
- The students self-learning with finishing the pre-task quiz related to the learning materials (Figure 4)

In class

- Teachers lead into the learning topic and emphasize the learning objectives with key and difficult language points (8 mins)
- Students are informed of the specific tasks (2 mins) (Figure 5)
- The teacher organises the discussion of the success criteria of the task and group task performance
- Students participate by brainstorming and vote about the success criteria (15 mins) (Figure 6)
- Students were divided into groups, with 5 students in each group (5 mins)

Task performing

- Students work in groups to prepare the task-performing (10 mins)
- Each group is randomly selected with an equal opportunity to present their group's working result. (30 mins)
- The teachers are only organizers; their roles are to guide students in performing tasks independently and to inspire students' enthusiasm for exploration.

After performed

- Teachers grade task performance with learners and peers based on the criteria discussed before the task (10 mins) (Figure 7)
- Teachers and students work together to conclude the learning results (10 mins)

Figure 3. The learning objective ( ), pre-class quiz ( ), and self-learning materials

Figure 4. The pre-task quiz related to the learning materials

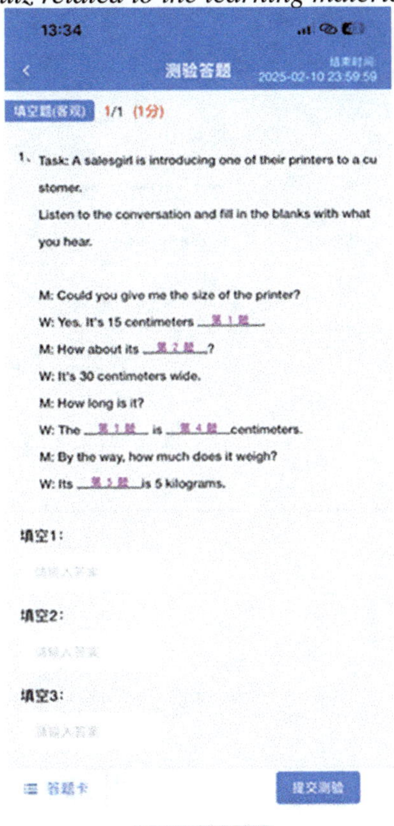

Figure 5. The specific tasks

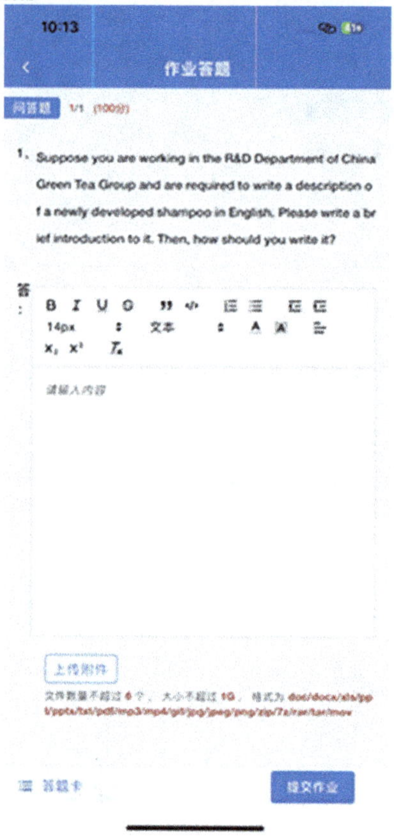

Figure 6. The brainstorming

Figure 7. The requirement of the class, self-evaluation ( ), learning process ( ), in-class evaluation ( )

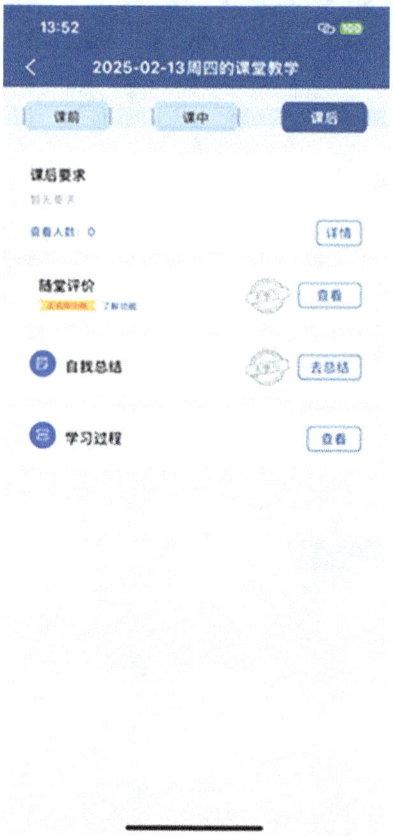

Three experts in instructional design and EOP education evaluated the SPOC using an instrument based on Ministry of Education quality standards. Feedback led to refinements in instructional flow, task complexity, and assessment alignment. Adjustments included improved task descriptions and a more equitable distribution of teaching time.

A small-scale pilot study involving 20 students (10 with task-based SPOC and 10 with content-based SPOC) was conducted over a three-week period. Results showed higher task performance and positive feedback in the task-based SPOC group. Suggestions such as enhancing multimedia and clarifying instructions were incorporated into the final version.

Implementation Phase

The final task-based SPOC and content-based SPOC courses were uploaded to the iCVE platform. Students accessed the platform independently and received minimal technical support via WeChat. Since all participants had prior experience with iCVE, no user manual was required.

A Task-Based SPOC Design Guide for English for Occupational Purposes

This guide synthesises the core principles, phases, and best practices derived from the design and development of a task-based SPOC (TB-SPOC) for English for Occupational Purposes (EOP). It offers a scalable framework for educators, instructional designers, and institutions seeking to implement similar blended learning models in Higher Vocational Colleges (HVCs).

1. Instructional Foundation

Theoretical Basis: Rooted in Task-Based Instruction (Ellis, 2003), Self-Determination Theory (Ryan & Deci, 2000), and ARCS Model of Motivation (Keller, 2010), the design centres on learner autonomy, competence, and real-world engagement.

Design Model: Follows the ADDIE instructional design cycle (Analysis, Design, Development, Implementation, Evaluation) enhanced by iterative refinement (Plomp, 2007; Reeves, 2006).

Transformation Approach: Utilises Chen & Yang's (2015) model to convert existing MOOC resources into contextually appropriate SPOC modules

2. Analysis Phase

Target Learners: First-year HVC students with heterogeneous academic backgrounds (high school vs. vocational).

Learning Needs: Identified key issues such as low language performance, poor motivation, and misalignment with occupational relevance.

Platform Selection: Chose iCVE for its compatibility, familiarity, and capability to support blended learning and track student performance.

3. Design Phase

Learning Objectives: Mapped to three communicative domains—comprehension, presentation, interaction—based on national curriculum standards.

Task Types: Selected five themes and matched each with a Thornbury (2007) task category (e.g., design, listing, survey, imaginative, research).

Motivational Structure: Embedded autonomy, competence, and relatedness across modules. ARCS principles applied to pre-task, in-class, and post-task elements

4. Development Phase

Lesson Planning: Structured each module with pre-task (independent learning), task-performing (collaborative communication), and post-task (peer/self-assessment).

Content Creation: Adapted high-quality MOOC resources into bite-sized, task-oriented instructional units enriched with multimedia.

Pilot Testing: Conducted a small-scale implementation with iterative feedback from learners and expert reviewers.

5. Implementation Considerations

Technology Integration: Ensure the platform supports synchronous/asynchronous activities, learner analytics, and multi-format communication (text, voice, video).

Teacher Facilitation: Teachers act as organisers and motivators, not lecturers, creating space for learner-led knowledge construction.

Support Mechanisms: Provide minimal but responsive tech support and use familiar platforms to lower learning curve and maximise autonomy.

6. Evaluation and Iteration

Evaluation Instruments: Use validated rubrics aligned with learning outcomes and task complexity.

Feedback Channels: Incorporate expert review, peer evaluation, and learner self-assessment.

Improvement Loop: Adjust complexity, pacing, and scaffolding based on pilot results and usage analytics.

7. Scalability and Transferability

Modular Structure: Each unit operates as a stand-alone instructional object that can be reused, adapted, or expanded across disciplines.

Policy Alignment: Designed to meet national curriculum standards and digital learning priorities.

Adaptability: Tasks and platforms can be localised for different vocational majors or even cross-disciplinary integration.

This guide serves as a roadmap for scaling task-based SPOCs in EOP instruction across diverse vocational contexts. By aligning theoretical insights with practical design strategies, it supports the delivery of learner-centred, performance-driven, and technology-enhanced vocational English education.

This part outlined the design and development of a task-based SPOC for EOP learning in HVCs. Utilizing the ADDIE model combined with iterative cycles and transformation methodology, the course was designed to address two critical challenges in vocational English instruction: low performance and weak perceived motivation. Through carefully selected MOOC materials, structured task types, motivational design, and technology-supported implementation, the task-based SPOC represents a pedagogically sound and contextually relevant intervention ready for evaluation in the next phase of this study.

METHODOLOGY

The methodology part presents a comprehensive overview of the research design and procedures employed to investigate the effectiveness of a task-based SPOC (TB-SPOC) in enhancing student performance and perceived motivation in English for Occupational Purposes (EOP) among Higher Vocational College (HVC) students in China. Given the practical constraints of educational settings and the need to maintain ecological validity, a quasi-experimental design was deemed most appropriate for this study. This approach enables the comparison of outcomes between two naturally occurring groups while acknowledging the limitations of random assignment in real-world educational contexts. The quasi-experimental framework enables researchers to examine causal relationships between instructional methods and learning outcomes while operating within the constraints of existing classroom structures and institutional policies (Rogers & Revesz, 2019). The study specifically compares the task-based SPOC (TB-SPOC) with an existing content-based SPOC (CB-SPOC) to determine their relative effectiveness in improving English language performance for occupational purposes.

Research Design

The research design incorporates a pretest-posttest comparison between two treatment groups, with educational background (high-school versus vocational) serving as a moderator variable. This 2×2 factorial design allows for examination of both main effects and interaction effects between the instructional approach and students' prior educational experiences. The TB-SPOC treatment group receives instruction focused on authentic occupational tasks and real-world language applications. In contrast, the CB-SPOC control group follows an existing curriculum organized around linguistic content and structures. Both groups complete identical pretest and posttest measures to assess performance, with testing instruments carefully aligned to the EOP curriculum standards and China's English Proficiency Scale. The IMMS questionnaire is used to measure students' perceived motivation towards the SPOCs. The quasi-experimental approach was selected over other potential designs due to its ability to balance methodological rigor with practical feasibility in educational settings where random assignment at the individual level is often impossible or unethical.

Several theoretical and practical considerations drove the selection of a quasi-experimental design. In educational research contexts, true experimental designs with random assignment are frequently impractical due to institutional constraints, ethical concerns about withholding treatments, and the natural grouping of students in classrooms. Quasi-experimental designs provide a viable alternative that maintains much of the rigor of true experiments while accommodating the realities of educational settings. This approach is particularly suitable for evaluating TB-SPOCs, as it enables researchers to study interventions as they would be implemented in practice. The design also enables examination of how different student populations (in this case, those with high-school versus vocational backgrounds) respond to the instructional approaches, providing valuable insights for differentiated implementation strategies.

Population and Sampling

The target population for this study consists of first-year students at a large public higher vocational college in Cangzhou, China. This population was selected because EOP is a compulsory course for all first-year students, ensuring a consistent academic context across participants. The accessible population includes approximately 6,454 freshmen aged 18-20 years old, providing a sufficiently large pool for sampling. The institution was chosen as the research site due to its reputation as a leading vocational college with a stable academic structure and experienced faculty, factors that enhance the reliability of implementation and the generalizability of findings. The large student population also allows for adequate representation of both high-school and vocational background students, enabling meaningful comparisons between these subgroups.

The total sample size of 360 participants (180 from each educational background) was determined based on power analysis considerations and guidelines from established sampling methodologies. First, according to Krejcie and Morgan (1970) in (Piaw, 2020), for a population size (N) of 6000, a sample size (S) of 361 is necessary to ensure statistical accuracy in the study. Given that the total number of students in this HVC in 2024 is 6454, a sample size of 360 is very close to this recommended number and ensures the validity and reliability of the results. Secondly, because the target population of this study consists of students with similar backgrounds (high school backgrounds or vocational backgrounds), the sample is relatively homogeneous, meaning that even with a smaller sample size, the standard error would be lower, still providing accurate results (Lakens, 2022). Finally, Aron, Coups, and Aron (2011) assert that a sample size of 30 is typically sufficient for most real-world research applications.

Sampling procedures employed a non-probability quota sampling method to ensure balanced representation of students from high-school and vocational backgrounds. Participants were recruited from 12 naturally occurring lecture groups, with 15 students from each educational background selected per group. This sampling approach acknowledges the practical constraints of educational research while still providing sufficient statistical power for detecting meaningful effects (Lakens, 2022). The quota sampling method helps ensure that both high-school and vocational background students are adequately represented in the study, allowing for valid comparisons between these subgroups. While non-probability sampling has limitations regarding generalizability, it represents a pragmatic solution given the institutional constraints of conducting research in authentic educational settings. The sample size exceeds minimum recommendations for quasi-experimental designs and provides adequate power for detecting moderate effect sizes in the planned analyses.

Research Instruments

The primary research instrument focuses on performance as the primary outcome variable, measured through standardized assessments developed by the English Teaching and Research department. These tests include both pretests (midterm exams) and posttests (final exams), designed to assess students' English proficiency in occupational contexts. The test items cover five key topics from the SPOC curriculum and incorporate various assessment formats, including individual presentations, role-plays, group discussions, and random questioning. Each test component is carefully timed to simulate real-world language use scenarios. Individual presentations are limited to five minutes, role-plays consist of four items within a five-minute timeframe, and group discussions involve three items over 6-8 minutes, with five students per group. See Appendix A for details. The performance tests underwent rigorous validation procedures to ensure their appropriateness for measuring the targeted constructs. Three content experts with over fifteen years of experience in English teaching and research evaluated the tests for content validity, resulting in an Item Content Validity Index (I-CVI) of 0.89, well above the acceptable threshold. Reliability was established through pilot testing with a subsample of 20 students, yielding strong internal consistency estimates (KR-20 coefficients of 0.918 for the pretest and 0.923 for the posttest).

The second research instrument adapted the Instructional Materials Motivation Survey (IMMS) by Ma and Lee in 2021 to assess students' perceived motivation towards the EOP course following their SPOC learning experiences. Adapted from Keller's (1993) ARCS model of motivation, the 18-item IMMS version developed by Ma and Lee (2021) evaluates four key motivational dimensions: Attention (4 items), Relevance (3 items), Confidence (3 items), and Satisfaction (8 items). The instrument utilizes a 5-point Likert scale (1 = Not True to 5 = Very True) with five strategically placed reverse-coded items to minimize response bias and enhance data quality. To ensure cultural and linguistic appropriateness for Chinese vocational students, the original English version underwent rigorous translation procedures including expert validation and back-translation, with all items presented in Mandarin. See Appendix B for details. While pilot testing revealed acceptable reliability for most subscales (α = .65- .94), the relatively lower alpha for Confidence (α = .65) suggests that this construct may represent a less cohesive dimension, although still within acceptable ranges for exploratory research (Nehring et al., 2015; Shrestha, 2021). The IMMS provides valuable supplementary data about learners' perceived motivation towards different SPOC formats, complementing the primary performance outcomes with insights into the psychological aspects of the learning experience. Convergent validity analyses showed strong results for Attention (AVE = 0.795, CR = 0.939) and Relevance (AVE = 0.703, CR = 0.875), supporting the instrument's effectiveness in capturing these motivational constructs within the vocational education context.

Validity of Experimental Design

Several measures were implemented to address threats to internal validity, which is particularly important in quasi-experimental designs where random assignment is not possible. Potential threats, including history, maturation, testing effects, instrumentation, statistical regression, selection bias, mortality, and selection-maturation interaction, were carefully considered and addressed through design features and procedural controls. The relatively short duration of the study (six weeks) helps minimize threats from history and maturation, while the use of equivalent but not identical pretest and posttest forms reduces testing effects. Instrumentation threats are addressed through standardized administration procedures and training for test administrators. Selection bias is mitigated by using intact groups from the same institution and controlling for educational background in the analysis. Attrition is closely monitored, with procedures in place to handle missing data effectively. The factorial design that crosses instructional method with educational background helps address selection-maturation interactions by allowing examination of whether different types of students respond differently to the treatments over time.

External validity concerns the generalizability of findings to other populations, settings, and conditions. Several features of the study design enhance external validity, including the use of a representative sample from a large vocational college, implementation in natural educational settings, and alignment with standard curriculum requirements. The selection of a well-established HVC with a diverse student population increases the likelihood that findings will generalize to similar institutions. The use of authentic classroom settings and standard academic procedures (e.g., regular course exams for assessment) rather than artificial laboratory conditions improves ecological validity. Detailed documentation of the research context, participant characteristics, and implementation procedures enables the evaluation of how the findings might apply to other settings. While no single study can establish universal generalizability, the design choices in this research maximize the potential for findings to inform practice in similar vocational education contexts.

Experimental Procedures

The experimental procedures were carefully structured across a six-week timeline to ensure consistent implementation while accommodating the practical realities of the academic calendar. The first week focused on pre-treatment activities including platform orientation (for the iCVE learning management system) and administration of the pretest. The subsequent four weeks comprised the treatment phase, during which students in the TB-SPOC condition completed five task-based modules, while the CB-SPOC group worked through equivalent content in an existing content-based format. Each topic followed a consistent sequence: pre-class preparation and orientation, task performance and assessment, followed by the next topic. The final week included posttest administration and data collection. Standardized protocols were developed for each phase to ensure consistency across groups and minimize variability in implementation. Facilitators received training on platform use, assignment administration, and observation procedures to promote treatment fidelity. Assignment descriptions and evaluation criteria were standardized across groups. The structured timeline and standardized procedures strike a balance between the need for experimental control and the practical requirements of conducting research in authentic educational settings.

Data Analysis

Data analysis procedures were designed to address the research questions while accounting for the quasi-experimental design. All analyses were conducted using

IBM SPSS Statistics software (Version 30). Descriptive statistics including means, standard deviations, and frequency distributions provide an overview of performance outcomes across groups and time points. Inferential analyses focus primarily on analysis of variance (ANOVA) techniques to compare performance between treatment groups while controlling for educational background. Mixed-design ANOVAs with time (pretest-posttest) as a within-subjects factor and treatment group as a between-subjects factor allow examination of performance changes over time and their interaction with instructional approach. Additional analyses explore whether educational background moderates the effectiveness of the different SPOC formats. Assumption testing including checks for normality, homogeneity of variance, and sphericity inform the selection of specific analytical approaches and potential need for adjustments or alternative procedures. Effect sizes are calculated to assess the practical significance of findings beyond statistical significance. The analytical approach provides a comprehensive evaluation of treatment effects while appropriately accounting for the study's quasi-experimental nature.

In summary, this study employed a quasi-experimental design to evaluate the effectiveness of task-based SPOCs English for Occupational Purposes (EOP) learning in Higher Vocational Colleges (HVCs). The design strikes a balance between scientific rigor and practical feasibility, incorporating multiple controls to mitigate validity threats while operating within real-world educational constraints. The focus on performance measured through standardized assessments aligned with vocational needs ensures the study addresses practical concerns of stakeholders in HVCs. The IMMS questionnaire is used to measure students' perceived motivation towards the SPOCs. Careful attention to sampling, instrumentation, implementation procedures, and analysis plans supports the generation of valid and actionable findings that can inform both practice and future research in this critical educational domain. The methodology provides a robust framework for examining how innovative SPOC learning approaches can enhance language skill development for occupational purposes among diverse student populations in HVCs.

RESULTS

The findings of this study provide compelling evidence regarding the effectiveness of Task-Based SPOCs (TB-SPOC) compared to Content-Based SPOCs (CB-SPOC) in teaching English for Occupational Purposes (EOP) to higher vocational college (HVC) students. The results demonstrate clear advantages of the task-based approach across multiple dimensions while also revealing important nuances related to students' educational backgrounds.

Beginning with performance, the data revealed statistically significant differences favoring TB-SPOC over CB-SPOC. Students who received instruction through the task-based SPOC achieved markedly higher post-test scores (M = 73.07, SD = 11.613) compared to their counterparts in the content-based SPOC (M = 68.35, SD = 10.637). This difference was not merely statistically significant ($F(1, 357) = 16.077$, $p < .001$) but also educationally meaningful, representing a substantial improvement in learning performance. The magnitude of this effect becomes particularly noteworthy when considering that both groups began with equivalent pre-test scores, as confirmed by initial homogeneity testing ($p = .699$). This finding strongly suggests that the pedagogical design of TB-SPOC, with its emphasis on practical, occupation-relevant tasks, more effectively facilitates language acquisition and application than existing content-based approaches.

Further analysis revealed important variations in treatment effects based on students' educational backgrounds before they are accepted by the Higher Vocational College (HVC) with qualification to study as HVC students. The performance advantage of TB-SPOC was especially pronounced among students with high-school backgrounds, who scored significantly higher in the task-based SPOC (M = 75.54) than in the content-based SPOC (M=68.57). This pattern suggests that HVC learners with high school educational backgrounds may be particularly well-suited to benefit from task-based SPOC. In contrast, students from vocational school backgrounds showed no statistically significant performance difference between the two SPOC modes ($p = .576$), indicating that their learning performance were less dependent on SPOC modes. extended

The study also examined performance differences between educational backgrounds within each SPOCs. Within TB-SPOC, students with a high-school background significantly outperformed their vocational background peers ($p = .034$), highlighting prior educational backgrounds continue to influence learning under the task-based SPOC. However, this performance gap disappeared in the CB-SPOC condition ($p = 1.000$), where both groups achieved similar results.

Turning to the perceived motivation of students, the results consistently favored the task-based SPOC. Students in TB-SPOC reported significantly higher levels of perceived motivation (M = 60.37) compared to those in CB-SPOC (M = 56.26), with this difference being highly statistically significant ($F(1, 358) = 20.737$, $p < .001$). Unlike performance, these perceived motivational benefits extended equally to students from both high-school and vocational backgrounds, with both groups showing significantly higher perceived motivation in TB-SPOC compared to CB-SPOC.

The analysis of interaction effects provided additional insights into how SPOC modes interact with student educational backgrounds. For performance, no significant interaction was found between SPOC mode and educational background ($F(1, 355) = 2.839$, $p = .093$), indicating that TB-SPOC's performance advantages operated similarly across students with different educational backgrounds. The same pattern held for perceived motivation ($F(1, 356) = 0.196$, $p = .658$), with TB-SPOC's benefits being equally distributed. These null findings are themselves meaningful, suggesting that while the absolute magnitude of TB-SPOC's effects may vary by student background (as seen in the performance results), the direction and significance of these effects remain consistent.

DISCUSSION

The study found that students in a task-based SPOC (TB-SPOC) significantly outperformed those in a content-based SPOC (CB-SPOC), supporting prior research on task-based instruction (TBI) in English for Specific Purposes (ESP) reading skills (Shabani & Ghasemi, 2014) and Brumfit's (1984) assertion that language learning is more effective when focused on meaning rather than form. These results align with Krashen's "Input Hypothesis" and Swain's "Output Hypothesis," which emphasize exposure to comprehensible input and real-world language use (quoted in Ellis, 2003). TB-SPOC's task-oriented approach—simulating real-life scenarios, such as writing emails or giving presentations—contrasts with CB-SPOC's content-driven method, where language acquisition is incidental. This aligns with Bărbuleţ's (2022) emphasis on naturalistic conditions for foreign language learning (FLL), thereby enhancing motivation.

The findings also corroborate Muhammad and Rahman's (2025) study on the effectiveness of TBI in SPOCs for writing proficiency, while extending its benefits to speaking skills. Similarly, Nitisakunwut et al. (2023) highlight the role of TBI in fostering communicative opportunities in EFL contexts. Critics, such as Seedhouse (2005), argue that TBI is flawed or limited to second-language settings, while Swan (2005) claims it's unsuitable for beginners. However, this study refutes these criticisms, demonstrating that TB-SPOC combines structured input with meaningful output, supported by Ellis (2018) and Solhi & Buyukyazi (2011). TBI's classroom-based real-world simulations address the limited external practice opportunities for EFL learners.

From a theoretical standpoint, TB-SPOC aligns with Piaget's constructivism and Vygotsky's sociocultural theory, positioning students as active knowledge constructors within their Zone of Proximal Development (ZPD). Collaborative tasks further enhance peer learning. While both TB-SPOC and CB-SPOC improved post-test scores, TB-SPOC yielded superior results, emphasizing its dynamic, socially constructed learning environment.

Additionally, the study examined SPOC effects across educational backgrounds (high-school vs. vocational). Both groups improved, but high-school students outperformed vocational students in TB-SPOC; however, the interaction effect was non-significant, suggesting that TBI's benefits are independent of prior educational background. This aligns with Moreno-Marcos et al. (2019), but highlights a research gap in SPOC design for learners with diverse backgrounds before they are accepted by the Higher Vocational College (HVC) and qualify to study as HVC students. Constructivist theory explains TB-SPOC's success through learner autonomy and active engagement, with social-guided learning further boosting performance. In conclusion, TB-SPOC's task-based framework proves more effective than CB-SPOC, particularly in fostering real-world language skills across varied educational backgrounds.

The study found that students in the task-based SPOC (TB-SPOC) exhibited significantly higher perceived motivation than those in the content-based SPOC (CB-SPOC). This aligns with prior research (Muhammad & Rahman, 2025) on the motivational benefits of TBI in language learning. The real-world relevance of TB-SPOC tasks—such as workplace simulations—enhanced learners' engagement by making lessons feel practical and meaningful. By initially avoiding excessive focus on linguistic accuracy, students gained confidence early on, which in turn fostered a sense of accomplishment and intrinsic motivation. This approach not only improved their communicative competence but also made learning more enjoyable, reinforcing attention, relevance, confidence, and satisfaction—key aspects of motivation.

The findings align with studies by Jiang (2022), Hu et al. (2022), and Xu et al. (2023), which underscore the role of SPOCs in enhancing satisfaction and motivation. However, this study uniquely emphasizes how task-based design specifically elevates perceived motivation compared to content-based methods. High-school and vocational background HVC students in TB-SPOC both reported higher motivation than their CB-SPOC counterparts, though high-school background students showed a slightly stronger response. This trend, although not statistically significant, suggests that TB-SPOC's structured, interactive tasks may better align with the preferences of high-school learners. Zhu's (2022) research supports this, noting the adaptability of SPOCs to diverse educational backgrounds.

Constructivist principles explain TB-SPOC's motivational advantages: active, autonomous learning and collaborative tasks foster deeper engagement. Jiang and Liang (2023) further link task readiness to motivation, underscoring how well-designed activities in TB-SPOC sustain student investment. In contrast, CB-SPOC's passive content delivery lacks similar motivational triggers. In summary, TB-SPOC outperforms CB-SPOC in enhancing perceived motivation across educational backgrounds, validating its role in fostering engaged, practical learning. Its success underscores the importance of task-based methodologies in SPOC design, particularly for vocational and higher education contexts where real-world applicability drives motivation.

The study's findings demonstrate that the Task-Based SPOC (TB-SPOC) approach significantly enhances student performance and motivation compared to Content-Based SPOC (CB-SPOC) in higher vocational education. These results provide important theoretical contributions by validating constructivist learning principles and extending task-based instruction into SPOC environments. The research shows how structured, real-world tasks in TB-SPOC create more effective learning conditions than passive content delivery in CB-SPOC, particularly benefiting students transitioning from high school to vocational education. The technological implications suggest SPOC platforms should prioritize interactive task design and adaptive learning features to optimize educational outcomes.

From a practical perspective, the study provides valuable guidance for curriculum designers in vocational education, particularly for skill-based subjects such as English for Occupational Purposes. The findings indicate that task-oriented digital learning experiences better support diverse student populations, with students from high school backgrounds showing robust performance gains. This highlights the need for differentiated instructional strategies in online learning environments. The research also identifies important areas for future investigation, including expanding studies across different disciplines and student demographics, examining additional cognitive and motivational factors, and exploring advanced technological integrations, such as AI-driven personalization and VR-enhanced learning.

The study makes a significant contribution to our understanding of blended learning effectiveness by providing empirical evidence that task-based approaches in SPOCs lead to superior learning outcomes. These findings have important implications for educational practice, suggesting that institutions should prioritize interactive, task-driven learning designs in their online and hybrid course offerings. Future research directions should focus on longitudinal studies to assess long-term knowledge retention, comparative analyses of different task types, and the development of more sophisticated learning analytics tools to track student progress in these environments. The study ultimately positions TB-SPOC as a promising model for the future of vocational and higher education, combining the scalability of digital learning with the benefits of task-based pedagogy.

CONCLUSION

This study examined the effectiveness of a task-based SPOC model in enhancing student learning outcomes in English for Occupational Purposes (EOP) within the context of Chinese Higher Vocational Colleges (HVCs). Grounded in Second Language Acquisition (SLA) theory and supported by constructivist and motivational frameworks, the study employed a quantitative research design to evaluate whether a task-based instructional model could outperform a content-based SPOC (CB-SPOC) in improving students' performance and perceived motivation.

The findings demonstrated that the task-based SPOC significantly enhanced both students' language performance and their perceived motivation toward the course. Compared to the CB-SPOC group, learners in the TB-SPOC group showed notably higher post-test scores, indicating improved communicative competence in vocational English. Moreover, students reported stronger motivational responses when engaged in structured, authentic tasks reflective of workplace scenarios. These outcomes validate the pedagogical value of task-based learning in digitally mediated environments and affirm the suitability of this model for vocational English instruction.

The study further revealed important nuances in the role of educational background. High school background students demonstrated greater gains in performance under the task-based condition than their vocational school background peers, although both groups benefited motivationally. While interaction effects between instructional mode and educational background were largely non-significant, the overall consistency of the task-based model's effectiveness across diverse learners underscores its generalisability and practical relevance.

In conclusion, this study makes a meaningful contribution to the growing body of literature on technology-enhanced language learning by empirically establishing that task-based SPOCs provide a more effective instructional alternative to content-based models for EOP learners in HVCs. The integration of real-world communicative tasks, scaffolded design, and motivational supports offers a scalable and pedagogically sound approach to blended learning. These findings have direct implications for curriculum developers, institutional leaders, and policy-makers seeking to improve vocational English instruction through digital innovation.

MANAGERIAL IMPLICATIONS

The findings of this study yield several managerial implications for academic administrators, curriculum planners, and decision-makers in Higher Vocational Colleges (HVCs), particularly in the context of English for Occupational Purposes (EOP). The empirical evidence supporting the task-based SPOC model underscores the value of redesigning traditional digital English instruction into more interactive, performance-oriented formats that reflect real workplace communication scenarios.

First, given that students in the task-based SPOC condition significantly outperformed their counterparts in the content-based SPOC condition ($F(1,357) = 16.077$, $p < 0.001$), academic managers should prioritise the adoption of task-based approaches in compulsory English curricula. The structure and authenticity of vocational tasks—such as simulated dialogues, report writing, and collaborative projects—not only facilitate improved communicative competence but also increase students' perceived value of the learning experience, as supported by the significant perceived motivation differences ($F(1,358) = 20.737$, $p < 0.001$). Institutions are therefore advised to realign course development strategies around task design and scenario-based learning.

Second, the results demonstrate that the performance benefits of the task-based SPOC are not evenly distributed. Students from a high school background showed stronger performance gains under the task-based model compared to their vocational background peers ($p = 0.034$), although both groups reported similarly enhanced perceived motivation. This suggests that institutional leaders should invest in differentiated support mechanisms, such as pre-module orientation, remedial language units, or study skills workshops, particularly for vocational school background learners who may require additional scaffolding to fully benefit from the task-based format.

Third, the implementation of task-based SPOCs requires institutional support in digital infrastructure and professional development. Managers should ensure that instructors are trained not only in task-based pedagogy, but also in the effective use of learning management systems such as iCVE. Ongoing investment in technical support and course design consultation is also essential to ensure that instructional staff can deliver context-rich, learner-centred content that aligns with institutional teaching goals.

Fourth, given that motivation was significantly enhanced across both educational background groups, the managerial focus should extend beyond academic outcomes to include learner satisfaction and retention. Administrative structures that encourage feedback collection, iterative course improvement, and recognition of effective digital teaching practices will help foster a positive learning environment that supports long-term institutional development.

Lastly, quality assurance units should establish a systematic evaluation process for SPOC-based instruction. The use of learning analytics, assessment tracking, and student perception surveys can inform evidence-based refinements to the TB-SPOC and its future iterations. Managers should also explore partnerships between departments, such as English language centres and career development offices, to align SPOC content more closely with occupational demands and employability outcomes.

In conclusion, this study provides a strong rationale for institutional managers to reconfigure vocational English delivery through scalable, task-oriented digital models. The task-based SPOC has proven to be not only pedagogically effective, but also practically implementable within HVC structures, offering a pathway for sustainable instructional reform in line with the goals of applied education.

PRACTICAL IMPLICATIONS

The results of this study yield several important implications for practitioners directly involved in English language instruction and course development within Higher Vocational Colleges (HVCs), particularly in the domain of English for Occupational Purposes (EOP). The clear advantages of task-based SPOC (TB-SPOC) over content-based SPOC (CB-SPOC) in improving both student performance and perceived motivation suggest that educators should reconsider conventional approaches to online and blended English teaching.

Firstly, EOP instructors should adopt a more task-oriented approach in course delivery, aligning instructional activities with real-world communicative demands found in the workplace. Rather than focusing on grammatical explanation or passive reading tasks, teachers should facilitate structured learning through simulations, problem-solving tasks, and goal-based assignments. For example, activities such as preparing product presentations, writing business emails, or participating in mock interviews offer practical opportunities for learners to develop both linguistic and professional competencies.

Secondly, the design of learning modules must emphasise authenticity and relevance to vocational contexts. The performance gains observed in the TB-SPOC group demonstrate that learners benefit from instruction that replicates real occupational communication. This implies that course developers need to collaborate with industry stakeholders and front-line educators to identify task types that reflect sector-specific English usage. The instructional content should be adapted accordingly, ensuring that it meets both pedagogical and professional expectations.

Thirdly, digital platforms such as iCVE must be used not only as content repositories but as active learning environments. Practitioners should be trained to use the platform's interactive functions—such as discussion boards, peer review, and formative quizzes—to support collaborative learning and foster learner autonomy. These tools can create a virtual learning space where students actively engage with tasks, receive meaningful feedback, and monitor their progress, thereby enhancing both competence and motivation.

Fourthly, the differing performance outcomes between high school and vocational background students highlight the necessity of differentiated instructional strategies. Educators must be prepared to tailor content delivery based on diagnostic assessments or early formative evaluations. For example, vocational-track students may require more scaffolded instructions or examples before completing independent tasks, while high school background students may be ready for more complex challenges. Practical guidance and task modelling can help bridge performance gaps and support inclusive teaching.

Lastly, teachers and academic support teams should adopt a reflective approach to SPOC delivery. Systematic collection of student feedback and outcome data should inform revisions to task design and instructional pacing. Teachers should be encouraged to share best practices, co-develop resources, and participate in peer observation to foster professional development centred on task-based instruction in online environments.

In summary, this study provides practical guidance for enhancing the quality of EOP instruction through the integration of task-based SPOCs. By focusing on authentic communication, learner-centred design, and differentiated support, educators can significantly improve students' language performance and motivation, thereby contributing to the overall effectiveness of vocational English education in the digital era.

THEORETICAL IMPLICATIONS

This study offers several key theoretical implications that contribute to the advancement of language learning theories, instructional design frameworks, and digital pedagogy within the field of English for Occupational Purposes (EOP). By empirically investigating the effects of task-based SPOC (TB-SPOC) on student performance and perceived motivation in Higher Vocational Colleges (HVCs), the research provides concrete support for the integration of task-based instruction into digitally mediated learning environments and validates several interrelated learning theories.

Firstly, the study reinforces the applicability of Krashen's Second Language Acquisition (SLA) theory in the design of online vocational English instruction. Krashen's emphasis on comprehensible input, low-anxiety environments, and meaningful communication is reflected in the TB-SPOC structure, where authentic tasks allow students to acquire language incidentally while focusing on workplace-relevant outcomes. The improvement in student performance observed in the TB-SPOC group provides empirical validation that task-based online environments can effectively simulate the conditions necessary for acquisition, even in English as a Foreign Language (EFL) settings.

Secondly, the study extends the principles of constructivist learning theory, particularly Piaget's cognitive constructivism and Vygotsky's sociocultural theory, to the domain of online EOP instruction. The TB-SPOC encouraged learners to build knowledge through active problem-solving, peer interaction, and scaffolded digital tasks, all of which align with the constructivist view that learning is constructed rather than transmitted. The improved motivation reported by students further suggests that learning environments grounded in student autonomy and social interaction are more likely to produce sustained engagement and deeper learning, thereby supporting the core tenets of sociocultural theory.

Thirdly, the study contributes to the theoretical development of task-based instruction (TBI) within SPOC contexts. While TBI has long been established as an effective classroom-based method in communicative language teaching (CLT), its integration into structured online modules for vocational learners has received limited attention. By operationalising Ellis and Shintani's (2013) criteria for task design and demonstrating measurable learning outcomes, the study validates the extension of TBI from traditional face-to-face settings to online blended formats. This confirms that the core mechanisms of TBI—gap-driven communication, meaning-focused input, and outcome-based interaction—remain effective when adapted into SPOC environments.

Fourthly, the findings affirm the relevance of Self-Determination Theory (SDT) in understanding learner motivation in online language education. Students in the TB-SPOC group reported significantly higher levels of perceived motivation, which supports the idea that well-structured tasks can satisfy learners' needs for autonomy, competence, and relatedness. These psychological dimensions, as proposed by Ryan and Deci (2000), are critical for sustained motivation and academic success. The presence of interactive, relevant, and progressively challenging tasks within the TB-SPOC provides an instructional model that operationalises these motivational constructs in a practical way.

Finally, the research also substantiates the use of Keller's ARCS model as a design framework for enhancing motivational appeal in SPOC environments. The incorporation of real-world relevance, structured task sequencing, confidence-building activities, and satisfaction through visible progress aligns closely with the Attention-Relevance-Confidence-Satisfaction dimensions of ARCS. The significant motivational gains among learners provide empirical evidence that these principles, when systematically embedded into course design, can positively influence learner attitudes and outcomes.

In summary, this study offers strong theoretical support for the convergence of SLA, constructivist, and motivational theories within the context of digital task-based instruction. It demonstrates that the integration of TBI and motivational design principles into SPOC-based EOP instruction can produce meaningful improvements in student performance and perception, thereby expanding the theoretical foundations of both language learning and digital pedagogy in vocational education settings.

RECOMMENDATION

Based on the findings of this study, several recommendations are proposed to enhance the effectiveness of English for Occupational Purposes (EOP) instruction through the wider adoption and optimisation of task-based SPOC (TB-SPOC) models in Higher Vocational Colleges (HVCs). These recommendations are addressed to different stakeholders, including institutional policymakers, curriculum designers, instructors, and educational researchers.

First, institutional leaders and academic committees in HVCs should prioritise the development and implementation of TB-SPOCs as a central component of digital vocational English education. The superior outcomes in both student performance and perceived motivation observed in this study provide a strong rationale for replacing passive, content-based instruction with more interactive, task-oriented models. This shift should be supported by policy frameworks that encourage innovation in curriculum development, blended delivery, and task-based pedagogy.

Second, curriculum designers should revise EOP course materials to integrate structured, authentic tasks aligned with students' future professional roles. The task types used in this study—including surveys, design tasks, and simulated workplace communication—proved effective in promoting both skill development and learner motivation. It is therefore recommended that future modules follow a similar model, ensuring that tasks are vocationally relevant, linguistically appropriate, and pedagogically scaffolded.

Third, teachers delivering EOP courses in HVCs should receive professional training in task-based instruction and digital facilitation strategies. While the task-based SPOC model offers clear pedagogical benefits, its success relies heavily on the instructor's ability to design, guide, and evaluate meaningful tasks. Training should focus on the design of communicative activities, use of SPOC platforms, facilitation of peer interaction, and implementation of formative assessment techniques.

Fourth, greater attention should be paid to the diversity of learners' educational backgrounds. While the task-based SPOC was effective across student groups, the findings indicate that students from vocational backgrounds may require additional support to achieve performance outcomes comparable to those of high school graduates. Therefore, diagnostic assessment at the beginning of the course, followed by differentiated instructional strategies, is recommended to ensure equity in learning outcomes.

Fifth, policymakers at the national or provincial level should consider incorporating TB-SPOC design principles into broader guidelines for digital and vocational education. Given the proven potential of this model, it could serve as a template for other skill-based language courses, especially in the context of China's continuing emphasis on education informatization and vocational curriculum reform.

Finally, future educational technology investment should be directed toward developing adaptive SPOC platforms that support task-based learning. Features such as real-time feedback, scenario-based simulations, and learner progress dashboards would further enhance the effectiveness and scalability of TB-SPOCs in vocational education.

In conclusion, to realise the full potential of TB-SPOCs in improving EOP instruction, coordinated efforts across policy, pedagogy, and practice are required. The recommendations outlined above are grounded in empirical evidence and offer a pragmatic roadmap for advancing digital language education in vocational institutions.

FUTURE DIRECTIONS

Looking ahead, several focused research directions are recommended to build on the current study's contributions and address its limitations. These directions seek not only to deepen the academic understanding of task-based SPOC (TB-SPOC) efficacy, but also to broaden its strategic and institutional relevance.

Firstly, while the present research concentrates on instructional design and learner outcomes, future studies should investigate the systemic support required for TB-SPOC to function effectively. This includes the role of teacher preparedness, digital pedagogical training, and institutional support mechanisms. Without sufficient teaching support, even well-designed task-based courses may fail to achieve their intended outcomes. Therefore, empirical research is needed to examine how teacher facilitation quality and technical assistance shape the success of TB-SPOC implementation across varied educational settings.

Secondly, there is a pressing need to examine the alignment between innovative pedagogical models like TB-SPOC and current policy frameworks. Despite national encouragement for blended and digital learning, there is often a lack of concrete policy instruments to guide or support sustainable SPOC adoption at scale. Future research should explore the extent to which institutional and governmental policies enable or inhibit the diffusion of SPOC-based innovation in vocational education, and propose more coherent policy-to-practice pathways.

Thirdly, future studies should examine the long-term effects of TB-SPOC participation on learning retention, skills transfer, and employability. While this study assessed immediate outcomes, it did not investigate whether knowledge and competence acquired through TB-SPOC are retained or applied in real-world settings over time. This is especially critical for vocational learners whose performance may vary widely. Special attention should be given to how TB-SPOC serves marginalised students, including those with lower academic ability, limited digital access, or from non-traditional educational backgrounds.

Lastly, the evolving role of educational technology opens promising avenues for future development. The integration of artificial intelligence (AI) to enable adaptive learning paths, personalised task sequences, and automated formative feedback could significantly enhance learner autonomy and instructional efficiency. Likewise, the use of virtual reality (VR) to simulate authentic occupational scenarios has potential to improve learner immersion and communicative competence. Future research should investigate how these tools can be ethically and effectively embedded in TB-SPOC ecosystems to support differentiated and scalable instruction.

These future directions call for a more interdisciplinary approach, combining instructional design, policy research, teacher development, and educational technology. Such integration is essential for ensuring that TB-SPOC evolves into a robust, equitable, and future-ready model for vocational English instruction.

REFERENCES

Abdullah, M., Husin, N. A., & Haider, A. (2020). Development of post-pandemic COVID19 higher education resilience framework in Malaysia. *Archives of Business Research*, *8*(5), 201–210.

Ali, W. (2020). Online and remote learning in higher education institutes: A necessity in light of COVID-19 pandemic. Higher education studies, 10(3), 16-25.

Aljohani, M. (2017). Principles of “constructivism” in foreign language teaching. *Journal of Literature and Art Studies*, *7*(1), 97–107.

Allen, M. (2017). Designing Online Asynchronous Information Literacy Instruction Using the ADDIE Model. In Maddison, T., & Kumaran, M. (Eds.), *Distributed Learning* (pp. 69–91). Chandos Publishing: Elsevier., DOI: 10.1016/B978-0-08-100598-9.00004-0

Almelhi, A. M. (2021). Effectiveness of the ADDIE Model within an E-Learning Environment in Developing Creative Writing in EFL Students. *English Language Teaching*, *14*(2), 20–36.

An, X., & Qu, C. (2021). A hierarchical learning model based on deep learning and its application in a SPOC and flipped classroom. [iJET]. *International Journal of Emerging Technologies in Learning*, *16*(9), 76–93.

Aron, A., Coups, J. E., & Aron, N. E. (2011). *Statistics for the behavioral and social sciences: A brief course* (5th ed.). Prentice Hall.

Bărbuleţ, G. (2022). Content based learning-Task based learning-Problem based learning in Teaching Romanian Language to Foreign Students. *Swedish Journal of Romanian Studies*, *5*(2), 241–250.

Brown, H. D. (2014). *Principles of language learning and teaching: A course in second language acquisition*. Pearson.

Brumfit, C. (1984). *Communicative methodology in language teaching*. Cambridge University Press.

Chen, C., & Meng, X. (2021). Exploring the relationship between student behavioral patterns and learning outcomes in a SPOC. [IJDET]. *International Journal of Distance Education Technologies*, *19*(1), 35–49.

Chen, J. (2020). SPOC-based flipped learning model applied in interpreting teaching. [iJET]. *International Journal of Emerging Technologies in Learning*, *15*(17), 4–13.

Chen, R., & Yang, C. (2015). Research on Design Model of SPOC Blended Learning. *Distance Education in China, 5*, 42–47.

Ding, Y., & Zhao, T. (2020). Emotions, engagement, and self-perceived achievement in a small private online course. *Journal of Computer Assisted Learning, 36*(4), 449–457.

Dong, Y., Ang, J., & Sun, Z. (2021). Designing Path of SPOC blended teaching and learning mode in post-MOOC Era. In 2021 10th International Conference on Educational and Information Technology (ICEIT) (pp. 24-28). IEEE.

Ellis, R. (2003). *Task-based language learning and teaching*. Oxford University Press.

Ellis, R. (2018). Taking the critics to task: The case for task-based teaching. New perspectives on the development of communicative and related competence in foreign language education, 28, 23.

Ellis, R., & Shintani, N. (2013). *Exploring language pedagogy through second language acquisition research*. Routledge.

Eriksson, T., Adawi, T., & Stöhr, C. (2017). "Time is the bottleneck": A qualitative study exploring why learners drop out of MOOCs. *Journal of Computing in Higher Education, 29*(1), 133–146.

Feng, L., & Liu, Y. (2022). Research and Practice of Online and Offline Blended Teaching based on MOOC and SPOC: A case study of computer foundation courses. *Educational Review, 11*(34), 68–70.

Fox, A. (2013). From moocs to spocs. *Communications of the ACM, 56*(12), 38–40.

Gu, Y. (2020). The Construction and Development of High Level Higher Vocational Colleges Driven by Innovation. *2020 International Conference on Social and Human Sciences (ICSHS2020)*. (pp.117-123). DOI: DOI: 10.38007/Proceedings.0000023

Guo, Y., Song, H., & Jiang, D. (2023). The construction and application of digital course on ICVE platform—Taking the course of health education and health promotion as an example. *Frontiers in Educational Research, 6*(4).

Gupta, V. (2020). Blended SPOC Teaching and Learning Model for Computer Programming Course: Insights and Defeating Challenges. In *2020 IEEE International Conference on Teaching, Assessment, and Learning for Engineering (TALE)* (pp. 251-257). IEEE.

Hu, T., Zhang, M., Liu, H., Liu, J., Pan, S., Guo, J., Tian, Z., & Cui, L. (2022). The influence of "small private online course + flipped classroom" teaching on physical education students' learning motivation from the perspective of self-determination theory. *Frontiers in Psychology, 13*, 938426. DOI: 10.3389/fpsyg.2022.938426

Hutchinson, T., & Waters, A. (1987). *English for specific purposes*. Cambridge university press.

Iranmehr, A., Erfani, S. M., & Davari, H. (2011). Integrating task-based instruction as an alternative approach in teaching reading comprehension in English for special purposes: An action research. *Theory and Practice in Language Studies, 1*(2), 142–148.

Javed, F. (2024). Digital Transformation in Teaching and Learning of English in Higher Education. In Digital Transformation in Higher Education, Part B: Cases, Examples and Good Practices (pp. 103-125). Emerald Publishing Limited.

Jiang, L. (2022). Factors influencing EFL teachers' implementation of SPOC-based blended learning in higher vocational colleges in China: A study based on grounded theory. *Interactive Learning Environments*. Advance online publication. DOI: 10.1080/10494820.2022.2100428

Jiang, L., & Liang, X. (2023). Influencing factors of Chinese EFL students' continuance learning intention in SPOC-based blended learning environment. *Education and Information Technologies, 28*(10), 13379–13404.

Jiang, W., Zhan, Y., Sun, D., Sun, J., & Tian, P. (2024). Exploring the effects of SPOC-based blended learning on students' learning performance at higher vocational education. *Interactive Learning Environments, 32*(10), 6949–6966.

Kavaliauskienė, G. (2005). Task-based learning and learning outcomes in the ESP classroom. *Kalbų Studijos*, (7), 66–70.

Keller, J. (1987). Development and use of the ARCS model of instructional design. *Journal of Instructional Development : JID, 10*(3), 2–10.

Keller, J. M. (1993). *Manual for instructional materials motivational survey*. IMMS.

Keller, J. M. (2010). *Motivational design for learning and performance: The ARCS model approach*. Springer.

Kim, B. K., & Jung, C. Y. (2012). The casual relationship among career decision-making self-efficacy, self-leadership, problem solving ability, and career motivation. *Journal of Agricultural Education and Human Resource Development, 44*(2), 49–71.

Krashen, S. (1981). Second language acquisition. *Second Language Learning*, *3*(7), 19–39.

Lakens, D. (2022). Sample size justification. *Collabra. Psychology*, *8*(1), 33267.

Li, F., Lu, Y., Ma, Q., Gao, J., Wang, Z., & Bai, L. (2023). SPOC online video learning clustering analysis: Identifying learners' group behavior characteristics. *Computer Applications in Engineering Education*.

Li, J. (2022). Domestic MOOC Learning Behavior Research: A Systematic Analysis of the Literature in the Last Decade. *New Generation of Information Technology*, *5*(3), 99–102.

Li, Z., & Jiang, W. (2022). Research on the Teaching Reform of Inorganic Chemistry Based on SPOC and FCM during COVID-19. *Sustainability*, *14*(9), 5707.

Liu, L. (2021). Research on IT English flipped classroom teaching model based on SPOC. *Scientific Programming*, *2021*, 1–9.

Ma, L., & Lee, C. S. (2021). Evaluating the effectiveness of blended learning using the ARCS model. *Journal of Computer Assisted Learning*, *37*(5), 1397–1408. DOI: 10.1111/jcal.12579

Ministry of Education of the People's Republic of China. (2018). Announcement of the Ministry of Education on issuing the "Education Informatization 2.0 Action Plan" [2018] No. 6.

Ministry of Education of the People's Republic of China. (2020). Action Plan for Improving the Quality of Vocational Education (2020-2023). Announcement of the Ministry of Education and nine other departments on issuing the Action Plan for Improving the Quality of Vocational Education (2020-2023). Faculty Cheng (2020) NO. 7. https://www.gov.cn/zhengce/zhengceku/2020-09/29/content_5548106.htm

Moreno-Marcos, P. M., De Laet, T., Muñoz-Merino, P. J., Van Soom, C., Broos, T., Verbert, K., & Delgado Kloos, C. (2019, March). Predicting admission test success using SPOC interactions. In *Proceedings of the 9th International Conference of Learning Analytics & Knowledge*, Tempe, AZ, USA (pp. 4-8).

Muhammad, S., & Rahman, M. (2025). Developing Students' Descriptive Writing Skills in terms of Content Knowledge at the Higher Secondary School Level: An Experiment with the Task-Based Writing Methodology. [DSSR]. *Dialogue Social Science Review*, *3*(1), 388–408.

Nitisakunwut, P., Nutayangkul, T., & Liang-Itsara, A. (2023). The sociocultural perspective on the use of L1 as a supporting tool for EFL learning. *English Language Teaching, 16*(2), 74–81.

Piaw, C. Y. (2020). *Mastering Research Methods* (2nd ed.). McGraw-Hill Education.

Plomp, T. (2007). Educational design research: An introduction. In Plomp, T., & Nieveen, N. (Eds.), *Educational design research: An introduction* (pp. 9–36). SLO.

Qiu, X. (2022). Blended Teaching Mode of Higher Vocational English Based on MOOC+ SPOC. *Wireless Communications and Mobile Computing*, •••, 2022.

Reeves, T. (2006). Design research from a technology perspective. In *Educational design research* (pp. 64–78). Routledge.

Reeves, T., & McKenney, S. (2015). Design-based research. In *The SAGE encyclopedia of educational technology* (pp. 189–191). SAGE Publications Inc.

Rogers, J., & Revesz, A. (2019). Experimental and quasi-experimental designs. In *The Routledge handbook of research methods in applied linguistics* (pp. 133–143). Routledge., https://discovery.ucl.ac.uk/id/eprint/10091265/7/Revesz_Rogers%20 Revesz_Experimental%20design%20book%20chapter.pd

Ryan, R. M., & Deci, E. L. (2000). Self-determination theory and the facilitation of intrinsic motivation, social development, and well-being. *The American Psychologist, 55*(1), 68–78.

Seedhouse, P. (2005). "Task" as research construct. *Language Learning, 55*(3), 533–570.

Shabani, M. B., & Ghasemi, A. (2014). The effect of task-based language teaching (TBLT) and content-based language teaching (CBLT) on the Iranian intermediate ESP learners' reading comprehension. *Procedia: Social and Behavioral Sciences, 98*, 1713–1721.

Solhi, M., & Büyükyazı, M. (2011, May). The use of first language in the EFL classroom: A facilitating or debilitating device. In Proceedings of the 1st international conference on foreign language teaching and applied linguistics, Sarajevo, Bosnia and Herzegovina.

Stern, H. H. (1983). *Fundamental concepts of language teaching: Historical and interdisciplinary perspectives on applied linguistic research.* Oxford university press.

Su, N. A. (2019). Research on the Teaching Practice of Task-based College English Writing Based on SPOC. *2nd Asia-Pacific Social Science and Modern Education Conference* (ISBN: 978-1-60595-678-7).

Sun, H. (2019). A SPOC teaching mode of college English translation based on" Rain Classroom [iJET]. *International Journal of Emerging Technologies in Learning, 14*(17), 182–193.

Swan, M. (2005). Legislation by hypothesis: The case of task-based instruction. *Applied Linguistics, 26*(3), 376–401.

Tang, H., Chiou, J. S., & Jarsaillon, O. (2015). Efficacy of Task-Based Learning in a Chinese EFL Classroom: A Case. *Study in English Language Teaching, 8*(5), 168–176.

Thamarana, S., & Narayana, T. (2016). A Critical Overview of Teaching English to Speakers of Other Languages. *First Language, 1*, L2.

Thornbury, S. (2007). *How to teach speaking*. Longma.

Valiathan, P. (2022). *Beginner's Guide to Instructional Design: Identify and Examine Learning Needs, Knowledge Delivery....* Methods, and Approaches to Design Learning Materia. Bhaktivedanta Book Trust.

Wei, L., Dew, T. P., & Said, N. (2024). The development of a SPOC platform for EFL listening instruction in Higher education. [IJELP]. *International Journal on E-Learning Practices, 7*(1).

Willis, J. (2013). *A Framework for Task Based Learning*. Longma.

Wuhue, J. (2023). Do SPOC Really Improve Student Learning in Vocational Schools? A Meta-Analysis of Studies in Chinese Contexts. *Turkish Online Journal of Educational Technology-TOJET, 22*(1), 49–59.

Xing, H. (2023). Current situation and research on English teaching in Higher vocational colleges under the information environment. *China New Communications, 25*(17), 221–223.

Xu, T., Xu, J., Xu, X., & Lu, J. (2023). Blended Learning on WeChat Platform-Based SPOC in Lower-Secondary School Science Teaching. *Journal of Baltic Science Education, 22*(4), 701–718.

Zeng, S., & Della, C. (2024). A Systematic Review of Professional Communication Skills in English for Specific Purposes in Vocational Education within the New Media Era. *Eurasian Journal of Educational Research, 114*, 226–249.

Zhang, H., Zhang, J., Wang, J., & Zhang, H. (2023). Integrating mobile learning and SPOC-based flipped classroom to teach a course in water supply and drainage science and engineering. *Computer Applications in Engineering Education.*

Zhang, L., Xuan, Y., & Zhang, H. (2020). Construction and application of SPOC-based flipped classroom teaching mode in Installation Engineering Cost curriculum based on OBE concept. *Computer Applications in Engineering Education, 28*(6), 1503–1519.

Zhang, X. M., Yu, J. Y., Yang, Y., Feng, C. P., Lyu, J., & Xu, S. L. (2019). A flipped classroom method based on a small private online course in physiology. *Advances in Physiology Education, 43*(3), 345–349.

Zhao, K. (2022). A Study on the Blending Learning Based on SPOC-Taking the Teaching Practice of "Practical English Writing" as an Example. *Journal of Educational Research and Policies, 04*(09), 132–135.

Zhu, Y. (2022). Research on mixed teaching practice of industrial English based on SPOC. *Overseas English, 7*, 228–230.

APPENDIX A

Figure 8.

Pertest and posttest

1. Exam Objectives:

The purpose of the exam is to assess students' overall oral English proficiency, emphasizing their discourse competence, including:

- Ability to organize and express ideas coherently and cohesively.
- Skill in managing and navigating conversations effectively in diverse communicative contexts.
- Use of appropriate language for specific purposes (e.g., explaining, inquiring, persuading, and negotiating).
- Confidence in engaging in real-life communication with clarity and fluency.

2. Exam Format:

a) Individual Presentation (5 minutes)

Students deliver a prepared short presentation on personal introduction. They should demonstrate logical structure, clear and concise ideas, smooth delivery, and clear and intelligible pronunciation.

item 1	personal introduction

b) Role Play (5 minutes)

Students participate in role-play with peers, simulating real-life communicative scenarios. The task emphasizes turn-taking, negotiation skills, and the ability to maintain topic coherence and solve a problem.

item 2	asking for direction
item 3	negotiating a purchase
item 4	in a restaurant
item 5	in a travel agent

c) 3. Group Discussion (6-8 minutes, 5 students per group)

Students engage in a collaborative discussion on a given topic. Each student should contribute actively, connect their ideas to others, and work towards shared understanding or solutions.

item 6	managing time
item 7	planning a school even
item 8	debating a product's benefits and drawbacks

d) Random Questioning (3-5 minutes)

The examiner asks students spontaneous questions related to daily life, studies, or interests. Students must provide detailed and relevant answers, demonstrating their ability to structure and expand their responses on the spot.

item 9	daily life
item 10	study
item 11	interests

Figure 9.

3. Scoring Criteria:

Item	Full Score	Scoring Criteria
Discourse Competence	35 points	Logical flow of ideas, coherence in maintaining topics, effective use of cohesive devices, and relevance of content.
Fluency and Adaptability	25 points	Smooth expression of ideas, minimal pauses, and ability to adapt language to context.
Interaction and Strategies	20 points	Active participation, use of conversational strategies like clarification and turn-taking.
Pronunciation and Clarity	20 points	Clear pronunciation, natural intonation, and speech comprehensible to listeners.

4. Grading Scale:

Excellent (A, 90-100 points): Exceptional discourse competence, clear and logical delivery, active interaction, minimal language or pronunciation errors.

Good (B, 80-89 points): Good coherence and interaction, logical responses with minor language or fluency issues.

Pass (C, 70-79 points): Adequate performance with some errors in organization, language, or fluency but generally understandable.

Fail (D, below 70 points): Frequent breakdowns in coherence, poor interaction, significant errors in language use, and difficulty maintaining communication.

5. Exam Schedule and Arrangements:

Each group will have 20 minutes, covering the individual presentation, role play, group discussion, and random questioning.

6. V. Notes:

- Preparation: Students should prepare their presentation topic in advance and practice organizing their ideas cohesively.
- Interaction Focus: Active participation and the ability to maintain and navigate discussions are key evaluation points.
- Language Use: Students should aim for clear and appropriate English, with a focus on logical and cohesive communication.
- Assessment: Scoring is based on the criteria outlined above, ensuring fairness and consistency in evaluation.

APPENDIX B

Figure 10.

Instructional Materials Motivation Survey (IMMS)

你对这些问题的回答将极大地帮助我们规划和设计有效、有趣的教学。你给出的答案不会影响你的成绩。

说明

1.在这个问卷中有 18 个陈述。思考每一个与你学习的课程有关的陈述，并指出它的正确性。给出真正适合你的答案，而不是你自己想要的答案，或者你认为别人想听的答案。

2.您给出的答案将是保密的，不会以任何方式影响您。

谢谢。

1= 不符合; 2=有点符合; 3=中度符合; 4 =多数符合; 5 =非常符合	1	2	3	4	5
1. 我对这门课感到相当失望					
2. 这门课几乎没有吸引我注意的东西					
3. 我认为我不会从这门课程中获益太多					
4. 在这门课上(或看这门课的视频)我经常做白日梦					
5. 这门课的主题似乎很重要					
6. 为了实现我的目标，我必须把这门课学好					
7. 我在这门课上学到的东西对我是有用的					
8. 因为我在上这门课，我相信如果我努力，我能成功					
9. 我相信我能学好这门课					
10. 这门课的主题对我来说太难了					
11. 我的好奇心经常被激发					
12. 我喜欢为这门课工作					
13. 我觉得这门课给了我很大的满足感					
14. 这个班的学生似乎对这个主题很好奇					
15. 我对这门课的设计很满意					
16. 我对我从这门课中学到的东西感到满意					
17. 这门课程的内容与我的期望和目标有关					
18. 教员采用了各种有趣的教学方法					

Figure 11.

Your answers to these questions will greatly assist us to plan and design effective and interesting instruction. The answers that you give not influence your grade.

INSTRUCTIONS

1. There are 18 statements in this questionnaire. Think about each statement in relation to the course you have just learned and indicate how true it is. Give the answers that truly apply to you, and not what you would like to be true, or what you think others want to hear.

2. The answers you give will be confidential and will not affect you in any way.

Thank you.

1 = Not True, 2=Slightly True, 3= Moderately True, 4 = Mostly True, 5 = Very True	1	2	3	4	5
1. I feel rather disappointed with this course					
2. This class has very little in it that captures my attention					
3. I do NOT think I will benefit much from this course					
4. I often daydream while in this class (or watching the video of this course)					
5. The subject matter of this course seems important					
6. To accomplish my goals, it is important that I do well in this course					
7. The things I am learning in this course will be useful to me					
8. As I am taking this class, I believe I can succeed if I try hard					
9. I feel confident that I will do well in this course					
10. The subject matter of this course is just too difficult for me					
11. My curiosity is often stimulated					
12. I enjoy working for this course					
13. I feel that this course gives me a lot of satisfaction					
14. The students in this class seem curious about the subject matter					
15. I am pleased with the design of this class					
16. I feel satisfied with what I am getting from this course					
17. The content of this course relates to my expectations and goals					
18. The instructor uses an interesting variety of teaching methods					

Chapter 13
Reimagining Instructional Design for Blended Learning in Chinese Higher Education:
A Self-Regulated Learning Perspective

Jingran Yang
https://orcid.org/0009-0005-3732-7706
Universiti Sains Malaysia, Malaysia

Wan Ahmad Jaafar Wan Yahaya
https://orcid.org/0000-0002-8605-0062
Universiti Sains Malaysia, Malaysia

ABSTRACT

Blended learning has rapidly expanded in Chinese higher education. Nevertheless, existing instructional designs do not fully exploit the potential of self-regulated learning (SRL), thereby constraining learner autonomy and limiting learning depth. This study reviews an SRL-driven framework for blended instruction that is tailored to the Chinese higher education context and aims to cultivate students' self-directed learning competence. Grounded in Zimmerman's SRL model and informed by empirical evidence and institutional case analyses. By integrating technological tools, cultural adaptation, and social interaction strategies, the framework seeks to bridge the gap between technological adoption and deep cognitive engagement, thus providing theoretical direction and practical guidance for instructional designers,

DOI: 10.4018/979-8-3373-7508-3.ch013

educators, and policymakers. Findings demonstrate that the systematic incorporation of SRL strategies into blended environments markedly enhances students' learning performance and self-regulatory skills.

INTRODUCTION

In recent years, the modernization and digital transformation of higher education in China have accelerated rapidly, making blended learning (BL) a central strategy for pedagogical innovation and reform (Ministry of Education of the People's Republic of China, 2019; Central Committee of the Communist Party of China & State Council of the People's Republic of China, 2024; Lim & Wang, 2016). National policy initiatives, such as China Education Modernization 2035 and the Plan for Building China into an Educational Powerhouse (2024–2035), have prioritized the integration of technology and student-centered approaches, with an explicit focus on cultivating learner autonomy and innovation.

Within this evolving landscape, self-regulated learning (SRL) theory, originally developed by Zimmerman and further enriched by subsequent scholars, has emerged as a key framework for understanding and enhancing student agency, metacognitive skills, and lifelong learning abilities (Zimmerman, 2002; Schunk & Zimmerman, 2011). Blended learning environments, by nature, offer increased flexibility, access to digital resources, and opportunities for personalized learning pathways (Wang, Han, & Yang, 2015). However, the successful realization of these advantages largely depends on the extent to which students are able to exercise self-regulation in their learning processes (Zimmerman, 2002; Broadbent & Poon, 2015). Research has shown that well-designed instructional frameworks and technological support can significantly promote SRL and improve academic outcomes (Broadbent & Poon, 2015). However, the practical integration of SRL strategies into blended instruction remains uneven across Chinese universities. Many current designs continue to rely on traditional teacher-centered paradigms, and formative assessment, peer collaboration, and digital scaffolding are often underutilized.

These challenges are further compounded by deep-rooted cultural traditions that emphasize teacher authority and examination-oriented learning, which can inhibit the development of student autonomy and adaptive learning strategies (Barnard-Brak, Lan, & Paton, 2010). Addressing these complex issues requires a localized, context-sensitive approach that not only draws on international models but also responds to the distinctive characteristics of Chinese higher education (Lim & Wang, 2016).

BACKGROUND OF STUDY

The transformation of Chinese higher education has been significantly shaped by national strategies aimed at educational modernization and digital integration (Ministry of Education of the People's Republic of China, 2019; Central Committee of the Communist Party of China & State Council of the People's Republic of China, 2024). With the implementation of initiatives such as China Education Modernization 2035 and the Plan for Building China into an Educational Powerhouse (2024–2035), universities across the country have embraced blended learning (BL) as a means to foster innovation, equity, and student-centered pedagogy (Lim & Wang,2016). As of 2024, China has launched over 76,800 MOOCs, serving more than 454 million users, and established upwards of 60,000 smart classrooms nationwide. Blended courses now reach over 70% of undergraduates, and targeted programs like the "MOOC Westward Action" have extended more than 93,600 hybrid courses to rural and under-resourced institutions, advancing both access and educational equity (China Education Informatization Network, 2024a; Ministry of Education of the People's Republic of China, 2024a).

Within this context, leading universities such as Tsinghua University have developed innovative platforms like "Rain Classroom" to promote blended and self-regulated learning (SRL), while institutions in central and western China have leveraged digital technologies to narrow regional disparities. These cases illustrate both the progress and the persistent implementation challenges: many blended courses still prioritize content delivery and summative assessment, with limited opportunities for students to engage in goal-setting, self-monitoring, or adaptive learning strategies. Cultural norms emphasizing teacher authority and examination-driven learning continue to constrain the systematic integration of SRL, resulting in passive student engagement and underdeveloped self-regulatory skills (Barnard-Brak, Lan, & Paton, 2010).

To unlock the transformative potential of blended learning, comprehensive reform is required in curriculum design, teacher professional development, and assessment policy (Broadbent & Poon, 2015). Creating genuinely student-centered and SRL-enhanced learning environments in Chinese higher education depends not only on technological infrastructure and policy vision but also on ongoing cultural shifts and the alignment of institutional practices with the needs of diverse student populations (Lim & Wang, 2016).

STATEMENT OF THE PROBLEM

Although extensive literature has confirmed that SRL abilities are critical for the effectiveness of blended learning (Broadbent & Poon, 2015), and while Chinese higher education continues to advance under the guidance of top-level policies and ongoing technological support, there remain significant gaps in the implementation of blended learning in China compared to other countries, particularly those in Europe, North America, and other developed regions of Asia, in areas such as instructional design, implementation outcomes, and the cultivation of students' self-regulated learning abilities.

Currently, leading international theories of blended learning and self-regulated learning, such as Zimmerman's model of self-regulation and Garrison's blended learning framework, are constructed based on Western social learning environments, cultural values, and educational policies (Zimmerman, 2002; Garrison & Kanuka, 2004). In contrast, Chinese higher education exhibits marked differences from Western contexts in areas such as instructional management, teacher roles, and student learning behaviors. Localization of blended learning and SRL theory in China remains limited; most research either directly adopts or superficially adapts Western theoretical models, lacking systematic innovations that deeply integrate local educational policies, management practices, cultural characteristics, and technological foundations. Although Chinese scholars have acknowledged the urgency of local innovation, systematic theoretical development of SRL in blended learning remains at an early stage. While some universities have introduced intelligent teaching platforms, many instructors still adhere to the traditional "lecture–assessment" model, which limits the effective use of these platforms for fostering SRL skills. Moreover, shaped by exam-oriented culture, collectivist traditions, and administrative management models, Chinese university students often demonstrate limited motivation and ability for autonomous learning, relying heavily on external incentives that constrain the enhancement of their SRL capacities (Barnard-Brak, Lan, & Paton, 2010).

The Chinese higher education system is characterized by significant diversity and hierarchical structures across multiple dimensions, including geographic regions (e.g., eastern coastal vs. central and western inland areas), institutional tiers ("Double First-Class" vs. local universities), and disciplinary fields. However, existing empirical research on blended learning and SRL tends to focus on top-tier universities and popular disciplines with abundant resources and advanced information infrastructure, such as Tsinghua University and Peking University, which benefit from better platforms, faculty, and policy support (China Education Informatization Network, 2024a). In contrast, ordinary undergraduate institutions, vocational colleges, and universities in central and western China face challenges such as limited digital infrastructure, insufficient teacher capacity, and a lack of curricular innovation, making it difficult to replicate the "leading experiences" (China Education Informatization Network, 2024b). The high degree of diversity in region, institution, and discipline, combined with disparities in equity and access compared to developed countries, means that most research and policy are centered on elite institutions, limiting the generalizability of findings and policy effectiveness.

As several scholars have observed, the understanding of the complex ecosystem of Chinese higher education remains insufficient, resulting in a lack of targeted policies and practical pathways for implementing SRL-oriented blended teaching reforms on a broad scale. Additionally, there are persistent disparities in equity and accessibility compared to developed countries, with uneven resources and support systems between urban and rural areas, regions, and institutions, which constrain large-scale, equitable blended learning and the development of SRL skills. While major policy documents and theoretical research emphasize "adapting to local conditions" and "differentiated promotion" (Central Committee of the Communist Party of China & State Council of the People's Republic of China, 2024; Ministry of Education of the People's Republic of China, 2019), in practice, it is often challenging to meet the diverse and personalized development needs of different institutions and students.

This chapter seeks to clarify the underlying causes of these persistent barriers by synthesizing the latest research, policy trends, and representative institutional cases. Through this analysis, the chapter aims to propose actionable recommendations for curriculum design, teacher training, and educational policy that can advance localized and sustainable integration of SRL and blended learning in the diverse landscape of Chinese higher education.

THEORETICAL FOUNDATIONS

The present study is grounded primarily in the theory of self-regulated learning (SRL), while also engaging with complementary frameworks such as Constructivism, the Community of Inquiry (CoI) model, Transformative Learning Theory, and Diffusion of Innovations Theory. Each theory offers a distinct perspective on the mechanisms and conditions that shape effective blended learning environments and self-regulation, particularly in contexts marked by resource and equity challenges, and specifically examines its relevance and applicability in the Chinese context.

Among these frameworks, Zimmerman's model of self-regulated learning is adopted as the primary theoretical lens for this study. This model directly addresses the core challenges of fostering learner autonomy, metacognitive awareness, and adaptive strategies in blended environments. Moreover, its compatibility with digital scaffolding and cyclical feedback makes it especially suitable for empirical research and instructional innovation in the context of Chinese higher education. Zimmerman (2002) defined SRL as "self-generated thoughts, feelings, and actions that are planned and cyclically adapted to the attainment of personal goals." The SRL framework identifies three cyclical phases: forethought (planning), performance (monitoring), and self-reflection (evaluation). Blended learning environments provide students with abundant learning resources, but whether students can effectively leverage these advantages depends largely on their self-regulated learning abilities. The introduction of the SRL perspective offers a more effective approach to addressing key challenges in Chinese higher education, such as large student populations, significant differences in abilities and backgrounds, the disconnect between technology and pedagogy, and high dropout rates in online courses. The SRL perspective provides both theoretical support and intervention pathways, enabling teachers to better design components such as self-monitoring, process feedback, and peer collaboration. This, in turn, enhances students' learning engagement and persistence, reduces attrition rates, and improves academic performance and self-discipline in blended learning environments. By aligning with national policy directives and the need to improve the quality of higher education, this approach also addresses practical shortcomings encountered in the implementation of blended learning in China.

Constructivist theory posits that knowledge is actively constructed by learners through interactions with their environment, content, and others, an idea that closely aligns with self-regulated learning (SRL), which emphasizes the active setting of goals, monitoring, and regulation of the learning process. Blended learning provides an ideal platform for integrating constructivism and SRL: online self-study components foster students' self-regulation, while offline interactions enhance knowledge construction and collaboration (Wang, Han, & Yang, 2015). In the context of blended learning in Chinese higher education, constructivism not only offers theoretical guidance for curriculum design but also encourages inquiry-based, collaborative, and project-based learning, prompting students to actively set goals and engage in continuous self-regulation across diverse tasks, ultimately achieving higher-order cognitive and skill development. Empirical studies have shown that, under constructivist guidance, the use of contextualized tasks and formative feedback can significantly improve Chinese students' self-management and learning outcomes. Moreover, constructivism directly addresses practical challenges in China's blended learning, such as excessive teacher dominance, insufficient student autonomy, and weak collaboration and reflection. For example, Zhu, Valcke, and Schellens (2010) found in their cross-cultural study that the introduction of constructivist concepts and collaborative projects promoted active exploration and peer collaboration, enhanced self-regulation abilities, and provided both theoretical and practical support for the transformation of blended teaching in Chinese universities.

EMPIRICAL LITERATURE REVIEW

The Impact of SRL on Learning Outcomes and Motivation

In the context of blended learning in Chinese higher education, "enhancing students' autonomous learning abilities and improving learning outcomes" has become a core goal. However, due to the deep-rooted traditions of content-centered teaching and exam-oriented culture, there are evident shortcomings in the cultivation and demonstration of students' SRL abilities in actual curriculum design, making it difficult to achieve a profound transformation toward blended learning models.

International empirical studies have consistently confirmed a close correlation between SRL levels and learning outcomes. For example, Broadbent and Poon (2015), in a meta-analysis examining the relationship between SRL strategies and academic performance in blended learning environments across 29 empirical studies and a total of 4,417 students, found that SRL strategies such as time management and self-monitoring were significantly and positively associated with academic achievement, especially in non-compulsory blended learning platforms. Puzziferro (2008), using structural equation modeling with 440 university students on a U.S. distance education platform, found that differences in SRL strategy use could effectively distinguish between high- and low-achieving groups.

In comparison, Zhang Xuelian et al. (2023) conducted surveys and follow-up interviews with students in blended courses at a university in China, finding a significant association between SRL levels and academic performance; however, most students exhibited weaknesses in goal management and reflection strategies. Large-scale empirical studies in China remain limited, with existing research mostly focusing on elite universities and single disciplines, lacking cross-regional and cross-disciplinary comparisons. Most data come from questionnaires, with insufficient longitudinal tracking and investigation of causal mechanisms.

SRL has a clear positive impact on the effectiveness of blended learning, but there is heterogeneity in its effects across different disciplines and student types. In China, further efforts are needed to deepen empirical research and policy development, especially in areas such as the localization of SRL theory, process-oriented assessment, and expanding interdisciplinary sample coverage.

The Role of Technology Empowerment and Digital Tools in SRL

With the widespread adoption of intelligent learning environments, technology-enabled SRL has become a major focus of empirical research. Sun and Rueda (2012) studied 227 students at a U.S. university and examined the impact of adaptive prompts on SRL behaviors in an online platform, finding that personalized feedback significantly increased students' use of strategies and levels of metacognitive reflection.

In China, intervention studies using AI-based learning platforms have reported that intelligent recommendations and automated feedback can enhance students' self-monitoring and learning motivation. However, these effects appear to vary across majors and grade levels, suggesting differential sensitivity to technological feedback. At the same time, much of the existing research relies heavily on platform data analysis, with limited long-term longitudinal tracking and insufficient application of complex behavioral modeling. As a result, the integration of technology and pedagogy in Chinese higher education remains in need of further development.

A typical process for integrating SRL and technology includes goal setting, behavior tracking, immediate feedback, and reflective improvement. Internationally, models such as "learning analytics + personalized scaffolding" have become mainstream. Chinese higher education should strengthen the deep integration of local platforms with course objectives. Technology empowerment provides new opportunities for visualizing and intervening in SRL behaviors, but it is urgently necessary to connect platforms, curriculum, and assessment into a complete chain in order to fully realize the potential of digital transformation in enhancing students' self-regulated learning abilities.

The Role of Instructional Design and Teacher Support in Promoting SRL

Although blended courses have become widespread, many still rely primarily on teacher-centered lectures and summative assessments, limiting the impact of instructional design and teacher support on SRL development. In fact, effective instructional design and teacher support are key to fostering students' SRL abilities. Kitsantas and Dabbagh (2010), through interviews and observations of blended courses in U.S. universities, found that scaffolded, phased instructional design (such as goal decomposition and formative assessment) helps stimulate students' self-regulation, deep reflection, and autonomous use of learning strategies. Van Laer and Elen (2017), in their review of attributes that support self-regulation in blended learning environments, emphasized the importance of metacognitive guidance and peer assessment in enhancing SRL. In the Chinese context, empirical studies using questionnaires and interviews have shown that university teachers often provide limited guidance on SRL in blended courses, and that course structures and evaluation systems do not adequately support students' self-regulation and deep reflection.

Research in China and other countries has tended to focus more on teachers' instructional behaviors, with insufficient attention to the causal mechanisms between course design and SRL outcomes. Additionally, most quantitative assessment tools are adapted from those developed in European countries, with limited cultural adaptation for the Chinese context. An ideal instructional process includes setting phased goals, implementing scaffolded tasks, teacher guidance, peer assessment, process reflection, and formative evaluation. This process requires localized innovation to be effectively implemented in the context of Chinese higher education.

The Moderating Role of Culture, Individual Differences, and Contextual Factors on SRL

Cultural background significantly influences both the choice and effectiveness of SRL strategies. Chinese higher education is characterized by diversity and hierarchical structures, with regional, disciplinary, gender, and other individual differences exerting a notable impact on SRL performance. Long-standing cultural authority and exam-oriented traditions continue to affect students' autonomy. (Barnard-Brak, Lan, and Paton (2010), in a comparative study of SRL behaviors among Chinese and American university students in blended learning environments, found that American students were more inclined toward active exploration and goal-setting, while Chinese students tended to rely more on external supervision and peer collaboration. Joosten and Cusatis (2020), in a study of students from different ethnic backgrounds in the United States, pointed out that socioeconomic status, learning culture, and autonomy orientation influence the application of SRL strategies. Empirical studies conducted at several Chinese universities have shown that region, gender, and disciplinary background can significantly moderate SRL performance. Nevertheless, comparative research between China and other countries remains limited, and contextual variables within China's diverse higher education ecosystem have not been sufficiently addressed. In particular, in-depth analyses of the multidimensional interactions among factors such as ethnicity, major, and grade level are still scarce.

Innovations in SRL Intervention Models and Long-Term Effect Tracking

Internationally, SRL intervention models are becoming increasingly diverse, encompassing blended approaches, mobile learning, and peer-assisted strategies. Zimmerman and Schunk (2011), through a systematic review, pointed out that phased interventions, formative assessment, and personalized feedback in blended environments can effectively enhance SRL abilities, but interventions must be adjusted to fit learners' actual needs and cultural contexts. Research has shown that short-term interventions alone are insufficient to sustain improvements in SRL, and that long-lasting effects require the systematic integration of curriculum, digital platforms, and teacher training. In the Chinese context, however, most innovative interventions remain short-term and isolated pilot projects, with limited longitudinal data and few multi-dimensional evaluations of effectiveness. As a result, the integration of theory and practice in SRL-oriented blended learning is still constrained.

Research findings differ across countries and regions, primarily due to significant differences in cultural adaptation, educational systems, the degree of technology integration, and the control of individual differences. For example, Western universities generally emphasize individual autonomy and reflection, resulting in more proactive use of SRL strategies and stronger outcomes, while Chinese university students, influenced by traditional teaching and exam culture, often demonstrate weaker goal-setting and reflection abilities, making technological empowerment and teacher guidance even more critical. On the other hand, limitations in research methods, the narrow sources of samples, and insufficient quantitative data also restrict theoretical innovation and cross-cultural comparisons. Future research in China should focus on deepening case studies, expanding cross-regional longitudinal tracking, and enhancing the integration of behavioral data with diverse evaluation methods. In particular, more attention should be given to the differentiated and sustainable mechanisms of SRL effectiveness across diverse student groups, course types, and technological platforms.

CONCEPTUAL FRAMEWORK

This study takes self-regulated learning (SRL) theory as its core and integrates the constructivist learning perspective, the Community of Inquiry (CoI) model, and the diffusion of innovation theory to construct a theoretical support system suitable for blended learning environments in Chinese higher education. This framework emphasizes the synergy between students' autonomous goal setting and reflection, digital support from teachers, deep integration of technology platforms, and the coordinated enhancement of cultural adaptation and diversity equity. This approach provides a clear theoretical foundation for subsequent instructional design innovation and empirical research.

RESEARCH METHODS

This study adopts a combination of scoping review and case analysis. First, it systematically reviews domestic and international empirical literature related to blended learning and SRL, summarizing mainstream theories and application trends. Second, it selects representative cases of blended courses, faculty development programs, and digital platform innovations from leading universities for comparative analysis and extraction of key elements. Third, it synthesizes effective pathways for implementing SRL strategies in blended learning environments. Methodologically, the study balances theoretical logic with the Chinese local context to ensure that the conclusions are both theoretically robust and practically applicable.

A Blended Learning Instructional Design Framework Based on Self-Regulated Learning (SRL) in Chinese Higher Education

Grounded in Zimmerman's self-regulated learning (SRL) theory (Zimmerman, 2002), and further extended by constructivist and blended learning models, this framework is designed to address the unique cultural, institutional, and technological characteristics of Chinese higher education. Previous research confirms that integrating SRL within blended learning environments enhances learner autonomy, motivation, and academic achievement (Broadbent & Poon, 2015). However, empirical evidence also reveals persistent challenges in China, including an over-reliance on teacher-centered pedagogy, limited formative assessment, and underutilized digital suppor. Therefore, the proposed framework deliberately incorporates contextual factors such as local educational culture, targeted teacher development, and technology-enabled analytics to maximize both the effectiveness and sustainability of SRL interventions.

The localized SRL and blended learning framework is organized into three interrelated phases, each supported by technology and adapted to local needs. In the forethought phase, students articulate personalized goals and develop structured learning plans, guided by digital templates and explicit instructor prompts. Research demonstrates that such structured goal setting and planning foster deeper engagement and more proactive learning, particularly in collectivist and exam-oriented environment. The framework, therefore, provides differentiated prompts and planning strategies to address the diversity among Chinese university students.

During the performance phase, learning management systems, analytics dashboards, and formative assessments deliver real-time feedback and facilitate ongoing self-monitoring and peer collaboration. The integration of technology-mediated feedback has been shown to significantly improve students' self-monitoring and metacognitive adjustment (Hadwin et al., 2017). The framework embeds culturally responsive scaffolding, including instructor check-ins and collaborative group activities, to balance learner autonomy with structured support, consistent with Chinese learner preferences and institutional practices.

In the reflection phase, students participate in reflective journals, self-assessment checklists, and group discussions, while mastery-based and formative assessments guide continuous improvement. Systematic reflection exercises and adaptive assessment strategies consolidate learning, enhance metacognitive awareness, and foster sustainable SRL skills (Van Laer & Elen, 2017). Reflection activities and assessment criteria are designed to be inclusive and sensitive to disciplinary and regional contexts.

This framework advances previous models by explicitly linking SRL, blended learning, and the Chinese cultural context in both design and practice. It provides detailed and actionable guidance for integrating digital tools, formative feedback, and reflective practices into curriculum and instruction. Furthermore, it addresses gaps identified in prior research, such as limited longitudinal data, regional disparities, and insufficient teacher support, by embedding mechanisms for continuous improvement and empirical monitoring. Empirical evidence from multi-institutional pilots and case studies validates the model's effectiveness, as shown by increases in student engagement, motivation, and academic achievement in SRL-enhanced blended learning courses.

Overall, this framework can be conceptualized as a cyclical process encompassing forethought, performance, and reflection, with each phase connected by ongoing feedback, digital analytics, and teacher support. Essential enabling systems, including professional development, technological scaffolding, and mechanisms for cultural adaptation, surround the core process. This model offers a dynamic, context-sensitive roadmap for designing and sustaining SRL-driven blended learning innovations across diverse settings in Chinese higher education.

DISCUSSION

The present study reinforces the growing consensus that self-regulated learning (SRL) integration is critical to maximizing the value of blended learning in Chinese higher education. Consistent with prior research, the analysis found that embedding SRL strategies, such as explicit goal-setting, ongoing formative assessment, and metacognitive scaffolding, leads to measurable improvements in students' autonomy, engagement, and learning outcomes, especially when supported by institutional commitment and digital infrastructure. This supports the positive findings from both Western and domestic studies, which have demonstrated that SRL-driven design enhances motivation, persistence, and achievement in blended environments (Broadbent & Poon, 2015; Schunk & Zimmerman, 2011).

However, several unique challenges specific to the Chinese context have also been identified. Unlike Western settings, where student-centered and constructivist pedagogies are the norm, Chinese higher education continues to be shaped by traditional cultural expectations, exam-driven practices, and hierarchical teacher–student relations. Consequently, the implementation of SRL frequently encounters barriers such as insufficient teacher training, resistance to pedagogical change, and unequal access to formative assessment and feedback technologies. These observations are consistent with previous studies, which highlight the "last mile" problem: despite substantial policy support and technological progress, the widespread and equitable adoption of SRL remains difficult to achieve, particularly in less-resourced or non-elite institutions.

A novel contribution of this study lies in the nuanced analysis of institutional and regional diversity in China. By comparing cases from leading and ordinary universities, and by incorporating multi-level data, it is evident that SRL success depends on a delicate balance of technological, cultural, and organizational factors, often requiring localized adaptation and continuous professional development. This contrasts with some previous literature that overemphasizes the universal transferability of SRL frameworks and underestimates the need for cultural and contextual adjustment.

The findings generally support existing theories that SRL strategies, if appropriately contextualized, are effective in improving blended learning outcomes. The results are consistent with the view that the core challenge now lies not in "whether" to adopt SRL, but in "how" to sustain and scale its implementation given China's vast educational heterogeneity and deep-rooted traditions. Rather than negating past research, this analysis advocates for a pragmatic and adaptive approach, emphasizing iterative innovation and localized experimentation as keys to long-term success.

Nonetheless, several limitations should be acknowledged. First, while this chapter employs a scoping review and case analysis, the lack of large-scale longitudinal and experimental data constrains causal inference and generalizability. Second, most available studies still focus on elite institutions or specific disciplines, resulting in potential sampling bias. Third, behavioral and qualitative data on students' SRL processes remain underexplored, and cross-institutional collaborations are still limited.

To address these gaps, future research should prioritize the following: (1) conducting longitudinal and experimental studies across a wider array of institutional types and regions; (2) integrating behavioral analytics and mixed-methods approaches to capture nuanced SRL processes; (3) exploring scalable, culturally responsive models of teacher training and curriculum innovation. These directions will help move the field from isolated "pockets of excellence" toward systematic, sustainable improvement.

CONCLUSION

This study was designed to answer the research question: How can blended learning in Chinese higher education be redesigned to effectively cultivate self-regulated learning (SRL) capabilities in students? Synthesizing national policy, empirical evidence, and institutional case studies, it is found that SRL-oriented blended teaching design, characterized by explicit metacognitive scaffolding, formative assessment, and contextual adaptation has significant potential to enhance student autonomy, motivation, and academic achievement. While the findings echo global research in affirming the benefits of SRL, persistent barriers in Chinese higher education related to cultural expectations, assessment practices, and resource disparities are also highlighted.

The significance of this research lies in its call for an adaptive, context-sensitive approach to SRL implementation, one that bridges the gap between policy vision and classroom reality. This entails fostering a culture of continuous teacher professional development, investing in digital infrastructure, and promoting cross-institutional collaboration for curricular and pedagogical innovation.

Based on these findings, it is recommended that universities and policymakers prioritize targeted investment in SRL-supportive environments, develop frameworks for scalable teacher training, and establish mechanisms for ongoing assessment and feedback. Ultimately, by embedding SRL at the heart of blended learning design, Chinese higher education can better prepare students for lifelong learning and success in an increasingly complex and digital world.

MANAGERIAL IMPLICATIONS

The findings of this study highlight that for university administrators and education managers, promoting SRL-oriented blended learning requires more than top-down digital transformation policies or generic teacher ICT training. Effective institutional support demands the targeted allocation of resources toward sustained faculty professional development in SRL pedagogy, as well as incentives for evidence-based instructional innovation. Data from leading Chinese universities show that the formation of interdisciplinary learning communities and the provision of collaborative curriculum co-design opportunities result in higher teacher engagement and more effective SRL implementation. Institutions should also prioritize the integration of advanced learning analytics into their LMS, enabling continuous formative assessment and data-driven decision-making. Furthermore, robust institutional frameworks that recognize and reward SRL-driven teaching innovation, particularly in under-resourced or non-elite settings, are critical to closing the equity gap and promoting scalable best practices across diverse educational contexts. This also indicates that, from the perspective of top-level policymakers, especially in resource-constrained regions and disciplines, clear policy guidance on curriculum reform, formative assessment, and digital infrastructure is crucial for aligning institutional priorities and accelerating systemic change.

PRACTICAL IMPLICATIONS

For instructors and instructional designers, this research underscores the necessity of deliberate, student-centered instructional planning to successfully embed SRL strategies into blended learning environments. Teachers should move beyond content transmission to design learning tasks that foster metacognitive awareness, such as explicit goal-setting, self-monitoring checklists, and structured opportunities for self-reflection and peer feedback. Evidence from empirical cases demonstrates that SRL integration is most successful when formative assessment and ongoing feedback are seamlessly woven into the learning process, rather than added as afterthoughts. To support these practices, faculty development programs must be discipline-specific, continuous, and collaborative, focusing on the practical use of digital tools for SRL, co-teaching models, and reflective teaching portfolios.

Moreover, integrating SRL in blended learning empowers students to develop transferable skills essential for lifelong learning, including self-directed problem-solving, critical thinking, and adaptability, skills highly valued in today's rapidly changing knowledge economy. For maximum impact, professional development programs for instructors should not only cover the technical aspects of blended learning platforms but also focus on evidence-based SRL instructional strategies and their impact on student learning trajectories.

By shifting instructional focus from knowledge delivery to the cultivation of self-regulatory capacity, blended learning environments can become powerful incubators of learner agency and resilience, fundamentally enhancing students' readiness for academic and professional success in a dynamic, digital future.

THEORETICAL IMPLICATIONS

From a theoretical perspective, this study advances the understanding of SRL and blended learning by demonstrating the critical importance of contextual and cultural adaptation in the Chinese higher education context. The analysis challenges the direct transplantation of Western-origin SRL frameworks, instead supporting the need for hybrid models that integrate core SRL principles with locally responsive instructional and assessment practices. These insights point toward the importance of developing localized theories of self-regulated learning and blended pedagogy that are empirically validated across diverse Chinese institutions.

RECOMMENDATION

Based on the synthesized findings, several targeted recommendations emerge for advancing self-regulated learning (SRL) within blended learning environments in Chinese higher education. Policymakers are encouraged to embed SRL as a core element in national and institutional education reform agendas, establishing clear standards, funding streams, and evaluation frameworks that prioritize SRL-supportive instructional innovation and professional development. Universities should facilitate interdisciplinary collaboration, expand teacher training programs focused on SRL strategies, and provide robust digital infrastructure to enable ongoing formative assessment and personalized learning pathways. For instructors, adopting evidence-based SRL pedagogies, including explicit goal-setting, process monitoring, and reflective activities, should be integral to course design, with a focus on fostering learner autonomy and adaptability. Continued research is needed to examine scalable intervention models, address regional and disciplinary disparities, and empirically validate context-sensitive SRL frameworks across diverse educational settings. Collectively, these efforts will help close the gap between policy ambition and classroom practice, ensuring that blended learning effectively cultivates lifelong learning capacities among students in China's rapidly evolving higher education system.

FUTURE DIRECTIONS

China's robust digital infrastructure, significant investment in artificial intelligence, and clear policy frameworks position the country as a global leader in advancing self-regulated learning (SRL) within blended learning environments. The capacity for large-scale pilot programs and rapid dissemination of best practices enables systematic reform and empirical validation across diverse higher education contexts. Moving forward, research should prioritize longitudinal and mixed-methods studies to assess the sustained impact of SRL interventions. Greater emphasis on interdisciplinary and international collaboration will enhance the generalizability and scalability of context-adaptive models. Systematic evaluation of SRL-driven reforms on student outcomes and educational equity will be essential for guiding future policy and practice.

REFERENCES

Barnard-Brak, L., Lan, W. Y., & Paton, V. O. (2010). Profiles in self-regulated learning in the online learning environment. *International Review of Research in Open and Distance Learning, 11*(1), 61–80.

Broadbent, J., & Poon, W. L. (2015). Self-regulated learning strategies & academic achievement in online higher education learning environments: A systematic review. *The Internet and Higher Education, 27*, 1–13.

Central Committee of the Communist Party of China & State Council of the People's Republic of China. (2024). Plan for building China into an educational powerhouse (2024–2035). Retrieved June 10, 2024, from https://www.gov.cn/zhengce/2024-01/19/content_6919883.htm

China Education Informatization Network. (2024a, May 15). Latest data on MOOCs and blended teaching in China. Retrieved June 10, 2024, from https://www.ictdedu.cn/news/jrgz/xxhdt/n20240515_84425.shtml

China Education Informatization Network. (2024b, April 17). Achievements of the "MOOC Westward Action" project. Retrieved June 10, 2024, from https://www.ictdedu.cn/news/jrgz/xxhdt/n20250417_86599.shtml

Garrison, D. R., & Kanuka, H. (2004). Blended learning: Uncovering its transformative potential in higher education. *The Internet and Higher Education*, *7*(2), 95–105.

Hadwin, A., Järvelä, S., & Miller, M. (2017). Self-regulation, co-regulation, and shared regulation in collaborative learning environments. In *Handbook of self-regulation of learning and performance* (pp. 83–106). Routledge.

Joosten, T., & Cusatis, R. (2020). Online learning readiness. *American Journal of Distance Education, 34*(3), 180–193.

Kitsantas, A., & Dabbagh, N. (2010). *Learning to learn with integrative learning technologies (ILT): A practical guide for academic success.* Information Age Publishing.

Lim, C. P., & Wang, L. (Eds.). (2016). *Blended learning for quality higher education: Selected case studies on implementation from Asia-Pacific*. UNESCO., https://unesdoc.unesco.org/ark:/48223/pf0000246851

Ministry of Education of the People's Republic of China. (2019, February 23). China education modernization 2035. Retrieved June 10, 2024, from https://www.gov.cn/zhengce/2019-02/23/content_5367987.htm

Ministry of Education of the People's Republic of China. (2024a, January 15). Statistical bulletin on the development of national education in 2023. Retrieved June 10, 2024, from http://www.moe.gov.cn/jyb_sjzl/s5990/202401/t20240115_1123112.html

Puzziferro, M. (2008). Online technologies self-efficacy and self-regulated learning as predictors of final grade and satisfaction in college-level online courses. *American Journal of Distance Education, 22*(2), 72–89.

Schunk, D. H., & Zimmerman, B. (Eds.). (2011). *Handbook of self-regulation of learning and performance*. Taylor & Francis.

Sun, J. C.-Y., & Rueda, R. (2012). Situational interest, computer self-efficacy and self-regulation: Their impact on student engagement in distance education. *British Journal of Educational Technology, 43*(2), 191–204.

Van Laer, S., & Elen, J. (2017). In search of attributes that support self-regulation in blended learning environments. *Education and Information Technologies, 22*(4), 1395–1454.

Wang, Q., Han, X., & Yang, S. (2015). Revisiting the blended learning literature: Using a complex adaptive systems framework. *Journal of Educational Technology & Society, 18*(2), 380–393. http://www.jstor.org/stable/jeductechsoci.18.2.380

Zhang, X., Li, H., Luo, Y., & Qian, C. (2023). [Exploration of online–offline blended teaching model for plant physiology experiments]. *New Education Era E-magazine (Teacher Edition),* (1). [in Chinese]

Zhu, C., Valcke, M., & Schellens, T. (2010). A cross-cultural study of teacher perspectives on teacher roles and adoption of online collaborative learning in higher education. *European Journal of Teacher Education, 33*(2), 147–165.

Zimmerman, B. J. (2002). Becoming a self-regulated learner: An overview. *Theory into Practice, 41*(2), 64–70.

KEY TERMS AND DEFINITIONS

Blended Learning: Blended learning combines in-person classroom instruction with online activities and digital tools, leveraging both settings to promote flexible, personalized, and interactive learning.

Cultural Adaptation: Cultural adaptation involves adjusting educational approaches and materials to fit local cultural values and learning traditions, ensuring relevance and effectiveness for diverse learners.

Formative Assessment: Formative assessment refers to ongoing feedback and evaluation during learning, aiming to guide student progress and instructional adjustments rather than only measuring final outcomes.

Instructional Design: Instructional design is the systematic development and alignment of objectives, content, methods, and assessments to optimize learning, especially in technology-enhanced and blended environments.

Learning Analytics: Learning analytics is the use of data from digital learning environments to provide insights and feedback, enabling personalized support and the improvement of learning processes.

Metacognitive Strategies: Metacognitive strategies are techniques learners use to plan, monitor, and reflect on their thinking and learning, supporting effective self-regulation.

Self-Regulated Learning (SRL): SRL is the process by which learners actively set goals, monitor their progress, use strategies, and reflect on outcomes to manage and improve their own learning.

Teacher Professional Development: Teacher professional development consists of structured activities to enhance educators' teaching skills, digital competencies, and capacity to support SRL in blended learning contexts.

Compilation of References

Abdullah, M., Husin, N. A., & Haider, A. (2020). Development of post-pandemic COVID19 higher education resilience framework in Malaysia. *Archives of Business Research*, *8*(5), 201–210.

Aberšek, B., Flogie, A., & Pesek, I. (2023). *AI and cognitive modelling for education*. Springer International Publishing., DOI: 10.1007/978-3-031-35331-4

Adaka, T. A., Adigun, O. T., Lalu, J., & Mngomezulu, T. P. (2022). Effect of mentorship on regular teachers' self-efficacy towards implementation of inclusive education at basic education level. *Special Education and Rehabilitation*, *21*(4), 233–253.

Adigun, O. T. (2021). Inclusive education among pre-service teachers from Nigeria and South Africa: A comparative cross-sectional study. *Cogent Education*, *8*(1), 1930491.

Adigun, O. T., & Mngomezulu, T. P. (2022). Occupational stress among teachers of learners with special needs. *Journal of Community Psychology*, *50*(2), 1185–1197.

Adigun, O. T., & Nzima, D. R. (2021). The fourth industrial revolution and persons with disabilities: Peeping into the future through the lens of the present. *Multicultural Education*, *7*(7), 113–118.

Adigun, O. T., Nzima, D. R., Maphalala, M. C., & Ndwandwe, N. D. (2022). COVID-19 and learners with disabilities: Towards divergent praxis in teacher preparation for equity and epistemic justice. *South African Journal of Higher Education*, *36*(4), 225–242.

Adigun, O. T., Vivekanantharasa, R., & Obosu, G. K. (2021). The Deaf or Hard of hearing population's attitude and information seeking behaviour towards COVID-19 in South Africa. *Journal of Human Ecology (Delhi, India)*, *75*(1-3), 16–26.

Adula, M., & Kant, S. (2025). Gamifying the Classroom by Mediation of Technological Innovations in Enhancing Student Engagement and Learning in Ethiopia. In *Enhancing Engagement With Gamification: Education, Business, and Healthcare Perspectives* (pp. 177-206). IGI Global Scientific Publishing.

Agyei, D. D. (2021). Integrating ICT into schools in Sub-Saharan Africa: From teachers' capacity building to classroom implementation. *Education and Information Technologies*, *26*(1), 125–144.

Ahdhianto, E., Barus, Y. K., & Thohir, M. A. (2025). Augmented Reality as a Game Changer in Experiential Learning: Exploring Its Role Cultural Education for Elementary Schools. *Journal of Pedagogical Research*, *9*(1), 296–313.

Ahir, K., Govani, K., Gajera, R., & Shah, M. (2020). Application on virtual reality for enhanced education learning, military training and sports. *Augmented Human Research*, *5*, 1–9.

Ahmad, F. K. (2015). Use of assistive technology in inclusive education: Making room for diverse learning needs. *Transcience*, *6*(2), 62–77.

Ahmad, M. I., Mubin, O., Shahid, S., & Orlando, J. (2019). Robot's adaptive emotional feedback sustains children's social engagement and promotes their vocabulary learning: A long-term child–robot interaction study. *Adaptive Behavior*, *27*(4), 243–266. DOI: 10.1177/1059712319844182

Ahmad, S. F., Rahmat, M. K., Mubarik, M. S., Alam, M. M., & Hyder, S. I. (2021). Artificial intelligence and its role in education. *Sustainability*, *13*(22), 12902. DOI: 10.3390/su132212902

Ahmed, A. (2018). Perceptions of using assistive technology for students with disabilities in the classroom. *International Journal of Special Education*, *33*(1), 129–139.

Ahmed, A. A. A., Sayed, B. T., Wekke, I. S., Widodo, M., Rostikawati, D., Ali, M. H., Abdul Hussein, H. A., & Azizian, M. (2022). An Empirical Study on the Effects of Using Kahoot as a Game-Based Learning Tool on EFL Learners' Vocabulary Recall and Retention. *Education Research International*, *9739147*. Advance online publication. DOI: 10.1155/2022/9739147

Ainscow, M., Booth, T., & Dyson, A. (2006). Inclusion and the standards agenda: Negotiating policy pressures in England. *International Journal of Inclusive Education*, *10*(4-5), 295–308.

Aiyeleso, M. M. (2016). The ideal special education teacher in Nigeria. *Asia Pacific Journal of Education, Arts and Sciences*, *3*(3), 1–5.

Ajuwon, P. M. (2008). Inclusive education for students with disabilities in Nigeria: Benefits, challenges and policy implications. *International Journal of Special Education, 23*(3), 11–16.

Akinradewo, O., Hafez, M., Aliu, J., Oke, A., Aigbavboa, C., & Adekunle, S. (2025). Barriers to the Adoption of Augmented Reality Technologies for Education and Training in the Built Environment: A Developing Country Context. *Technologies, 13*(2), 62.

Al Mamun, M. A., Azad, M. A. K., Al Mamun, M. A., & Boyle, M. (2022). Review of flipped learning in engineering education: Scientific mapping and research horizon. *Education and Information Technologies, 27*(1), 1261–1286. DOI: 10.1007/s10639-021-10630-z

Al-Aosail, A. B. F., Lamouchi, A., Ibrahim, S. A., Gafar, M. G., & Hafez, W. E. (2024). Digital Games for Learning Vocabulary: The Effects on Foreign Language Anxiety, Buoyancy, Online Engagement, and Vocabulary Learning. [Scopus.]. *CALL-EJ, 25*(4), 27–50.

Albahiri, M., & Almatrafi, M. (2025). THE FEASIBILITY OF USING ARTIFICIAL IN LIGENCE TECHNOLOGIES IN FLIPPED CLASSROOMS. INTED2025 Proceedings, 6919–6927. https://library.iated.org/view/ALBAHIRI2025FEA

Alemu, Z. K., Jio, W., & Kant, S. (2025). Developing Digital Leadership Skills for Managing a Tech-Driven Workforce Through Meta-Driven Human Resources in Africa. In *Transforming Organizational Culture Through Meta-Driven Human Resources* (pp. 61–90). IGI Global Scientific Publishing.

Algarni, B. (2021). Blended learning and the flipped classroom: The potential effect to enhance students' mathematical proficiency and self-efficacy: a mixed methods study from Saudi Arabia [PhD Thesis, University of York]. https://etheses.whiterose.ac.uk/29844/

Al-Hamidi, H. K., & Al-Rushidi, M. A. (2023). The effectiveness of blended learning in improving academic achievement and motivation to learn among students at the College of Basic Education in Kuwait. *Journal of Reading and Knowledge, 23*(255), 15–60.

Alharbi, K. (2024). Enhancing technical vocabulary acquisition: A multimedia strategic approach for English for specific purposes during COVID-19. *Interactive Learning Environments, 32*(9), 4812–4830. DOI: 10.1080/10494820.2023.2205902

Alhassan, A. I. (2024). Analyzing the application of mixed method methodology in medical education: A qualitative study. *BMC Medical Education*, *24*(1), 225. PMID: 38438987

Ali Elfa, M. A., & Dawood, M. E. T. (2023). Using artificial intelligence for enhancing human creativity. Journal of Art. *Design and Music*, *2*(2), 3. DOI: 10.55554/2785-9649.1017

Ali, W. (2020). Online and remote learning in higher education institutes: A necessity in light of COVID-19 pandemic. Higher education studies, 10(3), 16-25.

Aljohani, M. (2017). Principles of "constructivism" in foreign language teaching. *Journal of Literature and Art Studies*, *7*(1), 97–107.

Allen, I. E., & Seaman, J. (2015). *Grade level: Tracking online education in the United States.* http://www.onlinelearningsurvey.com/reports/gradelevel.pdf

Allen, M. (2017). Designing Online Asynchronous Information Literacy Instruction Using the ADDIE Model. In Maddison, T., & Kumaran, M. (Eds.), *Distributed Learning* (pp. 69–91). Chandos Publishing: Elsevier., DOI: 10.1016/B978-0-08-100598-9.00004-0

Almelhi, A. M. (2021). Effectiveness of the ADDIE Model within an E-Learning Environment in Developing Creative Writing in EFL Students. *English Language Teaching*, *14*(2), 20–36.

Andrade, M. S. (2015). Teaching online: A theory-based approach to student success. *Journal of Education and Training Studies*, *3*(5), 1–9. DOI: 10.11114/jets.v3i5.904

Antoniou, A. S., Efthymiou, V., Polychroni, F., & Kofa, O. (2020). Occupational stress in mainstream and special needs primary school teachers and its relationship with self-efficacy. *Educational Studies*, •••, 1–18.

An, X., & Qu, C. (2021). A hierarchical learning model based on deep learning and its application in a SPOC and flipped classroom. [iJET]. *International Journal of Emerging Technologies in Learning*, *16*(9), 76–93.

Aprizal, A. D., & Wachyudi, K. (2024). The Effectiveness of Memrise as a Vocabulary Learning Tool. *Jurnal Ilmiah Wahana Pendidikan*, *10*(4), 4. Advance online publication. DOI: 10.5281/zenodo.10499120

Areba, G. N., Gisore, B. N., Njurai, E. W., & Oranga, J. N. (2025). Re-Imagining Educational Leadership in Tech-Driven Environments: Challenges and Opportunities. *Leadership Paradigms and the Impact of Technology*, 319-340.

Arias-Pastor, M., Van Vaerenbergh, S., Fernández-Solana, J., & González-Bernal, J. J. (2023). Secondary education teacher training and emotional intelligence: Ingredients for attention to diversity in an inclusive school for all. *Education Sciences*, *13*(5), 519. DOI: 10.3390/educsci13050519

Arif, U. Q. (2025). The Influence of Gamification on English Vocabulary Retention in Online Learning Platforms. [JPPI]. *Jurnal Pendidikan Dan Pembelajaran Indonesia*, *5*(2), 2. Advance online publication. DOI: 10.53299/jppi.v5i2.1468

Armstrong, D. (2011). Students' perceptions of online learning and instructional tools: A qualitative study of undergraduate students' uses of online tools. *The Turkish Online Journal of Educational Technology*, *10*(3). http://www.tojet.net/articles/v10i3/10325.pdf

Aron, A., Coups, J. E., & Aron, N. E. (2011). *Statistics for the behavioral and social sciences: A brief course* (5th ed.). Prentice Hall.

Asgari, H., Gupta, R., Titiloye, I., & Jin, X. (2022). Challenges, perceptions, and future preferences for post-secondary online education given experiences in the COVID-19 outbreak. *Computational Urban Science*, *2*, 29. DOI: 10.1007/s43762-022-00058-7

Atanga, C., Jones, B. A., Krueger, L. E., & Lu, S. (2020). Teachers of students with learning disabilities: Assistive technology knowledge, perceptions, interests, and barriers. *Journal of Special Education Technology*, *35*(4), 236–248.

Athanasios, S., & Ioannidou, R. (2012). Artificial Intelligence in Special Education: A decade review. *International Journal of Engineering Education*, *28*(6), 1366–1372.

Aversa, E., & MacCall, S. (2013). Profiles in retention part 1: Design characteristics of a graduate synchronous online program. *Journal of Education for Library and Information Science*, *54*(2), 147–161. http://files.eric.ed.gov/fulltext/EJ1074122.pdf

Azuma, R. T. (1997). A survey of augmented reality. *Presence (Cambridge, Mass.)*, *6*(4), 355–385. DOI: 10.1162/pres.1997.6.4.355

Baek, Y., Zhang, H., & Yun, S. (2017). Teachers' attitudes toward mobile learning in Korea. *The Turkish Online Journal of Educational Technology*, *16*(1), 154–163.

Bahari, A. (2023). Challenges and Affordances of Cognitive Load Management in Technology-Assisted Language Learning: A Systematic Review. *International Journal of Human-Computer Interaction*, *39*(1), 85–100. DOI: 10.1080/10447318.2021.2019957

Bakić-Mirić, N., Butt, S., Dilparić, B., & Ashirimbetova, M. (2023). Teaching culture in the modern ESP classroom. *Journal of Teaching English for Specific and Academic Purposes, 0*, 0. Advance online publication. DOI: 10.22190/JTESAP230506037B

Bakti, I. K., Zulkarnain, Yarun, A., Rusdi, Syaifudin, M., & Syafaq, H. (2023). The role of artificial intelligence in education: A systematic literature review. *Jurnal Iqra'. Kajian Ilmu Pendidikan, 8*(2), 182–197. DOI: 10.25217/ji.v8i2.3194

Banditvilai, C. (2016). Enhancing students' language skills through blended learning. *Electronic Journal of e-Learning, 14*(3), 220–229.

Bandura, A. (1969). Social-learning theory of identificatory processes. *Handbook of socialization theory and research, 213*, 262.

Bandura, A. (1977). Self-efficacy: Toward a unifying theory of behavioral change. *Psychological Review, 84*(2), 191–215.

Bandura, A. (1991). Social cognitive theory of self-regulation. *Organizational Behavior and Human Decision Processes, 50*(2), 248–287.

Bandura, A. (1997). *Self-efficacy: The exercise of control.* W.H. Freeman.

Bandura, A., & Wessels, S. (1997). *Self-efficacy*. Cambridge University Press.

Banna, J., Grace Lin, M., Stewart, M., & Fialkowski, M. K. (2015). Interaction matters. Strategies to promote engaged learning in an online introductory nutrition course. *Journal of Online Learning and Teaching, 11*(2), 249–261. http://jolt.merlot.org/Vol11no2/Banna_0615.pdf

Baran, E., & Correia, A. (2014). A professional development framework for online teaching. *TechTrends, 58*(5), 95–101. DOI: 10.1007/s11528-014-0791-0

Barbieri, M., & Varvarigou, M. (2025). Developing learner-centred music theory resources: A case study from the Maltese Islands. *Music Education Research, 27*(2), 215–228. DOI: 10.1080/14613808.2025.2465264

Bărbuleţ, G. (2022). Content based learning-Task based learning-Problem based learning in Teaching Romanian Language to Foreign Students. *Swedish Journal of Romanian Studies, 5*(2), 241–250.

Barcroft, J. (2018). *Vocabulary in Language Teaching*. Routledge.

Barnard-Brak, L., Lan, W. Y., & Paton, V. O. (2010). Profiles in self-regulated learning in the online learning environment. *International Review of Research in Open and Distance Learning, 11*(1), 61–80.

Barr, B. A., & Miller, S. F. (2013). Higher education: The online teaching and learning Experience. *Online Teaching and Learning*. http://files.eric.ed.gov/Fulltext/ED543912.pdf

Barrett, B. (2010). Virtual teaching and strategies: Transitioning from teaching traditional classes to online classes. *Contemporary Issues in Education Research, 3*(12). http://files.eric.ed.gov/fulltext/EJ1072660.pdf

Basturkmen, H. (2022). Current trends in ESP research in the Asia Pacific region. *World Englishes, 41*(4), 512–522. DOI: 10.1111/weng.12601

Beaudoin, M. F. (2015). Distance education leadership in the context of digital change. *Quarterly Review of Distance Education, 16*(2), 33–44,148. https://go.gale.com/ps/i.do?p=AONE&u=googlescholar&id=GALE|A437059683&v=2.1&it=r&sid=AONE&asid=f1bdb7d7

Bellaiche, L., Shahi, R., Turpin, M. H., Ragnhildstveit, A., Sprockett, S., Barr, N., & Seli, P. (2023). Humans versus AI: Whether and why we prefer human-created compared to AI-created artwork. *Cognitive Research: Principles and Implications, 8*(1), 42. DOI: 10.1186/s41235-023-00499-6

Bell, P., Fainberg, J., Klejch, O., Li, J., Renals, S., & Swietojanski, P. (2021). Adaptation algorithms for neural network-based speech recognition: An overview. *IEEE Open Journal of Signal Processing, 2*, 33–66. DOI: 10.1109/OJSP.2020.3045349

Ben-Eliyahu, A., & Bernacki, M. L. (2015). Addressing complexities in self-regulated learning: A focus on contextual factors, contingencies, and dynamic relations. *Metacognition and Learning, 10*(1), 1–13. DOI: 10.1007/s11409-015-9134-6

Benvenuti, M., Cangelosi, A., Weinberger, A., Mazzoni, E., Benassi, M., Barbaresi, M., & Orsoni, M. (2023). Artificial intelligence and human behavioral development: A perspective on new skills and competences acquisition for the educational context. *Computers in Human Behavior, 148*, 107903.

Berestok, O. V. (2021). Synchronous and asynchronous e-learning modes: Strategies, methods, objectives. *Engineering and Educational Technologies, 9*(1), 19–27.

Bergmann, J., & Sams, A. (2012). Before You Flip, Consider This. *Phi Delta Kappan, 94*(2), 25–25. DOI: 10.1177/003172171209400206

Berk, R. A. (2013). Face-to-face versus online course evaluations: A "consumer's guide" to seven strategies. *Journal of Online Teaching and Learning, 9*(1), 140–148. http://jolt.merlot.org/vol9no1/berk_0313.htm

Bernard, R. M., Borokhovski, E., Schmid, R. F., Tamim, R. M., & Abrami, P. C. (2014). A meta-analysis of blended learning and technology use in higher education: From the general to the applied. *Journal of Computing in Higher Education, 26*, 87–122.

Berridge, G., Penney, S., & Wells, J. (2012). Formative assessment of classroom teaching for online classes. *Turkish Online Journal of Distance Education, 13*(1), 68–78. https://www.researchgate.net/publication/267425880

Bhagat, K. K., Yang, F.-Y., Cheng, C.-H., Zhang, Y., & Liou, W.-K. (2021). Tracking the process and motivation of math learning with augmented reality. *Educational Technology Research and Development, 69*(6), 3153–3178. DOI: 10.1007/s11423-021-10066-9

Bhatti, I., Mohi-U-din, S. F., Hayat, Y., & Tariq, M. (2024). Artificial Intelligence Applications for Students with Learning Disabilities: A Systematic Review. *European Journal of Science. Innovation and Technology, 4*(2), 40–56.

Bikanga Ada, M. (2018). Using design-based research to develop a Mobile Learning Framework for Assessment Feedback. *Research and Practice in Technology Enhanced Learning, 13*, 3. DOI: 10.1186/s41039-018-0070-3

Blanco-García, Y., Serrano, R. M., & Casanova, O. (2025). Toward a transversal education model: A review of digital and artistic-musical competencies (2014–2024). *Arts Education Policy Review, 0*(0), 1–15. DOI: 10.1080/10632913.2025.2459917

Bland, H. W., Melton, B. F., Welle, P., & Bigham, L. (2012). Stress tolerance: New challenges for millennial college students. *College Student Journal, 46*(2), 362–376. http://projectinnovation.biz/csj_2006.html

Bliuc, A.-M., Casey, G., Bachfischer, A., Goodyear, P., & Ellis, R. (2012). Blended learning in vocational education: Teachers' conceptions of blended learning and their approaches to teaching and design. *Australian Educational Researcher, 39*(2), 237–257. DOI: 10.1007/s13384-012-0053-0

Bloom, B. S. (1968). Learning for Mastery. Instruction and Curriculum. Regional Education Laboratory for the Carolinas and Virginia, Topical Papers and Reprints, Number 1. Evaluation Comment, 1(2), n2. https://eric.ed.gov/?id=eD053419

Boelens, R., De Wever, B., & Voet, M. (2017). Four key challenges to the design of blended learning: A systematic literature review. *Educational Research Review, 22*, 1–18.

Bolliger, D. U., Shepherd, C. E., & Bryant, H. V. (2019). Faculty members' perceptions of online program community and their efforts to sustain it. *British Journal of Educational Technology*, *50*(6), 3283–3299.

Bong, W. K., & Chen, W. (2024). Increasing faculty's competence in digital accessibility for inclusive education: A systematic literature review. *International Journal of Inclusive Education*, *28*(2), 197–213.

Bonnell, W., & Boehm, H. (2011). Improving feedback to students online: Teaching tips from experienced faculty. *Journal of Continuing Education in Nursing*, *42*(11). Advance online publication. DOI: 0.3928/00220124-20110715-02

Boston, W., Ice, P., & Gibson, A. (2011). *Comprehensive assessment of student retention in online learning environments.* http://www.westga.edu/~distance/ojdla/spring141/ boston_ice_gibson141.html

Boston, W., Ice, P., & Burgess, M. (2012). Assessing student retention in online learning environments: A longitudinal study. *Online Journal of Distance Learning Administration*, *15*(2). http://www.westga.edu/~distance/ojdla/summer152/boston_ice_burgess152.html

Bouchrika, I. (2023). 50 online education statistics: 2023 data on higher learning & corporate training. https://research.com/education/online-education-statistics

Boudadi, N. A., & Gutiérrez-Colón, M. (2020). Effect of Gamification on students' motivation and learning achievement in Second Language Acquisition within higher education: A literature review 2011-2019. *The EuroCALL Review*, *28*(1), 1. Advance online publication. DOI: 10.4995/eurocall.2020.12974

Boudjedra, A. R., & Khebbab, H. E. (2024). *Promoting EFL learners' self-regulated learning through the use of artificial intelligence applications* [Working Paper]. https://dspace.univ-guelma.dz/jspui/handle/123456789/16767

Boumediene, H., & Bouakkaz, M. (2025). Artificial intelligence in education: Emerging trends, ethical considerations, and future directions.*Next-Generation AI Methodologies in Education,*407–438.https://doi.org/DOI: 10.4018/979-8-3693-7220-3.ch014

Bourbina, J. (2024). Using a Flipped Course Design to increase positive outcomes in first year Science, Technology, Engineering, and Mathematics (STEM) courses. https://scholarworks.gvsu.edu/gradprojects/504/

Brito, S. M. (2019). *Active learning: Beyond the future*. BoD – Books on Demand.

Broadbent, J., & Poon, W. L. (2015). Self-regulated learning strategies & academic achievement in online higher education learning environments: A systematic review. *The internet and higher education*, *27*, 1–13.

Broadbent, J., & Poon, W. L. (2015). Self-regulated learning strategies & academic achievement in online higher education learning environments: A systematic review. *The Internet and Higher Education*, *27*, 1–13.

Brown, H. D. (2014). *Principles of language learning and teaching: A course in second language acquisition*. Pearson.

Brumfit, C. (1984). *Communicative methodology in language teaching*. Cambridge University Press.

Brummer, L., de Boer, H., Mouw, J. M., & Strijbos, J. W. (2024). A meta-analysis of the effects Of context, content, and task factors of digitally delivered instructional feedback on learning performance. *Learning Environments Research*, *27*, 453–476. DOI: 10.1007/s10984-024-09501-4

Buonviri, N. O. (2023). Educating Ears: The Role of Sound in Music Learning. *Music Educators Journal*, *110*(2), 30–36. DOI: 10.1177/00274321231202621

Cagıltay, K., Cakır, H., Karasu, N., Islım, O. F., & Cıcek, F. (2019). Use of educational technology in special education: Perceptions of teachers. *Participatory Educational Research*, *6*(2), 189–205.

Çakmak, F., Namaziandost, E., & Kumar, T. (2021). CALL-enhanced L2 cocabulary learning: Using spaced exposure through CALL to enhance L2 vocabulary retention. *Education Research International*, *5848525*. Advance online publication. DOI: 10.1155/2021/5848525

Cao, W. (2023). A meta-analysis of effects of blended learning on performance, attitude, achievement, and engagement across different countries. *Frontiers in Psychology*, *14*, 1212056. DOI: 10.3389/fpsyg.2023.1212056 PMID: 37502744

Carrim, N., & Bekker, T. (2022). Placing inclusive education in conversation with digital education. *South African Computer Journal = Suid-Afrikaanse Rekenaartydskrif*, *34*(2), 18–34.

Castle, S. R., & McGuire, C. (2010). An analysis of student self-assessment of online, blended and face-to-face environments: Implications for sustainable education delivery. *International Education Studies*, *3*(3). Advance online publication. DOI: 10.5539 /ies.v3n3p36

Cavalcanti, A. P., Barbosa, A., Carvalho, R., Freitas, F., Tsai, Y.-S., Gašević, D., & Mello, R. F. (2021). Automatic feedback in online learning environments: A systematic literature review. *Computers and Education: Artificial Intelligence*, *2*, 100027. Advance online publication. DOI: 10.1016/j.caeai.2021.100027

Central Committee of the Communist Party of China & State Council of the People's Republic of China. (2024). Plan for building China into an educational powerhouse (2024–2035). Retrieved June 10, 2024, from https://www.gov.cn/zhengce/2024-01/19/content_6919883.htm

Cetinic, E., & She, J. (2022). Understanding and creating art with AI: Review and outlook. [TOMM]. *ACM Transactions on Multimedia Computing Communications and Applications*, *18*(2), 1–22. DOI: 10.1145/3475799

Cetintav, G., & Yilmaz, R. (2023). The effect of augmented reality technology on middle school students' mathematic academic achievement, self-regulated learning skills, and motivation. *Journal of Educational Computing Research*, *61*(7), 1483–1504. DOI: 10.1177/07356331231176022

Chan, A. (2022). GPT-3 and InstructGPT: Technological dystopianism, utopianism, and "Contextual" perspectives in AI ethics and industry. *AI and Ethics*, *3*, 1–12.

Chang, D. H., Lin, M. P.-C., Hajian, S., & Wang, Q. Q. (2023). Educational design principles of using AI chatbot that supports self-regulated learning in education: Goal setting, feedback, and personalization. *Sustainability*, *15*(17), 17. Advance online publication. DOI: 10.3390/su151712921

Chassignol, M., Khoroshavin, A., Klimova, A., & Bilyatdinova, A. (2018). Artificial Intelligence trends in education: A narrative overview. *Procedia Computer Science*, *136*, 16–24.

Chatterjee, A. (2022). Art in an age of artificial intelligence. *Frontiers in Psychology*, *13*, 1024449. DOI: 10.3389/fpsyg.2022.1024449

Chen, X. (2023). Applying the Flipped Teaching Method in Group Piano Lessons to the First-Year Dance-Studies Undergraduate Students. Art and Design Review, 11(2), 140–149. https://www.scirp.org/journal/paperinformation?paperid=125251

Chen, C. Y. (2024). Flipped classroom with case-based learning for improving preservice teachers' classroom management learning outcomes. *Teaching and Teacher Education*, *152*, 104785. https://www.sciencedirect.com/science/article/pii/S0742051X24003184

Chen, C., Jamiat, N., Abdul Rabu, S. N., & Mao, Y. (2024). Effects of a self-regulated-based gamified interactive e-books on primary students' learning performance and affection in a flipped mathematics classroom. *Education and Information Technologies, 29*(18), 24143–24180. *Scopus.* Advance online publication. DOI: 10.1007/s10639-024-12789-7

Chen, C., & Meng, X. (2021). Exploring the relationship between student behavioral patterns and learning outcomes in a SPOC. [IJDET]. *International Journal of Distance Education Technologies, 19*(1), 35–49.

Chen, G., Gully, S. M., & Eden, D. (2001). Validation of a new general self-efficacy scale. *Organizational Research Methods, 4*(1), 62–83.

Chen, J. (2020). SPOC-based flipped learning model applied in interpreting teaching. [iJET]. *International Journal of Emerging Technologies in Learning, 15*(17), 4–13.

Chen, J., Mokmin, N. A. M., & Su, H. (2025). Integrating generative artificial intelligence into design and art course: Effects on student achievement, motivation, and self-efficacy. *Innovations in Education and Teaching International,* •••, 1–16.

Chen, K. C., & Jang, S. J. (2010). Motivation in online learning: Testing a model of self-determination theory. *Computers in Human Behavior, 26*(4), 741–752.

Chen, L., Chen, P., & Lin, Z. (2020). Artificial intelligence in education: A review. *IEEE Access : Practical Innovations, Open Solutions, 8,* 75264–75278. DOI: 10.1109/ACCESS.2020.2988510

Chen, R., & Yang, C. (2015). Research on Design Model of SPOC Blended Learning. *Distance Education in China, 5,* 42–47.

Chen, X., Xie, H., & Hwang, G. J. (2020). A multi-perspective study on artificial intelligence in education: Grants, conferences, journals, software tools, institutions, and researchers. *Computers and Education: Artificial Intelligence, 1,* 100005.

Chen, X., Zou, D., Xie, H., Cheng, G., & Liu, C. (2022). Two decades of artificial intelligence in education. *Journal of Educational Technology & Society, 25*(1), 28–47.

China Education Informatization Network. (2024a, May 15). Latest data on MOOCs and blended teaching in China. Retrieved June 10, 2024, from https://www.ictdedu.cn/news/jrgz/xxhdt/n20240515_84425.shtml

China Education Informatization Network. (2024b, April 17). Achievements of the "MOOC Westward Action" project. Retrieved June 10, 2024, from https://www.ictdedu.cn/news/jrgz/xxhdt/n20250417_86599.shtml

Chirobocea, O. (2018). Vocabulary acquisition in ESP: Perspectives, strategies and resources. *Studii Şi Cercetări Filologice. Seria Limbi Străine Aplicate*, *17*, 171–180.

Chitiyo, M., Hughes, E. M., Chitiyo, G., Changara, D. M., Itimu-Phiri, A., Haihambo, C., & Dzenga, C. G. (2019). Exploring Teachers' Special and Inclusive Education Professional Development Needs in Malawi, Namibia, and Zimbabwe. *International Journal of Whole Schooling*, *15*(1), 28–49.

Chiu, T. K. F. (2021). Applying the self-determination theory (SDT) to explain student engagement in online learning during the COVID-19 pandemic. *Journal of Research on Technology in Education, 54*(sup1), S14–S30. https://doi.org/DOI: 10.1080/15391523.2021.1891998

Chiu, M. C., Hwang, G. J., Hsia, L. H., & Shyu, F. M. (2024). Artificial intelligence-supported art education: A deep learning-based system for promoting university students' artwork appreciation and painting outcomes. *Interactive Learning Environments*, *32*(3), 824–842.

Chiu, T. K. F., Meng, H., Chai, C.-S., King, I., Wong, S., & Yam, Y. (2022). Creation and Evaluation of a Pretertiary Artificial Intelligence (AI) Curriculum. *IEEE Transactions on Education*, *65*(1), 30–39. DOI: 10.1109/TE.2021.3085878

Chiu, T. K., Xia, Q., Zhou, X., Chai, C. S., & Cheng, M. (2023). Systematic literature review on opportunities, challenges, and future research recommendations of artificial intelligence in education. *Computers and Education: Artificial Intelligence*, *4*, 100118.

Community College Research Center. (2013). Creating an effective online environment. *Teachers College, Columbia University*. http://ccrc.tc.columbiaEdu/media/k2/attachments/creating-effective-online-environment.pdf

Concina, E. (2023). Effective music teachers and effective music teaching today: A systematic review. *Education Sciences*, *13*(2), 107. https://www.mdpi.com/2227-7102/13/2/107

Conole, G., & Dyke, M. (2004). What are the affordances of information and communication technologies? *Research in Learning Technology*, *12*(2), 2. Advance online publication. DOI: 10.3402/rlt.v12i2.11246

Conrad, S. S., & Dabbagh, N. (2015). Examining the factors that influence how instructors provide feedback in online learning environments. *International Journal of Online Pedagogy and Course Design*, *4*(5), 47–66. DOI: 10.4018/IJOPCD.2015100104

Coxhead, A. (2024). *Technical vocabulary in government spoken communications: The team of five million in bubbles, PPE and CBACs*. https://doi.org/DOI: 10.25455/wgtn.26210741

Coxhead, A. (2025). Vocabulary and English for Specific Purposes. In *The Handbook of English for Specific Purposes* (pp. 107–123). John Wiley & Sons, Ltd., DOI: 10.1002/9781119985068.ch6

Crawford-Ferre, H. G., & Wiest, L. R. (2012). Effective online instruction in higher education. *Quarterly Review of Distance Education, 13*(1), 11–14. http://www.siue.edu/~lmillio/IT598/Resources/04_assessment/Effective%20Online%20I nstruction.pdf

Crogman, H. T., Cano, V. D., Pacheco, E., Sonawane, R. B., & Boroon, R. (2025). Virtual reality, augmented reality, and mixed reality in experiential learning: Transforming educational paradigms. *Education Sciences, 15*(3), 303.

Crompton, H., Burke, D., & Gregory, K. (2015). The effects of integrating mobile devices with teaching and learning: A meta-analysis. *Educational Research Review, 15*, 1–15. DOI: 10.1016/j.edurev.2015.10.001

Croxton, R. A. (2014). The role of interactivity in student satisfaction and persistence in online learning. *Journal of Online Learning and Teaching, 10*(2), 314–324. http://jolt.merlot.org/vol10no2/croxton_0614.pdf

Cui, Y., Schunn, C. D., & Gai, X. (2021). Peer feedback and teacher feedback: A comparative study of revision effectiveness in writing instruction for EFL learners. *Higher Education Research & Development*. Advance online publication. DOI: 10.1080/07294360.2021.1977692

Culver, S. (2010). Course grades, quality of student engagement, and students' evaluation of instructor. *International Journal on Teaching and Learning in Higher Education, 22*(3), 331–336. http://files.eric.ed.gov/fulltext/EJ938568.pdf

Curl, K. (2008). Assessing stress reduction as a function of artistic creation and cognitive focus. *Art Therapy: Journal of the American Art Therapy Association, 25*(4), 164–169.

D'Mello, S., & Graesser, A. (2012). Dynamics of affective states during complex learning. *Learning and Instruction, 22*(2), 145–157. DOI: 10.1016/j.learninstruc.2011.10.001

Dabbagh, N., & Kitsantas, A. (2012). Personal learning environments, social media, and self-regulated learning: A natural formula for connecting formal and informal learning. *The Internet and Higher Education, 15*(1), 3–8. DOI: 10.1016/j.iheduc.2011.06.002

Dalbani, H., Eissa, S., Syed-Ahmad, S. F., & Almusharraf, N. (2022). Transitioning to flipped classrooms: Instructors' perspectives. *Sustainability, 14*(20), 13426. https://www.mdpi.com/2071-1050/14/20/13426

Danesi, M. (2024). AI-Generated Art. In *AI-Generated Popular Culture: A Semiotic Perspective* (pp. 105–125). Springer Nature Switzerland.

Daniel, M. B., & Villanueva, H. D. (2023). Teachers' pedagogical practices in relation to students' motivation in blended learning. *ARRUS Journal of Social Sciences and Humanities, 3*(5), 612–620. DOI: 10.35877/soshum1719

Deci, E. L., & Ryan, R. M. (1985). *Intrinsic motivation and self-determination in human behavior*. Plenum Press.

Deci, E. L., & Ryan, R. M. (1985). The general causality orientations scale: Self-determination in personality. *Journal of Research in Personality, 19*(2), 109–134.

DeCosta, M., Bergquist, E., Holbeck, R., & Greenberger, S. (2016). A desire for growth: Online full-time faculty's perceptions of evaluation processes. *Journal of Educators Online, 13(*2), 19-52. http://www.thejeo.com/Archives/Volume13Number2/DeCostaBergquistHolbeckandGreenberger.pdf

Dede, C. (2009). Immersive interfaces for engagement and learning. *Science, 323*(5910), 66–69. DOI: 10.1126/science.1167311

Delialioglu, O., & Yildirim, Z. (2007). Students' Perceptions on Effective Dimensions of Interactive Learning in a Blended Learning Environment. *Journal of Educational Technology & Society, 10*(2), 133–146.

Demir, K., & Akpinar, E. (2018). The effect of mobile learning applications on students' academic achievement and attitudes towards mobile learning. *Malaysian Online Journal of Educational Technology, 6*(2), 48–68. DOI: 10.17220/mojet.2018.04.004

Demmer, T. R., Kühnapfel, C., Fingerhut, J., & Pelowski, M. (2023). Does an emotional connection to art really require a human artist? Emotion and intentionality responses to AI- versus human-created art and impact on aesthetic experience. *Computers in Human Behavior, 148*, 107875. DOI: 10.1016/j.chb.2023.107875

Deterding, S., Sicart, M., Nacke, L., O'Hara, K., & Dixon, D. (2011). Gamification. Using game-design elements in non-gaming contexts. *CHI '11 Extended Abstracts on Human Factors in Computing Systems*, 2425–2428. https://doi.org/DOI: 10.1145/1979742.1979575

Deterding, S., Dixon, D., Khaled, R., & Nacke, L. (2011). From game design elements to gamefulness: Defining gamification . *Proceedings of the 15th International Academic MindTrek Conference: Envisioning Future Media Environments*, 9–15. https://doi.org/DOI: 10.1145/2181037.2181040

Dignath, C., & Veenman, M. V. J. (2021). The Role of Direct Strategy Instruction and Indirect Activation of Self-Regulated Learning—Evidence from Classroom Observation Studies. *Educational Psychology Review*, *33*(2), 489–533. DOI: 10.1007/s10648-020-09534-0

Dikilitas, K., & Fructuoso, I. N. (2023). Conceptual framework for flexible learning design: The Context of flipped classroom. Conceptual Framework for Flexible Learning Design: The Context of Flipped Classroom. Https://Doi. Org/10.31265/Usps, 267. https://kudos.dfo.no/documents/77155/files/37244.pdf

Dinara, G. V., Irina, I. K., Elena, L. A., Natalya, V. K., & Jana, B. (2016). Enhancement of Students' Vocabulary Learning Through a Blended Learning Approach. *International Electronic Journal of Mathematics Education*, *11*(5), 1195–1203.

Ding, Y., & Zhao, T. (2020). Emotions, engagement, and self-perceived achievement in a small private online course. *Journal of Computer Assisted Learning*, *36*(4), 449–457.

Djiwandono, P. I. (2013). A Blended Learning Approach to Enhance College Students '. *Vocabulary Learning.*, *10*(2), 210–220.

Dolan, V. (2011). The isolation of online adjunct faculty and its impact of their performance. *International Review of Research in Open and Distance Learning*, *12*(2). http://www.irrodl.org/index.php/irrodl/article/view/793/1691

Dong, Y., Ang, J., & Sun, Z. (2021). Designing Path of SPOC blended teaching and learning mode in post-MOOC Era. In 2021 10th International Conference on Educational and Information Technology (ICEIT) (pp. 24-28). IEEE.

Dornyei, Z. (2009). The L2 Motivational Self System. In Dornyei, Z., & Ushioda, E. (Eds.), *Motivation, Language Identity and the L2 Self* (pp. 9–42). Multilingual Matters.

Doroudi, S. (2023). The intertwined histories of artificial intelligence and education. *International Journal of Artificial Intelligence in Education, 33*(4), 885–928. DOI: 10.1007/s40593-022-00313-2

Dou, A. Q., Chan, S. H., & Win, M. T. (2023). Changing visions in ESP development and teaching: Past, present, and future vistas. *Frontiers in Psychology, 14*. Advance online publication. DOI: 10.3389/fpsyg.2023.1140659

Dou, Y. (2023). Innovation of Flipped Classroom Teaching Mode in College Vocal Music Teaching. *Frontiers in Art Research, 5*(2). https://francis-press.com/uploads/papers/gYfqhDSyflcMvOtHhi0cmaGZM6lYoDjhAeF6WzlI.pdf

Drigas, A. S., & Ioannidou, R. E. (2013). A review on artificial intelligence in special education. *Information Systems, E-learning, and Knowledge Management Research: 4th World Summit on the Knowledge Society, WSKS 2011, Mykonos, Greece, September 21-23, 2011. Revised Selected Papers 4*, 385-391.

Drljević, N., Botički, I., & Wong, L. H. (2024). Observing student engagement during augmented reality learning in early primary school. *Journal of Computers in Education, 11*(1), 181–213.

Duffin, E. (2020a). *U.S. population targeted by online education programs 2019.* https://www.statista.com/statistics/731146/percentage-online-programs-that-were-designed-with-special-student-characteristics-in-mind-by-target-population-us/

Duffin, E. (2020b). *Reasons for online college selection among students in the U.S. 2019.* https://www.statista.com/statistics/956111/reasons-online-college-selection-students/

Ebadi, S., & Ghuchi, K. D. (2018). Investigating the Effects of Blended Learning Approach on Vocabulary Enhancement from EFL Learners' Perspectives. *Journal on English Language Teaching, 8*(2), 57–68.

Eccles, J. S., & Wigfield, A. (2002). Motivational beliefs, values, and goals. *Annual Review of Psychology, 53*(1), 109–132. PMID: 11752481

Ed-Dali, R. (2024). Enhancing EFL learning through multimodal integration: The role of visual and auditory features in moroccan textbooks. *Journal of World Englishes and Educational Practices, 6*, 38–48.

Edwards, M., Perry, B., & Janzen, K. (2011). The making of an exemplary online educator. *Distance Education, 32*(1). Advance online publication. DOI: 10.1080/01587919.2011.565499

Eichinger, J., & Woltman, S. (1993). Integration strategies for learners with severe multiple disabilities. *Teaching Exceptional Children, 26*(1), 18–21.

Eissa M A (2015). The effectiveness of a self regulated learning-based training program on improving cognitive and metacognitive EFL reading comprehension of 9th graders with reading disabilities. Online Submission 4(3), 49–59.

Elakiya, T. T., & Kalabarathy, S. (2022). Level of satisfaction on online teaching method among undergraduate students – A descriptive cross-sectional study. *Cardiometry,* (25), 1140-1145. https://doi.org/DOI: 10.18137/cardiometry.2022.25.11401145

Ellis, R. (2018). Taking the critics to task: The case for task-based teaching. New perspectives on the development of communicative and related competence in foreign language education, 28, 23.

Ellis, R. (2003). *Task-based language learning and teaching*. Oxford University Press.

Ellis, R., & Shintani, N. (2013). *Exploring language pedagogy through second language acquisition research.* Routledge.

El-Sofany, H. F., & El-Haggar, N. (2020). The effectiveness of using mobile learning techniques to improve learning outcomes in higher education. [iJIM]. *International Journal of Interactive Mobile Technologies, 14*(8), 131–148. DOI: 10.3991/ijim.v14i08.13125

Eriksson, T., Adawi, T., & Stöhr, C. (2017). "Time is the bottleneck": A qualitative study exploring why learners drop out of MOOCs. *Journal of Computing in Higher Education, 29*(1), 133–146.

Essary, M. (2014). Key external factors influencing successful distance education programs. *Academy of Educational Leadership Journal, 19*(3), 121–136. https://www.questia.com/library/journal/1G1-396615723/key-external-factors-influencing-successful-distance

Evmenova, A. S., & Regan, K. (2019). Supporting the writing process with technology for students with disabilities. *Intervention in School and Clinic, 55*(2), 78–85.

Fang, F., & Jiang, X. (2024). The analysis of artificial intelligence digital technology in art education under the internet of things. *IEEE Access : Practical Innovations, Open Solutions, 12*, 22928–22937.

Fedynich, L., Bradley, L. S., & Bradley, J. (2015). Graduate students' perceptions of online learning. *Research in Higher Education, 27,* •••. http://www.aabri.com/manuscripts/142108.pdf

Feng, L., & Liu, Y. (2022). Research and Practice of Online and Offline Blended Teaching based on MOOC and SPOC: A case study of computer foundation courses. *Educational Review, 11*(34), 68–70.

Fernandez, D. M., & Canado, L. P. (2001). Exploring The Student's Motivation in the EFL Class. *Present and Future Trends in TEFL*, 321-364.

Fernandez-Batanero, J. M., & Montenegro-Rueda, M., FernandezCerero, J., & Garcia-Martinez, I. (2022). Assistive technology for the inclusion of students with disabilities: A systematic review. *Educational Technology Research and Development, 70*(5), 1911–1930.

Fetaji, M., Ebibi, M., & Luma, A. (2024). Flipped Learning and Creativity: Fostering Innovation and Problem-Solving. Editorial Board, 31. https://seejsd.unt.edu.mk/wp-content/uploads/2024/06/SEEJSD-Volume-8_Issue-1-2024-2.pdf#page=31

Finnerty, M. S., Jackson, L. B., & Ostergren, R. (2019). Adaptations in general education classrooms for students with severe disabilities: Access, progress assessment, and sustained use. *Research and Practice for Persons with Severe Disabilities : the Journal of TASH, 44*(2), 87–102.

Fisher, D. P., & Southam, C. (2025). *The impact of timely formative feedback on university student motivation. Assessment & Evaluation in Higher Education*. Advance online publication. DOI: 10.1080/02602938.2025.2449891

Fish, W. W., & Wickersham, L. E. (2015). Best practices for online instructors. *Quarterly Review of Distance Education, 10*(3), 279–284. https://www.learntechlib.org/p/106758

Fitrianto, I., Setyawan, C. E., & Saleh, M. (2024). Utilizing artificial intelligence for personalized arabic language learning plans. *International Journal of Post Axial: Futuristic Teaching and Learning, 2*(1), 30–40. DOI: 10.59944/postaxial.v2i1.273

Fleischmann, K. (2020). Online design education: Searching for a middle ground. *Arts and Humanities in Higher Education, 19*(1), 36–57.

Fox, A. (2013). From moocs to spocs. *Communications of the ACM, 56*(12), 38–40.

Fraenkel, J., & Wallen, N. (2008). *How to design and evaluate research in education* (7th ed.). McGraw Hill.

Frattura, E., & Capper, C. A. (2006). Segregated programs versus integrated comprehensive service delivery for all learners: Assessing the differences. *Remedial and Special Education, 27*(6), 355–364.

Friborg, O., Barlaug, D., Martinussen, M., Rosenvinge, J. H., & Hjemdal, O. (2005). Resilience in relation to personality and intelligence. *International Journal of Methods in Psychiatric Research, 14*(1), 29–42.

Fu, J. (2020). Analysis on the piano teaching mode of flipped class in higher education. *Frontiers in Educational Research, 3*(14), 128–133. https://francis-press.com/uploads/papers/14fwlVlBkuLirc0mkNh0VsJjPeIVB3UHPhuscolQ.pdf

Gabelica, C., den Bossche, P. V., Segers, M., & Gijselaers, W. (2012). Feedback, a powerful lever in teams: A review. *Educational Research Review, 7*(2), 123–144. DOI: 10.1016/j.edurev.2011.11.003

Galindo-Dominguez, H. (2021). Flipped classroom in the educational system. *Journal of Educational Technology & Society, 24*(3), 44–60. https://www.jstor.org/stable/27032855

Gallego-Ortega, J. L., & Rodríguez-Fuentes, A. (2021). Teaching attitudes towards students with disabilities. *Mathematics, 9*(14), 1637.

Gandhi, A., Adhvaryu, K., Poria, S., Cambria, E., & Hussain, A. (2023). Multimodal sentiment analysis: A systematic review of history, datasets, multimodal fusion methods, applications, challenges and future directions. *Information Fusion, 91*, 424–444. https://www.sciencedirect.com/science/article/pii/S1566253522001634

Gardner, R. C. (1985). *Social Psychology and Second Language Learning: The Role of Attitudes and Motivation*. Edward Arnold.

Garrison, D. R., & Kanuka, H. (2004). Blended learning: Uncovering its transformative potential in higher education. *The Internet and Higher Education, 7*(2), 95–105.

George, D., & Mallery, P. (2010). *SPSS for Windows step by step*. Allyn & Bacon.

Gerges, E. (2025). Beyond Lectures: The Flipped Learning Model. In Best Practices and Strategies for Online Instructors: Insights From Higher Education Online Faculty (pp. 133–166). IGI Global Scientific Publishing. https://www.igi-global.com/chapter/beyond-lectures/361783

Ghofur, A., Kholis, M. N., Sodik, A. J., & Shiddiq, J. (2023). Students' Perceptions And Motivation Towards Teaching Arabic Vocabulary Through Gamification. *IJAZ ARABI JOURNAL OF ARABIC LEARNING, 6*(3), 682–694. DOI: 10.18860/ijazarabi.v6i3.18642

Ghosh, A., & Fossas, G. (2022). Can there be art without an artist? arXiv preprint arXiv:2209.07667. https://doi.org//arXiv.2209.07667DOI: 10.48550

Ghosh, A., Zhang, R., Dokania, P. K., Wang, O., Efros, A. A., Torr, P. H., & Shechtman, E. (2019). Interactive sketch & fill: Multiclass sketch-to-image translation. In *Proceedings of the IEEE/CVF International Conference on Computer Vision* (pp. 1171-1180).

Gibson, J. J. (1966). *The senses considered as perceptual systems*. Houghton Mifflin.

Giesbers, B., Rienties, B., Tempelaar, D., & Gijselaers, W. (2013). Investigating the relations between motivation, tool use, participation, and performance in an E-learning course using web videoconferencing. *Computers in Human Behavior, 29*(1), 285–292.

Giudici, P., Centurelli, M., & Turchetta, S. (2024). Artificial Intelligence risk measurement. *Expert Systems with Applications, 235*, 121220. DOI: 10.1016/j.eswa.2023.121220

Glassick, C. E., Huber, M. T., & Maeroff, G. I. (1997). *Scholarship assessed: Evaluation of the professoriate*. Jossey-Bass.

Gobinath, V. M., Ayyaswamy, K., Subramanian, C., & Kathirvel, N. (2024). Enhancing AI-Based Digital Technology Planning, Leadership, and Management to Transform Education. In *Cases on Authentic Assessment in Higher Education* (pp. 285–303). IGI Global.

Gómez-Ortiz, M.-J., Domínguez Romero, E., & Bobkina, J. (2023). Instagram as a learning tool to improve technical vocabulary for sports science students. *Journal of Hospitality, Leisure, Sport and Tourism Education, 32*, 100416. DOI: 10.1016/j.jhlste.2022.100416

Goodley, D., Cameron, D., Liddiard, K., Parry, R., Runswick-Cole, K., Whitburn, B., & Wong, M. E. (2020). Rebooting inclusive education? New technologies and disabled people. *Canadian Journal of Disability Studies, 9*(5), 515–549.

Goodyear, P., & Dudley, R. (2015). Enabling blended learning: A new approach to professional education. *Educational Technology, 55*(4), 23–28.

Gracia, R. W. C., & Perakaki, E. (2025). A seminar on music research in higher education and the flipped classroom: An action research project. Revista Electrónica Educare, 29(1), 4. https://dialnet.unirioja.es/servlet/articulo?codigo=10123058

Graham, C. R. (2013). Emerging practice and research in blended learning. In *Handbook of distance education* (pp. 333–350). Routledge.

Grájeda, A., Córdova, P., Córdova, J. P., Laguna-Tapia, A., Burgos, J., Rodríguez, L., & Sanjinés, A. (2024). Embracing artificial intelligence in the arts classroom: Understanding student perceptions and emotional reactions to AI tools. *Cogent Education, 11*(1), 2378271. DOI: 10.1080/2331186X.2024.2378271

Grasse, K. M., Kreminski, M., Wardrip-Fruin, N., Mateas, M., & Melcer, E. F. (2022). Using Self-Determination Theory to explore enjoyment of educational interactive narrative games: A case study of academical. *Frontiers in Virtual Reality, 3*. Advance online publication. DOI: 10.3389/frvir.2022.847120

Grobgeld, E., Teichman, -Weinberg Ariela, Wasserman, E., & Ben, -Av Mercedes Barchilon. (2020). Role perception among faculty members at teacher education colleges. *Australian Journal of Teacher Education (Online), 41*(5), 78–98. DOI: 10.3316/informit.094262645820831

Guan, C., Mou, J., & Jiang, Z. (2020). Artificial intelligence innovation in education: A twenty-year data-driven historical analysis. *International Journal of Innovation Studies, 4*(4), 134–147.

Guilherme, A. (2019). AI and education: The importance of teacher and student relations. *AI & Society, 34*, 47–54.

Guo, Y., Song, H., & Jiang, D. (2023). The construction and application of digital course on ICVE platform—Taking the course of health education and health promotion as an example. *Frontiers in Educational Research, 6*(4).

Gupta, V. (2020). Blended SPOC Teaching and Learning Model for Computer Programming Course: Insights and Defeating Challenges. In *2020 IEEE International Conference on Teaching, Assessment, and Learning for Engineering (TALE)* (pp. 251-257). IEEE.

Gustian, K., Aridah, A., & Rusmawaty, D. (2023). The benefits of flipped classroom model for Efl learners. *Journal of Education, 5*(4), 13918–13935. https://core.ac.uk/download/pdf/560351352.pdf

Gu, Y. (2020). The Construction and Development of High Level Higher Vocational Colleges Driven by Innovation. *2020 International Conference on Social and Human Sciences (ICSHS2020)*. (pp.117-123). DOI: DOI: 10.38007/Proceedings.0000023

Hachey, A. C., Wladis, C. W., & Conway, K. M. (2013). Balancing retention and access in online courses: Restricting enrollment. Is it worth the cost? *Journal of College Student Retention, 15*(1), 9–36. DOI: 10.2190/CS.15.1.b

Hadwin, A. F., Järvelä, S., & Miller, M. (2018). Self-regulation, co-regulation, and shared regulation in collaborative learning environments,*Handbook of self-regulation of learning and performance*. 83–106.

Hallinger, P., Banoğlu, K., & Gümüş, S. (2025). Scoping Review of Research on Digital Simulations and Serious Games in Educational Leadership and Management. *Leadership and Policy in Schools*, *24*(1), 178–199.

Hamari, J., Koivisto, J., & Sarsa, H. (2014). Does gamification work? – A literature review of empirical studies on gamification. *2014 47th Hawaii International Conference on System Sciences*, 3025–3034. https://doi.org/DOI: 10.1109/HICSS.2014.377

Hamid, A. E., Alasmari, A., & Eldood, E. Y. (2015). Attitude of pre-service educators toward including children with special needs in general classes case study of Education Faculty–University of Jazan. KSA. *International Journal of Scientific Research in Science and Technology*, *1*(3), 140–145.

Harder, J. T., & Abuhamdieh, A. H. (2015). The role of positive regard in self-regulated learning: An analysis of student evaluation data. *Journal of College Teaching and Learning*, *12*(2), 109–120. DOI: 10.19030/tlc.v12i2.9183

Hauser, R., Paul, R., Bradley, J., & Jeffrey, L. (2012). Computer self-efficacy, anxiety, and learning in online versus face-to-face medium. *Journal of Information Technology Education*, *11*, 141–154. http://www.jite.org/documents/Vol11/JITEv11p141-154Hauser0910.pdf

He, L. (2024). Students' Self-efficacy under the Blended Teaching Model: A Case Study of Hrastinski, S. (2019). What do we mean by blended learning? *TechTrends*, *63*(5), 564–569.

Hennessy, S., Wishart, J., Whitelock, D., Deaney, R., Brawn, R., & la Velle, L.. (2007). Pedagogical approaches for technology-integrated science teaching. *Computers & Education*, *48*(1), 137–152.

Herman, J. H. (2012). Faculty development programs: The frequency and variety of professional development programs available to online instructors. *Journal of Asynchronous Learning Networks*, *16*(5). http://files.eric.ed.gov/fulltext/EJ1000093.pdf

Herrington, C. D., & Summers, K. P. (2014). Global pressures on education research: Quality, utility, and infrastructure. *Asia Pacific Education Review*, *15*(3), 339–346.

Holmes, W., & Tuomi, I. (2022). State of the art and practice in AI in education. *European Journal of Education*, *57*(4), 542–570. DOI: 10.1111/ejed.12533

Hong, A. L. T., & Stapa, M. (2023). The Effect of Blended Learning Towards Pupils' Vocabulary Development and Motivation in an ESL Classroom. [JONUS]. *Journal of Nusantara Studies, 8*(1), 406–428. DOI: 10.24200/jonus.vol8iss1pp406-428

Hong, A. L. T., Stapa, M., & Tian, K. X. (2025). Malaysian Primary School Teachers' Self-Assessment of TPACK and their Blended Learning Practice. *International Journal of Instruction, 18*(1), 695–714. DOI: 10.29333/iji.2025.18139a

Honicke, T., & Broadbent, J. (2016). The influence of academic self-efficacy on academic performance: A systematic review. *Educational Research Review, 17*, 63–84.

Hopcan, S., Polat, E., Ozturk, M. E., & Ozturk, L. (2023). Artificial intelligence in special education: A systematic review. *Interactive Learning Environments, 31*(10), 7335–7353.

Horspool, A., & Lange, C. (2012). Applying the Scholarship of Teaching and Learning: Student Perceptions, Behaviours and Success Online and Face-to-Face. *Assessment & Evaluation in Higher Education, 37*, 73–88. DOI: 10.1080/02602938.2010.496532

Hossein-Mohand, H., Trujillo-Torres, J.-M., Gómez-García, M., Hossein-Mohand, H., & Campos-Soto, A. (2021). Analysis of the use and integration of the flipped learning model, project-based learning, and gamification methodologies by secondary school mathematics teachers. *Sustainability, 13*(5), 2606. https://www.mdpi.com/2071-1050/13/5/2606

Howard, S. K., Tondeur, J., Siddiq, F., & Scherer, R. (2021). Ready, set, go! Profiling teachers' readiness for online teaching in secondary education. *Technology, Pedagogy and Education, 30*(1), 141–158.

Hrastinski, S. (2019). What do we mean by blended learning? *TechTrends, 63*(5), 564–569.

Hsia, L., Lin, Y., & Hwang, G. (2021). A creative problem solving-based flipped learning strategy for promoting students' performing creativity, skills and tendencies of creative thinking and collaboration. *British Journal of Educational Technology, 52*(4), 1771–1787. DOI: 10.1111/bjet.13073

Hu, D. (2024). Research on the Impact of Music Aesthetic Education on the Cultivation of Students' Aesthetic Appreciation. Journal of Art, Culture and Philosophical Studies, 1(1). https://www.atlantic-press-journals.com/index.php/JACPS/article/view/17

Huang, F., Teo, T., Sánchez-Prieto, J. C., García-Peñalvo, F. J., & Olmos-Migueláñez, S. (2019). Cultural values and technology adoption: A model comparison with university teachers from China and Spain. *Computers & Education, 133*, 69–81.

Huang, Q. (2016). Learners' Perceptions of Blended Learning and the Roles and Interaction of f2f and Online Learning. *ORTESOL Journal*, *33*, 14–33.

Huang, X., & Dong, L., C, C. V., & D, P. K. (2022). Self-regulated learning and scientific research using artificial intelligence for higher education systems. [IJTHI]. *International Journal of Technology and Human Interaction*, *18*(7), 1–15. DOI: 10.4018/IJTHI.306226

Hu, B. (2022). Analysis of art therapy for children with autism by using the implemented artificial intelligence system. *International Journal of HR; Humanoid Robotics*, *19*(03), 2240002. DOI: 10.1142/S0219843622400023

Humble, N., & Mozelius, P. (2022). The threat, hype, and promise of artificial intelligence in education. *Discover Artificial Intelligence*, *2*(1), 22. DOI: 10.1007/s44163-022-00039-z

Hu, S. (2024). The effect of artificial intelligence-assisted personalized learning on student learning outcomes: A meta-analysis based on 31 empirical research papers. *Science Insights Education Frontiers*, *24*(1), 3873–3894. DOI: 10.15354/sief.24.re395

Hu, T., Zhang, M., Liu, H., Liu, J., Pan, S., Guo, J., Tian, Z., & Cui, L. (2022). The influence of "small private online course + flipped classroom" teaching on physical education students' learning motivation from the perspective of self-determination theory. *Frontiers in Psychology*, *13*, 938426. DOI: 10.3389/fpsyg.2022.938426

Hutchinson, T., & Waters, A. (1987). *English for specific purposes*. Cambridge university press.

Hutson, J., & Cotroneo, P. (2023). Generative AI tools in art education: Exploring prompt engineering and iterative processes for enhanced creativity. *Metaverse*, *4*(1). Advance online publication. DOI: 10.54517/m.v4i1.2164

Hu, Y., Chen, J., & Hwang, G. J. (2025). A ChatGPT-supported QIVE model to enhance college students' learning performance, problem-solving and self-efficacy in art appreciation. *Interactive Learning Environments*, •••, 1–14.

Hwang, G. J., & Tu, Y. F. (2021). Roles and research trends of artificial intelligence in mathematics education: A bibliometric mapping analysis and systematic review. *Mathematics*, *9*(6), 584.

Hwang, G.-J., Lai, C.-L., & Wang, S.-Y. (2015). Seamless flipped learning: A mobile technology-enhanced flipped classroom with effective learning strategies. *Journal of Computers in Education*, *2*(4), 449–473. DOI: 10.1007/s40692-015-0043-0

Hwang, G.-J., Rahimi, M., & Fathi, J. (2024). Enhancing EFL learners' speaking skills, foreign language enjoyment, and language-specific grit utilising the affordances of a MALL app: A microgenetic perspective. *Computers & Education*, *214*, 105015. DOI: 10.1016/j.compedu.2024.105015

Illeris, H. (2012). Aesthetic learning processes for the 21st century: Epistemology, didactics, performance. *Journal of the International Society for Teacher Education*, *16*(1), 10–19.

Iranmehr, A., Erfani, S. M., & Davari, H. (2011). Integrating task-based instruction as an alternative approach in teaching reading comprehension in English for special purposes: An action research. *Theory and Practice in Language Studies*, *1*(2), 142–148.

Ishengoma, F., Ngeze, L., & Ndibalema, P. (2024). Augmented Reality Applications in STEM Education: A Review. *International Journal of Open Information Technologies*, *12*(11), 48–57.

Ivan, J., & Krissh, P. (2021). Technical vocabulary acquisition using the online learning approach among aircraft maintenance learners. *International Conference on Multidisciplinary Innovation and Economics,* 8.

Jaggars, S. S., & Xu, D. (2010). *Online learning in the Virginia Community College system*. Columbia University, Teachers College, Community College Research Center., http://ccrc.tc.columbia.edu/media/k2/attachments/online-learning-virginia.pdf

Javed, F. (2024). Digital Transformation in Teaching and Learning of English in Higher Education. In Digital Transformation in Higher Education, Part B: Cases, Examples and Good Practices (pp. 103-125). Emerald Publishing Limited.

Jean-Berluche, D. (2024). Creative expression and mental health. *Journal of Creativity*, •••, 100083.

Jewell, M. E. (2008). No Child Left Behind: Implications for Special Education Students and Students with Limited English Proficiency. *Journal of the American Academy of Special Education Professionals*, *41*, 45.

Jhurree, V. (2005). Technology integration in education in developing countries: Guidelines to policy makers. *International Education Journal*, *6*(4), 467–483.

Jiang, L. (2022). Factors influencing EFL teachers' implementation of SPOC-based blended learning in higher vocational colleges in China: A study based on grounded theory. *Interactive Learning Environments*. Advance online publication. DOI: 10.1080/10494820.2022.2100428

Jiang, L., & Liang, X. (2023). Influencing factors of Chinese EFL students' continuance learning intention in SPOC-based blended learning environment. *Education and Information Technologies*, *28*(10), 13379–13404.

Jiang, W., Zhan, Y., Sun, D., Sun, J., & Tian, P. (2024). Exploring the effects of SPOC-based blended learning on students' learning performance at higher vocational education. *Interactive Learning Environments*, *32*(10), 6949–6966.

Jin, S.-H., Im, K., Yoo, M., Roll, I., & Seo, K. (2023). Supporting students' self-regulated learning in online learning using artificial intelligence applications. *International Journal of Educational Technology in Higher Education*, *20*(1), 37. DOI: 10.1186/s41239-023-00406-5

Jio, W., & Kant, S. (2025). Strategic Leadership Effect on Med-Tech Organization Citizenship Behavior With Mediation of Innovation Culture in the Horn of Africa. In *Strategic Management, Regulatory Challenges, and Global Governance of MedTech* (pp. 219-252). IGI Global Scientific Publishing.

Joosten, T., & Cusatis, R. (2020). Online learning readiness. *American Journal of Distance Education*, *34*(3), 180–193.

Kaelin, V. C., Valizadeh, M., Salgado, Z., Parde, N., & Khetani, M. A. (2021). Artificial intelligence in rehabilitation targeting the participation of children and youth with disabilities: Scoping review. *Journal of Medical Internet Research*, *23*(11), e25745.

Kalogiannakis, M., Papadakis, S., & Zourmpakis, A.-I. (2021). Gamification in science education. A systematic review of the literature. *Education Sciences*, *11*(1), 1. Advance online publication. DOI: 10.3390/educsci11010022

Kang, I. (2013). Factors of learner-instructor interaction which predict perceived learning outcomes in online learning environment. *Journal of Computer Assisted Learning*, *29*(3), 292–301.

Kant, S., & Adula, M. (2024). Human-Machine Interaction in the Metaverse in the Context of Ethiopia. In *Impact and Potential of Machine Learning in the Metaverse* (pp. 196–212). IGI Global.

Kant, S., Niguse, T., Adula, M., & Terefe, A. (2025). Integrating Simulation Tools Effect on Entrepreneurship Education by Mediation of Real-World Entrepreneurial Practices in the Horn of Africa. In *Integrating Simulation Tools Into Entrepreneurship Education* (pp. 525–548). IGI Global Scientific Publishing.

Kant, S., Toma, F., Niguse, T., & Adula, M. (2025). Transnational Higher Education Landscape Effect on Building a Global Vision for Staff Development by Navigating Cultural Diversity in Africa. In *Training and Development in Transnational Higher Education* (pp. 1–20). IGI Global Scientific Publishing.

Kaplan, S. N., Guzman, I., & Tomlinson, C. A. (Eds.). (2009). *Using the parallel curriculum model in urban settings, grades K-8.* Corwin Press.

Kapp, K. M. (2012). *The gamification of learning and instruction: Game-based methods and strategies for training and education.* John Wiley & Sons.

Kardan, S., & Conati, C. (2015). Providing adaptive support in an interactive simulation for learning: An experimental evaluation. *Proceedings of the 33rd Annual ACM Conference on Human Factors in Computing Systems*, 3671–3680. https://doi.org/DOI: 10.1145/2702123.2702424

Karkina, S., Mena, J., Valeeva, R., Yarmakeev, I., Dyganova, E., & Bhullar, M. (2023). Fostering future music teachers' professional skills: Developing a signature pedagogy using e-learning. *Frontiers in Education, 8*, 1162748. https://www.frontiersin.org/articles/10.3389/feduc.2023.1162748/full

Katemba, C. V. (2022). Vocabulary Enhancement through Presentation, Practice, Production(PPP) Method in the Rural EFL Classrooms. *Acuity: Journal of English Language Pedagogy. Literature and Culture*, *7*(1), 88–101. DOI: 10.35974/acuity.v7i1.2774

Kavaliauskienė, G. (2005). Task-based learning and learning outcomes in the ESP classroom. *Kalbų Studijos*, (7), 66–70.

Keengwe, J., & Kidd, T. T. (2010). Towards best practices in online learning and teaching in higher education. *Journal of Online Learning and Teaching*, *6*(2), 533–541. http://jolt.merlot.org/vol6no2/keengwe_0610.pdf

Keller, J. (1987). Development and use of the ARCS model of instructional design. *Journal of Instructional Development : JID*, *10*(3), 2–10.

Keller, J. M. (1993). *Manual for instructional materials motivational survey.* IMMS.

Keller, J. M. (2010). *Motivational design for learning and performance: The ARCS model approach.* Springer.

Kelly, K., & Heffernan, N. (2015). *Developing self-regulated learners through an intelligent tutoring system. Artificial Intelligence in Education.* Springer International Publishing., DOI: 10.1007/978-3-319-19773-9_128

Ke, M. F. (2023). Applications and challenges of artificial intelligence in the future of art education. *Pacific International Journal*, *6*(3), 61–65. DOI: 10.55014/pij.v6i3.405

Kertz-Welzel, A. (2022). *Rethinking music education and social change*. Oxford University Press., https://books.google.com/books?hl=zh-CN&lr=&id=KfhQEAAAQBAJ&oi=fnd&pg=PP1&dq=Rethinking+music+education+and+social+change&ots=qrJjGF8GZR&sig=_956gRn3GkZbGyPBoqf1sBf_KFs

Keung, H. (2021, October). Portable Interactive Meditation Mirror: A Novel Approach to Mindfulness Practice through Art and Technology. In *Proceedings of the 10th International Conference on Digital and Interactive Arts* (pp. 1-9). https://doi .org/DOI: 10.1145/3483529.3483696

Kexin, D., & Buang, N. A. (2024). Integrating Innovative Teaching Strategies: Assessing the Effectiveness of Flipped Classrooms, Blended Learning, and Task-Oriented Methods in Enhancing Academic Performance in Vocational IT Education. Journal of Digitainability, Realism & Mastery (DREAM), 3(05), 94–108. https://dreamjournal.my/index.php/DREAM/article/view/241

Khaleel, F. L., Ashaari, N. S., & Tengku Wook, T. S. M. (2020). The impact of gamification on students learning engagement. [IJECE]. *International Journal of Electrical and Computer Engineering*, *10*(5), 4965. DOI: 10.11591/ijece.v10i5.pp4965-4972

Kharbat, F. F., Alshawabkeh, A., & Woolsey, M. L. (2021). Identifying gaps in using artificial intelligence to support students with intellectual disabilities from education and health perspectives. *Aslib Journal of Information Management*, *73*(1), 101–128.

Khodaparast, F., & Ghafournia, N. (2015). On The Effect of Online / Offline Approaches on Vocabulary Achievement. *International Journal of Education and Research*, *3*(9), 269–280.

Kim, B. K., & Jung, C. Y. (2012). The casual relationship among career decision-making self-efficacy, self-leadership, problem solving ability, and career motivation. *Journal of Agricultural Education and Human Resource Development*, *44*(2), 49–71.

Kim, S. K., & Webb, S. (2022). The effects of spaced practice on second language learning: A meta-analysis. *Language Learning*, *72*(1), 269–319. DOI: 10.1111/lang.12479

Kintu, M. J., Zhu, C., & Kagambe, E. (2017). Blended learning effectiveness: The relationship between student characteristics, design features and outcomes. *International Journal of Educational Technology in Higher Education*, *14*(7), 1–20. DOI: 10.1186/s41239-017-0043-4

Kitsantas, A., & Dabbagh, N. (2010). *Learning to learn with integrative learning technologies (ILT): A practical guide for academic success.* Information Age Publishing.

Kizilcec, R. F., Piech, C., & Schneider, E. (2013). Deconstructing disengagement: Analyzing learner subpopulations in massive open online courses. *Proceedings of the Third International Conference on Learning Analytics and Knowledge*, 170–179. https://doi.org/DOI: 10.1145/2460296.2460330

Kohnke, L., & Ting, A. (2021). ESL students' perceptions of mobile applications for discipline-specific vocabulary acquisition for academic purposes. *Knowledge Management and E-Learning, 13*(1), 102–117. *Scopus.* Advance online publication. DOI: 10.34105/j.kmel.2021.13.006

Koleini, N., Boroughani, T., Eslami, Z. R., & Xodabande, I. (2024). Exploring the impacts of mobile-assisted learning on university students' technical vocabulary knowledge. *International Journal of Educational Research Open, 7. Scopus.* Advance online publication. DOI: 10.1016/j.ijedro.2024.100344

Kong, S.-C., & Yang, Y. (2024). A human-centered learning and teaching framework using generative artificial intelligence for self-regulated learning development through domain knowledge learning in K–12 settings. *IEEE Transactions on Learning Technologies, 17*, 1562–1573. DOI: 10.1109/TLT.2024.3392830

Koohang, A., & Weiss, E. (2003). Effect of prior experience with the internet on graduate students' perception toward courseware usability & web-based distance learning instruction: An exploratory study in a hybrid instruction environment. *Journal of Computer Information Systems*, *4*(2), 535–541.

Köpeczi-Bócz, T. (2024). The impact of a combination of flipped classroom and project-based learning on the learning motivation of university students. *Education Sciences, 14*(3), 240. https://www.mdpi.com/2227-7102/14/3/240

Krashen, S. (1981). Second language acquisition. *Second Language Learning*, *3*(7), 19–39.

Kukulska-Hulme, A. (2021). Reflections on research questions in mobile assisted language learning. *Journal of China Computer-Assisted Language Learning*, *1*(1), 28–46. DOI: 10.1515/jccall-2021-2002

Kumaraswamy, N. (2013). Academic stress, anxiety and depression among college students: A brief review. International review of social sciences and humanities, 5(1), 135-143.

Kumar, B. A., & Chand, S. S. (2019). Mobile learning adoption: A systematic review. *Education and Information Technologies*, *24*(1), 471–487.

Kuo, Y.-H. (2010). *Self-regulated learning: From theory to practice*. Online Submission.

Kurban, F. (2024). Evolution of pre-service mathematics teachers' spatial visualisation skills during a cognitive load theory-based education. *Problems of Education in the 21st Century, 82*(2), 202–235.

Kuvaeva, I. (2018). Teachers of special schools: stressors and manifestations of occupational stress. In *The Fifth International Luria Memorial Congress «Lurian Approach in International Psychological Science».—Ekaterinburg, 2018* (pp. 515-521). Knowledge E.

Kwong, R., Kwok, M. L. J., & Wong, H. (2024). Autonomous and controlled motivation in a flipped-classroom approach. *Asia Pacific Education Review*. Advance online publication. DOI: 10.1007/s12564-024-09983-0

Lai, S.-L., Hsu, H.-L., & Yang, H.-H. (2025). CALL and Vocabulary Learning. In *The Palgrave Encyclopedia of Computer-Assisted Language Learning* (pp. 1–11). Palgrave Macmillan., DOI: 10.1007/978-3-031-51447-0_293-1

Lakens, D. (2022). Sample size justification. *Collabra. Psychology*, *8*(1), 33267.

Lametti, D. (2022, December 7). A.I. could be great for college essays. https://slate.com/technology/2022/12/chatgpt-college-essay-plagiarism.html

Lan, X. LU, Z., & PENG, X. (2022). Cross-Cultural Adaptation of Chinese Students' Learning Thai Language Online in the Post-Pandemic Era—A Case Study of the Sino-Thai Co-operation Program at Guangxi University of Foreign Language. http://www.davidpublisher.com/Public/uploads/Contribute/6316e6c71c8b2.pdf

Larson, M. P., & Linnell, J. (2023). Are students coming to class prepared? The importance of pre-class learning in a flipped classroom. *Issues in Accounting Education*, *38*(3), 183–205. https://publications.aaahq.org/iae/article/38/3/183/10918

Laufer, B., & Hulstijn, J. (2001). Incidental vocabulary acquisition in a second language: The construct of task-induced involvement. *Applied Linguistics*, *22*(1), 1–26.

Lawter, L., & Garnjost, P. (2021). Cross-Cultural comparison of digital natives in flipped classrooms. *International Journal of Management Education*, *19*(3), 100559. https://www.sciencedirect.com/science/article/pii/S1472811721001087

Leakey, J., & Ranchoux, A. (2006). BLINGUA: A blended language learning approach for CALL. *Computer Assisted Language Learning*, *19*, 357–372.

LeCun, Y., Bengio, Y., & Hinton, G. (2015). Deep learning. *nature, 521*(7553), 436-444.

Lee, A., Lee, J. Y., & Jung, E. (2023). University students' experience of online space while engaging in synchronous learning via videoconferencing amidst the pandemic. *Frontiers in Psychology, 14*, 1083754. PMID: 36794081

Lee, R. S. P. (2020). Exploring the learning outcomes of flipped learning in a Second Language (L2) academic writing classroom for low proficiency pre-university students [PhD Thesis, Swinburne]. https://figshare.swinburne.edu.au/articles/thesis/Exploring_the_learning_outcomes_of_flipped_learning_in_a_Second_Language_L2_academic_writing_classroom_for_low_proficiency_pre-university_students/26282392

Lee, S. J., Srinivasan, S., Trail, T., Lewis, D., & Lopez, S. (2011). Examining the relationship among student perception of support, course satisfaction, and learning outcomes in online learning. *The Internet and Higher Education, 12*(3), 158–163. DOI: 10.1016/j.iheduc.2011.04.001

Lemi, K., Kant, S., & Jio, W. (2025). Greener Hospital Future in the Horn of Africa by Transactional Leadership: Outcome on Altruism Through Adaptability. In *Generation Alpha and Next Generation Leadership for Greener Futures* (pp. 1-22). IGI Global Scientific Publishing.

Lesica, N. A., Mehta, N., Manjaly, J. G., Deng, L., Wilson, B. S., & Zeng, F. G. (2021). Harnessing the power of artificial intelligence to transform hearing healthcare and research. *Nature Machine Intelligence, 3*(10), 840–849.

Lewis, C., & Adbul-Hamid, H. (2006). Implementing effective online teaching practices: Voices of exemplary faculty. *Innovative Higher Education, 31*(2). Advance online publication. DOI: 10.1007/s10755-006-9010-z

Liao, X., & Wang, W. (2025). A framework for designing immersive virtual reality learning environments based on the cognitive theory of multimedia learning. *Curriculum Learning and Exploration, 2*(5), 5. Advance online publication. DOI: 10.70711/cle.v2i5.6370

Li, B., & Peng, M. (2022). Integration of an AI-Based Platform and Flipped Classroom Instructional Model. *Scientific Programming, 2022*, 1–8. DOI: 10.1155/2022/2536382

Li, B., & Xu, X. (2025). Examining the intersectionality of learners' professional background and cultural diversity in Chinese ESP learners and its impact on students' engagement: A study on the application of communicative language teaching. *Current Psychology (New Brunswick, N.J.)*, *44*(7), 5854–5869. DOI: 10.1007/s12144-025-07479-7

Li, F., Lu, Y., Ma, Q., Gao, J., Wang, Z., & Bai, L. (2023). SPOC online video learning clustering analysis: Identifying learners' group behavior characteristics. *Computer Applications in Engineering Education.*

Li, J. (2022). Domestic MOOC Learning Behavior Research: A Systematic Analysis of the Literature in the Last Decade. *New Generation of Information Technology*, *5*(3), 99–102.

Li, L., Hew, K. F., & Du, J. (2024). Gamification enhances student intrinsic motivation, perceptions of autonomy and relatedness, but minimal impact on competency: A meta-analysis and systematic review. *Educational Technology Research and Development*, *72*(2), 765–796. DOI: 10.1007/s11423-023-10337-7

Lim, C. P., & Wang, L. (Eds.). (2016). *Blended learning for quality higher education: Selected case studies on implementation from Asia-Pacific*. UNESCO., https://unesdoc.unesco.org/ark:/48223/pf0000246851

Lin, C.-C., Huang, A. Y. Q., & Lu, O. H. T. (2023). Artificial intelligence in intelligent tutoring systems toward sustainable education: A systematic review. *Smart Learning Environments*, *10*(1), 41. DOI: 10.1186/s40561-023-00260-y

Lindner, K. T., & Schwab, S. (2020). Differentiation and individualisation in inclusive education: A systematic review and narrative synthesis. *International Journal of Inclusive Education*, •••, 1–21.

Lindsay, G. (2003). Inclusive education: A critical perspective. *British Journal of Special Education*, *30*(1), 3–12.

Ling, S. I. (2023). Music technology in the 21st century of global music education: Opportunities and challenges. The 14th Asia-Pacific Symposium for Music Education Research (APSMER 2023), 242–251. https://researchmap.jp/kazuwo_piano/presentations/43117806/attachment_file.pdf#page=246

Lin, H., & Chen, Q. (2024). Artificial intelligence (AI)-integrated educational applications and college students' creativity and academic emotions: Students and teachers' perceptions and attitudes. *BMC Psychology*, *12*(1), 487. DOI: 10.1186/s40359-024-01979-0

Lin, H., Dyer, K., & Guo, Y. (2012). Exploring online teaching: A three-year composite journal of concerns and strategies from online instructors. (English). *Online Journal of Distance Learning Administration, 15*(3), 1. http://www.westga.edu/~distance/ojdla/fall153/lin_dyer_guo153.html

Lin, P. Y., & Lin, Y. C. (2019). Understanding how teachers practise inclusive classroom assessment. *Studies in Educational Evaluation, 63*, 113–121.

Liu, D. (2024). The effects of segmentation on cognitive load, vocabulary learning and retention, and reading comprehension in a multimedia learning environment. *BMC Psychology, 12*(1). *Scopus.* Advance online publication. DOI: 10.1186/s40359-023-01489-5

Liu, G.-Z., Fathi, J., & Rahimi, M. (2024). Using digital gamification to improve language achievement, foreign language enjoyment, and ideal L2 self: A case of English as a foreign language learners. *Journal of Computer Assisted Learning, 40*(4), 1347–1364. DOI: 10.1111/jcal.12954

Liu, J., Cao, S., Liu, X., Ye, C., & Siano, P. (2024). Pre-class mode" flipped" again: Making videos instead of just watching them. *Heliyon, 10*(6). https://www.cell.com/heliyon/fulltext/S2405-8440(24)04136-7

Liu, L. (2021). Research on IT English flipped classroom teaching model based on SPOC. *Scientific Programming, 2021*, 1–9.

Liu, L. (2024). Impact of AI gamification on EFL learning outcomes and nonlinear dynamic motivation: Comparing adaptive learning paths, conversational agents, and storytelling. *Education and Information Technologies*. Advance online publication. DOI: 10.1007/s10639-024-13296-5

Liu, M., Zhao, G., Zhong, Z., Ma, J., & Wang, W. (2024). Theoretical Foundations for Blended Learning. In Li, M., Han, X., & Cheng, J. (Eds.), *Handbook of Educational Reform Through Blended Learning*. Springer., DOI: 10.1007/978-981-99-6269-3_1

Li, X., Sulaiman, N. A., & Aziz, A. A. (2025). Factors influencing Chinese Non-English majors' attitudes toward blended learning: The role of perceived relevance, online self-efficacy, and teachers' digital literacy. *Edelweiss Applied Science and Technology, 9*(5), 239–254.

Li, Y., & Hafner, C. A. (2022). Mobile-assisted vocabulary learning: Investigating receptive and productive vocabulary knowledge of Chinese EFL learners. *ReCALL, 34*(1), 66–80. DOI: 10.1017/S0958344021000161

Li, Z., & Jiang, W. (2022). Research on the Teaching Reform of Inorganic Chemistry Based on SPOC and FCM during COVID-19. *Sustainability, 14*(9), 5707.

Lo, C. K., Hew, K. F., & Jong, M. S. Y. (2024). The influence of ChatGPT on student engagement: A systematic review and future research agenda. *Computers & Education, 105100*. Advance online publication. DOI: 10.1016/j.compedu.2024.105100

Lo, K. W. K., Ngai, G., Chan, S. C. F., & Kwan, K. P. (2022). How Students' Motivation and Learning Experience Affect Their Service-Learning Outcomes: A Structural Equation Modeling Analysis. *Frontiers in Psychology, 13*, 825902. DOI: 10.3389/fpsyg.2022.825902 PMID: 35519642

Luckin, R., & Holmes, W. (2016). Intelligence unleashed: An argument for AI in education. *UCL Knowledge Lab: London, UK.* https://www.pearson.com/content/dam/corporate/global/pearson-dot-com/files/innovation/Intelligence-Unleashed-Publication.pdf

Lukes, L. A., Jones, Jason P., & and McConnell, D. A. (2020). Self-regulated learning: Overview and potential future directions in geoscience. *Journal of Geoscience Education, 69*(1), 14–26. DOI: 10.1080/10899995.2020.1820828

Luo, X., Zhang, A., Li, Y., Zhang, Z., Ying, F., Lin, R., & Huang, G. (2024). Emergence of artificial intelligence art therapies (AIATs) in mental health care: A systematic review. *International Journal of Mental Health Nursing, 33*(6), 1743–1760. DOI: 10.1111/inm.13384

Lv, H. Z. (2023). Innovative music education: Using an AI-based flipped classroom. *Education and Information Technologies, 28*(11), 15301–15316. DOI: 10.1007/s10639-023-11835-0

Ma, R. (2021). Stimulating students learning motivation: A case study of music education and pedagogy course based on flipped classroom. Psychology and Education Journal, 58(2), 109–114. https://www.researchgate.net/profile/Rui-Ma-133/publication/349281829_Stimulating_students'_learning_motivation_A_case_study_of_music_education_and_pedagogy_course_based_on_flipped_classroom/links/661faec8f7d3fc287467269b/Stimulating-students-learning-motivation-A-case-study-of-music-education-and-pedagogy-course-based-on-flipped-classroom.pdf

Maag Merki, K., Wullschleger, A., & Rechsteiner, B. (2023). Adapting routines in schools when facing challenging situations: Extending previous theories on routines by considering theories on self-regulated and collectively regulated learning. *Journal of Educational Change, 24*(3), 583–604. DOI: 10.1007/s10833-022-09459-1 PMID: 37560443

Magfirah, T., Roy, A., & Arridha, R. (2022). Improving Students' Technical English Vocabulary Using Readlang Platform at State Polytechnic of Fakfak. *Cebong Journal, 1*(3), 3. Advance online publication. DOI: 10.35335/cebong.v1i3.28

Mahmodi, M., & Ebrahimzade, I. (2015). The analysis of Iranian students' persistence in online education. *International Review of Research in Open and Distance Learning*, *16*(1). Advance online publication. DOI: 10.19173/irrodl.v16i1.1982

Mahmoud, C. F., & Sørensen, J. T. (2024). Artificial intelligence in personalized learning with a focus on current developments and future prospects. *Research and Advances in Education*, *3*(8), Article 8.

Mahraj, M., & Ouahani, N. (2024). Teaching Strategies of Technical Vocabulary: A Qualitative Approach. *Moroccan Journal of Quantitative and Qualitative Research*, *6*(3), 3. Advance online publication. DOI: 10.48379/IMIST.PRSM/mjqr-v6i3.49144

Makkar, N., & Sharma, R. (2022). Effect of blended learning on academic achievement in mathematics among ix grade students. *International Journal of Indian Psychology*, *10*(2). Advance online publication. DOI: 10.25215/1002.135

Makwana, V. (2025). A comparative analysis of AI-powered and teacher-led feedback: Investigating student perceptions and writing performance. *Journal of English Language Teaching*, *67*(1), 1.

Ma, L., & Lee, C. S. (2021). Evaluating the effectiveness of blended learning using the ARCS model. *Journal of Computer Assisted Learning*, *37*(5), 1397–1408. DOI: 10.1111/jcal.12579

Malau-Aduli, B. S., Adu, M. D., Alele, F., Jones, K., Drovandi, A., Mylrea, M., & Jennings, E. (2021). Adjusting to university: Perceptions of first-year health professions students. *PLoS One*, *16*(5), e0251634. DOI: 10.1371/journal.pone.0251634

Maphalala, M. C., & Adigun, O. T. (2021). COVID-19 and teacher preparation for learners with disabilities: The need for divergent praxis. *Psychology and Education*, *58*(5), 5228–5240.

Marella, V. C., Erukude, S. T., & Veluru, S. R. THE IMPACT OF ARTIFICIAL INTELLIGENCE ON TRADITIONAL ART FORMS: A DISRUPTION OR ENHANCEMENT?.DOI: DOI: 10.21817/indjcse/2025/v16i1/251603012

Marino, M. T., Vasquez, E., Dieker, L., Basham, J., & Blackorby, J. (2023). The future of artificial intelligence in special education technology. *Journal of Special Education Technology*, *38*(3), 404–416.

Marin, V. J., Pereira, T., Sridharan, S., & Rivero, C. R. (2017, April). *Automated personalized feedback in introductory Java programming MOOCs*. In *Proceedings of the 2017 IEEE 33rd International Conference on Data Engineering (ICDE)* (pp. 1259–1270). IEEE. https://doi.org/DOI: 10.1109/ICDE.2017.169

Marsh, D. (2012). *Blended learning: Creating learning opportunities for language learners*. Cambridge University Press.

Martínez, M. del V. D. M., & De Moya, M. del V. R. (2024). Sounds of Cultures: Strategies for Global, Intercultural, and Transformative Education Through Music. In Transformative Intercultural Global Education (pp. 209–231). IGI Global. https://www.igi-global.com/chapter/sounds-of-cultures/347094

Martin, F., Budhrani, K., & Wang, C. (2019). Examining faculty perception of their readiness to teach online. *Online Learning : the Official Journal of the Online Learning Consortium*, *23*(3), 97–119.

Martin, F., Polly, D., & Ritzhaupt, A. (2020). Bichronous online learning: Blending asynchronous and synchronous online learning. *EDUCAUSE Review*, •••, 8.

Mateos-Moreno, D., García-Perals, J., & Maxwell, T. W. (2025). Teaching to practice productively and consciously: An action-research study in one-to-one instrumental music teaching. *Music Education Research*, *27*(2), 203–214. DOI: 10.1080/14613808.2025.2465248

Mayer, R. E. (2014). Principles Based on Social Cues in Multimedia Learning: Personalization, Voice, Image, and Embodiment Principles. In *The Cambridge handbook of multimedia learning, 2nd ed* (pp. 345–368). Cambridge University Press. https://doi.org/DOI: 10.1017/CBO9781139547369.017

Mayer, R. E. (2005). Cognitive Theory of Multimedia Learning. In *The Cambridge handbook of multimedia learning* (pp. 31–48). Cambridge University Press., DOI: 10.1017/CBO9780511816819.004

Mayer, R. E. (2014). *Multimedia instruction. J. M. Spector, M. D. Merrill, J. Elen, & M. J. Bishop, Handbook of Research on Educational Communications and Technology*. Springer., DOI: 10.1007/978-1-4614-3185-5_31

McHone, C. (2020). Blended Learning Integration: Student Motivation and Autonomy in a Blended Learning Environment. *Electronic Theses and Dissertations*. 3750.

McKay, V. (2018). Introducing a parallel curriculum to enhance social and environmental awareness in South African school workbooks. *Balancing individualism and collectivism: Social and environmental justice*, 97-122.

McNamara, A. (2021). Flipping the creative conservatoire classroom. Theatre. *Dance and Performance Training*, *12*(4), 528–539. DOI: 10.1080/19443927.2020.1864462

McNamara, D. S. (2007). *Reading comprehension strategies: Theories, interventions, and technologies*. Psychology Press.

McNicholl, A., Casey, H., Desmond, D., & Gallagher, P. (2021). The impact of assistive technology use for students with disabilities in higher education: A systematic review. *Disability and Rehabilitation. Assistive Technology*, *16*(2), 130–143.

Means, B., Toyama, Y., Murphy, R., & Baki, M. (2013). The effectiveness of online and blended learning: A meta-analysis of the empirical literature. *Teachers College Record*, *115*(3), 1–47.

Messingschlager, T. V., & Appel, M. (2025). Mind ascribed to AI and the appreciation of AI-generated art. *New Media & Society*, *27*(3), 1673–1692. DOI: 10.1177/14614448231200248

Michinov, N., Brunot, S., Le Bohec, O., Juhel, J., & Delaval, M. (2011). Procrastination, participation, and performance in online learning environments. *Computers & Education*, *56*(1), 243–252. DOI: 10.1016/j.compedu.2010.07.025

Milgram, P., Takemura, H., Utsumi, A., & Kishino, F. (1995). Augmented reality: A class of displays on the reality-virtuality continuum. *Telemanipulator and Telepresence Technologies*, *2351*, 282–292. DOI: 10.1117/12.197321

Miller, T. W., & Miller, J. M. (2001). Educational leadership in the new millennium: A vision for 2020. *International Journal of Leadership in Education*. https://www.tandfonline.com/doi/abs/10.1080/13603120120806

Miller, G. (2015). Associations between learner interaction and achievement in an online course: A longitudinal study. *NACTA Journal*, *59*(3), 197–201. https://www.nactateachers.org/index.php/vol-59-3-sept-2015/2319-associations-between-learner-interaction-and-achievement-in-an-online-course-a-longitudinal-study

Minalla Alameen, A. (2024). Enhancing young EFL learners' vocabulary learning through contextualizing animated videos. *Theory and Practice in Language Studies*, *14*, 578–586. DOI: 10.17507/tpls.1402.31

Ministry of Education of the People's Republic of China. (2019, February 23). China education modernization 2035. Retrieved June 10, 2024, from https://www.gov.cn/zhengce/2019-02/23/content_5367987.htm

Ministry of Education of the People's Republic of China. (2020). Action Plan for Improving the Quality of Vocational Education (2020-2023). Announcement of the Ministry of Education and nine other departments on issuing the Action Plan for Improving the Quality of Vocational Education (2020-2023). Faculty Cheng (2020) NO. 7. https://www.gov.cn/zhengce/zhengceku/2020-09/29/content_5548106.htm

Ministry of Education of the People's Republic of China. (2024a, January 15). Statistical bulletin on the development of national education in 2023. Retrieved June 10, 2024, from http://www.moe.gov.cn/jyb_sjzl/s5990/202401/t20240115_1123112.html

Ministry of Education of the People's Republic of China. (2018). Announcement of the Ministry of Education on issuing the "Education Informatization 2.0 Action Plan" [2018] No. 6.

Miroshnychenko, I. (2024). Technical vocabulary in foreign language acquisition: Seeking effective methods for university students. *Collection of Scientific Papers «ΛΌΓΟΣ»*, Article May 24, 2024; Zurich, Switzerland. https://doi.org/DOI: 10.36074/logos-24.05.2024.058

Mishra, P. A., Hota, S., & Khamari, P. R. (2019). Curriculum adaptation in inclusive education. *International Journal of Applied Research*, *5*(8), 70–74.

Mohamed, A. H. H. (2018). Attitudes of special education teachers towards using technology in inclusive classrooms: A mixed-methods study. *Journal of Research in Special Educational Needs*, *18*(4), 278–288.

Mohammed, H. S., Aicha, B., & Rahil, M. (2023). EFL Students' Perceptions About The Effect Of Blended Learning On Their Learning Autonomy. *Journal of Language and Linguistic Studies*, *19*(3), 85–105.

Mohebbi, A. (2025). Enabling learner independence and self-regulation in language education using AI tools: A systematic review. *Cogent Education*, *12*(1), 2433814. DOI: 10.1080/2331186X.2024.2433814

Moher, D., Liberati, A., Tetzlaff, J., & Altman, D. G.PRISMA Group. (2009). Preferred reporting items for systematic reviews and meta-analyses: The PRISMA statement. *Annals of Internal Medicine*, *151*(4), 264–269. PMID: 19622511

Mokmin, N. A. M. (2020). The effectiveness of a personalized virtual fitness trainer in teaching physical education by applying the artificial intelligent algorithm. *International Journal of Human Movement and Sports Sciences*, *8*(5), 258–264.

Molinari, C. A., Freshman, B. L., & Rae, Y. T. (2015). Mindful awareness training in online and face-to-face learning environments: A comparative analysis. *The Journal of Health Administration Education*, *32*(4), 579–604. DOI: 10.12016/M2KM85

Moore, A., Nguyen, A., Rivas, S., Bany-Mohammed, A., Majeika, J., & Martinez, L. (2021). A qualitative examination of the impacts of financial stress on college students' well-being: Insights from a large, private institution. *SAGE Open Medicine*, *9*, 20503121211018122. DOI: 10.1177/20503121211018122

Moore, J. (2014). Effects of online interaction and instructor presence on students' satisfaction and success with online undergraduate public relations courses. *Journalism & Mass Communication Education*, *69*(3), 271–288. DOI: 10.1177/1077695814536398

Moore, M. G. (1993). Editorial. Three types of interaction. *American Journal of Distance Education*, *3*(2), 1–6. DOI: 10.1080/08923648909526659

Moore, M. G. (1997). Theory of transactional distance. In Keegan, D. (Ed.), *Theoretical principles of distance education*. Routledge.

Moore, M. G., & Kearsley, G. (2012). *Distance education: A systematic view of online learning* (3rd ed.). Wadsworth Cengage Learning.

Moreno-Marcos, P. M., De Laet, T., Muñoz-Merino, P. J., Van Soom, C., Broos, T., Verbert, K., & Delgado Kloos, C. (2019, March). Predicting admission test success using SPOC interactions. In *Proceedings of the 9th International Conference of Learning Analytics & Knowledge*, Tempe, AZ, USA (pp. 4-8).

Morin, J., & Willox, S. (2022). Closing the soft skills gap: A case in leveraging technology and the "flipped" classroom with a programmatic approach to soft skill development in business education. Transformative Dialogues: Teaching and Learning Journal, 15(1). https://journals.psu.edu/td/article/view/1707

Morrison, C., Cutrell, E., Dhareshwar, A., Doherty, K., Thieme, A., & Taylor, A. (2017, October). Imagining artificial intelligence applications with people with visual disabilities using tactile ideation. In *Proceedings of the 19th international acm sigaccess conference on computers and accessibility* (pp. 81-90).

Muchtar N. (2017). *An overview of mobile-assisted language learning*. 170–174. https://doi.org/DOI: 10.2991/iconelt-17.2018.38

Mueller, B., Mandernach, B. J., & Sanderson, K. (2013). Adjust versus full-time faculty: Comparison of student learning outcomes in the online classroom. *Journal of Online Learning and Teaching*, *9*(3), 341–353. http://jolt.merlot.org/vol9no3/mueller_0913.htm

Mueller, C., Mildenberger, T., & Lübcke, M. (2020). Do we always need a difference? Testing equivalence in a blended learning setting. *International Journal of Research & Method in Education*, *43*, 283–295. DOI: 10.1080/1743727X.2019.1680621

Muhammad, S., & Rahman, M. (2025). Developing Students' Descriptive Writing Skills in terms of Content Knowledge at the Higher Secondary School Level: An Experiment with the Task-Based Writing Methodology. [DSSR]. *Dialogue Social Science Review*, *3*(1), 388–408.

Muhati-Nyakundi, L. I. (2023). Teachers' Agency and Wellbeing in Inclusive Education: Challenges and Opportunities. *Journal of Educational Studies*, *2023*(si1), 365–379.

Murphy, T. R., Mannix-McNamara, P., Slattery, G., Masterson, M., O'Sullivan, M., & Corry, J. (2021). Teacher Well-being in an Inclusive Secondary School. *International Perspectives on Teacher Well-being and Diversity: Portals into Innovative Classroom Practice*, 145-162.

Nandi, D., Hamilton, M., & Harland, J. (2012). Evaluating the quality of interaction in asynchronous discussion forums in fully online courses. *Distance Education*, *33*(1). Advance online publication. DOI: 10.1080/01587919.2012.667957

Nandi, D., Hamilton, M., Harland, J., & Mahmood, S. (2015). Investigation of participation and quality of online interaction. *International Journal of Modern Education and Computer Science*, *7*(8), 25–37. DOI: 10.5815/ijmecs.2015.08.04

Nation, P. (2007). The Four Strands. *Innovation in Language Learning and Teaching*, *1*(1), 2–13. DOI: 10.2167/illt039.0

Nettleton, K. F., Kessinger, M. W., & Lennex, L. (2023). Engaging on Common Ground: Inclusion of the Gifted Student in the Classroom. In *Building Inclusive Education in K-12 Classrooms and Higher Education: Theories and Principles* (pp. 260-283). IGI Global.

Neville, D. O. (2015). The story in the mind: The effect of 3D gameplay on the structuring of written L2 narratives. *ReCALL*, *27*(1), 21–37. DOI: 10.1017/S0958344014000160

Nguyen A., Ilesanmi F., Dang B., Vuorenmaa E., J&#228, rvel&#228, & Sanna. (2024). Hybrid intelligence in academic writing: Examining self-regulated learning patterns in an AI-assisted writing task. *HHAI 2024: Hybrid Human AI Systems for the Social Good*, 241–254. IOS Press. https://doi.org/DOI: 10.3233/FAIA240198

Nikoletatos, P. (2020). Online learning has created challenges that universities and students must overcome. *Fenews*. https://www.fenews.co.uk/exclusive/online-learning-has-created-challenges-that-universities-and-students-must-overcome/

Nitisakunwut, P., Nutayangkul, T., & Liang-Itsara, A. (2023). The sociocultural perspective on the use of L1 as a supporting tool for EFL learning. *English Language Teaching*, *16*(2), 74–81.

Norman, D. A. (1999). Affordance, conventions, and design. *Interaction*, *6*(3), 38–43. DOI: 10.1145/301153.301168

Nuareni, C. (2020). Mobile-assisted language learning (MALL): Students' perception and problems towards Mobile learning in English language. *Journal of Physics: Conference Series, 1641*, 7.

Nur Fitria, T. (2021). *Artificial intelligence (AI) in education: Using AI tools for teaching and learning process.*

O'dea, X., & O'Dea, M. (2023). Is artificial intelligence really the next big thing in learning and teaching in higher education?: A conceptual paper. *Journal of University Teaching & Learning Practice, 20*(5), 1–17.

Ok, M. W., & Rao, K. (2019). Digital tools for the inclusive classroom: Google chrome as assistive and instructional technology. *Journal of Special Education Technology, 34*(3), 204–211.

Ok, M. W., Rao, K., Pennington, J., & Ulloa, P. R. (2022). Speech recognition technology for writing: Usage patterns and perceptions of students with high incidence disabilities. *Journal of Special Education Technology, 37*(2), 191–202.

Olagunju, A. T., Akinola, M. A., Fadipe, B., Jagun, O. O., Olagunju, T. O., Akinola, O. O., & Chaimowitz, G. A. (2021). Psychosocial wellbeing of Nigerian teachers in special education schools. *Journal of Autism and Developmental Disorders, 51*, 1131–1141.

Onderdijk, K. E., Bouckaert, L., Van Dyck, E., & Maes, P.-J. (2023). Concert experiences in virtual reality environments. *Virtual Reality (Waltham Cross), 27*(3), 2383–2396. DOI: 10.1007/s10055-023-00814-y

Osisanya, A., Oyewumi, A. M., & Adigun, O. T. (2015). Perception of parents of children with communication difficulties about inclusive education in Ibadan metropolis. *American Journal of Educational Research, 19*(1), 21–32.

Ouyang, F., Jiao, P., Alavi, A. H., & McLaren, B. M. (2022). Artificial intelligence in STEM education: Current developments and future considerations. In Artificial Intelligence in STEM Education (pp. 3-14). CRC Press. Audry, S. (2021). Art in the age of machine learning. Mit Press.

Ouyang, F., Zheng, L., & Jiao, P. (2022). Artificial intelligence in online higher education: A systematic review of empirical research from 2011 to 2020. *Education and Information Technologies, 27*(6), 7893–7925. DOI: 10.1007/s10639-022-10925-9

Oyewumi, A. M., & Adigun, O. T. (2013). Modifying learning and assessment techniques of accommodate students with hearing impairment. *Nigeria Journal of Speech/Language-Hearing Disorder and Rehabilitation, 1*(1), 33-38.

Padilla Rodriguez, B. C., & Armellini, A. (2015). Expanding the interaction equivalency theorem. *International Review of Research in Open and Distance Learning, 16*(3). Advance online publication. DOI: 10.19173/irrodl.v16i3.2085

Pagliari, L., Batts, D., & McFadden, C. (2009). Desired versus actual training for online instructors in community colleges. *Online Journal of Distance Learning Administration, 12*(4). https://www.learntechlib.org/p/76603

Panadero, E. (2017). A review of self-regulated learning: Six models and four directions for research. *Frontiers in Psychology, 8*. Advance online publication. DOI: 10.3389/fpsyg.2017.00422 PMID: 28503157

Panch, T., Szolovits, P., & Atun, R. (2018). Artificial intelligence, machine learning and health systems. *Journal of Global Health, 8*(2), 020303. PMID: 30405904

Pan, M., Guo, K., & Lai, C. (2024). Using artificial intelligence chatbots to support English-as-a-foreign language students' self-regulated reading. *RELC Journal, 00336882241264030*. Advance online publication. DOI: 10.1177/00336882241264030

Pannan, L. J., & Legge, K. A. (2016). A blended learning model and a design model combine to support academics in pedagogical redesign of the curriculum. *ASCILITE 2016 - Conference Proceedings - 33rd International Conference of Innovation, Practice and Research in the Use of Educational Technologies in Tertiary Education: Show Me the Learning.*

Paris, S. G., Lipson, M. Y., & Wixson, K. K. (1983). Becoming a strategic reader. *Contemporary Educational Psychology, 8*(3), 293–316. DOI: 10.1016/0361-476X(83)90018-8

Park, J., Choi, Y., & Lee, K. M. (2024). Research trends in virtual reality music concert technology: A systematic literature review. IEEE Transactions on Visualization and Computer Graphics. https://ieeexplore.ieee.org/abstract/document/10458432/

Park, H., & Choi, H. J. (2009). Factors influencing adult learners' decision to drop out or persist in online learning. *Journal of Educational Technology & Society, 12*(4), 207–217. https://pdfs.semanticscholar.org/152d/86fbe09ce4d476277b2dfacc38f85b2e2754.pdf

Passer, M. W. (2014). *Research methods: Concepts and connections.* Worth Publishers.

Pather, S. (2014). Evidence on inclusion and support for learners with disabilities in mainstream schools in South Africa: Off the policy radar? In *Disability, Poverty and Education* (pp. 57-71). Routledge.

Pedrelli, P., Nyer, M., Yeung, A., Zulauf, C., & Wilens, T. (2015). College students: Mental health problems and treatment considerations. *Academic Psychiatry*, *39*(5), 503–511.

Peláez-Sánchez, I. C., & Velásquez-Durán, A. (2023). The impact of duolingo in developing students' linguistic competence: An aspect of communicative language competences. *Educação e Pesquisa*, *49*, e252467. DOI: 10.1590/S1678-4634202349252467eng

Perrotta, C., & Selwyn, N. (2020). Deep learning goes to school: Toward a relational understanding of AI in education. *Learning, Media and Technology*, *45*(3), 251–269.

Peterson, S. G. (2018). *Epistemic beliefs and the innovation-decision process: A mixed methods analysis of faculty classroom assessment practice* (Doctoral dissertation, University of Nevada, Las Vegas).

Peterson, A. T., Beymer, P. N., & Putnam, R. T. (2018). Synchronous and asynchronous discussions: Effects on cooperation, belonging, and affect. *Online Learning : the Official Journal of the Online Learning Consortium*, *22*(4), 7–25.

Peterson, J. L. (2016). Formative evaluations in online classes. *The Journal of Educators Online*, *13*(1), 1–14. http://www.thejeo.com/Archives/Volume13Number1/Peterson.pdf

Pettersson, F. (2018). On the issues of digital competence in educational contexts–a review of literature. *Education and Information Technologies*, *23*(3), 1005–1021.

Phirangee, K., Epp, C. D., & Hewitt, J. (2016). Exploring the relationships between facilitation methods, students' sense of community, and their online behaviors. *Online Learning : the Official Journal of the Online Learning Consortium*, *20*(2), 134–154. https://tspace.library.utoronto.ca/bitstream/1807/73603/1/Exploring%20the%20Relationships%20Facilitation%20Methods.pdf

Piaw, C. Y. (2020). *Mastering Research Methods* (2nd ed.). McGraw-Hill Education.

Pina, A. A., & Bohn, L. (2014). Assessing online faculty: More than student surveys and design rubrics. *Quarterly Review of Distance Education*, *15*, 25–34.

Pintrich, P. R. (2000). *The role of goal orientation in self-regulated learning. M. Boekaerts, P. R. Pintrich, & M. Zeidner, Handbook of Self-Regulation*. Academic Press., DOI: 10.1016/B978-012109890-2/50043-3

Plomp, T. (2007). Educational design research: An introduction. In Plomp, T., & Nieveen, N. (Eds.), *Educational design research: An introduction* (pp. 9–36). SLO.

Poelhuber, B., & Anderson, T. (2011). Distance students' readiness for social media and collaboration. *International Review of Research in Open and Distance Learning*, *12*(6), 102–125.

Polakova, P., & Klimova, B. (2022). Vocabulary Mobile Learning Application in Blended English Language Learning. *Frontiers in Psychology*, *13*, 869055. DOI: 10.3389/fpsyg.2022.869055 PMID: 35592159

Popenici, S. A., & Kerr, S. (2017). Exploring the impact of artificial intelligence on teaching and learning in higher education. *Research and Practice in Technology Enhanced Learning*, *12*(1), 22. PMID: 30595727

Prasittichok, P., Jitprapaikulsarn, S., Sriprasertpap, K., & Hwang, G. J. (2024). Technological solutions to fostering students' moral courage: An augmented reality-based contextual gaming approach. *Cogent Education*, *11*(1), 2378276.

Preisman, K. A. (2014). Teaching presence in online education: From the instructor's point of view. *Online Learning : the Official Journal of the Online Learning Consortium*, *10*(3), 1–16. http://files.eric.ed.gov/fulltext/EJ1043166.pdf

Puzziferro, M. (2008). Online technologies self-efficacy and self-regulated learning as predictors of final grade and satisfaction in college-level online courses. *American Journal of Distance Education*, *22*(2), 72–89.

Qiang, F., Hirunrux, S., & Yukolthonwong, S. (2024). A Strategic Study on the Effective Application of Flipped Classroom Teaching Method in World Music Appreciation Classroom. *Journal of Roi Kaensarn Academi*, *9*(4), 819–826. https://so02.tci-thaijo.org/index.php/JRKSA/article/view/269933

Qindah, S. (2018). The Effects of Blended Learning on EFL Students ' Usage of Grammar in Context. [EPESS]. *The Eurasia Proceedings of Educational & Social Sciences*, *10*, 11–22.

Qiu, X. (2022). Blended Teaching Mode of Higher Vocational English Based on MOOC+ SPOC. *Wireless Communications and Mobile Computing*, **•••**, 2022.

Raes, A., Detienne, L., Windey, I., & Depaepe, F. (2020). A systematic literature review on synchronous hybrid learning: Gaps identified. *Learning Environments Research*, *23*, 269–290.

Rahmat, H., Mashudi, R., Hairul, M., Razak, A., Huda, N., Hamid, A., & Rahmat, N. (2019). the Readiness of MMU Lecturers Towards the Implementation of Blended Learning. *E-Bangi*, 16(1).

Rahsepar Meadi, M., Sillekens, T., Metselaar, S., van Balkom, A., Bernstein, J., & Batelaan, N. (2025). Exploring the ethical challenges of conversational AI in mental health care: Scoping review. *JMIR Mental Health, 12*, e60432. DOI: 10.2196/60432

Rainer, R. K., Prince, B., Sanchez-Rodriguez, C., Splettstoesser-Hogeterp, I., & Ebrahimi, S. (2020). *Introduction to information systems*. John Wiley & Sons.

Raji, N. R., Kumar, R. M. S., & Biji, C. L. (2024). Explainable Machine Learning Prediction for the Academic Performance of Deaf Scholars. *IEEE Access : Practical Innovations, Open Solutions, 12*, 23595–23612.

Rangel-de Lazaro, G., & Duart, J. M. (2023). You can handle, you can teach it: Systematic review on the use of extended reality and artificial intelligence technologies for online higher education. *Sustainability, 15*(4), 3507.

Reed, P., & Bowser, G. (2005). Assistive technologies and the IEP. In Edyburn, D., Higgins, K., Boone, R. (Eds.) *Handbook of Special Education Technology Research and Practice.* Knowledge by Design Inc. Whitefish bay.

Reeves, T. (2006). Design research from a technology perspective. In *Educational design research* (pp. 64–78). Routledge.

Reeves, T., & McKenney, S. (2015). Design-based research. In *The SAGE encyclopedia of educational technology* (pp. 189–191). SAGE Publications Inc.

Reimer, B. (2022). A philosophy of music education: Advancing the vision. State University of New York Press. https://books.google.com/books?hl=zh-CN&lr=&id=Q9eIEAAAQBAJ&oi=fnd&pg=PT9&dq=A+philosophy+of+music+education:+Advancing+the+vision&ots=B9vLhHbiZ2&sig=cMGCNYucLZa_xsGZGPumFFH0zwk

Revere, L., & Kovach, J. V. (2011). Online technologies for engaged learning: A meaningful synthesis for educators. *Quarterly Review of Distance Education, 12*(2), 113–124. http://citeseerx.ist.psu.edu/viewdoc/download?doi=10.1.1.466.7571&rep=rep1&type=pdf

Rico-Juan, J. R., Gallego, A. J., & Calvo-Zaragoza, J. (2019). Automatic detection of inconsistencies between numerical scores and textual feedback in peer-assessment processes with machine learning. *Computers & Education, 140*, 103609.

Rizzuto, M. (2017). Design recommendations for self-paced online faculty development courses. *TechTrends, 61*(1), 77–86. DOI: 10.1007/s11528-016-0130-8

Rodriguez, R. A. (2023). Competencies of modern musician entrepreneurs: The role of digitalization in the music industry [PhD Thesis, The University of Texas Rio Grande Valley]. https://search.proquest.com/openview/742693d86ebaacfd7ce21b59117f21b6/1?pq-origsite=gscholar&cbl=18750&diss=y

Rogers, J., & Revesz, A. (2019). Experimental and quasi-experimental designs. In *The Routledge handbook of research methods in applied linguistics* (pp. 133–143). Routledge., https://discovery.ucl.ac.uk/id/eprint/10091265/7/Revesz_Rogers%20Revesz_Experimental%20design%20book%20chapter.pd

Røkenes, F., & Krumsvik, R. (2016). Prepared to teach ESL with ECT? A study of digital competence inNorwegian teacher education. *Computers & Education*, *97*, 1–20.

Roll, I., & Wylie, R. (2016). Evolution and revolution in artificial intelligence in education. *International Journal of Artificial Intelligence in Education*, *26*(2), 582–599. DOI: 10.1007/s40593-016-0110-3

Romero, C., Espejo, P. G., Zafra, A., Romero, J. R., & Ventura, S. (2013). Web usage mining for predicting final marks of students that use Moodle courses. *Computer Applications in Engineering Education*, *21*(1), 135–146.

Rowe, M. (2019). Shaping our algorithms before they shape us. *Artificial intelligence and inclusive education: Speculative futures and emerging practices*, 151-163.

Runisah, R., Sudirman, S., Isnawan, M. G., Gunadi, F., Rosyadi, R., Son, A. L., & Assya, L. A. (2022). Impact of using augmented reality on students' cognitive and affective aspects in terms of education level. *International Journal of Science Education and Cultural Studies*, *1*(2), 2. Advance online publication. DOI: 10.58291/ijsecs.v1i2.51

Russo-Gleicher, R. J. (2013). Qualitative insights into faculty use of student support services with online students at risk: Implications for student retention. *The Journal of Educators Online*, *10*(1). Advance online publication. DOI: 10.9743/JEO.2013.1.4

Ryan, R. M., & Deci, E. L. (2000). Self-determination theory and the facilitation of intrinsic motivation, social development, and well-being. *The American Psychologist*, *55*(1), 68–78.

Ryan, R. M., & Deci, E. L. (2020). Intrinsic and extrinsic motivation from a self-determination theory perspective: Definitions, theory, practices, and future directions. *Contemporary Educational Psychology*, *61*, 101860. DOI: 10.1016/j.cedpsych.2020.101860

Ryan, R., & Deci, E. (2000). Self-determination theory and the facilitation of intrinsic motivation, social development and well-being. *The American Psychologist*, *55*(1), 68–78. DOI: 10.1037/0003066X.55.1.68

Saeedi, Z., & Najjarpour, M. (2025). Enhancing technical vocabulary acquisition in ESP context through virtual content development with Articulate Storyline. *Social Sciences & Humanities Open, 11*, 101539. DOI: 10.1016/j.ssaho.2025.101539

Safsouf, Y., & Mouachi, R. (2024). Empowering learners: GenIA and their impact on self-regulated learning. *ITM Web of Conferences, 69*, 01004. https://doi.org/DOI: 10.1051/itmconf/20246901004

Saint, J., Whitelock-Wainwright, A., Gašević, D., & Pardo, A. (2020). Trace-SRL: A framework for analysis of microlevel processes of self-regulated learning from trace data. *IEEE Transactions on Learning Technologies*, *13*(4), 861–877. DOI: 10.1109/TLT.2020.3027496

Samya, A. J. S. (2007). *Undergraduate Learners' Perceptions of Blended Learning and its Relationship with Some Demographic and Experiential Variables at the Arab Open University- Bahrain Branch*. University of United Arab Emirates.

Sanchez-Muñoz, R., Carrió, M., Rodríguez, G., Pérez, N., & Moyano, E. (2022). A hybrid strategy to develop real-life competences combining flipped classroom, jigsaw method and project-based learning. *Journal of Biological Education*, *56*(5), 540–551. DOI: 10.1080/00219266.2020.1858928

Sangsawang, T. (2020). An instructional design for online learning in vocational education according to a self-regulated learning framework for problem solving during the CoViD-19 crisis. *Indonesian Journal of Science and Technology*, *5*(2), 2.

Sansone, C., Fraughton, T., Zachary, J., Butner, J., & Heiner, C. (2011). Self-regulation of motivation when learning online: The important of who, why and how. *Educational Technology Research and Development*, *59*(2), 199–212. DOI: 10.1007/s11423-011-9193-6

Saraceni, G. (2023). Artificial Intelligence And Mental Health. *HUMANITIES AND RIGHTS GLOBAL NETWORK JOURNAL*, *5*(2). Advance online publication. DOI: 10.24861/2675-1038.v5i2.106

Scherer, R., Howard, S. K., Tondeur, J., & Siddiq, F. (2021). Profiling teachers' readiness for online teaching and learning in higher education: Who's ready? *Computers in Human Behavior*, *118*, 106675.

Schoenfeld. (2022). Why Are Learning and Teaching Mathematics So Difficult? In Handbook of Cognitive Mathematics (pp. 1–35). Springer International Publishing. https://doi.org/DOI: 10.1007/978-3-030-44982-7_10-1

Schunk, D. H., & Zimmerman, B. (2011). *Handbook of self-regulation of learning and performance*. Taylor & Francis.

Schunk, D. H., & Zimmerman, B. J. (2012). *Motivation and self-regulated learning: Theory, research, and applications*. Routledge.

Schunk, D. H., & Zimmerman, B. J. (2023). *Self-regulation of learning and performance: Issues and educational applications*. Taylor & Francis.

Schwab, K. (2017). *The Fourth Industrial Revolution*. Crown Business.

Seaba, V. E. S. (2023). Revolutionizing Education: Exploring the Potential of AI-Enabled Brain-Based Learning for Enhanced Cognitive Development. *OAlib*, *10*(10), 1–20.

Seedhouse, P. (2005). "Task" as research construct. *Language Learning*, *55*(3), 533–570.

Seibert Hanson, A. E., & Brown, C. M. (2020). Enhancing L2 learning through a mobile assisted spaced-repetition tool: An effective but bitter pill? *Computer Assisted Language Learning, 33*(1–2), 133–155. *Scopus*. Advance online publication. DOI: 10.1080/09588221.2018.1552975

Şen, N., & Akbay, T. (2023). Artificial intelligence and innovative applications in special education. *Instructional Technology and Lifelong Learning*, *4*(2), 176–199.

Seufert, S., Guggemos, J., & Sailer, M. (2021). Technology-related knowledge, skills, and attitudes of pre-and in-service teachers: The current situation and emerging trends. *Computers in Human Behavior*, *115*, 106552.

Seufert, T., Hamm, V., Vogt, A., & Riemer, V. (2024). The interplay of cognitive load, learners' resources and self-regulation. *Educational Psychology Review*, *36*(2), 50. DOI: 10.1007/s10648-024-09890-1

Shabani, M. B., & Ghasemi, A. (2014). The effect of task-based language teaching (TBLT) and content-based language teaching (CBLT) on the Iranian intermediate ESP learners' reading comprehension. *Procedia: Social and Behavioral Sciences*, *98*, 1713–1721.

Shafiee Rad, H. (2025). Reinforcing L2 reading comprehension through artificial intelligence intervention: Refining engagement to foster self-regulated learning. *Smart Learning Environments*, *12*(1), 23. DOI: 10.1186/s40561-025-00377-2

Shahloxon, B., & Yulduz, Q. (2024). Flipped Classroom Model. Analyze the Effectiveness of the Flipped Classroom Approach Compared to Tradition Teaching Methods in Various Subjects or Grade Levels. Yangi O 'zbekiston Ustozlari, 2(28), 128–134. https://cyberleninka.ru/article/n/flipped-classroom-model-analyze-the-effectiveness-of-the-flipped-classroom-approach-compared-to-traditional-teaching-methods-in

Shah, P. (2023). *AI and the Future of Education: Teaching in the Age of Artificial Intelligence*. John Wiley & Sons.

Shaikh, U. U., & Asif, Z. (2022). Persistence and dropout in higher online education: Review and categorization of factors. *Frontiers in Psychology*, *13*, 902070. DOI: 10.3389/fpsyg.2022.902070

Shao, H., & Yu, Z. (2025). Inclusive approaches to liberal arts education in the context of the creative economy: Integrating access, engagement, and technological literacy. *International Journal of Inclusive Education*, •••, 1–28.

Sharma, K., Nguyen, A., & Hong, Y. (2024). Self-regulation and shared regulation in collaborative learning in adaptive digital learning environments: A systematic review of empirical studies. *British Journal of Educational Technology*, *55*(4), 1398–1436. DOI: 10.1111/bjet.13459

She, M., Tan, Y., & Li, Z. (2024). Antecedents of college students' continuance behaviors in online fragmented learning: An empirical analysis from the extended ECM perspective. *Sustainability*, *16*(10), 10. Advance online publication. DOI: 10.3390/su16104138

Sheninger, E. C. (2016). *Uncommon learning: Creating schools that work for kids*. Corwin.

Sherman, M. (2014). The role of technology in supporting students' mathematical thinking: Extending the metaphors of amplifier and reorganizer. *Contemporary Issues in Technology & Teacher Education*, *14*(3), 220–246.

Shoaib, M., Sayed, N., Singh, J., Shafi, J., Khan, S., & Ali, F. (2024). AI student success predictor: Enhancing personalized learning in campus management systems. *Computers in Human Behavior*, *158*, 108301. DOI: 10.1016/j.chb.2024.108301

Shukla, A., Choudhari, S. G., Gaidhane, A. M., Syed, Z. Q., & Gaidhane, A. (2022). Role of art therapy in the promotion of mental health: A critical review. *Cureus*, *14*(8). Advance online publication. DOI: 10.7759/cureus.28026

Shuwen, L. E. I. (2024). Relevance of Music Education in the Cultural Program of Contemporary College Students. US-China Education Review, 14(1), 56–59. https://www.academia.edu/download/110947221/The_1st_issue_of_2024_Volume_14_Number_1_January_2024_Serial_Number_118_.pdf#page=61

Silverajah, V. G., Wong, S. L., Govindaraj, A., Khambari, M. N. M., Rahmat, R. W. B. O., & Deni, A. R. M. (2022). A systematic review of self-regulated learning in flipped classrooms: Key findings, measurement methods, and potential directions. *IEEE Access : Practical Innovations, Open Solutions, 10*, 20270–20294. https://ieeexplore.ieee.org/abstract/document/9684384/

Simones, L. (2024). Advancing Excellence in Teaching: Professionalizing Vocal and Instrumental Music Education. In The Applied Studio Model in Higher Music Education (pp. 34–60). Routledge. https://www.taylorfrancis.com/chapters/edit/10.4324/9781003426448-4/advancing-excellence-teaching-lilian-simones

Singh, J., Evans, E., Reed, A., Karch, L., Qualey, K., Singh, L., & Wiersma, H. (2021). Online, hybrid, and face-to-face learning through the eyes of faculty, students, administrators, and instructional designers: Lessons learned and directions for the post-vaccine and post-pandemic/COVID-19 world. *Journal of Educational Technology Systems, 50*(3), 301–326. https://journals.sagepub.com/doi/epub/10.1177/00472395211063754

Siyam, N. (2019). Factors impacting special education teachers' acceptance and actual use of technology. *Education and Information Technologies, 24*(3), 2035–2057.

Smalley, S. (2021). Half of all students take online courses. *Inside Higher Ed.* https://www.insidehighered.com/news/2021/10/13/new-us-data-show-jump-college-students-learning-online

Solhi, M., & Büyükyazı, M. (2011, May). The use of first language in the EFL classroom: A facilitating or debilitating device. In Proceedings of the 1st international conference on foreign language teaching and applied linguistics, Sarajevo, Bosnia and Herzegovina.

Somekh, B. (2008). Factors affecting teachers' pedagogical adoption of ICT. In Voogt, J., & Knezek, G. (Eds.), *International handbook of information technology in primary and secondary education* (pp. 449–460). Springer.

Stern, H. H. (1983). *Fundamental concepts of language teaching: Historical and interdisciplinary perspectives on applied linguistic research.* Oxford university press.

Sucaromana, U. (2013). The Effect of Blended Learning on the Intrinsic Motivation of Thai EFL Students. *English Language Teaching, 6*(5), 141–147.

Sun, Y., Loo, F. C., & Yeoh, P. S. (2025). APPLICATION OF FLIPPED CLASSROOM IN MUSIC EDUCATION: A SCOPING REVIEW. Arts Educa, 42. https://artseduca.com/submissions/index.php/ae/article/view/448

Su, N. A. (2019). Research on the Teaching Practice of Task-based College English Writing Based on SPOC. *2nd Asia-Pacific Social Science and Modern Education Conference* (ISBN: 978-1-60595-678-7).

Sun, A., & Chen, X. (2016). Online education and its effective practice: A research review. *Journal of Information Technology Education, 15*, 157–190. http://www.jite.org/documents/Vol15/JITEv15ResearchP157-190Sun2138.pdf

Sung, H. Y., Hwang, G. J., Lin, C. J., & Hong, T. W. (2017). Experiencing the analects of Confucius: An experiential game-based learning approach to promoting students' motivation and conception of learning. *Computers & Education, 110*, 143–153.

Sun, H. (2019). A SPOC teaching mode of college English translation based on" Rain Classroom [iJET]. *International Journal of Emerging Technologies in Learning, 14*(17), 182–193.

Sun, J. C.-Y., & Rueda, R. (2012). Situational interest, computer self-efficacy and self-regulation: Their impact on student engagement in distance education. *British Journal of Educational Technology, 43*(2), 191–204.

Sutherland, R., & Fischer, F. (2014). Future learning spaces: Design, collaboration, knowledge, assessment, teachers, technology and the radical past. *Technology, Pedagogy and Education, 23*(1), 1–5. DOI: 10.1080/1475939X.2013.870107

Svensson, I., Nordström, T., Lindeblad, E., Gustafson, S., Björn, M., Sand, C., & Nilsson, S. (2021). Effects of assistive technology for students with reading and writing disabilities. *Disability and Rehabilitation. Assistive Technology, 16*(2), 196–208.

Swan, M. (2005). Legislation by hypothesis: The case of task-based instruction. *Applied Linguistics, 26*(3), 376–401.

Swanwick, K. (2023). *Instrumental teaching as music teaching, in teaching music in secondary schools: A reader* (Sprace, G., Ed.).

Sweller, J. (1988). Cognitive load during problem solving: Effects on learning. *Cognitive Science, 12*(2), 257–285. DOI: 10.1016/0364-0213(88)90023-7

Sweller, J. (1994). Cognitive load theory, learning difficulty, and instructional design. *Learning and Instruction, 4*(4), 295–312. DOI: 10.1016/0959-4752(94)90003-5

Sweller, J., van Merriënboer, J. J. G., & Paas, F. (2019). Cognitive architecture and instructional design: 20 years later. *Educational Psychology Review*, *31*(2), 261–292. DOI: 10.1007/s10648-019-09465-5

Tabassum, B., Moin, M., Abbas, Q., Kumbhar, M. I., & Khan, M. H. N. (2024). The impact of blended learning on student performance. *Journal of Education and Social Studies*, *5*(2), 360–371. DOI: 10.52223/jess.2024.5217

Talbert, R., & Bergmann, J. (2023). Flipped learning: A guide for higher education faculty. Routledge. https://www.taylorfrancis.com/books/mono/10.4324/9781003444848/flipped-learning-robert-talbert-jon-bergmann

Tan, C. (2020). Digital Confucius? Exploring the implications of artificial intelligence in spiritual education. *Connection Science*, *32*(3), 280–291.

Tang, H., Chiou, J. S., & Jarsaillon, O. (2015). Efficacy of Task-Based Learning in a Chinese EFL Classroom: A Case. *Study in English Language Teaching*, *8*(5), 168–176.

Tang, Q., Zhang, T., & Jiang, L. (2023). Influence of blended instruction on students' learning effectiveness: The role of Flow. *Education and Information Technologies*, *28*(2), 1891–1909. PMID: 35967827

Tavassoli, K., & Beyranvand, S. (2023). How Instagram as a MALL tool impacts EAP learners' technical vocabulary learning and perceptions in an electronic context. *SN Social Sciences*, *3*(4), 70. DOI: 10.1007/s43545-023-00657-z

Taxipulati, S., & Lu, H. D. (2021). The Influence of Feedback Content and Feedback Time on Multimedia Learning Achievement of College Students and Its Mechanism. *Frontiers in Psychology*, *12*, 706821. DOI: 10.3389/fpsyg.2021.706821

Teimouri, M. (2024). Comparing Human and AI Emotion and Sentiment Analysis in Mixed Reality and Zoom Environments. https://www.utupub.fi/bitstream/handle/10024/178872/TeimouriBadelehDareh_Maryam_Thesis.pdf?sequence=1

Teng, L. S. (2022). *Self-regulated learning and second language writing: Fostering strategic language learners*. Springer Nature.

Teng, M. F. (2023). The effectiveness of multimedia input on vocabulary learning and retention. *Innovation in Language Learning and Teaching*, *17*(3), 738–754.

Teng, M., & Xu, J. (2025). Pushing vocabulary knowledge from receptive to productive mastery: Effects of task type and repetition frequency. *Language Teaching Research*, *29*(2), 588–606. DOI: 10.1177/13621688221077028

Terefe, A., Kant, S., Adula, M., & Gonfa, K. K. (2025). Reshaping Brand Interactions in the Experience-Driven Economy by Mediation of AI-Powered Marketing in the Horn of Africa. In *Leveraging AI-Powered Marketing in the Experience-Driven Economy* (pp. 181–202). IGI Global Scientific Publishing.

Thacker, E. S. (2017). "PD is where teachers are learning!" high school social studies teachers formal and informal professional learning. *Journal of Social Studies Research, 41*(1), 37–52.

Thamarana, S., & Narayana, T. (2016). A Critical Overview of Teaching English to Speakers of Other Languages. *First Language, 1*, L2.

Theide, R. (2012). Best practices with online courses. *US-China Education Review, 2*, 135–141. http://files.eric.ed.gov/fulltext/ED532176.pdf

Thornbury, S. (2007). *How to teach speaking*. Longma.

Tian, J., & Su, Y. (2023). The Role of Music Ethnography in Promoting Intercultural Art Education Communication and Cross-cultural Communication Sustainable Culturally Notch. Arts Educa, 36. https://artseduca.com/submissions/index.php/ae/article/view/59

Tichko, P., Kim, J. C., & Large, E. W. (2022). A dynamical, radically embodied, and ecological theory of rhythm development. *Frontiers in Psychology, 13*, 653696. https://www.frontiersin.org/articles/10.3389/fpsyg.2022.653696/full

Tigert, J. M., & Leider, C. M. (2022). Beyond the "core": Preparing art educators to meet the needs of culturally and linguistically diverse students. *TESOL Quarterly, 56*(1), 425–434.

Tirrel, T., & Quick, D. (2012). Chickering's seven principles of good practice: Student attrition in community college online courses. *Community College Journal of Research and Practice, 36*(8), 580–590.

Tomlinson, C. A. (2023). The parallel curriculum model: A design to develop potential & challenge high-ability learners. In *Systems and models for developing programs for the gifted and talented* (pp. 571–598). Routledge.

Tong, D. H., Uyen, B. P., & Ngan, L. K. (2022). The Effectiveness of Blended Learning on Students' Academic Achievement, Self-Study Skills and Learning Attitudes: A Quasi-Experiment Study in Teaching the Conventions for Coordinates in the Plane. *Heliyon, 8*, e12657. DOI: 10.1016/j.heliyon.2022.e12657 PMID: 36643330

Trach, Y. (2021). Artificial intelligence as a tool for creating and analysing works of art. Culture and arts in the modern world, 22, 164-173. DOI: 10.31866/2410-1915.22.2021.235907

Udaya, M. (2022). Using semantic maps as a teaching strategy for vocabulary development. *European Journal of English Language Teaching*, *6*(5), 5. Advance online publication. DOI: 10.46827/ejel.v6i5.4095

United Nations. (2008). *Convention on the rights of persons with disabilities*. United Nations.

Urbina, S., Villatoro, S., & Salinas, J. (2021). Self-regulated learning and technology-enhanced learning environments in higher education: A scoping review. *Sustainability*, *13*(13), 13. Advance online publication. DOI: 10.3390/su13137281

Valiathan, P. (2022). *Beginner's Guide to Instructional Design: Identify and Examine Learning Needs, Knowledge Delivery....* Methods, and Approaches to Design Learning Materia. Bhaktivedanta Book Trust.

van As, J., & Cooke, R. (2024). Immersive virtual community engagement: Unleashing the potential of AI avatars and virtual reality in education to enhance learning excellence. In *Integrating cutting-edge technology into the classroom* (pp. 162–183). IGI Global.

Van de Vord, R., & Pogue, K. (2012). Teaching time investment: Does online really take more time than face-to-face? *International Review of Research in Open and Distance Learning*, *13*(3). http://www.irrodl.org/index.php/irrodl/article/view/1190/2212

Van Laer, S., & Elen, J. (2017). In search of attributes that support self-regulation in blended learning environments. *Education and Information Technologies*, *22*(4), 1395–1454.

Van Lier, L. (Ed.). (2004). The Ecology and Semiotics of Language Learning: A Sociocultural Perspective. In L. Van Lier, M. C. Cavalcanti, H. Janks, C. Kramsch, & A. Pennycook (Eds.), *Theories of Language* (Vol. 3, pp. 23–53). Springer Netherlands. https://doi.org/DOI: 10.1007/1-4020-7912-5_2

van Merriënboer, J. J. G., & Sweller, J. (2005). Cognitive load theory and complex learning: Recent developments and future directions. *Educational Psychology Review*, *17*(2), 147–177. DOI: 10.1007/s10648-005-3951-0

Vargo, A., Yamaguchi, K., Iwata, M., & Kise, K. (2024). A Context-Based Multimedia Vocabulary Learning System for Mobile Users. *Informatics, 11*(1). *Scopus*. Advance online publication. DOI: 10.3390/informatics11010001

Vartiainen, H., & Tedre, M. (2023). Using artificial intelligence in craft education: Crafting with text-to-image generative models. *Digital Creativity*, *34*(1), 1–21.

Vaughan, N. D., Cleveland-Innes, M., & Garrison, D. R. (2013). *Teaching in blended learning environments: Creating and sustaining communities of inquiry*. Athabasca University Press.

Vaz, S., Wilson, N., Falkmer, M., Sim, A., Scott, M., Cordier, R., & Falkmer, T. (2015). Factors associated with primary school teachers' attitudes towards the inclusion of students with disabilities. *PLoS One*, *10*(8), e0137002.

Vekkot, S., Gupta, D., Zakariah, M., & Alotaibi, Y. A. (2020). Emotional voice conversion using a hybrid framework with speaker-adaptive DNN and particle-swarm-optimized neural network. *IEEE Access : Practical Innovations, Open Solutions*, *8*, 74627–74647. DOI: 10.1109/ACCESS.2020.2988781

Velastegui, D., Pérez, M. L. R., & Garcés, L. F. S. (2023). Impact of Artificial Intelligence on learning behaviors and psychological well-being of college students. Salud, Ciencia y Tecnologia-Serie de Conferencias, (2), 343. Scherer, L. A., & Leshner, A. I. (Eds.). (2021). Mental health, substance use, and wellbeing in higher education: Supporting the whole student.

Vijver, F. V. D. (1997). Meta-analysis of cross-cultural comparisons of cognitive test performance. *Journal of Cross-Cultural Psychology*, *28*(6), 678–709. DOI: 10.1177/0022022197286003

Von Keyserlingk, L., Yamaguchi-Pedroza, K., Arum, R., & Eccles, J. S. (2022). Stress of university students before and after campus closure in response to COVID-19. *Journal of Community Psychology*, *50*(1), 285–301. DOI: 10.1002/jcop.22561

Vrasidas, C. (2000). Constructivism versus objectivism: Implications for interaction, course design, and evaluation in distance education. *International Journal of Educational Telecommunications*, *6*(4), 339–362.

Vygotsky, L. S. (1978). Thought and language (Vol. 29). MIT press. https://books.google.com/books?hl=zh-CN&lr=&id=B9HClB0P6d4C&oi=fnd&pg=PR9&dq=thought+and+Language%EF%BC%8CVygotsky,+1978&ots=TuJaWag3Qs&sig=gaUdgsZqDveJxJMoxFdjextZrmw

Vygotsky, L. S. (1978). Interaction between Learning and Development. In Cole, M., John-Steiner, V., Scribner, S., & Souberman, E. (Eds.), *Mind and Society: The Development of Higher Psychological Processes* (pp. 79–91). Harvard University Press.

Walker, A., Gray, J., & Evans, K. (2025). Qualitative case study on virtual simulations engaging educational leadership candidates in ethical scenarios that positively impacted leadership skills. *International Journal of Research in Education Methodology, 15*(2024).

Walldén, R. (2024). Contextual elaborations and shifts when adult L2 learners present and discuss workplace-related vocabulary. *Linguistics and Education, 80*, 101272. DOI: 10.1016/j.linged.2024.101272

Wang, C., li, H., & Shang, J. (2017). Application and development prospect of educational games based on virtual reality and augmented reality.*Application and Development Prospects of Educational Games Based on Virtual Reality and Augmented Reality.*

Wang, C. K., Liu, W. C., Kee, Y. H., & Chian, L. K. (2019). Competence, autonomy, and relatedness in the classroom: Understanding students' motivational processes using the self-determination theory. *Heliyon, 5*, 1–6. PMID: 31372524

Wang, H. (2018). The application of flipped classroom in Colleges and Universities piano collective classes. *Creative Education, 9*(7), 1021–1026. https://www.scirp.org/journal/paperinformation?paperid=85100

Wang, J. (2024). Research on the Flipped Classroom + Learning Community Approach and Its Effectiveness Evaluation—Taking College German Teaching as a Case Study. *Sustainability, 16*(17), 17. Advance online publication. DOI: 10.3390/su16177719

Wang, J., & Abdullah, A. B. (2024). A summary of expressive arts therapy and painting therapy. *Creative Education, 15*(2), 278–288. DOI: 10.4236/ce.2024.152016

Wang, J., & Jou, M. (2023). The influence of mobile-learning flipped classrooms on the emotional learning and cognitive flexibility of students of different levels of learning achievement. *Interactive Learning Environments, 31*(3), 1309–1321. DOI: 10.1080/10494820.2020.1830806

Wang, L., Othakanon, L., & Saleewong, D. (2025). Development of Music Appreciation Course Based on Case Based Learning and Flipped Classroom to Enhance Music Appreciation Ability for First Year Students in Yan'an University. *International Journal of Sociologies and Anthropologies Science Reviews, 5*(1), 347–358. https://so07.tci-thaijo.org/index.php/IJSASR/article/view/5241

Wang, M., Zhang, D., Zhu, J., & Gu, H. (2025). Effects of incorporating a large language model-based adaptive mechanism into contextual games on students' academic performance, flow experience, cognitive load and behavioral patterns. *Journal of Educational Computing Research, 63*(3), 662–694. DOI: 10.1177/07356331251321719

Wang, Q., Han, X., & Yang, S. (2015). Revisiting the blended learning literature: Using a complex adaptive systems framework. *Journal of Educational Technology & Society, 18*(2), 380–393. http://www.jstor.org/stable/jeductechsoci.18.2.380

Wang, S., Wang, F., Zhu, Z., Wang, J., Tran, T., & Du, Z. (2024). Artificial intelligence in education: A systematic literature review. *Expert Systems with Applications, 252*, 124167.

Wang, T., & Lajoie, S. P. (2023). How does cognitive load interact with Self-Regulated learning? A dynamic and integrative model. *Educational Psychology Review, 35*(3), 69. DOI: 10.1007/s10648-023-09794-6

Wang, Z. (2025). Integrating mobile apps into vocal education: A study on accessibility and efficiency in learning. *Education and Information Technologies, 30*(9), 12179–12196. DOI: 10.1007/s10639-024-13301-x

Wan, Y. (2023). The impact and value of interdisciplinary collaboration on higher education art and design courses. *Frontiers in Educational Research, 6*(28), 186–192. DOI: 10.25236/FER.2023.062826

Warden, C. A., Yi-Shun, W., Stanworth, J. O., & Chen, J. F. (2022). Millennials' technology readiness and self-efficacy in online classes. *Innovations in Education and Teaching International, 59*(2), 226–236.

Ward, M., Peters, G., & Shelley, K. (2010). Student and faculty perceptions of the quality of online learning experiences. *International Review of Research in Open and Distance Learning, 11*(3). http://www.irrodl.org/index.php/irrodl/article/view/867/1610

Watts, L. (2016). Synchronous and asynchronous communication in distance learning: A review of the literature. *Quarterly Review of Distance Education, 17*(1), 23.

Webster, J., & Watson, R. T. (2002). Analyzing the past to prepare for the future: Writing a literature review. *Management Information Systems Quarterly, 26*(2), xiii–xxiii. https://www.jstor.org/stable/4132319

Weiger, E. A. (2021). Flipped Lessons and the Secondary-Level Performance-Based Music Classroom: A Review of Literature and Suggestions for Practice. Update. *Applications of Research in Music Education, 39*(2), 44–53. DOI: 10.1177/8755123320953629

Wei, L. (2023). Artificial intelligence in language instruction: Impact on English learning achievement, L2 motivation, and self-regulated learning. *Frontiers in Psychology, 14*. Advance online publication. DOI: 10.3389/fpsyg.2023.1261955 PMID: 38023040

Wei, L., Dew, T. P., & Said, N. (2024). The development of a SPOC platform for EFL listening instruction in Higher education. [IJELP]. *International Journal on E-Learning Practices, 7*(1).

Weiner, B. (2010). The development of an attribution-based theory of motivation: A history of ideas. *Educational Psychologist, 45*(1), 28–36.

Wenjing, X., & Cai, Z. (2023). Assessing the best art design based on artificial intelligence and machine learning using GTMA. *Soft Computing, 27*(1), 149–156.

Westelinck, K. D., Valcke, M., De Craene, B., & Kirschner, P. (2005). Multimedia learning in social sciences: Limitations of external graphical representations. *Computers in Human Behavior, 21*(4), 555–573. DOI: 10.1016/j.chb.2004.10.030

Willis, J. (2013). *A Framework for Task Based Learning*. Longma.

Wilson, M. (2024). The role of multimodal learning in enhancing language acquisition for bilingual learners. *Emerging Education Research, 2*, 1–11.

Wiratno, T. A., & Callula, B. (2024). Transformation of beauty in digital fine arts aesthetics: An artpreneur perspective. Aptisi Transactions on Technopreneurship (ATT), 6(2), 231-241. https://orcid.org/0009-0008-5662-4249

Wisniewski, B., Zierer, K., & Hattie, J. (2020). The power of feedback revisited: A meta-analysis of educational feedback research. *Frontiers in Psychology, 10*, 3087. DOI: 10.3389/fpsyg.2019.03087

World Health Organization, & United Nations Children's Fund. (2022). *Global report on assistive technology*. World Health Organization. Geneva.

Wuhue, J. (2023). Do SPOC Really Improve Student Learning in Vocational Schools? A Meta-Analysis of Studies in Chinese Contexts. *Turkish Online Journal of Educational Technology-TOJET, 22*(1), 49–59.

Xia, Q., Chiu, T. K. F., & Chai, C. S. (2023). The moderating effects of gender and need satisfaction on self-regulated learning through artificial intelligence (AI). *Education and Information Technologies, 28*(7), 8691–8713. DOI: 10.1007/s10639-022-11547-x

Xia, Q., Chiu, T. K. F., Chai, C. S., & Xie, K. (2023). The mediating effects of needs satisfaction on the relationships between prior knowledge and self-regulated learning through artificial intelligence chatbot. *British Journal of Educational Technology, 54*(4), 967–986. DOI: 10.1111/bjet.13305

Xing, B., & Zhang, H. (2025). A study of the effect of multimodal input on vocabulary acquisition: Evidence from online Chinese language learners. *Language Teaching Research, 13621688241313017*. Advance online publication. DOI: 10.1177/13621688241313017

Xing, H. (2023). Current situation and research on English teaching in Higher vocational colleges under the information environment. *China New Communications, 25*(17), 221–223.

Xodabande, I., Atai, M. R., & Hashemi, M. R. (2024). Exploring the effectiveness of mobile assisted learning with digital flashcards in enhancing long-term retention of technical vocabulary among university students. *Journal of Computers in Education*. Advance online publication. DOI: 10.1007/s40692-024-00347-6

Xu, D., & Jaggars, S. S. (2011). *Online and hybrid course enrollment and performance in Washington State Community and Technical Colleges*. Community College Research Center.

Xu, G., Lin, Y., Ye, Y., Wu, W., Zhang, X., & Xiao, H. (2024). Combination of concept maps and case-based learning in a flipped classroom: A mixed-methods study. *Nurse Education in Practice, 76*, 103918. https://www.sciencedirect.com/science/article/pii/S1471595324000477

Xu, J., Zhang, X., Li, H., Yoo, C., & Pan, Y. (2023). Is everyone an artist? A study on user experience of AI-based painting system. *Applied Sciences (Basel, Switzerland), 13*(11), 6496. DOI: 10.3390/app13116496

Xu, J., Zhang, X., & Li, W. (2023). Exploring user acceptance of AI-based painting systems in China: An extended TAM model approach. Preprint, 528 participants. https://doi.org/DOI: 10.20944/preprints202304.0593.v1

Xu, J., Zhang, Y., & Li, W. (2023). Exploring user acceptance of AI-based painting systems in China: An extended TAM model approach. *Computers & Education, 205*, 104786. DOI: 10.1016/j.compedu.2023.104786

Xu, T., Xu, J., Xu, X., & Lu, J. (2023). Blended Learning on WeChat Platform-Based SPOC in Lower-Secondary School Science Teaching. *Journal of Baltic Science Education, 22*(4), 701–718.

Xu, Y. (2022). An adaptive learning system for English vocabulary using machine learning. *Mobile Information Systems*, *2022*(1), 3501494. DOI: 10.1155/2022/3501494

Yadav, U., & Shrawankar, U. (2025). Artificial intelligence across industries: A comprehensive review with a focus on education. *AI applications and strategies in teacher education*, 275-320. Doi: DOI: 10.4018/979-8-3693-5443-8.ch010

Yang, M., Badger, R., & Yu, Z. (2006). A comparative study of peer and teacher feedback in a Chinese EFL writing class. *Journal of Second Language Writing*, *15*(3), 179–200. DOI: 10.1016/j.jslw.2006.09.004

Yang, W., Zhang, X., Chen, X., Lu, J., & Tian, F. (2024). Based case based learning and flipped classroom as a means to improve international students' active learning and critical thinking ability. *BMC Medical Education*, *24*(1). Advance online publication. DOI: 10.1186/s12909-024-05758-8

Yasmeen, Z., Mushtaq, I., & Murad, M. (2019). Intrinsic and extrinsic motivation of teachers in special education secondary school: A qualitative study. *The Journal of Educational Research*, *22*(2), 15–30.

Yee, C. H., & Ganapathy, M. (2017). To Investigate ESL Students' Instrumental and Integrative Motivation towards English Language Learning in a Chinese School in Penang: Case Study. *Journal of English Language Teaching*, *10*(9), 17–35.

Ye, Z., Sirivesmas, V., Joneurairatana, E., & Simatrang, S. (2025, January). Design and Application of Painting Teaching System based on Hyperlink-Induced Topic Search Algorithm. In *2025 International Conference on Intelligent Systems and Computational Networks (ICISCN)* (pp. 1-7). IEEE.

Yildirim-Erbasli, S. N., Gorgun, G., Bulut, O., Yildirim-Erbasli, S. N., Gorgun, G., & Bulut, O. (2023). *Enhancing self-regulated learning with artificial intelligence-powered learning analytics*.66-4.Ch004; IGI Global Scientific Publishing. https://doi.org/DOI: 10.4018/979-8-3693-0066-4.ch004

Yilmaz, H., & Zahal, O. (2023). Effects of Flipped Learning-Based Guitar Instruction on Motivation, Attitude, and Accompaniment Skills. *Journal of Pedagogical Research*, *7*(1), 307–321. https://eric.ed.gov/?id=EJ1381384

Yoon, M., Hill, J., & Kim, D. (2021). Designing supports for promoting self-regulated learning in the flipped classroom. *Journal of Computing in Higher Education*, *33*(2), 398–418. DOI: 10.1007/s12528-021-09269-z

York, T. T., Gibson, C., & Rankin, S. (2015). Defining and measuring academic success. *Practical Assessment, Research & Evaluation*, *20*(5), n5.

You, J. W. (2015). Examining the effect of academic procrastination on achievement using LMS data in e-learning. *Journal of Educational Technology & Society, 18*(3), 64–74. http://www.ifets.info/journals/18_3/5.pdf

Yu, A., & Trainin, G. (2022). A meta-analysis examining technology-assisted L2 vocabulary learning. *ReCALL, 34*(2), 235–252. DOI: 10.1017/S0958344021000239

Yu, D., Ding, M., Li, W., Wang, L., & Liang, B. (2019). Designing an artificial intelligence platform to assist undergraduate in art and design to develop a personal learning plans. In *Design, User Experience, and Usability. Application Domains: 8th International Conference, DUXU 2019, Held as Part of the 21st HCI International Conference, HCII 2019, Orlando, FL, USA, July 26–31, 2019* [Springer International Publishing.]. *Proceedings, 21*(Part III), 528–538.

Yüksel, H. G., Mercanoğlu, H. G., & Yılmaz, M. B. (2022). Digital flashcards vs. Wordlists for learning technical vocabulary. *Computer Assisted Language Learning, 35*(8), 2001–2017. DOI: 10.1080/09588221.2020.1854312

Yukselturk, E., & Bulut, S. (2007). Predictors for student success in an online course. *Journal of Educational Technology & Society, 10*(2), 71–83.

Yunkun, L. (2024). The Impact of Music Education on the Quality of Talent Cultivation. Transactions on Comparative Education, 6(1), 72–77. https://pdfs.semanticscholar.org/c047/d65f57261a2aece2889f7664c5e191a26634.pdf

Yusuf, B., & Taiye, M. A. (2021). A flipped learning environment: A disruptive approach for traditional classrooms. International Journal of Education, Psychology and Counseling, 6(42), 83–93. https://www.academia.edu/download/93937120/ijepc.pdf

Zainuddin, Z., Muluk, S., & Keumala, C. M. (2024). How do students become self-directed learners in the EFL flipped-class pedagogy? A study in higher education. *Indonesian Journal of Applied Linguistics, 8*(3), 678–690. https://researchnow.flinders.edu.au/en/publications/how-do-students-become-self-directed-learners-in-the-efl-flipped-

Zarei, S., & Mohammadi, S. (2022). Challenges of higher education related to e-learning in developing countries during COVID-19 spread: A review of the perspectives of students, instructors, policymakers, and ICT experts. *Environmental Science and Pollution Research International, 29*(57), 85562–85568. DOI: 10.1007/s11356-021-14647-2

Zawacki-Richter, O., Marín, V. I., Bond, M., & Gouverneur, F. (2019). Systematic review of research on artificial intelligence applications in higher education – where are the educators? *International Journal of Educational Technology in Higher Education, 16*(1), 39. DOI: 10.1186/s41239-019-0171-0

Zeng, S., & Della, C. (2024). A Systematic Review of Professional Communication Skills in English for Specific Purposes in Vocational Education within the New Media Era. *Eurasian Journal of Educational Research, 114*, 226–249.

Zeng, S., & Rahim, N., & Xu, S. (2025). Enhancing College Students' Achievement, Motivation and Engagement in Film Character Design through AI-Driven Smart sketchpad: A Personalized Interactive Learning Model for Art Education. *IEEE Access : Practical Innovations, Open Solutions*. Advance online publication.

Zhai, Q. (2022). Application of artificial intelligence in art design. In *2021 International Conference on Big Data Analytics for Cyber-Physical System in Smart City:* Volume 2 (pp. 981-986). Springer Singapore.

Zhang, M., & Fang, X. (2022). Exploring University EFL Teachers' Technological Pedagogical Content Knowledge and Teacher Efficacy in Technology-integrated Flipped Classroom. https://journals.sagepub.com/doi/full/10.1177/21582440221116105

Zhang, X., Li, H., Luo, Y., & Qian, C. (2023). [Exploration of online–offline blended teaching model for plant physiology experiments]. *New Education Era E-magazine (Teacher Edition),* (1). [in Chinese]

Zhang, C., & Lu, Y. (2021). Study on artificial intelligence: The state of the art and future prospects. *Journal of Industrial Information Integration, 23*, 100224. DOI: 10.1016/j.jii.2021.100224

Zhang, H. (2025). An action research on multimodal online teaching and vocabulary acquisition among chinese fifth-grade EFL learners. *International Journal of Social Science and Human Research, 08*(05), 3182–3199. DOI: 10.47191/ijsshr/v8-i5-63

Zhang, H. (2025). An Action Research on Multimodal Online Teaching and Vocabulary Acquisition Among Chinese Fifth-Grade EFL Learners. *International Journal of Social Science and Human Research, 08*(05), 3182–3199. DOI: 10.5281/zenodo.15469401

Zhang, H., Zhang, J., Wang, J., & Zhang, H. (2023). Integrating mobile learning and SPOC-based flipped classroom to teach a course in water supply and drainage science and engineering. *Computer Applications in Engineering Education.*

Zhang, L.-X., Leung, B.-W., & Yang, Y. (2023). From theory to practice: Student-centered pedagogical implementation in primary music demonstration lessons in Guangdong, China. *International Journal of Music Education, 41*(2), 271–287. DOI: 10.1177/02557614221107170

Zhang, L., Xuan, Y., & Zhang, H. (2020). Construction and application of SPOC-based flipped classroom teaching mode in Installation Engineering Cost curriculum based on OBE concept. *Computer Applications in Engineering Education*, *28*(6), 1503–1519.

Zhang, R., Zou, Di, & and Xie, H. (2022). Spaced repetition for authentic mobile-assisted word learning: Nature, learner perceptions, and factors leading to positive perceptions. *Computer Assisted Language Learning*, *35*(9), 2593–2626. DOI: 10.1080/09588221.2021.1888752

Zhang, T. (2025). Constructing and evaluating the effects of an immersive teaching mode for art education based on machine learning. *Journal of Computational Methods in Sciences and Engineering*, *25*(1), 355–369.

Zhang, X. M., Yu, J. Y., Yang, Y., Feng, C. P., Lyu, J., & Xu, S. L. (2019). A flipped classroom method based on a small private online course in physiology. *Advances in Physiology Education*, *43*(3), 345–349.

Zhang, Z. (2025). The Teaching Method of STEAM Education-based Audio-visual Aesthetics in College Vocal Music Teaching. *Frontiers in Educational Research*, *8*(2). Advance online publication. DOI: 10.25236/fer.2025.080216

Zhao, Y. (2023). Discussion on the Role of Basic Music Education in Cultivating Aesthetic Personality. Curriculum and Teaching Methodology, 6(15), 68–76. http://166.62.7.99/assets/default/article/2023/08/07/article_1691401000.pdf

Zhao, K. (2022). A Study on the Blending Learning Based on SPOC-Taking the Teaching Practice of "Practical English Writing" as an Example. *Journal of Educational Research and Policies*, *04*(09), 132–135.

Zhao, L., He, W., & Su, Y.-S. (2021). Innovative pedagogy and design-based research on flipped learning in higher education. *Frontiers in Psychology*, *12*, 577002. https://www.frontiersin.org/articles/10.3389/fpsyg.2021.577002/full

Zhu, C., Valcke, M., & Schellens, T. (2010). A cross-cultural study of teacher perspectives on teacher roles and adoption of online collaborative learning in higher education. *European Journal of Teacher Education*, *33*(2), 147–165.

Zhu, M., Berri, S., Koda, R., & Wu, Y. J. (2024). Exploring students' self-directed learning strategies and satisfaction in online learning. *Education and Information Technologies*, *29*(3), 2787–2803.

Zhu, Q., Jamaludin, K. A., Nasri, N. M., & Li, J. (2025). Flipped classroom for music theory course in Chinese universities: A conceptual framework of practice. *Cogent Education*, *12*(1). Advance online publication. DOI: 10.1080/2331186x.2025.2498146

Zhu, Y. (2022). Research on mixed teaching practice of industrial English based on SPOC. *Overseas English*, *7*, 228–230.

Zimmerman, B. J. (2009). Self-regulation: Where metacognition and motivation intersect. *In Handbook of metacognition in education*, 311–328.

Zimmerman, B. J. (2015). Self-regulated learning: Theories, measures, and outcomes. *International Encyclopedia of the Social & Behavioral Sciences*, 541–546. https://doi.org/DOI: 10.1016/b978-0-08-097086-8.26060-1

Zimmerman. (2002). *Becoming a self-regulated learner: An overview: Theory into practice: Vol 41, no 2*. https://www.tandfonline.com/doi/abs/10.1207/s15430421tip4102_2

Zimmerman, B. J. (1990). Self-regulated learning and academic achievement: An overview. *Educational Psychologist*, *25*(1), 3–17. DOI: 10.1207/s15326985ep2501_2

Zimmerman, B. J. (2000). Self-efficacy: An essential motive to learn. *Contemporary Educational Psychology*, *25*(1), 82–91. PMID: 10620383

Zimmerman, B. J. (2002). Becoming a self-regulated learner: An overview. *Theory into Practice*, *41*(2), 64–70. DOI: 10.1207/s15430421tip4102_2

Zubala, A., Kennell, N., & Hackett, S. (2021). Art therapy in the digital world: An integrative review of current practice and future directions. *Frontiers in Psychology*, *12*, 595536. DOI: 10.3389/fpsyg.2021.600070

Zubala, A., Pease, A., Lyszkiewicz, K., & Hackett, S. (2025). Art psychotherapy meets creative AI: An integrative review positioning the role of creative AI in art therapy process. *Frontiers in Psychology*, *16*, 1548396. DOI: 10.3389/fpsyg.2025.1548396

About the Contributors

Shaoxu Du is a Ph.D. candidate at the Centre for Instructional Technology and Multimedia, Universiti Sains Malaysia. His research interests include virtual reality, augmented reality, human-computer interaction, and cultural creativity.

Mageswaran Sanmugam acquired his B.Sc. (Hons) in Electrical Engineering from Universiti Teknologi Tun Hussein Onn in 2005 and Master's degree in Educational Management in 2012 from Universiti Utara Malaysia and Ph. D in Educational Technology in 2017 from Universiti Teknologi Malaysia. He worked as an Educator in both Primary and Secondary schools from 2008-2018, before being appointed as a Senior Lecturer in the Centre for Instructional Technology and Multimedia, Universiti Sains Malaysia, Pulau Pinang, Malaysia (from 2018- till 2021). Currently he is the Deputy Director of Research, Innovation and Networking in the Centre for Instructional Technology and Multimedia, Universiti Sains Malaysia, Pulau Pinang, Malaysia (from 2022- till now). His research interests encompass educational technology, ludology, game-based learning, gamification and game theory. He also serves as an exco-member in the Malaysian Educational Technology Association (META), and as a Senior Member under the Institute of Electrical and Electronics Engineers (IEEE).

Nurul Maziah Mohd Barkhaya acquired her B.IT. (Hons) in Software Engineering from Universiti Malaysia Terengganu in 2011 and Master's Degree in Education (TVET) in 2013 from Universiti Tun Hussein Onn Malaysia and Ph.D in Educational Technology in 2023 from Universiti Teknologi Malaysia. She worked as an educator in International Secondary schools from 2019 – 2023, before being appointed as a Senior Lecturer in the Centre for Instructional Technology and Multimedia, Universiti Sains Malaysia, Pulau Pinang, Malaysia started on 2024. Her research interests include the educational technology, creative multimedia, and e-Learning.

Chuang Chen is an Associate Professor at Zhengzhou University of Industrial Technology. He is also a Ph.D. graduate from the Centre for Instructional Technology and Multimedia, Universiti Sains Malaysia. His research focuses on virtual reality, augmented reality and instructional technology

Jia Wang obtained her Master's degree in Art Design from Peking University in 2014. She worked as a lecturer specializing in Digital Media at Nanyang Normal University, Henan, China, from 2016 to 2023. During this time, she published over ten academic papers on art education and research, guided students to win more than 30 awards in competitions, and received over ten awards in professional competitions herself. In 2023, she was awarded the Chinese Government Scholarship and began pursuing her Ph.D. in Cultural and Arts Management at Chung-Ang University, South Korea. Her research interests include art education, digital media, and cultural management.

***

Olufemi Timothy Adigun is a Senior Lecturer of inclusive education at the Department of Applied Educational Sciences, University of Namibia, Namibia. He holds a Doctoral degree in Special Education with a specialization in Deaf studies and deaf education from the University of Ibadan, Nigeria. Dr Adigun has served as Sign Language Interpreter to the deaf communities in several African countries. He is currently a Research Fellow with the Institute for Open Distance Learning, College of Education, University of South Africa, South Africa. He is C2 National Research Foundation (South Africa) rated researcher He has published over 68 articles on issues of Inclusive/Special need education, Deaf Education and Deaf studies, implication of technology in educational processes and psychosocial wellbeing of persons with disabilities. Dr Adigun is a recipient of the Shanghai Open University Visiting Scholar program (China); the University of Zululand (South Africa) Vice-Chancellor's Academic Award on Outstanding Achievements in Teaching and Research Community. He is also a beneficiary of the International Academic Forum (IAFOR) as well as the Stellenbosch University Postdoctoral Research Fellows conference funding.

Zerihun Alemu is an Associate Professor, Department of Management, Ethiopian Civil Service University, Ethiopia.

Feng Tian is a doctoral researcher in educational technology whose work focuses on digital game-based learning (DGBL), mobile-assisted language learning (MALL), and technical vocabulary acquisition. Her research integrates learning analytics, motivational theory, and instructional design to explore how digital tools can support professional language development in specialized domains.

Cynthy Haihambo is a Lecturer in the Department of Applied Educational Sciences at the University of Namibia School of Education. I am a teacher-educator, mostly teaching modules in Educational Psychology and Inclusive Education to teacher-education students. These include Inclusive Education 1 and 2; Guidance and Counselling 1, Life Skills, Comprehensive Sexuality Education, Gender and Disability Studies, HIV and AIDS among others.

Job Hengari is a Senior Lecturer of Inclusive education and educational Psychology.

Andy Lim Teik Hong is currently working as a Senior Lecturer in the Language Academy, Faculty of Social Sciences and Humanities, Universiti Teknologi Malaysia. Previously, he was a teacher in the state of Negeri Sembilan, Malaysia for almost 7 years. His research interests include teaching and learning pedagogy, blended learning and language teacher cognition.

Wako Jio is a PhD Scholar, in the Department of management, Bule Hora University, Ethiopia.

Yan Ju is a PHD student of the Center for Instructional Technology and Multimedia, Universiti Sains Malaysia, Malaysia.

Shashi Kant is an Associate Professor, Lovely Professional University, India.

Luqman Mahmud, Ph.D. is currently a Senior Lecturer in the Department of Human Resource Management, School of Business, at Universiti Utara Malaysia (UUM). His research interests primarily focus on green human resource management, environmental organizational citizenship behavior, and social capital.

Mariam Mohamad is the Senior Lecturer in Centre for Instructional Technology & Multimedia, Universiti Sains Malaysia, Penang, Malaysia. She can be contacted at email: mmohamad@usm.my. Scopus ID: 57214586750, Researcher ID: ABC-3218-2020, ORCID ID: 0000-0001-8498-4139, Google Scholar ID: vjuWOD8AAAAJ

Taralynn Petrites is a faculty member in the Department of Deaf and Sign Language Studies at Central Washington University, where she led the development of Washington's first BA in the field. She holds a Ph.D. in Higher Education Leadership and master's degrees in Adult Education and ASL Instruction. Her research focuses on linguistic equity, Deaf-led curriculum design, and institutional support for Deaf and Hard of Hearing faculty. Dr. Petrites also teaches graduate-level curriculum design, consults on state and national curriculum initiatives, and serves as an educational interpreter consultant to promote access and equity in learning environments.

Abhishek Sharma is an Assistant Professor in the Department of Marketing, Mittal School of Business, Lovely Professional University, India.

Melanie Shaw has spent the past two decades teaching and serving as an administrator in online higher education settings. She is a professor and academic program director in the Sanford College of Education at National University. She also serves as an adjunct faculty at several institutions and facilitates webinars for the Online Learning Consortium. In addition to her teaching roles, she trains faculty to develop and deliver courses online, conducts research on topics related to nontraditional education, and is involved in strategic leadership relative to the vision for online education. Melanie received a Ph.D. in Education with a specialization in Curriculum and Teaching, a master's degree in Education Administration, and a second master's degree in School Counseling. She holds teaching certificates in online teaching, elementary education, and school counseling.

Enock Simasiku is a Senior Lecturer and the Head of Department of the Department of Applied Educational Sciences, University of Namibia, Namibia

Irfan Naufal Umar is a professor at the Center for Instructional Technology and Multimedia, Universiti Sains Malaysia (USM), and currently serves as the Director of the Centre for Development of Academic Excellence (CDAE) at USM. His areas of expertise include educational technology and media, e-learning, and computer-based training. He has supervised more than 40 PhD candidates and numerous master's students in areas related to technology-enhanced learning, digital pedagogy, and instructional design.

Kazuvire Veii is a Lecturer of Inclusive Education and a Clinical Psychologist in Namibia.

Wan Ahmad Jaafar Wan Yahaya has been the Director of the Centre for Instructional Technology and Multimedia (PTPM) at Universiti Sains Malaysia (USM), Penang, since 2016. He also serves as the President of the Malaysian Educational Technology Association (META). Additionally, he is the Chairman of the Technical Committee on Audio, Video, Information Technology, and Communication Equipment at the Department of Standard Malaysia, Ministry of

International Trade and Industry Malaysia. He holds a PhD in Multimedia Education from the University of Leeds and a Master of Education (Computer in Education) from the University of Manchester, United Kingdom. Before that, he pursued a bachelor's degree at the University of Malaya, Malaysia. As the main supervisor, he has graduated 34 PhD students and has published more than 180 articles/papers in indexed journals such as Scopus, Web of Science (ISI), SCSI, SSCI, conference proceedings, and book chapters, primarily in the field of multimedia education. He has also presented over 18 speeches as a keynote and invited speaker, both nationally and internationally. Some of his innovative creations and projects have won gold awards and received special recognition in international innovation, invention, design, and technology competitions in Malaysia, Indonesia, Korea, and Geneva (Switzerland). In recognition of his outstanding contributions to the field of Educational Communications and Technology, he received the Thailand Association International Honor Award for the year 2023.

Wang Hanxu is a PHD student of Center for Instructional Technology and Multimedia, Universiti Sains Malaysia, Malaysia and a lecturer of School of International Education and Exchange, Cangzhou Technical College, Cangzhou, China

Jiaxin Wang was born in August 1999 in Shandong, China. She is currently a Master's student at the Centre for Instructional Technology and Multimedia (PTPM), Universiti Sains Malaysia, Penang. The research direction is e-learning and art education.

Jingran Yang is a PhD student at the School of Educational Technology, Universiti Sains Malaysia.

Huixin Zhen is the Phd of the Centre for Instructional Technology and Multimedia (PTPM). Unversiti Sains Malaysia(USM). Penang, Malaysia.

Index

I

M

N

O

P

S

T

V

www.ingramcontent.com/pod-product-compliance
Lightning Source LLC
LaVergne TN
LVHW062333300926
849161LV00007B/1674